T0293033

Get the eBook FREE!

(PDF, ePub, Kindle, and liveBook all included)

We believe that once you buy a book from us, you should be able to read it in any format we have available. To get electronic versions of this book at no additional cost to you, purchase and then register this book at the Manning website.

Go to https://www.manning.com/freebook and follow the instructions to complete your pBook registration.

That's it!
Thanks from Manning!

Outlier Detection in Python

Brett Kennedy

MANNING
SHELTER ISLAND

For online information and ordering of this and other Manning books, please visit www.manning.com. The publisher offers discounts on this book when ordered in quantity.

For more information, please contact

    Special Sales Department
    Manning Publications Co.
    20 Baldwin Road
    PO Box 761
    Shelter Island, NY 11964
    Email: orders@manning.com

Manning Publications Co.
20 Baldwin Road
PO Box 761
Shelter Island, NY 11964

Development editor:	Doug Rudder
Technical editor:	Aric LaBarr
Review editor:	Angelina Lazukić
Production editor:	Kathy Rossland
Copy editor:	Kari Lucke
Proofreader:	Keri Hales
Technical proofreader:	Ignacio Beltran Torres
Typesetter:	Tamara Švelić Sabljić
Cover designer:	Marija Tudor

ISBN 9781633436473
Printed in the United States of America

brief contents

contents

v

preface

This book is the result of many years of thinking about, and becoming fascinated by, the problem of outlier detection. I've worked in a number of jobs where outlier detection was a practical necessity of the work—for example examining financial data and performing social media analysis. So, there has been a very practical element to learning outlier detection. But outlier detection was also likely the most intellectually interesting area I worked on, even after many years of working in numerous other areas of data science.

The general idea of outlier detection is fairly simple: finding the items in a dataset that are most unlike the others. But, in practice, it's often quite difficult to do in an efficient and effective way, particularly where there are subtle outliers you're interested in. Once executed, it's difficult to determine if the items flagged as the most anomalous truly are the most anomalous. In fact, it can be difficult to even identify specifically why the items flagged are anomalous.

This is a very challenging, and also extremely interesting, area. I ended up reading probably a couple hundred journal papers and spending a lot of time experimenting with different techniques on different types of data. The main difficulty I found was the absence of interpretable models. Despite the importance of interpretability in outlier detection, there are actually very few methods to create interpretable results. So I developed a couple of tools I'm still maintaining today: Counts Outlier Detector and Data Consistency Checker.

I've continued to work with outlier detection and have been following advances in the field for some time, including recent progress in deep learning-based techniques for outlier detection.

I tried to distill this knowledge the best I could into this book. I hope you enjoy.

acknowledgments

I wish to thank my family, who've watched me sit in a room and write chapter after chapter for many, many, many months. And thanks to those on the Manning editorial team, especially acquisition editor Jonathan Gennick, development editor Doug Rudder, and technical proofreader Ignacio Beltran Torres, who have been very supportive from the beginning and made this a better book. A huge thanks also goes to the Manning production team for shepherding this book into its final format.

Thanks also to technical editor Aric LaBarr, who is a teaching associate professor in the Institute for Advanced Analytics. There he helps design the innovative program to prepare a modern workforce to wisely communicate and handle a data-driven future at the nation's first master of science in analytics degree program.

To all the reviewers: Adarsh Nair, Alejandro Cuevas Rivero, Anandaganesh Balakrishnan, Claudiu Schiller, Felipe Provezano Coutinho, Gabor Laszlo Hajba, George Carter, Graham Toppin, Jaromir D.B. Nemec, Jeremy Zeidner, Karan Gupta, Mariano Junge, Maxim Volgin, Michael Wang, Nguyen Tran Chau Giang, Oliver Korten, Peter Henstock, Rajiv Moghe, Sambasiva Andaluri, Sameet Sonawane, Sebastian Maier, Shantanu Neema, Siddharth Parakh, Srivathsan Srinivasagopalan, Thulasi Rangan Jayakumar, and Vidhya Vinay: your suggestions helped make this a better book.

about this book

This book will help you understand, first of all, the idea of outliers; it's a more subtle concept than is obvious at first. It will then help you identify outliers in data. The difficult part, which we'll also cover, is evaluating *how well* you're able to identify the outliers in the data.

We look at ways to try to find all (or as many as is practical) of the anomalies in a dataset. The book helps readers to look at data from different perspectives, to find the most relevant outliers for their needs. It also describes the main tools used today for outlier detection. It's not possible to describe everything, but this is quite comprehensive. It provides a solid background in the tools available and gives you the background to assess any other tools you may find—and to develop your own tools wherever necessary.

It's generally accepted that in outlier detection, no single algorithm will reliably detect all the outliers that may be useful to identify in any dataset. Consequently, it's common to use multiple detectors. This highlights the value in learning many outlier detection tools (which you will in this book), but it also means there's typically a need to create ensembles of detectors (which actually work a bit differently than with ensembles of predictive models). We go over the techniques to best create and use outlier detection ensembles.

Explainability is also very important in outlier detection—generally much more so than with predictive models. For example, if an outlier detection system identifies what may be a security threat, fraud, scientific discovery, failing machinery—or anything else that will require investigation—to investigate this, it's necessary to know what is unusual: why this was identified as anomalous. Despite this, there are few interpretable models available for outlier detection. The book, though, keeps interpretability [as well as explainable AI (XAI)] as a focus, so you can best understand why the items that were flagged as outliers by a detection system were flagged.

The book covers text, time-series, and image data, but focuses on tabular data, as this is the format where we tend to do the most work in outlier detection (though outlier detection with text, video, audio, and other formats is also very common and important). Other formats (for example, time-series or network data) can often be converted to table format to identify outliers, and so a solid understanding of tabular outlier detection is generally important when doing outlier detection work of any type.

Tabular data is also a very good format to work with when first working with outlier detection—it's a good place to learn to understand the main challenges of outlier detection and the solutions to these. We then build on this understanding and look at more advanced methods, including some of the most cutting-edge techniques developed to date. Outlier detection with image data, for example, requires deep learning-based approaches, which we cover, applying these as well to tabular and time-series data.

Who should read this book

Anyone doing work in machine learning or data science will benefit from this book. Outlier detection is a common task and likely something that will come up from time to time for anyone working in these fields; it's an important skill to have. Understanding outlier detection also helps practitioners better understand other areas of machine learning, such as prediction, clustering, and dimensionality reduction.

For anyone doing data analysis work, outlier detection can be very useful. In fact, it can be argued that the two main tasks when working to understand a dataset are to first understand the general patterns in the data and second to understand the exceptions to these: that is, the outliers.

In addition, anyone working in fields such as auditing, security, health care, bot detection, scientific research, or any other fields where it's useful to understand the data available and to understand the anomalies in it will find this book quite useful.

How this book is organized: A road map

The book is divided into four parts. Part 1 covers the basic ideas of outlier detection: what outliers are, some techniques to find them, and managing outlier detection projects.

- Chapter 1 covers the idea of outliers and some examples of where outlier detection may be used, along with high-level descriptions of how outlier detection may be applied to these cases. It looks at the subjective nature of outliers, provides some history of outlier detection, and describes the place of outlier detection in machine learning generally.
- Chapter 2 introduces outlier detection with simple statistical methods such as z-score, which can find rare or extreme values in sequences of values.
- Chapter 3 looks at tables of data and introduces some of the more common approaches to outlier detection, along with implementations in Python.
- Chapter 4 looks at how outlier detection projects can execute from start to finish. This can sometimes be left out of the discussion but is necessary for an effective outlier detection process.

Part 2 covers the main tools and algorithms for outlier detection in Python.

- Chapter 5 introduces outlier detection with scikit-learn and the tools it provides.
- Chapter 6 introduces the PyOD library, which is probably the most comprehensive library for outlier detection for numeric tabular data in Python.
- Chapter 7 describes several other libraries, tools, and algorithms. These are also very useful and effective but more difficult to find than those in scikit-learn or PyOD. These help readers understand outlier detection itself better, help readers see how to develop their own detectors, and provide a set of tools that are useful in themselves.

Part 3 covers the practical issues you'll likely encounter when performing outlier detection, such as working with different types of data, very large datasets, time constraints, and memory limits. It also covers techniques to evaluate individual detectors and the outlier detection system as a whole. This includes techniques to create synthetic data, create ensembles, and to process and interpret the results, even where large numbers of outliers are flagged.

- Chapter 8 covers techniques to identify the most useful detectors and best hyperparameters for any given project.
- Chapter 9 looks at working with specific types of data (e.g., text data, dates, addresses), encoding categorical data, binning and scaling numeric data, and the distance metrics that are used by many algorithms.
- Chapter 10 covers handling very large and very small datasets.
- Chapter 11 describes techniques to generate synthetic data, which is often necessary to tune and to evaluate outlier detection systems. The chapter also covers simulations, which is a useful outlier detection technique in itself.
- Chapter 12 introduces the idea of collective outliers: cases where no one item is necessarily unusual, but sets of items are collectively unusual. This includes where there are unusually many of certain things, where some things are completely absent, where events occur in unusual orders, and so on.
- Chapter 13 describes how to make outlier detection understandable so that the outliers flagged can be understood and efficiently investigated.
- Chapter 14 covers how to best use multiple detectors to identify the outliers in a dataset.
- Chapter 15 describes how to efficiently process the output of outlier detection routines.

Part 4 covers deep learning and two other modalities you may work with: image and time-series data.

- Chapter 16 describes deep learning-based methods for tabular and image outlier detection.
- Chapter 17 introduces outlier detection for time-series data.

The book proceeds from chapter to chapter, with some assumption that you're familiar with the material in the previous chapters, but you should be able to skip chapters that aren't germane to the work you're doing without any problems. I would recommend, though, reading at least the first five chapters to ensure the remaining chapters make sense. The exception is chapter 2, which you may skip if you're already familiar with the techniques covered there; as these are often covered in statistics courses, this is quite possible.

About the code

Other than chapter 1, all chapters have a good collection of code examples, both in numbered listings and in line with normal text (formatted in a `fixed-width font like this` to separate it from ordinary text), to help you understand the concepts and to have code ready to use in your projects.

Source code for the detectors and the longer examples is available at: https://github.com/Brett-Kennedy/OutlierDetectionInPython. You can get executable snippets of code from the liveBook (online) version of this book at https://livebook.manning.com/book/outlier-detection-in-python. The complete code for the examples in the book is also available for download from the Manning website at https://www.manning.com/books/outlier-detection-in-python.

Many of the source code examples require only NumPy and pandas, and many require scikit-learn or PyOD. These can all be installed with pip installs. Several other code listings use other libraries, but I've ensured that all are straightforward to install, either having a pip install or using a single .py file, and have included instructions on installing these.

In many cases, the original source code has been reformatted; we've added line breaks and reworked indentation to accommodate the available page space in the book. In rare cases, even this was not enough, and listings include line-continuation markers (➥). Additionally, comments in the source code have often been removed from the listings when the code is described in the text. Code annotations accompany many of the listings, highlighting important concepts.

liveBook discussion forum

Purchase of *Outlier Detection in Python* includes free access to liveBook, Manning's online reading platform. Using liveBook's exclusive discussion features, you can attach comments to the book globally or to specific sections or paragraphs. It's a snap to make notes for yourself, ask and answer technical questions, and receive help from the author and other users. To access the forum, go to https://livebook.manning.com/book/outlier-detection-in-python/discussion. You can also learn more about Manning's forums and the rules of conduct at https://livebook.manning.com/discussion.

Manning's commitment to our readers is to provide a venue where a meaningful dialogue between individual readers and between readers and the author can take place. It is not a commitment to any specific amount of participation on the part of the author, whose contribution to the forum remains voluntary (and unpaid). We suggest you try asking the author some challenging questions lest his interest stray! The forum and the archives of previous discussions will be accessible from the publisher's website as long as the book is in print.

about the author

BRETT KENNEDY is a data scientist with over 30 years of experience in software development and over 10 in data science. He has worked in outlier detection related to financial auditing, fraud detection, and social media analysis. He previously led a research team focusing on outlier detection. He lives in Toronto with his spouse and two children.

about the cover illustration

The figure on the cover of *Outlier Detection in Python,* titled "Créole de Cayenne," or "Cayenne Creole," is taken from a book by Louis Curmer published in 1841. Each illustration is finely drawn and colored by hand.

In those days, it was easy to identify where people lived and what their trade or station in life was just by their dress. Manning celebrates the inventiveness and initiative of the computer business with book covers based on the rich diversity of regional culture centuries ago, brought back to life by pictures from collections such as this one.

Part 1

Part 1 covers the basic ideas of outlier detection: what outliers are, some techniques to find outliers in data, and how to manage outlier detection projects.

In chapter 1, we cover the idea of outliers and provide some examples of where outlier detection may be used, along with high-level descriptions of how outlier detection may be applied to these cases. We look at the subjective nature of outliers, provide some history of outlier detection, and describe the place of outlier detection in machine learning generally.

In chapter 2, we introduce techniques for outlier detection with simple statistical methods (such as z-score and interquartile range), which can find rare or extreme values in sequences of values. These techniques are straightforward but are often all that is necessary for outlier detection projects. Where more sophisticated techniques are necessary, these often build upon the ideas presented in this chapter.

In chapter 3, we extend the discussion from one-dimensional series of values to tables of data and introduce some of the more common approaches to outlier detection for tabular data, along with implementations in Python.

In chapter 4, we look at how outlier detection projects can execute from start to finish. This can sometimes be left out of the discussion with outlier detection but is necessary for an effective process.

Introducing outlier detection

1

This chapter covers

- What outlier detection is
- Some examples of places where outlier detection is used
- A quick introduction to some approaches to outlier detection
- The fundamental problem of outlier detection

Outlier detection refers to the process of finding items that are unusual. For tabular data, this usually means identifying unusual rows in a table; for image data, unusual images; for text data, unusual documents, and similarly for other types of data. The specific definitions of "normal" and "unusual" can vary, but at a fundamental level, outlier detection operates on the assumption that the majority of items within a dataset can be considered normal, while those that differ significantly from the majority may be considered unusual, or outliers. For instance, when working with a database of network logs, we assume that the majority of logs represent normal network behavior, and our goal would be to locate the log records that stand out as distinct from these.

3

Outlier detection plays a pivotal role in many fields. Its applications include fraud detection, network security, financial auditing, regulatory oversight of financial markets, medical diagnosis, and the development of autonomous vehicles. Although outlier detection often doesn't garner the same attention as many other machine learning disciplines, such as prediction, generative AI, forecasting, or reinforcement learning, it holds a place of significant importance.

It's important to note that not all outliers are necessarily problematic, and in fact, many are not even interesting. But outliers often can be indicative of errors, hold special interest, or at least warrant further investigation. And it is a very common theme that, while many outliers may not be of interest—they are simply items that are statistically unusual—very often the converse is true: what we are looking for in data, possible fraud, errors, scientific discoveries, hardware failures, criminal activity, genetic variants, and so on, are outliers, and consequently specifically looking for outliers in data can be highly fruitful.

In this book, we'll go over examples of the uses for outlier detection, explain the various ways we can think about outliers, go through examples of identifying outliers in data, work through some of the challenges we often find in outlier detection, and describe how outlier detection projects typically work.

Conceptually, the notion of identifying unusual items is fairly straightforward. However, in practice, it proves to be a surprisingly difficult task. We will delve into the complexities later on, but for now, let's explore some of the applications of outlier detection.

1.1   *Why do outlier detection?*

Performing outlier detection is very often quite useful and can usually be applied anywhere we have a significant volume of data. As such, outlier detection is used broadly, so we cannot look at everywhere it's used, but we'll look at a few applications, which should provide some sense of how it works and where it can be used generally. One place where outlier detection is ubiquitous is finance, where it is used extensively by investors, fund managers, and regulators. It's used particularly to find fraud but also to help identify, for example, stocks or funds that are out of line with expectations or normal market trends.

Outlier detection is often used in video surveillance; it can be useful, for example, in situations where the same types of objects tend to be seen repeatedly and anything not normally seen may be of interest. With security video, this can relate to any unusual objects appearing where they are not normally seen; with traffic video, this may identify unusual trajectories, such as vehicles driving erratically. Outlier detection can be used to detect forgery, as forged documents may be unusual relative to legitimate documents. For years, e-commerce websites have been able to distinguish bots from legitimate users by looking at unusual behavior such as clicking at very high rates, viewing very large numbers of pages, or more subtle deviations from normal usage of the site, such as unusual mouse movements.

In the next few sections, we'll look closer at a few specific applications of outlier detection. This is, though, only a quick survey, and there are many other places where outlier detection is used. Nevertheless, outlier detection is probably still underutilized today, and many other fields can potentially benefit from its application. Going forward, we may see even greater use of outlier detection, as techniques to apply it to text, image, video, and audio have improved significantly over the past several years.

1.1.1 Financial fraud

There are many types of fraud. This section focuses on detecting financial fraud, but many of the techniques used to identify this are common to similar areas, such as tax or insurance fraud and anti-money laundering, as well as quite different types of fraud, for example with athletic performance or online games.

In general, there are two broad classes of financial fraud:

- The first is a lower level of fraud, where a company is bilked out of money or goods by staff or others, often suppliers or customers working in concert with staff.
- The second is a higher level of financial fraud, committed by senior management, or the company itself, primarily in the form of misrepresenting its financial position to defraud investors, its bank, or potential buyers. Fraud may also be perpetrated by senior managers seeking bonuses tied to stock prices, artificially inflating their company's earnings.

A large portion of fraud is undetected. Further, for companies, fraud entails a serious risk of financial loss, as well as a large reputational risk, and consequently, the great majority of fraud that is detected goes unreported. With respect to lower-level fraud committed against companies, a 2022 study by the Association of Certified Fraud Examiners estimated that organizations lose 5% of their annual revenue to fraud. If your company isn't checking for fraud, and specifically isn't using outlier detection for this purpose, there's a very good chance it could benefit from doing so.

With respect to high-level fraud, University of Toronto professor of finance Alexander Dyck and others published a study in January 2023 examining the pervasiveness of corporate fraud. They state: "We estimate that on average 10% of large publicly-traded firms are committing securities fraud every year, with a 95% confidence interval of 7%–14%. Combining fraud pervasiveness with existing estimates of the costs of detected and undetected fraud, we estimate that corporate fraud destroys 1.6% of equity value each year, equal to $830 billion in 2021." They also concluded only about a third of fraud is detected.

There are a large number of forms of high-level financial fraud; a few examples are:

- *Smoothing*—Smoothing seeks to make the year-after-year growth of the company more monotonically increasing, and often more linear, than it actually is, smoothing out the natural variations over time
- *Big bath fraud*—Senior managers, who often receive large bonuses on profitable years, but no penalties on years with losses, seek to direct all losses for several years to a single year, where they take a big bath this year and collect bonuses all other years

- *Round-tripping*—Goods are repeatedly bought and sold, or moved within the company, creating the illusion of there being more business activity than there is in reality
- *Bribery*— Bribery can manifest in many forms. For example, it may lead to special treatment for certain customers, overuse of certain suppliers, or cancellation of projects.

To detect fraud, audits are conducted on the financial records of the company, either by the company itself or by an external auditor. There are usually vastly too many records to check manually, so software tools are developed to check the records automatically, often using rules, which encode a number of simple tests that have been developed over the years. These include checking for rounded numbers (suggesting negotiated or estimated values), journal entries entered late at night, bulk entry of many identical entries, and so on. A slightly more complicated rule-based example may be: IF staff-level is "junior" and expense type is "meals and allowance" and amount > 100.00 THEN flag as suspicious.

Normally fraud increases over time as the perpetrators become more confident, and so many tests also check for escalations of certain behaviors. These tests work and continue to be useful, as older and less-sophisticated forms of fraud continue to be attempted.

However, fraud evolves over time, with people continuously developing new forms. And technology also keeps changing, which invariably creates new opportunities for fraud. One can never have a full set of rules that would catch everything. If we ever did, it would, in any case, soon become out of date. Thus, it's necessary to execute not just rules, which each check for specific, known patterns, but also outlier detection. Outlier detection can identify anything unusual and so catches the unknown patterns related to new forms of fraud, as well as to older forms not yet coded in the existing set of rules.

Outlier detection also allows audits to catch more subtle forms of fraud than can be realistically captured by rules. While forms of fraud such as smoothing may be suspected by simply checking if the year-after-year trend in earnings is unusually smooth, something like bribery may result in much more subtle deviations from previous behavior. These changes from the normal may also be gradual, taking place over extended periods of time. Outlier detection is often the only practical means to detect these.

When examining financial transactions, most unusual transactions will not be fraud; many will simply be rare transactions, such as annual payments (payments that are unusual solely because they are made only once per year) that are not problematic and may be understood by the analysts in any case. But most fraud, unless fraud is rampant, will be unusual, and so any unusual records, or unusual sets of records, are highly valuable to test for fraud. Similarly, testing for unusual records can be very effective to detect errors, inefficiencies, and other issues.

Another very powerful property of outlier detection is that it is capable of examining a dataset from thousands of angles exhaustively, without error and without bias. In the case of financial records, it's possible to check an enormous number of ways in which there can be usual patterns in the journals. For example, an outlier detection routine may find where certain staff have spikes in purchase records tied to a specific supplier at the end of each month that other comparable staff do not have. This would be infeasible to test manually or to encode with rules, as the number of such tests would be unworkable. Outlier detection allows for far more comprehensive checks of records, as it is not necessary to specifically code each test.

Still more advanced methods may be used to find more issues. Text analysis can examine memos, emails, contracts, patents, meeting minutes, and other documents. Time-series analysis can look for unusual trends or cycles in the data. Network analysis can examine the relationships and their evolution over time between staff, customers, suppliers, directors, related companies, and other entities. These can be difficult to set up and monitor but can also be necessary as fraud becomes more sophisticated over time. There has long been an arms race between those committing and those seeking to detect fraud, but outlier detection is a tool that can help tip the scales significantly toward identifying fraud, as it benefits greatly from data, which organizations now often possess an abundance of.

1.1.2 *Credit card fraud*

Credit card fraud refers to unauthorized use of a credit card, usually where the card was lost, stolen, or counterfeit. As the use of credit cards becomes more common, particularly for online purchases, credit card fraud has become correspondingly more frequent and is now surprisingly common. In the United States, approximately 7 cents of every $100 in transactions are fraudulent. Further, LexisNexis has reported a 140% increase in fraud since 2020. US retailers experience 1,740 fraud attempts each month on average, with slightly more than half of these attempts being successful. The year 2021 was the first in which successful fraud attempts outnumbered failed attempts. Given these trends, card fraud over the next 10 years is estimated to cost the industry $408 billion.

The bulk of losses are absorbed by credit card providers. As with companies risking financial fraud, credit card providers are highly dependent on outlier detection, in their case to detect unauthorized use of cards. And, as with financial fraud, there are certain known patterns that can be specifically looked for, but it's essential to also look for unusual behavior to flag anything the rules do not specifically cover. Outlier detection seeks to identify purchases, or sequences of purchases, that are somehow different from what is normal. As in most contexts, unusual behavior is not necessarily problematic, but problematic behavior will be unusual, at least in some way, making outlier detection an effective means to identify fraud.

Some tests for credit card fraud are defined in ways that are general and not specific to any cardholder, such as checking for two store purchases geographically far apart within a short time window or checking for people signing up for a card using a nonexistent address, invalid phone number, or nonsensical email address. Many tests are also relative to the cardholder, checking for purchases that are unusual given their history. Tests may also consider the history of the merchant and the time of purchase and allow for special events such as Christmas and Black Friday. As with financial fraud, credit card fraud tends to follow certain behaviors. Often people with stolen cards will test the card first with a few innocuous, small purchases in a short period, followed by progressively larger purchases, often at a small set of specific locations.

These tests are important, but it is impossible to write specific tests for every form of unusual behavior. Similar to financial fraud and the other areas we look at here, outlier detection is the only practical means to detect a very wide range of unusual patterns, including unusual patterns that have not yet been discovered or even conceived of. Having said that, an important application of outlier detection is discovering patterns that may be developed into rules. Although outlier detection is necessary, in many contexts (including where we wish to identify fraud), maintaining a good collection of rules is also important. Once relevant behaviors are identified by an outlier detection process, they may be encoded as rules to ensure the pattern is caught consistently going forward.

Fraud analysis is becoming more sophisticated. It used to be common to have to notify credit card providers when traveling; otherwise, the provider may have blocked any transactions. Outlier detection was simpler at the time and has since improved significantly, now having no trouble with cardholders traveling between cities. But it is also struggling to keep up. The volume, complexity, and often subtlety of fraud (for example, where only a small number of small fraudulent purchases are made) is challenging. Fraudsters also have access to modern machine learning technology, including outlier detection, though not the data that credit card providers and large retailers possess.

To further complicate matters, much of credit card fraud is done not by individuals but by organizations. Detecting this usually requires a sophisticated analysis, tracking the transactions of many cardholders and many merchants over time and searching for anything unusual. For this, we need to compare the set of transactions to either those of comparable groups of clients and merchants or the same clients and merchants for previous time periods. Outlier detection may detect unusual trends, spikes, or other anomalies. It may also detect where there are purchases that are each only slightly suspicious but where there are many of these, in some way related, within some time window.

What's important is to consider transactions in many different ways. As a simple example, we can check credit card transactions for unusual dollar values or unusual merchants, but a transaction may have neither. It may, however, have an unusual combination, such as hundreds of dollars at a restaurant where the cardholder would normally spend much less, possibly followed by other suspicious purchases. Modern outlier detection for fraud requires looking at substantially more complex relationships than this example, but the idea is similar: the more context, and the more history that is considered to assess the normality of a transaction, or set of transactions, the better we can identify anomalies.

1.1.3   *Network security*

Monitoring computer networks is necessary for a number of purposes, including security, detecting hardware and software failures, and detecting new trends in usage. Each of these is reliant on outlier detection. We consider, for the moment, specifically network intrusion, defined here as any unauthorized access to a network, usually with the goal of viewing, modifying, or deleting private data or disrupting the operations of the network. This, along with intrusion prevention (e.g., passwords, two-factor authentication) is the main tool to keep networks secure.

As in the fraud cases mentioned previously, much of intrusion detection is based on rules that check for known patterns. Rules are often developed by intuition and by post hoc examination of logs after an event. Both are useful, but they also leave a gap, as these cannot cover all current and future threats. Much like fraud, network security threats are constantly evolving, with new variations on previous threats and completely new threats regularly appearing. Security professionals are perpetually having to deal with what are called *zero-day threats*—threats with no history and no warning. In these cases, outlier detection can be the most effective way to identify the threats. Outlier detection removes both the manual process and the ad hoc nature of developing rules and is, as a result, much more flexible and comprehensive. It allows us to detect issues even before they are known.

Some threats are obvious from the beginning, such as denial of service attacks (where a service is sent massive numbers of requests, either shutting down the service or crowding out legitimate users), but many can be subtle and often unnoticed. As intrusion must be, in one manner or another, unusual, we are often best able to detect it by searching for activity deviating from the norm. Once any deviations are found, it's necessary to identify the root causes (for example, some excessive traffic patterns may be port scans performed by attackers and others simply unscheduled backups), but the first step is very often finding the anomalies.

Looking for anomalies, we can track hardware and operating system measurements such as processor temperature, number of processes, CPU usage, and disk requests. These can provide valuable information. In practice, all of these and much more could be relevant; much of outlier detection is examining data from many different angles, as records can appear normal in most senses and only stand out in specific contexts. But for simplicity, consider an analysis based simply on logs of system calls ordered by time.

Any given system call may be somewhat suspicious (for example, changing file permissions) but not likely enough to cause an alert: if so, the operations would not be possible. Much of what's being looked for is not individual actions but suspicious sequences of actions, usually within a short time window. Where there is a single suspicious system call, it is quite likely not an issue, but where there are many in a short time (or the sequence itself is very unusual), this is much more suspicious. This is more difficult to detect but is very often the only feasible way to identify inauthentic use of systems.

1.1.4 Detecting bots on social media

It is notoriously difficult to estimate the number of bots on any social media platform. For X (formerly known as Twitter), estimates have ranged greatly, with some estimates prior to Elon Musk's purchase as low as 5% (including from Twitter itself) and others as high as 9% to 15%. Even at the lower end, this is a very large number of accounts. And bot accounts can often produce a disproportionate amount of traffic. Social media companies are constantly removing bogus accounts using a combination of outlier detection, other machine learning tools, rules, and human inspection.

Though it is unknown how many bogus accounts are missed, as an indication that they were detecting a significant number, one project I worked on, analyzing Twitter (prior to being known as X) traffic through its public API, found that month after month, about 10% of the accounts we followed no longer existed. Some of these may have been closed by the users themselves, but we believed most were closed by Twitter.

Like a lot of cases covered here, this is an adversarial situation and consequently the specific methods used by the platforms need to be kept confidential. We can never know precisely how financial regulators or network security systems function, and we cannot know precisely how these bots are detected. We do know though, through statements platforms have made, the detection of unusual behavior is a part of the process. The sheer volume of traffic makes it impossible to monitor traffic manually. Given this and the fact that new and creative forms of inauthentic behavior on social media are constantly being developed, the only feasible way to detect a reasonable amount is to look for behavior that diverges from normal. As bots and paid operatives are using the system in atypical ways, they will stand out as unusual in some regard.

Despite the need for secrecy, Twitter was one of the most open of the major platforms, providing a free public API to collect tweets and making available a set of takedowns of information operations (operations where armies of bots or bogus accounts backed by real people are deployed for purposes such as propaganda, discrediting others, or stoking fear or distrust) publicly available. Takedowns are large collections of tweets by related accounts identified in specific operations (though without any indication of how these were identified), made available for researchers. Following these releases, there have been a significant number of academic papers on the subject, which present plausible and apparently effective ways to identify at least some inauthentic accounts. These include analysis of the user profiles, interactions with other users, the timelines of their actions, and the text content of their tweets, looking for outliers of various types.

Researchers have found many anomalies in the takedowns including cases of large numbers of accounts created at once with very similar profiles and each following each other and cases of multiple accounts that regularly send unusually similar tweet content at roughly the same time as each other. Researchers have also found accounts that, apparently being used for different purposes at different times, changed language multiple times. Other accounts became hyperfocused on specific topics for periods of time (presumably trying to attract followers interested in these topics) and then gradually inserted more and more political discussion into their tweets, usually on very specific topics. Some of these accounts would then later switch to another, unrelated topic, again becoming hyperfocused on this for some time before again switching to a specific political topic.

It is possible to specifically check for these patterns to identify bots, and it may be useful to encode checks for patterns similar to these as these specific patterns are found. However, it is not feasible to encode rules for every such possibility; it is far more practical to use outlier detection and take advantage of the fact that all of these behaviors are unusual.

1.1.5   *Industrial processes*

Outlier detection is common in many industrial processes such as manufacturing assembly lines, where it's necessary to maintain consistently high-quality output, well-running machinery, and a safe workplace. In this context, and particularly in just-in-time environments, there may be very little room for errors or unscheduled maintenance, so early detection of issues is imperative.

In industrial processes, unlike many other situations, the processes are normally stable and predictable. Anything unusual is quite likely a failure, or predictive of potential failures. Compared to other settings, there is much less of a concept of innocuous or irrelevant deviations; there is certainly no sense of deviations being potentially preferable to the norm. In these environments, outlier detection may capture, for example, unexpected levels of friction, leading to wearing down of parts, unusual voltages, or other anomalies that may lead to problems if left unattended. Where severe anomalies are detected, it may be necessary to send out alerts or, in more extreme cases, to slow down or stop the process. More often, though, any anomalies detected will be used to help predict when maintenance will be needed, so that this can be scheduled and conducted before there are risks of equipment failure.

A difficulty here is that these systems can become victims of their success. Part of the purpose of monitoring for anomalies is to predict time until failure. Learning to predict upcoming failures from the data requires historical data with examples of failures (and the data that was observed just prior to these failures). But many systems will have little history of failure, particularly where monitoring is in place. Further, even if there was a significant history of machine failures, it could not cover all the potential faults, and certainly not with many examples of each. As a result, looking for anomalies—anything unusual within the process—can be the most feasible way to monitor the system and keep it running smoothly. This won't flag imminent failures per se—only deviations from the norm—but in an environment where any deviations are suboptimal, checking for these is very important.

Industrial processes may collect video, audio, or other types of data to monitor the process, but much of what is collected will be sensor readings collected at regular time intervals. Machines often have many sensors, tracking metrics such as temperature and pressure. These sensors themselves have failures, which it is also necessary to monitor for. Sensors, when they are close to failure or stressed, may produce what are referred to as *data artifacts*, which are unusual values, or anomalies. Here the source is not the process being monitored but the collection process itself. This is a common theme in outlier detection: where we have anomalous values, it's not always clear at first if this is a data artifact or a truly unusual reading.

The anomalies may be what are called *point anomalies*—a single reading that is unusual, typically an unusually high or unusually low value. They may also be what are called *contextual anomalies* or *collective anomalies*. Here contextual anomalies refer to readings that are unusual given some context: the readings from other sensors or previous readings from the same sensor. Using multiple sensors and cross-referencing them can be useful to find some types of anomalies—for example, finding unusual combinations of readings. Or, where two sensors are normally independent, or normally in sync, finding unusual associations over time between the two would be an anomaly.

It's common to have one-time issues in industrial processes. These are not completely without concern, but given a large number of sensors, there will be many issues of some severity, but under a threshold, and these may not trigger any immediate action. They can, though, be logged. If these low-level anomalies become more common, they may then become a concern. Systems can monitor the number of point anomalies per minute, hour, or some appropriate period and set a threshold, beyond which alerts are sent or the process is halted. This threshold may be set based on a history of the normal number of point anomalies per period. Consequently, while it's not always feasible to address every anomaly, it is very useful to monitor for patterns in the unusual readings, such as periodicity or trends. Any unexpected but repeating or escalating pattern is particularly of interest. In addition, if there is an issue later, having these anomalies in the logs may help identify patterns to specifically monitor for going forward.

As the readings are effectively time-series data, outlier detection methods specific to time series can be effective at finding points of concern. An example may be a temperature reading rising and falling unusually often within a time interval, even where no individual temperature reading is itself necessarily unusual for that sensor. There are various ways to check for this, but one is to collect the temperature readings from a comparable sensor over a long period, or the same sensor over prior periods, and model what are normal fluctuations over time. See figure 1.1 as an example, showing both unusually high fluctuations (at 200 seconds) and low fluctuations (at 800 seconds). Both would be flagged as anomalies.

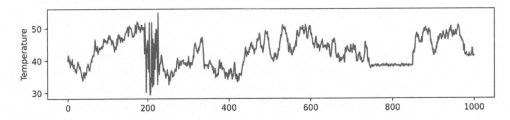

Figure 1.1 **Temperature readings from sensor data presented as a time series. The x-axis tracks time in seconds and the y-axis tracks the temperature. There is an unusually high level of fluctuation at 200 seconds and an usually low level at 800 seconds.**

To use outlier detection, there needs to be a set of data to compare against, which represents the ideal, or at least typical, functioning. This may be created, for example, immediately after maintenance, when it is known the processes are running normally. Given this, any readings, or sequences of readings, that diverge significantly are possibly of concern. How many to investigate is a question any time we work with outlier detection. In all contexts, this boils down to a question of balancing false positives (where we predict that there is an issue though there is none) with false negatives (where we predict none though there is an issue).

1.1.6 *Self-driving vehicles*

Unlike many other examples, self-driving vehicles are a case where mistakes can be catastrophic, and highly robust systems need to be put in place to ensure safety. Self-driving vehicles look for anomalies in different forms; one very important application of outlier detection is checking for anomalies with respect to vision. Autonomous vehicles have multiple cameras, which they use to help identify other vehicles, pedestrians, and other entities. A risk for these vehicles is that they may detect an object, misclassify it, and be overconfident in their classification. In the worst case, they may have high confidence that a person (perhaps wearing a costume or in some other way quite different from any of the images of pedestrians the vehicle was trained to identify) is an inanimate object with no chance of moving. Or they may see a vehicle of a type that has not previously been seen and believe it is something other than a vehicle.

The systems are trained to recognize many different types of objects and can do so with high accuracy when encountering these objects, but they can become confused when presented with different types of objects than they were trained to recognize. The systems may be trained well to recognize motorcycles, dogs, people on skateboards, people with baby strollers, trees, fire hydrants, traffic signs, and hundreds or thousands of other types of objects. But it isn't possible to train autonomous vehicles to recognize every type of object they may encounter. In one well-known example, one of Google's self-driving cars was fooled by a woman in an electric wheelchair chasing a duck with a broom. Not only is it infeasible to test every such possibility, it probably isn't even possible to think of more than a fraction of the possible things they may encounter.

In these cases, vehicles often predict that the object seen is an example of an object type they were trained on: the one that is most similar visually (though not necessarily similar in a practical way) to the actual object. But they can predict this with much higher confidence than is warranted. To address this, outlier detection systems can be run in parallel with the vision systems. The outlier detection process can flag any objects seen that are unusual relative to the data the system was trained on. This allows the vehicle to be more cautious and more open to other explanations of the objects identified visually.

1.1.7 *Healthcare*

Healthcare is another field where outlier detection has proven useful in research as well as in practice. A common application is analyzing 2D and 3D images—for example, to find tumors, cancerous masses, or other concerns. As these, fortunately, are not common in images, they can stand out as anomalies. In many cases, it is difficult to create a classifier to specifically look for issues such as these, but it can be feasible and productive to simply search for anything highly unusual in the images. Another application is examining time-series data from patient measurements, such as heartbeat, blood pressure, and blood sugar, identifying any irregularities in these as possibly concerning. Outlier detection can also be applied to checks for misdiagnosis, identifying cases that are outside the norm for the diagnosed condition.

Outlier detection is important in healthcare partially due to the vast amount we still don't understand in medicine, related, for example, to genetic dispositions, drug interactions, and the roles of bacteria. If these were perfectly understood, we would have specific things to look for in medical data; it may be a very long list, but we could nevertheless compile this and search for these. As it is, however, we often don't know exactly what to look for, and searching for anything anomalous may be the most tractable approach for research or diagnosis, or at least may be an important component. This is particularly true as there can be quantities of information far too large for people to manually inspect. Further, the data frequently contains subtle patterns that are difficult for people to reliably notice, especially when they are novel and people are not conditioned to looking for them. This is where outlier detection systems can perform especially well; this is what outlier detection is specifically designed to do and can perform with very large quantities of data.

1.1.8 *Astronomy*

Outlier detection is a useful tool in science and occasionally a source of scientific discovery. Often in scientific research, we are looking for very rare objects or rare events, as these are often the least-understood and most interesting. As such, many fields make use of outlier detection; it is used, for example, for examining results from the Large Hadron Collider. Astronomy is also an interesting example. Outlier detection tools can, for example, identify anomalies in images collected from telescopes: things we haven't seen before or rarely see, and these may lead to new discoveries or a better understanding of rare phenomena.

Historically, we've been able to identify anomalies manually. For example, pulsars were discovered by manually combing through observation data and recognizing there were outliers in the data. This led to the recognition of this new phenomenon—we had no concept of pulsars before this. But after many years of many people working in these areas, these types of discoveries are becoming much more difficult. What we do have, though, much like many other fields, is massive quantities of data—in this case, petabytes per day collected from telescopes around the world and in space. The volume of data is phenomenal. Single observations can be a terabyte, covering millions of galaxies. So, though manual inspection is largely no longer feasible to make new discoveries, automated processes are well situated to examine the data. In some cases, outlier detection can be the only practical means to process it. Other machine learning processes may be possible in principle, but very often we are interested in identifying the most unusual images as the data of the most interest, which outlier detection is perfectly suited for.

An example of one specific application of outlier detection in astronomy is processing images of transients: cases where the brightness of an object varies temporarily.

The great majority are routine, well-understood events, but they can also occasionally be very interesting. A single telescope may witness tens of millions of these per night. Consequently, an application of outlier detection is simply filtering these down to a more manageable number than can be analyzed by astronomers, keeping only the most unusual. This can help find rare but known events, such as neutron star mergers or, preferably, events that are completely unexpected. Often, we wish to do this in real time, in order to direct more resources to areas of the sky where there are observations, often short-lived, that may warrant the most interest.

1.1.9 *Data quality*

Data quality is a major issue in most organizations and affects many business processes and forms of analysis. Anecdotally, I've heard quite a number of stories of people attempting to work on machine learning projects for organizations and finding it all but impossible due to the state of the data. It's common for organizations to have huge collections of data, often in SQL or spreadsheet formats, created over long periods of time and with varying levels of consistency and documentation. Although there is very often a sufficient volume of data for useful analysis, it can be difficult to maintain a high level of data quality, and often data is not of sufficient quality to be useful for analysis.

Among the issues we may have are cases where the definitions of features, or code values within features, change over time; where there are errors from merging tables, normalizing, denormalizing, or aggregating data; or converting from long to wide (or wide to long) formats. The data may include missing or estimated values. Data may be collected from different divisions or regions that track and store data differently. Data that is manually entered inevitably has some rate of errors. Even data purchased from other firms can contain errors, or the meaning of the data may be misunderstood. Within spreadsheets particularly, the data quality can be questionable. It can be very difficult to review spreadsheets, and there are often coding errors, cases where formulas are not applied to all cells consistently, or other issues.

Given the data available, there are several tasks organizations may wish to do, including producing reports and dashboards, budgeting, basic benchmarking (e.g., comparing different subsets of the data to each other), data mining (more complex discovery of patterns in the data), or predictive machine learning. Where data quality is poor enough, these are impossible. Worse, the data may appear plausible, with the issues undetected, leading to invalid and misleading analysis.

The two most feasible ways to detect data quality issues are, as in the cases previously, to define rules and to run outlier detection. Writing rules consists of creating scripts specifying the valid range of values in each column, how the columns relate to each other, and so on, which requires a strong understanding of each feature in each table. Writing such rules can be far more time-consuming, error-prone, and difficult to maintain than it's worth. Outlier detection can be much more practical in some situations as it doesn't require any predetermined idea of what should be in the data. Outlier detection has some limitations here: it will flag many records that are not errors, just unusual, and it will miss errors if they are too common to be unusual, but it can be extremely useful to identify issues.

Checking for data quality can be done before running any analysis, but it's usually better, if possible, to run well before then, when the data is first collected or when it is first moved into its current form. At this point, any issues are much easier to assess, and also to fix. Over time, people tend to leave organizations or not remember how the data was collected and formatted. Some problems may persist over time, accumulating in the data and becoming more difficult to address, making correcting the data more difficult if outlier detection and other checks on the data are not performed early.

1.1.10 Evaluating segmentation

The last example we'll look at for now is evaluating the quality of data segmentation. This example is less obvious than the others, but hopefully it gives a sense of the range of problems outlier detection can be used for; outlier detection can very often be used effectively even in situations where we do not necessarily think of using it.

Data will often be divided into segments for more meaningful consideration. As an example, stocks or funds are routinely grouped together into segments to facilitate comparison. To assess a fund's performance in a meaningful way, it is useful to have a set of similar funds to compare to. A 2023 study by BlackRock concluded the segmentation done, even by prominent organizations such as Morningstar and Lipper, could be questioned. To determine this, the authors used an interesting outlier detection technique, useful for testing any kind of segmentation. They calculated, for each fund, its outlier score (an estimate of the "outlierness" of an item; in this case, a fund) relative to its assigned segment. That is, they measured how unusual each fund was relative to the segment it was placed in. They then considered if each of the funds were, instead, placed in other segments and measured their outlierness relative to these. Doing this, they found a number of funds that would be better placed in other segments (these funds were less unusual relative to these other segments than the segment they were actually placed in), at least using their measure of similarity. Based on this, it was reasonable to conclude that many were, and may still be, misclassified. Misclassified funds can lead to misleading evaluations of the funds, poorer choices for investments, and lost income. Interestingly, they also found that there was an inverse association between outlierness and returns: the more inappropriate a segment the stocks were placed in, the worse they performed relative to that segment.

Now that we've seen some examples of where outlier detection can be used and some of the considerations associated with outlier detection, we'll look at the discipline of outlier detection itself, particularly how it fits in with other areas of machine learning.

1.2   Outlier detection's place in machine learning

Outlier detection is a machine learning technique, which means it learns from data, as opposed to using rules crafted by people. More specifically, outlier detection is one of the main fields in an area of machine learning known as *unsupervised machine learning*. To explain what that means, we'll first explain another, better-known area of machine learning, called *supervised machine learning*. In that setting, we are given a set of data, possibly a spreadsheet of records, collection of text documents, time sequence of instrument readings, or audio files. What makes a problem supervised is the data includes what are called *labels*.

As an example, assume we have a collection of several hundred images, each with a label. The labels will in some way describe each of the images. For example, the images may be pictures of animals, and the labels may refer to the type of animal: cat, dog, and hamster. Given this, a supervised machine task would be to create a predictor. This predictor, more specifically, is referred to as a *classifier* if the labels represent categories (also known as classes); the classifier will learn to predict the class labels from the images (in this case predicting the type of animal in a given picture). And the predictor is referred to as a *regressor* if the labels are numeric values (for example, if we had labels representing a numeric quality of the pictures, such as the number of distinct animals in the picture); the regressor will learn to predict these numeric values from the images. The labels here are said to *supervise* the learning process.

However, often when we are working with data there are no labels, just the data itself. As a similar example, we may have a collection of images, again of animals, though without the labels and may wish to better understand this collection.

It is not possible with image data, but with tables of numeric data, such as accounting records or scientific measurements, we could use traditional statistics to analyze the data, which is essentially summarization: looking for the means, standard deviations, and other statistics that can concisely describe a dataset. These are very useful but can be limited. Beyond traditional statistics, we can do more sophisticated analysis, based on machine learning. In the absence of any labels for the data, this is the domain of unsupervised machine learning: providing advanced analysis on data using only the data itself. The main forms of unsupervised learning are clustering and outlier detection, though there are other forms as well.

When clustering data, we find sets of items that appear to be similar to each other. A clustering algorithm, given the collection of images of animals, would examine the pictures and divide them into some small set clusters, based on perhaps the animal's color, the background color, if their legs were visible, and other properties of the pictures. This would be done such that each cluster is internally consistent (the images in each cluster are similar to each other) and the different clusters are unlike each other.

Outlier detection, on the other hand, identifies the most unusual items in a dataset. This is based on something quite powerful: learning the fundamental patterns of a given set of data, what constitutes normal for this data, and what items diverge most strongly from these patterns.

Prediction and outlier detection do different things—both useful but quite different. Where labels are available, it can often be more useful to create a predictive model than to perform unsupervised analysis such as clustering or outlier detection. We can train a classifier to learn what types of images represent dogs, cats, and hamsters. Then, given any new pictures of a dog, cat, or hamster, the classifier can predict what type of animal it is. However, what a classifier cannot do well is recognize when it is given an unusual picture, perhaps a picture of something not in one of the three classes it was trained to predict, such as a parrot. A classifier will also not be able to recognize where it receives a picture of, say, a dog, but an unusual picture of a dog. These are problems outlier detectors can solve: recognizing what data we may be faced with, if any, is unusual.

Outlier detectors and predictors are two tools for two tasks, though we will explore cases where each can aid the other and where both can be used together to create more effective systems than either predictive models or outlier detectors could on their own. Many cases, though, including the previous examples, such as fraud detection, network security, advances in astronomy and other sciences, and many other tasks, are only feasible using outlier detection.

1.3 *Outlier detection in tabular data*

The main focus of this book is tabular data. In business contexts, this is the most common form of data, and it is likely the form of data that many data scientists will work with the most. It is also the type of data with the most history of outlier detection and with the richest and most mature set of tools available. We will, however, cover other modalities (forms of data), specifically text, time series, and image data in chapters 9, 16, and 17. While these modalities are quite different from tabular data, a common approach to outlier detection for other modalities is to convert the data to a tabular format and perform standard tabular data outlier detection on this. Other approaches, specific to deep learning, also exist and will be covered as well in chapter 16.

Where we work with other types of data, projects largely face the same general considerations and challenges as with tabular data, though these challenges and their solutions can be easier to understand with table data. So starting with tabular data will provide a good background for these modalities as well.

There is a wealth of tabular data worth examining, including scientific, weather, medical, economic, and server log data, to name only a few sources. Businesses often store vast quantities of (largely tabular) data that they know has more value than they currently get from it. There is far too much to go through manually, but there is useful information in there if we can get to it.

The purposes for examining data described earlier (fraud detection, security, identifying issues or possible future issues, data consistency, keeping vision systems and other machine learning systems running in a sensible manner, and so on) are very important. But it's also useful to simply extract human-understandable knowledge from the data available. This is important in many environments including business and scientific settings. To a large degree, this means identifying just two key things: the general patterns in the data and the unusual elements in it—the exceptions to the general patterns, the outliers. That is, outlier detection can be a useful step in understanding data. Outlier detection, by identifying the most unusual items present, gives a sense of the range of what's possible in the data. With some of the items discovered by outlier detection, we will be surprised that they exist at all. It can provide insights into a business (or other source of data) not otherwise possible.

1.4   Definitions of outliers

We've been discussing outliers, and you hopefully now have a good intuitive sense of what they are. In general, they are items that are significantly different from the majority of other items they may be compared to. (I'm generally using the term *anomaly* in this book synonymously though also often to indicate a single unusual property of an item: the individual oddities that make an item an outlier.)

We'll try to define here more precisely what outliers are, but as you'll see, this is only possible to a degree. Outliers are a nebulous concept. This has some advantages, as it allows us to approach outlier detection from many different vantages, but it also carries a lot of vagueness. Part of this stems from the fact that the context makes a great deal of difference. What is noise in one context is signal in another.

There are a few definitions that you will often see if you ever read the academic literature—each useful, but each a little hand-wavy. Grubbs in 1969 stated

> *An outlying observation, or outlier, is one that appears to deviate markedly from the other members of the sample in which it occurs.*

Barnett and Lewis (1994) used the following definition:

> *An observation (or subset of observations) which appears to be inconsistent with the remainder of that set of data.*

This broadens the concept of outliers as it adds the idea of collective outliers as well as single items (e.g., single credit card purchases) being unusual; a set of several (e.g., a series of credit card purchases over a few hours) may be an outlier, even if each item in the set is typical. One of the most-cited definitions of outliers is from Hawkins (1980):

> *An outlier is an observation which deviates so much from the other observations as to arouse suspicions that it was generated by a different mechanism.*

This definition can be debated, but it is based on an important idea: that there is some process, or set of processes, generating the data and that they operate within certain bounds. Other data, generated by other processes, can become included in a dataset and would then be considered anomalous. For example, consider the processes at a business, including purchasing office supplies and making rent payments. Each process will generate a set of expenses, which may be included in an expenses table. If the rent payments are much larger and far less common, they may be considered outliers, albeit completely legitimate. There may also be a staff member who is entering inaccurate records or possibly committing fraud. As these are distinct processes, they create records that are inherently different, even if only subtly so.

A central theme of outlier detection is that, despite the common need to identify unusual data points and despite these intuitive definitions, no universally accepted definition of specifically what qualifies as "unusual" exists. This means it's very difficult to nail down what items should be flagged as outliers. Consequently, one fundamental characteristic of outlier detection is that it's notoriously difficult. With no labels, there is no systematic way to evaluate any outliers flagged, and without a concrete definition, there is no definite way to create labels. Outlier detection is, then, highly subjective.

In practice, to identify outliers we use algorithms, known as *detectors*, specifically designed for outlier detection. Many of these are simple methods—for example, based on standard deviations (which can help flag unusually small or unusually large numeric values) and others that are more involved. Some are much more involved, based on behavioral analysis, time sequences, Markov models, neural networks, or other approaches. Many are available in Python libraries, including scikit-learn; some are described in academic literature or other sources. In the upcoming chapters, we'll go through several of these, but for now the main point is that most of these algorithms can be reasonably easily understood and each has a strong intuitive appeal, but each is different and each identifies different—and sometimes very different—items as outliers. Algorithms each have their own unique focus and approach. Each can be valuable within specific contexts, but none are definitive.

As we proceed through this book, I will try to make clear why a multitude of outlier detection algorithms exist; why this multiplicity is the most appropriate response to a problem that, by its very nature, lacks precise definition; and how you can effectively apply these algorithms to identify outliers within the datasets you work with. This is what makes outlier detection a fascinating problem as well as highly practical.

Based on this, I'd like to propose a practical definition of outliers, which I believe is quite useful. Similar to Einstein's definition of time, we can define an outlier as

An outlier is that which an outlier detector flags.

This is, of course, circular, but there is a logic to it. The idea is: for any sensible outlier detection algorithm that is implemented without errors, whatever it flags is, by definition, an outlier. This pragmatic approach puts the onus on the detection algorithms to define what they will flag, but the detectors are, in effect, doing this in any case, though they are guided by the general definitions cited previously.

Take figure 1.2 for example. This shows eight pictures of mugs. We can ask ourselves: which pictures are unusual? To say with any certainty, we would need many more examples than this, but just looking at eight pictures, we can start to see the many ways we could consider some as unusual. They differ in the color of the mug, the angle of the picture, the lighting, the position of the handle, and so on. Different people could look at these and reasonably come to different conclusions. Some may argue that they are all mugs, and so none are unusual. Others may say that the one in the bottom left is clearly a different mug than the others so could be considered unusual, and so on. An outlier detector, as a software application, may look at quite different things than a person would, possibly catching differences a person would miss or differences a person would see but not find relevant. The outliers, though, may in fact be very relevant if the outlier detection is being performed to prepare the data for another image-processing task.

Despite the diversity of legitimate ways to identify outliers in any collection, we have been able to develop well-functioning systems that can be used for important applications, often in a way that is essential.

Figure 1.2 **Eight images of mugs. Each is different, and a reasonable argument could likely be made for any one of them to be considered anomalous relative to the other seven.**

1.5 *Trends in outlier detection*

It is somewhat oversimplified, but we can think of outlier detection as having gone through three major stages, starting with traditional, simple statistical methods (for example, based on standard deviations) going back many decades. These were straightforward and could be computed by hand for small datasets but were limited to finding unusually small or large values in single sequences of numbers and don't extend well to tables of data.

These were followed by machine learning-based methods, largely from the last 30 or so years, developed as computer hardware improved, digitized data became common, and machine learning techniques improved. I'll refer to these here as *traditional machine learning* to distinguish them from the third major stage, which has advanced significantly in the last several years: the development of deep learning-based methods—methods based on deep neural networks. This has been crucial in some areas; outlier detection with vision, text, or audio would not be possible without deep learning. All three forms of outlier detection now play a valuable role in analyzing data and searching for anomalies and will be covered in this book.

Since their development, machine learning-based approaches have drastically changed outlier detection with tabular and time-series data, allowing for much more computationally expensive but sophisticated and powerful techniques. The examples described earlier, such as fraud detection, network security, bot detection, and so on, would not be feasible without machine learning methods.

Methods for time-series and tabular data have been largely stable for years. There have been steady, small improvements, but they have been fundamentally stable. As such, traditional machine learning-based outlier detection methods may also be considered reasonably mature. They have been used widely for many years, and we have a decent sense of their power and their limitations.

Where we have the most opportunity to improve traditional machine learning-based outlier detection with tabular data is with improving the collection and sharing of data. As outlier detection is based on data, it benefits from the explosion in data we are now producing and collecting. We now have a wealth of data to compare against, which allows us to develop a better sense of what is normal and what is not, which allows outlier detectors to be much more sensitive and accurate. A great deal of this data, though, is proprietary, owned by single organizations. The implication of this is larger organizations have the ability to perform outlier detection in a way smaller organizations cannot. Nevertheless, even smaller organizations can work with outlier detection in a very practical and useful way assuming a reasonable amount of data. For instance, there are many outlier detection algorithms available, and many of these are now well understood and have solid open-source implementations. So long as data is available, there are no real barriers to performing outlier detection.

As deep learning has advanced markedly in the last several years, largely focusing on vision and text, advances have spilled over to tabular, time-series, and network data, providing a new set of tools for these data modalities as well. While the preferred methods for tabular data remain traditional machine-learning methods, this may not always be true. With tabular data, we're starting to see deep learning methods become competitive with traditional methods, though they are much more computationally expensive and less interpretable. We may see further improvements in the near future, allowing them to surpass the current state of the art. I suspect, as would probably most, that most major advances in outlier detection in the next few years will be related to deep learning.

A major advantage of deep learning approaches is that they allow us to take advantage of much larger quantities of data that we could benefit from with traditional machine learning. Deep neural networks, by their nature, are able to continue to learn as larger and larger volumes of data are collected, while more traditional machine learning tools tend to level off at a certain point, learning little new information when given access to more data.

An area that has received some attention, though not as much as it deserves, is explainable artificial intelligence (XAI) for outlier detection. This is starting to improve as the need for XAI becomes more apparent and advances in XAI for predictive models are applied to outlier detection. It's an area we'll look into in this book. It's very important in many contexts as it answers the question: why did the outlier detector flag the items it flagged as anomalous?

1.6   *How does this book teach outlier detection?*

In this book, we'll go over in more detail what outliers are and how we can think about them. This is a more difficult question than we may suspect at first, but it is important to work through. We'll go through many coding examples, which will explain the concepts involved and how to apply them effectively for outlier detection. We'll cover a broad range of approaches, which should allow you to understand well the breadth of options available and be able to think even outside these, to other approaches where necessary. That is, we'll equip you with the knowledge to think through solutions to outlier detection problems even in the rare cases the standard tools aren't sufficient.

All examples are in Python, using some NumPy, pandas, and scikit-learn, though nothing advanced. If you're new to Python, you may want to check out chapters 3 to 6 of Manning's *Python for Data Science and Machine Learning* (https://mng.bz/4pVw). You may also wish to familiarize yourself, at least quickly, with NumPy and pandas if you have not already. Some background in statistics is also useful, but we assume only an understanding of basic concepts such as normal distributions, means, medians, and standard deviations. No other background is necessary, and we're assuming no previous knowledge of outlier detection.

The book starts with statistical methods, covers traditional machine learning, and finally covers deep learning approaches, applied to tabular data as well as to text, image, and time-series data. The book covers combining detectors into ensembles of detectors, evaluating outlier detection, applying XAI techniques to outlier detection, and running ongoing outlier detection projects.

We'll give you the background to develop your own outlier detection code where necessary but will focus on established open-source libraries, particularly scikit-learn and PyOD. These include the state-of-the-art models and will be, at least with tabular data, the ones you would use the most frequently.

Summary

- Outlier detection is an area of unsupervised machine learning, which involves extracting information and patterns from unlabeled data.
- Outliers are items significantly different from the majority of other items to which they can be compared.
- Outlier detection is a highly subjective notion with no precise definition, but it is nevertheless very useful.
- Outliers are not necessarily problems or interesting items, but usually problems and interesting items are outliers, making outlier detection a very useful process.
- Outlier detection can be applied to tabular data, images, text, video, audio, network, and other types of data.
- Outlier detection is used now in many fields and is likely applicable in many more.
- Python provides a rich set of tools for outlier detection.

Simple outlier detection 2

This chapter covers

- Statistical methods to find outliers in single columns
- More flexible methods based on histograms, kernel density estimation, and nearest neighbors measurements
- Methods to combine scores from multiple statistical tests
- An introduction to multidimensional outliers

In this chapter, we begin to take a look at specific methods to identify outliers. We start with statistical methods, defined here simply as methods that predate machine learning methods and that are based on statistical descriptions of data distributions, such as standard deviations and interquartile ranges. They are designed specifically to find extreme values, the unusually small and large values in sequences of numeric values. These are the easiest outlier tests to understand and provide a good background for the machine learning-based approaches we will focus on later. Statistical methods do have some significant limitations. They work on single columns of data and often don't extend well to tables. They also often assume specific data distributions, typically that the data is Gaussian, or at least nearly. At the same time, these methods are simpler to understand than methods we will look at later, but they still introduce well some of the complications inherent with outlier detection.

Another reason to look at statistical methods is that they are often sufficient to identify the outliers in a dataset, or at least the most significant outliers. For example, if a table contains several extremely small or large values, then the rows containing these are likely to be the most unusual rows in the table, and it may not be necessary to search for more subtle outliers.

Identifying the extreme values will also allow us to remove these before performing further outlier detection. Occasionally datasets have a few extreme values that overwhelm everything else, and it can often be worthwhile to check a dataset quickly for these values before going on to more thorough outlier detection, setting these aside as known outliers.

Within a table, each column will have a specific datatype, usually numeric, categorical, string, or date (or time or datetime). Categorical columns contain nonnumeric values that have no natural order. These are usually string values, but I'm distinguishing these from string columns, treating categorical features as having relatively low cardinality (a small set of distinct values, each repeated many times). A string column, on the other hand, tends to have longer text, and generally each value is unique. Table 2.1 shows an example of a table of staff expenses. The Staff ID, Department, and Account columns are examples of categorical columns, while the Amount column is numeric.

Table 2.1   Staff expenses

Row	Staff ID	Department	Account	Date of expense	Date submitted	Time submitted	Amount
1	9000483	Sales	Meals	02/03/2023	02/03/2023	09:10:21	12.44
2	9303332	Marketing	Travel	02/03/2023	02/03/2023	10:43:35	41.90
3	9847421	Engineering	Meals	02/03/2023	02/03/2023	10:56:04	643.99
4	9303332	Marketing	Supplies	02/03/2023	02/03/2023	11:12:09	212.00

For now we'll look primarily at the two most common types of data in tabular data—numeric and categorical—covering date and string values in chapter 9. There are statistical tests for numeric data, which may be applied to each numeric column, and tests for categorical data, which may be applied to each categorical column.

2.1   *One-dimensional numeric outliers*

The simplest form of outliers are one-dimensional outliers—that is, values that are unusual with respect to their column (simply considering each column as an unordered sequence of values) without considering any other columns. With numeric columns, these are usually the very large and very small values. In the Amount column of table 2.1, for example, the value 643.99 may be considered an outlier relative to that column if it is significantly larger than other values in that column.

2.1.1   *z-score*

Given a sorted sequence of values—say, 0, 1, 1, 1, 4, 5, 5, 6, 9, 34—it's straightforward to determine that 34 is unusually large. But how can we formalize this? Is there a set of guidelines we can use that will work generally on any sequence of numbers?

The simplest approaches are to flag any values over a predefined threshold or to flag any above a predefined percentile. In this example, we may set a fixed threshold value of, say, 20. This approach is not strictly data-driven, but realistically it would be based on our previous experience with similar data so would have some empirical basis. This can work well in many situations where we have reliable knowledge about what data to expect. This does, though, break down if we don't yet have a good baseline for what should be considered normal.

Using a predefined percentile, we could choose to select any in the top, say, 1% of values. Again, this would work well in some cases but would fail here as there are well under 100 items; it would also fail where the values are all fairly similar, with no real outliers. In that case, it would flag the top 1% of items, regardless of how normal or abnormal they are. Also, in cases where there are outliers, there may be a logical cutoff in the data, as with the case of 34 in our previous example, where we can reasonably say some values are outliers and the rest are not. If we choose a percentile without examining the data, the percentile chosen may be before the logical cutoff, resulting in some inliers being reported as outliers, or after the natural cutoff, resulting in some outliers being missed.

To address some of these issues, we can use the z-score test, which learns from the data itself which values are unusual relative to the others. This is very commonly used, and if you're familiar with any of the methods described here, chances are it's the z-score. Given a set of numeric values, we calculate the z-score of each value as the number of standard deviations from the mean. The z-score of each value is calculated as

$$\text{z-score} = \frac{\text{value} - \text{mean}}{\text{std dev}}$$

In the previous example, the mean is 6.6; the std dev is 10.04; and the z-scores of each item are –0.66, –0.56, –0.56, –0.56, –0.26, –0.16, –0.16, –0.06, 0.24, 2.73.

Using the z-score test, we identify any values where the absolute value of the z-score is over a given threshold. This does require setting a threshold, but as z-scores are unitless and widely used, we can draw on our experience using them in many other places. A common threshold is 3.0, though this is simply a convention, and other thresholds may suit your needs better. In this case, using 3.0 would flag none of the values, though 34 (with a z-score of 2.73) is close and would likely be flagged given a larger dataset if most values are still in the 0.0 to 10.0 range.

Figure 2.1 shows a set of ideal distributions: Gaussian, exponential, and beta, as well as one real-world distribution from the publicly available datasets on OpenML (https://openml.org), the Whole_weight column from the abalone dataset. This appears to have a roughly log-normal distribution, which is common in real-world data (log-normal distributions are somewhat similar to normal distributions but are more skewed so not symmetric, with longer tails to the right). The plots include vertical lines marking the thresholds where values would be flagged as outliers, using z-scores below −3.0 and above 3.0. Although z-scores may be applied to any distribution, the method does assume the data is reasonably close to a Gaussian distribution.

With asymmetric distributions such as beta or log-normal distributions, the coefficients used for upper limits may not be appropriate for lower limits. In the case of log-normal distributions, we may wish to take the log of all values and treat the data as normal before testing for outliers. In the case of exponential distributions with no negative values, there is no concept of unusually small values and only very large may be tested for.

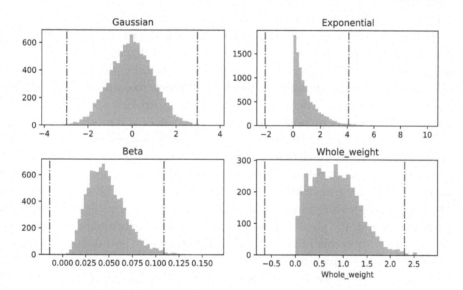

Figure 2.1 Four distributions with vertical lines indicating the points +/− 3.0 standard deviations from the mean

SWAMPING AND MASKING

A major issue with the z-score method is that it's not robust to outliers. The presence of outliers in the data affects the estimation of the mean and standard deviation and so affects the ability to find other outliers. Specifically, the z-score method allows for masking and swamping effects. See figure 2.2, which represents a single sequence of values in a swarm plot.

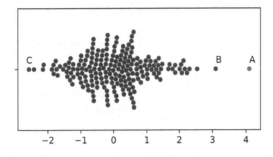

Figure 2.2   A swarm plot with at least one outlier, point A. Depending on the presence of A, points B and C may or may not be flagged as outliers, as A can affect the mean and standard deviation.

Masking occurs where the presence of one or more outliers causes other values to not be recognized as outliers, as the more extreme outliers skew the mean and standard deviations calculated. This is shown in figure 2.2, where point B is not flagged as an outlier but would be if A were not present. Swamping is the opposite effect: point A swamps point C here, as C is considered an outlier only given A in the dataset. Again, the extreme outlier affects the mean and standard deviation, this time such that values on the other side of the mean are more readily flagged as outliers.

Though the effects of swamping and masking can be particularly strong with z-score calculations, the effects may be seen with most outlier detection tools: the presence of outliers can undermine the ability to properly identify other outliers. Most other methods in common usage, though, are much more robust to outliers. We should be aware of these effects in outlier detection generally but particularly where we use means and standard deviations in our work. Although more robust and more general options are available, z-scores do have the appeal of simplicity, as well as a long history, so they will probably be in use for some time.

A similar but more robust measure uses the trimmed mean, where the mean and standard deviation are calculated after removing the top and bottom, for example, 1% of values, ideally leaving a more representative set, with the outliers removed. Alternatively, to deal with the possible presence of outliers, we may iteratively remove outliers one at a time (or in small batches), recalculate the mean and standard deviation, and continue with the remaining data. This, as you may assume, is prohibitive on large datasets and unnecessary with more modern outlier detection approaches. Outlier detection is often an iterative process, and often outliers are removed from a dataset to create a cleaner set to establish normal data more effectively, but iteratively removing in this manner (to identify one outlier at a time) is now seldom done.

EXPECTED AND UNEXPECTED OUTLIERS

For any given distribution, we can think of the outliers as being of two types. Some values are extreme but only to the extent we would expect to see, and some values are much more extreme than we would expect to see even once. Height, for example, follows a normal distribution. In most contexts, a record of a person having a height over 7' would be an outlier, but an outlier that would be expected given enough data points. A height of 70', on the other hand, is impossible and could only be a data error. With many distributions, including normal, values can only reach a certain distance from the mean.

In data science, we rarely assume any specific distribution in the data, but where data is reasonably believed to be Gaussian (the data appears to be unimodal, symmetric, and roughly bell-shaped), this does have the nice property that probabilities are associated with each z-score, and we can use these to help set appropriate thresholds given the context. Similarly, for example with log-normal distributions, we have established knowledge of the probabilities associated with each distance from the mean.

With other distributions as well, there are expected and unexpected values: there are extreme values that would be rare and considered outliers but are conceivable, and there are points beyond that that are either data errors or that indicate that our understanding of the data is incorrect. In fact, if we find any unexpected outliers, after examining these we may find that they are not data errors and such values are actually possible. A useful side effect of outlier detection is it can improve our understanding of what is conceivable in the data.

Given that we do not know the true distributions and must infer these from the data, we don't know which types of outliers we have when we encounter them, though in some cases we would be more interested in unexpected outliers, values beyond what may be normally presumed possible. In some cases, these may be possible to distinguish given some domain knowledge. Where it is possible to distinguish these, flagging only them will reduce overreporting and may flag only the truly interesting values. However, more often we are interested in any outliers in the data and, with respect to setting a threshold, are motivated more by balancing false positives and false negatives than distinguishing types of outliers; however, the distinction is also often very important.

If we are interested in flagging only values that are beyond what would be expected to ever occur in the data, where we do not have knowledge of any natural limits, only the data itself, we need to estimate the underlying distribution and take the data size into account. Given a Gaussian distribution, for example, and using an absolute z-score of 3.0 as the cutoff, we expect about 1 in every 370 observations to be beyond this. With Gaussian data, in a sample of 1,000 observations, we would expect about 3 values beyond 3.0 standard deviations, with even more being fairly likely. With large enough datasets, we would expect some values even 5 or 6 standard deviations from the mean, but with only 1,000 observations, we would not, and such values are more noteworthy. However, if any such values are found, this does not necessarily imply data artifacts or other unexpected anomalies; it is more likely that the estimate of the distribution was incorrect.

2.1.2 *Interquartile range*

A preferred, and also very standard, method to identify extreme values uses the interquartile range (IQR). The main appeal of IQR is that it is much more robust to outliers than z-scores. Like z-scores, the IQR method finds values far from the average, relative to the normal variance of the data, though it uses median for the average, as opposed to mean, and IQR for the variance, instead of standard deviation.

To calculate the IQR, we first calculate the first and third quartiles (that is, the values at the 25th and 75th percentiles). We then subtract these to get the IQR. See figure 2.3 (left). This indicates the quartiles as Q1 and Q3 and also shows the calculated thresholds for outliers.

The thresholds for outliers are defined as Q1 – (2.2 × IQR) and Q3 + (2.2 × IQR). The coefficient of 2.2 is now fairly standard, but other values may be used. In fact, John Tukey, who developed the test, used 1.5, and this was the norm for some time and is still often used. To calculate the thresholds, we can use code such as

```
import pandas as pd
import numpy as np

data = pd.Series(np.random.normal(size=10_000))
q1 = data.quantile(0.25)
q3 = data.quantile(0.75)
iqr = q3 - q1
iqr_lower_limit = q1 - (2.2 * iqr)
iqr_upper_limit = q3 + (2.2 * iqr)
```

Variations on the interquartile range are sometimes used, with a common one being the interdecile range (IDR). See figure 2.3 (right). Here, the IDR is calculated as D9 (the 9th decile, or 90th percentile) minus D1 (the 1st decile, or 10th percentile), with outliers defined as D1 – Φ IDR and D9 + Φ IDR. As with the IQR, coefficients (indicated here as Φ) may be used to avoid under- or overreporting, but a coefficient of 1.0 works reasonably well.

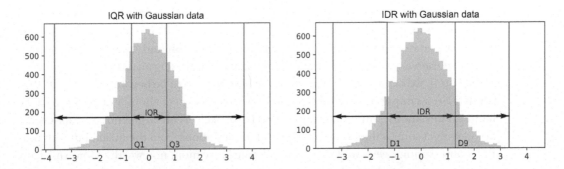

Figure 2.3   Gaussian data showing the IQR (on the left) and IDR (on the right), along with vertical lines indicating the points beyond which values would be considered outliers based on the IQR with a coefficient of 2.2 or the IDR with a coefficient of 1.0

2.1.3   *Median absolute deviation*

The median absolute deviation (MAD) is another measure of spread, similar to the IQR and more robust, again, to outliers. Though implementations are available, including in the popular SciPy library, the algorithm is simple, and I provide code to calculate this in listing 2.1. To get the MAD for a set of data, we first calculate the median for the data. We then take, for every point, the absolute difference from the median, and then take the median of these differences.

To determine if a point is an outlier using the MAD, we calculate how far the point is from the median (using the absolute difference). We then divide this by the MAD to determine how far from the median it is relative to the other points in the data. This gives us the MAD score for the point, which is the ratio of this point's deviation from the median to the normal deviation. To determine if a point is an outlier, we check if the MAD score is over a prespecified threshold. In this example, we again use the abalone dataset, with one inserted outlier, with a value of 4.0.

Listing 2.1 Calculating the MAD

```
import pandas as pd
import numpy as np
import statistics
from sklearn.datasets import fetch_openml
import matplotlib.pyplot as plt
```
Defines a general method to calculate the MAD for a list of data
```
def calc_MAD(data):
    median = statistics.median(data)
    deviations = [abs(x - median) for x in data]
    median_deviation = statistics.median(deviations)
    mad_scores = [abs(x - median) / median_deviation for x in data]
    return mad_scores
```
Collects the data
```
data = fetch_openml("abalone", version=1, parser='auto')
data = pd.DataFrame(data.data, columns=data.feature_names)

fig, ax = plt.subplots(nrows=1, ncols=3, figsize=(10, 3))
```
Plots the actual data
```
pd.Series(data['Whole_weight']).hist(bins=50, ax=ax[0])
ax[0].set_title("Whole_weight")
```
Plots the distribution of MAD scores
```
mad_scores = calc_MAD(data['Whole_weight'])
pd.Series(mad_scores).hist(bins=50, ax=ax[1])
ax[1].set_title("Distribution of MAD Scores")
```
Adds an outlier to the data
```
mad_scores = calc_MAD(np.concatenate([data['Whole_weight'], [4.0]]))
pd.Series(mad_scores).hist(bins=50, ax=ax[2])
ax[2].set_title("MAD Scores given an outlier")
```
Replots the distribution of MAD scores
```
plt.tight_layout()
plt.show()
```

Figure 2.4 presents the distribution values (left), of scores using the MAD calculation (center), and scores given an inserted outlier (right). There is a steady decrease in MAD scores as points become further from the median, with the outlier standing out with a score over 8.5. Often scores of 3.0 are used as the threshold for outliers, but this can vary.

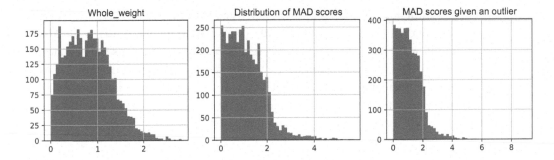

Figure 2.4   The distribution of MAD scores with and without one inserted outlier. The outlier receives the highest MAD score, slightly over 8.5.

2.1.4   *Modified z-score*

The modified z-score is generally considered a variation on the z-score but is actually much more similar to the MAD:

$$\text{modified z-score} = \frac{0.6745\,(\text{value} - \text{median})}{\text{MAD}}$$

The coefficient, 0.6745, is used to make the formula equivalent to the z-score for Gaussian data, as 0.675 is the 0.75^{th} quantile of the standard normal distribution. With the modified z-score, usually 3.0 or 3.5 is used as the threshold.

2.1.5   *Visualization for numeric outliers*

Examining plots, even without the previously discussed methods or other statistical methods, is actually a simple form of outlier detection in itself, where outliers are identified visually. This is less precise and more labor-intensive than statistical methods but can be good enough when there's a small number of series to examine. It does exacerbate the subjective nature of outlier detection, but it can also be more flexible when we are faced with unusual distributions. Figure 2.5 shows several distributions from OpenML datasets: att1 from the mfeat-karhunen table, A14 from credit-approval, Dattr from satimage, and Feature_9 from vowel. Visually examining these, one sensible choice may be to set 1,300 (or a similar value) as the threshold for A14 and to determine the others do not contain outliers. However, visualization is not intended to be precise, and different people looking at the same data will draw different thresholds.

It is also often useful to examine the data using a log scales, as this can provide another useful view of the data, especially as many real-world datasets are log-normal in nature.

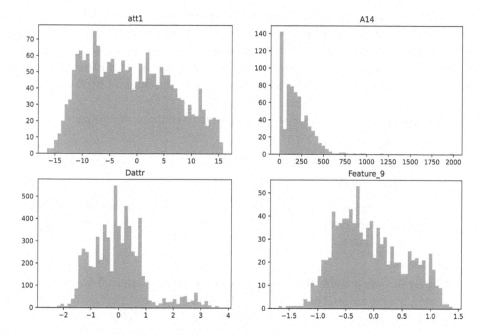

Figure 2.5   Examples of real-world data distributions

2.1.6   *Internal and external outliers*

The statistical methods discussed previously are intended to identify extreme values and will miss another type of outlier we may be interested in, known as *internal outliers*. See figure 2.6, which shows the hue-mean feature from the segment dataset on OpenML as an example. Internal outliers are less common than extreme values, as they can appear only in multimodal distributions or distributions with gaps. These do, though, occur fairly often, and the previously discussed methods, as they assume a single average and single variance, are not intended for multimodal distributions.

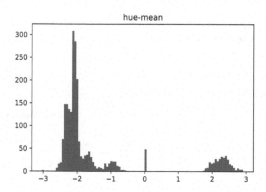

Figure 2.6   The hue-mean feature is bimodal and contains some values between the two main clusters, close to zero, which may be considered internal outliers.

While in some cases you may be interested only in external outliers (extreme values), in other cases, you may be interested in any unusual values. In fact, as extreme values can often be expected to some extent, internal outliers may actually be more interesting. For example, in a company where most purchases are for small items, in the $10 range, or larger items, in the $500 range, a rare purchase of $100 could stand out as unusual: quite likely legitimate but unusual.

There are a number of ways to detect internal outliers, including

- Histograms
- Kernel density estimation (KDE)
- Nearest neighbors calculations

These three methods are more flexible to unusual distributions than the previous methods and are often preferable generally, though each of z-score, IQR, and MAD are well used as well.

HISTOGRAMS

Histograms are possibly the easiest method to identify internal outliers and are useful generally with unusual distributions. The idea of histograms is to divide the space into a set of equal-width bins and calculate the count of each bin. This provides a concise description of any arbitrary distribution and can be used to determine outlier values; we may determine which bins have unusually low counts and flag any values within those bins as outliers. As most distributions have the lowest counts at their extremes, this tends to flag values in the left-most and right-most bins but, where appropriate, can flag bins in the middle as well. Using histograms does require determining an appropriate number of bins, which can be challenging.

An example using histograms is shown in listing 2.2. This uses panda's cut() method to create the bins, using 10 bins. For simplicity, it flags any bins with a count under 10. Pandas also provides a qcut() method, which provides equal-count bins. This is often useful as well; though it will provide bins with an equal number of items and the count method we are using here cannot be used, it is also possible to find the unusually sparse regions by comparing the bin widths.

Listing 2.2   Using histograms to identify outliers

```
import pandas as pd
from sklearn.datasets import fetch_openml
import statistics
import matplotlib.pyplot as plt

data = fetch_openml('segment', version=1, parser='auto')     ◁── Collects the data
data = pd.DataFrame(data.data, columns=data.feature_names)

histogram = pd.cut(
        data['hue-mean'], bins=10, retbins=True)[0]    ◁── Creates a histogram to represent one of the columns
counts = histogram.value_counts().sort_index()      ◁── Gets the count of values in each bin
```

```
rare_ranges = []
for v in counts.index:
    count = counts[v]
    if count < 10:
        rare_ranges.append(str(v))

rare_values = []
for i in range(len(data)):
    if str(histogram[i]) in rare_ranges:
        rare_values.append(data['hue-mean'][i])

fig, ax = plt.subplots()
plt.hist(data['hue-mean'], bins=10, density=True)
for rare_value in rare_values:
    ax.axvline(rare_value, color='red', linestyle='-.')
plt.xticks([statistics.mean([x.left, x.right]) for x in counts.index])
ax.set_xticklabels(range(10))
plt.show()
```

⟵ Creates a list of the bins with few values

⟵ Creates a list of the values in the bins with few values

⟵ Draws a red vertical line at the position of each outlier

Figure 2.7 displays the histogram. This is the same data as in figure 2.6 but fit into 10 bins. From the histogram, we can see the relative frequency of each bin. Bin 1 has many records, and values here would be strong inliers. Bins 4, 6, and 7 have few records, and values here can likely be considered outliers. Values in bin 0 may be mild outliers. Figure 2.7 also draws a dashed vertical line at each point in the data that is flagged as an outlier using the code in listing 2.2 (this flags records appearing in bins with counts under 10). We can see it flagged the internal outliers but missed the external outliers. This can be adjusted by using different numbers of bins and a more robust calculation of the threshold than a predefined value.

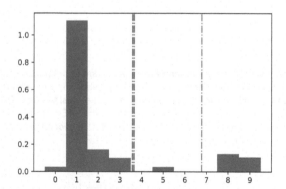

Figure 2.7 The segment data divided into 10 histogram bins. The x-axis indicates the bins. The height of each bar indicates the number of records in the bin. Dashed vertical lines indicate values flagged as outliers: those in bins with unusually low counts. We can see a number of outliers in bin 4 and in bin 7 (both bins with quite low counts). Bin 6 has no records and so no outliers. This method can identify internal outliers though it is sensitive to the number of bins.

KDE

KDE works similarly to histograms, but instead of dividing the space into bins, it attempts to estimate the density as a continuous function at each point along the number line. To calculate the KDE, the algorithm creates a small kernel, which is a small shape such as a triangle, box, or Gaussian where each datapoint is located. These are then summed up vertically along the range. So where there are several data points close to each other, their kernels will overlap, and when summed together, this region will have high probability density estimates. In more sparse regions, where there are few points, only a small number of kernels will be summed together, giving low probability estimates. Where there are no datapoints, there will be no kernels, and the probability estimate will be zero. This is more robust than histograms, as it is based on many small kernels, each centered on a data point, as opposed to a relatively small set of bins. It also avoids the need to set the number of bins, though it is sensitive to the width of the kernels used.

An example is shown in figure 2.8 using KDE to estimate the distribution given 10 points (drawn along the x-axis). The three panes show examples using three different widths for the kernels. In each case, a Gaussian is drawn, centered on each point, so there are 10 Gaussians. These are summed to give the KDE estimate, shown as the dashed line in each case. The wider the bandwidth (the width of each kernel), the smoother the final KDE. In the left pane, a narrow bandwidth is used, and the final KDE is variable. The middle pane uses a wider bandwidth and the right pane a bandwidth that is wider still, which results in a very smooth KDE—likely too smooth, as it loses any sense of the sparse regions between the points.

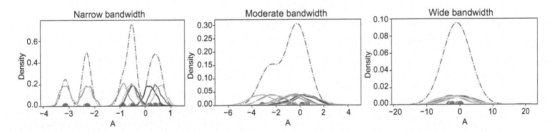

Figure 2.8 Given a dataset, here containing 10 points, KDE can estimate the distribution by creating a small kernel—in this case, a Gaussian shape—at each point and summing these. The three panes show the effect of adjusting the widths of the kernel. With narrow kernels, there is less summing of the kernels; the final KDE estimate resembles the individual kernels and fits the data tightly. With wider kernels, the KDE estimate becomes smoother. We wish to find a balance with an appropriate bandwidth. In this case, the first or second panes or somewhere in between may work best.

The code in the following listing gives an example of plotting a histogram using seaborn, which has an option to include a KDE estimate of the distribution.

Listing 2.3   Seaborn histplots with KDE enabled

```
import pandas as pd
from sklearn.datasets import fetch_openml
import matplotlib.pyplot as plt
```

```
import seaborn as sns

data = fetch_openml('segment', version=1, parser='auto')
data = pd.DataFrame(data.data, columns=data.feature_names)
sns.histplot(data['hue-mean'], kde=True)
plt.show()
```

The output is shown in figure 2.9. The KDE is a smooth, continuous estimation of the distribution.

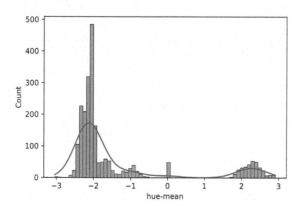

Figure 2.9 Using seaborn to draw a KDE estimate of a data series

An example using KDE for outlier detection is provided in listing 2.4. We use the `KernelDensity` class provided by scikit-learn, and Gaussian as the kernel shape. Once we create a `KernelDensity` object, we can use it to estimate the density at any point along the line, which we do for each point in the data.

Once we have a KDE estimate for each data point, we again have the challenge of determining which of these are unusually low. In this example, we take the IQR of the scores. This is an example of another important application of statistical methods; they are often used to identify the unusually large scores produced by other outlier detection tools.

Listing 2.4 Using KDE to identify outliers

```
import pandas as pd
from sklearn.datasets import fetch_openml
from sklearn.neighbors import KernelDensity
import matplotlib.pyplot as plt                           ┐ Collects
                                                          │ the data
data = fetch_openml('segment', version=1, parser='auto')  ◄──┘
data = pd.DataFrame(data.data, columns=data.feature_names)   ┐ Creates a KDE
                                                             │ estimate of
X = data['hue-mean'].values.reshape(-1,1)                 ◄──┘ one feature
kde = KernelDensity(kernel='gaussian', bandwidth=0.2).fit(X)
kde_scores = pd.Series(kde.score_samples(X))
```

```
q1 = kde_scores.quantile(0.25)
q3 = kde_scores.quantile(0.75)
iqr = q3 - q1
threshold = q1 - (2.2 * iqr)
rare_values = [data['hue-mean'][x] for x in range(len(data))
               if kde_scores[x] < threshold]

fig, ax = plt.subplots()
plt.hist(data['hue-mean'], bins=200)
for rare_value in rare_values:
    ax.axvline(rare_value, color='red', linestyle='-.')
plt.show()
```

Calculates a threshold for KDE estimates using IQR

Draws the distribution of the data

Draws vertical lines at each point in a region with an unusually low KDE estimate

Figure 2.10 shows the points identified as outliers using this method, drawing vertical bars at these points.

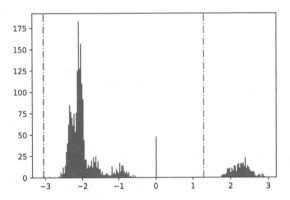

Figure 2.10   Data from the segment data set with outliers found using KDE scores shown with dashed vertical lines. The outliers are in low-density areas, far from most other data.

K-NEAREST NEIGHBORS

The k-nearest neighbors (KNN) method is based on the idea that outliers are farther from most other points than is normal. To identify outliers, KNN measures the distance from each point to the set of points nearest to it. It doesn't normally consider the distance of each point to all other points, as this is computationally expensive and actually may not work well in all distributions. It instead calculates the distance to a small number, defined as k, other points. The reasoning is: if there are two points close to each other but very far from the majority of other points, we'd probably still consider them outliers, even though they each have one other point they are close to—similarly for a group of three or four points. But if a point is close to many other points, we would likely consider it an inlier. In the segment dataset, there are 2,310 points in total, so if a point is close to 100 other points, it may reasonably be considered an inlier, even without calculating its distance to the 2,210 other points—similarly (probably) for a point close to 50 other records. What threshold we set is a judgment call. In listing 2.5, we set k to 25.

To implement this, we use a data structure provided by scikit-learn called `BallTree`, which is an efficient structure to calculate and store the distances between each pair of points in a dataset. Here we simply provide the `BallTree` the full dataset and then call `query()` to get the pairwise distances. The `query()` method returns, for all points, an array of distances to their k nearest points. It also returns the indexes of the nearest neighbors, but for this task, we just need the distances. We set k = 26, as the `query()` method will always return an array with the first element representing the distance of the point to itself, which will always be zero; as we're interested in the distance to 25 other points, we set k one higher.

Given the array of distances, we wish to convert this into a single number, which will represent the outlierness of the point. Usually, to do this, we take either the mean or max distance, though other functions are sometimes used as well. In this case, we use the max function, which means we're calculating the distance to the kth nearest point for each point. Doing this, we're actually using a distance metric sometimes referred to as *kth-nearest neighbor* (k[th]NN). Here a point close to even 24 points, but far from its 25th closest neighbor, would receive a high score. Given this, if there are any small, isolated clusters, with 1 to 24 points, the points in them will receive high outlier scores. But any larger clusters (of 25 or more points) will receive low scores.

Listing 2.5 Using k nearest neighbors to identify outliers

```
import pandas as pd
from sklearn.datasets import fetch_openml
from sklearn.neighbors import BallTree

data = fetch_openml('segment', version=1, parser='auto')      Creates a BallTree
data = pd.DataFrame(data.data, columns=data.feature_names)     and calculates the
X = data['hue-mean'].values.reshape(-1, 1)                     distances between
tree = BallTree(X, leaf_size=2)                                each pair of records
dist, ind = tree.query(X, k=26)                         Retrieves the distances to
max_dist_arr = pd.Series([max(x) for x in dist])        the 25 nearest neighbors
                                                        for each record
```

For each record, finds the distance
to the 25th nearest neighbor

As with histogram counts and KDE estimates, this returns a set of scores that are well ranked but aren't immediately interpretable, and it's not clear what the best cutoff is. Figure 2.11 (left) shows the distribution of k[th]NN scores. To save space, we did not show the distribution of scores for the histograms or KDE scores, but normally we would examine the distribution of scores for any outlier test. As is normal, most scores are close to zero, as most points are not outliers. It is difficult to see the full distribution, so we focus just on the tail in the center plot by drawing only those records with a k[th]NN score over 0.05. Here we can see a reasonable cutoff probably around 0.2. Using this, the final set of values flagged are shown in the right plot.

A similar approach to k-nearest neighbors (KNN) is to cluster the data and flag any points far from the nearest cluster center. In fact, k-means clustering is a quite similar algorithm, used for clustering, as is KNN, used for prediction; $k^{th}NN$ may be viewed as the outlier detection version of these.

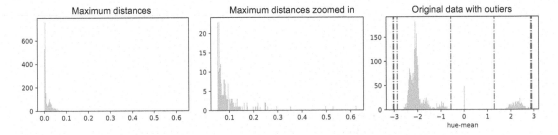

Figure 2.11   The distribution of scores using KNN with k = 26 (left), the scores again, showing only those over 0.05 for clarity (center), and the locations of outlier values based on the KNN scores (right)

2.1.7   Scoring outliers

As opposed to setting a threshold and providing a binary label (inlier/outlier) for each value, we could instead simply give each value a score. In the previous methods, this is straightforward: we simply return the z-score, KDE estimate, and so on depending on the method used. It is then up to the consumer of the outlier detection routine to choose a suitable threshold if binary labels are needed. This can be a useful approach and is what is done by most machine learning outlier detectors. An obvious benefit of this is that calling routines receive a ranked order of the outliers, and so some sense of their outlierness, even where their scores aren't easily interpretable. Another benefit is it can facilitate combining the scores of many detectors, as is very common in outlier detection. Using the scores, we have more information to work with.

We now have a decent introduction to outlier detection with sequences of numeric values and are ready to take a look at categorical columns.

2.2   One-dimensional categorical outliers: Rare values

Categorical columns are actually treated quite a bit differently than numeric columns, and you may find them a little easier or a little trickier to work with. The goal is to find values that are unusually rare. Unlike numeric features, there is no concept of internal outliers, so we are simply looking for values that are both rare and rarer than most other values.

Instead of working with each individual value, we work with the counts of each distinct value. Let's take a look at the distributions of a few categorical features from the SpeedDating table on OpenML, the dining, age_o, importance_same_religion, and pref_o_attractive columns, shown in figure 2.12. These have a bar for each unique value (the specific values are not listed here), sorted from most to least frequent, and display the count of each on the y-axis. These are fairly representative of the sort of shapes we see with real-world data, with a significant difference between the most and least frequent classes. More uniform distributions are rare, though they can be seen at times as well. Working with count values, there is no concept of clusters or gaps: there is simply a single count for each distinct value. We may, though, where the values are sorted, see significant drops in frequencies from one value to the next.

The question here is: where do we set a threshold: at what point do we say that any values having a count less than this threshold are outliers?

A naïve first approach may be to flag any value occurring less than some predefined number times, say with counts of 10 or less. This can work well where the counts of each value can be estimated well ahead of time but would not work in the general case where we do not know in advance how many of each distinct value to expect.

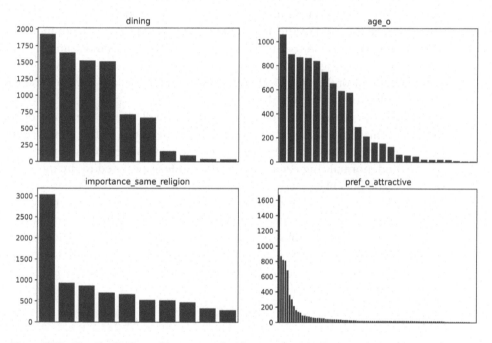

Figure 2.12   The distributions of four categorical features from the SpeedDating dataset

We could also consider flagging the N rarest values—say the three least-common values. This can also break down easily, as we cannot know ahead of time how many rare values there will be. In the cases shown in figure 2.12, we can see where this may under- or overreport for different distributions of counts. With importance_same_religion, for example, likely all of the values are reasonably common and none are outliers, making it odd to flag the N rarest values for any N. The others probably do have outliers, but there may not be any value of N that will work consistently for any distribution. Any overly simple system to set a threshold would likely break down for at least one of the four example distributions.

We could flag any value representing less than 1% of the rows. This has some appeal, as we likely do not wish to report any values occurring more than about 1% of the time, but it can overreport, as there may be numerous values with counts under 1%. In the pref_o_attractive case in figure 2.12, such a test may flag many values, possibly many more than we would wish. With features with higher cardinality, this problem becomes more common: there will be many values that are somewhat rare—so much so that having a rare value doesn't qualify a point as an outlier. If there are, say, 2,000 rows with 1,000 unique values, all about equally common, and so each with a count of about 2, this method may flag almost every value. We wish to flag values that are both rare and unusually rare. While those methods are intuitive, they do fail to work in the general case. We'll look next at some more viable options.

To start, we may calculate the number of unique values and then consider what the count would be for each value if these were evenly distributed. Doing this, for each value, we take the ratio of the actual count over the count expected under a uniform distribution. This gives a useful normalized score for each value, similar to the count but in a more meaningful format. It does still require a threshold if we wish to label each value as inlier or outlier, but, as this is a unitless value, we may set a general threshold, not dependent on the current data.

We may also compute the count of each value relative to the count of the mode value. This may appear unstable, as it relies on the count of the most frequent value being meaningful, but it actually works fairly well. This method is similar to the previous method, normalizing each value by the mode as opposed to the mean. Using the median is also possible.

Another approach is to evaluate the cumulative counts. We start by sorting the unique values from least to most frequent and then calculate the cumulative sum (the sum of all smaller counts plus the current count) for each value. We then flag values under some threshold, such as 1%. This is a robust method that often works quite well. An example is provided in listing 2.6 using the age_o feature and 0.5% as the threshold for the cumulative count.

Listing 2.6   Determining the count threshold for outliers using cumulative counts

```
import pandas as pd
import numpy as np
from sklearn.datasets import fetch_openml
import matplotlib.pyplot as plt
import seaborn as sns

data = fetch_openml('SpeedDating', version=1, parser='auto')      ← Collects the data
data = pd.DataFrame(data.data, columns=data.feature_names)

col_name = 'age_o'                                                 Fills null values
data[col_name] = \
    data[col_name].fillna(data[col_name].median()).\
        astype(np.int64)                                           ← Gets the count of each unique value

vc = data[col_name].value_counts()                                 ←
```

```
cumm_frac = [vc.values[::-1][:x+1].sum() / len(data)
             for x in range(len(vc))]
cumm_frac = np.array(cumm_frac)
num_rare_vals = np.where(cumm_frac < 0.005)[0].max()
cut_off = vc.values[::-1][num_rare_vals]
min_count = vc[cut_off]
```
Gets the cumulative count of each unique value

Finds the values with low cumulative counts

```
plt.subplots(figsize=(10, 2))
s= sns.barplot(x=vc.index, y=vc.values, order=vc.index, color='blue')
s.axvline(len(vc) - num_rare_vals - 0.5)
s.set_title(col_name)
plt.show()
```

The results are shown in figure 2.13. This flags all values such that their cumulative sum is under 0.5%.

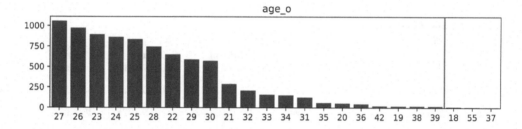

Figure 2.13 The counts of each value of age_o sorted most-to-least frequent, with a cutoff for unusual values calculated based on cumulative sums, drawn between the fourth and third last values

Another effective method is to apply a statistical test, such as MAD, to the set of counts and use this to flag any unusually small counts. This can break down, though, where there are very few distinct values, which can occur even in very large tables: the cardinality of some columns can be quite small. In these cases, setting a minimum percentage may be the most appropriate approach.

For more reliable solutions, we may wish to employ multiple checks—for example, requiring for any value to be flagged: a MAD score under a given threshold and its cumulative count also under a threshold.

2.3 Multidimensional outliers

The previously discussed techniques are useful to identify and score the unusual values within a single set of values. However, in data science we typically work with tables of data and wish to flag not unusual values but unusual rows. Outliers based on single features are an important element of finding unusual rows and are referred to as *univariate* outliers, but also very important are outliers based on multiple features, referred to as *multivariate* outliers. These are combinations of values that are not unusual on their own but their combination is rare. Nailing down univariate outliers, as we've seen, is surprisingly difficult—multivariate outliers are, as one might expect, even more so. This is due to several reasons, including that there is an explosion in the number of combinations to consider and that associations between the features need to be taken into consideration.

In the expenses in table 2.1 (repeated here as table 2.2), our goal is to identify not the unusual times, amounts, or accounts per se but the unusual purchases. Doing this requires assessing each of these features both individually and together. We may flag each of the rows shown due to having unusual single values (univariate outliers): unusual amounts, times, and so on, as shown in bold. We can also look for unusual combinations of values (multivariate outliers)—for example, dollar values that are normal generally but not normal for the account, or dollar values that are normal for the account, say meals, but not for the time of day, with lunch expenses possibly being normally more moderate than dinner expenses. In this example, we may have rows that are not unusual when considering any single, or even pair of features, but only when considering all three of account, time, and amount.

Table 2.2   Staff expenses

Row	Staff ID	Department	Account	Date of expense	Date submitted	Time submitted	Amount
1	**9000483**	Sales	Meals	02/03/2023	02/03/2023	09:10:21	12.44
2	9303332	Marketing	Travel	02/03/2023	02/03/2023	10:43:35	41.90
3	9847421	Engineering	Meals	02/03/2023	02/03/2023	10:56:04	**643.99**
4	9303332	Marketing	**Supplies**	02/03/2023	02/03/2023	**21:12:09**	212.00

2.3.1   *Types of multidimensional outliers*

Given a table, there are, ultimately, only two reasons to flag a row:

- The row contains one or more unusual values.
- The row contains one or more unusual combinations of values.

That is, a row may contain univariate or multivariate outliers. In figure 2.14 we see a pair of scatter plots with the outlier values identified. In the left plot, point A has been flagged as having two univariate outlier values: it has an unusual value in both the x and y dimensions. In the right plot, point B has been flagged, though it has values that are unusual in neither the x nor the y dimensions, but the combination is rare. This sort of phenomenon can occur with categorical data as well. Imagine a table containing descriptions of animal species. There may be many rows for mammals and many for egg-laying species but only a small number (platypus and echidna) with that combination.

When working with tabular data, we may flag rows that have very rare single values or very rare combinations of values. We may also flag rows that have neither but do have several values that are moderately rare or several combinations of values that are moderately rare.

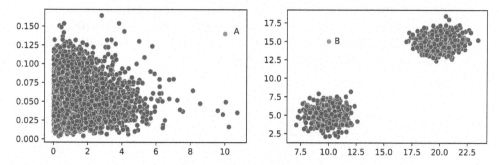

Figure 2.14 Point A is an example of an outlier in two single dimensions (left pane). Point B is an example of a rare combination of values (right pane).

2.3.2 *Visualization for multidimensional data*

As with one-dimensional data, a common method for identifying outliers in tables is visualization. The general approach is to look at each single feature as discussed previously, plotting numeric columns as histograms and categorical columns as bar plots and then also looking at each pair of features. Examining sets of three or more features in single plots is possible but more difficult and less common.

This does limit examination to unusual single values and unusual pairs of values, missing cases where there are unusual combinations of three or more features, so it is not recommended as the sole form of outlier detection in most cases; it can, however, be a good first step to identify any clear outliers. And, as with any data science project, it's useful to start with exploratory data analysis (EDA) to get a sense of the data and determine if there are any errors with the data before proceeding further. Good tools that provide this sort of visualization include Sweetviz (https://github.com/fbdesignpro /sweetviz) and Autoviz (https://github.com/AutoViML/AutoViz). To describe this in some more detail, though, we'll go through some quick examples ourselves.

Usually, for two categorical features we would use a heatmap, for two numeric features a scatterplot, and for one categorical and one numeric, a boxplot. Figure 2.15 shows examples of a heatmap and boxplot based on two pairs of features from the eucalyptus dataset on OpenML. With heatmaps, we can see any combinations that are nonzero but low compared to other combinations. For this plot, I colored the lowest values in the darkest shades and removed the zero counts for clarity.

Boxplots allow you to see anything unusual in either dimension: if one category is different from the others (having a different range or distribution of values in the numeric column) or if some numeric values in one category are unusual relative to that category.

One property of boxplots is that they include whiskers (the short, perpendicular ends to the lines), which indicate the extent of the inliers. That is, with boxplots, the decision as to which points are outliers has already been made. In seaborn, for example, the whiskers are drawn using an IQR-based threshold, using 1.5 as the coefficient. Any points outside this range are drawn as single dots. This is not entirely a negative, however, and having predefined thresholds allows more consistent and objective examination of the data. We have all manner of biases in how we think about data and how we look at plots that can affect our ability to determine what are outliers, and a consistent, predetermined threshold can be helpful.

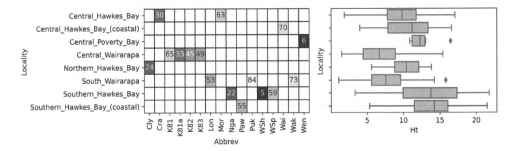

Figure 2.15   Examples of visualization for two-dimensions, with two categorical features (left) and one categorical and one numeric feature (right)

Boxplots can be misleading where the data is multimodal, as, with multiple modes (especially if the clusters are some distance apart), it is not meaningful to measure how far from the first or third quartile a point is. But, for unimodal data, they provide a useful, concise representation of the distribution.

In practice, visualizations are used more to understand and double-check the scores given by outlier detectors than to actually set the outlier scores for values. For example, we can see how the records with high scores compare to those with lower scores, at least within each two-dimensional view of the data. We should note, though, that this can be misleading where rows are flagged due to anomalies spanning three or more dimensions, which will not be possible to see in these plots.

2.4   *Rare combinations of categorical values*

With multiple categorical columns, we can apply the same techniques to identify unusual combinations as we do with single columns. See listing 2.7, which takes three categorical columns from the eucalyptus dataset and displays the count of each combination using the `value_counts()` method. Taking the list of counts, we can identify any that are unusually small.

Listing 2.7   Determining the counts for a pair of features

```
from sklearn.datasets import fetch_openml
import pandas as pd

data = fetch_openml('eucalyptus', version=1, parser='auto')
data = pd.DataFrame(data.data, columns=data.feature_names)
print(data[['Abbrev', 'Locality', 'Sp']].value_counts())
```

This outputs the count of each combination, ordered from most to least common:

```
Abbrev  Locality              Sp
Mor     Central_Hawkes_Bay    am    18
                              nd    15
Puk     South_Wairarapa       re    15
Mor     Central_Hawkes_Bay    te    12
Puk     South_Wairarapa       ov    12
                              ..
K82     Central_Wairarapa     pu     1
                              fr     1
                              el     1
K81a    Central_Wairarapa     br     1
Wen     Central_Poverty_Bay   te     1
```

2.4.1 *Rare combinations using their absolute count*

With single features, it is possible to encounter cases where there are enough rare values that it is not meaningful to flag any values as unusual. In extreme cases, even values with only a single count are common, so there is no sense of any values being unusually rare. While this can occur in single columns, it isn't the norm. With multiple columns, though, it can be much more likely.

However, this isn't as frequent in practice as might be expected. Where a table has, say, 5 categorical columns, each with a cardinality of 10, there are 10^5 (100,000) possible combinations. If all occur equally frequently, in a table of 1 million rows, we expect roughly 10 instances of each, with some natural variation, which can be modeled with a Poisson distribution. But generally with real-world data, many combinations will be far more frequent, and some will not occur at all, as in the heatmap of eucalyptus data. Many cases may be nonsensical combinations or just very unlikely. So the number of actually occurring combinations may be small enough that many have significant counts, and those with low counts can be meaningfully said to be outliers. The more features considered and the higher the cardinalities, however, the less true this will be.

2.4.2 *Combinations that are rare given their marginal probabilities*

We can, as we've been discussing, identify rare combinations simply by considering their counts relative to the counts of other combinations. This is a useful method, but there is also another method that may be used to identify outliers, albeit a different form of outliers, based on what are known as the *marginal probabilities* of each feature.

Simply taking the count of each combination will detect combinations that are rare for two reasons. Some are rare simply because all feature values involved are rare, so the combination is naturally rare as well (this is still clearly an outlier, as it contains multiple rare values). Others are rare in cases where all feature values are common but the combination is rare. These are strictly rare combinations and can be specifically detected using the marginal probabilities of each feature.

In table 2.3 we have two features: one with values A, B, C, D, and E and the other with values V, W, X, Y, and Z. The counts of each combination are given in the cells. The right-most column and bottom row (that is, the *margins*) give the overall counts for each value. In table 2.3, we see there are 975,257 rows in all and, for example, that there are 1,513 of these with value A in the first feature, 3,014 with value W in the second feature, and 2 with the combination of both. Given this combination of values is very rare, the two rows having this combination may be considered outliers, but these are not the second type of outlier—outliers considering marginal probabilities—as both A and W are rare, so the combination naturally is rare as well.

Table 2.3   Example data, showing the marginal counts for each value in two features

	A	B	C	D	E	Sum
V	1	2	10	500	1,000	1,513
W	2	4	8	1,000	2,000	3,014
X	10	20	200	5,000	10,000	15,230
Y	500	1,000	50,000	250,000	50,000	351,500
Z	1,000	2,000	100,000	500,000	1,000	604,000
Sum	1,513	3,026	150,218	756,500	64,000	975,257

From the counts in the margins of table 2.3 we can calculate the marginal probabilities (a complex term for a simple idea: it's just the probabilities for a feature not considering other features), which are shown in the margins of table 2.4, in the Fraction row and column. For example, there are 3,014 rows with value W in the second feature, which out of 975,257, is 0.003 as a fraction. Table 2.4 also contains the counts we would expect for each combination based on the marginal probabilities and the total count. This is found by multiplying the fractions together and multiplying this by the full row count. (This does require using the full fractions and not the rounded values shown here.)

Table 2.4   The counts we would estimate using the marginal probabilities

	A	B	C	D	E	Fraction
V	2.3	4.6	233.0	1,173.6	99.2	0.001
W	4.6	9.3	464.2	2,337.9	197.7	0.003
X	23.6	47.2	2,345.8	11,813.8	999.4	0.016
Y	545.3	1,090.6	54,141.2	272,656.0	23,066.7	0.360
Z	937.0	1,874.0	93,033.6	468,518.5	39,636.7	0.619
Fraction	0.001	0.003	0.154	0.776	0.066	1.000

Table 2.5 provides the ratio between the actual and expected values. Any that are unusually low (well below the expected ratio of 1.0), such as the combination of E and Z in this example, with a ratio of 0.02, may be flagged as an outlier of this type. As the count is still fairly high, at 1,000, we may wish to flag only combinations that are both rare and rarer than expected given the marginal probabilities, such as the combination of C and V, with a count of 10 and ratio of actual to expected of 0.04.

Table 2.5   The ratio between the actual and expected counts

	A	B	C	D	E
V	0.42	0.42	0.04	0.42	10.07
W	0.42	0.42	0.01	0.42	10.11
X	0.42	0.42	0.08	0.42	10.00
Y	0.91	0.91	0.92	0.91	2.16
Z	1.06	1.06	1.07	1.06	0.02

2.5   *Rare combinations of numeric values*

Explanations of outlier detection typically present scatterplots of two-dimensional numeric datasets—for example, figure 2.16, which is an excellent place to begin but can be misleading, as it side-steps the many difficulties that occur with outlier detection, particularly those with finding outliers in high-dimensional spaces. These plots are not feasible to draw beyond two dimensions, while many modern datasets have dozens or hundreds of features.

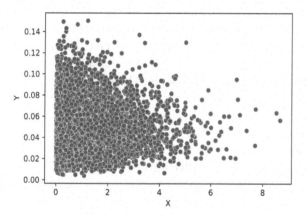

Figure 2.16   Two-dimensional scatterplot of data. Some points at the right side of the plot can be considered outliers in the x dimension. Any such outliers will automatically also be outliers in any higher-dimensional space that includes this dimension.

We'll explore the issues that come with high-dimensional spaces later, but examining two-dimensional spaces does allow us to introduce a lot of the important concepts in outlier detection. One of the key points is that when a point is an outlier in any dimensionality, it will be in higher dimensions as well but will not necessarily be in lower dimensions. To see this, consider figure 2.16. Any point unusual in any single dimension will be at least somewhat unusual when viewed in two (or more) dimensions. The points at the far right are not unusual in the y dimension, but they are in the x dimension and so remain unusual when viewing both features together. This is true as we consider three and more dimensions as well, though the effect becomes less pronounced if the other features have more typical values for this point.

While in theory we can consider a dataset looking at the single features or pairs of features and can extend this idea to consider triples of features and so on, in practice, few outlier detectors actually do this. It is, though, a useful way to think about outlier detection, as we can picture outliers more easily in this manner. In practice, most outlier detectors consider all features at once so examine a single, high-dimensional space covering every feature. This can be more efficient than examining large numbers of subsets of features and will ultimately tend to find the same things. Given that points that are unusual in any subspace of features will also be in larger subspaces, examining all features at once can be quite effective (though, as we'll see in later chapters, this does break down with enough features).

2.6   *Noise vs. inliers and outliers*

"Noise" is an overloaded term in machine learning, taking on many meanings. In the context of outlier detection, it is sometimes used to refer to points that are not quite inliers and not quite outliers. However, noise is also sometimes regarded as an outlier, referred to as a *weak outlier*, distinguishing some points from what are referred to in this sense as *strong outliers*. So "noise" can refer to either points we wish to flag as outliers, though with a lower score than strong outliers, or points we wish to exclude, even if not considering them as fully inliers either.

At times with data, there are clear, tight clusters of points and a few points that are distinctly separate. But very often the dataspace simply becomes less and less dense as we move away from the clear inliers, until eventually we can take the points as outliers. See figure 2.16. Some points to the far right can be safely considered outliers, but it's not clear where the inliers end and the outliers begin. The data is noisy, which is quite common.

It is challenging when data is noisy and you wish to flag only the strong outliers. Most likely this will come down to setting a threshold that works well for your situation. As with the statistical metrics we discussed earlier, most outlier detectors also require setting a threshold or other parameters that will control how many records they return. Doing this, you are, at least in cases where the data is noisy, controlling how much noise is flagged and how much is not.

Noise also highlights an example where scoring outliers is open to a number of decisions. Different detectors can quite reasonably give significantly different scores to different records. Consider figure 2.16: while it's likely fairly agreeable that the points well outside the main cluster should all be flagged as outliers, it's not clear what their scores, or even relative scores, should be. The noise points may receive slightly lower scores than the strong outliers or may receive scores substantially lower.

2.7   *Local and global outliers*

In outlier detection, one of the fundamental distinctions is between what are called *local* and *global* outliers. These usually only apply when working with data of at least two dimensions, so they do not appear normally with the statistical methods discussed earlier (though they can if the data appears in clusters). The distinction is important to understand when doing outlier detection; they are actually quite different types of outliers. The idea is easiest to picture with numeric data but occurs with categorical data as well.

In figure 2.17 we can see two outliers, point A and point B. Point A is a local outlier. In terms of processes generating the data, point A was likely generated by the same process as the points in the nearby cluster but is somewhat different. Point B, on the other hand, is a global outlier, as it is distinct from the majority of other data points. Point B is a unique type of record, likely generated by a distinct process.

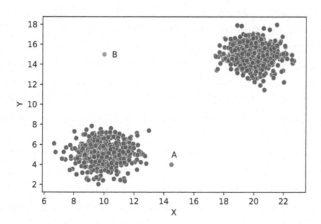

Figure 2.17   Point A is a local outlier and point B is a global outlier. Point A appears to be the same type of record as the cluster it is near but is distinct from it, while point B is not comparable to other points at all.

In the case of vision, these are often referred to as *in-distribution* and *out-of-distribution* outliers. Given a collection of pictures of animals, for example, with almost all being either dog, cat, or hamster, a picture of a parrot would be out-of-distribution, or a global outlier. It is a distinct type of item compared to the majority of the others. A picture of a dog wearing a hat taken at an unusual angle or with unusual lighting would be an in-distribution, or local outlier: it is of a common type but is different from other examples of this type. With financial tabular data, we may have transactions that are primarily purchases, sales, and payroll, with a small number of cash disbursement records, which would be global outliers. Local outliers would include purchase records that are different from the majority of the other purchases.

Very often we are more interested in global outliers than local outliers, but it is also common to be interested in both. They are both relevant though, at least conceptually, quite different. Much of selecting the appropriate detectors and tuning their parameters comes down to flagging global versus local outliers. In practice, though, many outliers are somewhere in between and not perfectly classifiable as either.

One thing to note with outlier detection as well, making it a challenging task, is that where data of different types are mixed together, for example sales and purchase records, the records may not actually be comparable. It may be quite sensible to have them in a single table, as for most purposes we would wish to treat them together, but for the purposes of outlier detection, it can be difficult to work with a mixed bag. If the distinct types of records can be identified and separated, they may more reasonably be compared. However, this isn't always feasible, and even where it is, there is likely a hierarchy of types of ever-more-specific records we could separate and compare, eventually leading to sets too small to compare in a stable way. Hence, detectors that test for local outliers can be the most useful option, as they allow working with heterogeneous data and will attempt to compare each record to the most comparable set of other records.

2.8   *Combining the scores of univariate tests*

The easiest form of outlier detection for tables is to simply run statistical, or similar tests such as histogram tests, on each feature, which will provide an outlier score for each cell in the table relative to their columns. The final outlier score of each row is, then, the sum of the scores for each cell. This misses unusual combinations but detects what are, arguably, the most relevant outliers, or at least among the most relevant. It is also very fast and relatively interpretable. This is, in fact, often done with tabular data, though more often the machine learning methods described in later chapters are used.

It turns out scoring in this way is actually very difficult to do in a fair way, as the scores given for one feature may not be comparable to those for another. A clear example is scores for numeric columns versus those for categorical columns, which would likely use completely different tests. Even where the same tests are used, as the distributions will be different, the scores may have different meanings. However, with univariate scoring methods such as the ratio to the MAD and several others, the scores are often (but not always) comparable and may reasonably be summed. This is an advantage we do not have with the output of most machine learning-based detectors, which can be much more difficult to combine.

One technique to adjust for different scales of scores between the features, where this is an issue, is to scale the scores in each column to the same range, usually between 0.0 and 1.0, so that all features have the same importance. This isn't ideal, as some features may contain stronger outliers than other features; we'll look at alternatives later. It does, though, provide a simple system to flag the most unusual rows in terms of those with the most, and the most extreme, univariate outliers.

It's also not clear if a row that received a high score for one value should be scored higher or lower overall than a row that received lower scores but in two values. Table 2.2 shows three rows with flagged values. Row 4 has two flagged values, while the others have one each. How can we compare these? This is another place where outlier detection is subjective. Where we look at multidimensional outliers, we also have questions such as: how do we score local outliers versus global? Or noise versus strong outliers? Intuitively, everything else equal, we should score global outliers higher than local outliers and strong outliers higher than noise, but how much higher?

Some of this can be addressed, when combining the scores, in the choice of function used to combine them. I suggested the sum is the most straightforward to use. It is also possible to use the maximum, to privilege very high scores over multiple moderate scores, or to sum over the squares of each score, to weight higher scores more heavily but not ignore the moderate scores.

Figure 2.18 shows examples of two features from the segments dataset on OpenML. The top-left and bottom-left plots show the distribution of values and the top-right and bottom-right the distribution of MAD scores.

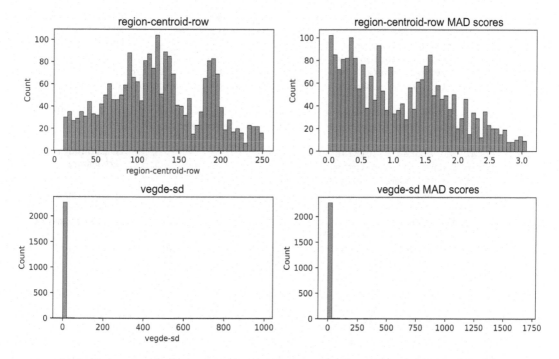

Figure 2.18 The distribution of values and MAD scores for two features in the segment dataset. Region-centroid-row is well-behaved with the maximum MAD score around 3.0. vegde-sd has extreme values, with a maximum MAD score of about 1750.

As there is an extreme range in MAD scores, they cannot simply be summed. To support combining the scores, we scale the MAD scores first, using a min-max scaler as shown in listing 2.8. The code uses an updated `calc_MAD` function that handles where the median deviation is zero, using the mean deviation in this case. This does treat some features somewhat differently, but in this dataset the results are similar, and taking the min-max of the scores for each feature helps ensure these are comparable. Doing this makes each feature of equal importance in the final scores. In practice, if some features are more relevant to the task at hand, we may wish to weight them higher in the final calculation, but without knowledge of this, it is safest to weight each feature equally.

Listing 2.8   Creating outlier scores using univariate tests

```
import pandas as pd
import numpy as np
import statistics
from sklearn.preprocessing import MinMaxScaler
from sklearn.datasets import fetch_openml

def calc_MAD(data):
    median = statistics.median(data)
    deviations = [abs(x - median) for x in data]
    median_deviation = statistics.median(deviations)
    if median_deviation == 0:
        mean_deviation = statistics.mean(deviations)
        return [abs(x - median) / mean_deviation for x in data]
    return [abs(x - median) / median_deviation for x in data]

data = fetch_openml('segment', version=1, parser='auto')
df = pd.DataFrame(data.data, columns=data.feature_names)

total_mad_scores = [0]*len(df)
for col_name in df.columns:
    if df[col_name].nunique() == 1:
        continue
    mad_scores = calc_MAD(df[col_name])
    mad_scores = np.array(mad_scores).reshape(-1, 1)
    transformer = MinMaxScaler().fit(mad_scores)
    col_mad_scores = transformer.transform(mad_scores).reshape(1, -1)[0]
    total_mad_scores += col_mad_scores
print(total_mad_scores)
```

- Uses the mean for features with median deviations of 0
- Collects the data
- Loops through each feature
- Scales the MAD scores for each feature to be between 0.0 and 1.0

This example used MinMaxScaler, which scales all scores to be between 0.0 and 1.0. This is common in outlier detection both for scaling the data and scaling the scores produced by outlier detectors. A number of other scalers are also commonly used, including StandardScaler and RobustScaler. These and others are covered in chapter 9. Once completed, the total scores for each row will be the sum of the scores for each element in the row so may be much higher than 1.0 (at most 1.0 times the number of features).

Summary

- Outlier detection has a long history in statistics, and many well-established simple methods exist, but they are usually univariate and often assume specific data distributions, usually Gaussian.
- Statistical methods to identify outliers in a sequence of numbers include tests based on z-scores, IQR, IDR, and MAD.
- These methods can be applied to individual table columns.
- Statistical methods can work well in some cases but have significant limitations.
- These are also useful to evaluate the scores of other outlier tests, identifying the extreme scores.

- In some projects, identifying internal outliers may be more important, and in other projects, external outliers (extreme values) may be more important. Usually both are relevant.

- Many other methods for finding univariate outliers may also be used, including histograms, KDE, and k^{th}NN, which are able to find internal outliers and to work with asymmetric and multimodal distributions.

- With categorical features, we look at the counts of each unique value and score values based on the frequency of the value.

- To set thresholds with categorical data, it can be useful to look at the cumulative counts.

- Visualization can also be useful but is limited.

- In outlier detection, we usually wish to distinguish noise from strong outliers and global from local outliers.

- It is nontrivial and often subjective to determine outlier scores even for simple cases involving a single feature.

- Complications are multiplied when we work with full tables of data.

- Though it is commonly done, it can be difficult to fairly combine the results of many tests—for example when performing univariate tests on each column and combining the results into a final score per row.

Machine learning-based outlier detection

This chapter covers

- An introduction to unsupervised machine learning-based outlier detection
- The curse of dimensionality
- Some of the broad categories of outlier detection algorithms used
- Descriptions and examples of some specific algorithms
- The properties of outlier detectors

If you are working on a challenging data problem, such as examining tables of financial data in which you wish to identify fraud, sensor readings that may indicate a need for maintenance, or astronomical observations that may include rare or unknown phenomena, it may be that the statistical techniques we've looked at so far are useful but not sufficient to find everything you're interested in.

We now have a good introduction to outlier detection and can begin to look at machine learning approaches, which allow detection of a much wider range of outliers than is possible with statistical methods. The main factor distinguishing machine learning methods is that the majority, with some exceptions, are multivariate tests: they consider all features and attempt to find unusual records, as opposed to unusual single values. These make more subtle outliers, like fraud, machine failure, or novel telescope readings, much more feasible to detect.

Some are extensions of the ideas in the previous chapter, applying them to multidimensional spaces—for example kernel density estimation (KDE) estimates of multidimensional data, multidimensional histograms, and multidimensional kth-nearest neighbors calculations. Others are based on completely different concepts, such as trees (similar to decision trees), neural networks, clustering, compression, and Markov models.

Although there are many techniques in common usage (and many more that have been proposed in the academic literature), they can be placed into a relatively small number of general categories. There are, though, many ways of categorizing outlier detection algorithms, and some sources use different terminology, or are even somewhat contradictory. This is not a concern though: knowing the categories of algorithms isn't necessary in itself. It's simply a way to help make sense of the myriad algorithms you may encounter, as some are based on the same high-level ideas or are just variations on each other. For any given algorithm, knowing the broad category it fits into also helps make clear the properties it will have and what makes it suitable for some problems and unsuitable for others. Different types of detectors perform well on different types of data and produce different results. Some, for example, are designed more for speed than completeness and can be more useful in real-time environments, some scale to larger datasets well, others are more interpretable, and so on.

Thinking of the general categories of detectors can also be helpful in that, in some cases, we may specifically wish to use a number of detectors that are very different from each other in an ensemble—to help identify a broader set of outliers than can be found by a single detector, or by two similar detectors. Using two very different detectors—detectors that can be considered to be in two different categories—can help achieve this; as they take different approaches, they often flag different records, and are usually more able to complement each other well than detectors in the same category.

3.1 The curse of dimensionality

Before we get into the general approaches to outlier detection, it's important to understand the issues involved with very high-dimensional data—in particular what is known as the *curse of dimensionality*, which is among the main challenges in outlier detection. Working with large numbers of features introduces difficulties that don't exist with lower dimensionalities. Many data mining and machine learning techniques, including some outlier detectors, lose their effectiveness in high dimensions; they simply weren't intended for high-dimensional data, though in data science we're now often faced with tables with hundreds or thousands of features. At the same time, some outliers may be subtle and only detectable when examining many features, so we need some means to examine high-dimensional data when working with such datasets.

Some approaches to outlier detection are much more susceptible to the curse of dimensionality than others, and this can be one of the primary qualities distinguishing detectors from each other, at least where you have data with large numbers of features. Some detectors can, in fact, become ineffective in analyzing tabular data with enough columns, sometimes with as few as 10 or 20 features and very often with 50 or more.

It's important to note that very few outliers require many features to describe them. We may need to examine many features to identify the outliers, but the outliers themselves will typically be outliers because they have an unusual single value or an unusual combination of 2, 3, 4, or perhaps more features but very unlikely of 10 or more features. Outliers related to many features tend to be less interpretable and less relevant than outliers based on few features. Further, any outlier based on many features would likely be statistically difficult to identify reliably; in fact, this is generally only possible with working with an enormous dataset. If an outlier is based on, say, eight features, there are probably many combinations of values in these eight columns. In the case of an enormous dataset, inliers will possibly have substantially higher counts, and the outliers can then be reliably distinguished. However, more often, each of the combinations will have very low counts, similar to those of the outliers, and outliers will be difficult to identify correctly. Consequently, working with smaller subsets of features can be very important and is covered in chapter 10. However, in practice, most detectors will simply work with all features at once, relying on high-dimensional analysis of the data, which means this is something we need to be careful with. When working with datasets with many features, we may need to either reduce the number of features used or use detectors suitable for the number of features.

Some of the other major issues we see with high-dimensional datasets are

- The data space becomes very sparse.
- Almost all data points are in the margins of the data in at least some dimensions—almost no datapoints are in the center of the data in every dimension. That is, every data point starts to become unusual in one sense or another.
- Eventually, distance measures, such as Euclidean distance, become unreliable, with all points becoming roughly the same distance from each other.
- Calculations can become very slow.
- Outlier detection can become a data dredging exercise, where many anomalies are found simply because there are many places in which to look for them.

We'll describe these in more detail here, as many of these effects are quite unintuitive.

3.1.1   Data sparsity

Data sparsity is a result of the data space becoming extremely large, while the number of points available (the records in the training data at hand) can fill only a minute proportion of the space, leaving the bulk of the space empty.

To describe the problem we'll take, as an example, a dataset with 10,000 rows and 20 categorical columns, with 4 distinct values per column. Even in this simple example, the number of possible combinations of values is astronomical. To simplify the analysis, we also assume, for the moment, that the four values in each column have roughly equal counts and that the columns are independent, with no associations. These are not realistic assumptions, but they will, temporarily, make the analysis easier. We would expect, given these assumptions, that their joint probabilities will roughly match the product of their marginal probabilities. That is, the probability of each combination of values can be estimated by taking the probabilities of each individual value and simply multiplying them. Given that all four values are about equally common, each would appear in about 25% of the rows. The probability of one specific value in column 1 is 0.25. The probability of one specific value in column 1 combined with one specific value in column 2 is 0.25^2. The probability of any specific set of 20 values is 0.25^{20}, which is extraordinarily unlikely. We would require a dataset many orders of magnitude larger than 10,000 rows to expect any given unique set of values to appear even once.

In practice, we have two advantages that typically appear in real-world data. One is the data is correlated; the features are not completely independent, so some combinations will occur more than others. And the data within any given column will be skewed, with some values much more likely than others, as in figure 2.12 in the previous chapter.

If we consider where the features are still independent but the marginal probabilities are very skewed, it may still be the case that we cannot consider this many features at once. If, in each of the 20 columns the most frequent value occurred 75% of the time, then even with the most likely combination, where all 20 features have their most common value, the expected frequency would be 0.75^{20}, or 0.32%. Given 10,000 rows, we would expect only about 32 instances, with much fewer also being quite likely. For any other combination of values, we would expect well less than 32 instances. This means that any set of 20 specific values that actually appear at all in the data would appear more often than anticipated, making it impossible, in this manner, to flag any records as outliers. That is, given even 20 features, some forms of analysis for outlier detection break down.

The issue is mitigated significantly by the fact that most features are actually well-associated and not independent, so some combinations do, despite the number of dimensions, occur reasonably frequently. In fact, it is argued that most data points do not live in the full dataspace defined by the features in any given dataset but instead within a much lower-dimensional manifold (some regions are fairly dense, while others are empty). Given that, the curse of dimensionality, while reduced, is not eliminated. We still face significant challenges when working with high-dimensional data, though this is less true the more associated the features are. Given even 20 features, there may still be a very large number of specific combinations that occur only once. In fact, it's common for every row in a table to be unique, with zero perfect duplicates, even with fewer than 20 features. The implication is that it is likely impossible to flag any combination of 20 values as unusual: we simply cannot do outlier detection in this way.

The same phenomena occur with numeric data as well and can be more pronounced in this case. With numeric data, it's common to view the data as points in high-dimensional space. For example, if a table has 1,000 rows and 20 numeric columns, we can view the data as 1,000 points in 20-dimensional space. In fact, many of the outlier detection algorithms we'll cover in this book explicitly treat data in this way.

In low-dimensional spaces, these algorithms can work very well. The interesting (and problematic) thing, though, is that high-dimensional spaces can behave quite differently than we are used to in lower-dimensional spaces.

If we consider each region of a dataspace in a similar way as we view categorical values, for example dividing the 20-dimensional dataspace into many bins, as with a histogram, we can see that the number of such bins is enormous. Even dividing each dimension into only two, with 20 features, we have 2^{20} bins—far more than the number of data points. Again, finding bins with only one record does not indicate anything unusual about that single record, as we expect all the bins to have well less than even one record.

You may be thinking that it sounds crazy to even try to consider all 20 features at once—possibly more so when thinking about categorical data. And, with categorical data, in practice, few detectors do consider all features at once. Most instead seek to find associations between small sets of features. With categorical detectors, we tend to avoid the curse of dimensionality by working with these small sets of features. But, with numeric data, it is common for detectors to consider all features at once, particularly those that picture the records as points in high-dimensional spaces.

3.1.2 *Data appearing in the margins*

An interesting property of high-dimensional data is that almost all data will appear along the margins of the data space and not near the center, even if almost all the data is close to the center in each individual dimension. This can be hard to picture, as it just doesn't happen in low dimensions. If you can imagine a 2D square with points clustered around the center in both dimensions, the majority of points will be close to the center of the square, with only a small fraction along the margin, which is to say close to one of the four edges of the square. Similarly, in a 3D cube with data centered in all three dimensions, most points will be close to the cube's center with only some on the margins—that is, close to one of the six faces at the edge of the cube.

As we add dimensions, a larger and larger fraction of the data ends up on the margin, close to one of the edges of the space. As an example, assume again 20 dimensions, here all numeric. And assume in each dimension 90% of the data is close to the center and 10% close to one of the two edges. To be in the center of the hypercube representing the data space, it's necessary to be in the center in all 20 dimensions; 0.9^{20} is 0.12, meaning only about 12% of the data will be in the center, with 88% on the edge. With 40 features, we have only 0.9^{40} or 1.5% of the data in the center of the dataspace, with about 98.5% on the margin.

The implication of this is that almost all data is unusual in some way, and some tests for abnormality, depending how they are constructed, can break down, flagging virtually every record as unusual in some way.

3.1.3 *Distance calculations*

These issues are important, but the main issue here haunting outlier detection is the effect of the curse of dimensionality on the distance calculations that many detectors depend on. To assess how unusual a point is, many detectors examine the distance from the point to other points. This is intuitive and useful—points that are very far from most other points can reasonably be considered outliers. But these distance measurements, unfortunately, become unreliable in high dimensions.

Consider a point in a dataset with four dimensions, as in figure 3.1. This shows plots of two pairs of the features. We can see one point (drawn as a star), though not unusual in the other three dimensions, is unusual in feature A. Its distance in 4D space to all other points will be large, and given this, we can reliably identify it as an outlier. But imagine that instead of four dimensions there were 100 dimensions and that all dimensions (other than feature A) have fairly uniform distributions, similar to those of B, C, and D. This point is clearly an outlier, even if only in one dimension. However, in 100-dimensional space, its distance to the other points will become about the same as the distances between any two other points. As in lower dimensions, the distance between points is calculated using the Pythagorean formula as shown here, where f1 and f1′ are the values of the first feature, f2 and f2′ for the second feature, and so on up to the 100th feature, for the two records:

$$\sqrt{(f1 - f1')^2 + (f2 - f2')^2 + (f3 - f3')^2 + \ldots + (f100 - f100')^2}$$

The gap in space between the point and the other points in feature A becomes irrelevant as the distances in 99 other dimensions are included in the formula.

The implication of this is: as we add features to a dataset, the distances between any two points become about the same; all points become roughly equidistant from each other. This is true no matter how far apart each pair of points is in any one dimension. Any detectors dependent on distance calculations can become unusable given a large number of dimensions, unless features are removed or dimensionality reduction (such as PCA) is performed.

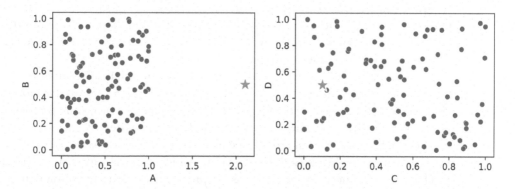

Figure 3.1 A scatterplot of features A and B (left) and scatterplot of features C and D (right). A point (drawn as a star) is shown that is an outlier in A, though is normal in features B, C, and D. Its distance to the other points in 4D space will separate it well from the other points, but this could fail in much higher dimensional spaces.

3.2   *Types of algorithms*

I've tried to stick with the conventional ways of classifying unsupervised machine learning outlier detection algorithms and have included here what are, I believe, the largest categories of detectors. However, many popular algorithms, including one of the most popular, known as Isolation Forest (covered in chapter 5), do not fit neatly into any of these, and so this should not be taken as a complete list of the categories of algorithms, but simply as a set of categories that each have multiple specific algorithms and that provide a good introduction to some of the major high-level ideas of outlier detection. In addition, this chapter covers only approaches specific to tabular data, with methods for other types of data covered later.

The first categories of algorithms discussed here—distance-based, density-based, and cluster-based—assume that all features are numeric (any categorical features must be numerically encoded—that is, converted to numeric values) and are easiest to understand picturing each row as a point in space. Each of these methods is based on the pairwise distances between points and, due to the curse of dimensionality, can struggle with very high-dimensional datasets.

Each also requires scaling the numeric features such that each is on the same scale, usually using min-max scaling or standardization (converting to z-scores). Otherwise, any distance calculations will be dominated by features that happen to be on larger scales than others. It is possible to scale some features to slightly smaller or lower ranges if we wish to decrease or increase their influence in the detector, though this is seldom done in practice. Setting the scales well is virtually impossible without the ability to assess the scaling empirically by testing against a labeled dataset, which we normally do not have in outlier detection problems. Consequently, we almost always put all numeric features on the same scale.

3.2.1   *Distance based*

Distance-based algorithms seek to find records that have few similar records. Viewing the records as points in high-dimensional space, these are records with few other records near them. If we imagine a dataset where most points have many other points fairly close to them, these points would be inliers. If we also have some points that have only a few other points near them (or where the points nearest to them are relatively far), then we can say these are outliers.

The most basic and, to my knowledge, first proposed distance-based outlier test is to flag any records for which more than p percent of the other records are more than d distance away, for some specified p and d. This does require providing two parameters so can be difficult to tune and is less used now than some other distance-based tests.

The best known and most widely used example of a distance-based approach is likely the kth-nearest neighbors (k^{th}NN) algorithm, which requires only a single parameter, k. This was introduced in the previous chapter when looking for outliers in a single sequence of numbers. The idea can be extended to any number of dimensions and, in fact, is much more commonly used in multidimensional spaces than in single features.

As in the single-dimension case, records are scored based on their distance to the kth-nearest neighbor. A variation on this, sometimes called KNN, where their average distance to all k nearest neighbors is used, can actually be more robust. Although using a single value of k will produce a stronger detector if the optimal k can be determined, in most cases, as there is no labeled data, the k value cannot be tuned. Given this, averaging over a reasonable range of values of k can produce the strongest detector in a practical way.

To identify the distances to the kth-nearest neighbors for each point, in principle, it's necessary to calculate the distance between every pair of points, but in practice techniques are used to avoid this as it can become computationally infeasible. In the example here, we implement k[th]NN with the `BallTree` class, a data structure provided by scikit-learn that makes these calculations much more efficient. There are implementations of k[th]NN available in open-source libraries, but the ideas are important to understand, so it's worth going through a coding example here, at least at the level of using the `BallTree` class, as this is used routinely in outlier detection.

We first look at the pairwise distances themselves. Consider where we have a table of inventory items, with two rows of the table shown in table 3.1.

Table 3.1   Inventory records

Inventory ID	Weight	Cost	Age in inventory	Maximum storage temperature
1002	43.12	2,848.94	156	34.0
1023	54.22	34.22	233	60.3

To calculate the distances between points, we first need to scale the data. Assuming there are hundreds of rows, with only two shown here, we can't know precisely what the scaled values will be, but let's assume they are scaled to be between 0.0 and 1.0 and are as shown in table 3.2. As the Inventory ID is not used for outlier detection, there is no need to scale it.

Table 3.2   Inventory records after min-max scaling

Inventory ID	Weight	Cost	Age in inventory	Maximum storage temperature
1002	0.21	0.91	0.82	0.32
1023	0.25	0.04	0.89	0.77

We can now calculate the distance between the first two rows. If we use the Euclidean distance, this is

$$\sqrt{(0.25 - 0.21)^2 + (0.04 - 0.91)^2 + (0.89 - 0.82)^2 + (0.77 - 0.32)^2}$$

The distance measurements are taken care of by the `BallTree` object that we use in this example. We seldom calculate the distances directly, but it is important to understand how they work.

This example, shown in listing 3.1, uses random synthetic data, which can be somewhat unrealistic. We shouldn't take any findings using synthetic data as necessarily applying the same to real-world data, but using simple, controlled data can be an excellent place to start with outlier detection; it allows us to understand the process and confirm if the process works well with simple data where a ground truth is known (we know which records are outliers). This allows us to remove any obvious bugs (such as reversing the labels for inliers and outliers, or not scaling). Using synthetic data also allows us to adjust the data distributions and the parameters used by the models and see what effects these have. Among other things, this gives us a better sense of the purpose of the parameters, how they affect the results, and how they can be tuned. This will not indicate the optimal parameters to use on real-world data (the optimal parameters can be quite different from one dataset to another) but at least provides a good idea of how to set them to adjust to different datasets.

We look here at a simple, two-dimensional dataset with 1,000 rows (two clusters of 500 points each), shown in figure 3.2 (top left). In this example, the data is on the same scale, so we can skip the step of scaling it for now. We create the `BallTree` and fit it using the full dataset. We then call query with k = 3, getting the distances to the nearest three points (that is, the nearest two points other than the point itself). We take the average of these distances as the outlier score for each point.

Listing 3.1   Example of a KNN outlier detector

```
import numpy as np
import pandas as pd
from sklearn.neighbors import BallTree
import matplotlib.pyplot as plt
import seaborn as sns

np.random.seed(0)
n_per_cluster = 500

data_a = pd.Series(
        np.random.laplace(size= n_per_cluster))          Creates first
data_b = pd.Series(np.random.laplace(size= n_per_cluster))   cluster
df1 = pd.DataFrame({"A": data_a, "B": data_b})

data_a = pd.Series(
        np.random.normal(loc=5, size=n_per_cluster))        Creates
data_b = pd.Series(np.random.normal(loc=15, size=n_per_cluster))  second cluster
df2 = pd.DataFrame({"A": data_a, "B": data_b})

df = pd.concat([df1, df2])

fig, ax = plt.subplots(nrows=2, ncols=2, figsize=(8, 6))

s = sns.scatterplot(data=df, x="A", y="B", alpha=0.4, ax=ax[0][0])

tree = BallTree(df, leaf_size=100)                 Creates a BallTree
dist, _ = tree.query(df, k=3)                      object representing
dist = [x.mean() for x in dist]                    the data
df['Score'] = dist
```

```
s = sns.scatterplot(data=df, x="A", y="B", s=50*df['Score'],
                    alpha=0.4, ax=ax[0][1])

cutoff = sorted(df['Score'])[-6]
df['Outlier'] = df['Score'] > cutoff
sns.scatterplot(data=df[df['Outlier']==False], x="A", y="B",
                alpha=0.4, ax=ax[1][0])
sns.scatterplot(data=df[df['Outlier']==True], x="A", y="B", s=100,
                alpha=1.0, marker='*', ax=ax[1][0])

cutoff = sorted(df['Score'])[-16]
df['Outlier'] = df['Score'] > cutoff
sns.scatterplot(data=df[df['Outlier']==False], x="A", y="B",
                alpha=0.4, ax=ax[1][1])
sns.scatterplot(data=df[df['Outlier']==True], x="A", y="B", s=100,
                alpha=1.0, marker='*', ax=ax[1][1])

plt.show()
```

Finds the top five outliers

Finds the top 15 outliers

Figure 3.2 shows the original data in the top left and the same data using the point size to represent the outlier scores in the top right. It's common to use either color or size to represent outlier scores. Where binary labels are used to distinguish inliers from outliers, marker symbols may also be used. We show examples of this in the bottom left (indicating the top 5 outliers), and the bottom right (indicating the top 15 outliers), with the outliers shown as stars.

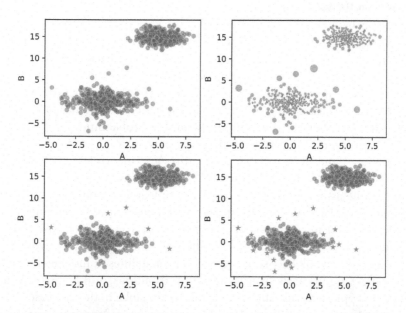

Figure 3.2 Synthetic data in two clusters (top left) and the same data with the size of each point corresponding to its outlier score based on a KNN calculation using k = 3 (top right). Binary outlier labels are also shown for the top 5 outliers (bottom left) and for the top 15 (bottom right).

In practice, we almost always keep k relatively low for KNN detectors, often between about 2 and 50. In cases where there are many records, we will usually use larger values of k than with smaller datasets, but we usually still keep k fairly small. Intuitively, setting k equal to N, the number of rows in the dataset, has appeal, but calculating the distances between all pairs of points is computationally expensive and can actually provide less meaningful results. Somewhat similar to the curse of dimensionality, taking the average distance to all other points can tend to lead to all records having roughly the same score. Here, using k = 3 works quite well, flagging the values on the fringes of the less-dense cluster—the points that are far from their nearest neighbors.

3.2.2 *Density based*

Density-based methods are somewhat similar to distance-based methods. Instead of looking specifically at the distances between points, density-based detectors try to identify regions within the space that have low density and flag any of the few items that are in these areas as outliers. In practice, although numerous other methods are also used, this is often done by computing the pair-wise distances between points; areas where the distances between points tend to be large can be taken as low-density regions.

Possibly the most widely used density-based algorithm is known as *local outlier factor* (LOF), which we'll cover later. LOF is an example of a density method that uses distances to estimate density. To introduce the idea, though, we will look at three other methods to estimate density. These are variations of methods we've already seen: z-scores, a variation on KNN often called Radius, and multidimensional KDE.

MULTIDIMENSIONAL GAUSSIAN DATA

A simple density-based method is to simply assume that each feature has a Gaussian distribution. Using this approach, we calculate the mean and standard deviation of each column. Then, for each row, we can calculate the z-score of each value in the row (relative to the mean and standard deviation for their columns). Z-scores correspond to probabilities, so we can calculate the probability of each value in each row. We can then calculate the probability of each row by multiplying the probabilities of each value in the row. Outliers are then the rows with unusually low probabilities.

This, however, relies on several assumptions, particularly that the data is close to Gaussian in every dimension and that the features are uncorrelated—that is, that the data is effectively a single high-dimensional Gaussian cluster.

In practice, the assumption of independence of features is unlikely. And while the assumption of Gaussian distributions in any one dimension can be tenuous, it is much more so when multiplying the probabilities of many features. Given distributions somewhat similar to Gaussian, measuring the numbers of standard deviations from the mean for any given value may still have some value, but probabilities cannot be inferred where the data diverges significantly from Gaussian distributions, and errors can multiply. Given that, this approach is usually too unstable to be viable. In the rare cases where it is usable (where there are a small number of features, they are largely independent, and they all follow Gaussian distributions well), this is a very convenient method and has the appealing property that probabilities can be estimated.

As this method is usually inapplicable, we do not explore it further, though do look later at variations on this, such as one called *Gaussian mixture models*.

RADIUS

Radius is quite similar to KNN, with the difference analogous to that between scikit-learn's KNeighborsClassifer and RadiusNeighborsClassifer. With the Radius method, instead of finding the distances to a specified number of points, we determine how many other points are within a specified radius. This then indicates how dense the space (in this case, a hypersphere of the specified radius) around each point is. Using a radius measure can be more stable than KNN, but choosing an appropriate radius is far less intuitive and realistically needs to be found experimentally.

In the example shown in listing 3.2, we use the same dataset created in the previous KNN example and again use a `BallTree` to calculate and store the pairwise distances between points. We use the `query_radius()` method, which returns the count of points within the given radius, and use 2.0 for the radius (which was found experimentally).

Listing 3.2   Radius outler detection

```
tree = BallTree(df)
counts = tree.query_radius(df, 2.0, count_only=True)

fig, ax = plt.subplots(nrows=1, ncols=3, figsize=(8, 4))

s = sns.histplot(counts, ax=ax[0])
s.set_title(f"Number of Points within Radius")

min_score = min(counts)
max_score = max(counts)
scores = [(max_score - x)/(max_score - min_score) for x in counts]
s = sns.histplot(scores, ax=ax[1])
s.set_title(f"Scores")

df['Score'] = scores
threshold = sorted(scores, reverse=True)[15]
df_flagged = df[df['Score'] >= threshold]
s = sns.scatterplot(data=df, x="A", y="B", ax=ax[2])
s = sns.scatterplot(data=df_flagged, x="A", y="B", color='red',
                    marker='*', s=200, ax=ax[2])

plt.tight_layout()
plt.show()
```

Plots a histogram of the counts of records with different numbers of points within radius 2.0

Reverses the scores so the more outlierish points have higher scores

Plots the data, highlighting the points with the 15 highest scores

Implementations of this, as well as several other detectors covered by this book are provided on GitHub at https://github.com/Brett-Kennedy/OutlierDetectionInPython/tree/main.

Figure 3.3 (left) shows the distribution of counts (the number of points with one other point within the radius, with two points, with three points, and so on). This is actually a measure of how normal a point is, so it is reversed, as well as normalized, to create an outlier score, shown in the middle plot. Due to space constraints, we do not always show the distribution of scores, but I would recommend always looking at this with any outlier detection work you do: it gives you a better sense of how well the outliers are being separated and if there are clear cutoffs for outliers. Figure 3.3 (right) shows the flagged outliers using this method. For simplicity, we simply show the top 15 scores as outliers.

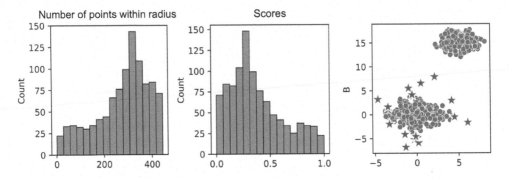

Figure 3.3   Given the synthetic dataset shown in figure 3.2, we calculate the number of points within radius 2.0 from each point. The distribution of these counts is shown (left). These are converted directly to outlier scores (middle). The top 15 outliers are shown (right).

KDE

We've seen KDE used in 1D data (a single series of values), but it can actually be used with any number of dimensions. With 1D data, we can picture small 2D kernels being stacked along the number line to create the KDE estimate. With 2D data, we can picture 3D kernels being stacked along the 2D plane, creating a 3D representation of the density in the 2D plane, similar to a topographic map. The same is true for higher dimensions: though it becomes impossible to picture in our minds beyond 3D, the idea is the same.

KDE is often used, as well as for outlier detection, for visualization, and we start with an example of this. This example plots two features from the wall-robot-navigation dataset from OpenML using seaborn's `kdeplot` class. We can see the majority of points, by definition, are in high-density areas (those areas with a dark background), with a few in lower-density areas, which can quite possibly be considered outliers. Listing 3.3 presents the code used to create this image, with the image shown in figure 3.4 (left). This places a scatterplot on top of the kdeplot, showing both the data and the data density.

Listing 3.3   Example of 2D KDE plot

```
import pandas as pd
from sklearn.datasets import fetch_openml
import matplotlib.pyplot as plt
import seaborn as sns

data = fetch_openml('wall-robot-navigation', version=1, parser='auto')
data_df = pd.DataFrame(data.data, columns=data.feature_names)
```

```
sns.kdeplot(data=data_df, x="V6", y="V19", fill=True)
sns.scatterplot(data=data_df, x="V6", y="V19", alpha=0.2)
plt.show()
```

It is also possible use KDE to estimate the outlierness of each point by calculating the density of its location, as in listing 3.4, For this, we use scikit-learn's `KernelDensity` class (useful tools for KDE are also provided in the SciPy and statsmodels libraries). As KDE is based, behind the scenes, on distance measures between points, it is vulnerable to the curse of dimensionality and so can support only a limited number of features.

Here we may specify two parameters for the `KernelDensity` class. The kernel, or shape of the kernels, is specified as Gaussian. The bandwidth, or size of each kernel, may be specified as well or set to "silverman," which allows the `KernelDensity` class to estimate the best width.

Listing 3.4 Using scikit-learn's `KernelDensity` class for outlier detection

```
from sklearn.neighbors import KernelDensity

X = data_df[['V6', 'V19']]
kde = KernelDensity(kernel='gaussian').fit(X)
log_density = kde.score_samples(X)
data_df['KDE Scores'] = -log_density
cutoff = sorted(data_df['KDE Scores'])[-30]
data_df['Outlier'] = data_df['KDE Scores'] > cutoff

sns.scatterplot(data=data_df[data_df['Outlier']==False], x="V6", y="V19",
                alpha=0.1)
sns.scatterplot(data=data_df[data_df['Outlier']==True], x="V6", y="V19",
                s=200, alpha=1.0, marker="*")
plt.show()
```

The results are shown in figure 3.4 (right). The outliers correspond to the low-density regions in the data.

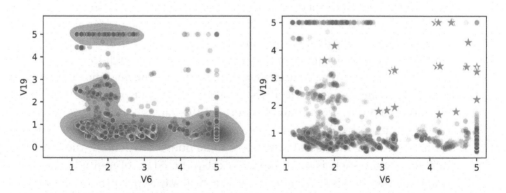

Figure 3.4 KDE plot of two features from OpenML's wall-robot-navigation dataset (left) and the top 30 outliers identified using a KDE-based outlier detector (right)

3.2.3   *Cluster based*

Cluster-based outlier detection works based on the idea that there is a strong correspondence between clustering and outlier detection: inliers are the points close to the centers of large, dense clusters, and outliers are the points distant from these centers.

With cluster-based methods, records are first divided into clusters. Once this is done, we can identify any global outliers: the points not placed in any cluster. These are the records that are not similar to any other rows (or not enough that other rows form a cluster). And we can identify local outliers: the points on the edges of clusters. These are the records that may be similar to some other rows but are still notably distinct from them.

Where data fits well into clusters, these methods can provide a very meaningful way to identify outliers, but effective clustering can be difficult, and much real-world data does not fit well into clusters. In this regard, distance-based and density-based methods can be more reliable, as they do not rely on meaningful clustering of the data.

Where the data is well-clustered, though, this can provide a useful frame of reference for each record to be compared to. If clusters correspond, say, to different types of financial transactions, the clusters may not be comparable to each other. It may make sense to compare a sales record to other sales records (assuming the clustering algorithm is able to cluster these together well) but not to purchase or payroll records (which are ideally in other clusters). The clusters may have quite different densities, with the transactions in some clusters being, for example, fewer in number, more spaced out in time, and having larger dollar values. Consequently, comparing a record to its cluster, and not the full dataset, can provide the most meaningful comparison.

Clustering algorithms are an example of algorithms that compare each point not to the full dataset but to a relevant subset of the data or subset. KNN and Radius are also examples of this: they evaluate each point relative to their neighborhood. With KNN, neighborhoods are defined as the k nearest neighbors; with Radius, the neighborhood is the hypersphere around each point with a specified radius. In principle, comparing records to their clusters is more meaningful than comparing to their neighborhoods. Each cluster, if well-formed, will be reasonably large and reasonably internally consistent and may provide the best basis for comparison for each record.

Distance and density methods, on the other hand, can look at neighborhoods or regions that are somewhat arbitrary and can be small enough to be less stable to compare to than full clusters. Consider figure 3.5, showing the neighborhoods of two points, A and B. As methods such as KNN usually look only at perhaps 10 or 20 neighbors around each point, they will tend to cover, if the data is clustered, only a small portion of one cluster, possibly near the center, and possibly, as with point A, near the fringe. At the same time, the neighborhoods of some points, particularly those not fitting well into any cluster, such as point B, may overlap the edges of multiple clusters. Though using neighborhoods is often the most practical way to perform outlier detection, this does suggest that, if the data is well clustered, these neighborhoods may not be the best frame of comparison; they may be somewhat suboptimal compared to the cluster.

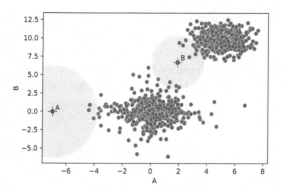

Figure 3.5 **Example of two neighborhoods. For point A, the neighborhood includes the edge of one cluster, which is likely unrepresentative of the cluster. For point B, the neighborhood includes portions of two clusters.**

Once data is clustered, we can identify outliers by examining

- *If a row is in a cluster or not*—Any records outside of the clusters may be considered outliers, assuming most records are included in clusters.
- *The size of the cluster*—Everything else equal, the larger the cluster, the more normal the records. Points in relatively small clusters may be flagged.
- *The distance of points to the cluster center*—Points farther from the center are more unusual than points near the center.
- *The distance of points to the cluster center, relative to other points in that cluster*—Different clusters may have a different sense of what is a normal distance from their cluster center, and this may be more relevant for points to compare to than a global average of the distances of points to their cluster centers.
- *The distance to the center of the nearest large cluster*—This may be calculated to avoid penalizing points in small clusters that are also close to large clusters.

Cluster-based outlier detection uses standard clustering algorithms such as k-means clustering, k-prototypes, Birch, and so on. scikit-learn provides a good collection of clustering methods (and clustering evaluation metrics) that are sufficient for most purposes. For this example, we will use DBSCAN. DBSCAN is sometimes also considered a density-based approach due to the way in which it discovers clusters; here, though, as it is a clustering algorithm, we will categorize it as a clustering-based approach.

Other slightly more elaborate examples of cluster-based outlier detection are provided in later chapters, but here we take a simple approach of simply considering each point in a cluster an inlier and all other points as outliers, as DBSCAN has the convenient property of allowing some points to not be included in clusters. scikit-learn also provides an implementation of another clustering algorithm, HDBSCAN, which can be used in the same way and which I've also found to work well for outlier detection. HDBSCAN is similar to DBSCAN, but supports hierarchical clustering and is generally more robust to noise.

As is the case with most outlier detectors, most clustering algorithms (with a few exceptions, such as k-modes and k-prototypes) assume purely numeric data, requiring categorical columns to be dropped or numerically encoded. Also like outlier detectors, most clustering algorithms require the null values to be replaced and the numeric features to be scaled. This example works with numeric data, where all features happen to be on the same scale and where there are no null values, so these steps can be skipped here.

Listing 3.5 loads the wall-robot-navigation dataset from OpenML and takes two features (which allows us to visualize the data). We cluster the data using DBSCAN and take the rows not in clusters as outliers.

Listing 3.5   Using DBSCAN for outlier detection

```python
from sklearn.cluster import DBSCAN
import pandas as pd
import numpy as np
from sklearn.datasets import fetch_openml
import matplotlib.pyplot as plt
import seaborn as sns

data = fetch_openml(
        'wall-robot-navigation', version=1, parser='auto')    ← Collects the data and selects two features
data_df = pd.DataFrame(data.data, columns=data.feature_names)
X = data_df[['V6', 'V19']]

clustering = DBSCAN().fit_predict(X)    ← Determines the cluster for all datapoints

data_df['DBScan Outliers'] = \
        np.where(clustering < 0, 1, 0)
sns.scatterplot(data=data_df[data_df['DBScan Outliers']==False], x="V6",    ←
                y="V19", alpha=0.2, color='blue')
sns.scatterplot(data=data_df[data_df['DBScan Outliers']==True], x="V6",
                y="V19", marker='*', s=200, color='red')
plt.show()
```

Takes any points outside a cluster as an outlier

In this example, DBSCAN clustered the data into three clusters, which allows identifying small clusters as well. But, for simplicity, we simply flag any values with cluster id −1 (indicating they are not in any cluster) as an outlier and consider all others as inliers. The results are shown in figure 3.6 with the outliers as stars.

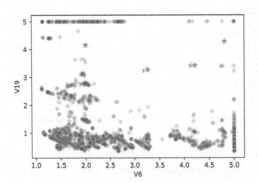

Figure 3.6 The results of using DBSCAN for outlier detection on two features from the wall-robot-navigation dataset. The majority of points were placed in three clusters, with some points being placed in no cluster, which we flag here as outliers, shown as stars.

Using DBSCAN, at least where we simply identify outliers as data points that are not placed in clusters, can also be effective even where the data is not well clustered—for example where data is in a single cluster or is bunched along the x- and y-axes as in figure 3.7. Regardless of the data distribution, points some distance from the other points will tend to not be included in a cluster and consequently will tend to be flagged as outliers.

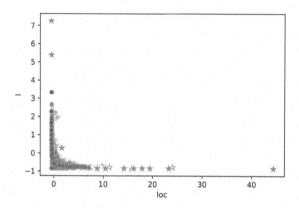

Figure 3.7   Evaluating outliers using two features from the jm1 dataset from OpenML, loc, and l, scaled with StandardScaler. Here several points far from the main cluster are flagged as outliers as they are not placed in a cluster.

One nice property of clustering-based outlier detection is that, regardless of how the clustering is done and how the clusters are used to identify outliers, the general idea of clustering for outlier detection extends beyond tabular data to virtually all modalities, including time-series, text, and image data. For any type of data, there will be some concept of similar and dissimilar items, and there will be some meaningful way to form sets of items that are similar to each other, but different from other sets. Though the implementation details vary for other modalities, the ideas are the same: we find items that don't fit well into any cluster, that *are* in a cluster but in a very small cluster, or that are different from most others in their cluster, and can take these to be outliers.

Another advantage of at least of some forms of cluster-based outlier detection is they can be very efficient in production. For example, if we take each point's distance to the nearest cluster center as its outlier score and assume there is a relatively small number of clusters, we can evaluate each point very quickly. To implement this, we first cluster the data in the training set and identify the corresponding set of cluster centers. Each new point, then, needs to be compared only to this small set of cluster centers, taking the minimum distance as their outlier score (that is, the distance to the closest cluster center). Any points close to at least one cluster center are inliers and any points not close to any of these centers may be considered outliers. The scores may also, optionally, be weighted by the sizes of the clusters in the training data to take this into consideration, without significantly affecting efficiency.

Cluster-based outlier detection does, though, require good clustering, which can be difficult to find, even where the data is logically clustered. It may be necessary to try multiple clustering algorithms and multiple parameters for these before finding a good clustering. There are a variety of metrics, such as the Silhouette score (proved by scikit-learn) that make it possible to evaluate each clustering. These allow us to compare the clusterings and select the clustering that received the best score. While this allows us to select the best clustering, the scores can still be difficult to interpret, and it can be difficult to determine if we have a meaningful clustering. This is a major challenge of clustering-based algorithms.

A similar idea to clustering data is to explicitly segment the data. That is, instead of relying on clustering algorithms to divide the data into subsets, it is possible to divide the data ourselves. For example, instead of clustering financial records, we can explicitly segment these into sales, expenses, payroll, and so on. Doing this may actually separate records created by the various mechanisms better than a clustering algorithm. Depending on the data, this can be done based on one or a small number of features—for example, simply by taking the unique values in a categorical column or binning values in a numeric column and taking these as representing distinct processes. In the case of financial transactions, if we can separate sales, purchases, payroll, and so on, this can be more reliable than hoping a clustering algorithm will do this. It will also certainly be more interpretable.

If we are able to, through either clustering or segmenting, divide the data into meaningful subsets, this allows us to perform outlier detection separately on each, without having the different clusters affect the sense of what's normal in the other clusters. This can be a plus if the clusters are completely distinct, but it loses some signal where there are, for example, some features that are consistent among the clusters; in these cases, we may benefit from assessing the complete dataset to get the best sense of what is normal, at least in these features.

It is also the case that, while dividing the data has benefits, it's possible to repeatedly subdivide the data into progressively more and more specific subsets of records. This can create extremely relevant subsets for comparison for each record but can also create very small subsets that may not be large enough to compare to in a statistically sound way. Normally, we would divide the data into about 2 to 10 clusters and rarely more unless the data is very large.

3.2.4   *Frequent item set based*

The detectors we've seen so far assume numeric data, and this is true of the majority of outlier detector algorithms. It's possible to use numeric detectors with tables that have one or more categorical columns, but the categorical values will need to be encoded as numbers. This is quite possible, and we'll look in later chapters at ways to do this. Where your data is primarily categorical, though, working with categorical outlier detectors (detectors that assume the features are categorical) can be more convenient and avoids the difficulties of creating good numeric encodings. Unfortunately, there are relatively few categorical outlier detectors; frequent item set-based methods are among the few examples. The two main frequent item sets-based methods are frequent pattern outlier factor (FPOF) and association rules. FPOF is the simpler of these, and we'll cover it here, with association rules covered in chapter 7.

Frequent item sets (FISs) are very common values within a column, or sets of values from two or more columns that frequently appear together. For example, in the expenses table in the previous chapter, repeated here and showing more rows as table 3.3, we may see certain staff IDs frequently appearing with certain accounts. We see three records for Staff ID 9000483 and Account Meals, which may then be a frequent pattern.

FPOF is based on the idea that, as long as a dataset has many frequent item sets (which almost all do, as almost all tables have some associations between the features), then most rows will contain multiple frequent item sets and inlier records will contain significantly more frequent item sets than outlier rows. We can take advantage of this to identify outliers as rows that contain much fewer, and much less frequent, FISs than most rows.

Table 3.3 Staff expenses

Row	Staff ID	Department	Account	Date of expense	Date submitted	Time submitted	Amount
1	9000483	Sales	Meals	02/03/2023	02/03/2023	09:10:21	12.44
2	9303332	Marketing	Travel	02/03/2023	02/03/2023	10:43:35	41.90
3	9847421	Engineering	Meals	02/03/2023	02/03/2023	10:56:04	643.99
4	9303332	Marketing	Supplies	02/03/2023	02/03/2023	11:12:09	212.00
5	9000483	Sales	Meals	02/03/2023	02/03/2023	11:43:43	33.65
6	9000483	Sales	Meals	02/03/2023	02/03/2023	12:05:37	41.77

To perform FIS-based outlier detection on this data, it is necessary to first convert the date and numeric values to categories. For this we use binning: placing each date or numeric value into a single bin. Binning can be done in various ways, with different advantages and disadvantages. In this example, we will put the emphasis on interpretability; for dates, we use the day of the month, the times will be converted to one of 24 categories based on the hour, and the amounts are based on the order of magnitude (number of digits). This results in the values shown in table 3.4.

Table 3.4 Staff expenses with binned values

Row	Staff ID	Department	Account	Date of expense	Date submitted	Time submitted	Amount
1	9000483	Sales	Meals	2	2	9	2
2	9303332	Marketing	Travel	2	2	10	2
3	9847421	Engineering	Meals	2	2	10	3
4	9303332	Marketing	Supplies	2	2	11	3
5	9000483	Sales	Meals	2	2	11	2
6	9000483	Sales	Meals	2	2	12	2

For a real-world example of using FPOF, see listing 3.6, which runs on the SpeedDating set from OpenML. Executing FPOF begins with mining the dataset for the FISs. A number of libraries are available to support this. For this example, we use mlxtend (https://rasbt.github.io/mlxtend/), a general-purpose library for machine learning. It provides several algorithms to identify frequent item sets; we use apriori here. To install this, we can call

```
pip install mxltend
```

We first collect the data from OpenML. Normally we would use all categorical and (binned) numeric features, but for simplicity here we will use only a small number of features.

Listing 3.6 Executing FPOF on the SpeedDating dataset

```
from mlxtend.frequent_patterns import apriori
import pandas as pd
from sklearn.datasets import fetch_openml
import warnings

warnings.filterwarnings(action='ignore', category=DeprecationWarning)

data = fetch_openml('SpeedDating', version=1, parser='auto')          ← Collects the data
data_df = pd.DataFrame(data.data, columns=data.feature_names)

data_df = data_df[['d_pref_o_attractive', 'd_pref_o_sincere',
                   'd_pref_o_intelligence', 'd_pref_o_funny',        ← Selects a subset
                   'd_pref_o_ambitious',                               of the features
                   'd_pref_o_shared_interests']]
data_df = pd.get_dummies(data_df)          ← Converts the data
data_df = data_df.replace(1, True)           to binary format
data_df = data_df.replace(0, False)

frequent_itemsets = \                                               ← Identifies the
        apriori(data_df, min_support=0.3, use_colnames=True)          frequent item sets

data_df['FPOF_Score'] = 0
                                                                   ← Loops through each
for fis_idx in frequent_itemsets.index:                              FIS found in the data
    fis = frequent_itemsets.loc[fis_idx, 'itemsets']
    support = frequent_itemsets.loc[fis_idx, 'support']            ← Finds the support
    col_list = (list(fis))                                           for the current FIS
    cond = True
    for col_name in col_list:
        cond = cond & (data_df[col_name])
                                                                   ← Updates the score for
    data_df.loc[data_df[cond].index, 'FPOF_Score'] += \              each record based on
        support                                                      the support of each
                                                                     FIS it contains
min_score = data_df['FPOF_Score'].min()          ← Reverses the scores to have higher
                                                   values for more outlierish records
```

```
max_score = data_df['FPOF_Score'].max()
data_df['FPOF_Score'] = [(max_score - x) / (max_score - min_score)
                         for x in data_df['FPOF_Score']]
```

The apriori algorithm requires all features to be one-hot encoded. For this, we use pandas's `get_dummies()` method. We then call the apriori method to determine the frequent item sets. Doing this, we need to specify the minimum support, which is the minimum fraction of rows in which the FIS appears. We don't want this to be too high or the records—even the strong inliers—will contain few FISs, making them hard to distinguish from outliers. We also don't want this to be too low or the FISs may not be meaningful and outliers may contain as many FISs as inliers. With low minimum support, apriori may also generate a very large number of FISs, making execution slower and interpretability lower. In this example, we use 0.3. It's also possible, and sometimes done, to set restrictions on the size of the FISs, requiring they relate to between some minimum and maximum number of columns, which may help narrow in on the form of outliers you're most interested in.

The FISs are then returned in a pandas dataframe, with columns for the support and the list of column values (in the form of the one-hot encoded columns, which indicate both the original column and value). We then loop through each frequent item set and increment the score for each row that contains the frequent item set by the support. This can optionally be adjusted to favor frequent items sets of greater lengths (with the idea that a FIS with a support of, say 0.4 and covering five columns is, everything else equal, more relevant than a FIS with support of 0.4 covering, say, two columns), but here we simply use the number and support of the FISs in each row. This actually produces a score for normality and not outlierness, so when we normalize the scores to be between 0.0 and 1.0, we reverse the order. The rows with the highest scores are now the rows with the least and the least common frequent item sets.

One weakness of this algorithm is that the frequencies of the item sets can be difficult to compare fairly, as each column has its own distribution and each set of features has their own joint distributions. This is a common theme in outlier detection, even within single outlier detectors: where multiple tests are performed on the data, it is necessary to combine the scores in a meaningful way, and this can be difficult. The approach here is simple (simply adding the support for each FIS found) and avoids any complications scaling the individual scores, but we should note that varying the scoring may suit your needs better.

To interpret the results, we can first view the `frequent_itemsets`. To include the length of each FIS we add

```
frequent_itemsets['length'] = \
    frequent_itemsets['itemsets'].apply(lambda x: len(x))
```

There are 24 FISs found, the longest covering three features. Table 3.5 shows the first 10 rows, sorting by support.

Table 3.5   The frequent item sets found in SpeedDating using 0.3 as minimum support

support	itemsets	Length
0.797326	(d_pref_o_ambitious_[0-15])	1
0.726307	(d_pref_o_shared_interests_[0-15])	1
0.593817	(d_pref_o_ambitious_[0-15], d_pref_o_shared_interests_[0-15])	2
0.509907	(d_pref_o_intelligence_[16-20])	1
0.461924	(d_pref_o_funny_[16-20])	1
0.455956	(d_pref_o_sincere_[16-20])	1
0.380520	(d_pref_o_funny_[0-15])	1
0.365839	(d_pref_o_sincere_[0-15])	1
0.359274	(d_pref_o_attractive_[21-100])	1
0.347577	(d_pref_o_ambitious_[0-15], d_pref_o_funny_[0-15])	2

Adding the score column to the original dataframe and sorting by the score, we see the most normal row in table 3.6:

Table 3.6   The most inlier row

d_pref_o attractive	d_pref_o sincere	d_pref_o intelligence	d_pref_o funny	d_pref_o ambitious	d_pref_o shared interests	FPOF Score
[21-100]	[16-20]	[16-20]	[16-20]	[0-15]	[0-15]	0.0

We can see the values for this row match the FISs well. The value for d_pref_o_ attractive is [21-100], which is a FIS (with support 0.36); the values for d_pref_o_ ambitious and d_pref_o_shared_interests are [0-15] and [0-15], which is also a FIS (support 0.59). The other values also tend to match FISs.

The most unusual row is shown in table 3.7. This matches none of the identified FISs.

Table 3.7   The most outlier row

d_pref_o attractive	d_pref_o sincere	d_pref_o intelligence	d_pref_o funny	d_pref_o ambitious	d_pref_o shared interests	FPOF Score
[0-15]	[21-100]	[21-100]	[0-5]	[16-20]	[16-20]	1.0

As the FISs themselves are intelligible, this method has the advantage of producing reasonably interpretable results, though this is less true where many frequent item sets are used. Also, the interpretability can be reduced, as outliers are identified not by containing FISs but by not containing them, which means explaining a row's score amounts to listing all the FISs it does not contain. However, it is not strictly necessary to list all missing FISs to explain each outlier; listing a small set of the most common FISs that are missing will be sufficient to explain outliers to a decent level for most purposes.

One variation on this method uses the infrequent, as opposed to frequent, item sets, scoring each row by the number and rarity of each infrequent item set they contain. This can produce useful results as well but is significantly more computationally expensive, as many more item sets need to be mined, and each row is tested against many FISs. The final scores can be more interpretable, though, as they are based on the item sets found, not missing, in each row.

A similar idea, used in time series data, is known as *frequent episode mining* (see, for example, https://github.com/chuanconggao/PrefixSpan-py), where we identify sets of events that tend to occur together within a given time window, either in a specific order (event A tends to precede event B) or simply together. Again, where we can identify these patterns and they are frequent, then any series that matches these patterns well is more normal than one that does not.

I am not aware of an implementation of FPOF in Python, though there are some in R. The bulk of the work with FPOF is in mining the FISs, and there are numerous Python tools for this, including the `mlxtend` library used here. The remaining code for FPOP is fairly simple. Some variation on the previous code may suit your needs well and is not difficult to implement or test. This does also provide an example, along with some other detectors in this chapter (KNN, Radius, and DBSCAN), that shows that implementing outlier detections algorithms can often be straightforward. The bulk of the work with outlier detection is typically in assessing and tuning the detectors, but implementing the detectors themselves can be relatively simple.

3.2.5 *Model based*

A common theme with outlier detection is to take techniques developed for other purposes, such as some we've seen already (frequent item set mining, clustering) or others we'll see later (including compression, entropy, forecasting) and apply these to outlier detection. These techniques each attempt to model, in some way, the data in a dataset. In practice, they usually tend to model well only the majority of data, and will not perfectly cover the outliers, which means outliers can be picked up as records where these models do not quite fit. With the previous models, this is where points don't fit into clusters, or can't be described well by any set of FISs. With compression, this relates to records that don't compress well. In this section, we look at predictive models, using the same general idea: outliers are values that cannot be predicted well by a model that is otherwise accurate.

There are several methods to identify outliers based on predictive models, including some covered in later chapters. For an example here, we use the approach of creating a synthetic dataset, similar to the real data, and then training a binary classifier to distinguish real records from fake. This approach is known by various names, but for this book I refer to it as a Real versus Fake outlier detector.

Listing 3.7 uses a real dataset provided by scikit-learn, the `breast_cancer` set. In this example, to generate the synthetic data, we simply calculate the mean and standard deviation of each feature in the real data and then randomly create values from a normal distribution for each column using this. More sophisticated techniques are examined in chapter 11, but in this case, we were able to create a decision tree that largely distinguishes the real from fake while still flagging some real rows as appearing to be fake. A variation on this, classifier adjusted density estimation (CADE) works almost identically, though it uses a uniform distribution instead of a normal distribution, so will tend to generate slightly less realistic data, which allows the real and the fake to be separated somewhat more easily.

Listing 3.7   Predicting real vs. synthetic data

```
import pandas as pd
import numpy as np
from sklearn.datasets import load_breast_cancer
from sklearn.tree import DecisionTreeClassifier
from sklearn.metrics import confusion_matrix
from sklearn.tree import export_text

np.random.seed(0)
                                                         ◄──┐ Collects
data = load_breast_cancer()                                 │ the data
data_df = pd.DataFrame(data.data, columns=data.feature_names)
data_df['Real'] = True

synth_df = pd.DataFrame()                      ◄──┐ Generates similar
for col_name in data_df.columns:                  │ synthetic (fake) data
    mean = data_df[col_name].mean()
    stddev = data_df[col_name].std()
    synth_df[col_name] = np.random.normal(
        loc=mean, scale=stddev, size=len(data_df))
synth_df['Real'] = False

train_df = pd.concat([data_df, synth_df])          ┐ Creates a
                                                   │ predictive model
clf = DecisionTreeClassifier(                      │ to distinguish the
        max_depth=7, random_state=0)           ◄──┘ real from fake
clf.fit(train_df.drop(columns=['Real']), train_df['Real'])
pred = clf.predict(train_df.drop(columns=['Real']))    ┐ Outputs the accuracy
confusion_matrix(train_df['Real'], pred)           ◄──┘ of the model
```

This does take some tweaking, both in generating the fake data and in tuning the classifier. In this example, I adjusted the `min_samples_per_leaf` and `max_depth` of the tree parameters, settling on using the default for `min_samples_per_leaf` and 7 for `max_depth`. This found, of the 569 real records, that 544 were correctly identified as real and 25 were predicted as fake. Of the 569 fake records, 561 were correctly identified as fake, and 8 were predicted as real (this is expected, as the data is random and some fraction will naturally be very realistic).

This looks good. As the decision tree was generally accurate but not able to distinguish 25 real records from synthetic data, we can consider these as outliers. This works well here and required creating only semi-realistic synthetic data: the features each had realistic values, but the associations between the features were not maintained. Creating good synthetic data for outlier detection purposes, including this, is difficult (as covered in chapter 11). The general idea is to create data as realistic as necessary and then tune a model until it is very accurate but not perfect. The model will then capture the strongest patterns in the data and will misclassify (predict to be synthetic) any rows not matching these patterns. The process can be tuned to focus on obvious outliers (such as single extreme values) or subtle outliers (such as combinations of multiple columns), as is more relevant.

This type of outlier detector has the major advantage that, where an interpretable classifier is used to distinguish real from fake records, we have, then, an interpretable outlier detector. In this case, we use a fairly shallow decision tree, which we can examine by calling the `export_text()` method. Given that, for any records flagged as outliers (predicted to be fake), we can compare these against the tree to determine why the prediction was made as it was. We take a closer look at this in chapter 13.

In this example, if we are simply looking for records that are different from the majority of other records, it's not necessary to create a robust model that can reliably generalize well to unseen data. We can simply evaluate the decision tree and confirm if this appears sensible to identify outliers. However, where this will run long term as an outlier detector on unseen data, we should cross-validate the predictor to ensure it can generalize well.

Interestingly, this approach is close to the opposite of something commonly done in vision. There, we often train models to be robust to perturbations, so rotate, crop, discolor, and otherwise modify the images, training the models to recognize that, despite these modifications, these are still the same objects, and are not anomalies. In vision, it's normally the case that any perturbations of this sort do not fundamentally change the nature of the image, as we're usually interested in identifying the objects themselves and not properties of the picture. With tabular data, on the other hand, perturbations like these very often result in data that's unusual and possibly nonsensical, as there are many more constraints related to the relationships between columns.

3.3 Types of detectors

As well as there being different algorithms, there are other properties that distinguish detectors. These include

- How sensitive/robust they are to being trained with contaminated data
- If they work with numeric or categorical data
- If they are able to detect global and/or local outliers
- If the output is a score or a binary label
- The training time required
- The inference time required
- Interpretability
- The number of parameters and how sensitive the detector is to the parameters
- Robustness to the curse of dimensionality

3.3.1   *Clean vs. contaminated training data*

A distinction sometimes made, for example by scikit-learn, is between *outlier detection* and *novelty detection*. In some cases, the term *anomaly detection* may be used as an umbrella term for both, but often, as in this book, the three terms are used interchangeably. The distinct ideas are important though. In the sense scikit-learn uses the terms, *novelty detection* implies that the detector has been trained on very clean data, with no outliers. There is no concept of checking this data for outliers—only any subsequent data that may be collected. In this case, the detector is looking for anything different from what it was trained on. That is, novelties are records that are novel compared to the training data.

On the other hand, with *outlier detection* (in this sense of the term), the detector is trained on contaminated data—data with some outliers—and so will attempt to model the majority, but not all, data as well as possible. It is able to flag outliers within this, as well as any subsequent data collected. Some detectors may only be able to support novelty detection, though most are able to support being trained with some outliers present in the data.

3.3.2   *Numeric vs. categorical*

The majority of detectors assume entirely numeric data, with some assuming entirely categorical data. Very few support mixed data, though the majority of real-world data contains a mix of numeric and categorical columns; and usually both types are equally relevant, or nearly, for outlier detection. Consequently, for most outlier detection work, we must either use a numeric detector and numerically encode all categorical features (for example, using one-hot or ordinal encoding) or use a categorical detector and bin the numeric features.

3.3.3   *Local vs. global detectors*

Local and global outliers are quite different, and some detectors are more suited to find one than the other. In addition, some algorithms can detect both but may tend to favor one or the other based on parameter settings.

The concept of local and global *detectors* is closely related to the concept of local and global *outliers*. As we've seen, some detectors compare records to all other records and some to only a subset of other records. With KNN and Radius, for example, points are compared to their neighborhoods. With Real vs Fake, on the other hand, we do not divide the data in this way. However, what makes a detector a local or a global detector is not this but how the scores are evaluated. With global detectors, there's a global sense of what is normal that all points are compared to. With local detectors, there's a local sense of what's normal that points are compared to. Local detectors not only compare the points to only a subset of the data, but they also gauge their outlierness against only a subset of the data.

KNN, for example, evaluates each point with respect to its neighborhood (its k nearest neighbors) so is local in this regard, but there's a global standard of what distances are normal, and so the KNN detector is actually considered a global outlier detector; records are scored high if there's a large distance to their kth-nearest neighbor relative to the full dataset, even where this is a typical distance in that region. This may be desirable, as k^{th}NN then puts more emphasis on global outliers, but it may provide less meaningful scores for local outliers.

KDE detectors are also global detectors: each point is evaluated based on the density of its location, and we compare this density to the density of all other points in the dataset to identify the points in the most sparse spaces. (KDE does not compare the density of records to only those of their neighbors.) FPOF is also a global detector: rows are evaluated based on the number of FISs they contain relative to all other rows in the data.

Local detectors compare each point to a small set of other points, usually their neighborhood or their cluster, and will gauge how unusual a record is in comparison to this subset of the data. Some cluster-based methods may be considered local detectors—for example, where records are evaluated based on the distance to their cluster center compared to the average distance to the center for that cluster. We may also create a similar but global detector, where records are evaluated based on the distance to their cluster center compared to the average distance of all points in the dataset to their cluster centers.

With local detectors, the idea is to compare like with like (for example, comparing payroll records to other payroll records), while with global detectors, the idea is to find the most anomalous records overall.

The distinction, though, is not as strict as it may seem. While local detectors evaluate each record against a local standard of what's normal, they will still tend to flag records that are globally unusual. Global detectors, however, as they evaluate each record only against a global standard of normal, will not detect records that are globally normal but locally unusual.

3.3.4 Scores vs. flags

Some detectors return binary labels distinguishing inliers from outliers, while others return numeric scores, estimating how unusual each record is. Most modern detectors are capable of providing both, so the distinction is less relevant than it once was, though you may still find some detectors that return only binary labels or only scores. One example is the DBSCAN method described previously (at least as it is defined there), which simply returned –1 for outliers—without any score (though it is possible to use DBSCAN to produce scores as well).

The difference may seem minor as, where detectors return only scores, labels can be easily created from scores given a threshold, but setting an appropriate threshold can actually be quite difficult. And, where the detectors return only labels, this can lose valuable information, as the specific score is an important part of understanding the outliers (in some cases there is no other information provided to assess the outliers— we have only the detector's estimate of how outlierish the record is). Also, in situations where you wish to collect the top, say, 50 outliers, this is impossible where binary labels are used and we have more, or less, than 50 records flagged by the detector. In this case, it is necessary to tune the detector until there is roughly the desired number, while with scores, we can simply take those with the top 50 scores, even if it is not clear from the scores if all of these are reasonably outliers.

In most cases, there is no truly meaningful cutoff between inliers and outliers. In some cases, there may be, such as where we are looking strictly for data artifacts, and some entries are clearly correct and some clearly incorrect and there is a large distinction in outlier scores. More often, though, there is a spectrum from the strongest inliers to the strongest outliers, with no clear demarcation and labels are actually somewhat of a false dichotomy. See figure 3.8 for the distribution of outlier scores from previous examples, the distribution of FPOF scores on the SpeedDating dataset, and the distribution of KDE scores on the wall-robot-navigation dataset. These show both the histograms of scores and a rank plot, plotting the scores against their rank order. With the FPOF scores, there is a roughly normal distribution, with no clear specific cutoff. The KDE scores are more exponential—still with no clear specific cutoff—but it appears at least easier to set a reasonable point, likely somewhere between 4 and 6.

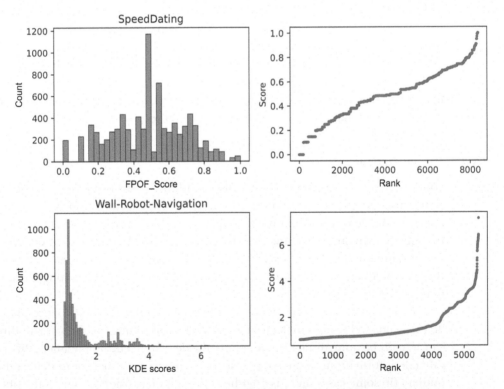

Figure 3.8   The distribution of outlier scores using FPOF on the SpeedDating dataset and KDE on the wall-robot-navigation dataset. In some cases, such as the KDE scores from the robot navigation dataset, we can identify a reasonable cutoff to separate inliers from outliers, while with the FPOF scores from SpeedDating, there is no clear cutoff.

In most contexts, only some manageable set of outliers will be investigated or acted upon, and it's necessary to pick some sensible threshold, either in terms of score, or number of outliers, to be pragmatic. The best way to do this will vary. For example, where we wish to investigate up to 50 outliers, the detector is able to output both binary labels and scores, and the binary labels are meaningful, then one reasonable option may be: where the detector assigns a binary outlier label to more than 50 labels, take those with the top 50 scores, and where the detector assigns a binary outlier label to less than 50, take only those.

It is, however, more difficult to tune a detector to create binary labels that match your interests than scores, as setting the binary labels for many detectors still requires scoring the records, followed by setting a threshold, and so two stages of tuning.

3.3.5 *The time required for training and predicting*

The ability to scale to large volumes of data is an important distinction, as some detectors are designed for smaller data sets and cannot function well beyond this. Some, with large numbers or rows, or, depending on the algorithm, large numbers of features, can become too slow to be practical.

With outlier detectors, we need to consider both the time to fit a model as well as inference time: the time to score a set of records once the model is fit. In most situations, the time to fit the model is not overly relevant, as it can be done outside of the production environment and may be done relatively infrequently, while the time required for inference, particularly in real-time environments, can be crucial. In other environments we may constantly receive new data and need to evaluate the most recent data relative to a current sense of what is normal; in these cases, training new models quickly may also be important.

When experimenting with outlier detectors, it can be useful to start with small numbers of rows and columns and then try using larger numbers, both for training and for predicting (where these are separate steps). You may find some algorithms too slow to be practical. There are several ways to speed up algorithms, which we look at later, but it may be more practical to use other algorithms. The methods that scale the best are those based on performing simple univariate tests on each column and aggregating the results. There are, as well, detectors that provide multivariate tests and can scale sufficiently in most contexts, for example, Isolation Forest, which we'll see in chapter 5.

3.3.6 *The ability to process many features*

Some detectors, including most distance-, density-, and clustering-based methods, can see their accuracy degrade with large numbers of features due to the curse of dimensionality. Again, where there are many features, univariate tests may be the most practical, as they avoid the curse of dimensionality completely. In general, detectors that avoid distance calculations will tend to scale better to larger numbers of features. Where your data has a very large number of features, this may limit the set of feasible detectors. It may also be possible to execute outlier detection on subsets of features, which we will describe in chapter 10.

3.3.7   *The parameters required*

Setting the parameters appropriately can be much more difficult for some detectors than for others. As we indicated, distance-based detectors that require specifying p and d (such that at least p percent of rows are within distance d) are more difficult to tune than, say, KNN, which requires setting only a single parameter, k. In addition, even where only a small number of parameters are required, in some cases these can be difficult to set, as with Radius, where setting an appropriate value for the radius is unintuitive and can realistically only be set experimentally.

As well as the difficulty in determining the most appropriate parameters, some detectors are much more sensitive than others to the choice of parameters: some detectors can score the records significantly differently based on the choice of parameters. For example, KNN is very sensitive to the k used (though less so if the distances to the k nearest neighbors are averaged, as opposed to taking the maximum). More difficult still to tune can be detectors based on neural networks, which may require selecting an appropriate architecture as well as learning parameters. On the other hand, some detectors (for example, one we'll see later called ECOD), require no parameters, and others, such as Isolation Forest, do require parameters but are reasonably robust to these, returning similar results for different values passed.

Summary

- There are numerous machine learning approaches to outlier detection. These can be placed in categories, including categories such as covering distance, density, clustering, frequent item set, and predictive model-based outlier detection.
- There are also many outlier detection algorithms that do not fit into these categories.
- Most detector algorithms support only numeric data, while others support only categorical data, with very few, unfortunately, natively supporting both.
- Coding outlier detection algorithms can often be surprisingly simple, with many requiring very few lines of code.
- One of the most difficult challenges in outlier detection is the curse of dimensionality.
- Where datasets have many features, the ability to handle the curse of dimensionality is one of the most relevant criteria determining which detectors are feasible to use, though using subsets of features is also possible.
- Methods based on calculating distances between points are most vulnerable to the curse of dimensionality.
- There are several other properties of outlier detectors that can make them more or less feasible or convenient for different outlier detection projects, including their ability to train on contaminated data, the time required to train and predict, and the ease of tuning the parameters.

The outlier
detection process

4

This chapter covers

- Working on an outlier detection project in production
- The types of problems we may work with
- Where outlier detectors are actually the best option
- Collecting and preparing data as well as fitting the models
- Evaluating and combining models

We now have a good sense of how outlier detection works generally and how some specific algorithms to identify anomalies work, including statistical and machine learning-based methods. There are, though, a number of steps involved with effectively executing an outlier detection project, which, now that we have a good foundation, we should look at.

In this chapter, we'll go through the main steps typically involved in outlier detection projects, though they will, of course, vary. If you're familiar with other areas of machine learning, such as prediction, the steps with outlier detection will be very similar. Each of these steps is important, and each has some subtle points, often a little different than the corresponding steps for prediction projects.

4.1   Outlier detection workflow

The general steps for a fairly typical outlier detection project will, more or less, be

- Determine what type of outliers we wish to identify
- Choose the type of model(s) to be used
- Collect the data
- Clean the data if possible (removing any obvious outliers)
- Feature selection
- Feature engineering
- If necessary, encode categorical values/bin numeric values
- If necessary, scale numeric values
- Fit one or more models
- Evaluate the models as well as is feasible
- Take the best model created or create an ensemble of models
- Reformat the data to additionally locate collective outliers
- Reformat, where applicable, into time-series or other formats to help identify further outliers.
- If necessary, set up the model to run in production on an ongoing basis
- As the model runs in production, collect and log the results
- Follow up with the outliers found
- Evaluate the results and tune the detectors to run better going forward

Some of these steps may not be clear now, but we'll go through each of these, at least briefly, in this chapter. Several steps, including evaluation, creating ensembles of detectors, and identifying collective outliers, are significant issues in themselves that require more attention than we can give here, but will receive further discussion in later chapters. We cover here the early steps in detail, particularly assessing the type of problem, collecting the data, and fitting a model, to get you on your way to working with outlier detection.

Many of these steps will be unnecessary for some projects. For example, where we have a one-off project, without the need to run outlier detection on an ongoing basis, steps related to ongoing monitoring will not apply. And using time-series analysis will not lend itself to all projects or be worth the effort in all cases, though it is very powerful where it is applicable and is often worth examining. We provide some introduction to this in chapter 17.

Figure 4.1 shows the main steps for a simple one-off project. One key point is that the process can be very iterative. Once the data is collected and preprocessed, we will

typically loop between trying different models and parameters, trying different combinations of models, and evaluating the system. However, this diagram is only one possible workflow, and very often we loop back and collect more data, try different feature
selection, feature engineering, and preprocessing as well until we get results that are
useful for the task at hand.

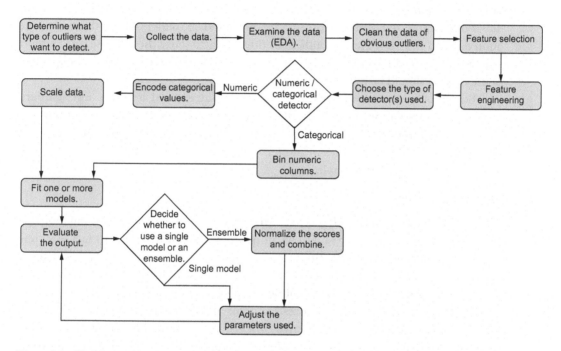

**Figure 4.1 Workflow outlining the basic steps in an outlier detection project. This assumes a one-time analysis
(as opposed to ongoing monitoring) and skips tests for collective outliers and time-series analysis, which may
also often be done. Note the loop between tuning and evaluating the model, which may continue for any number
of iterations. Additional loops may also be present in some projects, as any of the steps may be repeated as
necessary.**

Determining which steps are relevant, and often how to perform each step, relates to
the problem we are trying to solve, which largely comes down to identifying which type
of outliers we wish to identify, so this is where we start.

4.2   *Determining the types of outliers we are interested in*

The term *outlier detection* can be used in different ways, which can relate to quite different types of problems. In some cases, this refers to searching for what may be called
statistical outliers: here we are looking for anything statistically unusual, without necessarily a preconceived idea of what we are interested in. These are the types of outliers
we focus on in this book: outliers that are found with methods such as univariate tests,
distance, density, frequent item set-based detectors, and other such tests. These are

records that are simply statistically different than the majority of other rows and may or may not all be of interest for any given project.

In other cases, there may actually be something specific we are looking for, which we'll refer to here as *specific outliers*. For example, it may be data entry errors, fraud, network intrusion, certain chemical reactions, or some other object or event that we wish to locate in a collection of data. If this type of item is rare, or of unique interest, it may sometimes be referred to as an *outlier*, regardless of whether it is statistically unusual or not. For example, data entry errors may be referred to as outliers even if these are common enough that they are not outliers in the statistical sense. In this case, the outliers are unusual, not with respect to a given dataset, but compared to an ideal, or expected, sense of what should be in the data.

The terms "statistical outlier" and "specific outliers" used here are not standard terms, so it's not important to learn the terminology, but the concepts are important. There are different types of records you may be interested in finding, and different tools will return different types of outliers. It's important to create a system that best detects what you are interested in.

4.2.1 Statistical outliers

Very often when working with data, we know there may be issues in the data, or that there may be points of interest, but we don't know specifically what. In fact, it's common in business and scientific situations to collect a large volume of data—far more than can be assessed manually—and then to wish to search it for any nuggets. Even where we are aware of, or can think of, some specific things to look for, it may be clear that there could easily be other interesting items in the data. In a scientific context, we have to be careful to not quickly derive conclusions from anything found, but outlier detection can be a useful process to identify points to investigate or to help develop hypotheses, which can then be verified, if they turn out to be correct, through a more rigorous scientific process.

In other cases, there may be specific items we are looking for in the data, but if these items are rare and different from most other records, they will also be statistical outliers and so should be flagged by an outlier detector. An outlier detector may be an effective means to find these, though the detector will also flag anything else that is rare, so will likely also flag records we are uninterested in. Ideally, we will be able to filter the results down to the outliers we are interested in.

4.2.2 Specific outliers

Where the goal is to find specific outliers (a specific type of issue, which may or may not be statistically unusual), using rules or classifiers, as opposed to outlier detectors, may be the most viable option, though even here it may be that outlier detectors will work the best. The main distinction is that with specific outliers, it is at least possible to use tools other than detectors. Which is the best option will vary. It can be the case that running outlier detectors may not find the specific outliers we are interested in—for example, if these items are too common to be statistical outliers, are swamped by other records that are more statistically unusual, or are unusual but in a way too subtle for an outlier detector to identify, at least without also identifying many false positives as well.

If outlier detection does not find the records that you are interested in, in many cases you can tune the outlier detection process until it works better, trying different detectors and different hyperparameters, and creating collections of multiple detectors (possibly combined with rules). If the specific outliers you're interested in are truly rare and different, it is likely some detector will be able to find these. Outlier detection is often an experimental process that can require some trial and error. Having said that, if the specific outliers are too common to be considered statistical outliers, it may be best to use other methods, most likely rules or classifiers, discussed later.

4.2.3 *Known and unknown outliers*

We may also think of outliers in terms of *known* and *unknown outliers*, where *known* outliers refer to types of records we may expect to see, at least potentially (either records we've seen before or that we can anticipate), and *unknown* outliers refer to types of records we haven't even considered. An example of known outliers may be where data follows a Gaussian distribution and we may reasonably expect data five or six standard deviations from the mean on occasion. With autonomous vehicles, this may include other vehicles travelling at extremely high speeds—something we expect to see only very rarely if at all but that we can imagine.

Unknown outliers are outside these cases. In the case of image data, this may include types of objects we've not expected to see. For example, in astronomy, this may be an unanticipated shape of galaxy; or with autonomous vehicles, it may be an unknown type of object appearing on the road. In tabular data, unknown outliers may be types of financial transactions or sensor readings we've not previously thought about. These can often be the most interesting outliers, though they can also be tangential your purpose for outlier detection.

The concepts (statistical versus specific and known versus unknown) are related, though slightly different. Statistical outliers, which are anything statistically unusual, may include both known and unknown outliers. That is, both things we expect to see and things we do not anticipate may be statistically unusual if present.

Specific outliers will generally include only known outliers, but may actually include unknown outliers if the type of specific outlier is defined broadly enough. For example, if we are trying to detect data entry errors (a specific but fairly broad type of outlier) and are singularly concerned with finding these, these errors may still include cases we have not previously thought of.

Often multiple people are involved in outlier detection projects—for example, domain experts, data experts, data scientists, or others. Putting our heads together, we may have different ideas about what's possible to look for and what's useful, and we can often get a better sense, when discussing this, of what's most relevant. Coming out of this, even where there are specific outliers we are interested in, it's often the case that we see the utility in finding other types of outliers. Or we may find the opposite: we may conclude the greatest value is in focusing on the most relevant outliers.

Where we use outlier detectors and the system runs over a period of time, we will collect the set of statistical outliers found—the records that are unusual in some way. These will usually be assessed manually, or at least spot-checked, and in these we may find some records that are interesting or useful in some other way, and it may be worth looking for these going forward. Over time, your idea of what's relevant may change, possibly becoming more or less specific, or changing focus to other types of issues.

4.3   *Choosing the type of model to be used*

As there are different types of goals with outlier detection, different types of models will be appropriate in different cases. The first questions are: are you looking for statistical outliers or specific outliers, and are you looking for unknown or known outliers? There are then a few approaches we can take:

- Define a set of rules
- Train a classifier to distinguish normal from abnormal
- Use an outlier detector

That is, using an outlier detector is actually just one option, and rules-based and classifier-based approaches can be used for outlier detection as well and, in many cases, may work as well or better. Some types of outliers lend themselves more to each of these, though often two or all three of these approaches will be used together in a project.

The majority of the steps involved with a project, including gathering and preparing the data, creating one or more models, evaluating and combining these models, running the model(s) in production, and following up on the results, are largely the same regardless of the type of outlier we are interested in, and if we use rules, classifiers, or detectors as our models, though there are some differences we should be mindful of.

In many domains, including security, fraud detection, log monitoring, scientific research, auditing, and numerous others, we will be interested in statistical outliers (anything that is unusual), and we may be especially interested in unknown outliers (anything unanticipated). In other domains, we will be interested in specific anomalies (reasonably well-defined events that occur rarely). Where we are interested in statistical outliers, we will almost always use outlier detectors, as this is what they are designed for. Rules may be able to detect some statistically unusual records and may also be useful, but we will almost always want to use detectors as at least part of the system. Where we are interested in specific issues, we may use detectors, classifiers, or rules.

4.3.1   *Selecting the category of outlier detector*

Where we wish to use an outlier detector, as the whole or as part of the solution, there are specific types we can consider, as we saw in the previous chapters, such as k nearest neighbors (KNN), Radius, histogram-based, frequent pattern outlier factor (FPOF), etc. We will continue to look at specific algorithms as well in later chapters, which should help to develop our understanding of the strengths and weaknesses of each and the types of outliers they can detect. However, you will see in practice, much of outlier detection is experimentation.

Differences from one dataset to another (e.g., the number of rows, number of features, distribution of data, and so on) and the types of outliers you're interested in can make a large difference in terms of which tools are most useful, often in ways that may be difficult to predict. But it is good to have a sense of why tools may be, or may not be, able to detect what you are interested in. For example, clustering-based methods may break down if the data is not well-clustered, distance-based detectors may work poorly if the number of neighbors selected is inappropriate, and local outlier detectors may give poor results if we are interested primarily in global outliers.

Each detector will produce results that are meaningful in some sense, but they may not be relevant for the purpose at hand. There is often some tuning involved, primarily adjusting the specific models used and the hyperparameters. As there are many options available for outlier detection, it is common to try many; ideally this is done in a disciplined way, looking at forms of outlier detector that logically should be relevant.

Where these still do not give the results you wish, it may be because you have a clear sense of specific outliers you wish to find, and it may be useful to also look at rules or classifiers. We've looked at detectors already and will focus on these for the majority of the book but should take a closer look at using rules and classifiers, which we do next.

4.3.2   *Rules-based approaches*

Rules are simple scripts that assess the data row by row and flag any items that are specifically identified by the tests. These may be set up to run sequentially (so that the first rule to fire for a row is the only rule) or in parallel (so that each row is checked against each rule and multiple rules may fire). As an example, consider table 2.1 from chapter 2, repeated here as table 4.1 (with additional columns added to further support generating useful rules). Taking the approach where any number of rules may fire per row, we may have rules such as

```
score = 0
if Account not in (Meals, Travel, Supplies, Payroll, Inventory, Rent)
    return True
if Time before 7:00am or after 8:00pm
    return True
if Count in Prev. Hour > 10:
    score += 4
if Count in Prev. Hour <= 10 and > 5:
    score += 3
if Amount > 200.00
    score += 2
if Account is Meals and Amount > 100.00
    score += 5
if Account is Meals and Amount > 80.00
    score += 4
if score > 6:
    return True
return False
```

Table 4.1   Staff expenses

Row	Staff ID	Department	Account	Time	Amount	Count in prev. hour	Count in prev. minute
1	9000483	Sales	Meals	09:10:21	12.44	44	1
2	9303332	Marketing	Travel	10:43:35	41.90	12	12
3	9847421	Engineering	Meals	08:56:04	643.99	1	1
4	9303332	Marketing	Supplies	03:12:09	212.00	1	2

We see here examples of both where rows will be immediately flagged as outliers (the first two rules) and where rows will be flagged as outliers if their total score is over a defined limit. Each individual rule can be as simple or complex as necessary, but usually most are very simple.

Most descriptions of outlier detection are fairly negative about the idea of using rules to identify even specific outliers—never mind statistical outliers. I'm much more open to the idea and find rules often work very well, though they do have real limitations, which means they should often be used in conjunction with outlier detectors. Nevertheless, rules can be a valuable tool for finding specific, and even statistical, outliers. When working with specific outliers especially, the outliers may be well defined enough that creating rules to identify them is straightforward. The rules may even be sufficient—the rules may be able to detect every anomaly you're interested in. Considering the expense report in table 4.1, it may be that the set of cases we wish to flag is captured well by the set of rules shown. Given that, flagging anything else would simply produce false positives.

In general, using rules has some strong advantages. They can be fast to execute and are deterministic—they will do exactly what is specified every time (some outlier detectors are stochastic, which is a negative where we wish to reproduce results, though most can be made deterministic by setting a seed).

Another major advantage of rules is they are interpretable. This is, unfortunately, not true of most outlier detectors (though we will look later at ways to make detectors more interpretable). This means that when a record is flagged by one or more rules, we know exactly why. This can make follow-up much more practical. In this example, there is likely a team assigned to check the expenses, that may not be able to evaluate each individually. If a transaction is flagged and a list of the rules flagging it can be presented, it makes that job a lot easier. Further, this allows outliers to be processed in bulk, as the similar outliers (those flagged by the same rules) can be found and considered together, allowing much more efficient analyses of the outliers found.

Another advantage is that rules lend themselves better to unit testing than do detectors. Though detectors can also be unit tested (this is covered in chapter 15), and there are significant advantages in this as with any software, rules are more straightforward in this regard. Each rule can be trivially converted into a unit test. In addition, by crafting the unit tests we may be able to define more precisely what we want flagged, and we can tweak the rules to ensure this is the case.

In regulated environments, rules may be the best approach simply because they can be audited. Where it must be fully understood how the system will behave given any potential input, this can preclude using most classifiers or detectors, making rules the only viable option, though some classifiers and detectors are interpretable and may be permissible in some cases as well.

Rules also have some significant disadvantages. They need to be written by hand, which can be error prone and time consuming, and they will never catch anything other than what is specifically coded. Further, if these rules constitute our complete system for monitoring the data, we won't know when we're missing anything else important. From time to time, we may wish to run an outlier detection routine, separate out anything flagged by the existing rules, and examine the remaining outliers. We may then decide to add additional rules. In the case of table 4.1, a detector may find additional outliers we wish to detect going forward—for example, for invalid staff IDs or very high values of Count in Prev. Minute.

What's commonly cited as a major problem with using rules is that in some environments, though the individual rules tend to be simple, there may be an explosion of rules created, and the sheer number may become an issue in itself. It may be necessary to create many hundreds of rules to reliably catch all the cases we're interested in. Given this, it's common to end up with sets of rules that are no longer interpretable or easy to tweak, often with many overlapping and contradictory rules and sometimes no history of why they were added or why thresholds are set as they are. With good coding practices, though, including code reviews, documentation, and unit tests, these issues can be well mitigated.

Another distinction between rules and detectors is in how they handle data changes. In many contexts, data will inevitably change over time. This is not true in all situations, such as with monitoring industrial processes that remain stable over time (unless changes are specifically made to the input or machinery), but it is often the case. For example, when monitoring web applications, we expect user behavior to change over time. Where rules are used, we will need to manually update the rules, which can be very time consuming. It can also be difficult to even detect when we need to update the rules: it is easy to detect where we start encountering more false positives (items erroneously flagged as outliers), but it can be difficult to detect where we have false negatives (items that should now be flagged as outliers but are not). There may be no way to notice this is occurring other than running outlier detectors from time to time.

Detectors also have challenges with shifting data patterns, but they are easier to update than rules: they simply have to be fit to more recent data. This has nuances we will look at later, but the process is at least easy and automatic. To make rules similarly flexible, and to adjust for changes in the data over time, the rules can be constructed to test, not for fixed thresholds, but for thresholds defined in terms of interquartile range, median absolute deviation, or other values, which are based on assessing the data over some recent period. For example, a rule shown previously is

```
if Time before 7:00am or after 8:00pm.
```

We could update this to remove the hard-coding of the times and base the thresholds instead on recent data—for example:

```
if Time before [the minimum time in the last 3 months] or after
    [the maximum time in the last 3 months]:
```

This provides a more robust system that allows the rules to adjust to recent changes in data.

Overall, rules provide clear, reliable, interpretable tests, but they will miss anything not specifically coded. Detectors will flag some records we are not concerned with and may miss some records we are concerned with, but they have the advantage that they will also detect outliers whether we anticipated them or did not (we do not need to specifically code for each type of outlier). Using both rules and outlier detectors together allows us to benefit from both.

Thus using both allows us to catch items that may be missed when using only rules or only detectors. It also allows us to create stronger scoring systems, especially where many rules and many outlier detectors are used. Where each rule and each detector score each record, the records are given a more robust overall score, based on many factors. This allows us, for example, to score records flagged by both rules and detectors higher, as these can reasonably be considered likely the most anomalous.

4.3.3 *Classifier-based approaches*

As with rules, classifiers (for example, Random Forests, boosted machines, or neural networks) may also be used to identify outliers. Normally this would be done only for *specific outliers*: cases where we have a clear idea of what we are looking for. For example, we may have cases where machinery has failed a number of times in the past and where we have logs both prior to these times and prior to the (vastly more common) times where the machinery worked normally. Where we can create simple rules, we would likely do so, but the patterns may be too difficult to identify well in this way. Where we cannot necessarily manually assess the logs to identify rules, we may be able to train a classifier to learn to distinguish these cases.

Classifiers do require a good set of labeled data. This can be the biggest point precluding using classifiers to identify rare items, even where the rare items are reasonably well defined. Normally in outlier detection settings, we have no, or almost no, labeled data. Classifiers can struggle to learn in contexts where there are few examples of the minority class. It is, however, not always the case that we have few examples of the rare event: even where events are relatively rare (say, 1 in every 5,000 records), with a large collection of data, such as a million rows or more, it may be possible to collect enough examples of these to train a strong classifier. In many cases, though, this is impossible. Where there are numerous specific things we are looking for, this can be especially difficult. In the case of looking for data entry errors, for example, this would require a decent number of examples of each possible such error, which is likely infeasible.

At least this is usually the case initially. If the system runs long term, we may accumulate labeled data over time, as detectors flag records and people assess and label these as being points of interest or not. Once there is sufficient labeled data, we then have a supervised machine learning problem and may be able, at that point, to use classification. Given that, there are some benefits from doing so: we can take advantage of state-of-the-art classifiers, such as boosted models or AutoML tools. We also have, where this is useful, more options in terms of interpretable models with classifiers as compared to outlier detectors.

Where it is possible to create an interpretable classifier, such as a shallow decision tree, it may also be possible to convert the model to rules. That is, training a classifier may simply be an intermediate step to create rules. This has an advantage where the classifier is used in a system with existing rules, as the rules can then be tweaked and simplified and the redundant rules removed, maintaining a single, clean set of rules. Some other interpretable models, such as generalized additive models, do not tend to convert as easily to rules, though they remain accurate and interpretable and are also useful to help identify specific outliers.

Another challenge we may have with training a classifier is that it's quite likely there are some number of unlabeled outliers mixed in with the data assumed to be inliers, which can result in unreliable classifiers. Over time, though, if we iteratively apply an improved process to the data, this may be eventually reduced. That is, classifiers may become more viable over time if the system runs long term.

Classifiers have some appealing advantages over rules. They can be more flexible, as they will flag not just records exactly matching one or more rules but any records similar to the records in the training data labeled as outliers. Classifiers will create a decision boundary that (though possibly difficult to understand) can be broad enough to cover some outliers that would not have been quite flagged by the rules, though this does lead to records also being incorrectly flagged in this way (flagged as outliers when they are in fact not).

Classifiers also have an advantage in that they can produce probabilities. The probabilities are not necessarily well calibrated (representing true probabilities), but at a minimum, if well fit, the probabilities will be at least well-ranked. If a classifier predicts one record is an outlier with a probability of 0.89 and another record with a probability of 0.6, we know the first record is more likely an outlier, even though we cannot say precisely how much more likely. In fact, working with probabilities in outlier detection contexts will usually work better than binary labels, as labels can be more difficult to tune well.

Although often useful for specific outliers, classifiers are unable to flag statistical outliers. We look further at this in chapter 15, but classifiers are inherently unable to determine which records are statistically unusual. Once trained, the classifier's purpose would strictly be to detect records similar to the specific type(s) of outlier they were trained on. To detect anything else (records anomalous in any other way), a detector will be necessary.

For the most part, the remainder of this chapter assumes the use of detectors, as opposed to rules or classifiers. There are some differences in how the steps are done depending on which is used. For example, with rules-based systems, feature selection is not as pressing; we do not need to remove irrelevant features and can simply not create rules related to these. The majority of the steps, however, are largely the same. We would, for example, engineer features in the same way, reformat date and string features the same, and so on.

4.4   Collecting the data

Realistically, once you are looking at an outlier detection project and are able to determine the types of outliers you are interested in, you already have at least some data at hand. But you may not have all the data that will be useful to train and evaluate the system, so it may be necessary to collect this data.

In most cases, the data collected will act both as the training data (the data that establishes what normal data looks like) and the predicted data (the data in which we search for outliers). So the data collected here likely serves two distinct purposes. If the outlier detection process is ongoing, this data will also establish the sense of normal that future data is compared against, at least until the model is refit. That is, the data collected, along with the models generated from it, will define what we evaluate all current and subsequent records against.

The model or models used can be one or more of the univariate statistical tests covered in chapter 2, multivariate tests such as those covered in chapter 3, rules, classifiers, or other types of models. With any of these, fitting a model is the act of determining the predominate patterns in the training data and creating a model to represent this. As we've seen, this can be simple, such as taking the mean and standard deviation of each feature, or more involved, such as determining the clusters and cluster centers for the data or the frequent item sets.

In the case of distance- and density-based models, such as KNN or Radius, though, this process works a little differently. The models are actually not such concise descriptions of the data, but are the training data itself, making the training data used particularly important. With Python detectors of these types, the fitting process usually consists of simply storing these points in a `BallTree` or similar structure.

One of the powerful qualities of outlier detection is that, as it is based on data, it will learn on its own (given just the training data) what constitutes normal and abnormal for data of this type, without the need for anyone to specify. This does imply, though, that outlier detectors need good training data that represents well the population it's modeling. As with machine learning generally, the more data, everything else equal, the better, though there will be diminishing returns beyond some point. In addition, the more typical the data used for training, the better we will be able to establish what normal data looks like.

Here, it's important that the data collected is typical—not just in the sense that each row is reasonably normal, but in the sense that the distribution of the data represents the true distribution well. This is much truer than with prediction models, where it is more important to cover all relevant cases well, without normally worrying about maintaining any distribution in the training data. But with outlier detection, the training data will establish not just what are normal rows, but the normal patterns. If we collect data for training and all the records in the data are typical but some segments of the data are over- or underrepresented, we may not be able to train a completely reliable detector. For example, if we used a simple detector such as one based on z-scores, it will rely on estimates of the mean and standard deviation of each column. If the data is skewed relative to the true population, this will skew the estimated mean and standard deviation and affect our ability to gauge how outlierish the data is. Where the data is skewed, we also develop a poor sense of what the frequent items sets are, the normal distances between points, the sparse regions, and so on.

When collecting the data, it's also important to include a sufficient set of features—the set of features we will need to assess properly which records are the most unusual. When first examining the data, it may be clear that more context is needed to identify what is of interest and what is not of interest. For example, with financial data, it may be useful to include macroeconomic data to provide context; it may be that fluctuations in company or industry performance can be explained, at least partially, by the economic climate, and the relevant outliers are the times when companies did well in poor economic conditions or poorly in good conditions.

Where rules are exclusively used, it is not necessary to collect data to train a model; there is, in fact, no training step in this case (unless we analyze the data to set thresholds and whitelists of valid categorical values based on the training data). Nevertheless, it is still necessary to collect data for testing, as the rules will need testing before being put in production and will need retesting from time to time. We may find, for example, that the rules flag far too few or far too many records, execute too slowly, are less interpretable than we wish, or otherwise need to be improved.

4.5 *Examining the data*

As with any machine learning project, starting with exploratory data analysis (EDA) is important to ensure the data collected is correct and to identify any insights we can from the data that may be useful for the outlier detection process. This is difficult in high dimensions and is usually restricted to examining single features and pairs of features at a time, but this does provide some context.

In this example, shown in listing 4.1, we'll load the baseball dataset from OpenML, which has career statistics for several players. We assume, for the example, we are looking for players that are highly unique but not in any specific way. Looking at the data, we can see the table has 1,340 rows and 16 columns and is primarily numeric, with only one categorical column. The dataset contains the following features: `Number_seasons`, `Games_played`, `At_bats`, `Runs`, `Hits`, `Doubles`, `Triples`, `Home_runs`, `RBIs`, `Walks`, `Strikeouts`, `Batting_average`, `On_base_pct`, `Slugging_pct`, `Fielding_ave`, and `Position`.

> **Listing 4.1 Loading and examining the baseball dataset from OpenML**

```
import pandas as pd
import numpy as np
from sklearn.datasets import fetch_openml
import matplotlib.pyplot as plt
```

```
import seaborn as sns
data = fetch_openml('baseball', version=1, parser='auto')
df = pd.DataFrame(data.data, columns=data.feature_names)
print(df.shape)
print(df.head())
print(df.dtypes)

for col_name in df.columns:
    if (df[col_name].dtype in ['int64', 'float64']):
        sns.histplot(data=df[col_name])
        plt.show()
```

Identifies the numeric types found in this dataset. Other datasets may require a more thorough list.

This code also generates a histogram of each numeric feature. Three examples are shown in figure 4.2. Each feature has a reasonable distribution. Some features, such as `Triples`, have what may be considered outliers but nothing unexpected. None of the features include internal outliers—only extreme values, if any outliers.

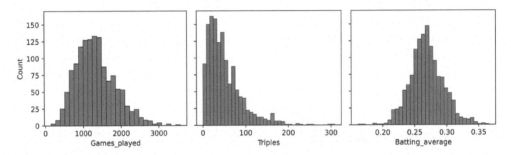

Figure 4.2   Distribution of the `Games_played`, `Triples`, and `Batting_average` features from the baseball dataset

We can also plot the distribution of each categorical feature. In this case, there is only one categorical feature, `Position`, which may be plotted as

```
sns.countplot(data=df, y='Position', orient='h', color='blue')
plt.show()
```

The results are shown in figure 4.3. The `designated_hitter` category is rare, though not likely enough to be considered anomalous. We may then plot the features pairwise, with code such as

```
for col_idx_1, col_name_1 in enumerate(df.columns):
    for col_idx_2 in range(col_idx_1+1, len(df.columns)):
        col_name_2 = df.columns[col_idx_2]
        if (df[col_name_1].dtype in ['int64', 'float64']) and \
            (df[col_name_2].dtype in ['int64', 'float64']):
            sns.scatterplot(data=df, x=col_name_1, y=col_name_2)
            plt.show()
```

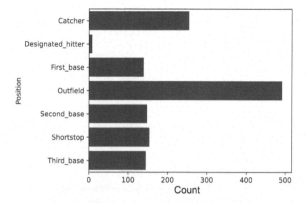

Figure 4.3 Distribution of the `Positions` feature

This creates a large number of plots; three examples are displayed in figure 4.4. We can see that the data has some correlations between the features and that there do not appear to be multiple clusters.

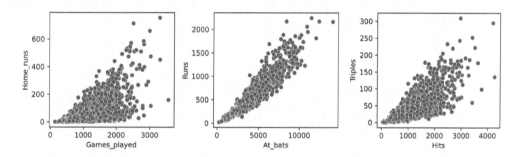

Figure 4.4 Scatterplots showing three pairs of features. We can see there are correlations between the features, with some players being somewhat unusual with respect to the patterns, but no large variations.

We should be cautious with the last observation though. Given the data appears in a single cluster in all 2D projections, we can assume this is likely true in the full data space as well, but it may not be. See figure 4.5 which shows an example of two clusters that can be seen in 2D but not in any 1D view. The same may occur here: there may be multiple clusters visible only in higher dimensions that are invisible in 1D or 2D views. Given this, it may still be worthwhile to try clustering the data to determine if there are clusters.

If there are multiple categorical columns, we can plot each pair as a heatmap, though this dataset has only one. We can also plot each pair of categorical and numeric features as boxplots. The code may be

```
for col_name_1 in df.columns:
    if (df[col_name_1].dtype in ['int64', 'float64']):
        sns.boxplot(data=df, x=col_name_1, y='Position', orient='h')
        plt.show()
```

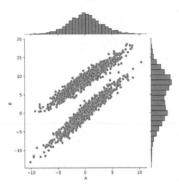

Figure 4.5   Example of data with multiple clusters that can be seen in one dimensionality (2D) but cannot be seen in lower dimensions. The histograms indicate the distributions in 1D, which show no indication of clustering.

The values of three features, conditioned on the Position feature, are shown in figure 4.6. This shows the position—at least the catcher position—is relevant. The designated hitter position also appears different, but this has too few examples to say anything with certainty.

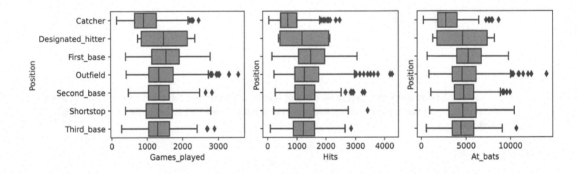

Figure 4.6   Boxplots of three numeric features with Position. The designated hitter category is small so cannot be compared reliably to the others. The catcher position is, though, distinct from the others. Most other positions appear to be comparable to each other.

4.6   Cleaning the data

As with any machine learning task, preprocessing the data before training the model can actually take a large portion of the total time—often well over half—but it can also be very important. The main steps here are cleaning the data (removing any obvious outliers), encoding categorical columns (in the case of numeric detectors), or binning numeric columns (in the case of categorical detectors), scaling the numeric features, handling null values, feature engineering, and feature selection.

The first step, removing strong outliers, is one that doesn't normally exist with prediction models (though it may be done with some regression models, such as linear regression). For some outlier detectors, this is necessary, as they support only novelty detection and require the training data to be free of outliers. For others, this is not strictly necessary but may allow the detector to perform better, as it will allow the detector to form a more accurate model of normal data.

Ideally, instead of cleaning the data, we would use data that is well-assessed and known to be clean. In most contexts, though, this is not practical. Usually, we have very little data that has been checked and determined to be free of outliers. Where we do have some, it may not be appropriate to use for training a detector for at least two reasons. There may be too little data to develop a good sense of what is normal and abnormal, and the small amount of labeled data may not follow the same distributions as the full population from which it was taken. Most of the time, we will need to work with the data we have, first removing the strongest outliers from this.

There are different ways to do this, but one is to simply run one or more detectors, either univariate statistical tests or machine learning tests, and take a small number of the strongest outliers found with these. For example, if we run 5 detectors for this purpose and take the top 10 outliers from each, this removes a total of 50 records, minus duplicates, from the training data. Once the model is fit, we may add these records back to be scored as normal.

Removing outliers in this way will help expose better any other outliers that were masked by these. For example, with a KNN detector, where remote points are removed, any remaining points that would have had these strong outliers as neighbors will now have larger distances to their remaining neighbors. With DBSCAN, any remaining points near the removed points may now be more easily isolated and flagged as outliers. With a clustering-based detector, strong outliers may be removed from very small clusters, leaving the remaining points in these clusters now in even smaller clusters, which are then easier to detect.

This process may be run iteratively any number of times, so long as the remaining data remains large. However, if we run it too many times, we will start to remove records that are weak outliers, such as the noise points between inliers and outliers, or even start to remove inliers. In this case, we may, when predicting, erroneously flag some inliers as outliers, though we can mitigate this by considering how many iterations were executed before they were scored highly. Most likely, though, this process would be run only on a small number of iterations.

Even before removing the strong outliers, we will need to fill the null values if there are any. The detectors used to remove the strong outliers, and the detectors used for the main outlier detection work, usually cannot support null values. To identify these values, we can call

```
df.isna().sum()
```

This indicates there are 20 null values, all in the Strikeouts column. There is no logical reason for this column to ever be null. The values may be zero but should be nonnegative integers for all players. For this, we would need to investigate, but it would appear to most likely be a data artifact of some type. The nulls will not help us identify unusual players, so for now we can simply fill the values with typical values, for example with

```
df['Strikeouts'] = df['Strikeouts'].fillna(df['Strikeouts'].median())
```

We are now ready to remove some extreme values before modeling, such as in listing 4.2, which continues from the previously shown code. This uses interquartile range, removing any rows with values over the upper limit, using a coefficient of 3.5 (which is often used to identify strong outliers). This reduces the data size from 1,340 to 1,312 rows. A similar method can be used to remove any very small values.

Listing 4.2   Removing extreme values from the data

```
limit_dict = {}

for col_name in df.columns:
    if (df[col_name].dtype in ['int64', 'float64']):
        q1 = df[col_name].quantile(0.25)
        q3 = df[col_name].quantile(0.75)
        iqr = q3 - q1
        limit = q3 + (3.5*iqr)
        limit_dict[col_name] = limit

cond = [True]*len(df)
for key, limit in limit_dict.items():
    cond = cond & (df[key] <= limit)

print(len(df))
clean_df = df[cond]
print(len(clean_df))
```

4.7   Feature selection

Feature selection is likely considerably more important with outlier detection than with prediction. Part of the reason for this is that, while many predictors, such as tree-based models and neural nets, can learn which features are relevant and can, to some extent, ignore the irrelevant features, outlier detection cannot. When training a classifier or regressor, it is preferable to remove any irrelevant or redundant features, but the model can still function with these, albeit with some reduction in accuracy. And with enough data, the reduction can, though not always, be fairly small.

Outlier detectors are different in this way; they treat all features equally, and because they are unsupervised, they have no way to learn from a target column which features are most relevant. With distance-based models, for example, the distances between points are measured treating all dimensions equally. The implication is that any features not relevant for outlier detection should be removed.

This has a few benefits. It helps mitigate the curse of dimensionality, can remove some noise from the results, and can allow the detectors to run more efficiently. To identify the irrelevant features, you can simply ask for each feature: if I found a rare or extreme value in this column, would this be interesting? Or: if I found a rare combination involving this column, with any other, would I be interested? As an example, take the staff table shown in table 4.2.

To start, we may wish to check the staff IDs for valid IDs. If any were outside of the normal values, this may indicate a data error, or perhaps an issue such as a ghost employee—a fictitious employee created in some forms of fraud. It may be worth doing some univariate tests on the staff ID, such as checking they are within a reasonable range of values or that there are no duplicates.

Table 4.2 Staff listing

Staff ID	Start date	Prior experience	Salary	Bonus	Department
847337	May 7, 2019	5	50,500	Y	Sales
847432	Jun 19, 2019	2	75,090	N	Engineering
847471	Jan 8, 2020	6	110,439	Y	Marketing
847511	Jan 23, 2020	13	98,000	Y	Sales

In this example, the Staff ID and Start Date columns may be related, and we may wish to check those two columns together as another simple test. This may be checking that the Staff ID values match, or at least roughly match, the rank order of the Start Date values. The following code will check for an exact match in terms of rank and will output the number of rows matching and not matching in this regard:

```
df['Staff Rank'] = df['Staff ID'].rank()
df['Start Date Rank'] = df['Start Date'].rank()
df['Ranks Match'] = df['Staff Rank'] == df['Start Date Rank']
df['Ranks Match'].value_counts()
```

We can probably (after flagging any suspicious IDs and any exceptions to this two-feature test) remove the Staff ID column. So, although we may wish to check the Staff ID column in some ways, it may not be useful in the multivariate tests. For these, we should use as few features as are useful. It may be harmless, in this example, to include Staff ID in any multivariate tests, but it's better to remove any noise we can from the results. In addition, in a more realistic example, the table may have many more features, and removing irrelevant features may be more necessary to produce the most meaningful results.

It may make sense to leave the Start Date column, as this may help identify relevant multivariate outliers—for example, unusual combinations of Start Date, Department, and Salary (which may be viewed as staff with unusual salaries given their start date and department).

In the case of the baseball dataset, the features all appear relevant for outlier detection. However, there are enough features that distance calculations can start to become somewhat suspect. Though distances between rows with 15 columns will not necessarily be meaningless, it is preferable to perform any outlier detection on subsets of features.

4.8   Feature engineering

With prediction models, we tend to do any feature engineering before feature selection so that the engineered features may be evaluated along with the original features, keeping only the most useful set for predicting the given target. Here this is less necessary as there is no target column that we can use to guide feature selection—only our own judgment. Feature engineering may, then, be done before or after feature selection. As with prediction projects, feature engineering will be based on modifying or combining one or more original features.

Feature engineering may be done to make use of features that otherwise would be dropped, or to combine two or more features into more useful features. It also may be done to get data into a format usable by an outlier detector, which is almost always either a numeric or a categorical format, requiring we reformat any date and string (and possibly other) features. In table 4.2 (describing staff), we'd wish to convert the Start Date column to a format that outlier detectors can accept—likely a numeric format. To cross-reference with the Staff ID, we converted it to rank order, which works well in that situation but is not how we would normally transform a date column for general outlier detection (though rank order can be a valid transformation too and may sometimes be used, it does lose significant information). We look closer at date features in chapter 9, but for now we may convert this to a format such as number of days since an epoch date, possibly since the minimum date in the dataset. We may also extract the day of the week to help catch data errors, such as where recorded start dates are weekends or other days that may be uncommon in the data. We can use

```
df['Start DOW'] = df['Start Date'].dt.dayofweek
df['Start Date'] = (df['Start Date'] - df['Start Date'].min()).dt.days
```

In the staff expenses table, repeated here as table 4.3, we see two examples of engineered features: the running count by hour and by minute for each staff. These help to identify outliers that may be impossible to detect without these. The more relevant features of this sort that we can create, the more ways we can identify the records that are anomalous and the greater our likelihood of finding truly interesting records.

Table 4.3   Staff expenses

Row	Staff ID	Account	Time	Amount	Count in prev. hour	Count in prev. minute
1	9000483	Meals	09:10:21	12.44	44	1
2	9303332	Travel	10:43:35	41.90	12	12
3	9847421	Meals	08:56:04	643.99	1	1
4	9303332	Supplies	03:12:09	212.00	1	2

Examining the data can help determine how best to transform the data or engineer features that will help identify anomalies. In table 4.2 (staff table with salaries), some engineered features we may wish to add if prior salary values are available may be, for example, related to changes in salary, durations without changes in salary, and so on. This may help to highlight where staff have unusual salaries given their history or unusual changes in salary.

Another common technique is to engineer features that represent arithmetic relationships between two or more features, such as the ratio between the width and height of an object or the ratio of the pretax and with-tax dollar amounts: it may be that some records have normal pretax values and normal with-tax values but the combination is anomalous.

In the baseball data, we can examine the sums or ratios between many of the statistics. One may be to add the doubles, triples, and home runs to produce a feature representing where the player had any of these. The following listing gives an example of another engineered feature, the ratio of home runs to at bats.

Listing 4.3 Engineering a feature to represent home runs per at bats

```
new_feat = 'Home_runs per at_bats'
feat_1 = 'Home_runs'
feat_2 = 'At_bats'
df[new_feat] = df[feat_1] / df[feat_2]

fig, ax = plt.subplots(nrows=1, ncols=2, figsize=(8, 3))
sns.scatterplot(x=df[feat_2], y=df[feat_1], ax=ax[0])
sns.histplot(df [new_feat], bins=100, ax=ax[1])
plt.show()
```

A scatterplot of the two original features shows their relationship in figure 4.7 (left). A histogram of the engineered feature is shown in figure 4.7 (right), indicating there are some outliers in this feature.

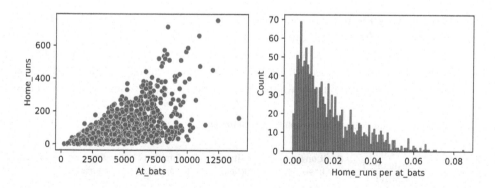

Figure 4.7   The left pane shows a scatterplot of home runs and at bats, indicating there is a relationship between the two. The right pane shows the distribution of an engineered feature created as the ratio of these. This feature may intuitively make sense and exposes some players as strong outliers.

Engineered features often capture patterns that the detector can identify in any case, but adding some additional features can aid this, possibly allowing more accurate detectors. Creating engineered features can also allow us to create single features that can, by themselves, identify useful outliers using simple univariate outlier detectors, which can be a major advantage; these can be faster, more reliable, and more interpretable than multivariate outlier tests. In addition, these features may better support the creation, at some time, of rules to identify points of interest.

4.9   *Encoding categorical values*

One form of preprocessing that is almost always necessary is converting categorical values to numeric format. This is necessary whenever we use a numeric outlier detector and the data contains (relevant) categorical features. We examine the options in more detail in chapter 9, but in general, the choices are the same as for prediction models where the predictors require strictly numeric data (for example, scikit-learn's RandomForest).

The most common encoding methods are one-hot and ordinal encoding, with count encoding also being common—much more so than with prediction. Ordinal encoding works by replacing each value in a column with numeric values. For example, if a column named Color contains the values [Red, Red, Blue, Blue, Green, Red], we may map Red to 0, Blue to 1, and Green to 2. The column would then be encoded as [0, 0, 1, 1, 2, 0]. Count encoding is similar but uses the count of each value as the encoding. Here Red appears three times, Blue twice, and Green once, so the column may be encoded as [3, 3, 2, 2, 1, 3]. One-hot encoding will create a series of binary columns for each unique value. In this case, the original Color column would be replaced with three columns: `Color_Red`, `Color_Blue`, and `Color_Green`. The first value, red, would be encoded to have a 1 in `Color_Red` and a 0 in `Color_Blue` and in `Color_Green`.

To use one-hot encoding with the baseball data, we can simply call

```
df = pd.get_dummies(df)
```

This will leave the numeric features as-is and replace the categorical column(s) with a binary column for each unique value. In this case, seven features are created: `Position_Catcher`, `Position_First_Base`, `Position_Outfield`, and so on. A sample set of rows for the last seven columns of the dataframe, after calling `get_dummies()`, is shown in table 4.4. For each row, there will be exactly one 1, and all other columns will have 0.

Table 4.4   One-hot columns created by the call to get_dummies

Position Catcher	Position designated hitter	Position first base	Position outfield	Position second base	Position shortstop	Position third base
0	0	0	0	1	0	0
0	0	1	0	0	0	0
0	0	0	0	0	0	1

4.10 Scaling numeric values

The other preprocessing step that is necessary with numeric features, for most detectors, is scaling. Distance, density, and clustering-based detectors all require this step, as they rely on calculating distances between pairs of points. In figure 4.8 (left), we see a set of points in two dimensions, the `Games_played` and `Triples` features, with `Games_played` ranging from 1 to 3,562 and `Triples` ranging from 1 to 309. Taking the Euclidean distance between any two points would effectively give their distance solely in terms `Games_played`, almost ignoring their difference in `Triples`—the scale of games played is large enough to make triples nearly irrelevant.

Min-max, z-score scaling, and robust scaling are all common. Min-max scaling will scale all values to be between 0.0 and 1.0. z-score scaling (also called standard scaling) will calculate the z-score for each value: the number of standard deviations it is from the mean for that feature. Robust scaling is similar but is done in a way that is more robust to outliers (using the median and interquartile range instead of mean and standard deviation). These are described in more detail in chapter 9.

This example uses robust scaling, which puts all values on comparable scales, but the distribution of the points remains unchanged. This allows meaningful distance calculations, considering all features equally.

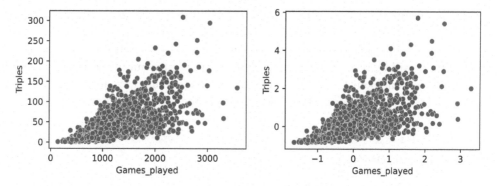

Figure 4.8 Data before (left) and after (right) scaling. Robust scaling was used in this example. The distributions are identical, but the scales are adjusted.

To scale the baseball data using RobustScaler, we may use code such as

```
from sklearn.preprocessing import RobustScaler
scaler = RobustScaler()
df = pd.DataFrame(scaler.fit_transform(df), columns=df.columns)
```

The scaling is only possible with numeric data, so the categorical encoding shown earlier is necessary before performing this step. Table 4.5 shows a sample of the data prior to scaling.

Table 4.5   Sample of baseball data set prior to scaling

Number seasons	Games played	At bats	Runs	Hits
23	3,298	12,364	2,174	3,771
13	1,165	4,019	378	1,022
13	1,424	5,557	844	1,588

The code transforms the data from a format as shown in table 4.5 to that in table 4.6.

Table 4.6   The same sample after scaling

Number seasons	Games played	At bats	Runs	Hits
2.5	2.91	2.84	3.27	3.07
0.0	–0.17	–0.01	–0.40	–0.17
0.0	0.20	0.44	0.55	0.49

4.11   *Fitting a set of models and generating predictions*

Normally we would try several outlier detectors with each outlier detection project. If we ran only one or two detectors, whether they find some significant outliers or not, we would realistically have no way to know if there are more significant outliers remaining in the data. The best way to determine if there are additional outliers that are of interest in the data is to run many detectors and manually assess the results. If this is a one-time project, our work may be done there; if we are setting up an ongoing process, there will be some additional work determining the models used in the final system (which will likely be only a subset of the detectors that were tested). With the baseball data, we try first using DBSCAN as shown in the following listing.

Listing 4.4   Running DBSCAN on the baseball data

```
import pandas as pd
import numpy as np
from sklearn.datasets import fetch_openml                    Collects
from sklearn.preprocessing import RobustScaler              the data
from sklearn.cluster import DBSCAN
                                                            Fills null
                                                            values
data = fetch_openml(
        'baseball', version=1, parser='auto')
df = pd.DataFrame(data.data, columns=data.feature_names)     One-hot
df['Strikeouts'] = \                                         encodes the
        df['Strikeouts'].fillna(df['Strikeouts'].median())   categorical
df = pd.get_dummies(df)                                      values
scaler = RobustScaler()                                     Scales
df = pd.DataFrame(scaler.fit_transform(df), columns=df.columns)   the data

df['DBSCAN Outliers'] = np.where(              Identifies the points not in
    DBSCAN(eps=2.0).fit_predict(df) < 0, 1, 0)  clusters after executing
                                               DBSCAN clustering
```

If run on the full data (with all columns) and using default parameters, DBSCAN will flag a very large number of records—more than is useful (HDBSCAN performs similarly in this case). This can be adjusted using the hyperparameters, particularly the eps parameter with DBSCAN. Setting this to 2.0, as is used in listing 4.4, will result in 1,255 inliers and 85 outliers, which appears reasonable.

It is useful to examine different hyperparameters. In listing 4.5 we look at an example calling DBSCAN with a range of values of eps, treating each equally and summing the number of times each row is outside of any cluster given the current eps setting. This allows the detector to be more robust to the parameters used and, also importantly, for us to use this form of test to generate numeric scores for each record; otherwise, tests that produce binary labels can be somewhat blunt instruments.

Listing 4.5   Looping through the eps parameter for DBSCAN

```
df['DBSCAN Score'] = [0] * len(df)
for eps in np.arange(0.1, 5.0, 0.1):
    df['DBSCAN Score'] += \
        np.where(DBSCAN(eps=eps).fit_predict(df) < 0, 1, 0)
sns.histplot(df['DBSCAN Score'])
plt.show()
```

The distribution of scores is shown in figure 4.9.

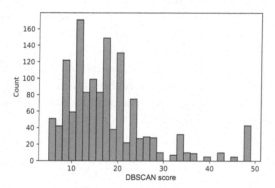

Figure 4.9   The distribution of scores after calling DBSCAN multiple times varying the eps parameter

In listing 4.6, we execute the KNN algorithm on the same data. This uses k = 4, but in practice we should vary this as well, as KNN can be very sensitive to the k specified. We set a binary label here (the "KNN Outliers" feature), which is used for plotting.

Listing 4.6   Running KNN on the baseball data

```
from sklearn.neighbors import BallTree

tree = BallTree(df)
dist, ind = tree.query(df, k=4)
```

```
dist = [x.mean() for x in dist]
df['KNN Score'] = dist
df['KNN Outliers'] = df['KNN Score'] > 2.3

sns.histplot(df['KNN Score'])
plt.show()
```

Figure 4.10 displays the distribution of KNN scores produced here.

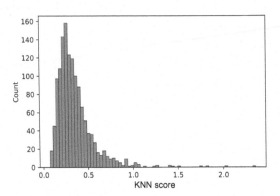

Figure 4.10   The distribution of KNN scores on the baseball dataset using k = 4. We do not know if it is flagging the most interesting rows, but the distribution appears good.

To get a sense of what is being flagged, we can examine the data rows and plot out the outliers, both as univariate and bivariate plots. Figure 4.11 shows just a few pairs of features. The other 2D plots look similar. What is being flagged is more extreme values than unusual combinations, which is fair given these appear to be the type of outliers that are stronger in this dataset. We should not be too influenced by 1D and 2D plots, as there may be more interesting phenomena in higher dimensions, but in this case, we can see that virtually every record flagged is, while possibly interesting in other ways as well, an extreme value. Flagging unusual combinations will likely require more

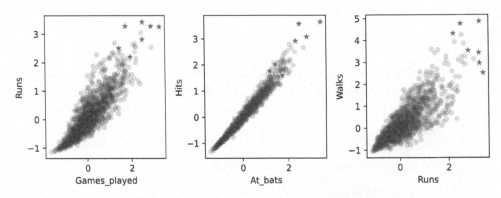

Figure 4.11   Three scatterplots showing the points flagged as outliers by the KNN test

emphasis on engineered features. I also tested several other detectors, including Radius and kernel density estimation (KDE), which produced similar-looking plots. Some of the detectors we'll look at in later chapters may be better suited to flag points along the edges of the data and at the low values, which may or may not better match our interests.

4.12 Evaluating the models

Given the lack of a ground truth and the inherently subjective nature of outlier detection, it is very difficult to evaluate outlier detection processes. If we are very focused in what we are looking for, we may miss other anomalies in the data that are just as interesting or relevant. But being very focused does make evaluation easier: in this case, if we can label the data, we can measure the false positives and false negatives. On the other hand, if we are interested in statistical outliers, and especially unknown outliers, it is difficult to evaluate if the outliers found are interesting. It's even more difficult to determine if what was not flagged is more interesting.

For outlier detection, it's important to understand a concept referred to as the "myth of average." The main idea is that very few examples of anything are completely average, an idea related to the curse of dimensionality. The idea is normally traced back to work done by the US Air Force. They had been fitting cockpits to fit the average pilot, considering average height, arm length, and several other dimensions. What they ended up discovering is that, while most pilots are average in most dimensions, not even one pilot in the force at the time was average in every dimension: no one was completely average. This is something we can see with almost any type of data. As with the mugs in chapter 1, we can find something unusual about each. None are completely average, which makes it possible to argue that each is, in some way, an outlier.

With any tabular data, if there are enough features, we can see the same phenomena, where every row is somewhat unusual in some way. An implication of this is almost any records can be considered, at least slightly, unusual in some sense if we look at the data from enough different angles. And, in fact, it may be quite legitimate for an outlier detector to give almost every row some non-zero score. Given the possible presence of noise in the data, where inliers slowly turn to noise and then outliers, there may not be a clear break between the scores, but the outlier scores should, at minimum, be higher for clear outliers than clear inliers.

As there are many completely orthogonal, but also completely reasonable, ways to look for outliers, it may be that many detectors, when evaluating the same dataset, will produce quite different scores. Some may score rows with extreme values more highly than internal outliers, while others score these the same, or score rows with unusual combinations of two features higher than unusual combinations of three features, while other detectors may do the opposite. Which is preferable depends on the outliers that are most useful to flag for your work. There is no definitive answer generally, but there is a sense of what's most relevant for your data and your goals.

Taking an example with tabular data, imagine a dataset with 10 million rows. Outliers need not be distinct from absolutely all other rows in the dataset; it's possible for there to be a small number, say 5 or 10 of very similar (or even identical) records, and to reasonably still consider these outliers if they are sufficiently different from all other rows. Given, for example, a set of 5 identical records, all very distinct from the majority of rows, and another set of 10 nearly (but not quite) identical records, also very distinct from the majority of rows, some detectors may score the records in the set of 5 higher (as this is a smaller set) and some the records in the set of 10 (as these are each more unique). Inspecting the data, we may determine one is more relevant than the other for our purpose. We may also find that neither are relevant; it may be, for example, that the data contains many such small sets, almost as unusual as these, and that these are not, in fact, noteworthy given our goals. In this example, we may be able to get more useful results using different hyperparameters or possibly different detectors.

This demonstrates a couple of things. First, outlier detection completely depends on context—what you are most interested in—and second, outlier detection is often an iterative process, where we examine the results and either filter down the results in some way or tweak the process, using a different algorithm, preprocessing, or parameters, and repeat until we have results that make sense and appear to miss little of importance.

We'll go through techniques to do this later in the book, but for now, let's look at a high level at a simple example, where we have an algorithm that appears to work well: we have 10 million rows and it flags 10 rows that are like each other, but unlike all other rows, and no other rows were flagged. We would have to inspect the records flagged to say if they are useful for the current project. Ideally, we would also spot-check some records not flagged, to check that these are, in fact, not of interest and that those flagged are of greater interest. For this, we would first check the records that were not quite flagged (that received moderate scores). As this may be a small number of records, these will be relatively easy to check.

Then the hard question remains: are any of the other rows not flagged actually as strong of outliers as those flagged? Spot-checking records with low scores is worth doing but has very limited ability to find any issues with the outlier detection system—given the outliers are, by definition, rare, it is usually impossible to inspect the data sufficiently to determine if they are being detected well. To determine this, there are two main approaches: test with synthetic data (covered later) and run many detectors. If we run many detectors, we will likely find many duplicates and likely many records that are of no interest, but we will also tend to flag anything that can be realistically found with outlier detection, so will have a pseudo-ground truth we can compare the detectors against.

In terms of the number of outliers flagged, having 10 does seem reasonable generally, though it may be low or high in some situations. What if, instead, it returned 100 such rows? Or 1,000? Or 10,000? One thousand seems like an impossible number of outliers: can something that frequent really be considered unusual? Or 10,000? But, out of 10 million rows, this is still only 1 in every 1,000 rows, so potentially we could consider these unusual. At least we may reasonably consider them statistically unusual, though they may not be useful for your situation.

If they will be manually inspected, this is almost certainly too many. But if they are well-scored and we can inspect the top, say, 50, this may work well. Or it may work if we can develop some simple rules to filter the output down to the cases we're most interested in (covered in chapter 15).

The main point is that the outliers flagged will usually need to be inspected manually, especially where the data is changing over time. Where the numbers of outliers are too large to fully inspect, we may be better off spot-checking them or developing tools to sort them, even running outlier detection processes on the outliers themselves. Even where the system contains only rules, we may find the thresholds or the scoring used is suboptimal and should be adjusted occasionally.

Inspecting the outliers can be difficult depending on how the outliers are flagged. Everything else equal, interpretable models should be used, but in some cases, you may find you can only get the results you need from uninterpretable processes.

We'll cover the use of synthetic data later. This can be helpful for testing, as it effectively creates a labeled dataset we can evaluate against, but it can be unclear how well we can extrapolate from performance on synthetic data to real data. Synthetic data, despite this, can be invaluable in cases where there is no other reliable means to test the system, and while not as useful as real data (at least where there is a large, diverse, and well-labeled collection of the relevant outliers in the real data), it is much preferred to no data.

Looking at the example of the baseball data, we saw previously that that results for the KNN detectors looked reasonable, though they were limited largely to extreme values. I also experimented with DBSCAN, HDBSCAN, Radius, and KDE. In figure 4.12 we plot the relationships between three of the detectors, KNN, Radius, and KDE. There is a significant correlation but not complete agreement between them, suggesting that, while some may produce results you're less interested in, none are redundant.

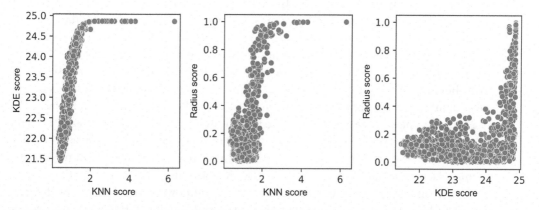

Figure 4.12 **The relationship between the scores of the KNN, Radius, and KDE detectors on the baseball dataset. There is some agreement, particularly between KNN and KDE, but the scores do not perfectly match between the three.**

The next steps would be to examine the top output of each detector and determine the most relevant outliers. In the case of a one-off project, it may not be relevant which detectors flagged the rows if we are simply collecting a set of the records that appear, based on our judgment, to be the most unusual. With ongoing projects, we will wish to determine which detectors tend to produce the most relevant results. This is the set of detectors we will use going forward.

In this example, it may be a reasonable decision to rely on univariate tests for extreme values, including those performed on some engineered features, such as the earlier example of home runs per at bat. This has the advantage of providing clean, interpretable results that may be similar to the results produced by multivariate tests in any case. It may, though, also be useful to incorporate some multivariate tests as these will flag some records missed otherwise.

4.13 *Setting up ongoing outlier detection systems*

We've covered here a number of the steps involved with detecting outliers. We'll look at preprocessing the data further later as there are nuances related to that, which may be clearer after we have explained how some of the other common detectors work. We'll also look at each of the steps that occurs after training a model in later chapters. These are complex areas in themselves, but they are important, so will receive some more attention than we can give them here. I will, though, provide some explanation here of what these refer to, specifically creating ensembles of detectors, finding collective outliers, performing time-series analysis, and running detectors on an ongoing basis.

A common theme with outlier detection is to combine many detectors into an ensemble: a collection of detectors. It's generally accepted that no single detector will identify all the anomalies in a dataset, as there are numerous ways in which rows may be considered anomalous and each detector will search only in one such way. Using many detectors can help identify a larger set of outliers. In addition, much like with prediction, using many detectors allows us to combine the scores, averaging out better where some detectors under- or overscore records, returning a more reliable final score for each record.

Collective outlier detection and time-series analysis may also be used to find more, or more relevant, outliers. It's common with datasets to wish to identify not just unusual rows but any unusual patterns in the data. This may include unusual numbers of rows of certain types, rows appearing in unusual orders, and so on. With the staff table (table 4.2), an example may be where there are records that all individually appear normal but where there are multiple staff with the same ID or many staff on the same starting date (or within a few days of each other). In other cases, it may be the absence of records that is unusual, such as gaps in staff IDs or gaps in time with no staff starting. To detect these sorts of anomalies, we need to examine the data in other ways—they cannot be detected simply by looking for unusual single rows in the original table. Often this means simply reformatting the data into a different table format, which can be used to detect collective outliers. For example, we may transform the table to have a row for each month, with the rows listing aggregate information about that month, such as the numbers of hires in each department, etc. This will allow us to detect anomalous months. In other cases, we may format the data as a time series, which can help identify different types of anomalies.

There is a major distinction between one-off and ongoing outlier detection projects. In the former case, we need only find the records that are most relevant in the current data, with no further work required. In the case of the baseball dataset, we wished only to find the most anomalous records in that collection. Running multiple univariate and multivariate tests could allow us to find and assess these, with nothing else necessary.

But in other cases, such as monitoring sensor data, scientific instrument readings, financial transactions, network activity, web traffic, and so on, there's an ongoing need for outlier detection. In these cases, we need to set up a system that can run long term and that will reliably detect any outliers we may be interested in that may eventually appear in the data. For this, we will usually use a much larger and more diverse set of detectors than may be necessary to detect the outliers present in the training data.

In either case, usually evaluation will include experts manually evaluating the outliers that are flagged (even where the outliers are used to trigger automatic actions such as shutting down assembly lines, as opposed to being given to experts to assess, these outliers will usually be logged and later manually assessed). In ongoing systems, this will give us the opportunity to tune, over time, the outlier detection process to score the types of outliers we are most interested in higher and the outliers we are not, lower, allowing for a better-functioning system. This allows us, to some extent, to overcome the major difficulty in outlier detection: the challenge of evaluating the systems, as we will now have some labeled data to evaluate against.

If run over time, as the output of the detectors is assessed and classified, the numbers of known anomalies will tend to increase, while the unknown anomalies found will decrease, though never disappear. These can be the most interesting outliers—the outliers rare enough to not be discovered for some time. These will be, at least in some sense, the most unusual—they are outliers among the outliers. That is, where we are interested in unknown outliers, they become more rare but more interesting over time.

4.14 *Refitting the models as necessary*

Although it is possible to fit and predict on the same data, and this is common, the processes of fitting and predicting are actually distinct. With ongoing systems, it's common to fit only occasionally, but to evaluate data as it arrives. For example, if we are collecting sensor data, we may wish to run outlier detection on this on an ongoing basis. Before setting up the outlier detection system, we may have some data collected where we are reasonably confident the readings are fairly normal (i.e., the data is of good quality). We can then fit a model using this data. That data would then define what's normal (though with the understanding that it likely does contain some outliers). Then, as we then collect new data, we can compare it against the model, finding outliers in this new data—in this case outliers relative to the prior period.

This can work well, but it can also raise a question about whether it is meaningful to compare new data to old data. A key question when performing outlier detection is: unusual compared to what? That is, for a given set of data, what is it most relevant to compare against? The commonly used reference points in outlier detection are the dataset itself, and equivalent datasets for a prior period. Ideally, we have available a perfectly representative dataset to compare to, but in practice, we rarely do. Although learning from data is powerful, it also has limitations, as we can create a frame of reference that may not always be the most appropriate—where the training data is skewed relative to the true population of data. More commonly, if trained some time ago, the model may be skewed relative to more current data.

For example, in financial auditing, auditors examine (and evaluate) a company for a specific period, usually a year. They may look for unusual transactions that occurred during that year (that are unusual relative to that year, or relative to prior years) or may compare the year in aggregate to prior years. These are useful tests, but we do have to be mindful that they can be misleading if this or the prior years were not typical years. This is difficult, because every year is different to some extent—some much more so than others—while some processes within a company should normally be stable even during atypical periods.

In the example of monitoring web traffic, as we collect data, we can examine it in real time in order to detect issues quickly. The question is, again, what do we compare this to? If we examine, for example, the number of clicks in the last minute, what is a good reference to compare this to? We could identify (taking into consideration the time of day, day of week, time of year, and so on) a typical number of clicks from prior periods to compare to, but there may be a new normal for the website, and comparing to old data may not be relevant. Conversely, if we compare to more recent behavior on the site, the recent period may be atypical and not a good reference point. Often there is no one good single point of comparison in these situations and comparing against multiple points of reference may be the most meaningful.

A lot relies on a judgment call: does recent data represent the new norm or is it, itself, an anomalous set, and is it more relevant to be distinct from newer data or from another, established reference set? This is another case, as is a running theme in outlier detection, where there are no definitive answers and it's necessary to work through what works best for the problem at hand.

Using an established reference set may be used in situations where we specifically wish to identify how different a new set of data is from the prior data, such as when monitoring for data drift or when data is arriving frequently. This includes streaming environments, where constantly retraining a detector on the new data is infeasible, as well as where new data arrives very slowly, making the recent data too small to develop a reliable sense of what is normal.

An established reference set may also be used where people have verified the reference set as being of good quality, either checking by hand, or from the experience of working with it. For example, there may be a long period in an industrial process known to have no defects, during or long after this period, which can allow us to say with some confidence the data was good during this time, which may not be an advantage you have with more recent data.

The question, then, is how best to choose the set of data we use to fit the model(s). Where the system is stable over time, it may be that using more data is strictly better, though also has diminishing returns. In other situations, where things change over time, this is a difficult question. Often a rolling window is used, as in financial audits, where it's common to compare against the previous three, four, or five years but only rarely go back further, with the idea that anything older usually isn't comparable.

Another option is to create a progressively larger reference dataset over time, sampling data from different time periods, but this can be difficult to do. It is easy to collect a set of typical records, but representing the true distributions in this way is challenging. It may be more practical, again, to maintain multiple reference datasets. This can be too much overhead for many situations, but it does have some advantages: it provides more context, as we can see where new data is considered unusual relative to some, but possibly not all prior datasets.

Summary

- There are standard steps that we usually use on outlier detection projects, which are similar to those on prediction projects.
- It's very important to determine what types of outliers you are looking for. Specifically, are you looking for something specific, or for anything that is unusual or unexpected in the data?
- It's also important to determine if you will use rules, classifiers, detectors, or some combination to find the type of items you're interested in.
- The type of model selected depends largely on the type of outliers you are looking for.
- Rules-based models and classifiers trained to predict outliers have their limitations but can be useful, especially if combined with outlier detectors.
- Detectors are very useful in most situations where we wish to find anomalies and will usually form at least part of the solution.
- It's important to collect representative data for outlier detection—that is, data where the rows are each fairly normal but also where the distributions match the true distributions. Everything in the data should be in proportion to the true population.
- Removing strong outliers from the data, such as those with one or more extreme values, can be helpful before looking for additional outliers.
- In most cases, we will use a numeric detector and will need to encode categorical features and scale numeric features.
- In other cases, we will use a categorical detector and need to bin numeric features.
- It's difficult to evaluate outlier detectors and it usually requires manual inspection.
- There are additional steps that may be performed to find outliers other than single rows. One method is to reformat the data in various ways to allow the discovery of collective outliers.
- In some cases, we will run the outlier detection on a long-term basis and will need to monitor and tune this over time.
- Running outlier detection on an ongoing basis is more difficult as it requires being prepared to detect outliers not in the training data.

Part 2

Part 2 covers the main algorithms and libraries for outlier detection in Python.

In chapter 5 we introduce outlier detection with scikit-learn. In chapter 6 we introduce the PyOD library, which is probably the most comprehensive library available for outlier detection for numeric tabular data in Python. In both chapters 5 and 6, we cover the algorithms provided (each of these libraries provides several tools for outlier detection), explain how they work, and describe how they may be used in your projects.

In chapter 7 we describe several other algorithms, tools, and libraries. These are also very useful and effective but are more difficult to find than those in scikit-learn or PyOD. They will help you understand outlier detection itself better (examining them provides a fuller understanding of the breadth of approaches available to identify outliers), help you see how to develop your own detectors where necessary, and provide a set of tools that are useful in themselves. They also include some detectors suited for categorical data, which is not directly supported by scikit-learn or PyOD.

5

Outlier detection using scikit-learn

This chapter covers

- An introduction to the scikit-learn library
- A description and examples of the Isolation Forest, local outlier factor, one-class Support Vector Machine, and Elliptic Envelope detectors
- A description of three other tools provided by scikit-learn: `BallTree`, `KDTree`, and Gaussian mixture models
- How to most effectively use these
- Where it is most appropriate to use each

We now have a good general understanding of outlier detection, some specific algorithms, and how outlier detection projects proceed. We will now look at the standard libraries for outlier detection, which will provide the majority, if not all, of the tools you will need for most outlier detection projects, at least for tabular data. Understanding these libraries well will be a major step toward being able to effectively execute outlier detection projects.

123

Researchers, over the past 30 years or so, have proposed dozens of outlier detection algorithms, many now with open-source implementations. In general, Python provides implementations of many of these, likely as many as any other language (though the support for outlier detection in R is also very good). Given there are many tools available for outlier detection and that none will detect all outliers, in most outlier detection projects it's useful to use several detectors. This allows us to reliably detect a greater number and variety of outliers than can be found with a single detector. Consequently, it's worthwhile to learn how best to use many detectors. It's not possible to cover all outlier detection algorithms, but in the next few chapters we'll cover a significant number of the most important algorithms. Many are included in the standard libraries, scikit-learn and PyOD, which we cover in this and the next chapter.

In this book, we hope to provide you with enough understanding of outlier detection that you can develop your own code where necessary, but more often in outlier detection, we use libraries such as scikit-learn, at least as much as possible. These have the obvious, and substantial, advantage that the bugs have been worked out. In addition, a lot of the benefit of using these is in the optimization. Some may run faster than you can realistically match without a significant time commitment. Where your datasets are small, this may not be an issue, but where they are large, it may be important. Much of scikit-learn is written in Cython and runs extremely efficiently.

Established libraries have some other advantages as well. scikit-learn and PyOD not only cover a good number of the important algorithms, but they also make working with multiple detectors easy, as they provide simple, consistent APIs. There is also a history of use, so an idea, often from many years of use by many people, of the appropriate preprocessing and hyperparameters to use (the libraries also provide sensible defaults for the hyperparameters). scikit-learn is also very well documented, which can make a real difference. Outlier detection can be easy to do in a way that's ineffective or misleading (as there is usually no ground truth, it can be difficult to assess if the records scored highest are actually the most anomalous in a meaningful way), and so it is important to have both a solid general background in outlier detection and an understanding of the specific detectors used, which is much more feasible with established and documented libraries.

In your projects, you may or may not use all the detectors covered here, but in either case, there is value in understanding how they work. Learning these algorithms provides a fuller picture of the challenge of outlier detection and provides more ways to think about outliers. It provides a better understanding of the range of tactics we can use to try to assess what's anomalous, and it can help us appreciate why there are so many detectors. It's useful to be cognizant that however we look for outliers, there are still other ways records could be considered anomalous—some matching the task at hand well and some not. A good understanding of the detectors also helps us understand the strengths and limitations of each and which best match our current task.

In this chapter, we look first at the four detectors provided by scikit-learn. We also look at some other tools provided by scikit-learn that are valuable for outlier detection. We've looked at scikit-learn's KernelDensity class already but cover here Gaussian mixture models, and take a closer look at the BallTree class, as well as a similar class, the KDTree.

5.1   *Introducing scikit-learn*

scikit-learn (https://scikit-learn.org/stable/) can be an excellent place to begin and potentially may cover all your needs for outlier detection. If you're doing any other machine learning work in Python, you're almost certainly familiar with scikit-learn. It is likely the most popular package for machine learning with tabular data. It provides models for classification, regression, clustering, and outlier detection, as well as numerous tools to preprocess and postprocess data, evaluate models, and a fair amount more.

scikit-learn provides four outlier detectors, including two of the most reliable and well-used detectors, Isolation Forest and LocalOutlierFactor. Journal papers proposing new algorithms compare themselves to these two, as well as k nearest neighbors (KNN), probably more than any others. For researchers, these are the ones to beat. And, as data scientists, these can be our go-to algorithms and, where we try many algorithms, the ones we try first.

The four detectors provided by scikit-learn are all numeric detectors, so any categorical columns will require encoding. All, other than Isolation Forest, also require scaling, as they operate based on distances calculated between the points. As with predictors, scikit-learn provides a standard API for outlier detection, though there are some variations in the methods provided by the detectors. Each is able to return both scores and labels (with –1 indicating outliers and 1 indicating inliers).

5.2   *Isolation Forest*

The first detector provided by scikit-learn that we look at is Isolation Forest (IF). Although the detectors we've looked at previously [KNN, Radius, kernal destiny estimation (KDE), DBSCAN, frequent pattern outlier factor (FPOF), classifier-based detectors] and the others covered in this chapter and later in the book are all well used and often excellent choices for projects, IF is probably the most generally applicable detector, at least for numeric tabular data. It will usually be at least one of the detectors used in outlier detection projects.

Isolation Forest uses an elegant algorithm, which is fairly unique among outlier detectors. Instead of attempting to model the data and then find exceptions to the normal patterns, Isolation Forest seeks to isolate the anomalous points from the remainder of the data. It works by recursively subdividing the data in a way similar to a set of decision trees. Given this, Isolation Forest is often likened to RandomForest, though it is actually more similar to ExtraTrees: it works by creating multiple trees, each subdividing the feature space in a way that's completely random. Where RandomForests are guided in their splits by the goal of maximizing information gain, Isolation Forests are unsupervised and simply randomly divide the data space into smaller and smaller regions.

As with almost all detectors, IF has separate train and predict steps. The train step creates a series of Isolation Trees, each built on a small random selection of the data; each tree uses a different random set of data in order to increase diversity among the trees. As with decision trees, each node in an Isolation Tree represents some region of the data, with the root node representing the full data and each child node a portion of its parent's data.

An example is given in figure 5.1, which shows a collection of points in two dimensions. The set of plots shows the first few steps creating a single tree. To grow the trees, the algorithm repeatedly picks, for each node, a random feature and split point (within the range of values in that region for that feature) and divides the data into progressively smaller regions. It proceeds until each region contains either a single (isolated) point or exact duplicates or it reaches a predefined maximum depth. The maximum tree height is configurable but by default is the log of the number of samples, which equals the full depth of the tree if the tree were perfectly balanced, and about half the full height in an average case if the tree were grown until every point was actually isolated.

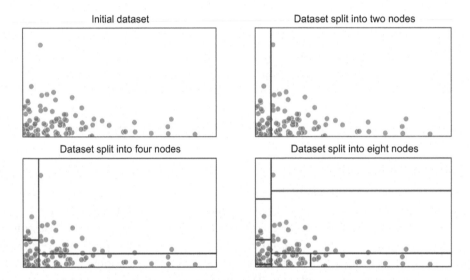

Figure 5.1   The training data for an Isolation Forest is divided randomly in each Isolation Tree. This shows the first three steps, resulting in eight nodes, each covering some subregion of the full dataspace. At this point (in the bottom right pane), one point (in the top right region) has already been isolated.

The top left pane shows the full data, which corresponds to the root node. In this example, it first randomly chooses the x dimension, which is split at a random split point, creating two smaller regions (each corresponding to a node in the tree one level below the root), as shown in figure 5.1 (top right). It then recursively divides each of these regions in two. Figure 5.1 (bottom left) shows the next step and figure 5.1 (bottom right) the result of the following random splits. The tree is, then, three levels deep, so it contains eight leaf nodes. At this point we can see one point, in the top-right region, has already been isolated. This node will no longer be split in this tree (as it contains a single point), though the other nodes will be split further.

The main idea of Isolation Trees is that outliers will be isolated earlier than inliers, in nodes closer to the root. With strong inliers (points in dense regions), it may take many iterations before they are isolated, and in fact the Isolation Forest algorithm, by setting a maximum tree depth, doesn't necessarily actually isolate these; once a region is established to strictly contain inliers, it is unnecessary to calculate exactly how many steps it would take to isolate them, and this is simply estimated.

Note that the training step does not actually evaluate the outlierness of any records. This is impossible, as the trees are each trained on only a small sample of the data. The training step simply creates the trees, which tend to represent the sparse regions in higher leaf nodes and the dense regions in lower leaf nodes.

During the predict step, after the trees are built, IF estimates an outlier score for every record tested. To do this, each record is passed through each Isolation Tree, and we determine which leaf node each ends in, in each tree. There are two types of leaf nodes: those where a single point was isolated in the sample data during construction and those nodes that were not subdivided due to containing strictly duplicates or reaching the maximum tree depth. For these, an estimate of the depth for the passed record is calculated based on the number of sample points remaining in that node when creating the tree. The final outlier score for each record is based on the average tree depth of each leaf node it ends in.

The use of sampling to train the models has a few advantages. The sample size by default is 256, which, being very small, allows the trees to be trained extremely quickly. Using small samples also reduces swamping and masking effects, where the presence of outliers can affect the ability to properly distinguish other points as inliers and outliers. If very large samples were used, it may allow, for example, tight clusters of outliers, which can be slow to isolate. As it is, some researchers have found this remains a limitation of Isolation Forests, but using smaller samples for each tree does reduces this. The original paper used sampling without replacement, though scikit-learn's implementation makes this configurable.

Isolation Forest is stochastic, so it can give different results from one run to another but is generally fairly stable. It is also robust to the parameters used. It's possible to control the number of trees, the number of samples used to train each tree, and the number of features that may be selected from at each node. The number of trees is set, by default, to 100, though the authors and subsequent researchers have found the results tend to converge given just 10 or 20 trees, and so using any additional trees will tend to return consistent results. Isolation Forests are robust as well to the other parameters, with their performance being affected usually only slightly. The default parameters can usually be safely used.

Isolation Forest is among the most useful and well-used detectors. It provides a number of advantages: it does not require scaling the data (as it is tree-based) or defining a distance metric between rows, and it has few parameters. And it is very fast—often much faster than other detectors. It executes in linear time ($O(n)$, where n is the number of rows), while many detectors are quadratic or worse in the number of rows or number of features. Its main advantage over many other numeric outlier detectors is likely that it can handle far more features. It is still vulnerable to the curse of dimensionality, but because it does not rely on distance calculations between points, it can scale to more dimensions than distance or density-based algorithms.

One drawback is that the results are uninterpretable, which can be a limitation in some cases. The scores are interpretable on some level: it's easy to understand the outlier points were more easily isolated, but the relevant set of features for each record that receives a high score can't be determined.

5.2.1   *The KDD Cup dataset*

For many of the examples in this chapter, we use a dataset available with scikit-learn, the KDD Cup dataset, related to intrusion detection and very commonly used (along with several other datasets) in outlier detection research, even for deep learning-based algorithms. Other datasets related to intrusion detection are also available and are sometimes used, but the KDD Cup dataset is frequently used as a baseline test: as it's known to be solvable by outlier detection methods, it often serves as a basic test for detectors. It's worth taking a quick look at the dataset here.

Table 5.1 shows a sample of the dataset. There are actually 41 features, so this is only a sample of the features. Each record represents one connection, each of which consists of multiple packets sent from the sender to the host and back.

Table 5.1   Sample of KDD Cup dataset

duration	protocol type	service	src bytes	dst bytes	logged in	su attempted	num file creations	num access files	serror rate
0	tcp	http	234	5450	1	0	1	1	0.00
0	icmp	http	256	487	1	0	0	0	0.00
3	tcp	private	158	1535	0	0	0	0	0.07
5	udp	smtp	199	2363	1	0	0	0	0.00
0	icmp	other	310	2361	1	1	0	0	0.00

A description of the features shown in table 5.1 is as follows:

- `duration`—Length of the connection in seconds
- `protocol type`—IP protocol (e.g., tcp, udp)
- `service`—Network service (e.g., http, telnet)
- `src-bytes`—Number of bytes from source to destination
- `dst-bytes`—Number of bytes from destination to source
- `logged in`—1 if logged in; 0 otherwise
- `su attempted`—1 if the super user (su) command was attempted; 0 otherwise
- `num file creations`—Number of file creation operations
- `num file access`—Number of file access operations
- `serror rate`—Percent of connections with SYN errors

There are also features related to other errors, the numbers of connections to this and other hosts and services within the last two seconds, and so on. The dataset has about 4.8 million rows in total. The data is labeled, with the target column containing either "normal" or the name of an attack type. About 99.7% of the rows are the normal class, while the remaining represent various network attacks. There are 24 attack types in all, including smurf attacks, port sweeps, buffer overflows, and so on. As outlier detection is essentially a form of binary classification, these may be grouped into a single class, representing nonnormal use of the network.

The scikit-learn API supports collecting different subsets of the data as it is quite large. Most subsets include only three or four features. We use the SA subset in this example, which has about 1 million rows and 41 features. scikit-learn also provides an option to collect just 10%, which will reduce only the normal class collected. The attacks are about 0.3% of data if the full SA subset is collected and about 3.5% if only 10% of the normal data is collected.

One of the major advantages of the dataset is that it is labeled. This allows us to evaluate outlier detectors with realistic data in an environment where the minority class (the attacks), are truly anomalous and detectable: many outlier detectors are able to detect the attacks with very high accuracy. Where detectors do not perform well on the KDD Cup dataset, though, this does not indicate they are generally poorly performing—only that they are not suited for this type of data.

In general, it's common to use classification datasets with large imbalances, such as this, in outlier detection research. The idea is that very rare classes can be considered outliers and ideally would be picked up by outlier detectors. With real-world outlier detection problems, labels are usually not available, but it is convenient to be able to demonstrate and test algorithms on labeled data where we can. Working with labeled classification datasets provides similar advantages and limitations as working with synthetic datasets: they may not represent your real data well, but they can be very valuable to help get you started.

Interestingly, having a high imbalance can make classification more difficult (the data is labeled and so classification is possible with this problem), but it can make outlier detection easier: as the outliers are rarer, they are easier to identify as outliers (though there is still the risk of labeled outliers being masked by other statistical outliers). More importantly, though, for network security, classifiers can learn only to recognize the attack forms they are specifically trained on (the attack forms covered in this dataset), and novel attacks appear regularly, effectively necessitating outlier detection.

A frustrating side of intrusion detection is that anomaly detection systems are vulnerable to learning to recognize anomalies as normal behavior. If attackers gradually introduce certain behavior patterns (that should be considered anomalies) in benign ways, and if eventually these become common enough, the systems will learn to consider these as normal. In other domains, something similar may occur, though usually naturally and not maliciously.

5.2.2 Using Isolation Forest on the KDD Cup dataset

Listing 5.1 gives an example using Isolation Forest with the KDD Cup dataset (specifically the SA subset). As with all detectors provided in scikit-learn and PyOD, the process is fairly simple but particularly so for IF, as we can skip scaling the features and setting the hyperparameters, requiring only encoding the categorical features. The SA subset of KDD Cup has three categorical columns. There are several options for encoding categorical columns; scikit-learn recommends OrdinalEncoding for Isolation Forest, which we use here.

> **Listing 5.1   Example using Isolation Forest on the KDD Cup dataset**

```
import numpy as np
import pandas as pd
from sklearn.datasets import fetch_kddcup99
from sklearn.ensemble import IsolationForest
from sklearn.preprocessing import OrdinalEncoder
from sklearn.metrics import confusion_matrix
from sklearn.metrics import roc_auc_score
import matplotlib.pyplot as plt
import seaborn as sns

np.random.seed(0)

X, y = fetch_kddcup99(subset="SA", percent10=True, random_state=42,
                      return_X_y=True, as_frame=True)
y = (y != b"normal.").astype(np.int32)

enc = OrdinalEncoder()                          Encodes the
X = enc.fit_transform(X)                         categorical columns

                                                Creates and fits an
det = IsolationForest()                          IsolationForest detector
det.fit(X)
                                                Calls predict() to get a binary
pred = pd.Series(det.predict(X))                 prediction for each record
pred = pred.map({1: 0, -1: 1})
print(confusion_matrix(y, pred))                Evaluates the model using
                                                 the labels in the dataset

pred = det.score_samples(X)                     Calls scores_samples() to get a
min_score = pred.min()                           numeric prediction for each record
max_score = pred.max()
pred = [(x - min_score) / (max_score - min_score) for x in pred]
pred = [1.0 - x for x in pred]
roc_auc_score(y, pred)                          Evaluates again, using
                                                 the numeric predictions
```

Calling the `predict()` method, we get a binary score for each record. The number set as outliers is based on the contamination parameter set—the fraction of records to be flagged as outliers. `IsolationForest` first creates a numeric score for each record and then sets a binary label for the specified number of the top-scored of these, as is standard among the scikit-learn detectors. In this example, we use the default contamination level (the default is actually to use a formula to determine the contamination rate, and not a fixed fraction), which results in the confusion matrix shown in figure 5.2.

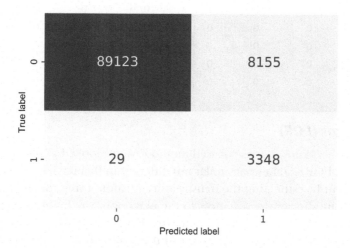

Figure 5.2 Results of using Isolation Forest to detect network events on the KDD Cup dataset. The Isolation Forest detector is working here similarly to a classifier as there is a ground truth we can test against in this case, which is rare. In this case, most predictions are correct, but there are 8,155 cases where the record is not an attack but was predicted to be an outlier and 29 cases where it was an attack but was not predicted to be an outlier.

By calling the `score_samples()` method, we get a score for each record. The example also includes code to normalize the scores and then evaluate using the AUROC metric, which evaluates how well ranked the scores are compared to the ground truth. Normalizing the scores isn't necessary but can be convenient to help interpret the scores. Executing this results in an AUROC score of about 0.95, though if the example code is run repeatedly, as IF is stochastic, you will see (if removing the seed from the code) some variation, with scores usually between about 0.93 and 0.98. This also fits and predicts on the same data as is common in outlier detection.

In this example, if we instead fit on only clean data (the data in the normal class), the scores will be somewhat higher—about 0.98. Although this is not normally possible, it is an example where training on clean data is preferable where it is possible.

The top five highest-scored records are shown in table 5.2. The columns shown here mostly look innocuous, and in fact most of the 41 features are fairly typical other than the features related to error rates. Whether they are responsible for the high scores given by IF is, unfortunately, impossible to determine. We will cover explainability later, but here will have to either simply accept the results, or try to replicate them with simpler tests, such as univariate tests on each feature or by running IF with small numbers of features to determine if we are able to get similar results.

Table 5.2   The highest-scored records using Isolation Forest

duration	protocol type	service	src bytes	dst bytes	logged in	su attempted	num file creations	num access files	serror rate
0	tcp	private	0	0	0	0	0	0	1.00
0	tcp	other	0	0	0	0	0	0	0.21
0	tcp	private	0	0	0	0	0	0	1.00
0	tcp	private	0	0	0	0	0	0	1.00
0	tcp	private	0	0	0	0	0	0	1.00

5.3   *LocalOutlierFactor (LOF)*

LOF is probably the best-known density-based method. We've looked at two others so far: KDE and Radius. LOF is somewhat similar but different in that it is a local method. It evaluates each point by estimating the density at its location, using the distances to the nearest points. The shorter the distances to the neighbors, the higher the density where the point is located; the longer the distance, the lower the density. To score each point, LOF compares the density at each point to the density of the other points in the neighborhood (defining neighborhood in the same way as KNN). That is, it uses a local, not a global, standard of what level of density is normal.

LOF is based on the idea that different regions of the data have different densities. Taking the example of financial transactions, if a record is a specific type of purchase transaction, then to determine if it's anomalous in a local sense (significantly different from comparable transactions), we compare it to nearby transactions, which will be other purchases of that type. This can be more relevant than the overall average densities, as different types of purchase transactions, in the high-dimensional space we may picture them in, may be spaced closer or further apart from each other than other types of transactions. For example, for different types of transactions, there may be a narrower or wider range of dollar values, dates, tax rates, or other fields.

LOF is particularly useful in situations of this type, where we have regions with different densities. Figure 5.3 is similar to a plot provided in the original paper introducing LOF. This shows two clusters, C1 with 400 points and C2 with 100 very dense points. We can also see two points that may be reasonably considered outliers, O_1 and O_2, while the other points would likely not be. Taking a distance-based approach, for example, where we flag records where more than p percent of the values are more than d distance away, there are actually no values that can be set for p and d that would achieve this. C1 has more points, so does the most to establish the normal distance between closest points, which is quite different than in C2. Using the normal distances within C1, O_2 would be very normal—its distance from the other points in C2 is normal going by the average distances in C1. And when using the normal distances between points in C2, O_1 would be an outlier, but so would many other points around C1. There is no universal sense of normal distance that would capture O_1 and O_2 but nothing else.

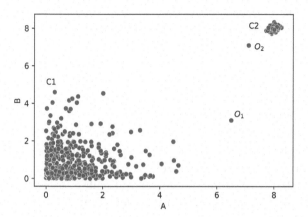

Figure 5.3 Example motivating the LOF algorithm. Two points can reasonably be considered outliers: O_1, and O_2, with O_1 an outlier of the C1 cluster and O_2 an outlier of the C2 cluster. Using the normal distances between points in C1, O_2 would be considered normal, and using the normal distances between points in C2, many points in C1 besides O_1 would be outliers.

As a sketch of how the algorithm works, LOF calculates, for each point, the distances to its k nearest neighbors and takes the average of these distances. It then compares this value to the average distances of each of its neighbors to each of their neighbors, taking the ratio of these. For points that are very normal—for example, points inside a dense cluster (other than those on the fringe of the cluster)—this will be roughly 1.0: they are about the same distances to their neighbors as their neighbors are to theirs and so will be considered inliers. Any score over 1.0 indicates being, at least slightly, more of an outlier than is normal for the immediate neighborhood.

The complete algorithm is actually more nuanced, and the paper describes some interesting details to the algorithm, including a smoothing technique it uses to handle variations in the distances to close neighbors. Where there are very dense regions, the distances between the points can be very small, but the ratios of the average distances can be very large. This would result in high outlier scores even for points in these dense regions without the smoothing. The precise algorithm is worth looking into for any who are interested. Note, though, many second-hand accounts actually describe it slightly incorrectly—the full description is a bit subtle, though manageable.

Given how LOF works, it can struggle to highlight global outliers. It will identify these, but may not score global outliers any higher than local outliers. If your primary focus is global outliers, LOF may not be appropriate—at least not as the sole detector.

LOF is sensitive to the value of k used. The authors indicate that values below 10 result in statistical fluctuations, stemming from the variances in the very small distances common with very close neighbors. They found with k under 10, even with uniform data (where there are no outliers), it's possible for some points to get scores well over 1.0. Conversely, if k is set too large, it fails to consider well the local densities. The authors recommend using a range of k values, based on estimates of cluster sizes. However, in most cases we have no reliable estimates of cluster sizes, so we have to estimate a reasonable value, or range of values. scikit-learn recommends using a k of around 20.

LOF can support either outlier detection (where the training data may be contaminated, and outliers will be found in the same data) or novelty detection (where the training data is clean and the model will be used on separate data), but it is necessary to specify which is being done. By default, scikit-learn's LOF assumes outlier detection, which is what we use in the example in listing 5.2.

In this case, we use RobustScaler to scale the numeric features, which scikit-learn recommends. LOF, as well as many numeric detectors, can be quite sensitive to the scaler used, and using others, such as min-max, can at times provide lower-quality results, though this will vary and trying others can be useful.

This tests on the same dataset as the previous Isolation Forest example, the KDD Cup set, but it performs noticeably worse. As scikit-learn's documentation indicates, IF and LOF can each do well or poorly on different datasets, as we may expect given that they use quite different approaches. Unfortunately, it's very difficult to estimate ahead of time which will perform better, though generally LOF will focus more on local outliers so may perform better in that regard.

This code also provides an example of adjusting k to find the highest accuracy, which is not normally possible but is in this case as we have labeled data. As k is increased, the number of neighbors each record is compared against increases, shifting from very local but possibly unstable predictions, to larger regions of neighbors for comparison, which may include a mix of local and nonlocal points. scikit-learn's implementation uses the n_neighbors parameter to represent k. To determine the best value for this dataset, we try here a range of values, from 10 to 80, including the default 20. This can take several minutes to execute.

Listing 5.2   Example using LOF (including tuning k)

```python
import numpy as np
import pandas as pd
from sklearn.datasets import fetch_kddcup99
from sklearn.neighbors import LocalOutlierFactor
from sklearn.preprocessing import OneHotEncoder
from sklearn.metrics import roc_auc_score
from sklearn.preprocessing import RobustScaler
import matplotlib.pyplot as plt
import seaborn as sns

X, y = fetch_kddcup99(subset="SA", percent10=True, random_state=42,
                      return_X_y=True, as_frame=True)
y = (y != b"normal.").astype(np.int32)

cat_columns = ["protocol_type", "service", "flag"]      # Encodes the categorical
X_cat = pd.get_dummies(X[cat_columns])                  # columns using one-hot
col_names = [x.replace("'", '_') for x in X_cat.columns] # encoding
X_cat.columns = col_names
X_cat = X_cat.reset_index()

numeric_cols = \
        [x for x in X.columns if x not in cat_columns]   # Scales the numeric
transformer = RobustScaler().fit(X[numeric_cols])        # columns using the
X_num = pd.DataFrame(transformer.transform(X[numeric_cols])) # RobustScaler class
X_num.columns = numeric_cols
```

```
X_num = X_num.reset_index()

X = pd.concat([X_cat, X_num], axis=1)

scores = []
for k in [5, 10, 20, 30, 40, 50, 60, 70, 80]:
    print(f"Executing loop for k={k}")
    det = LocalOutlierFactor(n_neighbors=k)
    pred = det.fit_predict(X)
    pred = 1.0 - det.negative_outlier_factor_
    r = roc_auc_score(y, pred)
    scores.append(r)

s = sns.lineplot(
        x=[5, 10, 20, 30, 40, 50, 60, 70, 80], y=scores)
s.set_ylabel("AUROC Score")
s.set_xlabel("k")
plt.title("AUROC given k")
plt.ylim(0.0, 1.0)
plt.show()
```

Loops through values of k to determine the optimal value of k for this dataset

Creates a LOF predictor, fits to the data, and collects the predictions on the training data

Evaluates the LOF using the current value for k

Outputs a plot of the AUROC scores vs k

The AUROC was highest at n_neighbors=40, which resulted in a score of 0.63, higher than the 0.56 achieved with n_neighbors=20. A plot of the scores vs n_neighbors is shown in figure 5.4.

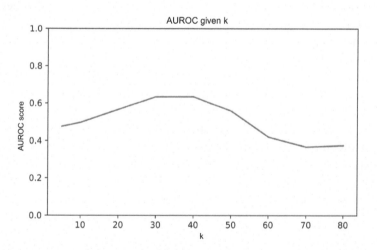

Figure 5.4   The AUROC score for various values of k

LOF is now one of the most well-used detectors for tabular outlier detection. Although it's common for other detectors to outperform LOF in some tests, it is generally quite competitive overall. Since the publication of its paper, there have been numerous variations on LOF proposed, including Local Outlier Probability (LoOP), connectivity-based outlier factor (COF), local correlation integral (LOCI),

Influenced Outlierness (INFLO), and subspace outlier detection (SOD), each claiming to perform better than LOF, at least in some circumstances. Many of these we'll cover in chapters 6 and 7.

5.4   One-class SVM (OCSVM)

One-class SVM (OCSVM) is an example of a concept known as *one-class* methods. These are based on an interesting idea: that we can create a classifier that models a single class, being trained only on data of that class. One-class methods, given some set of training data, create a model to describe the data they receive as tightly as possible. A simple example would be a model that, given a list of integers as training data, finds the minimum and maximum values and uses these to define the normal class. With OCSVMs, a more complex but similar process occurs: the model creates a decision boundary around the data (or the majority of the data), making the decision boundary as small as possible but also leaving as few points outside as possible.

Once a one-class model is fit, any subsequent data can be tested against it; if it fits with the model, we can assume it is normal, and if it does not, it is a novelty. In the case of the model based on minimum and maximum integer values, we can simply test the outlierness of subsequent data by checking if they are within this range, and in the case of the SVM, if points are within the decision boundary.

In principle, any model type may be used as a one-class model. There have been proposals to use Random Forests, and in the past Naïve Bayes models were sometimes used. But in practice, at this point, only SVMs and deep neural networks (one-class deep networks are covered in chapter 16) are used. SVMs are what is commonly used, and this is what scikit-learn supports.

Listing 5.3 gives an example of working with an OCSVM, similar to an example provided in the scikit-learn documentation. This uses synthetic data, which helps us understand the behavior of the detector more clearly. The example plots the decision boundary, which is possible with all scikit-learn detectors in this way. Though plotting is limited to two dimensions, and it can be tenuous to extend the ideas to high dimensions, this does provide some insight into how the detectors work. In this example, we create training data consisting of two clusters with 100 points each. The OCSVM is fit to these points, so it generates a decision boundary around them. The code then generates additional test data, which is evaluated against the fit model.

Listing 5.3   OCSVM with decision boundary plotted

```
import pandas as pd
import numpy as np
from sklearn import svm
import matplotlib.pyplot as plt

min_range = -5                                          Defines the range
max_range = 5                                           used for plotting
xx, yy = np.meshgrid(np.linspace(min_range, max_range, 1000),
                     np.linspace(min_range, max_range, 1000))
```

```
x_data = np.random.normal(loc=2.0, scale=0.5, size=100)
y_data = np.random.normal(loc=2.0, scale=0.5, size=100)
cluster_1_df = pd.DataFrame(({'A': x_data, 'B': y_data}))
x_data = np.random.normal(loc=-2.0, scale=0.5, size=100)
y_data = np.random.normal(loc=-2.0, scale=0.5, size=100)
cluster_2_df = pd.DataFrame(({'A': x_data, 'B': y_data}))
X_train = pd.concat([cluster_1_df, cluster_2_df]).values

x_data = np.random.normal(loc=2.0, scale=0.4, size=20)
y_data = np.random.normal(loc=2.0, scale=0.4, size=20)
X_test_normal = pd.DataFrame(({'A': x_data, 'B': y_data})).values

x_data = np.random.normal(loc=0.0, scale=4.0, size=20)
y_data = np.random.normal(loc=0.0, scale=4.0, size=20)
X_test_outliers = pd.DataFrame(({'A': x_data, 'B': y_data})).values

clf = svm.OneClassSVM(nu=0.1)
clf.fit(X_train)

y_pred_train      = clf.predict(X_train)
y_pred_normal     = clf.predict(X_test_normal)
y_pred_outliers   = clf.predict(X_test_outliers)
n_error_train     = y_pred_train.tolist().count(-1)
n_error_normal    = y_pred_normal.tolist().count(-1)
n_error_outliers  = y_pred_outliers.tolist().count(-1)

dec_func = clf.decision_function(np.c_[xx.ravel(), yy.ravel()])
dec_func = dec_func.reshape(xx.shape)

plt.title("OCSVM")
plt.contourf(xx, yy, dec_func,
             levels=np.linspace(dec_func.min(), 0, 7), cmap=plt.cm.PuBu)
a = plt.contour(xx, yy, dec_func, levels=[0], linewidths=2, colors="red")
plt.contourf(xx, yy, dec_func, levels=[0, dec_func.max()], colors="green")

train_points = plt.scatter(X_train[:, 0], X_train[:, 1],
                           c="grey", s=40, marker='.')
normal_points = plt.scatter(X_test_normal[:, 0], X_test_normal[:, 1],
                            c="blue", s=50, marker="*")
outlier_points = plt.scatter(X_test_outliers[:, 0], X_test_outliers[:, 1],
                             c="red", s=50, marker='P')

plt.axis("tight")
plt.xlim((min_range, max_range))
plt.ylim((min_range, max_range))
plt.legend(
    [a.collections[0], train_points, normal_points, outlier_points],
    ["Decision Boundary", "Training data", "Subsequent normal points",
        "Subsequent outlier points"],
    bbox_to_anchor = (1.6, 0.6),
    loc="center right",
)
plt.xlabel(
    (f"Errors in training: {n_error_train}/200\n"
     f"Errors novel normal: {n_error_normal}/20\n"
     f"Errors novel outlier: {n_error_outliers}/20"))
plt.show()
```

Creates the training data

Creates test data similar to the training data

Creates test data unlike the training data

Creates and fits a OCSVM detector

Predicts for the train and test data

Plots the data and the decision boundary

The code generates a 2D plot (figure 5.5) that shows the training data, the decision boundary drawn around this data, and the subsequent data, which is tested against this model. We see some training data is slightly outside the decision boundary, which is controlled by the parameters used. In this example, we set the nu parameter to 0.1, which allows 10% of the training data to appear outside. This may be set lower (any value from 0.0 to 1.0 may be used), which will create a larger decision boundary, shifting from more false positives to more false negatives (with the decision boundary larger, more outliers will fall within it and hence will not be flagged as outliers, resulting in more false negatives). In this case, we use synthetic data, so we can safely set this to 0.0, but with real-world data—even clean data—we may wish, at least for some problems, to create a tight decision boundary to represent the core of the data well.

The background color indicates the scores given in each part of the space, and we can see that the scores generated by the OCSVM increase with greater distances from the decision boundary.

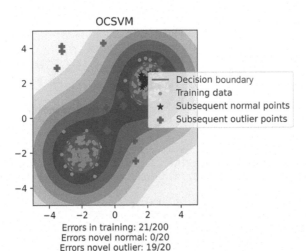

Figure 5.5   The training data and subsequent data used on an OCSVM detector. This also shows the decision boundary created around the training data and a contour indicating the distance from the decision boundary. Some training points and normal subsequent points fall outside the decision boundary, though only slightly. Most generated outliers are well outside the boundary, though some randomly fall within it.

Due to the nature of one-class models, they are recommended only for novelty detection, and their performance can suffer if trained with contaminated data or if they are executed with the same data used for training. Any outliers included in the training will be considered normal data, and the model will attempt to include these points within the decision boundary, expanding the boundary to do so. This may not always preclude the OCSVM functioning well, though, particularly if the nu parameter is set appropriately for the data. We see in figure 5.5 that the decision boundary does not necessarily include all training data. Adding a small number of additional outliers in the training data may not always move the decision boundary significantly. However, including outliers in the training data can often affect the decision boundary, and this does make it quite possible these outlier points will not be flagged as outliers (if we predict on the same data that we trained on). Further, when testing subsequent data, any outliers similar to those used in training will also not necessarily be flagged, as these will usually be included within the decision boundary. Only novelties (data unlike the training data) will be reliably flagged.

Unfortunately, it is not normally the case that completely clean data is available, but it can nevertheless be worth trying OCSVM models. While the models may not flag outliers similar to those included in the training data, they will still detect well any outliers that are different from these. In addition, it is usually possible to clean the data, removing strong outliers, before fitting the OCSVM. In fact, almost all outlier detectors will benefit from this, and it is generally worth doing in any outlier detection work regardless of the models used.

Another limitation of SVM models generally is that if not well-tuned, they can execute very slowly. With one-class models, it is possible to train on samples, which can help a great deal when the available data is larger than necessary. Sampling can work very well, though we should be cautious to create a sample that spans the full normal class. A risk with sampling is that it is possible to exclude some records that may be better to include, in the sense that they, while being rare enough to potentially be excluded from a sample (and so reasonably considered outliers, at least in a statistical sense), may be considered normal for the task at hand. We need to cover the full range of normal data (data you do not wish flagged as outliers) in the training set or there may be false positives later when executing the model. As well as sampling, the scikit-learn documentation provides advice on scaling one-class SVM models, which is useful where large datasets may be used.

The one scenario where one-class models may be the best option available is where we have clean data and wish to test for the possible appearance of anomalies, but it's not clear what anomalies may look like. In this scenario, there may be no real outliers to test with or base synthetic data on, and it may not be feasible to write rules given the lack of clarity about what outliers may appear. OCSVM models can work quite well here, as they will simply flag anything different from the training data.

5.4.1 OneClassSVM class

An example using OCSVM with the KDD Cup dataset is shown in listing 5.4. Here we fit to a small sample to allow the process to execute more quickly, which works well in this case. We ensure clean data for training by taking advantage of the labels available and filtering out any rows not marked normal. As with other scikit-learn models, we create an instance of the detector—a `OneClassSVM` object in this case. We divided the data into separate train and test subsets so fit on the training data and predict, calling `score_samples()` on the test data.

This achieves an AUROC score of 0.999—almost perfect. In this case, even without filtering the training data (and using the default nu of 0.5), a very high AUROC can still be achieved—around 0.98. In other datasets where SVM does not perform as well, however, it can be difficult to tune, as the parameters are somewhat unintuitive, many relating to kernel methods that can be difficult to understand.

Listing 5.4   Using OneClassSVM on the KDD Cup dataset

```python
import pandas as pd
import numpy as np
from sklearn.datasets import fetch_kddcup99
from sklearn.model_selection import train_test_split
from sklearn.svm import OneClassSVM
from sklearn.preprocessing import OneHotEncoder, RobustScaler
from sklearn.metrics import roc_auc_score

X, y = fetch_kddcup99(
    subset="SA",  percent10=True,
    random_state=42, return_X_y=True, as_frame=True)
y = (y != b"normal.").astype(np.int32)

cat_columns = ["protocol_type", "service", "flag"]         ◀── Encodes the
X_cat = pd.get_dummies(X[cat_columns])                          categorical columns
col_names = [x.replace("'", '_') for x in X_cat.columns]
X_cat.columns = col_names
X_cat = X_cat.reset_index()

num_cols = \                                               ◀── Scales the
        [x for x in X.columns if x not in cat_columns]         numeric columns
transformer = RobustScaler().fit(X[num_cols])
X_num = pd.DataFrame(transformer.transform(X[num_cols]))
X_num.columns = num_cols
X_num = X_num.reset_index()
                                                           Splits the data into train
                                                           and test portions
X = pd.concat([X_cat, X_num], axis=1)

X_train, X_test, y_train, y_test = train_test_split(X, y, test_size=0.90,
    random_state=42)
y_train = y_train[y_train == 0]        ◀── Finds the normal examples
X_train = X_train.loc[y_train.index]       in the train in the y feature

                                       Uses the same subset of records
det = OneClassSVM()          ◀──       (the normal records) for the X
det.fit(X_train)                       features as for the y feature

                                 Evaluates the
pred = det.score_samples(X_test)  ◀──  model on the     Creates and fits a OCSVM detector
min_score = pred.min()                 test data        on the normal train data
max_score = pred.max()
pred = [(x - min_score) / (max_score - min_score) for x in pred]
pred = [1.0 - x for x in pred]
roc_auc_score(y_test, pred)
```

Interestingly, the records scored highest by OCSVM tend to receive high, but not the highest, scores from the Isolation Forest detector. There is a difference in the records each scores highest, highlighting that even accurate detectors can flag different records.

5.4.2   *SGDOneClassSVM*

For larger datasets, scikit-learn also provides a similar class called SGDOneClassSVM, which uses stochastic gradient descent to fit the model. This can produce a similar decision boundary as `OneClassSVM` but will execute in time linear to the number of training rows, so can be considerably faster for larger datasets. Using this class, as opposed to `OneClassSVM`, is recommended for datasets over about 10,000 rows.

The `SGDOneClassSVM` class may be used simply as is, but it is recommended to use a kernel approximation technique, at least to obtain results similar to those you would get with `OneClassSVM` on the same data. This requires using a scikit-learn pipeline. Listing 5.5 provides a simple example using a kernel approximation provided with scikit-learn called `Nystroem`. This process works similarly to using a detector directly, though calls are made to the pipeline class as opposed to the detector. The code is the same as listing 5.4, with only the differences shown here.

Listing 5.5 Example using `SGDOneClassSVM` with a kernel approximation

```
import numpy as np
from sklearn.kernel_approximation import Nystroem
from sklearn.linear_model import SGDOneClassSVM
from sklearn.pipeline import make_pipeline

...

transform = Nystroem(random_state=42)
clf_sgd = SGDOneClassSVM()
pipe_sgd = make_pipeline(transform, clf_sgd)
pipe_sgd.fit(X_train)
pred = pipe_sgd.score_samples(X_test)
```

For the KDD Cup dataset, though, using a kernel approximation is not necessary, and we can simply use the same code as in listing 5.4 and replace the call to create the detector from det = `OneClassSVM()` to det = `SGDOneClassSVM()` and remove the code to reverse the scores:

```
pred = [1.0 - x for x in pred]
```

This returns an AUROC of 1.0.

5.5 *Elliptic Envelope*

Elliptic Envelope detectors work by evaluating each point with respect to their distance from the data center. Where the data is in a single large cluster, this is a logical approach: points close to the data center would be considered inliers and points far away outliers.

A similar idea as Elliptic Envelope is to take the mean of each feature (taken across all features, this gives us the data center) and determine how far from the means each of the values in a row are. Assuming the data is scaled so that all features are on the same scale, this gives us the distance of each point to the data center. Summing the distances for each feature from that feature's mean gives the Manhattan distance. Squaring the distances, summing, and taking the square root gives the Euclidean distance.

This can be intuitive but actually often works poorly in practice. The issue with this method is it ignores the variance of each feature and the correlations between the features. Elliptic Envelopes, and related methods, address this, taking the variances and correlations into consideration, which creates a more meaningful distance metric between points and the data center than when treating every dimension equally and independently.

In figure 5.6, we see an example of a skewed dataset and two points, A and B, where point A, considering the distribution of the data, is more anomalous than point B. To evaluate points A and B, it is possible to examine the distances between them and the data center, using a plain Euclidean distance (middle pane) though this may not be meaningful, as this does not consider the nature of the data. The right pane shows the distances used by the EllipticEnvelope detector, which takes the shape of the data into consideration and results in point A being recognized as more anomalous than point B.

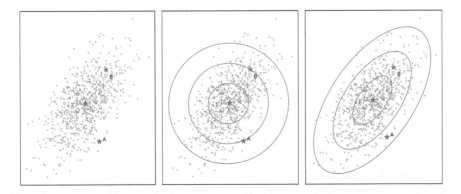

Figure 5.6   The middle pane is an example of using Euclidean distance from the center of a dataset to measure the outlierness of datapoints. Here, point A is a stronger outlier than point B but is the same distance from the center using Euclidean distance. The right pane is an example using distances based on fitting an ellipse to the data and provides more meaningful distance measures, allowing us to consider A farther from the center than B.

The Elliptic Envelope detector is an elliptic estimator: it tries to fit the tightest multidimensional ellipse it can around the available data, flagging any points significantly outside this ellipse. Elliptic Envelope is also an example of a parametric model, which is to say that it assumes the data follows a certain distribution that can be described with a small set of parameters, in the same way Gaussian distributions can be described with the mean and variance, or Poisson distributions with lambda. In this case, the assumption is that the data is in a single cluster with each dimension roughly Gaussian, where the features may vary in their variances and where there may be correlations between the features. Fitting a model in this case is a matter of estimating as well as possible the parameters to describe this.

We cannot describe the data well simply using the mean and standard deviation of each dimension. Instead, we use a similar, but more sophisticated model—a multivariate

Gaussian distribution, which describes the data distribution with two parameters: the data center and what's called the *covariance matrix*. This is a d × d matrix (where d is the number of dimensions) that includes the variance of each feature as well as the covariance between each pair of features. It's a concise summary of the shape of the data and a rough approximation of a scatterplot of the data, which allows us to construct ellipses around the data. The idea is closely related to a distance metric called the *Mahalanobis* distance, which is also very often used in outlier detection and so is described next.

5.5.1 *Mahalanobis distance*

The Mahalanobis distance is a distance measure used to compare points to a data distribution that does so by incorporating the covariance matrix. That is, the Mahalanobis distance is the distance from a point to the data center, considering the shape of the data. By doing this it avoids the limitations of using a plain Euclidean distance. In fact, the right pane of figure 5.6 shows concentric rings of Mahalanobis distances from the center.

To calculate the Mahalanobis distance, we use a formula very similar to the formula for Euclidean distances but include the inverse covariance matrix. Including this matrix in the formula effectively transforms the data to a space where the features are uncorrelated and have equal variance, where the Euclidean distance may then be used. If you're familiar with principal component analysis (PCA), this is the same idea and, in fact, PCA can be used to calculate Mahalanobis distances.

Using this method does assume the data is in a single cluster and that each dimension is roughly Gaussian, or at least unimodal. These are not always safe assumptions, but I've found the Mahalanobis distance to frequently work quite well in practice.

The first step, then, is to calculate the covariance matrix. scikit-learn provides several tools to do this, including implementations of two of the best-known algorithms, minimum covariance determinant (MCD) and minimum volume ellipsoid (MVE). Some of the methods available in scikit-learn are not robust and may be affected by outliers: there may be some swamping and masking effects. MCD and MVE, however, are both robust methods that are not significantly affected by outliers.

Estimating this covariance matrix is straightforward. Given a dataset, we can simply use one of the covariance estimators provided by scikit-learn and fit it to the data. In listing 5.6, we create a random dataset with three correlated features, based on Laplacian, normal, and exponential distributions. Using the `MinConvDet` class, we are able to get the covariance matrix. The class also allows us to determine the center of the data using the `location_` attribute. All covariance estimators in scikit-learn include a `mahalanobis()` method, which can be used as well to test for outliers.

Listing 5.6 Example using MCD

```python
import numpy as np
import pandas as pd
from sklearn.covariance import MinCovDet

np.random.seed(0)
a_data = np.random.laplace(size=1000)
```

```
b_data = np.random.normal(size=1000) + a_data
c_data = np.random.exponential(size=1000) + a_data + b_data
X = pd.DataFrame({"A": a_data, "B": b_data, "C": c_data})

cov = MinCovDet(random_state=0).fit(X)
print(cov.covariance_)
```

In this example, we get the following covariance matrix:

1.57	1.50	3.02
1.50	2.33	3.81
3.02	3.81	6.98

The main diagonal contains the variances for each feature: 1.57, 2.33, and 6.98 (as we might expect, column C, which includes an exponential component, has the highest variance) and the other cells contain the pairwise covariances between features. The table is symmetric across the main diagonal, as the covariance between, for example, A and B is the same as between B and A. We can then access the Mahalanobis distances from the data center calling

```
cov.mahalanobis(X)
```

Once we have the Mahalanobis distance from each point to the data center, we effectively have a measure of the outlierness of each point. We should note that using the Mahalanobis distance in this manner, while typically more relevant than the Euclidean, is more expensive. However, it is still a very fast outlier detection method relative to most, and it can typically scale to more dimensions while producing meaningful distances than approaches based on Euclidean distances.

Another limitation of the method is, although it can detect outliers that are extreme values or outliers that are unusual combinations of values, it will miss internal outliers, as it assumes the data is a single cluster.

There are several other useful methods in Python for Mahalanobis distances other than the tools in scikit-learn, including SciPy and the alibi-detect library (https://github.com/SeldonIO/alibi-detect).

5.5.2 *Example using the EllipticEnvelope class*

Although it's possible to use Mahalanobis distances directly to evaluate outliers, scikit-learn also provides, as we've seen, the EllipticEnvelope class, which makes this even a little easier as it follows the same format as other scikit-learn outlier detectors. Internally, it uses MCD and Mahalanobis distances (and also provides a `mahalanobis()` method). In some cases, you may find that using other covariance estimators will produce slightly different results, but as long as you're using a robust estimator, the differences will tend to be small.

This is likely the most limited of the detectors provided by scikit-learn. The conditions for effective use can be hard to meet with many dimensions: the assumption of near-Gaussian distributions in all dimensions becomes harder to maintain with more features. At the same time, the method is fast and can work very well where the data is in a single, well-formed cluster. Testing with the KDD Cup data, taking listing 5.1 and simply substituting EllipticEnvelope for Isolation Forest results in an AUROC score of 0.77, better than LOF but not as strong as OCSVM or IF. A snippet of the updated code is shown in listing 5.7. If used, it may be useful to identify subsets of features where the Gaussian distribution holds well and where there are strong correlations between features.

Listing 5.7   Using EllipticEnvelope on the KDD Cup dataset

```
from sklearn.covariance import EllipticEnvelope
det = EllipticEnvelope()
pred = det.fit_predict(X)
r = roc_auc_score(y, pred)
```

To provide another example, where we may more easily picture the elliptic envelope drawn around the data, we use another dataset, shown in listing 5.8. This uses a real-world dataset from OpenML, though only two dimensions, to allow us to plot easily. The method is easy to use and works quite well in this instance. The data in this example is a single blob, which EllipticEnvelope is very good at working with, and which is relatively common in real-world data, though is certainly not everywhere. Mapping the scores to 0 and 1 values is done to simplify plotting.

Listing 5.8   Example of the EllipticEnvelope detector

```
import pandas as pd
import numpy as np
from sklearn.covariance import EllipticEnvelope
from sklearn.datasets import fetch_openml
import matplotlib.pyplot as plt
import seaborn as sns

data = fetch_openml(                                      ← Collects the data
        'mfeat-karhunen', version=1, parser='auto')          from OpenML
df = pd.DataFrame(data.data, columns=data.feature_names)

cov = EllipticEnvelope(                                   ← Creates and fits an
        random_state=0).fit(df[['att6', 'att7']])           EllipticEnvelope detector
pred = cov.predict(df[['att6', 'att7']])

df['Elliptic Score'] = pred

df['Elliptic Score'] = \                                  ← Plots the results
        df['Elliptic Score'].map({-1: 1, 1: 0})
sns.scatterplot(data=df[df['Elliptic Score']==0], x="att6", y='att7',
            alpha=0.3)
sns.scatterplot(data=df[df['Elliptic Score']==1], x="att6", y='att7',
            alpha=1.0, s=200, marker='*')
plt.show()
```

The output is shown in figure 5.7, with a sensible selection of outliers.

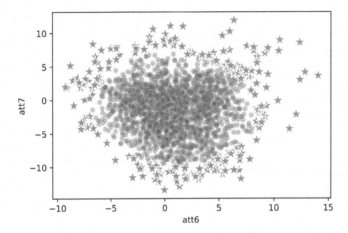

Figure 5.7   **The output of the EllipticEnvelope detector on two dimensions of a real-world dataset. As the data is in a single cluster, EllipticEnvelope is able to effectively flag points on the fringe and outside this cluster.**

5.6   *Gaussian mixture models*

Gaussian mixture models (GMMs) are similar to the ellipse estimation method but are more general in that they represent data with a series of multivariate Gaussians, as opposed to a single one. GMMs handle where data is clustered by creating a multivariate Gaussian for each cluster. When using a single cluster, they perform essentially the same covariance estimation and Mahalanobis distance calculations as elliptic estimators, so they work equivalently to an Elliptic Envelope detector in that case. Where the data is in multiple clusters, however, GMMs can perform significantly better, as they can model each cluster. GMMs often model datasets very well.

GMMs are used normally for clustering, but often for outlier detection as well. We've looked previously at clustering algorithms, such as DBSCAN, that perform what's called *hard clustering*. That is, they place each record in exactly one (or sometimes no) cluster. Other clustering algorithms, including GMMs, use *soft clustering* and instead give each record a series of scores, one for each cluster, indicating how well they match each of the clusters.

The idea is that each multivariate Gaussian (that is, each center point and shape of data around it) ideally represents a process generating the data. In the example of financial data, there may be one or more processes generating sales records and others generating purchase, payroll, and other records. It may be possible to represent each of these as a multivariate Gaussian, each with a certain center, variance in each dimension, and correlation between the features.

An example is shown in figure 5.8, where the data can be modelled with three Gaussians. Data near one or more centers is probable, and data far from any centers (or close only to centers that appear to generate little data) is unlikely. Points where Gaussians overlap (points that could plausibly have been produced by any one of multiple processes) are, everything else equal, more likely than points near only one Gaussian. GMMs can, given this, be viewed as similar to KDE: as another tool provided by scikit-learn to create probability density estimates from data.

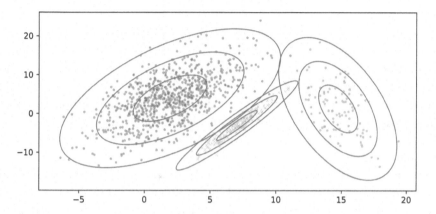

Figure 5.8 Data with three clusters, each captured by a multivariate Gaussian. Each location in the space has a probability, which can be estimated by the sum of the probabilities of it being generated by any one of the Gaussians, weighted by the size of each Gaussian.

Like Elliptic Envelope, GMM is an example of a parametric model. That is, it assumes a certain structure of data (in this case a series of multivariate Gaussians) and seeks to find the best parameters to describe this model. On the other hand, most of the models we've looked at (including KNN, Radius, frequent pattern outlier factor (FPOS), KNN, IF, LOF) are nonparametric: they make no assumptions about the data. There are advantages to both. Parametric models can be more restrictive, as the assumptions may not hold, and the models will not always be applicable. At the same time, parametric models can also be very effective where the assumptions do match the data. With GMMs, the parameters are the number of clusters, the center and covariance matrix of each cluster, and a weight parameter for each cluster, indicating the likelihood of any point being in that cluster.

GMM uses expectation maximization (EM) to find the best parameters. This is an iterative process where, repeatedly, a set of parameters are selected, evaluated, and then adjusted to create a progressively better fit to the data. The process begins with a random set of values for the parameters. At each step, it evaluates the parameters by calculating how likely the data is given these parameters, which is done by calculating the probability of each row (that is, how likely the row is to have been generated by the set of Gaussians) and multiplying the probabilities for each row together (to estimate the probability of the training set as a whole). The parameters are then adjusted, and the process repeats until the evaluations converge or some other stopping criteria is met.

Doing this, we find the set of parameters that describe the GMM most likely to have generated the given training data.

Once fit, we treat the model as a generative model and assume the data was, in fact, generated by this process. With this, we can determine the probability of each record tested against the model. This is the probability of it being generated by any one of the clusters, multiplied by the weights for each cluster. Outliers are the significantly unlikely points.

GMM is best suited for cases where there are multiple clusters and they can be represented reasonably well with multivariate Gaussians. This can become difficult in high dimensions: the more dimensions at play, the better the chances of a good number being distinctly non-Gaussian.

GMM also requires reasonably large datasets to model the multiple Gaussians well. The covariance matrixes particularly have a large number of parameters each, which are easy to overfit. scikit-learn does, though, allow limiting the number of parameters to fit, making limiting assumptions about the covariance matrixes—to reduce overfitting and to allow for faster execution. By default, each cluster may have any shape and size, but the fitting process may be restricted so that all have the same shape (share the same covariance matrix) or, further, such that all must be hyperspheres. Restricting the models in this way, the range of options is reduced, and while the fit may be more approximate, the GMM can be calculated faster and in a manner that is possibly more stable.

Where clustering algorithms are used for outlier detection, GMM can often be one of the better choices. K-means clustering is probably used more often, as it can be faster than most other clustering algorithms, and it's straightforward to evaluate the clustering (for example, using the Silhouette score). But k-means does have an implicit assumption that all clusters are about the same size, while GMM does not require this. In fact, GMM specifically tries to determine the size (and shape) of each cluster individually, making GMM more effective in these cases.

Listing 5.9 shows an example using GMM to identify outliers in a synthetic dataset containing three dense clusters as well as additional points outside these clusters. Here, the clusters are well-separated, but they can also be overlapping in space. This uses scikit-learn's `make_blobs` API to generate 2D data.

The `score_samples()` method returns the log likelihood of each point, providing low likelihoods for points not near any cluster centers or in very small clusters. The `score_samples()` API doesn't require a real record per se; it takes the values passed as locations in the data space and returns the likelihood of that location.

While the results are likelihoods and not true probabilities, using some calculus and selecting small regions, it is possible to determine the actual probabilities. If we integrate over the full dataspace, the total probability will be 1.0.

This code includes a loop to determine the best number of components for the GMM using the Bayesian information criterion (BIC) measure, which balances the accuracy of the model (in this case the probability of the passed data, given the model) with the complexity of the model (the number of components).

Listing 5.9 Example of GMMs for outlier detection

```
from sklearn.datasets import make_blobs
import numpy as np
import pandas as pd
import matplotlib.pyplot as plt
import seaborn as sns
from sklearn.mixture import GaussianMixture
from scipy import stats

np.random.seed(0)

vals, _ = make_blobs(n_samples=500, centers=3, n_features=2,
                  cluster_std=1, random_state=42)
df_inliers = pd.DataFrame(vals, columns=["A", "B"])

vals, _ = make_blobs(n_samples=15, centers=2, n_features=2,
                  cluster_std=10, random_state=42)
df_outliers = pd.DataFrame(vals, columns=["A", "B"])

df = pd.concat([df_inliers, df_outliers])
X = df[['A', 'B']]

best_n_components = -1
best_bic = np.inf
for n_components in range(1, 8):
    gmm = GaussianMixture(n_components=n_components, n_init=5,
                       random_state=42)
    gmm.fit(X)
    bic = gmm.bic(X)
    if bic < best_bic:
        best_bic = bic
        best_n_components = n_components

gmm = GaussianMixture(n_components=best_n_components,
                   n_init=5, random_state=42)
gmm.fit(X)

score = gmm.score_samples(X)
df['Score'] = score

pct_threshold = np.percentile(score, 3.0)
df['Outlier'] = df['Score'] < pct_threshold

sns.scatterplot(data=df[df['Outlier'] == False], x='A', y='B', alpha=0.3)
sns.scatterplot(data=df[df['Outlier'] == True], x='A', y='B',
             s=150, marker='*')
plt.show()
```

Creates
synthetic data

Creates a set of GMMs
with a range of values
for n_components

Creates a final GMM
using the best
n_components

Sets a threshold
on the scores to
support plotting

Interestingly, this actually selected four (and not three) as the optimal number of components, though one of the four components is quite minor, as can be seen accessing the means_ and weights_ attributes. The weights of the four clusters are [0.03, 0.32, 0.32, 0.3]. The first has very low weight and, as it happens, even points very close to its center are estimated as having low likelihood. The results are shown in figure 5.9 when taking the top 3% of outliers. This model does a good job of identifying the most outlierish points.

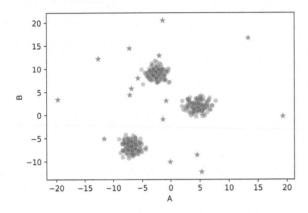

Figure 5.9 **Synthetic data in three clusters, along with the outliers identified**

GMM is stochastic and can create better models in some executions than others. The `n_init` parameter indicates how many attempts should be made to fit the data, keeping the best fit. This is 1 by default, but it's preferable to set higher, for example to 5 or 10 or even higher if feasible.

Working with the KDD Cup data, the GMM class, having a similar API, can be used the same as the previous examples. The same code as used for LOF can be used with GMM, replacing the one line:

```
det = GaussianMixture(n_init=5)
```

Using GMM for the KDD Cup dataset produces a very high AUROC score of 0.99.

5.7   *BallTree and KDTree*

We've used the `BallTree` class a few times already to implement KNN and Radius detectors. In general, if you work with outlier detection using methods based on distances, you'll likely work with `BallTree`. It's also used internally by scikit-learn to implement several other tools, including KDE and LOF. scikit-learn provides another similar structure as well, called `KDTree`. Both are designed for fast nearest neighbors queries (finding the nearest points in the training data to a given location), though, depending on the situation, one or the other may be more efficient.

SciPy (https://scipy.org/) also provides an implementation of `KDTree`, as well as a structure called *Rectangle*, used to represent subspaces of a dataspace as hyperrectangles. These classes can all be useful to model your data and help identify anomalous points, in the sense of points with few close neighbors or as points in especially low-density regions.

A `BallTree` is fit on a set of training points, which essentially involves storing their locations in a way that allows fast lookup. Once the `BallTree` is fit, it's possible to call its `query()` method with a set of points and parameter k, which will return, for each point passed to query, the k nearest points from the training set and the distances to each. This is why, as we saw earlier, if the same data is used to train the model as for the call to `query()`, the method will include the distance of each point to itself. That is, the `query()` API can be called passing the same data used to fit the model or with different data. In either case, each record passed will be evaluated in terms of its distance to the nearest k points from the training set. The `query_radius()` API works similarly, finding the number of points from the training data within the specified radius for each record passed to the query.

The `BallTree` class takes a couple of parameters. One is the `leaf_size`, which affects the efficiency of the lookups but not the results. The other is the distance metric. By default, `BallTree` uses Euclidean distance, but other options are available. With outlier detection (as well as clustering and other applications of nearest neighbors searches), the results found using Euclidean, Manhattan, Mahalanobis, or other distance metrics can be different, and one may better match the type of outliers you are more interested in. Usually, some experimentation is needed.

`BallTree` and `KDTree` are both tree data structures that recursively divide the dataspace into smaller regions, somewhat similar to decision trees, so as to group points that are close within the full multidimensional space. `KDTree`s are very fast for low-dimensional dataspaces but can suffer in higher-dimensional spaces, which `BallTree` was developed to address. `BallTree` achieves this by dividing the data space into hyperspheres, as opposed to hyperrectangles, which actually allows more efficient lookups. `BallTree` is also somewhat less vulnerable to the curse of dimensionality than `KDTree` but is still limited in the number of dimensions it can support (any distance metrics in high-dimensional space will eventually break down). With any detectors based on `BallTree` or `KDTree`, calculations will benefit from removing any unnecessary features. Scikit-learn provides some guidance on when to use `KDTree` or `BallTree` and how to set the `leaf_size`, which are worth looking into if you have larger volumes of data to work with.

scikit-learn also provides the `NearestNeighbors` class, which is a wrapper for either `BallTree` or `KDTree` (though also supports a brute-force algorithm), which can also be convenient to use for outlier detection work. It can also be used for Mahalanobis distance comparisons.

Summary

- The Python language includes implementations of a very large number of outlier detectors, possibly more than any other language.
- scikit-learn provides implementations for four detectors, including two of the most common and useful: Isolation Forest and LOF.
- IF and LOF are both useful for most outlier detection problems on tabular data.

- The other two detectors provided, OCSVM and EllipticEnvelope, work well in some specific cases but are not always appropriate.
- OCSVM is intended for training with clean data and predicting on separate data, though you may find good results training and testing on the same data.
- Elliptic Envelope works well when the data is in a single cluster but may not otherwise.
- It is not always clear ahead of time which detector will work the best on a given data problem.
- The Mahalanobis distance is an important concept in outlier detection and is often more relevant than the Euclidean distance between points.
- scikit-learn also provides additional tools to support outlier detection, notably `BallTree`, `KDTree`, and GMM.
- `BallTree` and `KDTree` are similar, but their efficiency can be different on different datasets.
- Usually, `KDTree` is more efficient with few features and `BallTree` with more features.
- GMM is a clustering algorithm that is very useful for outlier detection and is commonly used.
- GMM works similarly to Elliptic Envelope but supports multiple clusters.

The PyOD library 6

This chapter covers

- The PyOD library
- Several of the detectors provided by the library
- Guidance related to where the different detectors are most useful
- PyOD's support for thresholding scores and accelerating training

The PyOD (Python Outlier Detection) library (https://github.com/yzhao062/pyod) provides the largest collection of outlier detectors available in Python for numeric tabular data, covering both traditional machine learning and deep learning-based methods. PyOD is probably the most effective tool for working with outlier detection in Python. As well as a large collection of detectors, PyOD provides several other tools. And, similar to scikit-learn, it provides a simple, consistent API for the detectors, making it efficient to work with.

In all, depending on how similar detectors are counted, there are about 29 detectors based on traditional unsupervised machine learning and eight based on deep learning (most are forms of Generative Adversarial Network (GAN) or

AutoEncoder-based detection). We cover the former here and deep-learning methods in chapter 16. It's not feasible to cover all the traditional detectors in PyOD, so we'll just provide a sample of several. This will provide a good introduction to PyOD and will help further present some of the diversity of methods to identify outliers in tabular data that exists today.

Some are variations on each other; for example, connectivity-based outlier factor (COF, described later) is really a variation on local outlier factor (LOF) and two others, empirical cumulative distribution (ECOD) and copula-based outlier detection (COPOD, also described later) are both based on a concept known as *empirical cumulative distributions*. However, most are quite distinct and cover a wide swath of the range of algorithms proposed in academic papers for outlier detection.

As we've seen, a large portion of outlier detection algorithms are adaptations of algorithms designed for other purposes, such as frequent item set mining and clustering. This is true of many of the detectors in PyOD as well. One detector, QCMD, for example, is based on space-filling curves; another, LUNAR, is based on graph neural networks; with others building on principal component analysis (PCA), sampling methods, and a number of other ideas. The algorithms range from very simple, such as histogram-based outlier score (HBOS) and Cook's Distance (based on linear regression), to very sophisticated, particularly the deep learning approaches. As with the other detectors we've looked at, even where you do not use these specific detectors, understanding them will help you understand outlier detection generally.

PyOD provides, for all detectors, references to the original papers, which makes looking deeper into them manageable, if not the most convenient. The most popular detectors, such as k nearest neighbors (KNN), Isolation Forest, and LOF, have numerous explanations online, but many of the detectors supported by PyOD, unfortunately, have few sources of explanation other than academic papers. However, the papers in this field are generally very readable, with only rare exceptions. Journal papers in some areas of computer science can be challenging, but outlier detection papers tend to be clear even if the reader does not have a prior background in the area. I will, nevertheless, try to provide a sufficient background on these for most purposes. The PyOD implementations are, in any case, often somewhat different from the referenced papers.

PyOD provides implementations of many algorithms not available elsewhere. It also provides wrappers for the main outlier detection tools provided in scikit-learn, though not Elliptic Envelope. PyOD provides Isolation Forest, LOF, One-class Support Vector Machine (OCSVM), KNN, Gaussian mixture models, and kernel density estimation (KDE). In most cases these are simple wrappers, though with Isolation Forest (included in PyOD as IForest), PyOD also provides an attribute called `feature_importances_` (available only for the IForest detector), which is a convenient way to determine the overall importance of each feature to the final scores (this is over the full data—the feature importances are not provided per record).

PyOD does have some limitations. At present, for example, PyOD does not provide categorical detectors, and many detectors worth trying for projects are not supported by PyOD, so PyOD will not always provide all the tools you will need. Having said that,

PyOD is currently the most comprehensive library available for outlier detection in Python.

The PyOD detectors not covered in this chapter are, on average, going to be just as useful for your projects, and I'd encourage you to look into these as well. After looking at these, you'll understand PyOD well and will be well-equipped to use the other detectors it provides.

We start by looking at the API used by all detectors, then at several detectors provided by PyOD, and finally at some of the tools provided, which support faster model training and thresholding the results. PyOD also provides tools for combining detectors, which are covered in chapter 14. The tools provided are quite useful; even where using detectors outside of PyOD, it may be useful to use PyOD in order to access these tools.

6.1 *The PyOD common API*

In PyOD, there's a simple and consistent way we use each detector, which usually requires only a few lines of code. We first create an instance of the detector, fit the data, and then predict either the outlier scores or labels, either using the same data used to train or other data. We can also, optionally, collect the confidence of each outlier score.

The common API makes PyOD straightforward to use and experiment with. The detectors do, though, all have different hyperparameters, which take some time to understand. We'll go through several in this chapter but cannot cover them all. PyOD provides sensible defaults for these that let you get working right away, but it is worth looking into these for each detector, as some settings may be suboptimal for your data or for your goal for performing outlier detection.

Before using PyOD, it's necessary to install it, which can be done with

```
pip install pyod
```

We introduce the common API in listing 6.1. This uses PyOD's implementation of a detector you're already familiar with, KNN. Here we import the class, create an instance, fit the data, and use the `decision_scores_` attribute to access the scores for each record in the training data. This is a very basic example but is often all that is necessary. This assumes the `data` object contains a set of data to evaluate.

Listing 6.1 Basic example using PyOD with the KNN detector

```
from pyod.models.knn import KNN

clf = KNN()
clf.fit(data)
scores = clf.decision_scores_
```

As another example, the KDE class provided by PyOD is a simple wrapper around scikit-learn's `KernelDensity` class. Using the detector again follows the standard PyOD format and can be used such as in listing 6.2.

> **Listing 6.2   Basic example using PyOD with the KDE detector**

```
from pyod.models.kde import KDE

clf = KDE()
clf.fit(data)
scores = clf.decision_scores_
```

In PyOD, the main methods are

- `fit()`—This fits the model to the provided training data.
- `predict()`—The test data is passed as a parameter. This returns a predicted binary label for each record in the test data; it is used if the test data is separate from the training data.
- `decision_function()`—Similar to `predict()` but returns a numeric score for each record in the test data.
- `predict_proba()`—By default, this simply processes the results of `decision_function()` using min-max scaling (to put all scores between 0.0 and 1.0). Other scaling methods are also available. These are not true probabilities but can be treated similarly. The results are returned as a 2D array: for each record, we have both the probability of the record being an inlier and the probability of it being an outlier. These will sum to 1.0.

As well as the common methods supported by all detectors, two attributes may also be used to collect results on the training data:

- `labels_`—Returns a binary label for each row in the training data.
- `decision_scores_`—Returns a numeric score for each row in the training data. This was used in listings 6.1 and 6.2.

Where different data is used to fit and predict, these allow us to separate the scores easily; and where the same data is used, these allow us to simply fit the data, automatically getting the outlier scores through these attributes.

As with all numeric detectors, it is necessary to encode categorical features and to fill any None or NaN (not a number) values. Almost all PyOD detectors also require scaling the numeric features.

We now take a look at a longer example in listing 6.3, which uses more of the available APIs and includes an example scaling the numeric features. This code also provides another example of PyOD's KNN detector. As with all detectors, KNN has limitations (it is limited by the curse of dimensionality and does not allow for differences in density in different regions) but also works very well in many cases. KNN is still actively studied in outlier detection research.

Previously we've used scikit-learn's `BallTree` class to implement both KNN and Radius detectors. It is, though, slightly easier to use PyOD's KNN class, which supports both tests. In practice, the difference is small; internally, PyOD uses either scikit-learn's `BallTree`, `KDTree`, or a brute-force algorithm to calculate and store the distances between points, but the PyOD implementation is easier to use as it is already constructed as an outlier detector (BallTree on the other hand, is a tool tool to build other tools like outlier detectors) and uses PyOD's standard API. PyOD's implementation of KNN supports using the mean, median, or max of the k nearest neighbors, using max by default.

The code in listing 6.3 first creates random data, consisting of 1,000 inlier points in a single Gaussian cluster, five outliers on the edge of this, and five outliers in a more distant space. These are shown in figure 6.1 (left). In this chapter, we provide several examples of synthetic data such as this that may be created for quick tests of the detectors. This data is not intended to test the detectors rigorously, but to provide simple examples that can highlight what different detectors do well and do not do well. Creating such data, as well as more complex synthetic data, is a common practice in working with outlier detection, particularly when first working with new detectors.

We then create a KNN object and fit this to the data. We call predict() to return a binary prediction for each row. As with scikit-learn, this simply applies a threshold on the numeric scores based on the specified contamination rate. In this case, we know the true contamination level but in most cases would not, so the contamination rate is left as the default value.

Listing 6.3 Example of the standard PyOD API using KNN

```
import pandas as pd
import numpy as np
from pyod.models.knn import KNN
from sklearn.preprocessing import RobustScaler
import matplotlib.pyplot as plt
import seaborn as sns

np.random.seed(42)

x_data = np.random.normal(loc=10, scale=1.0, size=1000)      Creates
y_data = np.random.normal(loc=10, scale=1.0, size=1000)      normal data
df1 = pd.DataFrame({'A': x_data, 'B':y_data})
df1['Ground Truth'] = 0

x_data = np.random.normal(loc=8, scale=1.0, size=5)      Creates outliers
y_data = np.random.normal(loc=8, scale=1.0, size=5)      around the edge of
df2 = pd.DataFrame({'A': x_data, 'B':y_data})            the normal data
df2['Ground Truth'] = 1

x_data = np.random.normal(loc=1, scale=3.0, size=5)      Creates outliers outside
y_data = np.random.normal(loc=1, scale=3.0, size=5)      the normal data
df3 = pd.DataFrame({'A': x_data, 'B':y_data})
df3['Ground Truth'] = 1

df = pd.concat([df1, df2, df3])
df = df.reset_index()
df = pd.DataFrame(RobustScaler().fit_transform(df), columns=df.columns)

fig, ax = plt.subplots(nrows=1, ncols=4, sharey=True, figsize=(10, 3))

sns.scatterplot(data=df[df['Ground Truth'] == False], x='A', y='B',
```

```
                   alpha=0.1, ax=ax[0])
s = sns.scatterplot(data=df[df['Ground Truth'] == True], x='A', y='B',
                   alpha=1.0, s=100, marker='*', ax=ax[0])
s.set_title('Ground Truth')
```
Plots the ground truth

```
clf = KNN()
clf.fit(df[['A', 'B']])
```
Fits the model to the data
Plots the predictions

```
df['KNN Binary Prediction'] = clf.predict(df[['A', 'B']])
sns.scatterplot(data=df[df['KNN Binary Prediction'] == False], x='A',
                   y='B', alpha=0.1, ax=ax[1])
s = sns.scatterplot(data=df[df['KNN Binary Prediction'] == True], x='A',
                   y='B', alpha=1.0, s=100, marker='*', ax=ax[1])
s.set_title('Binary Predictions')
```

```
df['KNN Decision Scores'] = clf.decision_scores_
s = sns.scatterplot(data=df, x='A', y='B', hue='KNN Decision Scores',
                   size='KNN Decision Scores', ax=ax[2])
s.get_legend().remove()
s.set_title('Training Decision \nScores')
```

```
df['KNN Decision Function'] = clf.decision_function(df[['A', 'B']])
s = sns.scatterplot(data=df, x='A', y='B', hue='KNN Decision Function',
                   size='KNN Decision Function', ax=ax[3])
s.get_legend().remove()
s.set_title('Decision Function \nScores')
```

```
plt.tight_layout()
plt.show()
```

The results of calling `predict()` are shown in figure 6.1 (second pane). This includes more points than were specifically created as outliers but does show a reasonable selection—the points outside the main cluster and along the edges.

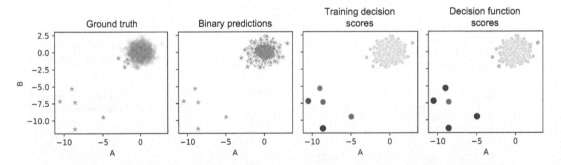

Figure 6.1 **An example of running PyOD's KNN detector on synthetic data. The left plot indicates the ground truth, the next the binary predictions, and the right two the numeric scores. The scores are shown using both color and size of point. Training scores (third pane) are calculated on the training data and the decision function scores (fourth pane) on the test data. In this case, the same data was used, and the scores are (almost) the same. The scores are noticeably higher for the five outliers outside the main cluster than for points in or near the cluster.**

We also collect the values in `decision_scores_` to get numeric scores for each point from the training process (shown in the third pane) and call `decision_function()` to get the scores from the test process (shown in the fourth pane). The scores are numeric, so we use size here to indicate the magnitude of the scores. The `predict_proba()` API (not shown) returns the equivalent results, though normalized, so on a scale from 0.0 to 1.0.

To examine this more closely, we next look at the specific scores returned. In this case, we know the outlier records were added in the last 10 rows and so these should receive the highest outlier scores. Figure 6.2 shows the results of plotting `decision_scores_` for the full 1,010 records. The scores are noticeably higher for the last rows, but it's hard to see specifically what is being flagged.

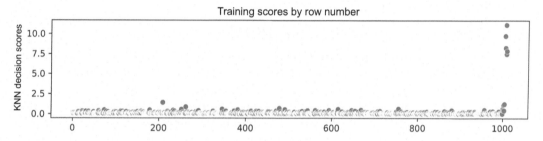

Figure 6.2   Distribution of training scores from the KNN detector

In the next plot, figure 6.3, we use markers to distinguish the known outliers, and we zoom in and show the scores just for the last 30 records, including the 10 outliers, in this case using `decision_function()`. The results are slightly different from using `decision_scores_`. KNN uses `BallTree` and some distances are approximate, so it's possible to get slightly different scores on the training and test data even where the data used for fitting and predicting are identical. For deterministic detectors such as COPOD (described later), this does not occur. In this case, we can see slightly higher

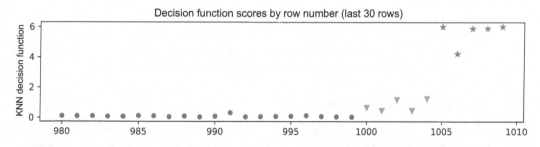

Figure 6.3   Distribution of testing scores for the last 30 rows. The last five (shown as stars) are the points outside the main cluster and have the highest outlier scores. The previous five (shown as triangles) are the points on the edge of the main cluster and have the next highest outlier scores, though closer to the scores of the inliers.

than average scores for the five points next to the main cluster and significantly higher scores for the five points well outside the cluster, which is reasonable.

PyOD also provides the ability to determine the confidence in each prediction. In this example, the data was simple, and the confidence is close to 1.0 for almost every row. This can be accessed with code such as

```
clf.predict_confidence(df[['A', 'B']])
```

In this example, we demonstrated a number of the APIs available, but in most cases only a few of these need to be used, as in listings 6.1 and 6.2. If fitting and predicting on the same data, it's possible to simply create the detector, call fit, and then use the values provided by the `decision_scores_` attribute. The identical process can be used for almost all detectors.

6.2   *Histogram-based Outlier Score (HBOS)*

Histogram-based Outlier Score (HBOS) is a detector we've not seen previously but is based on a very interesting idea. HBOS is designed, above all else, to be fast. It considers each feature completely individually and so will detect only univariate outliers, not outliers based on rare combinations. HBOS is not appropriate to detect subtle outliers but is excellent in environments where the data must be examined extremely quickly or where there are a huge number of features and testing multiple features together is not feasible. HBOS (and other detectors based on univariate tests) may also work best where there is little association between the features in any case, which is rare but does occur. And, as we've indicated earlier, univariate outliers can often, though certainly not always, be the most relevant outliers. In addition, in many situations where people manually follow up with each outlier flagged, univariate tests may detect as many strong outliers as it's feasible to examine in any case, and there is little benefit in identifying additional outliers.

Listing 6.4 gives an example of using HBOS. This uses the speech dataset from OpenML. A sample of the data is shown in table 6.1. The dataset actually has 400 features, so only a fraction is shown here. The data represents spoken English, with each of the 400 features representing a segment of speech, each in a format called *i-vectors*, which are often used for spoken language. Accents with low representation in the data can be considered outliers. Unfortunately, the features are not intuitive, as was the case with the baseball or even KDD Cup datasets. This can reduce our ability to reliably detect outliers, as it's difficult to gauge how truly unusual they are. Unfortunately, this is a realistic scenario and a common occurrence in outlier detection. Usually, domain experts will be needed to help ensure the outliers identified are sensible.

Table 6.1   Sample from the speech dataset

V1	V2	V3	V4	V5	V6	V7
−0.35069	0.52721	−1.62470	−1.334000	−1.03020	1.24750	−0.98067
−0.42537	−0.08818	0.84575	0.881570	1.35690	0.74894	−1.68620
−1.22100	0.43960	-0.06303	0.709530	0.95079	−0.21874	−1.24850

In this case, HBOS may be a better choice than many detectors as, with 400 features, it's not likely feasible to perform any multivariate tests (unless we can work with small sets of features at a time). Also, given the data is inscrutable, it's preferable to use a simpler, safer detector such as HBOS, since it may be difficult to assess which multivariate outliers are meaningful. Listing 6.4 provides code to execute HBOS on the speech dataset. This simply calculates the outlier scores and displays a histogram of the scores.

Listing 6.4   Using HBOS with the speech dataset

```
import pandas as pd
from pyod.models.hbos import HBOS
from sklearn.datasets import fetch_openml
import matplotlib.pyplot as plt
import seaborn as sns

data = fetch_openml("speech", version=1, parser='auto')
df = pd.DataFrame(data.data, columns=data.feature_names)
print(df.head())

det = HBOS()
det.fit(df)
pred = det.decision_scores_

sns.histplot(pred)
plt.show()
```

The distribution of scores is shown in figure 6.4. This appears reasonable. The scale and shape of the scores varies from one detector to another, but PyOD consistently uses higher scores for rows that are more likely outliers.

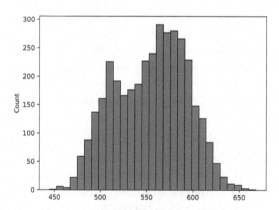

Figure 6.4   Distribution of scores using the HBOS detector on the speech dataset from OpenML

HBOS works by creating a histogram for each feature, dividing each numeric feature into a set of equal-width bins. Each bin for each feature will have a count based on the training data: the number of records in the training data in that bin. The lower the counts, the more outlierish values in that bin are. This allows HBOS to detect internal outliers as well as extreme values (any bin in the histogram may have low counts).

To evaluate a row, HBOS determines the score for each value in the row and sums these together. For example, if a table has three features and a row has values [10.0, 453.1, 0.003], HBOS would determine the score for the first value (10.0), the score for the second value (453.1), and the score for the third value (0.003) and then sum these three scores together. The histograms may appear as in figure 6.5.

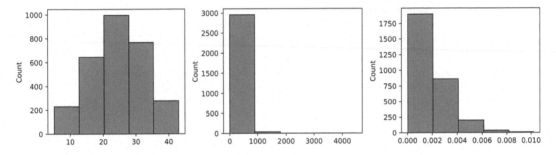

Figure 6.5   Example histograms for a dataset with three features

To determine the score for the first value, 10.0, it would first determine which bin this value appears in. If the first feature has values ranging from, say, 5.0 to 43.0 and five bins are used, then each bin will have a width of 7.6. A value of 10.0 will appear in the first bin (the first bin covers 5.0 to 12.6). All values appearing in the first bin will receive the same score (similarly for all other bins). This score is based on how many records from the training data appeared in this bin. If this bin had few records from the training data, then values appearing in this bin during prediction can be considered rare and will be given high scores. If this bin had many records from the training data, then values appearing in this bin during prediction can be considered common and will be given low scores. We repeat this for the second and third values in the row. Outliers are then rows that have many rare values, and very rare values, relative to their columns.

A limitation of HBOS is that it's not possible to determine why rows received the scores they did. Explanations are missing from most PyOD detectors (and most detectors outside of PyOD as well). HBOS does have the advantage that it's conceptually simple, which allows us, to some extent, to reverse-engineer what it does. Here we show one technique to help understand the output of an outlier detector. In listing 6.5 we provide an example of code to determine, on the level of the detector (not for scores on individual rows), which features are the most relevant, on average, for the outlier scores HBOS assigns. This creates a pair of boxplots for each feature, comparing the distribution of values for records with HBOS scores in the top 0.5% (for this purpose, outliers) to those in the lower 99.5% (inliers).

Listing 6.5 Plotting the relationship between features and HBOS scores

```
df['HBOS Score'] = pred
df['Outlier'] = (df['HBOS Score'] > df['HBOS Score'].quantile(0.995))

fig, ax = plt.subplots(nrows=20, ncols=20, sharey=True, figsize=(65, 65))

for i in range(20):
  for j in range(20):
    col_name = f"V{(i*20) + j + 1}"
    sns.boxplot(data=df, x=col_name, orient='h', y='Outlier', ax=ax[i][j])
plt.show()
```

We can then examine all 400 features and can see some features are, on average, more relevant than others to the HBOS scores. We can't show all here, but figure 6.6 shows six of the features. Of the six shown, all other than V1 appear to have different values for inliers compared to outliers. In the case of the other five shown, despite the outliers covering only 0.5% of the rows, they have larger interquartile ranges than the inliers, which is to say, more range in their values. V368 even has lower minimum values for the outliers than the inliers despite having far fewer rows.

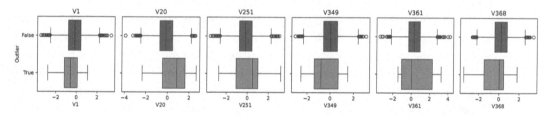

Figure 6.6 Comparison of the distributions of values for six features for inliers versus outliers. Of the six shown, all other than V1 show different, though not drastically different, distributions for the outliers and inliers.

This form of analysis is applicable to any dataset and detector, though it will be the most useful for detectors such as HBOS that tend to flag extreme values. Similarly, histograms may be used instead of boxplots to see where internal outliers are and aren't captured well by the detectors.

This particular process is useful, but it also has limitations. It helps us understand how the detector scored as it did, though not how it *should* have scored. It also captures only how the detector scored on the whole, and does not capture how individual rows are scored—particularly, how the detector combines the univariate scores from each feature. It can be difficult to gauge situations where, for example, one row had a very rare value and another row had two moderately rare values. Where greater interpretability is needed, it may be necessary to use or implement a similar detector that best suits your needs. For most cases, however, HBOS detectors can work well.

HBOS will automatically bin any numeric features provided. By default, HBOS uses 10 bins per feature; it also allows setting n_bins to "auto," which will estimate an optimal number of bins. HBOS can be sensitive to the number of bins used. We'll discuss this further in chapter 9, but it can be worthwhile to try different values for the n_bins parameter.

The PyOD API allows seeing the edges used to define the bins for each feature with the bin_edges_ attribute and the density of each histogram with the hist_ attribute.

Categorical values can be treated equivalently as bins from numeric columns, though PyOD's implementation requires categorical data be numerically encoded. This is common in outlier detection (and machine learning generally), as numeric data is more efficient to process. To encode categorical values, we can simply use ordinal encoding, which will usually directly map the feature from string to numeric values. The exception is where there are more unique values than bins specified, in which case some distinct values will be placed in the same bins. As with the numeric features after binning, there is no order among the values—only a frequency for each bin/ordinal value.

Given its speed, HBOS is often used in real-time environments where it's more pressing to identify outliers quickly than to catch all outliers. In these environments, it may still be possible to create and store logs of the data encountered, which may then be evaluated in a more comprehensive way offline. But for real-time monitoring, evaluation often has to be very fast, and HBOS is among the fastest detectors available.

HBOS is also much more robust to large numbers of features than most detectors. There are always issues with checking many features, and HBOS will inevitably flag some rows due to chance appearances of rare values, but the highest-scored records will be those that have multiple rare values, and very rare values, and so this effect will tend to be minimal.

Despite its limitations, HBOS often performs quite well in comparison to other detectors. Though it is not the strongest, it does compare well. There are many situations where simply identifying univariate outliers in each feature is the most effective method, and, in these cases, HBOS can be an effective tool.

6.3   *Empirical Cumulative Distribution Function (ECOD)*

Empirical Cumulative Distribution Function (ECOD) is not as well-known of an outlier detection algorithm as many but is actually one of the stronger detectors provided by PyOD. In fact, when getting started with outlier detection PyOD recommends trying Isolation Forest and ECOD first. ECOD has some major advantages as a detector, but possibly the largest is that it has no parameters; there is no tuning involved with using ECOD, which is very appealing given the difficulties associated with tuning parameters with unlabeled data.

Like HBOS, ECOD treats each feature individually, so it cannot detect unusual combinations. And, like HBOS, ECOD is very fast, deterministic and can scale to many features. The independence assumption (the assumption that each feature is independent from the other features and can be examined separately) allows the base detectors to run in parallel, which is not possible for all detectors, though it is for some others, including HBOS and IForest.

HBOS has one advantage over ECOD in that it can detect internal outliers, while ECOD is able to find only extreme values. At the same time, ECOD addresses one short-coming in HBOS, which is that HBOS can be sensitive to the number of bins used. In general, ECOD, by not requiring users to specify the number of bins or other parameters, tends to be more robust.

ECOD works based on a concept known as the empirical cumulative distribution function (ECDF). The "empirical" here refers to the fact that we work with the actual data, not an ideal distribution. Cumulative distributions are quite frequently used in statistics and data science. For a given sorted set of values, they indicate, for each unique value in the set, what portion of the data has a value up to and including that value. For an example plotting an ECDF, see listing 6.6. This loads in a dataset, the `breast_cancer` dataset from sklearn, then plots three histograms and an ECDF plot of the fourth column, using seaborn's `histplot()` and `ecdfplot()` methods. To show the effect of the number of bins, we plot with different numbers of bins.

Listing 6.6   Example using an ECDF plot from seaborn

```
from sklearn.datasets import load_breast_cancer
import matplotlib.pyplot as plt
import seaborn as sns

data = load_breast_cancer()['data']
col = 3

fig, ax = plt.subplots(nrows=1, ncols=4, figsize=(11, 2))
sns.histplot(data[:, col], ax=ax[0], bins=5)
sns.histplot(data[:, col], ax=ax[1], bins=20)
sns.histplot(data[:, col], ax=ax[2], bins=200)
sns.ecdfplot(data[:, col], ax=ax[3])
plt.tight_layout()
plt.show()
```

Displays column 3 using a histogram with five bins

Displays column 3 using a histogram with 20 bins

Displays column 3 using a histogram with 200 bins

Displays column 3 using an ECDF plot

In figure 6.7, the first three panes show histograms (with 5, 20, and 200 bins) and the right-most pane the corresponding ECDF plot. ECDF can be viewed as an alternative representation to histograms. ECDF plots are less intuitive, but avoid bias due to binning; histograms can appear different given different numbers of bins and can be more or less effective for outlier detection. The ECDF, however, is consistently a reliable representation of the distribution. In this example, looking at the second pane, a histogram with 20 bins, we can see the shape fairly well (though the other histograms are equally valid) and can use this to match to the ECDF plot. High points in the histogram correspond to steep sections of the ECDF (where the cumulative count increases rapidly) and low points in the histogram to flat sections of the ECDF (where the cumulative count does not significantly increase). We can identify the sparse regions in the data as the flat areas in the ECDF plot.

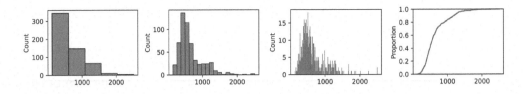

Figure 6.7 The first three panes show a histogram of one feature from the breast cancer dataset. The right pane shows the corresponding ECDF. We see a steep section in the ECDF plot, indicating many data points, and flatter sections later in the plot, indicating few data points.

Looking at the ECDF plot in figure 6.7 (the right-most pane), we can easily see, for any value in the data, the probability of a value that is either of that value or smaller. Taking a value on the x-axis, we find the point on the curve and identify the corresponding point on the y-axis. The probability of a larger value is simply 1.0 minus this value.

Using ECDF to identify outliers is similar to an idea we used in chapter 2 to identify the rare values in categorical columns using cumulative counts. ECOD identifies the flat tail areas in each feature's ECDF. Given this, we can identify the extreme values in both tails. During prediction, it calculates the tail probabilities (as ECOD tests data only for extreme values, it needs only to estimate how likely each value is in the tails) for each value in each feature and aggregates these together, simply multiplying them. This final score is not actually a true probability but is a representative score for each record.

For features that have a unimodal and symmetric distribution, such as a roughly Gaussian shape, the rare values are on the tails. For some skewed distributions, though, such as log-normal distributions, it may not be meaningful to describe one of the tails as having outliers—only the other, which ECOD takes into consideration: for some features, ECOD may only consider one tail as opposed to both. Figure 6.7 is an example of this, where there likely is no concept of outliers in the left tail—only the right.

ECOD is called in the same way as other PyOD detectors. It does provide an additional API, `explain_outlier()`, which is available in PyOD only for ECOD and one other detector, COPOD. An example is shown in the following listing, again looking at the speech dataset.

> **Listing 6.7   ECOD with the speech dataset**

```
import pandas as pd
import numpy as np
from pyod.models.ecod import ECOD
from sklearn.datasets import fetch_openml

data = fetch_openml("speech", version=1, parser='auto')
df = pd.DataFrame(data.data, columns=data.feature_names)

det = ECOD()
det.fit(df)
pred = det.decision_scores_

det.explain_outlier(np.argmax(pred))
```

Provides a visual explanation of the row that is given the highest score by ECOD

In figure 6.8, we see an explanation of the ECOD score assigned to a single row, the row given the highest score. This is difficult to view in detail, but it does demonstrate that the specified row has many features that are in the tail regions of their features. The features are listed along the x-axis (though do not render with a larger number of features such as here), and each triangle represents the evaluation of one feature, with two cutoff bands shown. Values higher above the cutoff bands are more extreme relative to their column, being more likely in the tails.

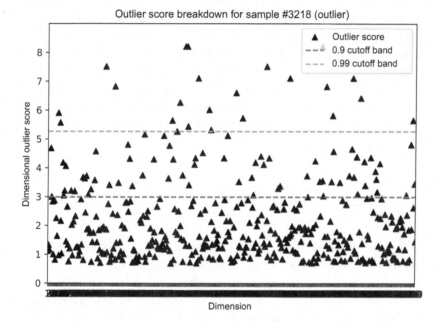

Figure 6.8   The results of running ECOD on the speech dataset. The plot is less clear with 400 features, but we can see that a very high fraction of the values for the specified row (row 3218) are above one or both cutoff bands.

6.4   *Copula-based outlier detection (COPOD)*

Copula-based outlier detection (COPOD) is a similar detector to ECOD, proposed by largely the same group of authors, and is also based on empirical cumulative distributions, though it is somewhat more complex in its design. Like ECOD, COPOD was designed to avoid distance calculations and so scale to very large numbers of features. It also makes no assumptions about the data distribution, is very fast, and can provide explanations for the outlier scores. As with ECOD, the most appealing property of COPOD may be that it is parameter-free.

COPOD is based on a concept known as *copulas*, a clever way to describe the joint distribution between features with marginal distributions in a way that allows reconstructing the original joint distribution. COPOD creates a copula representing the training data and then identifies points on the tail of this copula as points of low probability and so outliers. As it uses empirical cumulative distributions (based on the actual data and not theoretical distributions), the copulas are referred to as *empirical* cupolas. COPOD executes using three main steps:

1 Produce the empirical cumulative distribution functions (ECDFs) for each feature.
2 Use these to produce an empirical copula.
3 Use the empirical copula to estimate the tail probabilities of each record.

The idea is to estimate, for each record, the probability of seeing a point at least as extreme (containing as unusual a set of very low/very high values). The estimates are adjusted to consider the number of dimensions; without this, every row becomes extremely improbable in high dimensions. Like ECOD, COPOD also corrects for data skew.

Along with IForest and ECOD, COPOD is the only detector within PyOD that provides an explanation of the outlier scores, with COPOD and ECOD providing explanations per record (as opposed to the aggregate feature importances provided by IForest). The explanations are presented in the same format as with ECOD.

Calling COPOD is the same as other PyOD detectors, adding an additional import:

```
from pyod.models.copod import COPOD
```

and changing only the line creating the class:

```
det = COPOD()
```

With the speech dataset, the same row (row 3218) is the highest scored, though based a somewhat different evaluation of each feature, as shown in figure 6.9.

Here we also provide a simple example using synthetic data (listing 6.8), which can help clarify the behavior of the COPOD detector. We create a dataset with random normally distributed data and an extreme value in the first column of the last row.

Listing 6.8   Example of COPOD with synthetic data

```
import pandas as pd
import numpy as np
from pyod.models.copod import COPOD

np.random.seed(42)
a_data = np.random.normal(loc=10, scale=1.0, size=1000)
b_data = np.random.normal(loc=10, scale=1.0, size=1000)
df = pd.DataFrame({"A": a_data, "B": b_data})
df.loc[999, 'A'] = 15

clf = COPOD()
clf.fit(df)
clf.explain_outlier(999)
```

We can plot the explanation for the known outlier (figure 6.10) and can see clearly here that COPOD correctly identified the first feature as extreme but not the second

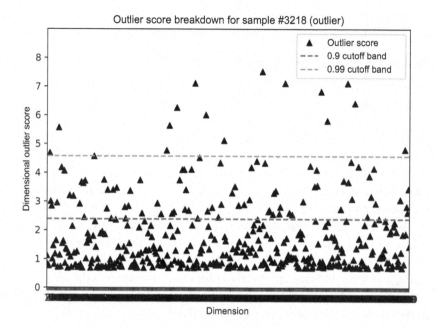

Figure 6.9 **The results of running COPOD on the speech dataset. The explanation is different than for ECOD, but the same row is scored highest for both detectors.**

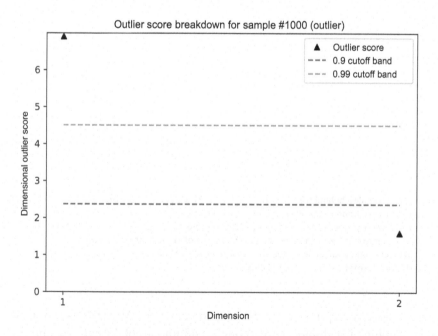

Figure 6.10 **Explanation of COPOD with synthetic data on row 999 (row 1000 in the display, which is 1-based), where the first feature is known to have an extreme value and the second feature does not, as displayed in the plot**

feature. Again, it can be useful to start with simple data like this and proceed to increasingly complex data, as well as work with real data, to understand the detectors well.

6.5 *Angle-based outlier detection (ABOD)*

Angle-based outlier detection (ABOD) is another detector designed to work with datasets with high dimensionality. As many numeric detectors use, in one way or another, distance measures between points, they can suffer from the curse of dimensionality, with distance measures becoming increasing less meaningful as features are added. ABOD addresses this by calculating the angles, instead of the distances, between points, which the authors argue allows ABOD to scale to many more features.

ABOD is based on the insight that for points that are centrally located, the angles to other pairs of points can vary greatly, while for those more outside the main body of points, the angles will vary less. In figure 6.11, in the left and center panes, we see examples of two angles centered on a point (point A) inside the main cluster. For this point, we can see that, for any two other points selected, some angles will be very narrow, some very wide, and some in between: there will be a large variation in the angles. The right pane shows an angle centered at a point outside the main cluster (point B). For this point, the angles to all other pairs of points will be fairly consistent. For points on the edge of the cluster, the angles to other points will vary less than for those inside the clusters but more than for the point well outside the clusters. In this way, ABOD is able to distinguish between these cases.

Figure 6.11   **The idea behind ABOD is shown with a 2D dataset. ABOD works by, for each point, finding the angle between it and every other pair of points. Inliers will have a large variance of angles, while outliers will have a narrow variance of angles. The left and middle pane show two angles formed around point A in the center of the data. This point is the center of angles with a diverse range of sizes. The right pane shows an example of an angle formed around an outlier point, point B. The set of angles formed with this point at the center will have a small range of sizes.**

Though this is based primarily on the variation in angles, ABOD does also consider distances to points. The distances are, though, a minor part of the equation and so render ABOD less vulnerable to the curse of dimensionality than many algorithms. Distance is used to distinguish between strong outliers, where the variances between angles may be very similar, though some are, in fact, farther from the majority of other points than others.

The full implementation calculates, for each point, the angle between it and every other pair of points. This is $O(n^3)$, which is quite slow compared to, say $O(n^2k)$ for LOF, where n is the number of rows and k the number of neighbors used by LOF. The authors also proposed a variation of ABOD, fastABOD, based on samples of the data. PyOD's implementation, by default, uses a sample and runs efficiently on most datasets.

The original paper compared ABOD to LOF (as an example of a detector based on distance measures between points) and found ABOD started performing better at around 50 features, with a stronger improvement at 100 features or more. Other researchers, however, have found ABOD to scale only slightly better or, in fact, no better than LOF with high numbers of features. This is intuitive as ABOD is based on cosine calculations, which can degrade in high dimensions as readily as Euclidean distance calculations.

Another limitation is that ABOD cannot transform the data space, as may be done with Mahalanobis distances. Many detectors that use distances measures use Euclidean distances by default but can also use Mahalanobis distances. With many scikit-learn and PyOD detectors (for example, KNN, KDE, LOF), the distance metric can be specified as a parameter and easily set to Mahalanobis distance or other appropriate distance measures. However, there is no equivalent to this with angle measurements.

ABOD can also produce infinite values in the scores, which have to be cleaned before using for any downstream tasks. This is straightforward to do, though, setting them to the maximum values found.

In terms of accuracy, in comparisons done by some researchers, ABOD does not typically do as well as IF or LOF, and in my experience it can produce some unintuitive results—for example, scoring points on the edges of clusters higher than those well outside clusters. As with any detector, though, it can be useful in many cases and will often be worth trying. All detectors can be the among the most useful detectors for some outlier detection projects. More likely, though, detectors such as ABOD that tend to work well, but not as well as some others, are most useful in an ensemble of detectors.

To use ABOD, we can again use code similar to listing 6.4 (from the HBOS example), simply updating the import and substituting `det = ABOD()` to create the detector.

6.6 *Clustering-based local outlier factor (CBLOF)*

Clustering-based local outlier factor (CBLOF) is likely, along with DBSCAN and Gaussian mixture models, among the most commonly used clustering-based approaches for outlier detection. To execute, CBLOF first clusters the data such that each point is in exactly one cluster. Any clustering algorithm may be used for this. K-means clustering is usually used as it is among the more efficient clustering algorithms. It is the default in PyOD's implementation, though the original CBLOF paper used a clustering algorithm called *Squeezer*, also developed by the paper's authors.

Once the data is clustered, the clusters are each labeled as either large or small clusters, relative to the sizes of the other clusters. There are parameters (alpha and beta) that allow tuning this. The main idea is that normal points are either in relatively large clusters and reasonably close to the center, or are in small clusters but still relatively close to a large cluster. Due to the quirks of clustering, some points that may be reasonably considered part of a large cluster may actually be placed in a smaller cluster (where this smaller cluster may be considered a subcluster of the larger cluster).

The original paper proposed generating the outlier score for each record based on two variables. For points in large clusters, the score would be based on the size of the cluster and the distance to the center of that cluster. For points in small clusters, it would be based on the size of the cluster and the distance to the center on the nearest large cluster. To provide more stable behavior, however, PyOD's implementation uses, by default, only the distance to the center of the nearest large cluster. PyOD's CBLOF may be set to include the cluster sizes, though, with the use_weights parameter.

As, by default, PyOD does not use the cluster sizes, using the distances to the nearest large cluster center (as opposed to the nearest cluster center) can be more sensible. Figure 6.12 shows three clusters. The points in C3 are all very close to the center of C3 but should still, as there are few of them, receive higher outlier scores than most in C2. This is achieved by measuring the points in C3 with respect to their distance to the center of C2, the nearest large cluster.

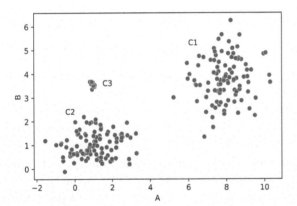

Figure 6.12   The idea behind CBLOF. The data is divided into three clusters, C1, C2, and C3. As C3 is a small cluster, it can be more reasonable to evaluate the points in C3 relative to the closest large cluster, C2. Given a different clustering of this data, these points could have been included in C2 in any case.

Although CBLOF is a local algorithm, in the sense that points are compared to their local cluster (or local large cluster in the case of points in small clusters), there is a global standard for the sizes of clusters and for distances from the centers. Given this, it can struggle where clusters have different sizes and different densities.

6.7   *Local correlation integral (LOCI)*

Local correlation integral (LOCI) is a local outlier detector quite similar to LOF, but using a given radius, as opposed to a given number of neighbors, to define the neighborhood around each point. LOCI can also be viewed as a local variation on the Radius method, introduced in chapter 3. LOCI estimates the density at the location of each point based on the number of other points within a given radius and compares this to the densities of its neighbors. As with LOF, it flags records that appear unusual relative to their neighborhood.

LOCI actually works with two radii: these are referred to as the counting radius and the sampling radius. LOCI calculates, for each point, the number of points within the counting radius. This provides a measure of how dense the space around each point is. Next, for all points in the sampling radius, it calculates the average number of points within their counting radii. This provides a measure of the normal density for the neighborhood. Similar to LOF, the outlier scores are then based on the ratios of these. Also, like LOF, the details are somewhat complicated, but the general idea is appealing. In practice, though, LOCI is generally very slow and can fail to finish within reasonable time frames for even modestly sized datasets.

The original paper provides a strong argument for the use of LOCI and includes a technique to run it parameter-free and methods to provide some interpretability. These are not currently included in the PyOD implementation. PyOD's implementation, for example, requires setting the radius (though only a single radius and not two), which can be difficult to tune. As with other radius methods, the radius can be a very meaningful definition of the neighborhood but can be unintuitive to set well. This is one of the few detectors within PyOD you may wish to be cautious using. However, other than speed, it works well. Where it can operate efficiently, it can be an effective detector.

6.8 *Connectivity-based outlier factor (COF)*

Connectivity-based outlier factor (COF) was designed as an improvement over LOF. It's actually very similar but uses a different method to identify the local neighborhood. Instead of finding the k nearest neighbors based on the Euclidean distances from each point, it uses a chaining method. This is more expensive to calculate than LOF's method but captures better where there are associations between features in the data, so it can provide more relevant outliers in some cases.

As LOF defines each point's neighborhood as the k nearest points, it tends to define the neighborhood around each point as roughly a hypersphere, depending on how the data is distributed. COF, on the other hand, iteratively builds a chain from one point to the next, finding the closest point to the previous points at each step. The neighborhoods around each point appear more as longer filaments than hyperspheres. COF also uses a different distance measure, called the chaining distance. Using this, distances between points represent the minimum of the lengths of each path linking the neighbors.

Like LOF, COF compares each point to its local neighborhood, so it compares the average chaining distance of each point to its neighbors to the average chaining distance of the neighbors to their neighbors. The details of how this work can get complicated, but like most PyOD detectors, the source code is actually quite short and is manageable to read if there is a need. Like LOF, COF would be used where we wish to focus on local outliers. Again, this can be called as in previous examples, simply updating the import statement and creating the detector with: `det = COF()`.

6.9   *Principal component analysis (PCA)*

Principal component analysis (PCA) is commonly used in data science, generally for dimensionality reduction (and often for visualization), but it is also very useful for outlier detection. PCA uses the same ideas as we've seen with elliptic estimators and the Mahalanobis distance but in a way that's possibly more useful for outlier detection. The idea is that most datasets have much more variance in some columns than others and also have correlations between the features. This means, to represent the data, it's often not necessary to use as many features as we have; we can often approximate the data quite well using fewer features—often far fewer. To achieve this, PCA transforms the data into a different coordinate system, where the dimensions are known as components. An example is shown in listing 6.9. Here we create a simple synthetic dataset, with the data highly correlated. There are two outliers, one following the general pattern but extreme (point A in figure 6.13) and one with typical values in each dimension but not following the general pattern (point B in figure 6.13). We then use scikit-learn's PCA class to transform the data. This is placed in another pandas dataframe, which can then be plotted (as shown), or examined for outliers.

> **Listing 6.9   Example using scikit-learn's PCA class to transform 2D data**

```
import numpy as np
import pandas as pd                              ◄── Creates two arrays of 100
from sklearn.decomposition import PCA                random values, with high
                                                     correlation between them
x_data = np.random.random(100)        ◄───────┘
y_data = np.random.random(100) / 10.0
                                                   Creates a dataframe
                                                   with this data plus
data = pd.DataFrame({'A': x_data, 'B': x_data + y_data})  ◄── two additional points
data= pd.concat([data,
    pd.DataFrame([[1.8, 1.8], [0.5, 0.1]], columns=['A', 'B'])])

pca = PCA(n_components=2)                  ◄────── Uses PCA to transform the
pca.fit(data)                                     data to another 2D space
print(pca.explained_variance_ratio_)

new_data = pd.DataFrame(pca.transform(data), columns=['0', '1'])  ◄──┐

                                              Creates a dataframe with
                                              the PCA-transformed data
```

The original data is shown in figure 6.13 (left). The data tends to appear along a diagonal. Drawing a line from the bottom left to the top right, we can create a new, single dimension that represents the data very well. In fact, executing PCA, this will be the first component, with the line orthogonal to this (also shown in the left pane) as the second component, which represents the remaining variance. The right pane shows the data in the new space created by the PCA transformation, with the first component on the x-axis and the second on the y-axis. In the case of 2D data, a PCA transformation will simply rotate and stretch the data. The transformation is harder to visualize in higher dimensions but works similarly. Often the components would be examined one at a time, but in this example, we use a scatterplot, which saves space as we can view two at a time.

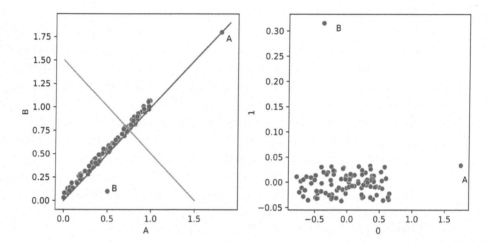

Figure 6.13 The left pane shows the original data, which contains two outliers, one (point A) that keeps with the general pattern of the data but is extreme and one that has typical values in both dimensions but does not keep with the general pattern (point B). The right pane shows the two components after PCA transformation, with the first component (which captures most of the variance) on the x-axis and the second component (which captures the remaining variance) on the y-axis. The outliers stand out as extreme values in the two components.

Printing the explained variance indicates component 0 contains 0.99 of the variance and component 1 contains 0.01, which matches the plot well.

PCA works by first finding the line through the data that best describes the data. This is the line where there squared distances to the line, for all points, is minimized. This is, then, the first component. The process then finds a line orthogonal to this that captures the most of the remaining variance. Figure 6.13 shows only two dimensions so only one choice for direction of the second component, at right angles with the first component. The process continues until all variance in the data is captured, which will create as many components as the original data had dimensions. Given this, PCA has three properties:

- All components are uncorrelated.
- The first component has the most variation, then the second, and so on.
- The total variance of the components equals the variance in the original features.

PCA has some nice properties that lend themselves well to outlier detection. As we can see in figure 6.13, the outliers become separated well within the components, which allows simple univariate tests to identify them. We can also see another interesting result of PCA transformation: points that are in keeping with the general pattern tend to fall along the early components but can be extreme in these, while points that do not follow the general patterns of the data tend to not fall along the main components and will be extreme values in the later components.

There are two common ways to identify outliers using PCA:

- We can transform the data using PCA and then use a set of univariate tests, one on each component, to score each row. This is straightforward to code, though using HBOS or ECOD to evaluate the transformed data may be simpler.
- We can look at the reconstruction error. In figure 6.13, we can see that using only the first component describes the majority of the data quite well. The second component is necessary to fully describe all the data, but by simply projecting the data onto the first component, we can describe well where most data is located. The exception is point B; its position on the first component does not describe its full location well and there would be a large reconstruction error using only a single component for this point, though not for the other points. In general, the more components necessary to describe a point's location well (or the higher the error given a fixed number of components), the stronger of an outlier a point is.

Another method is possible where we remove rows one at a time and identify which rows affect the final PCA calculations the most significantly. Although this can work well, it is often slow and not commonly used.

PCA does assume there are correlations between the features and provides little value if there are not. But, given most datasets have significant correlation, it is very often applicable. As with Elliptic Envelope and some other techniques we looked at earlier, PCA works by creating a covariance matrix representing the general shape of the data, which is then used to transform the space. In fact, there is a strong correspondence between elliptic envelope methods, the Mahalanobis distance, and PCA.

One limitation of PCA is, it is sensitive to outliers. It's based on minimizing squared distances to the components, so it can be heavily affected by outliers. To address this, robust PCA is often used, where the extreme values in each dimension are removed (similar to the trimmed mean method described in chapter 2) before performing the transformation. Similarly, values with high Mahalanobis distances from the center may be removed.

Another limitation of PCA, as well as Mahalanobis distances and similar methods, is they can break down if the correlations are in only certain regions, which is frequently true if the data is clustered. These methods may not work well, or it may be necessary to cluster or segment the data first and then perform PCA on each subset of the data.

6.9.1   *Univariate tests on the components*

I indicated earlier that univariate tests on data can be very useful and are often sufficient, but they do miss the unusual combinations of values (points that don't follow the main patterns of the data). However, once data is transformed using PCA, as the components are all (by construction) independent, there is no association between them, and univariate tests become very powerful. Using PCA and univariate tests on the components allows you to tune the process fairly easily to get the types of outliers (extreme values versus deviations from patterns) that are most germane for your problem. We can select and weight the components until we get the results we want. This can take some trial and error, but over time, as outliers are flagged by the system and we determine which are relevant for our needs and which are not, we also learn which components scored them high and which did not. Some applications tend to favor the first, middle, or last components. Weighting all equally can be a reasonable starting point, but this is relatively easy to tune. Some researchers examining the KDD Cup using PCA have found both the major (the first components) and minor (the later) components were useful, with some outliers found by just one or just the other. Examples using univariate tests on PCA-transformed data are shown in chapter 10.

Now that we've gone over how PCA works and how it can be applied to outlier detection, we can look at the detectors provided by PyOD. PyOD actually provides three classes based on PCA: PyODKernelPCA, PCA, and KPCA.

6.9.2 *PyODKernelPCA*

PyOD provides a class called PyODKernelPCA, which is simply a wrapper around scikit-learn's KernelPCA class. Either may be more convenient in different circumstances. This is not an outlier detector in itself, and provides only PCA transformation (and inverse transformation), similar to scikit-learn's PCA class, which was used in the previous example. The KernelPCA class is different than the PCA class in that KernelPCA allows for nonlinear transformations of the data and can better model some more complex relationships. Kernels work similarly in this context as with SVM models: they transform the space (in a very efficient manner) in a way that allows outliers to be separated more easily. scikit-learn provides several kernels. These are beyond the scope of the book but can improve the PCA process where there are complex, nonlinear relationships between the features. If used, outlier detection works, otherwise, the same as with using the PCA class.

6.9.3 *The PCA detector*

PyOD provides two PCA-based outlier detectors: the PCA class and KPCA. The latter, as with PyODKernelPCA, allows kernels to handle more complex data. PyOD recommends using the PCA class where the data does contain linear relationships and KPCA otherwise. Both classes use the reconstruction error of the data, using the Euclidean distance of points to the hyperplane that's created using the first k components. The idea, again, is that the first k components capture the main patterns of the data well, and any points not well modeled by these are outliers.

As with PCA generally, it's best to remove any obvious outliers before calling. We've looked previously at ways to do this. ECOD is also an effective tool to clean data, where we wish to trim off extreme values. An example is shown in listing 6.10, removing the top 1% of rows identified by ECOD before fitting a PCA detector.

Listing 6.10   Using ECOD to clean data before using PCA for outlier detection

```
import pandas as pd
from pyod.models.pca import PCA
from pyod.models.ecod import ECOD
from sklearn.datasets import fetch_openml

data = fetch_openml("speech", version=1, parser='auto')      ◄─────┐ Collects the data
df = pd.DataFrame(data.data, columns=data.feature_names)
scores_df = df.copy()
                                                             ┌───── Creates an ECOD detector
clf = ECOD(contamination=0.01)                               │      to clean the data
clf.fit(df)                                                 ◄┘
scores_df['ECOD Scores'] = clf.predict(df)                  ┌───── Creates a clean version of
                                                            │      the data, removing the top
clean_df = df[scores_df['ECOD Scores'] == 0]               ◄┘      outliers found by ECOD

clf = PCA(contamination=0.02)                              ◄┐
clf.fit(clean_df)                                          ─┤ Fits a PCA detector
pred = clf.predict(df)                                     ◄┘ to the clean data
                                                            │
                                                            └── Predicts on the full data
```

6.9.4   *KPCA*

The KPCA detector works very much the same as the PCA detector, with the exception that a specified kernel is applied to the data. This can transform the data quite significantly. The two detectors can flag very different records, and, as both have low interpretability, it can be difficult to determine why. As is common with outlier detection, it may take some experimentation to determine which detector and parameters work best for your data. As both are strong detectors, it may also be useful to use both. To create a KPCA detector using a linear kernel, we use code such as

```
det = KPCA(kernel='linear')
```

KPCA also supports polynomial, radial basis function, sigmoidal, and cosine kernels.

6.10   *Subspace outlier detection*

When working with datasets with many features, even after removing the features not relevant for outlier detection, there may be too many features to effectively execute many outlier detectors, including KNN, Radius, LOF, COF, CBLOF, and others. In these cases, it's worth focusing on models that can scale to more features, such as Isolation Forest, HBOS, and ECOD, but it's also worthwhile to investigate using subspaces: subsets of the features. For example, given a dataset with 300 features, we may create a set of 50 detectors, each using only 8 features. This allows each detector to work with a small number of features, which allows the distance calculations to be reliable. It also takes advantage of ensembling, a practice well-established to improve the performance of predictive models. In fact, the strongest predictive models for tabular data tend to all be ensembles, including CatBoost, LGBM, XGBoost, and RandomForest. Ensembling is also very useful in outlier detection.

Using multiple subspaces often also allows us to more easily tune the model over time, as the weights can be increased or decreased on the subspaces (sets of features) that produce the most and least relevant output. PyOD does not support this, but the idea is easy to implement where useful.

We've seen previously that most detectors tend to use either a single feature at a time (which misses unusual combinations of values) or all features (which can suffer from the curse of dimensionality and can treat less relevant features equivalently as the more relevant). At the same time, most outliers require only a small number of features to identify them. That is, outliers can usually be identified using fairly small subspaces, though the relevant subspaces can be different for different outliers. It is, consequently, desirable to try to find useful subsets of features to identify outliers. We look at this in more depth in chapter 10, but for now, we look at two detectors provided by PyOD that work with subspaces: subspace outlier detection (SOD) and FeatureBagging.

The idea is shown in figure 6.14. This shows two outliers, points A and B. Point A is an outlier in feature A but not in the other dimensions. Evaluating it in even two dimensions, as with the left pane, may fail to identify it as an outlier, as its Euclidean distance from the other points is fairly typical. It is clearly identified, though, if using only feature A—similarly with point B, which stands out as an outlier in features C and D (the middle pane) but not in features E or F (the right pane). Using additional features actually hinders our ability to identify these, which is a significant issue. Given that very few outliers are unusual in all features, it can be difficult with many features to identify outliers that are anomalous only in small numbers of features.

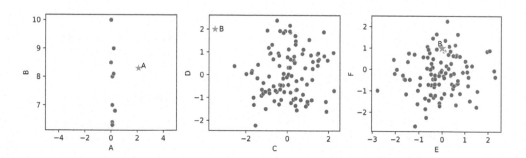

Figure 6.14 The left pane shows point A in a 2D dataspace. The point is unusual considering feature A but not if using Euclidean distances in the full 2D dataspace. Using additional features can be counterproductive. In the middle and right panes, we see another point, point B, which is an outlier in the C—D subspace but not in the E—F subspace. We need only features C and D to identify this outlier.

SOD works, similar to KNN and LOF, by identifying a neighborhood of k neighbors for each point, known as the reference set. The reference set is found in a different way, though, using a method called *shared nearest neighbors* (SNN). This is based on the idea that if two points are generated by the same mechanism, they will not only be close but will have many of the same neighbors. So neighborhoods can be identified by using, not the points with the smallest Euclidean distances, but the points with the most shared neighbors. This tends to be robust even in high dimensions and even where there are many irrelevant features: the rank order of neighbors tends to remain meaningful, so the set of nearest neighbors can be reliably found even where specific distances cannot. Once we have the reference set, we use this to determine the subspace, which is the set of features that explain the greatest amount of variance for the reference set. Once we identify these subspaces, SOD examines the distances of each point to the data center.

We'll use, as an example, a synthetic dataset that will help explain how SOD works. By varying this, adjusting the parameters, and comparing with other detectors, you can get a sense of the strengths and limits of SOD. Listing 6.11 provides an example of working with 35 features, where 2 features (features 8 and 9) are correlated and the other features are irrelevant. A single outlier is created as an unusual combination of the two correlated features. SOD is able to identify the known outlier as the top outlier. We set the contamination rate to 0.01 to specify to return (given there are 100 records) only a single outlier. Testing this beyond 35 features, though, SOD scores this point much lower. This example specifies the size of the reference set to be 3; different results may be seen with different values.

Listing 6.11 Testing SOD with 35 features

```
import pandas as pd
import numpy as np
from pyod.models.sod import SOD

np.random.seed(0)
d = np.random.randn(100, 35)
d = pd.DataFrame(d)
d[9] = d[9] + d[8]         ◄── Ensures features 8 and 9
                               are correlated, while all
                               others are irrelevant
d.loc[99, 8] = 3.5
d.loc[99, 9] = -3.8        ◄── Inserts a single outlier

clf = SOD(ref_set=3, contamination=0.01)   ◄── Executes SOD, flagging
d['SOD Scores'] = clf.fit (d)                   only one outlier
d['SOD Scores'] = clf.labels_
```

We display four scatterplots in figure 6.15, showing four pairs of features. We can see features 8 and 9 in the second pane, and we can see the point as a clear outlier, and flagged as such, though it is typical in all other dimensions.

6.11 FeatureBagging

FeatureBagging was designed to solve the same problem as SOD, though takes a different approach to determining the subspaces, and additionally subsamples the rows for each base detector. A specified number of base detectors are used (10 by default), each of which selects a random set of rows and features. For each, the maximum number of

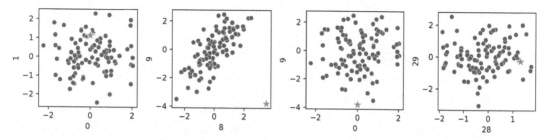

Figure 6.15 Testing SOD with 35-dimensional data. One outlier was inserted into the data and can be seen clearly in the second pane for features 8 and 9. Although the point is typical otherwise, it is flagged as the top outlier by SOD. The third pane also includes feature 9, and we can see the point somewhat unusual here, though no more so than many other points in other dimensions. The relationship in features 8 and 9 is the most relevant, and SOD appears to detect this.

features that may be selected is specified as a parameter, defaulting to all. So, for each base detector, FeatureBagging

- Determines the number of features to use.
- Chooses this many features randomly.
- Chooses a set of rows randomly. This is a bootstrap sample of the same size as the number of rows.
- Creates an LOF detector (by default; other base detectors may be used) to evaluate the subspace.

Once this is complete, each row has been scored by each base detector and the scores must be combined into a single score for each row. PyOD's FeatureBagging provides two options for this: using the maximum score and using the mean score. As we saw in figures 6.14 and 6.15, points can be strong outliers in some subspaces and not in others, and averaging their scores in the subspaces where they are typical can water down their scores and defeat the benefit of using subspaces. In other forms of ensembling with outlier detection, using the mean can work well, but in this case, using the maximum will typically be the better of the two options.

Any detector can be used within the subspaces. PyOD uses LOF by default, as did the original paper. LOF is a strong detector and a sensible choice, though you may find better results with other base detectors.

In the original paper, subspaces are created randomly, each using between d/2 and d − 1 features, where d is the total number of features. Some researchers have pointed out that the number of features used in the original paper is likely much larger than is appropriate. If the full number of features is large, using over half the features at once will allow the curse of dimensionality to take effect. And using many features in each detector will result in the detectors being correlated with each other (for example, if all base detectors use 90% of the features, they will use roughly the same features and tend to score each record roughly the same), which can also remove much of the benefit of creating ensembles. PyOD allows setting the number of features used in each subspace, and it should be typically set fairly low, with a large number of base estimators created.

6.12 *Cook's Distance*

Cook's Distance is a unique detector in PyOD in that it is not based on any journal paper, other than the original paper from 1977 explaining Cook's Distance itself (without any reference to outlier detection). Cook's Distance is the measure of the *influence* or *leverage* a point has on a regression model. For example, in figure 6.16 (left) we see a set of points and the regression line calculated from them using ordinary least squares. In the right pane, we see the same data with point P1 added and show new regression line as well as the previous. As the line has moved significantly, we can consider P1 to have high leverage and therefore to be a form of outlier.

Using Cook's Distance for outlier detection is based on the more general idea that records that affect how models are fit or that negatively affect the accuracy of models must be outliers, at least in some sense.

The Cook's Distance detector loops through each feature in the data and creates an instance of sklearn's `LinearRegression` class to predict the feature (using all other features), identifying the Cook's Distance for each record for each linear regression. That is, Cook's Distance specifically looks for the points that negatively affect regression models, though it also considers residuals for the regression models fit on the data.

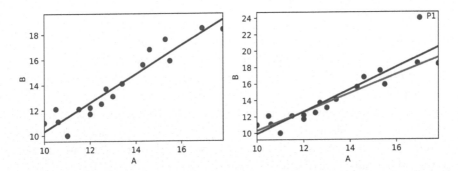

Figure 6.16   The left pane shows a regression line through a set of points that contain no outliers. The right pane shows the same points along with the addition of an outlier point, P1. We see the original regression line and the line given the presence of P1. As the addition of P1 causes the regression line to move significantly, P1 has a large Cook's Distance, and so can be considered an outlier.

Cook's Distance is useful where the data has linear relationships, which is common. Where there are nonlinear relationships, it may be useful to transform the data first— for example, taking the square or log of some features. Cook's Distance is also an example of a simple algorithm that is usually best to use within PyOD but can be quite reasonably implemented from scratch where necessary—for example, to provide more interpretability or to automate transforming the data.

6.13 Using SUOD for faster model training

Outlier detection can be slow, and this can particularly be an issue when first setting up a system, as it may be necessary to run many detectors in many different ways before a good set of detectors and parameters is found. Scalable Framework for Unsupervised Outlier Detection (SUOD) is a library for accelerating outlier detection. It maintains its own GitHub page (https://github.com/yzhao062/SUOD), which is part of the same GitHub account as PyOD. The GitHub account has several other repositories worth looking at to learn more about outlier detection as well. SUOD is tightly integrated into PyOD, though it does require a separate install. This is done with

```
pip install suod
pip install pyod
```

SUOD allows training multiple PyOD detectors at once. Also, SUOD uses numba to optimize the code and provides options to use dimensionality reduction to allow for faster execution. Using SUOD can be significantly faster than fitting the models one at a time. See listing 6.12 for an example similar to one on the SUOD website. This trains several detectors including four KNN detectors. SUOD can also be viewed as a tool for combining models, as well as for executing them more efficiently. The results are combined into a single set of scores using the specified combination method, in this case averaging. The n_jobs parameter will need to be set to match your hardware, though as is standard, −1 indicates to use all resources available.

Listing 6.12 Using SUOD to train multiple models at once

```
import pandas as pd
from pyod.models.iforest import IForest
from pyod.models.pca import PCA
from pyod.models.knn import KNN
from pyod.models.copod import COPOD
from pyod.models.abod import ABOD
from pyod.models.cblof import CBLOF
from pyod.models.suod import SUOD
from sklearn.datasets import fetch_openml

data = fetch_openml("speech", version=1, parser='auto')      ◁─────┐ Collects the data
df = pd.DataFrame(data.data, columns=data.feature_names)

detector_list = [IForest(), PCA(),
                KNN(n_neighbors=10), KNN(n_neighbors=20),
                KNN(n_neighbors=30), KNN(n_neighbors=40),     Defines the detectors
                COPOD(), ABOD(), CBLOF()]                     used by SUOD

clf = SUOD(base_estimators=detector_list, n_jobs=2, combination='average',
          verbose=False)
                                                             Creates an instance
                                                             of SUOD
clf.fit(df)
scores = clf.decision_scores_          Collects the final scores in the same
                                       way as when using a single detector
```

6.14   *The PYOD thresholds module*

Where you wish to identify a specific number of outliers, it's possible, as we've seen, to set the contamination level (or let PyOD use a default), fit a model and access the `labels_` attribute, or to call `predict()` with a test dataset. These will return binary labels with a fixed percentage of the records as outliers. Using PyOD's thresholds module (under pyod.models.thresholds) provides a more robust option, which allows a statistical algorithm to, given a set of scores, determine how many of the top scores should be considered outliers. As we saw in chapter 2, this can be a difficult problem.

The thresholds module's tools are actually wrappers around another very useful library, PyThresh (https://github.com/KulikDM/pythresh), which provides more than 30 methods for thresholding the scores from outlier detectors. The PyThresh library also provides documentation, links to the original papers, and examples of each thresholding tool.

It can be difficult to determine which thresholding algorithm is preferable for your project, but most will likely work well. An appealing property of these is that none require any parameters—only the choice of which algorithm to use. Most are also nonparametric: they make no assumptions about the distribution of scores. Many are effectively outlier detection routines themselves and run on the scores of other outlier detectors.

Similar to the way different outlier detectors are each valid but different (and some will match the task at hand better), the thresholding algorithms are each valid but different. Most are also quite complex, though many simple methods are also included; some of these we've seen before, based on z-scores, IQR, MAD, or histograms. Methods included also use clustering and OCSVM applied to distributions of outlier scores. One included method (CPD) is based on change point detection, a common task in time series analysis (covered in chapter 17). Others use matrix decomposition, deep neural networks, gradient descent, and so on. The PyThresh documentation recommends using FILTER (based on distinctions in the frequencies of anomalies versus inliers), CLF (based on linear models), or META (based on meta learning) algorithms. There is also the option to use a method called COMB, which combines the results of multiple thresholders. This can be the safest option where it's not clear if one method is the most appropriate.

Listing 6.13 shows an example using one thresholding algorithm, FILTER, to threshold the scores produced by a KNN detector. Before this may be executed, it is necessary to install PyThresh with

```
pip install pythresh
```

> **Listing 6.13   Example using thresholds with a single detector**

```
import pandas as pd
from pyod.models.knn import KNN
from pyod.models.thresholds import FILTER
from sklearn.datasets import fetch_openml
```

```
data = fetch_openml("speech", version=1, parser='auto')
df = pd.DataFrame(data.data, columns=data.feature_names)

clf = KNN()
clf.fit(df)
decision_scores = clf.decision_scores_

thres = FILTER()
labels = thres.eval(decision_scores)
print(labels.tolist().count(0), labels.tolist().count(1))
```

Collects the data

Uses a KNN detector to assign scores to each record

Uses a FILTER thresholder to determine a threshold to distinguish low from high scores

This indicates 745 were labeled as outliers. In the following listing, we use the COMB method with default parameters. This is imported from PyThresh as opposed to PyOD.

Listing 6.14 Example using the COMB method

```
import pandas as pd
from pyod.models.knn import KNN
from pythresh.thresholds.comb import COMB
from sklearn.datasets import fetch_openml

data = fetch_openml("speech", version=1, parser='auto')
df = pd.DataFrame(data.data, columns=data.feature_names)

clf = KNN()
clf.fit(df)

decision_scores = clf.decision_scores_

thres = COMB()
labels = thres.eval(decision_scores)
print(labels.tolist().count(0), labels.tolist().count(1))
```

Listing 6.15 shows an example of thresholding the combined scores of three detectors—in this case, KNN, IForest, and PCA, combined here using the OCSVM thresholding algorithm. That is, we use a single thresholder but use it to combine the predictions of multiple detectors. This can be a convenient way to combine the scores of multiple detectors.

Listing 6.15 Example using thresholds with multiple detectors

```
import pandas as pd
import numpy as np
from pyod.models.knn import KNN
from pyod.models.iforest import IForest
from pyod.models.pca import PCA
from pyod.models.thresholds import OCSVM
from sklearn.datasets import fetch_openml

np.random.seed(0)
```

```
data = fetch_openml("speech", version=1, parser='auto')          ◄────┐ Collects the data
df = pd.DataFrame(data.data, columns=data.feature_names)

knn_det = KNN()                          ◄────┐ Creates three detectors
iforest_det = IForest()
pca_det = PCA()

scores = []                                                      ◄────┐ Collects the scores
scores.append(knn_det.fit(df).decision_function(df))                  │ from all three
scores.append(iforest_det.fit(df).decision_function(df))              │ detectors on all rows
scores.append(pca_det.fit(df).decision_function(df))

scores = np.vstack(scores).T                        ◄────┘ Transposes the set of scores

thres = OCSVM()                                                  ◄────┐ Creates a OCSVM
labels = thres.eval(scores)                                           │ thresholder to create
print(labels.tolist().count(0), labels.tolist().count(1))             │ binary labels based on
                                                                      │ all three numeric scores
```

This results in 12 records being labeled as outliers. Also note that although these are normally used to determine a threshold between the inliers and outliers given the scores, they may also be used as univariate tests on the original data.

Summary

- PyOD covers a large number of detectors, likely as many as you will need for the majority of projects on numeric tabular data. Though there are many useful detectors not covered by PyOD, PyOD supports a sufficient number of detectors that, working strictly with PYOD, is a feasible option in many projects.

- PyOD does not support categorical data well, providing only numeric detectors.

- PyOD provides some, but only minimal, support for interpretability. IForest provides feature importances at the detector level; ECOD and COPOD provide plots presenting which features had exceptional values for a given record. This is very useful but is missing for other detectors.

- PyOD wraps detectors available in scikit-learn, allowing users to work with these within the PyOD interface, which is convenient when also using other PyOD detectors.

- PyOD provides a consistent interface to each detector, making it easy to use and to experiment with other detectors, though additional APIs are available for some detectors.

- PyOD provides confidence estimates for each outlier score as well as the scores themselves.

- Some detectors have a large number of parameters, which makes tuning sometimes difficult, but the default values are good to get started.

- HBOS and ECOD are very fast detectors, though they will perform only univariate tests.

- PyOD provides CBLOF, a very effective means to work with clustering, though there are other outlier detection methods based on clustering as well.
- There are many variations on LOF, including LOCI and COF, both included in PyOD.
- PCA is a very useful concept for outlier detection. PyOD provides two tools to work with PCA based on reconstruction error, but using PCA to identify univariate outliers (in the transformed space) is also very useful.
- There are several ways to define the neighborhood of a point, including the k nearest neighbors, Radius, connectivity, and shared neighbors.
- SOD and FeatureBagging provide methods that work with subspaces (subsets of the features), which allows for working with large numbers of features and identifying outliers that may appear in only some subspaces.
- PyOD supports SUOD for accelerating outlier detection and combining detectors.
- PyOD also supports PyThresh for applying meaningful binary labels to the scores.
- Where necessary, it is quite feasible to implement the detectors provided by PyOD—for example, to provide more interpretability—but PyOD is well-implemented and good to use where possible.

Additional libraries and algorithms for outlier detection

7

This chapter covers

- Additional Python libraries that support outlier detection
- Additional algorithms not found in libraries
- Three algorithms that support categorical data
- An interpretable outlier detection method, association rules
- Examples and techniques you'll need to develop your own outlier detection code where necessary

Although scikit-learn and PyOD cover a large number of outlier detection algorithms, there are many algorithms not covered by these libraries that may be equally useful for outlier detection projects. In addition, the detectors provided in these libraries cover only numeric and not categorical data, and may not be as interpretable as may sometimes be necessary. Of the algorithms we've looked at so far, only frequent pattern outlier factor (FPOF) and histogram-based outlier score (HBOS) provide good support for categorical data, and most have low interpretability. We'll introduce in this chapter some other detectors better suited for categorical and mixed data: Entropy, association rules, and a clustering method for categorical data. Association rules detectors also have the benefit of being quite interpretable.

The algorithms covered in this chapter may also be useful in many projects simply because they allow the use of more detectors. Given the nature of outlier detection, where each detector examines data differently and no detector can be definitive, using more detectors can provide additional coverage, identifying more, and different, outliers than can be detected with a smaller set of detectors. If you have a sense of what you wish to flag and not all are being detected reliably, you may want to try other detectors. Or if you are more interested in finding unknown outliers and can't determine if you will catch everything you would be interested in, it may be wise to cast a wider net and utilize more detectors.

Researchers creating general-purpose outlier detectors focus on the question, "How can we identify the records that are the most statistically distinct from the others?" Each tool addresses this in a quite different way, and some may suit your needs for a given task much better than others. For your project, though, you would be asking a very different, and more specific, question: How can I identify the records in this specific dataset that I would be most interested in examining? It may be that your data, and your reasons for looking for outliers, are such that none of the detectors in the major libraries exactly meet all your needs.

In almost all outlier detection projects, we would use a set of standard detectors, either from scikit-learn or PyOD or from repositories such as GitHub. To find the relevant outliers, the customization we need for our projects will be mostly in the form of feature engineering and other preprocessing, as well as parameter tuning. When these tools are not sufficient, though, it's possible to locate additional techniques in the academic literature. Outlier detection is still a very active area of research, with new ideas appearing regularly. The website arXiv (https://arxiv.org/) is an excellent resource for this. Many papers provide source code; all will provide at minimum the algorithm, which are often surprisingly easy to implement.

In other cases, you may find methods to look for anomalous records in ways useful to you but not covered well by existing algorithms, and it may be best to develop a detector from your own algorithm, coding this yourself. When it is necessary to create your own detector, having a strong understanding of outlier detection generally, including points related to combining and evaluating detectors we'll cover later, will help you develop an effective system. You may create something unique to your project, but you may also create a tool that is useful as a general-purpose outlier detector, and it may be beneficial to the community to post this on GitHub to allow others to use and experiment with it.

Whether developing your own algorithm or implementing a published algorithm, some coding will be involved, but usually this will be manageable, and writing your own code can have some real advantages. It allows you to understand well what is being checked and so understand the coverage and limitations on the algorithms.

It allows you to tweak the code as you need, such as filtering out irrelevant cases or adding logging—for example, tracking statistics about what is in the data (in terms relevant to the algorithm) to get a better sense of what is normal. This chapter includes implementations of several detectors, which will provide some examples to help you create your own detectors where appropriate. Nevertheless, there are also several algorithms presented in this chapter that have established implementations, and, everything else equal, these will be easier to use in most cases.

In this chapter, we start with two libraries beyond scikit-learn and PyOD that can be useful for outlier detection: alibi-detect and PyCaret. We then look at some other algorithms that are not in any library; these may be more difficult to discover otherwise but can actually be as useful as those in the libraries. In some cases, there are no Python implementations. For these, source code is provided to help get you started using these and to provide some examples of coding outlier detectors. In many cases, you may be able to use the code as is, though may also need to support logging, include visualizations, optimize the code to scale to larger datasets, or make other modifications, possibly combining these with other techniques presented in the book.

7.1   *Example synthetic test sets*

To simplify presenting and testing the libraries and detectors covered in this chapter, we provide two very simple 2D synthetic test sets. The first (listing 7.1) creates a single Gaussian cluster, which is likely the simplest case for outlier detection. Here there are no strong outliers, though some points along the edges of the data can reasonably be considered outliers. This is a form of smoke test for outlier detection but is also the case some outlier detectors are specifically designed for, where data is in a single cluster, such as ellipse estimation methods (covered in chapter 5) and one shown later called Convex Hull.

> **Listing 7.1 Creating the first set, a single Gaussian cluster**

```
import numpy as np
import pandas as pd

def create_simple_testdata():
    np.random.seed(0)
    a_data = np.random.normal(size=100)
    b_data = np.random.normal(size=100)
    df = pd.DataFrame({"A": a_data, "B": b_data})
    return df
```

The second listing (listing 7.2) creates four clusters, each with a different size and density and with one cluster having some correlation between the features and thus an oblong shape. This represents a more challenging case for outlier detection. Here there are known outliers: the first five rows, which form a very small cluster, and the last three rows, which are global outliers, outside the clusters and close to no other points. These are used in the following examples to help describe what the detectors flag.

Listing 7.2 Creating the second set, with four clusters

```
import numpy as np
import pandas as pd

def create_four_clusters_test_data():
    np.random.seed(0)

    a_data = np.random.normal(loc=25.0, scale=2.0, size=5)
    b_data = np.random.normal(loc=4.0, scale=2.0, size=5)
    df0 = pd.DataFrame({"A": a_data, "B": b_data})

    a_data = np.random.normal(loc=1.0, scale=2.0, size=50)
    b_data = np.random.normal(loc=19.0, scale=2.0, size=50)
    df1 = pd.DataFrame({"A": a_data, "B": b_data})

    a_data = np.random.normal(loc=1.0, scale=1.0, size=200)
    b_data = np.random.normal(loc=1.0, scale=1.0, size=200)
    df2 = pd.DataFrame({"A": a_data, "B": b_data})

    a_data = np.random.normal(loc=20.0, scale=3.0, size=500)
    b_data = np.random.normal(loc=13.0, scale=3.0, size=500) + a_data
    df3 = pd.DataFrame({"A": a_data, "B": b_data})

    outliers = [[5.0, 40],
                [1.5, 8.0],
                [11.0, 0.5]]
    df4 = pd.DataFrame(outliers, columns=['A', 'B'])

    df = pd.concat([df0, df1, df2, df3, df4])
    df = df.reset_index(drop=True)
    return df
```

- Creates a very small cluster of five elements
- Creates a small, but not anomalous, cluster of 50 elements
- Creates a cluster of 200
- Creates a cluster of 500, with correlation
- Creates a set of three global outliers

The two datasets are shown in figure 7.1. The right pane labels the four clusters and three global outliers. Cluster A is very small and can be considered outliers.

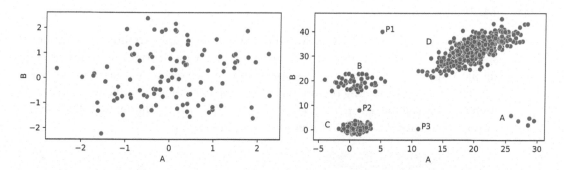

Figure 7.1 The two main test datasets used in this chapter. The first contains a single cluster. The second contains four clusters: A, B, C, and D, as well as three global outliers: P1, P2, and P3.

7.2   *The alibi-detect library*

The alibi-detect library (https://github.com/SeldonIO/alibi-detect) is a well-regarded Python library with a collection of tools for outlier detection and drift detection. It supports tabular, text, image, and time series data. Outlier detection and drift detection are actually similar problems, though they are different in some ways as well. Outlier detection involves looking, usually, for unusual single records, while drift detection refers to determining if the recent overall distribution is anomalous relative to prior data. It is fairly natural for a single library to support both. Often when machine learning applications (or other such software systems) are put into production, outlier detection and drift detection systems (as well as log monitoring systems) are deployed alongside these to help monitor both the application's behavior and the data it is processing. In addition, drift detection is actually an important use of outlier detection. Outlier detection can be used to determine if recent data has drifted from its earlier distribution if it contains a higher-than-expected proportion of outliers.

The alibi-detect library provides, for tabular data, a number of deep learning-based methods that we will cover in chapter 16, as well as Isolation Forest (IF) and Mahalanobis distance. IF is simply a wrapper around scikit-learn's implementation, while their Mahalanobis distance implementation provides a convenient wrapper on a Mahalanobis method provided by PyTorch.

7.3   *The PyCaret library*

PyCaret (https://github.com/pycaret/pycaret) is a Python library that simplifies machine learning by providing easy-to-use wrappers around other tools (for prediction, clustering, time series analysis, and outlier detection) and automating many of the steps in machine learning work. It's particularly useful as an autoML tool and for creating ensembles, and is well integrated with MLFlow. In terms of the outlier detectors supported, PyCaret simply provides a wrapper around detectors provided by PyOD and supports only a subset of these. How PyCaret is very useful, though, is the ease it allows in preprocessing data and feature engineering. Before using, we must first install PyCaret with

```
pip install pycaret
```

The outlier detection methods provided by PyCaret are similar to those for scikit-learn and PyOD. They have a different signature, but the idea is the same; they are also very simple and consistent from one detector to another. An example is provided in listing 7.3. This starts with creating the test data. Once we have the data to be used, we would then typically call the `setup()`, `create_model()` (specifying a model type, KNN in this example) and `predict_model()` methods, as in this example.

> **Listing 7.3   Example using PyCaret on test data using the KNN detector**

```
from pycaret.datasets import get_data
from pycaret.anomaly import *
```

```
df = create_four_clusters_test_data()
setup(data=df)
knn = create_model('knn')
knn_predictions = predict_model(model=knn, data=df)
```

This produces an output dataframe, which is effectively the original dataframe with Anomaly and Anomaly Score columns added, shown in table 7.1. As with scikit-learn and PyOD, the binary labels are applied to the scores based on a specified (or defaulted) contamination level, here set in the `create_model()` method.

Table 7.1   Output of `predict_model()`

A	B	Anomaly	Anomaly score
28.52	2.04	1	4.722
25.80	5.90	1	4.722
26.95	3.69	1	2.526

Most of the additional power of PyCaret is provided as options in the `setup()` method. Some examples are included here, starting with an option that will create a set of features equivalent to using sklearn's `PolynomialFeatures` module, multiplying each pair of features (a useful technique to capture feature interactions) and raising each feature to the power of 2. This can help identify records that are different in ways that cannot easily be determined with the original features:

```
setup(data=df, polynomial_features=True)
```

There is an option to group features that will, while keeping the existing features, create an additional set based on the groups specified. Here we specify one group, called Group1, which is comprised of features A and B. This will result in new features representing the min, max, mean, standard deviation, median, and mode of the specified Group1: there will be a new column for the minimum of columns A and B, a new column for the maximum of A and B, and so on:

```
setup(data=anomaly, group_features={"Group1": ['A', 'B']})
```

This can help identify unusual combinations of values in the sense of records having unusual min, max, mean, or other relationships between the features. Another option allows cleaning the data, removing any strong outliers first using an IsolationForest:

```
setup(data=anomaly, remove_outliers=True)
```

Other options also simplify encoding categorical and date columns, imputing missing values, and other preprocessing. PyCaret's integration with MLFlow is also a significant advantage, as it helps track experiments, which can become difficult to keep straight with outlier detection, as we often try many experiments, each producing different sets of outliers.

7.4   *Local outlier probability (LoOP)*

In chapter 5, we introduced the local outlier factor (LOF) algorithm, which is among the more powerful and commonly used detectors for outlier detection. There are a number of variations of LOF, which behave somewhat differently and may provide results more suitable to certain projects. In the next two sections, we look at two of these: Local Outlier Probability (LoOP) and local distance-based outlier factor (LDOF).

LoOP is part of the PyNomaly library (https://github.com/vc1492a/PyNomaly). Like LOF, it is a local density model and also scores based on the density of each point relative to its neighborhood, defining the neighborhood as the k nearest points and using distances to estimate densities. LoOP provides an advantage over LOF in the scoring. LoOP generates scores that may be interpreted as probabilities, in the range 0.0 to 1.0. This is a very nice property; it means scores are interpretable and comparable from one dataset to another.

LoOP works by assuming the distances to the k nearest neighbors follow a Gaussian distribution (as the distances are all positive; this is actually a half-Gaussian). Given that, the distances can be evaluated in probabilistic terms, which allows the probability for the density of each record to be estimated.

The implementation in PyNomaly also provides the option to use numba (a tool for high-performance Python) for calculations, which can accelerate execution.

An example is shown in listing 7.4. The detector is easy to use. This example uses the default parameters, but different parameters may work better for some datasets. As with LOF, the optimal parameters are difficult to tune, and it's usually best to use a number of parameter values and combine the results. We look at techniques to find suitable parameters in chapter 8.

LoOP also supports passing cluster labels for each record if the data has been clustered; in this case, LoOP will be run separately on each cluster. In the following listing, we simply run the detector and plot the results. Before this is executed, we must install the package using:

```
pip install PyNomaly
```

Listing 7.4   Example using LoOP

```
from PyNomaly import loop
import numpy as np
import pandas as pd
import matplotlib.pyplot as plt
import seaborn as sns

sns.set_style("whitegrid", {'axes.grid' : False})

df = create_simple_testdata()                              ⟵  Creates a test dataset
m = loop.LocalOutlierProbability(df, use_numba=True,
                        progress_bar=True).fit()           ⟵  Creates a LoOP detector
```

```
scores = m.local_outlier_probabilities
df['LoOP Scores'] = scores

fig, ax = plt.subplots(nrows=1, ncols=2, figsize=(8, 3))
sns.scatterplot(data=df, x='A', y='B', hue='LoOP Scores',
                size='LoOP Scores', ax=ax[0])
ax[0].legend().remove()

df = create_four_clusters_test_data()
m = loop.LocalOutlierProbability(df, use_numba=True,
                                 progress_bar=True).fit()
scores = m.local_outlier_probabilities
df['LoOP Scores'] = scores

sns.scatterplot(data=df, x='A', y='B', hue='LoOP Scores',
                size='LoOP Scores', ax=ax[1])
sns.move_legend(ax[1], "upper left", bbox_to_anchor=(1, 1))
plt.show()
```

Collects the outlier
scores for each record

Plots the results

Repeats the above for
the 2nd test dataset

The results are shown in figure 7.2 for both test datasets, with scores shown using size and color. In the legend we see all scores are between 0.0 and 1.0. LoOP scores the points quite reasonably in these cases and can be a strong outlier detector generally.

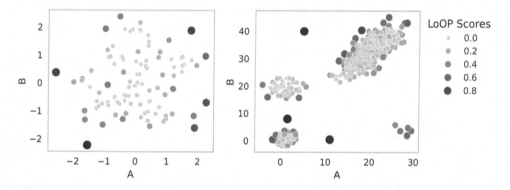

Figure 7.2 The output of LoOP. These are simple tests, but LoOP performs quite well here. In the left pane, it scores highest the points on the edge of the data. In the right pane, it scores highest the three global outliers, the small cluster of five, and some points on the edges of the three larger clusters.

7.5   *Local distance-based outlier factor (LDOF)*

LDOF is another variation of LOF. It will often produce similar results but in some cases may produce preferable results, or at least results that are different, and so may be worthwhile combining with LOF or other detectors. The major difference from LOF is in how the density of each point is compared to the densities of its neighbors. LOF considers, for each point, the distance to its k nearest neighbors compared to the distances of these points to *their k nearest neighbors*. LDOF instead considers, for each point, the distance to its k nearest neighbors compared to the distances of these points *to each other*. In a sense, LDOF may be considered more local than LOF, as each point is concerned strictly with its k nearest neighbors and not their neighbors, so it works with a smaller, more local set of records. As with all variations of LOF, it can be difficult to set k. The authors of the original paper recommend k be at least equal to the number of dimensions (i.e., features).

I'm not aware of an implementation of LDOF, but the algorithm is quite simple, and a code example is presented here (listing 7.5). LDOF does not have the intricacy of LOF, so it may encounter some issues that LOF was designed to address, related particularly to points in dense spaces where using the ratios of distances between points can be unstable. This implementation uses BallTree to store the data and perform nearest neighbors queries. The array `knn_distances` stores, for each record, the average distance to its k nearest neighbors, and the array `inner_distances` tracks, for each record, the average distance between the k nearest neighbors. We return the ratio of these as the score for each record.

Listing 7.5   LDOF outlier detection

```
import numpy as np
import pandas as pd
from sklearn.neighbors import BallTree
from sklearn.preprocessing import RobustScaler

class LDOFOutlierDetector:
    def __init__(self):
        pass

    def fit_predict(self, df, k):
        balltree = BallTree(df)
        dist, ind = balltree.query(df, k=k)
        knn_distances = [x.mean() for x in dist]

        inner_distances = []
        for i in df.index:
            local_balltree = BallTree(df.loc[ind[i]])
            local_dist, local_ind = balltree.query(df.loc[ind[i]], k=k)
            inner_distances.append(local_dist.mean())

        return np.array(knn_distances) / np.array(inner_distances)

df = create_four_clusters_test_data()
df = pd.DataFrame(RobustScaler().fit_transform(df), columns=df.columns)

clf = LDOFOutlierDetector()
df['LDOF Score'] = clf.fit_predict(df, k=20)
```

Annotations:
- Calculates the KNN distances: the average distances to the k nearest neighbors for all records
- Loops through each record in the data
- Calculates the average distances from the k nearest neighbors to each other
- Takes the ratio of these

For brevity, listing 7.5 skips the code to execute and display the results for both test sets, but this is the same as in listing 7.4. The output for both test sets is shown in figure 7.3.

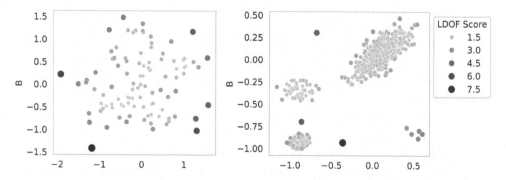

Figure 7.3 Output of LDOF on the two test data sets. LDOF performs well in both cases. With the single cluster, it scores high points in the margin. With four clusters, it scores high the small cluster of five, the three global outliers, and little else.

7.6 Extended Isolation Forest (EIF)

As Isolation Forest is a popular and effective tool for outlier detection, a number of variations have been proposed. There are several but not nearly as many variations on LOF. One of the stronger is Extended Isolation Forest (EIF; https://github.com/sahandha/eif). This tends to work similarly as IF, but often provides more intuitive scores. As with scikit-learn's IF, this implementation of EIF uses Cython and is also performant on large datasets. EIFs do, though, require more trees than standard IFs and EIF is not as fast as IF.

The authors of the original EIF paper argue that EIF is more flexible than IF, which allows it to be more consistent and reliable in its scoring. As shown in figure 7.4 (left), IF is limited to axis-parallel splits: for each split, a single feature, and a single value for that feature, is selected, which ensures all splits are parallel to one of the axes. Given this, in each tree, IF effectively divides the space into hyperrectangles, which may not represent the sparse and dense regions optimally. EIF's splits, in contrast, are hyperplanes through the full dataspace and may divide the data at any angle, as in figure 7.4 (right). This additional flexibility allows the algorithm to better separate dense from sparse regions where the regions have odd shapes.

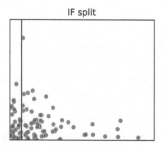

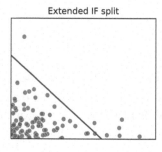

Figure 7.4 Examples of splits possible with IFs and EIFs. With IF, the splits are limited, in that they are always parallel to one of the axes. With EIFs, the splits are not limited and may isolate points more effectively, particularly where the data has clusters or unusual shapes.

The EIF project on GitHub provides good documentation and is easy to use. For ease of installation, though, I actually often use another implementation (https://mng.bz/9o6j), which I use in listing 7.6 and to generate the figures here. This is a single Python file, which needs to be copied and included in your projects. Copying in the code, you get a class called iForest, which can be used similarly to other outlier detectors.

An example comparing the decision boundaries created by IF and EIF on the test data with four clusters is shown in figure 7.5. In this case, EIF does tend to score records somewhat preferably to IF. I've found this generally to be true when comparing IF and EIF: they evaluate datasets similarly, but EIF can be favorable in its scoring.

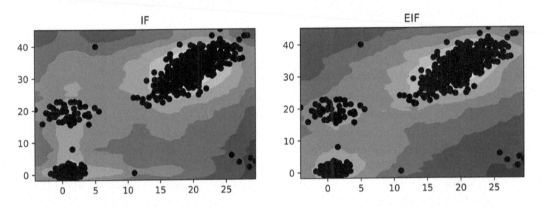

Figure 7.5   The decision boundaries created by IF (left) and EIF (right) on the test data. EIF is more able to score highly the regions outside the three large clusters.

The API works slightly differently than other outlier detectors we've seen, scoring the records one at a time instead of in bulk. Here we create a single array of scores using a list comprehension. We again test on the two test sets created earlier. Listing 7.6 includes code to execute on one of these. If the EIF code is placed in a separate file, an import statement will also be required.

Listing 7.6   Example using EIF

```
df = create_four_clusters_test_data()
forest = iForest(df.values)
df['EIF Scores'] = [forest.anomaly_score(point) for point in df.values]
```

The output of this is shown in figure 7.6, along with output running the algorithm on the dataset with a single cluster. Again, the output is reasonable, though somewhat different than with LoOP, LDOF, or other algorithms. EIF is another effective algorithm and is also quite simple to use. As with IF, it may be used with any numeric dataset.

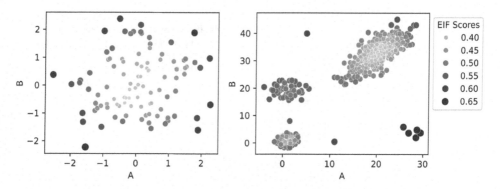

Figure 7.6 The output of EIF. The left pane shows the output on the single-cluster dataset and the right pane on the dataset with four clusters. In both cases, EIF performs quite well. In the right pane, the small cluster of five are scored higher than the three global outliers, which is reasonable but different from other detectors.

7.7 Outlier Detection Using In-degree Number (ODIN)

Outlier Detection Using In-degree Number (ODIN) is a variation on KNN, working in the opposite direction. As opposed to looking at the distances to the nearest neighbors, ODIN is based on the idea that outliers are records that are the nearest neighbors of few other records. This is referred to as *reverse KNN*. Here we use the in-degree of each record (the number of other records that point to this record as a nearest neighbor), which may be viewed as, though different than the standard KNN measure, equally relevant.

This is a useful outlier detector but also provides another example of coding detection algorithms. An implementation of ODIN is provided in listing 7.7. In this implementation, the matches are weighted: each case where the point is a nearest neighbor of another point, we count this highest if the point is the closest neighbor, second highest if the second nearest neighbor, and so on. You may wish to adjust this to favor closer neighbors more or less strongly than is done here. As with all nearest neighbors methods, this is sensitive to the choice of k.

Listing 7.7 ODIN outlier detection

```python
import pandas as pd
import numpy as np
import matplotlib.pyplot as plt
import seaborn as sns
from sklearn.neighbors import BallTree
from collections import Counter

class ODINOutlierDetector:
    def __init__(self):
        pass

    def fit_predict(self, df_in, k):
```

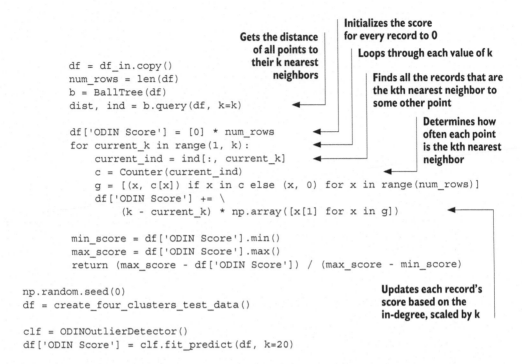

```
df = df_in.copy()
num_rows = len(df)
b = BallTree(df)
dist, ind = b.query(df, k=k)

df['ODIN Score'] = [0] * num_rows
for current_k in range(1, k):
    current_ind = ind[:, current_k]
    c = Counter(current_ind)
    g = [(x, c[x]) if x in c else (x, 0) for x in range(num_rows)]
    df['ODIN Score'] += \
        (k - current_k) * np.array([x[1] for x in g])

min_score = df['ODIN Score'].min()
max_score = df['ODIN Score'].max()
return (max_score - df['ODIN Score']) / (max_score - min_score)

np.random.seed(0)
df = create_four_clusters_test_data()

clf = ODINOutlierDetector()
df['ODIN Score'] = clf.fit_predict(df, k=20)
```

The output of this for both test datasets can be seen in figure 7.7. The results are reasonable though, again, different from the previous detectors.

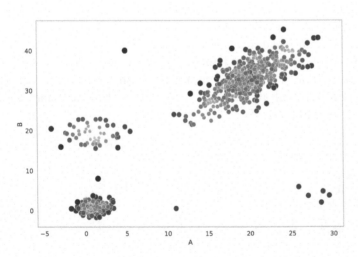

Figure 7.7   The output of ODIN on the two test sets. Here points along the margins of the clusters are scored similarly as the small cluster and three global outliers.

Another variation on this you may wish to investigate is called INFLO, which is based on both the distances to the k nearest neighbors and the in-degree. I'm not aware of a Python implementation, but the algorithm is also quite practical to implement.

7.8   *Clustering*

Using clusters is natural in outlier detection and can be especially convenient when you're already performing clustering on the data—for example, where the clustering and outlier detection are both performed to better understand the data. Clustering is also very useful in outlier detection where the data is strongly clustered, as it's often more meaningful to assess the outlierness of records relative to their clusters than relative to the full dataset.

In chapter 3, we introduced the idea of outlier detection based on clustering and have looked, so far, at systems where outliers are points not placed in any cluster (using DBSCAN or other clustering algorithms that allow unassigned records), Gaussian mixture models (GMM; where outliers are points in low-probability regions), and clustering-based local outlier factor (CBLOF; where outliers are points far from the closest large cluster center).

Additional forms of outlier detection using clustering can also be useful. In this section, we take a look at a couple of examples where data is clustered and global outlier detection algorithms are applied to each cluster. We also provide an example of clustering with categorical data.

7.8.1   *Mahalanobis distance per cluster*

Where data is in multiple clusters, even where each cluster has its own unique shape and size, the Mahalanobis distance for each point relative to its cluster is an intuitive measure of outlierness. This is similar to the idea of simply taking the Mahalanobis distance of each point, as we did when introducing the Mahalanobis distance in chapter 5, but does not assume, as we did there, that the data is in a single cluster.

This is also somewhat similar to CBLOF, though CBLOF uses Euclidean distances, which ignore the shape of the data, and CBLOF distinguishes small from large clusters, which this method does not (though it could be enhanced to do so where desired).

Code is provided in listing 7.8. In this example, we use GMM for clustering, as it handles well where the size, density, and correlations of the clusters vary. To aid the clustering, we also use an Isolation Forest to first remove any strong outliers, removing the rows with the top 50 highest scores before fitting the GMM. Many clustering algorithms are sensitive to outliers, and using outlier detection to clean data prior to clustering is an important use of outlier detection in itself, though here it is simply a step in a larger outlier detection process.

The code then tests clustering using different numbers of clusters and takes the number of clusters associated with the best Bayesian information criterion (BIC) score. Once the clustering is complete, we determine the cluster sizes (and apply a min-max scaling to the sizes so that they range from 0.0 to 1.0), which is optionally used as part of the final scores for each record. We include cluster sizes in the outlier scores with the idea that records in small clusters are, everything else equal, more outlierish than points in large clusters. This is a simple means to incorporate the cluster size, but other options are available that you may find more favorable; it can work well to use the log of the cluster sizes or the ratio of the cluster size to the size of the largest cluster.

The main part of the scores is based on the Mahalanobis distance of each point to its cluster center. Specifically, we use the ratio of this distance to the average Mahalanobis distance for this cluster, which provides a meaningful measure of how unusual each point is relative to its cluster. Using the ratio also creates a useful score in the sense that the scores from records in different clusters are comparable, which would not be the case using their raw Mahalanobis distances (given the cluster sizes and densities may be quite different, the sense of what a normal Mahalanobis distance for each cluster may also be quite different).

The final score is based on the cluster sizes and the relative Mahalanobis distances to the cluster center. The weight given to the cluster size is specified as a parameter.

Listing 7.8 Clustering and calculating Mahalanobis distances

```python
import pandas as pd
import numpy as np
import matplotlib.pyplot as plt
import seaborn as sns
from sklearn.mixture import GaussianMixture
from sklearn.preprocessing import MinMaxScaler, RobustScaler
from sklearn.covariance import MinCovDet
from sklearn.ensemble import IsolationForest

def cluster_based_outliers(df, sizes_weight=0.05):
    clf_if = IsolationForest()                          # Filters the strong
    clf_if.fit(df)                                      # outliers using an IF
    pred = clf_if.decision_function(df)
    trimmed_df = df.loc[np.argsort(pred)[50:]]

    best_score = np.inf                                 # Finds the best
    best_n_clusters = -1                                # number of clusters
    for n_clusters in range(2, 10):
        gmm = GaussianMixture(n_components=n_clusters)
        gmm.fit(trimmed_df)
        score = gmm.bic(trimmed_df)
        if score < best_score:
            best_score = score
            best_n_clusters = n_clusters

    gmm = GaussianMixture(n_components=best_n_clusters)  # Performs the
    gmm.fit(trimmed_df)                                 # clustering
    X = df.copy()
    X['Cluster ID'] = gmm.predict(df)                   # Finds the sizes
                                                        # of the clusters
    vc = pd.Series(X['Cluster ID']).value_counts()
    cluster_counts_dict = {x: y for x, y in zip(vc.index, vc.values)}
    size_scores = [cluster_counts_dict[x] for x in X['Cluster ID']]
    scaler = MinMaxScaler()
    size_scores = scaler.fit_transform(
        np.array(size_scores).reshape(-1, 1))
    size_scores = np.array(size_scores).reshape(1, -1)[0]
    size_scores = np.array([1.0 - x for x in size_scores])  # Finds the actual vs.
                                                            # average Mahalanobis
                                                            # distances
    dfs_arr = []
```

```
for cluster_idx in range(best_n_clusters):
    cluster_df = X[X['Cluster ID'] == cluster_idx].copy()
    cov = MinCovDet(random_state=0).fit(cluster_df[df.columns])
    cluster_df['Mahalanobis Dist'] = \
        cov.mahalanobis(cluster_df[df.columns])
    cluster_df['Mahalanobis Dist'] = \
        (cluster_df['Mahalanobis Dist'] /
        cluster_df['Mahalanobis Dist'].mean())
    dfs_arr.append(cluster_df)
maha_scores = pd.concat(dfs_arr).sort_index()['Mahalanobis Dist']
scaler = MinMaxScaler()
maha_scores = scaler.fit_transform(
    np.array(maha_scores).reshape(-1, 1))
maha_scores = np.array(maha_scores).reshape(1, -1)[0]
return (sizes_weight * size_scores) + maha_scores

df = create_four_clusters_test_data()
df = pd.DataFrame(RobustScaler().fit_transform(df), columns=df.columns)
df['Cluster-Based Scores'] = cluster_based_outliers(df)
```

The results are shown in figure 7.8 using both test sets. The code works well in both cases but does depend on the clustering and will behave poorly whenever clustering cannot be performed well. For example, k-means clustering tends to work poorly on these datasets.

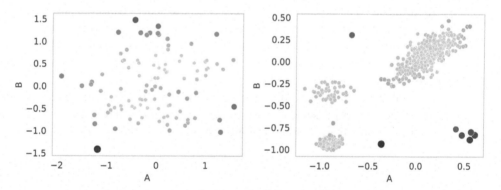

Figure 7.8 The results using outlier detection based on cluster size and Mahalanobis distance relative to the cluster. With a single cluster (left) it performs well, scoring highest the points on the margins. With multiple clusters (right), it also does well, scoring the very small cluster and the three global outliers the highest.

It may be desirable at times to increase or decrease the influence of the size of the clusters on the scores. However, it's not generally useful to use only the cluster size for the scores, as this will result in all records in each cluster receiving the same score. Doing this may, though, be useful at times, when we are not concerned about distinguishing records within clusters and wish only to identify small clusters.

7.8.2   *Kernel density estimation per cluster*

As a second example (listing 7.9), we modify the `cluster_based_outliers()` method to use multiple clusterings, and we apply a different test, here using kernel density estimation (KDE) instead of Mahalanobis distance. As with Mahalanobis distances, KDE is normally used in global tests for outliers, but this can be suboptimal if different regions have different densities. Again, it may be more reasonable in these cases to compare points to their cluster than to the full dataset. We also, to keep the example simple, remove the code to clean the data prior to clustering and to optionally weight by the cluster size, though these would normally be included in a full implementation.

In this example, we use k-means clustering as opposed to GMM. Multiple numbers of clusters and multiple clusterings for each are used here, averaging the results over each clustering, to provide more stable results. Relying on a single clustering can be unsafe, as clustering-based outlier detection is dependent on high-quality clustering, and clustering processes are not always reliable. In some cases, data can reasonably be divided into different numbers of clusters, often with only small differences in the Silhouette scores (or for other clustering metrics used), suggesting there is no definitive clustering for the data. Also, clustering may vary from one execution to another with stochastic clustering algorithms, such as k-means.

We take the KDE of each point relative to the average KDE for each cluster, creating a ratio. As with the previous example, the ratio can be more meaningful than the raw KDE score, as it gauges each point against what is normal for its cluster. Here we also would need to be mindful of combining the scores from different executions of the loop, particularly where different numbers of clusters are used, as the raw scores in these cases may not be comparable. Ratios, however, are comparable. For example, indicating that a point is in a location twice as dense as is normal for its cluster has meaning regardless of the number and size of clusters.

As well as varying the number of clusters, it's preferable, though for simplicity not shown here, to vary the set of clustering algorithms used. scikit-learn makes this straightforward as it provides implementations of numerous clustering algorithms.

Listing 7.9   Clustering using KDE and multiple clusterings

```
from sklearn.neighbors import KernelDensity
from sklearn.cluster import KMeans

def cluster_based_outliers(df, min_n_clusters=1, max_n_clusters=20,
                           n_trials=10):
    scores_df = pd.DataFrame()
    scores_col_name = 0
    X = df.copy()
    for n_clusters in range(                         ◀── Loops through each
        min_n_clusters, max_n_clusters+1):                number of clusters
        for trial_idx in range(n_trials):            ◀── Loops through
            seed = n_clusters * 100 + trial_idx            each trial
            np.random.seed(seed)
            kmeans = KMeans(n_clusters=n_clusters, random_state=seed,
```

```
            init='random', n_init="auto").fit(df)     ◄─ Uses k-means to cluster
    X['Cluster ID'] = kmeans.labels_                       the data with the
                                                           specified number of
                                                           clusters and random seed
    dfs_arr = []
    for cluster_idx in range(n_clusters):          ◄─ Loops through
        cluster_df = X[X['Cluster ID'] == cluster_idx].copy()   each cluster
        kde = KernelDensity(kernel='gaussian'). \
    fit(cluster_df[df.columns])
        kde_scores = (-1) * \                      ◄─ Calculates the
            kde.score_samples(cluster_df[df.columns])   KDE for the
        cluster_df['KDE Score'] = \                     current cluster
    kde_scores / kde_scores.mean()        ◄─ Finds the KDE for each point
        dfs_arr.append(cluster_df)            relative to the average KDE
                                              for this cluster
    scores_col_name += 1
    scores_df = pd.concat([scores_df,
        pd.concat(dfs_arr).sort_index()['KDE Score']], axis=1)
    return scores_df.mean(axis=1)

df = create_four_clusters_test_data()
df = pd.DataFrame(RobustScaler().fit_transform(df), columns=df.columns)
df['Cluster-Based Scores'] = cluster_based_outliers(df)
```

Figure 7.9 shows the results of running the algorithm on the two test datasets. It's not shown here, but repeating this, passing the true number of clusters (one for the first dataset and four for the second) produces similar results. That is, on these datasets, the function does as well if the true number of clusters is known or if it simply (as by default) loops over each possible number of clusters between 1 and 20. We may, though, wish to enhance the code to evaluate the clusterings. For example, we may use the Silhouette score or other metric and weight the scores using the quality of each clustering: we may increase the importance of the KDE scores for iterations where we had strong clustering and decrease the importance of the KDE scores on iterations where the clustering was poor.

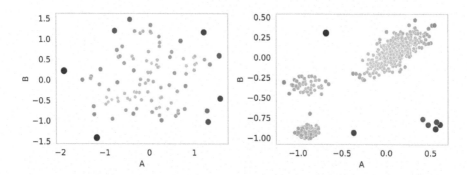

Figure 7.9 The results of the second version of `cluster_based_outlilers()`, using KDE. In both cases, we see good results, though in the right pane only two of the three global outliers receive high scores.

Here we see decent results despite k-means not being as effective as GMM to cluster the data for the test set with four clusters. This is largely due to looping over many clusterings and taking the average result.

Using this general approach to identifying outliers—running global tests on each cluster—you may also wish to use global tests other than Mahalanobis distances or KDE on the clusters, such as angle-based outlier detection, principal component analysis, or HBOS, but may otherwise use some combination of the techniques used in these two examples.

7.8.3 *Clustering with categorical data*

The clustering examples so far have all used numeric clustering algorithms, which are possible to use with categorical data, given that categorical data may be encoded, but this isn't ideal. Here we show an example of categorical outlier detection using the kmodes clustering library (https://pypi.org/project/kmodes/). This library provides kmodes clustering for categorial data and kprototypes for mixed data. An example of using this for outlier detection is shown in listing 7.10. As this requires categorical data, we cannot use the test data we've been using so far in this chapter. The code in listing 7.10 creates random synthetic data with a clear pattern and specifically adds an outlier in the last row, row 99. Columns F1 and F2 each have random values with three unique values each, creating nine combinations. Normally, data would have F3 repeat F2 and F4 would be a concatenation of F1 and F2, but row 99 follows neither of these patterns. Given the consistency (other than row 99), we have nine clear clusters in the data.

The algorithm works by clustering the data and then, for each record, determines its cluster, the center of that cluster, and the distance from the center. Before executing this, you must install kmodes:

```
pip install kmodes
```

Listing 7.10 Outlier detection using the kmodes clustering algorithm

```
import pandas as pd
import numpy as np
from kmodes.kmodes import KModes

class kmodesOutlierDetector:
  def __init__(self, n_clusters):
    self.n_clusters = n_clusters

  def fit_predict(self, df):
    km = KModes(n_clusters=self.n_clusters,          ◄─── Clusters the data
      init='Huang', n_init=5)                              using kmodes
    clusters = km.fit_predict(df)
    df_copy = df.copy()
    df_copy['Cluster'] = clusters

    scores = [-1] * len(df)                          ◄─── Loops through
    for cluster_idx in range(self.n_clusters):            each cluster
```

```
         cluster_df = df_copy[df_copy['Cluster'] == cluster_idx]
         center = km.cluster_centroids_[cluster_idx]          ◄──── Gets the center of
         for i in cluster_df.index:                                  the current cluster
            row = cluster_df.loc[i]
            num_diff = 0
            for j in range(len(center)):          Loops through all
               if row[j] != center[j]:            records in this
                  num_diff += 1                    cluster and calculates
            scores[i] = num_diff                   their distance from
      return scores                                the center


np.random.seed(0)
data = np.random.choice(['A', 'B', 'C'], (100, 2))   ◄──── Creates a synthetic dataset
df = pd.DataFrame(data, columns=['F1', 'F2'])               with clear patterns
df['F3'] = df['F2']                                         between the features
df['F4'] = df['F1'] + df['F2']
df.loc[99] = ['A', 'A', 'B', 'CC']     ◄──── Creates a single outlier
                                             row that does not
                                             follow the patterns
clf = kmodesOutlierDetector(n_clusters=9)
scores = clf.fit_predict(df)
df['KModes Scores'] = scores
df.tail()
```

The output for the last five rows is shown in table 7.2. In this case, we know all rows, other than Row 99, are typical and they, correctly, receive low scores (specifically, zero), as shown in the KModes Scores column. Row 99 has a high score, representing its unusual distance from its cluster's center.

Table 7.2   The last five rows of the test data (including the known outlier) and their scores

Row	F1	F2	F3	F4	KModes scores
95	A	A	A	AA	0
96	A	A	A	AA	0
97	C	A	A	CA	0
98	A	C	C	AC	0
99	A	A	B	CC	2

This is a simple example to demonstrate working with categorical data and simply takes the number of clusters as a parameter. As with the previous examples, it is preferable to loop over many different numbers of clusters than to require specifying a given number.

As another simplification, this uses a simple measure of the distance between each row and its cluster center, counting the number of cells with the same value and treating every cell as either a match or not a match. Row 99 has values, [A, A, B, CC], and the cluster center for row 99 has values, [A, A, A, AA], giving row 99 two values different from the center. We will look at more sophisticated means to measure distances with categorical data in chapter 9, but even as is, this code can work well for outlier detection with data that is well-clustered and predominantly categorical.

7.9   *Entropy*

Entropy is another interesting method, used at times to detect outliers. As with HBOS and empirical cumulative distribution function (ECOD), this calculates a univariate score for each cell value in a row and combines these for a total score per row, not considering associations between features. Entropy is possible to calculate with numeric data using some calculus, but it is much easier to describe and work with categorical data and so Entropy-based detectors are, in most cases, categorical detectors, requiring binning any numeric data.

Entropy measures the degree of uncertainty in data. Although it is most associated with thermodynamics and information theory, entropy is used in a number of places in machine learning as well, the best known probably being in the construction of classification decision trees. Usually, though, decision trees actually use a similar measure called Gini impurity; this is because Gini is based on squaring operations, while entropy is based on log operations, which are slower to calculate. Where entropy is used, decision trees are constructed such that as each node is split, we try to minimize the total entropy, which is achieved by trying to get each child node as pure as possible, ideally with only a single target value in each child node.

As a simpler example, looking at the content of a dataset, consider three categorical features, each representing the colors of items. If the table has 300 rows and Feature A contains 100 red, 100 blue, and 100 green values, we would say this feature has high entropy, as there is high uncertainty (it's hard to guess a value); the value of Feature A could equally be any of three values. If Feature B contains 50 red, 50, blue, 50 green, 50 white, 50 yellow, and 50 brown, then this is even higher entropy; here there is more uncertainty as the value could here be equally any one of six values. If Feature C contains 290 red and 10 blue, then there is low entropy, as there is low uncertainty. We can be reasonably confident a random value from Feature C is red, and if not, there is only one other possibility.

Given a dataset with 300 rows, a feature has the maximum possible uncertainty (and maximum entropy) if all 300 values are all distinct. It has the minimum uncertainty (and minimum entropy) if all contain the same, single value. One interesting point is, outliers increase the entropy of a set of values significantly, while inliers do not. In fact, adding strong inliers to a dataset will actually reduce the entropy, making the data overall more consistent (and so predictable), while adding outliers will increase the entropy.

We can take advantage of this in order to estimate the outlierness of any value in a column, not by adding values, but by removing values. Removing some values will cause the total entropy of the feature to decrease more than removing any other value would. For example, if we have 299 red and one blue, then removing the one blue value (which we can consider an outlier) allows us to have 100% red values, with minimal entropy. Removing any one of the red values does not result in as large a drop in entropy. So, after testing removing each value and examining the new value for the entropy of the feature, we can determine the blue ball is the strongest outlier.

The formula for entropy is a bit involved to explain, but we can take here the formula as given:

$$\text{Entropy} = -\sum p(x) \log(p(x))$$

That is, for each unique value in a set, we find its probability and the log of its probability, multiply these, and sum over all unique values. In this example, we start with 299 red and one blue, with probabilities 299/300 and 1/300 and entropy 0.0322. If we remove the blue to have 299 red only, this has entropy of 0.0 (the minimum possible entropy). If we remove any red value, to have 298 red and one blue, we have an entropy of 0.323, actually increasing the entropy. So, removing the one blue, in this example, does the most to reduce the entropy for this feature out of the 300 rows we could remove, and is therefore the strongest outlier for this feature.

However, there are usually multiple features in a table, and to find the row, such that removing it will result in the largest total drop in entropy, we have to sum the drops in entropy over all features.

Entropy-based outlier detection is performed by iteratively removing one row at a time from the dataset, each time finding the next most outlier-ish record, until a specific number of outliers have been found. If we wish to find, say, 50 outliers in a table of 10,000, then the first iteration, we would test removing, one at a time, all 10,000 rows, determine the one that would result in the largest drop in entropy, and then actually remove it. For the next iteration, there are 9,999 rows remaining. We again test removing each of these, and again remove the one resulting in the largest drop in entropy, and so on for 50 iterations.

This may sound very inefficient, but for each entropy calculation, as we're only considering removing one row, the probabilities (and the logs of the probabilities) remain constant for all classes in each feature other than the class for the row currently being tested, which will result in the count of that one class being decreased by one. For simplicity, the code example in listing 7.11 recalculates the counts of all values for each feature each iteration, but in practice, we would calculate the counts of each value for each feature at the beginning and maintain the current count of these as rows are removed. This can, then, be calculated very quickly.

As with any detector that assumes independence between the features, this cannot detect rare combinations or local outliers. Entropy, overall, has roughly the same strengths and weaknesses as HBOS or ECOD, though these are better established and have solid implementations in PyOD and should, everything else equal, normally be tried before Entropy, though you may find useful results with Entropy as well. Similar to HBOS, Entropy requires specifying a number of bins for any numeric features. An implementation is shown in listing 7.11, which provides a useful example when you do wish to try entropy. To keep the example simple, it is not optimized and assumes the dataset has two features. It does, though, present the idea and can be expanded and optimized where needed.

Listing 7.11   Example of outlier detection using Entropy

```
class EntropyOutlierDetector:
  def __init__(self, num_outliers, num_bins=7):
    self.num_outliers = int(num_outliers)
    self.num_bins = num_bins

  def calculate_entropy(self, values):          ◀── Calculates the entropy
      vc = values.value_counts(normalize=True)       of an array of values
      entropy = 0.0
      for v in vc.values:
          if v > 0:
              entropy += ((v) * np.log2(v))
      entropy = (-1) * entropy
      return entropy

  def fit_predict(self, df):
    df = df.copy()
    df['A binned'] = pd.cut(                    ◀── Transforms all numeric
        df[df.columns[0]], bins=self.num_bins)      features into a set of bins
    df['B binned'] = pd.cut(
        df[df.columns[1]], bins=self.num_bins)

    temp_df = df.copy()                         Each iteration of the loop
    scores = [0]*len(df)                        removes one record.
    for iteration_num in range(self.num_outliers):  ◀── Loops through each
        lowest_entropy = np.inf                      remaining row and
        lowest_entropy_row = -1                      determines the drop
        for i in temp_df.index:                      in entropy if it were
            a_entropy = self.calculate_entropy(temp_df['A binned'].drop(i))  removed
            b_entropy = self.calculate_entropy(temp_df['B binned'].drop(i))
            total_entropy = a_entropy + b_entropy  ◀── To determine the drop in
            if total_entropy < lowest_entropy:       entropy, we can actually look
                lowest_entropy = total_entropy       simply at the entropy of the
                lowest_entropy_row = i               data with the record removed.

        scores[lowest_entropy_row] = (self.num_outliers - iteration_num)
        temp_df = temp_df.drop(index=lowest_entropy_row)
    return scores

df = create_four_clusters_test_data()
df = pd.DataFrame(RobustScaler().fit_transform(df), columns=df.columns)
df['Entropy Scores'] = EntropyOutlierDetector(num_outliers=10, num_bins=10).
    fit_predict(df)
```

The results are shown in figure 7.10. This is a univariate test, so it finds results that are valid but different from a multivariate test.

To address the limitation that rare combinations are missed, it is possible to group the columns—for example, in pairs. Given d columns, this creates $d(d-1)/2$ pairs of columns, which can then replace the original d features. The algorithm may then be executed as normal. This is much more expensive to execute but can catch outliers that would otherwise be missed.

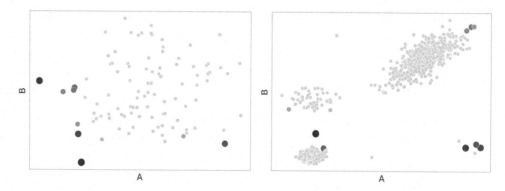

Figure 7.10 **The output of the entropy detector on the test datasets. Here we can see quite different results than previous detectors as the algorithm works very differently, focusing on univariate outliers.**

7.10 *Association Rules*

Association rule-based outlier detection is one of the more interpretable outlier detection methods and handles categorical data well. This is a frequent item set (FIS)-based method. As with FPOF, it starts with mining the data for FISs and then performs what is called *Association Rule mining*. That is, it looks for rules of the form X → Y, where X and Y are both FISs. It finds patterns that describe, where a row contains a given FIS, what other FISs also tend to appear in the row. A FIS may span one or more columns, so a simple example may be where the telephone area code column has 416, the city column tends to contain Toronto.

There are two broad approaches to evaluating the outlierness of records using association rules. The first is to evaluate each row by the number of association rules that hold true: the more rules that hold true, the more normal the data, and the fewer rules that hold, the more outlierish the rows. This approach will find outliers similar to those found by FPOF. In fact, depending on how the parameters are set when mining for FISs and rules, any rule could be treated as a FIS.

The other approach is to evaluate the rows by exceptions to the rules: cases where the left-hand side FIS is present but the right-hand side FIS is not—for example, where the area code is 416 but the city is not Toronto. This discussion and the code examples here take the second approach, but both are valid and often useful.

With this approach, we identify a quite different type of anomaly than what FPOF finds. This starts with records that contain at least one FIS so are to some degree normal, at least in this sense (though some may still have far fewer FISs than is typical). Given that testing for exceptions to association rules does not check for rows with few FISs (and will actually skip rows with zero FISs), it's often useful to also run FPOF. This depends, though, on the types of outliers that are useful for the current task.

This form of outlier detection is quite interpretable, as it is possible for each outlier to simply list the relevant association rules (the rules where the left-hand side is true but the right-hand side is not), along with some statistics about these rules. It is straightforward, for example, to indicate the city and area code do not match as is normal. Where many association rules are violated for a row, it may be sufficient to provide statistics about this, along with a small number of the association rules, to avoid long explanations.

In listing 7.12 we demonstrate the first step, FIS mining. This uses the SpeedDating dataset from OpenML, as was used in the FPOF example earlier. This works the same as with FPOF. As with using FPOF, it is necessary to install mlxtend, using

```
pip install mlxtend
```

Listing 7.12   Creating frequent item sets

```
from mlxtend.frequent_patterns import apriori
import pandas as pd
from sklearn.datasets import fetch_openml
import matplotlib.pyplot as seaborn                          Collects
                                                             the data
data = fetch_openml('SpeedDating', version=1, parser='auto')
data_df = pd.DataFrame(data.data, columns=data.feature_names)   Selects a small
data_df = data_df[['d_pref_o_attractive', 'd_pref_o_sincere',    number of
                   'd_pref_o_intelligence', 'd_pref_o_funny',    features
                   'd_pref_o_ambitious', 'd_pref_o_shared_interests']]
data_df = pd.get_dummies(data_df)
frequent_itemsets = apriori(data_df, min_support=0.3, use_colnames=True)

                                             Collects the frequent item sets

                                                      One-hot encodes
                                                        the columns
```

As with frequent item set mining, we can use mlxtend for the next step, association rule mining. This is very easy, though setting the min_threshold parameter may take some tuning. This is shown in the following listing.

Listing 7.13   Creating and testing association rules

```
from mlxtend.frequent_patterns import association_rules

assoc_rules = association_rules(frequent_itemsets, metric="confidence",
                                min_threshold=0.7)
```

Once the FISs and association rules are found, there are a number of metrics associated with each. Table 7.3 shows part of the assoc_rules table returned in listing 7.13. There are actually more metrics than can fit in this page, and we show only four metrics here. The antecedents and consequences (left-hand and right-hand sides of the rules) are both FISs and can each cover multiple columns. The second row here is an example where the antecedent covers two features; the third row is an example where the consequence covers two columns.

Table 7.3　Sample of the association rules found in the SpeedDating dataset

antecedent	consequences	Antecedent support	Consequent support	support	confidence
d_pref_o attractive [21-100]	d_pref_o ambitious [0-15]	0.35	0.79	0.34	0.96
d_pref_o attractive [21-100], d_pref o_ambitious [0-15]	d_pref_o shared interests [0-15]	0.34	0.72	0.31	0.89
d_pref_o attractive [21-100]	d_pref_o ambitious [0-15], d_pref_o shared interests [0-15]	0.35	0.59	0.31	0.86

Once we have the association rules, we can evaluate each record with respect to them. In this example, we check for violations of rules and score each by the support of the rule. Note though that other metrics such as lift, leverage, conviction, Zhang's metric, or surprise may work better for your tasks. Code for this is provided in the following listing.

Listing 7.14　Evaluating records based on association rules

```
data_df['Assoc Rules Score'] = 0
for assoc_rule_idx in assoc_rules.index:
    antecedents = assoc_rules.loc[assoc_rule_idx, 'antecedents']
    consequent = assoc_rules.loc[assoc_rule_idx, 'consequents']
    support = assoc_rules.loc[assoc_rule_idx, 'support']
    cond = True
    col_list = (list(antecedents))
    for col_name in col_list:
        cond = cond & (data_df[col_name])
    fis_true_list = data_df[cond].index
    col_list = (list(consequent))
    for col_name in col_list:
        cond = cond & (data_df[col_name])
    assoc_rule_true_list = data_df[cond].index
```

Initializes the score for each record to zero

Loops through each association rule

Finds the set of records where the left-hand side of the rule is true

Finds the set of records where the right-hand side of the rule is true

```
rule_exceptions = list(set(fis_true_list)-set(assoc_rule_true_list))
data_df.loc[rule_exceptions, 'Assoc Rules Score'] += support
```

Updates the scores for these records based on the support of the association rule

Finds the set or records where the left-hand side is true and the right-hand side is false

In this example, the row with the highest score is row 5650. Examining this row, we can see the following values:

d_pref_o_attractive_[0-15]	False
d_pref_o_attractive_[16-20]	False
d_pref_o_attractive_[21-100]	True
d_pref_o_sincere_[0-15]	True
d_pref_o_sincere_[16-20]	False
d_pref_o_sincere_[21-100]	False
d_pref_o_intelligence_[0-15]	True
d_pref_o_intelligence_[16-20]	False
d_pref_o_intelligence_[21-100]	False
d_pref_o_funny_[0-15]	False
d_pref_o_funny_[16-20]	True
d_pref_o_funny_[21-100]	False
d_pref_o_ambitious_[0-15]	False
d_pref_o_ambitious_[16-20]	False
d_pref_o_ambitious_[21-100]	True
d_pref_o_shared_interests_[0-15]	True
d_pref_o_shared_interests_[16-20]	False
d_pref_o_shared_interests_[21-100]	False

It's then possible to examine each association rule and identify rules where the left-hand side is true but the right-hand side false for this record, such as

```
d_pref_o_attractive_[21-100] → d_pref_o_ambitious_[0-15]
d_pref_o_sincere_[0-15] → d_pref_o_ambitious_[0-15]
```

This, along with the statistics about the rules in table 7.3, describe each outlier.

A key distinction from FPOF is that association rule-base outlier detection (in this form) is a local method, while FPOF is a global method. FPOF finds the rows that have the least coverage by the most common FISs, using a global standard of what is normal, while association rules outlier detection compares each row only to the other records where the FIS on the left-hand side of the rule is also true. However, rows will tend to actually be evaluated based on many association rules so will use multiple local contexts.

With any FIS-based outlier detection system, where features have high cardinality, it may be useful to group together some values in a column. For example, if a column contains the unique values black, white, red, yellow, light blue, light green, dark blue, and dark green, it may make sense to combine light blue with dark blue and light green with dark green, reducing the number of unique values in the column. This may allow FISs to be found more easily and may possibly support more useful association rules.

For example, if Weight = High tends to be associated with either Color = light blue or Color = dark blue, it may be that neither has the support to be recognized as an association rule but Weight = high → Color=blue may be.

7.11 Convex Hull

Convex Hull is an established method in outlier detection. The idea is to identity the points most distant from the main body of points, remove these, find the next set of most distant points, and so on until all points are removed or some stopping condition is met, such as executing a predetermined number of iterations or identifying a predetermined number of outliers. At each iteration, the most distant points are those identified on a Convex Hull drawn around the full set of data. An example is shown in figure 7.11 covering the first three iterations. Each point on the outermost hull is given the highest outlier score, each point on the second hull the second highest, and so on. The process is also referred to as convex peeling, as in each step, a layer of points is effectively peeled off, revealing the points removed in the next step.

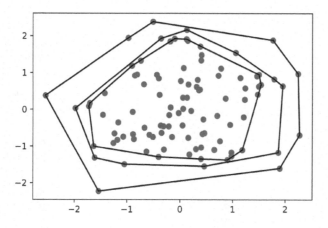

Figure 7.11 The first three layers of convex peeling on a dataset. At each stage, the outermost points on a Convex Hull are removed, leaving all other points. The process continues until all points are removed or a prespecified number of layers or outliers is reached.

The algorithm is intuitive and reasonably robust to the shape of the data and to outliers: as the algorithm works by repeatedly removing small numbers of points, there are few masking or swamping effects. The algorithm does assume the data is in a single cluster and can be ineffective where this is not the case.

The algorithm can also be slow, though in many cases it is only necessary to run for a small number of iterations, as this may identify a sufficient set of outliers. Executing beyond this will simply measure points that are, in any case, inliers.

The major limitation of the Convex Hull outlier detection method is that it does not scale to more than a small number of features. Some researchers have even recommended it for no more than four or five. Convex Hull operations are heavily limited by the curse of dimensionality—not in the sense of distance measures becoming meaningless but in the sense that, where there are enough dimensions, almost all points end up on the edge of at least one dimension. When this occurs, we can see many points being removed each iteration, including many that should likely be considered inliers. Even where all points removed are actually outliers, if many points are removed each iteration, it is impossible to give each a distinct score: all points removed in the same iteration will receive the same score, though some may be drastically farther from the data center than others.

In listing 7.15, we provide an example of code that executes Convex Hull outlier detection for a fixed number of iterations. This code uses the `ConvexHull` method provided by SciPy.

Listing 7.15 Example code for `ConvexHull` outlier detector

```
from scipy.spatial import ConvexHull
import numpy as np
import pandas as pd
from sklearn.preprocessing import RobustScaler

class ConvexHullOutlierDetector:
  def __init__(self, num_iterations):
    self.num_iterations = num_iterations

  def fit_predict(self, df):
    scores = [0] * len(df)                          # Initializes the score
    remaining_df = df.copy()                        # for all records to zero
    remaining_df['Row Idx'] = remaining_df.index

    for iteration_idx in range(self.num_iterations):   # Loops through a specified
        hull = ConvexHull(                             # number of iterations
        remaining_df[[df.columns[0], df.columns[1]]])   # Finds the set of
                                                        # points on the
        simplex_idxs = [y for x in hull.simplices for y in x]  # Convex Hull of the
        simplex_idxs = list(set(simplex_idxs))          # remaining data
        for idx in simplex_idxs:                        # (initially the full
            orig_row_idx = remaining_df.loc[idx, 'Row Idx']  # data)
            scores[orig_row_idx] = \
                (self.num_iterations - iteration_idx)   # Sets the score for
            remaining_df = remaining_df.drop(index=idx)  # any points on the
        remaining_df = remaining_df.reset_index(drop=True)  # Convex Hull

    return scores                                       # Removes the points on
                                                        # the hull from the data
df = create_four_clusters_test_data()
df = pd.DataFrame(RobustScaler().fit_transform(df), columns=df.columns)
df['ConvexHull Scores'] = \
    ConvexHullOutlierDetector(num_iterations=2).fit_predict(df)
```

The results are shown in figure 7.12. Convex Hull does not consider clustering so flags only values on the extremes of the full dataspace. Where data is clustered, it can be useful to first cluster the data and run Convex Hull on each cluster, similar to the previous examples using Mahalanobis distance and KDE. Where the data contains many features, it will be useful to find subspaces using techniques such as subspace outlier detection (SOD) or FeatureBagging, to identify subspaces with few features, where Convex Hull can be quite effective.

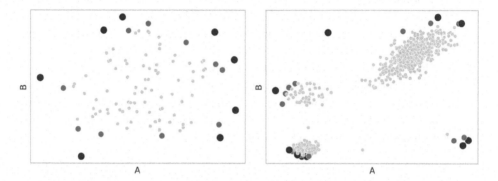

Figure 7.12 The output of Convex Hull on the two test datasets. This flags the points on the extremes of the full dataspace and does not consider local outliers or internal outliers but provides strong results with respect to the full dataspace. It is more appropriate in cases such as the first dataset than the second, as the first is in a single cluster.

Although Convex Hull is limited in its application, it can be useful where data is of low dimensionality and in a single cluster. It can work somewhat similarly to other detectors that use the distance to the center of the data, though it uses a unique (but useful) distance metric and so produces distinct results.

7.12   *Distance metric learning (DML)*

So far, we've been working with a number of detectors that work on the premise that rows that are similar to many other rows are inliers and rows similar to few other rows are outliers. While this is clearly a useful idea, it can be difficult to determine, in a meaningful way, which rows are similar to each other and which are not. Most of the time we use, at least with numeric data, Euclidean, Manhattan, Mahalanobis, or other such distance measures. These distance metrics are simple but may not capture well how similar rows really are. These are each based on the premise that records are points in high-dimensional space, which may not always be the optimal way to view data.

Here we use another way to measure their similarity based on the idea that, if we have a predictor (to predict some target) and two rows are similar to each other, they will not only result in the same prediction but will generally be treated similarly by the predictor. To test for similarity in this sense, we construct a RandomForest and pass each record in the data through this. For each record, we examine within each tree in the RandomForest which leaf node it ends in. If two records, when passed through the random forest, often end in the same leaf nodes, we can say they are similar to each other; if two rows rarely end in the same leaf nodes, they are different in this regard.

As outliers are records that are similar to few other rows, outliers can be identified as rows that end in the same leaf nodes as few other rows. An efficient way to determine this is to simply examine the count of other records ending in the same leaf nodes. Records that tend to end in nodes with few other records may be considered outliers. An implementation of this idea is shown in listing 7.16.

When creating the random forest, we need some target for it to predict. This can be anything relevant, but in this case, we create a RandomForest to distinguish the training data from similar synthetic data, which is generated here as well. This simply uses the mean and standard deviation of each feature, similar to the technique to generate synthetic data as we used in chapter 3 to predict real versus fake data. This algorithm can work very well but may require some tuning with respect to the synthetic data used and the parameters of the RandomForest. In this case, we set the RandomForest to use a `max_depth` of 5 and use default parameters otherwise. We use the `apply()` method to determine the leaf node each record ends in for each tree.

Listing 7.16 Distance metric learning outlier detection

```
from sklearn.ensemble import RandomForestClassifier
from collections import Counter

class DMLOutlierDetection:
    def __init__(self):
        pass

    def fit_predict(self, df):
        real_df = df.copy()
        real_df['Real'] = True

        synth_df = pd.DataFrame()                       ◄─┐ Generates synthetic data that
        for col_name in df.columns:                       │ is similar to the real data
            mean = df[col_name].mean()
            stddev = df[col_name].std()
            synth_df[col_name] = np.random.normal(loc=mean,
                scale=stddev, size=len(df))
        synth_df['Real'] = False

        train_df = pd.concat([real_df, synth_df])

        clf = RandomForestClassifier(max_depth=5)
        clf.fit(train_df.drop(columns=['Real']), train_df['Real'])

        r = clf.apply(df)                  ◄─┐ Gets the leaf node each record ends in

        scores = [0]*len(df)               ◄─┐ Initializes the score for all records to 0

        for tree_idx in range(len(r[0])):                  ◄─┐ Loops through each tree
            c = Counter(r[:, tree_idx])                    ◄─┘ in the Random Forest
            for record_idx in range(len(df)):     ◄─┐
                node_idx = r[record_idx, tree_idx]         Gets the count of
                node_count = c[node_idx]                   each leaf node
```

Loops through each record and updates its score based on the frequency of the node it ends in

```
        scores[record_idx] += len(df) - node_count

    return scores

df = create_four_clusters_test_data()
df = pd.DataFrame(RobustScaler().fit_transform(df), columns=df.columns)
clf = DMLOutlierDetection()
df['Scores'] = clf.fit_predict(df)
```

As with the preceding examples, we can use this to evaluate both test datasets. The results are shown in figure 7.13. The results are, again, different than those from other detectors. In the case of the second test dataset, emphasis was put on all points outside the center of the largest cluster.

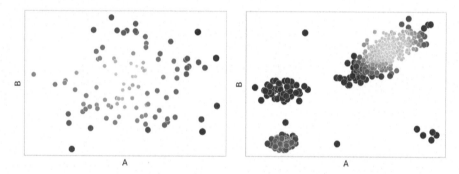

Figure 7.13 Output of distance metric tearning on the two test datasets. With the first, the points along the edge are scored highest. With the second, the points outside the center of the large cluster are scored highest.

Although this is presented here as an outlier detector in itself, distance metric learning can also be combined with other detectors. For example, using commonality in the RandomForest leaves as a means to measure the distance between points for distance or density-based outlier detectors. It may also be performed, as in the previous examples, separately on each cluster where the data is well-clustered.

7.13 *NearestSample*

Working with outlier detection, there have been cases where I wished to use an approach similar to KNN or LOF but found the process more affected by the value of k specified than I wished and so developed the NearestSample algorithm, which is presented here. This is, again, a useful detector in itself but also an example of code that may be created to get the types of results you may need. After first working with NearestSample, I found it to be generally useful; it is fast and effective, though it is based on distance calculations between points so suffers from the curse of dimensionality in the same way as any distance or density detector. The algorithm is very similar to the sampling detector provided by PyOD.

NearestSample works by testing the distance of each point to a small random sample of points from the data. The idea is: inliers are close to many other points and outliers are far from most points. Given that, inliers will usually be close to at least one point from a small random sample of points from the data, and outliers will usually be far from all points in the sample. To be more robust, the process is repeated several times, each time taking a different random sample of points, and for all points (including those in the sample), finding the minimum distance to any of the sample points. Figure 7.14 presents the general idea. Each iteration, a set of random points is selected as the samples, and all other points are measured by their distance to the closest of these.

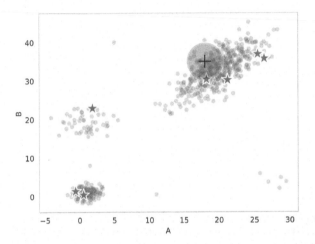

Figure 7.14   An example of NearestSample outlier detection. For each iteration, a set of samples is selected from the data. Here we select seven, shown as stars. For each other point, we measure the distance to the nearest sample. For a typical point, such as the point drawn as a + sign, in most iterations, there will be at least one sample point fairly close. Here we show a circle whose radius represents the distance to the nearest sample. For outlier points, such as the three global outliers or the five points in the small cluster, most iterations will have no sample near them, as in this case.

NearestSample benefits from having only two parameters, both of which are fairly intuitive. The n_iterations is straightforward: this is the number of times the process is repeated, and more is strictly preferable in terms of accuracy. The n_samples parameter controls the number of points taken in the sample each iteration. This can be less intuitive, but the model is also robust to the choice. As long as the number is significantly larger than the number of clusters (enough that in most iterations most clusters have at least one sample point) and not very large, the model tends to work well, and the defaults can usually be used.

An implementation is provided in listing 7.17. This captures local behavior well, as sample points in each region are usually selected in proportion to the population of each region. So long as n_samples is set reasonably large (such as the default of 100), each dense region will have multiple sample points, allowing points in these regions to have small distances to the closest of these. Sparse regions will tend to have few or no sample points, and so records in these areas have longer distances to the nearest sample point and tend to get higher outlier scores.

Listing 7.17 NearestSample outlier detection

```python
import numpy as np
import pandas as pd
from tqdm import tqdm
from sklearn.neighbors import BallTree

class NearestSampleOutlierDetector:
    def __init__(self, n_iterations=10, n_samples=100,
                 show_progress=False):
        self.n_iterations = n_iterations
        self.n_samples = n_samples
        self.show_progress = show_progress
        self.training_df = None
        self.orig_cols = None
        self.tree = None

    def fit(self, df):
        self.training_df = df.copy()
        self.orig_cols = df.columns
        return self

    def decision_function(self, df_in):
        df = pd.DataFrame(df_in).copy()
        self.balltree = BallTree(df)

        if self.show_progress:
            for iteration_idx in tqdm(range(self.n_iterations)):
                scores = self.execute_iteration(df)
                self.df[f'Scores_{iteration_idx}'] = scores
        else:
            for iteration_idx in range(self.n_iterations):
                scores = self.execute_iteration(df)
                df[f'Scores_{iteration_idx}'] = scores

        score_cols = [f'Scores_{x}' for x in range(iteration_idx)]
        df['Score'] = df[score_cols].sum(axis=1)

        return df['Score'].values

    def execute_iteration(self, prediction_df):
        sample_idxs = np.random.choice(range(len(self.training_df)),
                                       self.n_samples)

        distances_arr = []
        for sample_idx in sample_idxs:
```

Creates a BallTree representing the full dataset

Loops through a specified number of iterations (optionally showing progress at each step)

Executes this function each iteration

Selects a random sample of records

Loops through each sample record

```
        row = self.training_df.iloc[sample_idx: sample_idx+1]
        dist, ind = self.balltree.query(row[self.orig_cols],
                        k=len(prediction_df))
        dist = dist[0]
        ind = ind[0]
        ordered_idxs = np.argsort(ind)
        dist = pd.Series(dist)
        distances_arr.append(dist.loc[ordered_idxs].values)

    distances_df = pd.DataFrame(distances_arr).T
    return np.array(distances_df.min(axis=1))
df = create_four_clusters_test_data()
df = pd.DataFrame(RobustScaler().fit_transform(df), columns=df.columns)
df['NearestSample Scores'] = \
    NearestSampleOutlierDetector().fit(df).decision_function(df)
```

Gets the distance of all points to this sample

Sets distances_arr to the minimum distance to a sample point for each record

The results of using NearestSample outlier detection on the test datasets is shown in figure 7.15. In the case of the single cluster dataset, this uses n_samples=5, as the dataset is very small with only 100 records.

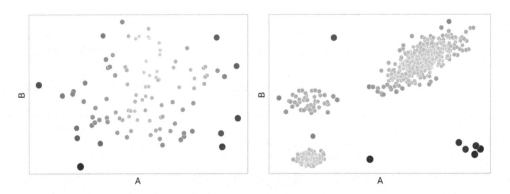

Figure 7.15   The output of NearestSample outlier detection on the test datasets

Summary

- Though scikit-learn and PyOD are the most popular and useful Python libraries for tabular outlier detection, there are other libraries that can also be worth looking at.
- PyCaret is a convenient tool for preprocessing data before outlier detection and also provides integration with MLFlow.
- A very large number of algorithms are proposed in academic literature, some with implementations on GitHub or elsewhere, and many are quite manageable to code if no implementations are available.

- LoOP and EIF are not included in scikit-learn or PyOD but are available on GitHub and are simple to install.
- Association Rules, clustering based on kmodes, and Entropy can support categorical data well.
- Association Rules is useful as an interpretable outlier detector.
- There are many ways to take advantage of clustering for outlier detection, including running global outlier detection methods on each cluster.
- Executing Mahalanobis distance and KDE tests on each cluster can be an effective way to identify outliers.
- The idea of running global outlier tests on each cluster can be applied to other tests as well, such as ABOD, PCA, HBOS, Convex Hull, and others.
- LDOF, ODIN, Entropy, Association Rules, Convex Hull, distance metric learning, and NearestSample are straightforward to implement and can all be effective algorithms for outlier detection.
- Convex Hull is possibly the most limited detector presented here, as it cannot scale to more than a small number of dimensions, though it can work well with small numbers of features.

Part 3

P art 3 covers the practical issues you'll likely encounter when performing outlier detection, such as working with different types of data, very large datasets, time constraints, and memory limits. Part 3 also covers techniques to evaluate individual detectors and the outlier detection system as a whole, including techniques to create synthetic data; it explains how to create ensembles and how to process and interpret the results of outlier detection processes, even where large numbers of outliers are flagged.

In chapter 8, we go over techniques to identify the most useful detectors and best hyperparameters for any given project. Often there are many approaches possible to identify outliers in a dataset, and it can be quite nontrivial to identify the most appropriate tools and settings for your needs.

In chapter 9, we look at working with specific types of data (for example, text data, dates, addresses), encoding categorical data, binning and scaling numeric data, and the distance metrics that are used by many algorithms. Decisions related to these can significantly affect the outliers flagged, so it is important to understand how to set these appropriately.

In chapter 10, we look at handling very large and very small datasets.

In chapter 11, we describe techniques to generate synthetic data, which is often necessary to tune and evaluate outlier detection systems. This also covers simulations, which can be an effective technique to generate high-quality synthetic data for testing but is also a useful outlier detection technique in itself.

In chapter 12, we introduce the idea of collective outliers: cases where no one item is necessarily unusual but sets of items are collectively unusual—for example, where there are unusually many of certain things, where some things are completely absent, where events occur in unusual orders, and so on.

In chapter 13, we describe how to make outlier detection comprehensible so that the outliers flagged can be understood and efficiently investigated.

This presents both outlier detection algorithms that are inherently interpretable and explainable AI techniques to help describe the behavior and output of black box outlier detection tools.

In chapter 14, we cover how to best use multiple detectors (combined in ensembles) to identify the outliers in a dataset.

In chapter 15, we describe how to efficiently process the output of outlier detection routines. Often large numbers of outliers are flagged (even if only a small fraction of the original data). And, even where only moderate numbers of outliers are flagged, it can be advantageous (and sometimes necessary) to be able to evaluate the outliers quickly, to determine which indicate real issues, points of interest, or other things worth investigating further or acting upon.

Evaluating detectors and parameters

This chapter covers

- The effect of the k parameter used with k nearest neighbors and local outlier factor
- Techniques to evaluate detectors
- Evaluating the similarity in scores between detectors
- Using synthetic data to test outlier detectors
- Comparing the train and predict times for detectors under different workloads

Now that we've described a number of outlier detection algorithms, the question you'll face is: Which is the best detector, or the best set of detectors, to use for your projects? We can't answer this completely, as each detector will be more appropriate in some circumstances than others, but we will go through some methods to help compare outlier detectors.

We start, though, by looking not at comparing detectors but at a related and equally important problem: comparing the parameters used for a given detector.

As a specific example, we look at the `n_neighbors` (or k) parameter used by k nearest neighbors (KNN), local outlier factor (LOF), and similar detectors. We then look at evaluating detectors, examining how we can understand what outliers they will find, estimating their accuracy, and examining the level of agreement between detectors. For this, we start with simple (1D and 2D) visualizations and proceed to working with more realistic synthetic datasets. We then examine the time required for different detectors, as this can vary significantly and can be a limiting factor when working with large volumes of data or in environments where data needs to be evaluated very quickly.

8.1   The effect of the number of neighbors

Setting the parameters well for outlier detectors can be difficult but is often important to generate useful results. For this, it's important to understand how the detectors work in terms of their algorithms, but it may also take some experimentation. We take the number of nearest neighbors parameter here as an example. We've seen that KNN, LOF, and variations of these can be excellent detectors, but they also require setting k to an appropriate value. We look at six detectors (introduced in chapters 3, 5, and 6) that require specifying the number of neighbors—KNN, LOF, connectivity-based outlier factor (COF), Local Outlier Probability (LoOP), local distance-based outlier factor (LDOF), and outlier detection using in-degree number (ODIN)—and see how they are affected by the value of k selected.

For this, we use the same synthetic data used in chapter 7. Using synthetic data is less realistic than real-world data but also has major advantages: it allows us to understand the data very clearly and to understand what is and is not being flagged. It also allows us to adjust the data, creating more or fewer clusters, adjusting the relationships between features, the distributions of values, and so on. For this example, we hold the data constant and adjust the k parameter, but the general idea can be applied to other experiments that may help you understand the detectors you are working with.

Adjusting the value of k changes the set of neighbors that points are compared to, and any given point may be more, or less, typical when compared to different sets of neighbors. Using very small values for k can result in high variance (making the model somewhat arbitrary), as the evaluation of each point is based on very few other points. Using a very large k can result in comparing to points that are in different regions and not meaningful to compare to.

8.1.1   2D plots of results

We start by executing each of the six detectors with five different values for k—5, 10, 20, 50, and 100—and plotting the results in 2D scatterplots. This uses a simple 2D dataset, which is useful to start with, but we should be careful as many detectors have parameters, including the `n_neighbors` parameters used for these detectors, which must be tuned to the number of features and/or number of rows. So, while working with 2D datasets is useful to help understand the parameters, it cannot usually be used to tune them. We'll look at this soon, but for now look at the effect of adjusting the parameters in a situation that is easy to understand.

The results are shown in figures 8.1a and 8.1b, showing the top 25 outliers for each detector and value of k. This uses method = "mean" for KNN, which tends to be consistently reliable. The default "largest" (which takes the distance to the kth-nearest neighbor, as opposed to the average distance to the k nearest neighbors) can do very well if k is set optimally but often poorly otherwise.

Good results would likely score the three global outliers and the cluster of five highest, followed by some points along the edges of the three larger clusters, with none in the centers of the clusters scored high.

With KNN we can see sensible, though different, results for most values of k. The other detectors generally do well with k set to at least 20, and using k set between 20 and 50 appears to work best for all detectors. As we have a cluster of 5 that should likely be scored high and a cluster of 50 that should not, any values of k between these will tend to perform better than values outside this range.

In practice, we will not know what sizes of clusters are present, but we can know what sizes of clusters, *if present*, we would consider a small cluster of outliers and which sizes of clusters, by virtue of the clusters being large enough, we would consider inliers. In this case, we may feel that a cluster of perhaps 10 or fewer points could be considered outliers while a cluster of 11 or more could be considered inliers. In this case, setting k to 11 may work well. This heuristic will usually provide some guidance for setting k, though the specific effects of the choice of k can be unintuitive, especially in high dimensions.

Considering ODIN, we see poor results with k = 5. ODIN will flag any records that are among the k nearest neighbors of few other records, and this can be unstable with low values of k. For example, in dense areas such as the center of the largest cluster, we see many records flagged that are close to other records but not within the closest five to any.

The six different detectors work differently, and we expect different results from each. For example, KNN and ODIN use a global measure of outlierness, while LOF, COF, LoOP, and LDOF use a local sense. The global detectors may tend to focus more on the smaller clusters, while the local detectors may focus more on the points on the edges of the clusters. Some may be more suited to your goals or just work better on your data. In all cases, though, we can see that the choice of k affects how the detectors behave, and some values of k produce more sensible results than others.

The optimal values for k for KNNs can be low, even 1 or 2, but for most detectors will rarely be below 10. Less obviously, the optimal values for k will also rarely be high, though intuitively it may make sense to set k very high, even to the full size of the data, with the idea that outliers are points far from most other points, and so it may work to test each point against all other points. However, this tends to not work well in practice, other than where data is a single, consistent cluster. Otherwise, we can see outliers with similar average distances as inliers, as points are compared to points in different clusters, often some distance apart. In this case, the three global outliers and the five points in the small cluster in the bottom-right have about equal average distances to the other points as the inliers do.

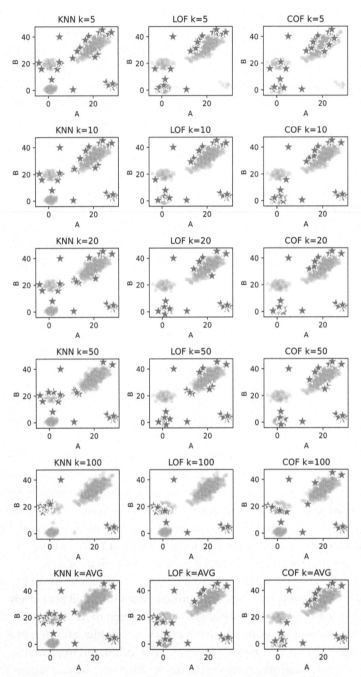

Figure 8.1a   The effect of varying k with the KNN, LOF, and COF outlier detectors. Most detectors do well for most values of k, but all do well when averaging over multiple value of k, even though this includes some poor choices of k, which is inevitable when the ideal k cannot be well estimated.

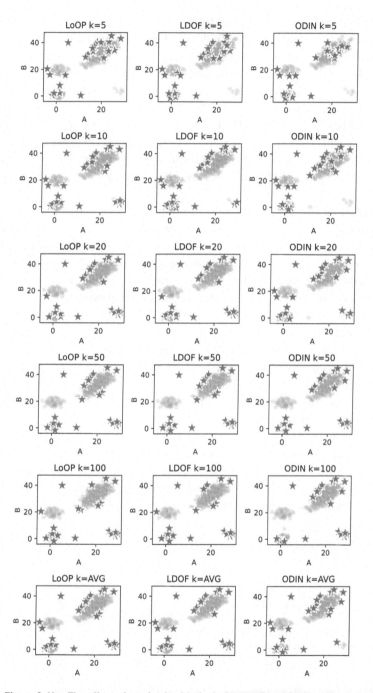

Figure 8.1b   The effect of varying k with the LoOP, LDOF, and ODIN outlier detectors

Using k = 100 produced poor results for KNN (in the sense that it missed two of the three global outliers), though LoOP, LDOF, and ODIN still performed well. It is not shown here, but this dataset also shows, for these detectors, further degradation in performance with higher values of k; all perform poorly by k = 500. Calculating the distances between many pairs of points, as is required with large values of k, is also computationally expensive.

The last row of figures 8.1a and 8.1b shows the results when we use the average over each value of k instead of using a single value of k—that is, where we average the outlier scores calculated when using k = 5, 10, 20, 50, and 100. For all six detectors, we can see strong results in this case, although not necessarily as ideal as some specific values of k used.

Given that plotting the results has only a limited ability to explain the behavior of the detectors (it can be error-prone and will not be able to determine well if outliers in three or more dimensions are detected well), we cannot rely on visualization to best set the parameters and usually need to ensure we use robust means to detect outliers. This is achieved best by averaging over multiple detectors and over multiple parameters for each. In fact, this is the reason that using the "mean" method over the "largest" method tends to work better for KNN: the results are averaged over multiple values of k, which will not usually be optimal but will be robust.

The detectors perform similarly to each other once averaged. They are not precisely the same: KNN emphasized outliers near the cluster in the bottom-left less than the others, for example, but they are very similar. This is however a simple example, and robust detectors in this case will tend to agree more here than in more complex and realistic scenarios, including those with many features.

In listing 8.1, we provide a code snippet with an example of averaging values for a single detector—in this example, the KNN detector. This loops over each value of k, tracks the scores for each iteration, places these in a pandas dataframe, and sums across the rows. Note this, and the following code snippets, are simply examples of code that may be used and are missing some setup so not complete examples.

> **Listing 8.1   Averaging over multiple values of k for the KNN detector**

```
scores_arr = []
k_vals = [5, 10, 20, 50, 100]
for k in k_vals:
    clf = KNN(n_neighbors=k, method='mean')
    clf.fit(df)
    scores_arr.append(clf.decision_scores_)
s_df = pd.DataFrame(scores_arr)
scores_df['KNN Scores'] = s_df.sum(axis=0)
```

Averaging over multiple detectors is also very useful with outlier detection. Listing 8.2 provides an example averaging over all six detectors. This uses a MinMax scaler to put the scores of all detectors on the same scale. This assumes the scores from each detector are placed in a dataframe called `scores_df`.

Listing 8.2   Averaging over multiple detectors

```
scaler = MinMaxScaler()
for col_name in scores_df.columns:
  scores_df[col_name] = \
    scaler.fit_transform(np.array(scores_df[col_name]).reshape(-1, 1))
scores_df['Avg Score'] = scores_df.sum(axis=1)
```

The result of averaging over all six detectors is shown in figure 8.2. This identifies the three global outliers, the small cluster of five, and points around each of the three large clusters, though they have different sizes and densities. While this is true as well for many of the examples in figure 8.1, results will tend to be more reliable when averaging over many detectors rather than using a single detector.

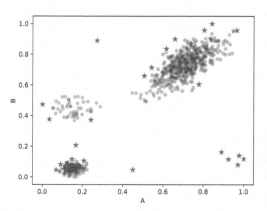

Figure 8.2   The results of averaging over all parameter values for all detectors. The results are quite strong. This scores highest the three global outliers, the small cluster of five, and points around each of the larger clusters.

Playing with this, you may find similar effects varying the number of clusters, relative size and densities of the clusters, associations between features, and the number of dimensions. Some detectors will do better than others, but most can do well as long as the results are averaged over a reasonable range of parameter values. In addition, averaging over many detectors will usually be the most reliable, though we will look at other ways to combine multiple detectors besides averaging, which can be preferable at times, in chapter 14.

8.1.2   1D plots of results

Visualization can be applied to 1D spaces as well, plotting histograms of each numeric feature and count plots of each categorical feature, and highlighting what is flagged in each dimension. Similar to 2D plots, which can only explain outliers in one or two dimensions and not outliers in three or more, 1D plots can only explain outliers in one dimension and not those in two or more. Listing 8.3 shows an example of code to render histograms of feature A in the test data, along with vertical lines to indicate the outliers found. Feature B can be plotted in the same way and is included in figure

8.3. The code assumes the scores for the detectors are averaged in a dataframe called `scores_df` and that a binary field "Outlier" indicates the top 15 outliers.

> **Listing 8.3   Histogram of feature A along with the flagged values**

```
s = sns.histplot(df['A'])
sub_df = scores_df[scores_df['Outlier'] == True]
for i in sub_df.index:
  a_val = df.loc[i, 'A']
  s.axvline(a_val, color='red', linestyle='-.')
plt.show()
```

The output, along with similar output for the "B" feature, is shown in figure 8.3. This shows the top 15 outliers after averaging over the 6 detectors. While the results are clear in higher dimensions (2D in this example, shown in figure 8.2), the outliers cannot be explained by looking at these plots. In this case, all outliers are outliers in two dimensions, and inspecting the data in lower dimensions will be unable to explain the outlier scores. Some appear in the bins on the edges, which may suggest these are 1D outliers, but in figure 8.2 we can see this is not the case. Although plotting can be very useful, this is a limitation of visualization with outlier detection.

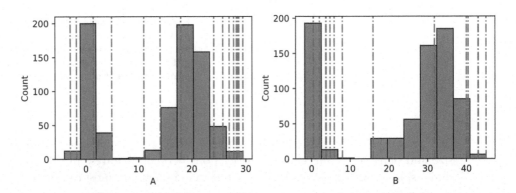

Figure 8.3   Histograms of the two features in the test data, with vertical lines indicating where rows were flagged as outliers. As all outliers in this dataset are multivariate outliers, they have no relationship to the 1D distributions and may appear nonsensical when viewed in this way.

In this example, although 1D plots were not useful, 2D plots were sufficient to explain the outliers, and the visualization process, overall, was quite useful. Similarly, with pairs of categorical features, heatmaps may be created to indicate the proportion of outliers for each pair of unique values in each pair of categorical features. Again, this will work well for outliers in one or two categorical features but will not explain outliers in higher dimensions.

Given this dataset contains only 2D outliers, to better demonstrate 1D plots, we next look at the baseball dataset, introduced in chapter 4. As you may remember, it tended to contain more 1D than multidimensional outliers. In figure 8.4 we show the results on the baseball dataset using an empirical cumulative distribution function (ECOD) detector and plotting the top fifteen outliers in the context of two of the features, RBIs and Home_runs. As the baseball dataset contains some extreme values, and this is what ECOD focuses on, 1D plots are much easier, and more reliable, to analyze here. There are, however, a couple of outliers that are unusual in neither feature shown—vertical lines shown in a fairly typical region of RBIs and again in Home_runs. It would be necessary to examine each feature to fully understand the scores, which is quite manageable for this dataset as there are not very many features.

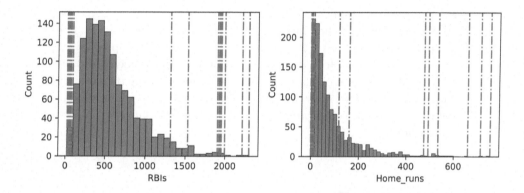

Figure 8.4 Outliers shown along with histograms of two features from the baseball dataset, RBIs and Home_runs. Outliers are shown as dashed vertical lines. In this case, the outliers were detected with ECOD, which flags extreme values, and the outliers are largely at the two extremes for these two features, though not perfectly, as other features also contribute to the outlier scores.

This process of creating simple test data and visualizing it can be quite useful to help understand how outlier detectors work. It can be difficult to extrapolate from here to the real-world data you will work with, but it does allow you to start understanding the detectors and their parameters. It is also possible to adjust the test data to test specific forms of outliers, as was shown in chapter 7, or to be more similar to the real data you have. Creating fully realistic synthetic data can be more difficult, though, and is covered in chapter 11.

8.2 Contour plots

We next look at another method to help understand the behavior of detectors—rendering contour plots, which help make the decision boundaries for detectors clearer. We've seen these before when describing One-class Support Vector Machine (OCSVM) and Extended Isolation Forest, but look now at the code used to generate these. Again, this is limited to 2D spaces, so we should not extrapolate into higher dimensions, but it does help describe how the detectors model data and consequently how they distinguish normal from anomalous regions. For example, we see how detectors score internal outliers compared to extreme values, local compared to global outliers, and so on.

8.2.1 *Examining parameter choices with contour plots*

Many parameters with outlier detectors can be unintuitive—for example, the bandwidth with kernel density estimation (KDE) detectors, the kernel with kernel principal component analysis (KPCA), eps with DBSCAN, nu with OCSVM, and number of bins with histogram-based outlier score (HBOS). Examining contour plots with simple test data can be very helpful in understanding the parameters (though, as with other plots, this cannot usually be used to tune the parameters). For this example, we look again at k. In listing 8.4 we provide an example of code to render the decision boundary of a KNN detector for a wide range of values for k: k = 3, 10, and 300. This uses the same test data as before. The code to create this is provided in chapter 7.

Creating contour plots uses a process where we fit a detector and then pass, instead of actual data, a mesh of a large number of points covering the same range as the data. This allows us to determine the detector's prediction at each location in this space and color the contour to indicate this. We then draw the data on top of the contour as a scatterplot.

Listing 8.4 Code to render a contour plot of a detector

```python
from pyod.models.knn import KNN
import matplotlib.pyplot as plt

def plot_scatterplot(k, ax):
    clf = KNN(n_neighbors=k, method='mean')
    clf.fit(df)

    Z = clf.decision_function(np.c_[xx.ravel(), yy.ravel()])
    Z = Z.reshape(xx.shape)

    ax.contourf(xx, yy, Z, cmap='Blues')
    ax.scatter(data=df, x="A", y='B', color='black')
    ax.set_title(f"k={k}")

df = create_four_clusters_test_data()         ◀──┤ Creates test data
fig, ax = plt.subplots(nrows=1, ncols=3, figsize=(10, 3))

xx, yy = np.meshgrid(                          ◀──┤ Creates a mesh of points
    np.linspace(df['A'].min(), df['A'].max(), 50),    within the range of the data
    np.linspace(df['B'].min(), df['B'].max(), 50))

plot_scatterplot(3, ax[0])                     ◀──┤ Renders contour and scatterplots
plot_scatterplot(10, ax[1])                       of different values of k
plot_scatterplot(300, ax[2])

plt.axis('tight')
plt.legend().remove()
plt.show()
```

In figure 8.5, the contour (background coloring) indicates the regions considered normal and abnormal by the detector, with lighter colors indicating more normal (low outlier scores) regions and the darker colors more abnormal (high outlier scores) regions. We can see that with k = 3, the small cluster of 5 in the bottom right is considered inliers, as each has three close neighbors, while with k = 300 even the cluster of 50 is considered somewhat outlierish given that none of these have 300 close neighbors. This suggests a value for k close to 10 may work best here, though which is preferable depends on your interests, particularly how desirable it is to score the points in a cluster of 50 higher than those in the larger clusters.

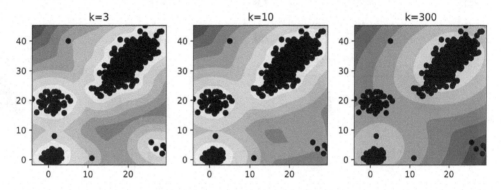

Figure 8.5 Contour plot of the decision boundary of a KNN model using k = 3, 10, and 300. We can see the regions around the small cluster in the bottom-right are considered normal when k = 3 (as each point has this many close neighbors) but not when k is higher. When k is very high, such as 300, even fairly large clusters may receive moderate outlier scores.

8.2.2 Examining detectors with contour plots

The choice of the best detectors for a project is affected heavily by the number of features, distributions, correlations, clustering, and other properties of the data, which can be understood, to some extent, by viewing contour plots for the detectors.

Figure 8.6 shows the results of drawing contour plots using 15 different detectors on the same test dataset. This dataset is clustered, which some detectors are naturally more able to handle. We can see here that Isolation Forest (IF), LOF, OCSVM, KDE, KNN, and Nearest Sample are all able to model the data well. Several other detectors not shown here, such as LDOF, ODIN, Radius, Extended Isolation Forest, distance metric learning, and the clustering methods described in chapter 7 are also able to work well with clustered data.

The Gaussian mixture model (GMM) has fit the data to a single cluster, which results in a suboptimal though usable model. The main finding, though, is that HBOS, ECOD, copula-based outlier detection (COPOD), Cook's Distance (CD), Mahalanobis, and principal component analysis (PCA) are not suited for this data; they were designed for different types of data, where the data is in a single cluster or has strong linear associations.

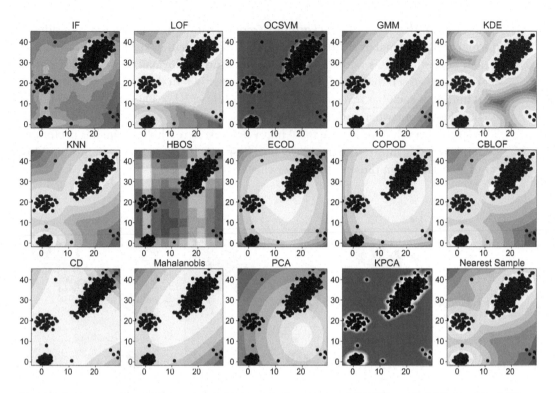

Figure 8.6   Contour plots of 15 detectors (all using default parameters). OCSVM and KPCA fit the data tightly enough that most of the other space is considered highly outlierish. CD and PCA are linear models and do not work well with clustered data. HBOS works based on bins, which can be seen in the checkerboard pattern. ECOD and COPOD test for distance from the overall data center, not considering clusters. This also helps present the similarity in ECOD and COPOD. KNN, CBLOF, and Nearest Sample appear particularly well suited for this data though they are also very similar to each other.

As well as being limited to 2D spaces, contour plots are limited to detectors with separate fit and predict methods. For some detectors, though, there isn't a clear separation. For example, with Convex Hull, the outliers are found by peeling off layers from a specific dataset, and there is no concept of predicting with separate data; it is not possible to pass the detector a mesh of points to evaluate. Entropy, similarly, can evaluate only a given dataset and cannot be fit on one dataset and applied to another. However, almost all detectors have distinct fit and predict steps, and this is rarely a problem otherwise.

8.3   *Visualizing subspaces in real-world data*

Visualization can be used with synthetic data, as in the previous examples, to help describe what the detectors can find in different scenarios, but, more usefully, it can also be used with the actual data: when evaluating detectors on a given dataset, it is possible to plot out pairs of features in the same way. While we should be cautious about assuming any behavior of the detector holds in higher dimensions, it can be a useful way to gain some sense of how well the detector fits the data.

Given that univariate and bivariate outliers (outliers based on pairs of features) will usually be among the most relevant outliers, this has some real value. The visualizations can be tricky to examine, though. When viewing the 1D and 2D plots, there may be values, as in figure 8.3, that are flagged as outliers but appear to be typical: in these cases, they may be flagged erroneously, or they may be outliers in other 1D or 2D spaces or in higher dimensions. Conversely, there may be strong outliers in higher dimensions, and it will not be possible to determine, viewing 1D and 2D plots, if they are detected by any of the detectors.

These plots are most valuable where there are strong outliers visible in 1D and 2D plots; we can see clearly here if these points are scored highly by each detector. Though this will not be the best way to evaluate the detectors (for that, using synthetic data, described shortly, is usually the best), this will be useful to help understand what is working well and what is not with the detectors.

For this, and most of the rest of the chapter, we'll use a dataset we've seen before: the abalone dataset from OpenML. This provides an example of using outlier detection for analysis of biological data. The abalone dataset contains information about the sizes of marine snails. The target column is the age of each specimen, but we leave this out for these examples, using only the independent features and simply searching for anomalous specimens. To collect the data, we may use

```
import pandas as pd
from sklearn.datasets import fetch_openml

data = fetch_openml('abalone', version=1)
df = pd.DataFrame(data.data, columns=data.feature_names)
```

8.3.1 *2D plots of results on real-world data*

Running outlier detectors on the abalone dataset, we are able to plot the results, which can help us get some sense of how well the process is working. See figure 8.7 for a set of plots related to one pair of features, `Diameter` and `Shell_weight`. Ideally, similar plots would be examined for all features and for each set of parameters for each detector. In this case, we show the results for 8 detectors (each using default parameters), with the top 20 outliers found by each. Examining these can help us see where detectors are useful. There are some outliers at the top of the image and one outside the cluster (shown with a circle to highlight this point), which we can see some detectors scoring high and others not. The circled point is flagged in the top 20 by LOF and GMM in this example and not the other detectors. Although detectors score these strong outliers low, they may still be useful for other 2D spaces or for detecting outliers in higher dimensions, and we should not necessarily dismiss these detectors immediately. More important is that each point that is visibly a strong outlier is scored high by at least one detector.

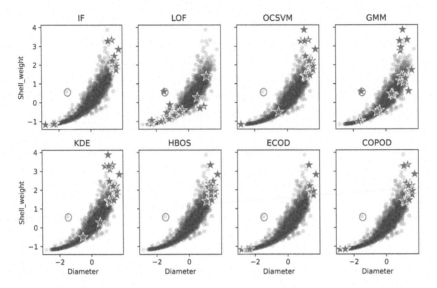

Figure 8.7   2D plots of two features, `Diameter` and `Shell_weight` from the abalone dataset, tested with eight detectors. There are some points that appear to be the strongest outliers, including a point outside the main cluster (circled), which is flagged only by LOF and GMM. In addition, the largest point in the `Shell_weight` dimension, at the top of the plot, which is flagged only by OCSVM, GMM, and KDE. Some detectors, including LOF, GMM, and KDE, flag points within the main cluster, which may be legitimate as they may be outliers in other spaces.

We may, at times, wish to use visualizations like these to understand why specific rows were scored as they were. This may be done either to test the detection process (checking that each row scored highly was visibly anomalous in some subspace) or (once we have confidence in the outlier detection system) simply to see why rows are anomalous. One approach to help see the results more clearly is to take a single record, flagged highly by at least one detector, and examine the point in the context of each 2D space. While this will not explain points that are outliers in higher dimensions, it will explain clearly any outliers that are anomalous in any one or two dimensions.

Plotting pairs of features can be infeasible where there are many features. If the number of features is d, then $d(d-1)/2$ plots would be necessary to visualize every pair of features. In these cases, a sample of the 2D spaces may be plotted to give some insight into what is being scored high and what is not. This can form a basic smoke test to ensure the results are sensible. As these plots are simply useful tools and not definitive tests of the detectors, testing a sample of 2D spaces can be sufficient. Our main purpose is to ensure that, at minimum, all strong univariate and bivariate outliers are scored highly by at least some detectors.

8.3.2   *Contour plots on real-world data*

Here we examine a set of contour plots created on the abalone dataset using the same 15 detectors used for the synthetic dataset in figure 8.6. This is done only for a single

2D space so does not indicate how the detectors perform on the full dataspace; the process is more similar to debugging than to testing but does give some indication of how suited the detectors are for 2D spaces within the dataset.

The abalone dataset appears to have a single cluster and near-linear relationships, which means different detectors are appropriate here than with the synthetic data used earlier. PCA, ECOD, COPOD, and CD work better with this data and appear to be more usable, if not optimal. Again, Nearest Sample performs similarly to KNN and ECOD similarly to COPOD.

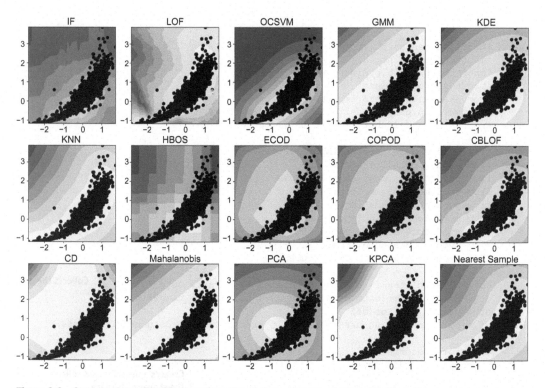

Figure 8.8 Contour plots of two features from the abalone dataset using 15 detectors. Here we can see most detectors working well, though some may be more suitable than others given the types of outliers we are interested in.

8.4 *Correlation between detectors with full real-world datasets*

While visualization is very useful, it is time consuming and limited to lower dimensions. Visualization is also subjective, and so it is important to also use objective measures of the performance of outlier detectors. Given a lack of ground truth and a possibly evolving sense of which outliers are relevant, this is difficult. There are, however, some objective tests we can perform, including measuring the correlations between detectors, accuracy in identifying synthetic outliers, and execution times.

We start here with correlations, continuing with the abalone dataset. The data is collected and evaluated as shown in listing 8.5. We use Spearman correlation, which measures the Pearson correlation between the rank order of the scores. Pearson correlations of the raw scores may not be as useful of a measure, as the distributions of scores can be very different for different detectors, and there is often a strong rank correlation even where there is little linear correlation. This uses a random set of nine detectors. To save space, only the code to collect the scores for IF and LDOF are shown. The others are also in PyOD so are used in the same manner as IF. The LDOF detector is defined as in chapter 7.

Listing 8.5   Testing for correlations in output

```
import pandas as pd
import numpy as np
import matplotlib.pyplot as plt
import seaborn as sns
from sklearn.datasets import fetch_openml
from sklearn.preprocessing import RobustScaler
from sklearn.neighbors import BallTree

from pyod.models.iforest import IForest
from pyod.models.lof import LOF
from pyod.models.ocsvm import OCSVM
from pyod.models.gmm import GMM
from pyod.models.kde import KDE
from pyod.models.knn import KNN
from pyod.models.hbos import HBOS
from pyod.models.ecod import ECOD
from pyod.models.copod import COPOD

data = fetch_openml('abalone', version=1, parser='auto')      ◀── Collects the data
df = pd.DataFrame(data.data, columns=data.feature_names)
df = pd.get_dummies(df)
df = pd.DataFrame(RobustScaler().fit_transform(df), columns=df.columns)

def score_records():
    scores_df = df.copy()
                                                  Creates a detector and collects
    clf = IForest()                         ◀──   the scores it produces
    clf.fit(df)
    scores_df['IF Scores'] = clf.decision_scores_

    # (similar code for LOF, OCSVM, GMM, KDE, HBOS, ECOD, and COPOD
    #  as for IF)

    clf = LDOFOutlierDetector()
    scores_df['LDOF Scores'] = clf.fit_predict(df, k=5)

    return scores_df

scores_df = score_records()

fig, ax = plt.subplots(figsize=(10, 10))
```

```
scores_cols = [x for x in scores_df.columns if "Scores" in x]
m = sns.color_palette("Blues", as_cmap=True)
sns.heatmap((scores_df[scores_cols].corr(method='spearman')),
            cmap=m, annot=True)
plt.show()
```

Finds the
set of
columns
with the
scores

Plots a heatmap
of the correlations

This will find the correlations between the scores. However, finding a meaningful measure of correlation is actually a little more complicated than this. Simply taking the Spearman correlation between the scores of a set of detectors includes the scores that are very low and so includes a lot of irrelevant scores. For example, if two detectors scored a row as 0.02 and 0.42 (both on a scale from 0.0 to 1.0), then the difference is large, but it is not relevant: both consider the record to be an inlier. What's really relevant is the degree of agreement regarding the outliers, not regarding the inliers. This is the agreement as to which records are outliers and agreement in the actual ranking of the outliers.

There are several ways to test this, though there is no single best way. One method is to take only the rows where at least one detector scored the row in their top 5% (or at some such cutoff). We can then calculate the correlation in scores on this subset of the data.

Another method is to take the scores from each detector, determine the rank order, and set any scores below the top 5% (or some cutoff) to 0.0. An example of this is shown in listing 8.6. These will consider the actual rank for any high scores and will treat all low scores equivalently, simply as inliers with rank zero. This assumes the scores_df dataframe contains a row for each row in the data and a column for each detector used.

Listing 8.6   Cleaning the outlier scores to calculate their correlation

```
top_scores_df = scores_df[scores_cols].copy()
for col_name in top_scores_df.columns:
  top_scores_df[col_name] = top_scores_df[col_name].rank()
  top_scores_df[col_name] = top_scores_df[col_name].apply(
      lambda x: x if x > (len(df) * 0.95) else 0.0)
```

In listing 8.7, we look at another method. Here we apply RobustScaler to the scores from all detectors so that the scores are on the same scale. Scaling preserves more of the distribution of scores than using rank order. In this case, MinMax scaling works poorly as some detectors, particularly LOF, can generate a small number of scores far higher than others, and MinMax scaling will push all other values to zero. Here we set all scaled values below 2.0 to 0.0.

Listing 8.7   Alternative approach using RobustScaler

```
from sklearn.preprocessing import RobustScaler

top_scores_df = scores_df[scores_cols].copy()
for col_name in top_scores_df.columns:
  scaler = RobustScaler()
  top_scores_df[col_name] = scaler.fit_transform(
      np.array(top_scores_df[col_name]).reshape(-1, 1))
```

```
  top_scores_df[col_name] =\
    top_scores_df[col_name].apply(lambda x: x if x > 2.0 else 0.0)

fig, ax = plt.subplots(figsize=(10, 10))
m = sns.color_palette("Blues", as_cmap=True)
sns.heatmap(top_scores_df.corr(method='spearman'), cmap=m, annot=True)
plt.show()
```

The output of the robust scaling method is shown in figure 8.9. The results are somewhat similar to when using the full set of scores but are more meaningful. All detectors have some correlation with each other, though with some of it is very weak and approaching zero. ECOD and COPOD have a correlation of 0.75, which highlights the similarity of the two algorithms. HBOS also checks for univariate outliers and is, as expected, also very similar to ECOD and COPOD. LOF and LDOF have the least correlations with the other detectors shown here and have a Spearman correlation of only 0.49 with each other.

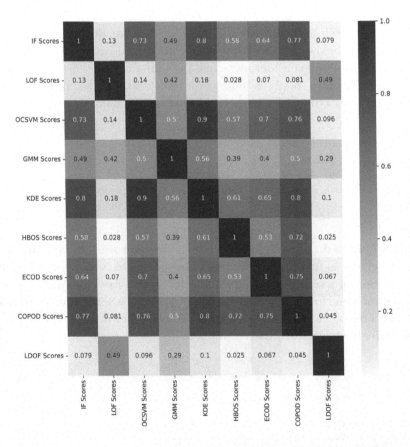

Figure 8.9   Correlations of detector scores taking only the top scores of each detector. Many detectors are highly correlated with each other, though none perfectly. Some, such as LOF and LDOF, are quite different from the others, though all are at least partially correlated.

Where outlier detectors disagree, it's not necessarily that one is more correct than the other, though it may be that one is more suitable for the project at hand. It's also quite possible that they each identify both useful outliers and not-useful outliers, but that they simply identify different of these.

Examining the correlations among detectors can help us create a useful ensemble of detectors where it is not practical to use all detectors. We will take a closer look at creating ensembles of detectors in chapter 14, but in general, we want a set such that each is accurate but different, and that they cover well the range of outliers we are interested in. Assuming reasonably accurate detectors, everything else equal, we would normally take the most diverse detectors, which are those with the lowest correlations between them. Even with sets of detectors that have high correlations, they will not agree completely, and there is likely some value in keeping each, at least when well-tuned for the data for the current project, but there is less value than with diverse detectors. In this case, it may be redundant to include HBOS, ECOD, and COPOD and sufficient to keep only one of these. The same is true of OCSVM and KDE, which have a correlation of 0.90 for this dataset.

8.5 Modifying real-world data

In general, to evaluate machine learning systems, we need some reference, either external or internal to the data, that we can use to gauge the results. With prediction problems, we have an external reference in the labels associated with each record (external in the sense that the labels are not used in the predictions but only to evaluate them). With clustering, we have internal references in the measures of similarity within clusters and dissimilarity between clusters. Usually, though, neither of these is possible with outlier detection—we have no labels and no internal reference to gauge the outliers found. Given this, it can be difficult to evaluate outlier detection systems.

Even where some hand labeling has been performed and labels are available, there will often be too few to accurately measure the accuracy of the detectors. We've seen that visualizing the data can be helpful, but it doesn't provide a complete picture of how well detectors perform, and it is impractical when evaluating dozens of different detectors, each with many different combinations of preprocessing and parameters. Correlations are useful as well but only in combination with estimates of the accuracy.

Further, visualizations and measuring the correlations between detectors can help give a sense of how the detectors perform on the current data but may not suggest well how they will perform on future data, particularly where you are interested in detecting any statistical outliers, as opposed to a more restricted, specific type of outlier.

In most projects, using synthetic data can be the best means to evaluate the system—to test that the system both covers the sorts of outliers you wish to find and that it ranks them as you would wish. Using a good collection of synthetic data can also test if the system can be expected to do so with future data. Using synthetic data, we deliberately insert outliers of the sort we would be interested in into the data and test if they are detected well. This can cover a wide range of outliers, including outliers based on three or more features (which are impossible to test for using visualization techniques). We will take a look now at how synthetic data can be created and used for this purpose.

8.5.1 Adding known anomalies

We've looked already at one method to generate synthetic data, where we determine the mean and standard deviation for each feature and generate random data from a Normal distribution based on these (a similar method may be used for categorical features, selecting each class proportional to its frequency in the training data). In chapter 3, we saw an example of a Real versus Fake detector, where the fake data was generated in this way. The same technique was also used to generate the synthetic data used by the distance metric learning outlier detector in chapter 7.

For those (and for the current purpose) testing detectors, many other methods to generate synthetic data may be used, which we will look at in chapter 11. Here we introduce another simple and very effective method. For this, we take a copy of the real data and modify each row in some way. This process is sometimes referred to as *doping*. One tool to support this process is the DopingOutlierTester (https://mng.bz/j0Ka). However, the process is straightforward, and we provide a simple example here, shown in listing 8.8.

In this case, we modify one cell in each row, selected randomly. If the value is above the median value, it is set to a random value below the median and if below, to a random value above the median. With this form of modification, the individual values remain typical, but the values will deviate from the normal associations between the features. This is only an example; the data may be modified in any way that can simulate outliers you may be interested in identifying. Three detectors, IF, LOF, and ECOD, are fit with the real data and tested on both the real and doped data. This tests the ability of a detector to catch anomalies that are similar to the doped records in future data. Ideally, during testing the detectors will score the doped records consistently higher than the real records.

It is also possible to use the doped data in another manner, which is to train and test on data that includes some small number of doped records (using the same data for training and testing). This is a different form of test but also very useful; it allows us to test our ability to detect outliers in the current data. When doing this, it is important to not include more than a few doped records in the training data, as we do not wish to affect the overall distributions of the data. Taking this approach, we would check that the doped versions of records are scored higher than their original versions.

In this example, we create an equal number of doped records as there are real, but, as the doped data is used here for testing only, any large number of test records will work well.

Listing 8.8 Evaluation of detectors using a doping process

```
import pandas as pd
import numpy as np
from sklearn.datasets import fetch_openml
from sklearn.preprocessing import RobustScaler
import matplotlib.pyplot as plt
```

```
import seaborn as sns
from pyod.models.iforest import IForest
from pyod.models.lof import LOF
from pyod.models.ecod import ECOD

data = fetch_openml('abalone', version=1)                    ◄──┘ Collects the data
df = pd.DataFrame(data.data, columns=data.feature_names)
df = pd.get_dummies(df)
df_orig = df.copy()
df = pd.DataFrame(RobustScaler().fit_transform(df), columns=df.columns)

clf = IForest()                                    ◄───┐ Uses an IF to
clf.fit(df)                                            │ clean the data
if_scores = clf.decision_scores_
top_if_scores = np.argsort(if_scores)[::-1][:10]
clean_df = df.loc[[x for x in df.index if x not in top_if_scores]].copy()

doped_df = df.copy()                               ◄───┐ Creates a set
for i in doped_df.index:                               │ of doped records
  col_name = np.random.choice(df.columns)
  med_val = clean_df[col_name].median()
  if doped_df.loc[i, col_name] > med_val:
    doped_df.loc[i, col_name] = \
      clean_df[col_name].quantile(np.random.random()/2)
  else:
    doped_df.loc[i, col_name] = \
      clean_df[col_name].quantile(0.5 + np.random.random()/2)

def test_detector(clf, title, df, clean_df,
        doped_df, ax):                             ◄───┐ Tests a specified
  clf.fit(clean_df)                                    │ detector
  df = df.copy()
  doped_df = doped_df.copy()
  df['Scores'] = clf.decision_function(df)
  df['Source'] = 'Real'
  doped_df['Scores'] = clf.decision_function(doped_df)
  doped_df['Source'] = 'Doped'
  test_df = pd.concat([df, doped_df])
  sns.boxplot(data=test_df, orient='h', x='Scores', y='Source', ax=ax)
  ax.set_title(title)

fig, ax = plt.subplots(nrows=1, ncols=3, sharey=True, figsize=(10, 3))  ◄──┐
test_detector(IForest(), "IForest", df, clean_df, doped_df, ax[0])         │
test_detector(LOF(), "LOF", df, clean_df, doped_df, ax[1])                 │
test_detector(ECOD(), "ECOD", df, clean_df, doped_df, ax[2])     Plots each │
plt.tight_layout()                                                detector │
plt.show()
```

The results are shown in figure 8.10, which shows how the detectors score the doped compared to the real records. We can see that for this type of outlier, LOF performs the best, as it is best able to assign consistently higher scores to doped than to real records. IF works well, though not as well, and ECOD is not useful here. This is as expected, as no extreme values were added in this example.

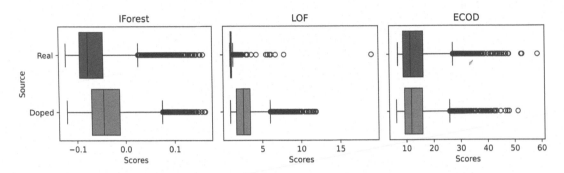

Figure 8.10   Scores for real versus doped records when tested on IF, LOF, and ECOD. For this form of doping, LOF performs very well and IF reasonably well. As no extreme values were added in this example, ECOD makes no distinction between the real and doped data.

We can continue in this way, testing other forms of doping, such as modifying the cells to a larger or smaller degree, modifying more cells per row, modifying specific features, and so on. One advantage of doping is it allows us to focus on the sorts of outliers we are most interested in detecting.

To analyze more closely how each detector is able to distinguish real from doped records, we can again use 2D plots, similar to the previous examples. In figure 8.11, we examine one detector, LOF, and two features, Length and Diameter. In the first three plots, we show the real data, and the next three show the doped data. In both cases, we plot both those flagged (using 0.5 as the contamination rate, as we tested with an equal number of real and doped records) and not flagged. With the real data, a fair number are flagged, and it's not clear from this if they are reasonably outliers in another space or not. What's more relevant is the doped data. We see that some doped data strays from the main diagonal pattern between these two features and that they are consistently flagged, though some along the main diagonal are flagged as well, possibly erroneously. As in the previous cases, the main goal is to determine if the points that should be considered strong outliers are, in fact, flagged. The most important plot here is the Doped Unflagged plot; we want to check that there are few points here other than in regions that are typical for real data, which is the case.

Testing with doping will provide a strong sense of which outliers are being detected and which are not. For example, running repeatedly with specific forms of doping (such as focusing on a specific set of features, modified in a specific way), we can see which detectors (and parameters) score the doped records highest and which do not. This method also allows us to deliberately modify data to have outliers in any number of dimensions and with any degree of deviation from the norm. Experimenting with doping in this way can take some time, though in most cases we would use visualization, if at all, only for spot checking and not extensively. An exception may be where the data is particularly difficult to model.

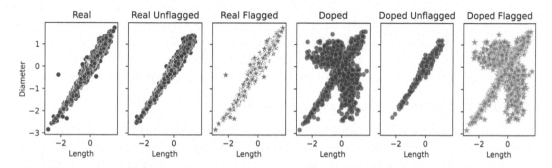

Figure 8.11 Examining 2D plots of the rows flagged for real vs doped data. The first three panes show the real data. Of these, some are flagged, which may be due to anomalies in other features. One flagged point is off the main diagonal and is likely correct to flag. The doped data includes many values similar to the real data but also unusual combinations of Length and Diameter. Of the more typical records within the doped data, some are flagged and some are not, but the unusual points are consistently flagged, which is the most important to check.

8.5.2 Evaluation metrics

As with prediction problems, it's important to be able to determine the most accurate detectors for a given problem using a single numeric score. This is possible where we create synthetic data that can be assumed to be anomalous, as is the case of doping. That is, using synthetic data provides a ground-truth label we can use to evaluate detectors.

Although the real data remains unlabeled (we don't know which records within it are outliers), we do know the majority of the real data are inliers and that the majority of the doped records are outliers. This allows us to assign a binary label to the data and test the detectors using an objective measure, as is routinely done with prediction models. The same set of metrics used for binary classification may then be used for outlier detection: precision, recall, F1 score, Brier score, and so on. The most commonly used metric for outlier detection is the area under an ROC curve (AUROC). This tests that the scores are well-ranked, with the scores for outliers higher than those for inliers. A detector that perfectly ranks all outliers higher than all inliers will have a score of 1.0. One behaving randomly (half the time giving outliers higher scores than inliers and half the time the reverse) will have a score of 0.5.

Another metric that is often useful for outlier detection, though not provided by scikit-learn, is the precision at k. This is useful, for example, where people will investigate the records that are given the top k scores; in this case, we would be concerned with how many of these k records actually are outliers, with this being, ideally, all k. A variation on this, which may be more suitable depending on the importance of false positives compared to false negatives, is to determine the number of records that must be examined to identify k true outliers.

In general, it is usually best to tune a system to have a strong AUROC score, with the scores being well-ranked for the records, before tuning the system to optimize metrics related to binary labels, such as precision, recall, F1 score, and precision at k. Once the system has records ranked well, appropriate thresholds can then be set on the scores to provide the most useful binary labels for your context, if any are needed. An exception may be for precision at k where k is quite small. In this case, it may not be as relevant how well the records are ranked overall, given only a small number will be investigated.

8.5.3   *Evaluating detectors using accuracy metrics*

An example using doped data to evaluate two detectors, IF and LOF, is shown in listing 8.9, taking the AUROC scores. This provides an objective measure of the detectors and is often the best means to select detectors, as well as to tune the hyperparameters, select the preprocessing, feature engineering, and other decisions. This assumes listing 8.8 has been executed.

Listing 8.9   Evaluating detectors using AUROC

```
from sklearn.metrics import roc_auc_score

test_df = pd.concat([df, doped_df])
y_true = [0]*len(df) + [1]*len(doped_df)

clf = IForest()
clf.fit(clean_df)
y_pred = clf.decision_function(test_df)
if_auroc = roc_auc_score(y_true, y_pred)

clf = LOF()
clf.fit(clean_df)
y_pred = clf.decision_function(test_df)
lof_auroc = roc_auc_score(y_true, y_pred)
```

This produces a score of 0.69 for IF and 0.93 for LOF. Consistent with the boxplots in figure 8.10, IF is moderately accurate and LOF very accurate, though not perfect. However, as the doped data is not necessarily strictly more anomalous than the original data (some real data will be anomalous, and some doped data will be typical), we do not expect doped scores to be entirely higher than the original records.

When using this means to identify the best hyperparameters, we will usually want to find a range, not a single value, where the detector appears to perform well. Anomalous real data may not be entirely the same as the doped data, and it is best to create a robust system using a range of hyperparameters where possible.

8.5.4   *Adjusting the training size used*

Often in outlier detection we have a very large collection of data, and it may be slow and unnecessary to fit the model using all the data. We may also have situations where the detector will need to be updated in production regularly to model more recent data and we wish to limit the time required for this. The more data used, the stronger the model will be, but there can be diminishing returns after a moderate amount of data is used, and the training times for some detectors can be significant. In addition, with detectors such as KNN and LOF that use lazy evaluation (that compare each record during the predict step to the set of records stored during training), the fewer records stored during training, the faster prediction will be.

Given this, we may wish to evaluate the effect of reducing the training size on the model. As part of this, we can view a collection of 2D plots, either scatterplots with results shown or contour plots, covering each pair of features and check at which levels of training data the plots are sensible. This can only form part of the evaluation, and objective tests using synthetic data will be the best test, but this can help us understand how the detectors perform when trained on different amounts of data.

Figure 8.12 shows contour plots of the decision boundary created by an LOF trained on 50, 100, and 500 rows of the test dataset. In this case, there is a noticeable improvement as we increase the training size, though the accuracy when using 100 may be sufficient for some purposes.

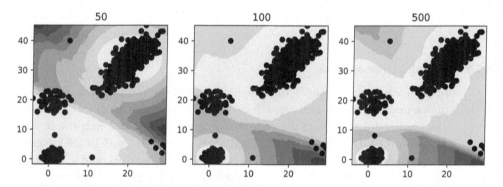

Figure 8.12 The decision function for LOF given training sizes of 50, 100, and 500 records. The quality improves with more training records, but it is possibly useable at 50 or 100 depending on the accuracy required.

The best way to determine the effect of adjusting the training size is to test with synthetic data. The following listing provides a function that can be used to train the model on a sample of the `clean_df` dataframe (created in listing 8.8) and then test the accuracy of the model on the full set of real and doped data, measuring the AUROC.

Listing 8.10 Testing adjusting the training set size

```
def test_training_size(n_rows):
  clf = LOF()
  clf.fit(clean_df.sample(n=n_rows))
  y_pred = clf.decision_function(test_df)
  lof_auroc = roc_auc_score(y_true, y_pred)
  return lof_auroc
```

The results, calling this function with n_rows set to 50, 100, 250, 500, 1,000, and 2,000, are plotted in figure 8.13. At 50, the AUROC is only 0.55 (slightly better than chance). At 100, it is 0.62. By 500 it reaches 0.89, with only small (though possibly important) increases given 1,000 or 2,000 rows for training.

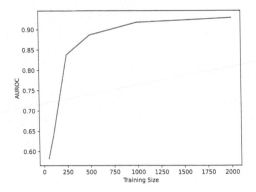

Figure 8.13   AUROC versus training size for the abalone dataset using LOF with default parameters

8.5.5   *Adding extreme values*

In some cases, the presence of extreme values in the training data can create swamping or masking effects and can affect the ability to ability to detect other outliers. We can test for this by varying the code in listing 8.8, in this case keeping IF and LOF but replacing ECOD with clustering-based local outlier factor (CBLOF). Executing this, we get AUROC scores of 0.71 for IF, 0.93 for LOF (as before), and 0.79 for CBLOF. We can repeat this, adding the following code prior to fitting the detectors:

```
for i in range(10):
    col_name = np.random.choice(df.columns)
    max_val = clean_df[col_name].max()
    clean_df.loc[i, col_name] = max_val * 100.0
```

This will add 10 extreme values into the training data. After adding this and again executing the code, we get AUROC scores virtually the same for IF and LOF, but the AUROC for CBLOF drops to 0.52, which is equivalent to a random guess. CBLOF is dependent on clustering, which can be severely affected by outliers. In most cases cleaning the data (removing strong outliers) prior to fitting will ensure the models are robust in this way. However, it is worth testing this to ensure the cleaning process is sufficient and that the detectors are robust.

8.6   *Testing with classification datasets*

A method commonly used to evaluate outlier detectors is to test with datasets that were originally intended for classification, as we saw with the KDD Cup dataset in chapter 5. These are usually datasets with one or more minority classes that are far less frequent than the majority classes and so may be considered outliers. It's also possible to use more balanced datasets and down-sample one or more classes such that they are made rare enough to be considered outliers. The idea is that, given these classes are rare, they should be detectable by outlier detectors. This will not work perfectly; often there are rows in the majority classes that are, in some senses, as rare or rarer than the rows in the minority classes. But it works surprising well and is often used in research to compare detectors. In fact, any reports you may see indicating how detectors compare to each other were most likely created using this form of testing.

While this is a reasonable (if somewhat flawed) way to determine if outlier detectors work well generally and is likely the most objective (using synthetic data is open to abuse when there is an incentive to publish results), it will not usually be the most relevant test for any specific outlier detection project. For this, what's necessary are not the detectors that usually work best but the detectors that work best for your current problem.

For that, hand-labeling data and experimenting with doping the data will usually be your best approach. Your dataset and your interest in finding outliers will be unique, and any detector that performs well, even if not among the top-performing generally, may be the most suitable for your project.

Evaluation on classification datasets, though, does indicate which detectors tend to, on average, perform best, which can be a good starting point, especially when it is only practical to test a small number of detectors. This is particularly true when the detectors have been tested on many datasets (and usually many variations on each dataset: using different down-sampling, different feature selection, adding random noise features, and so on). For example, on most projects, if you work with standard detectors that require little tuning, such as IF and ECOD, you will likely tend to do reasonably well, though may still miss many outliers that may be more relevant for you.

A good resource for classification datasets used to evaluate outlier detectors is the Outlier Detections DataSets dataset collection (https://odds.cs.stonybrook.edu/). The tabular datasets there are all found in the OpenML collection in any case, but this is a well-curated set, and the tables here are often used in research.

Another good resource for comparisons of detectors is the Anomaly Detection Benchmark project (https://github.com/Minqi824/ADBench), which was created to evaluate many detectors on many datasets in a consistent and comparable way. Their main finding is that none of the evaluated detectors is clearly better-performing than the others. The detectors are limited to those in PyOD, and so other detectors, for example those described in chapter 7, may perform better in some cases, though, again, none would consistently outperform the others.

8.7   *Timing experiments*

In many scenarios, the time to fit and to execute the models can be very relevant. Time is not always a concern: some datasets are small, and the time required is insignificant regardless, and in some cases, finding a complete and accurate set of outliers is significantly more important than the time required. For one-off outlier detection projects as well, time may be less of a concern as it needs only to be incurred once. But for projects where it will be necessary to predict on new data as it arrives, especially in real-time environments—where data may arrive rapidly, and it may be necessary to generate predictions quickly—time can be a very important consideration.

In environments where it is necessary to evaluate all data quickly, it may be reasonable to trade off some accuracy for speed or to limit the system to detecting simple outliers, such as univariate extreme values. Balancing accuracy with performance requires some estimation of the accuracy (likely best found from doping experiments) and estimates of the execution times under different, realistic workloads.

In ongoing projects, it can also be necessary to retrain from time to time, though this is typically done far less frequently than predicting and can be done offline, where the time required is likely still relevant but much less so than the prediction times.

Here we look at one method to estimate the time required for different potential workloads taking the current dataset and duplicating it several times. Given estimates of how much data will arrive and be used by the model, we can then estimate both the fit and predict times for future workloads.

In this example, shown in listing 8.11, we time 12 detectors (the identical process can be done with any other set of detectors), with 6 different sizes of data, though more sizes would typically be tested for a more complete picture of the times required. This helps us see how the detectors vary from each other in terms of fit and predict times and how they are affected by the number of rows.

Listing 8.11   Sample of code to time fit and predict times

```python
import time
from pyod.models.iforest import IForest
from pyod.models.lof import LOF
from pyod.models.ocsvm import OCSVM
from pyod.models.gmm import GMM
from pyod.models.kde import KDE
from pyod.models.knn import KNN
from pyod.models.hbos import HBOS
from pyod.models.ecod import ECOD
from pyod.models.copod import COPOD
from pyod.models.abod import ABOD
from pyod.models.cblof import CBLOF
from pyod.models.pca import PCA

def time_detector(clf):
    start_time = time.process_time()
    clf.fit(test_df)
    iteration_fit_results_arr.append(time.process_time() - start_time)

    start_time = time.process_time()
    clf.decision_function(test_df)
    iteration_predict_results_arr.append(time.process_time() - start_time)

data = fetch_openml('abalone', version=1)          ◀——┘ Collects the data
df = pd.DataFrame(data.data, columns=data.feature_names)
df = pd.get_dummies(df)
df = pd.DataFrame(RobustScaler().fit_transform(df), columns=df.columns)
```

```
fit_results_arr = []
predict_results_arr = []

for multiplier in [1, 5, 10, 15, 20, 25]:
  test_df = pd.concat([df]*multiplier)
  iteration_fit_results_arr = [len(test_df)]
  iteration_predict_results_arr = [len(test_df)]

  time_detector(clf = IForest())
  time_detector(clf = LOF())
  time_detector(clf = OCSVM())
  time_detector(clf = GMM())
  time_detector(clf = KDE())
  time_detector(clf = KNN())
  time_detector(clf = HBOS())
  time_detector(clf = ECOD())
  time_detector(clf = COPOD())
  time_detector(clf = ABOD())
  time_detector(clf = CBLOF())
  time_detector(clf = PCA())

  fit_results_arr.append(iteration_fit_results_arr)
  predict_results_arr.append(iteration_predict_results_arr)

col_names = ['Number Rows', 'IF', 'LOF', 'OCSVM',
             'GMM', 'KDE', 'KNN', 'HBOS', 'ECOD',
             'COPOD', 'ABOD', 'CBLOF', 'PCA']
fit_results_df = \
        pd.DataFrame(fit_results_arr, columns=col_names)
display(fit_results_df)

predict_results_df = pd.DataFrame(predict_results_arr, columns=col_names)
display(predict_results_df)
```

Initializes arrays of fit and predict times

Loops through different sizes of data

Creates a dataset of the specified size

Times both fit and predict using each detector

The training times are shown in table 8.1 and the predict times in table 8.2, measured in seconds and running on Google Colab. In all cases, the times do increase as the row counts increase, but in most cases for the detectors shown remain small. There are some exceptions. Particularly in the last rows, where we have larger numbers of rows, we can see significantly larger fit and predict times for OCSVM and KDE compared to the others. As indicated in chapter 5, OCSVM can be tuned to execute more quickly; this is simply using the default settings for each detector.

Table 8.1 Fit times for 12 detectors on 6 sizes of data

# Rows	IF	LOF	OCSVM	GMM	KDE	KNN	HBOS	ECOD	COPOD	ABOD	CBLOF	PCA
4,177	0.8	0.2	1.9	0.1	2.1	0.1	0.0	0.0	0.0	0.7	1.4	0.0
20,885	1.9	1.3	42.6	0.1	55.9	0.7	0.0	0.1	0.1	2.3	2.4	0.0
41,770	3.2	3.2	152.7	0.3	235.6	1.1	0.0	0.1	0.1	3.9	3.1	0.1
62,655	3.8	5.5	350.5	0.4	819.5	1.2	0.0	0.2	0.2	7.3	3.6	0.1
83,540	5.5	8.5	605.5	0.4	1361.8	1.9	0.1	0.4	0.3	8.7	4.0	0.1
104,425	6.7	5.5	1049.1	0.5	2055.5	2.8	0.1	0.4	0.3	11.9	4.5	0.1

Table 8.2   Predict times for the same cases

# Rows	IF	LOF	OCSVM	GMM	KDE	KNN	HBOS	ECOD	COPOD	ABOD	CBLOF	PCA
4,177	0.2	0.2	0.5	0.0	2.0	0.4	0.0	0.0	0.0	0.5	0.0	0.0
20,885	0.8	1.0	13.9	0.0	54.5	1.8	0.0	0.2	0.1	2.0	0.0	0.0
41,770	1.5	2.3	55.3	0.1	234.9	4.1	0.0	0.3	0.3	5.1	0.0	0.0
62,655	2.2	4.6	119.9	0.0	777.3	7.0	0.0	0.5	0.5	6.1	0.0	0.0
83,540	2.4	3.1	204.2	0.0	1382.5	9.3	0.0	0.7	0.6	9.1	0.0	0.1
104,425	3.1	4.0	318.6	0.1	2111.9	12.1	0.0	0.8	0.8	12.0	0.0	0.1

It is interesting that for some detectors, such as KNN, predict times are longer than training times, while for others, such as IF and CBLOF, the training time is longer. This is as expected, as KNNs do little during the fit process but evaluate many distances between records during predictions. IF and CBLOF, on the other hand, both do significant up-front work during training, with IF constructing the trees and CBLOF performing the clustering. During prediction, IF simply passes the records through the trees and CBLOF simply compares the points to the nearest large cluster center.

The prediction times of 10 of the detectors are shown in figure 8.14. OCSVM and KDE are not shown here as they are considerably slower for this data and the current parameters and would obscure the results for the other detectors. For those shown, some are slower than others, but none are excessively slow.

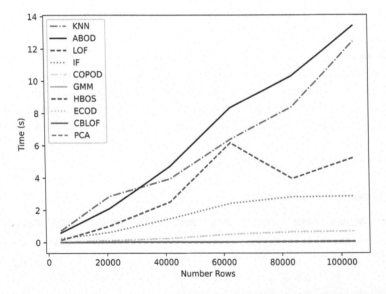

Figure 8.14   Predict times for 10 detectors on various sizes of the abalone dataset run on Google Colab. Times are in seconds. Of these, the times are either constant or linear in the number of rows. The legend is ordered from slowest to fastest. For these, the times remain short, with the largest, KNN and ABOD, taking only 12s.

Where the time required is important, it may be useful to perform experiments such as these, though in a manner most relevant to your project. For other datasets, we may see quite different results; the number and type of the features can make a large difference, along with the parameters used. For example, with KNN, LOF, and other detectors that specify the number of nearest neighbors, the more used, the slower the process will be. OCSVM and KDE were the slowest in this experiment, with KDE requiring over 2,000s (about 35 minutes) to predict with the largest dataset. The time for KDE is affected by the `leaf_size` and bandwidth parameters, and the times can be reduced by adjusting these. PyOD does not allow setting the shape of the kernel, though scikit-learn's `KernelDensity` class does, which also affects fit and prediction times.

As well as estimating train and predict times, it is also useful to perform similar tests (adjusting the size of the training data and performing train and predict) to help tune the parameters. Many parameters, including the `n_neighbors` parameter used by KNN, LOF, and so on, depend on the number of rows in the training data so will need to be tuned to match this. For example, if a good range of values for k for 10,000 rows is 40 to 70; then for 20,000 rows, the preferable range may be closer to 80 to 140 (where the number of rows doubles, the number of rows best to compare to approximately doubles), but this is best to determine experimentally, testing both the effect on accuracy metrics with doped data and the execution times. As previously, plots may be used to assist with this.

In general, to estimate the accuracy and the time required for your system, it's useful to run experiments such as those covered in this chapter. These sorts of tests can be used to help assess other steps in the outlier detection process as well in terms of how the detectors work, the estimated accuracy, the agreement between detectors, and the estimated times required under high loads. We can test, for example, the results of other modeling decisions, including filling null values, encoding categorical features, binning, and scaling data.

Summary

- The parameters used by detectors, such as the k value used by KNN, LOF, COF, LoOP, LDOF, and ODIN, can make a significant difference in the accuracy of a detector.

- To make a model more robust, it is preferable to use multiple parameter values and average over these.

- Using synthetic data can be useful to get a general sense of how outlier detectors behave, as we can create very controlled test scenarios and test cases that we believe may be faced by the detector but are not necessarily present in the current data.

- Examining the detectors in 2D subspaces can be useful, but we need to be careful not to overemphasize any insights from this, as they will not necessarily extend to higher dimensions.

- Contour plots are also useful but also apply only to 2D spaces, so they have limited, but real, value in understanding the detectors and parameter choices.

- Using visualization is more akin to debugging than evaluating, though it can be a part of the evaluation process where we check that visibly strong outliers are detected.

- It can be useful to measure the correlations between detectors. In doing so, we should be careful not to include the scores for inliers in the calculations. The correlations between the highest scores are the most relevant.

- Synthetic data created by modifying (doping) real data can be particularly useful to test outlier detectors, and it allows us to evaluate in a meaningful way how well the detectors work on the current data.

- The AUROC metric is widely used in outlier detection but can only be used where there is a ground truth, which is often only possible with synthetic data.

- The time required for fitting and/or predicting can limit the set of detectors, parameters, number of training rows used, or other decisions.

- In assessing execution times, we need to consider fit and predict times separately.

- Some outlier detectors are considerably faster than others. The parameters also affect the fit and predict times.

- If the model will be put in production and may face larger workloads than the data currently available, it is important to test fitting and predicting with large datasets.

- When fitting the models with different numbers of rows, there may be different ranges for the parameters that should be used, which can be determined through testing with doped data.

Working with specific data types

This chapter covers

- Handling null values
- Working with email addresses, phone numbers, and other special data types
- Working with dates and text data
- Encoding categorical data
- Binning and scaling numeric data
- Distance metrics for numeric and categorical data

Different types of data require handling in different ways. The data we've looked at so far has been primarily either numeric or categorical, but much real-world data can be of other types, such as dates or text, and often quite specific data types, such as phone numbers, addresses, URLs, IP addresses, and so on. These provide opportunities for identifying outliers that don't tend to exist with categorical or numeric data, but to work with them, we do need to process them into a format that outlier detectors can work with, which usually means converting them to numeric or categorical formats.

Once all the features are in these formats, we have decisions related to how to best further preprocess the data, which usually consists of categorical encoding, binning numeric fields, and scaling. We've seen examples of these previously. However, it can be tricky to determine the appropriate preprocessing method in most cases. We take a closer look at these here.

We start by looking at handling missing data. Most detectors require that any None or NaN values be filled, but it's not always clear the best way to do this. We then look at some examples of specific data types that are fairly common to see in tabular data, followed by examining various preprocessing methods. We end with a look at distance metrics and how to best represent the distances between rows.

9.1   *Null values*

Handling null values in outlier detection is very much like with other machine learning tasks, though it can sometimes be more important in outlier detection, as the presence of nulls may have some significance. For example, if null values are very rare, or the combination of null values in one column with certain other values in another column is very rare, this may be a useful form of outlier.

There are two common sources of null values. The first is where the values are legitimately null. For example, where a table has features for "Number of Children" and "Age of Eldest Child," if the number of children is 0, we would expect the age of the eldest child to be null. In fact, any other value may suggest a data quality problem. Here, the null value simply means "not applicable." If rare, it may still be a statistical outlier, but it does not suggest a data error.

The second source is data collection problems. In these cases, there is a true value, but it is missing from the data. For example, if the number of children is three, but the age of the eldest child is stored as Null, there is a true age of the eldest child, but it is unknown. This can occur when creating the dataset if it was impossible to access certain information, or it may result from an error processing data—for example, in joining or appending tables.

With this type of null value, there may be some bias in where they appear: it may be nonrandom where data is missing. For example, temperature sensors may tend to fail at very low or very high temperatures, leading to a disproportionate number of missing values in these cases. There is, then, information value in the null values themselves, although the actual temperature is still unknown. Even though we will need to fill the null values, it is useful to keep a record that they were there.

How outlier detection projects execute can vary, but often we may wish to first identify the data artifacts (where the values stored in the data are not the true values), and then separate these and identify the statistical outliers in the remaining data. In this case, we may wish to first separate the cases where the nulls are the results of data artifacts. These rows may be removed or simply noted and kept in the data in order to identify any other anomalies in these rows.

With both not-applicable cases and nulls due to errors, the null values will need to be replaced for most outlier detectors for any further outlier detection. In the case of numeric outlier detectors, these would be replaced with numeric values, and for categorical detectors with categorical values. How we replace the null values, though, may vary depending on what we believe the source is. For this, we will usually, as with all data science projects, require some exploratory analysis and likely some input from domain experts.

Examining the data for nulls, and patterns with the nulls, is a good place to begin any examination of data. Useful packages include missingno (https://github.com/ResidentMario/missingno) and DataConsistencyChecker (https://mng.bz/WV5g).

Note that if you are using pandas, there is a distinction between None and NaN values, and your data may contain both. It may be worth distinguishing between the two if they indicate different sources or different types of issues. In addition, missing data may appear in the form of empty strings, zero values, or special values people have inserted in the data to indicate unknown values. You may see "n/a," "none," "XXXXX," or similar values, which may be worth flagging.

Usually we will leave the dataset as is, simply replacing the null values with valid values, though we may remove some entire rows or features if we feel they will bias the outlier detection process. For example, if a feature has many null values and these appear to be random, but do not suggest data quality problems in the other features, this feature may not help, and may even hinder, our ability to find the unusual records. We can simply note this, remove the feature, and proceed with outlier detection in the other features.

In terms of what we replace null values with, there are two main choices:

- Use a value very distinct from the other values to maintain the uniqueness of the null value. In the case of categorical columns, this can be a new value not used otherwise. In the case of numeric columns, it is possible to use a very small or very large value.
- Use a typical value, such as the mode or median value in the feature. This may be done, for example, if we've already identified the null as an outlier and we wish to effectively remove this anomaly from the data to proceed with finding other outliers.

It's also common to add a second, binary column mirroring each original column to indicate if the original value was null or not. Here the nulls in the original column would be filled with a typical value. This allows us to keep the signal in the null values while still replacing them with values the detector can accept. We may further wish to add a column to indicate the number of null values per row, which can help flag rows where there are an unusual number of nulls. An example is shown in listing 9.1. This uses pandas's `isna()` method, which checks for both None and NaN.

Listing 9.1 Filling None and NaN values

```
import pandas as pd
import numpy as np

df = pd.DataFrame({"A": [1, 2, np.NaN, 4, 5, None],
                   "B": ['A', 'B', None, "B", "B", "F"]})
```

```
df_filled = df.copy()
df_filled['A Null'] = df['A'].isna()
df_filled['B Null'] = df['B'].isna()
df_filled['Num Null'] = df.isna().sum(axis=1)
df_filled['A'] = df['A'].fillna(df['A'].median())
df_filled['B'] = df['B'].fillna(df['B'].mode()[0])
print(df_filled)
```

If there are many null values and there may be some pattern to the nulls, one form of outlier detection that may be executed quickly, in addition to other tests, is to convert the data to a set of binary columns indicating if the data is missing or not and perform standard outlier detection on this. One nice quality of purely binary data is that it's possible to use both numeric and categorical detectors. Listing 9.2 has an example. This creates a new dataframe with the same rows and columns as the original dataframe but with each cell simply containing a binary value indicating if the original data was null or not null, as provided by the isna() method. Often, we see in data cases where two or more columns tend to have null in the same rows (for example "Age of Eldest Child" and "Age of Youngest Child") or have nulls in the opposite rows, and exceptions to these patterns may be useful outliers.

> **Listing 9.2   Converting data to binary indicator of null values**

```
import pandas as pd
import numpy as np

df = pd.DataFrame({"A": [1, 2, np.NaN, 4, 5, None],
                   "B": ['A', 'B', None, np.NaN, "E", "F"]})
df_filled = df.isna()
print(df_filled)
```

9.2   *Special data types*

In the next few sections, we'll go through some common data types found in tabular data: phone numbers, addresses, email addresses, and ID/Code values. These are just examples, though, and what's most relevant is the general idea that when data follows a specific pattern, it's often productive to examine it more closely and identify ways to locate unusual values. Usually this is done by removing the original feature and replacing it with one or more engineered features that can help highlight the most unusual values.

9.2.1   *Phone numbers*

As with many special data types, phone numbers cannot be used in their original form for outlier detection, as they cannot be treated as categorical or numeric. Phone numbers would have too many unique values to be handled as categorical data and have no meaning as numeric values (the values do not imply any order or magnitude). To use the feature, we will need to engineer features that capture relevant properties of the phone numbers.

A useful technique to identify feature engineering methods is to ask: when would I identify a value as wrong? In this case, we can ask: when would a telephone number be invalid? Although we're looking for any unusual values and not strictly wrong values, the relevant engineered features may largely be the same. With phone numbers, depending on the location(s), we expect a certain number of digits, so engineering a feature to count these may be useful, as in listing 9.3. Here we create a simple test dataset containing phone numbers and then engineer two features to describe these, taking their total number of characters and number of digits. To collect the number of digits, we define a function that counts the number of characters matching the isdigit() method.

Listing 9.3 Extracting features from phone numbers

```
def num_digits(x):
    return len([c for c in x if c.isdigit()])

df = pd.DataFrame({'Phone': ['123-456-9890', '555-555-5555', '555-555']})
df['Num Characters'] = df['Phone'].str.len()
df['Num Digits'] = df['Phone'].apply(num_digits)
print(df)
```

The product is shown in table 9.1.

Table 9.1 Engineered features generated from phone numbers

Phone	Num characters	Num digits
123-456-9890	12	10
555-555-5555	12	10
555-555	7	6

In cases where most are in the form XXX-XXXX, XXX-XXX-XXXX, and 1-XXX-XXX-XXXX, anything other than 7, 10, or 11 digits would be unusual in this regard. Unusual numbers of total characters can be tested for here as well.

If most are in these formats, or some other format consistently, it may be possible to create a regular expression matching this and create a binary column to indicate phone numbers matching and not matching the expression. This may capture, for example, characters other than digits, hyphens, parentheses, and any other commonly used characters.

Separating out the area codes may also be useful where there are a relatively small number of these; this will help flag any unusual area codes, as well as unusual combinations of other values with the area codes. As with the example with association rules, we can check for cases such as where the area code is 416 but the city is not Toronto. Sample code to collect the area codes, assuming that any with 10 digits has the area code first and any with 11 digits have the area code after the 1-digit country code:

```
def area_code(x):
    digits_only = ''.join([c for c in x if c.isdigit()])
```

```
if len(digits_only) == 10:
    return digits_only[:3]
if len(digits_only) == 11:
    return digits_only[1:4]
return ''
```

Another useful test with data of this type is to check for values that may be entered as placeholders—for example 555-5555. For this, we may add a feature to capture the number of unique digits. This may be implemented with code such as

```
def num_unique_digits(x):
    return len(set([c for c in x if c.isdigit()]))
```

9.2.2 Addresses

Often in tabular data we have address information neatly separated into distinct columns—for example, with features for unit number, street number, street, city, postal code, and so on. It's also common to have all of these in a single column with values such as "432-34 West 3rd Street, Monroe County"; these require parsing to separate into their components to effectively perform outlier detection using the address information.

There are several tools for this, including usaddress (https://github.com/datamade/usaddress) and libpostal (https://github.com/openvenues/libpostal). In my experience, most work well with addresses in Western countries but can struggle with addresses in other parts of the world. It may be necessary in these cases to use multiple tools.

Once the addresses are broken into specific parts, we can look for unusual values or combinations of values. For example, we may be able to look for unusual combinations of city and rental rates, country and currency (e.g., dollars for United States and euros for Germany would be normal, and exceptions may be outliers), or any other values that may be associated with location.

The other common approach with address data is to convert locations to latitude and longitude values. One popular library for this is geopy (https://github.com/geopy/geopy), which includes several other tools. With most tools for geolocating, it's not necessary to format the address; most will be able to accept the address strings in any reasonable format.

Once we have the latitude and longitude, it is easy to test for locations that are far from the others by simply using standard outlier detection methods such as Isolation Forest, k-nearest neighbors (KNN), or Radius on these two features. For very large distances, in the thousands of miles, it can be useful to use the Haversine, as opposed to Euclidean, distance, which is designed for geographic locations and considers the spherical shape of the earth in the distances calculated.

It may be more productive to cross-reference other values (such as rental rates) with the latitude and longitude rather than with the address fields, as the exact location can often better capture the properties of the area than, say, the city or state features. For example, latitude and longitude may be better for distinguishing between neighborhoods within cities and for representing areas not quite within but near cities.

9.2.3 Email addresses

Email addresses are much easier to work with than postal addresses, though they typically have less information value. Email addresses do, though, require a specific format, so it's possible to check for invalid email addresses, which may catch data artifacts. We can also test for nonsense values such as xxx@xxx.com by engineering features for the number of characters, number of unique characters, presence of invalid characters, presence of "@" and "." characters, and so on. While the existence of nonsense email addresses in some datasets may not be interesting, unusual patterns in these may be—for example, suggesting bulk creation of bogus accounts.

In some tables, we may find most records use the same or a small number of domains, so separating these out will leave a small number of distinct values, which can be treated as categorical data. In Python, this can be done using split('@') and taking element [1] of each email address. Given this, we can identify any rare domains where this may be informative.

9.2.4 ID/Code values

Tabular data often contains data with ID or Code values, which may have some pattern that we can check for deviations. In some cases, there may be a natural order to the values. For example, employee IDs may be assigned sequentially but starting from a point other than 1, so converting these to a rank order may be useful for some processing.

Code values are also sometimes comprised of distinct elements, with values such as "A-504," where the prefix "A" and the suffix "504" both have some meaning. In this case, separating these into distinct values (creating two new columns to replace the original column) may be useful to identify unusual values or combinations with other columns. It also may reduce the number of distinct values in each column to a more workable level.

9.2.5 Dates

Tabular data also often contains date values, as in the staff expenses table from chapter 2, repeated here as table 9.2.

Table 9.2 Staff expenses

Row	Staff ID	Department	Account	Date of Expense	Date Submitted	Time Submitted	Amount
1	9000483	Sales	Meals	02/03/2023	03/03/2023	09:10:21	12.44
2	9303332	Marketing	Travel	03/03/2023	05/03/2023	10:43:35	41.90
3	9847421	Engineering	Meals	04/03/2023	05/03/2023	10:56:04	643.99
4	9303332	Marketing	Supplies	04/03/2023	07/03/2023	11:12:09	212.00

We've seen before where dates may be converted into their rank value or as the number of days (or seconds, hours, months, or dates, depending on which period is appropriate) from the minimum date in the data. In listing 9.4, we look at some other examples of feature engineering, generating a column for the day of the week (DOW), day of the month (DOM), a Boolean feature indicating if the date is in the first or second half of the month (often in business, certain processes tend to occur at the beginning or end of each month but not necessarily on specific days), and a column for the number of days between the two original date columns.

Checking for shorter or longer periods between dates is very often useful. We can examine here the gaps between the Date of Expense and Date Submitted columns. Very long gaps may be of interest, as would negative gaps, assuming these are rare, where the expense is submitted prior to the purchase. In listing 9.4, we drop the original date columns as they cannot be used by most outlier detectors.

Listing 9.4   Engineering features related to dates

```
import datetime
import pandas as pd
import numpy as np

df['DOW 1'] = df['Date of Expense'].dt.dayofweek
df['DOM 1'] = df['Date of Expense'].dt.day
df['Beg. of Month'] = df['DOM 1'].apply(lambda x: x < 15, 1, 0)
df['Gap'] = (df['Date Submitted'] - df['Date of Expense']).dt.days
df = df.drop(columns=['Date of Expense', 'Date Submitted'])
print(df)
```

This replaces the two date columns with the engineered features as shown in table 9.3.

Table 9.3   Staff expenses with engineered features

Row	Staff ID	Department	Account	DOW 1	DOM 1	Beg. of month	Gap	Time submitted	Amount
1	9000483	Sales	Meals	3	2	1	1	09:10:21	12.44
2	9303332	Marketing	Travel	4	3	1	2	10:43:35	41.90
3	9847421	Engineering	Meals	5	4	1	1	10:56:04	643.99
4	9303332	Marketing	Supplies	5	4	1	3	11:12:09	212.00

Checking for holidays is also useful. An example of collecting holidays into an array using pandas is shown in listing 9.5. Note that this covers only US holidays. Another library that may also be useful for this purpose and covers international holidays is python-holidays (https://github.com/vacanza/python-holidays).

Listing 9.5   Collecting holiday dates

```
from pandas.tseries.holiday import USFederalHolidayCalendar

cal = USFederalHolidayCalendar()
holidays = cal.holidays(
    start='2023-01-01', end='2023-12-31').to_pydatetime()
```

9.2.6 *High-cardinality categorical columns*

Often in tabular data there are features that are essentially categorical (the values are short strings) but that have a very large number of distinct values. For example, a table with 1,000 rows may have a feature with 600 unique values. This can make working with the values as categorical impractical. It may be that most, or even all, of the unique values are rare, and therefore there is no sense of unusually rare values or of unusual combinations with other features. Given this, these features usually cannot be used as-is for outlier detection.

In some cases, as with phone numbers, addresses, code values, and other data types, we may be able to extract features with small numbers of unique values from the original features, which will allow us to treat them as categorical. In the case of addresses, it may be that every address value in a table is unique, but if we extract the city, we have a manageably small number of unique values. Or we may be able to extract numeric features as we did with phone numbers. Often, though, the best approach in these cases is to map the set of values to a smaller set. This is the same idea as in the example mapping "dark blue" and "light blue" to "blue" we saw when discussing association rule mining.

The first part of this process may be to attempt to deduplicate the data, finding sets of values that are not just similar but actually equivalent. Where there are many unique values, it is often the case that many are variations of the same thing—for example, with different spellings or as synonyms, creating what is called *dirty* data.

A useful tool for identifying duplicates, in the form of spelling variations, is skrub (https://github.com/skrub-data/skrub). This has several tools that work with high-cardinality data, including vectorizing the data. Here, though, we will look at the deduplication tool it provides, with an example in listing 9.6. This uses skrub's `make_deduplication_data()` method to create test data (a good way to get started with the tool), which creates variations on the values passed, simulating values in a feature for staff expenses with various typographical errors. Before executing this, it is necessary to install skrub with

```
pip install skrub
```

The main method is `deduplicate()`, which suggests a correct value for each simulated value. That is, the tool helps consolidate similar values into single values.

Listing 9.6 Using skrub for deduplication

```
from skrub.datasets import make_deduplication_data
from skrub import deduplicate

duplicated_names = make_deduplication_data(
    examples=["online course", "seminar", "conference", "in-person class",
              "lecture series"],
    entries_per_example=[500, 500, 500, 500, 500],
    prob_mistake_per_letter=0.1,
    random_state=42,
)
deduplicated_data = deduplicate(duplicated_names)
```

This will detect where sets of string values are similar, which is useful where we can assume a similar meaning is implied most of the time. It won't detect where the values have similar meanings but dissimilar strings, such as "seminar" and "conference," which is a much harder problem. Tools such as wordnet from NLTK (https://www.nltk.org/) can be used to check for synonyms, at least where the words follow their normal meanings. Listing 9.7 shows an example. However, in tabular data, string values often have domain-specific values, and it may be best to work with a domain expert to find a mapping to a smaller set. To install nltk, execute

```
pip install nltk
```

Listing 9.7   Identifying synonyms using NLTK's wordnet

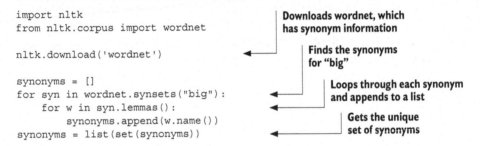

```
import nltk
from nltk.corpus import wordnet

nltk.download('wordnet')

synonyms = []
for syn in wordnet.synsets("big"):
    for w in syn.lemmas():
        synonyms.append(w.name())
synonyms = list(set(synonyms))
```

Downloads wordnet, which has synonym information
Finds the synonyms for "big"
Loops through each synonym and appends to a list
Gets the unique set of synonyms

Using methods like these, we can often reduce, though not necessarily drastically, the number of unique values. Unfortunately, in these cases, it may not be possible to use high cardinality features if we cannot consolidate the values or extract other features from them.

9.3   Text features

Often in tabular data we see text features, such as comment or description columns, which may be of value for identifying outliers. In table 9.4 we see an example of this, with another view of the staff expenses table including a comments column.

Table 9.4   Staff expenses with comments

Row	Staff ID	Department	Account	Date of expense	Date submitted	Time submitted	Amount	Comments
1	9000483	Sales	Meals	02/03/2023	03/03/2023	09:10:21	12.44	Lunch
2	9303332	Marketing	Travel	03/03/2023	05/03/2023	10:43:35	41.90	Taxi airport to hotel
3	9847421	Engineering	Meals	04/03/2023	05/03/2023	10:56:04	643.99	Dinner with clients (ACME) at hotel restaurant
4	9303332	Marketing	Supplies	04/03/2023	07/03/2023	11:12:09	212.00	Printer toner

It may be that "printer toner" is an unusual expense, or an unusual expense for the marketing department, or unusual for $212. Having access to the comments allows us to identify anomalous expenses in a much more meaningful way. But text is also much more difficult to work with than most other types of data. This column is not numeric and has too many distinct values to treat as categorical. To extract information from the text, we will need to use text processing methods, which can generate a new set of features to describe the comments. There are several ways to do this, including some we look at here: natural language processing (NLP), topic modeling, and clustering. It is also possible to use large language models to convert the text to embeddings, though this is difficult to do for outlier detection. We look more at embeddings in chapter 16.

9.3.1 *Extracting NLP features*

Very often it's useful to simply create a set of features to describe the length of the strings or some other basic properties, such as the number of unique characters, which helps identify missing, extreme, or nonsensical values (for example, during data entry people may enter values such as "zzzzzz" in lieu of actual values). In some cases, such as forgery detection (where forgeries will stand out as outliers relative to other documents for the same author), we may wish to examine the data in a much more sophisticated way to find more subtle outliers, but for many purposes, we simply wish to identify the most obvious outliers. Using simple, interpretable features supports this and also allows us to easily tune the model to identify the most relevant outliers. These simple features may not be sufficient, but they are often a very good place to start.

For this example (listing 9.8), we use a dataset frequently used in data science for working with text: the 20 Newsgroups dataset. This is a collection of approximately 11,000 messages posted on 20 different newsgroups; each newsgroup has a specific topic, such as computer graphics, baseball, medicine, or space. To extract features, we use an NLP tool called spaCy (https://spacy.io/), a powerful and efficient tool supporting 73 languages, most common NLP tasks, and large language models.

To execute this code, it is necessary to first install spacy and download the en_core_web_lg model (or another model, though this example uses en_core_web_lg). This may be done with

```
pip install spacy
python -m spacy download en_core_web_lg
```

We first collect the data and then loop over each value in the data. Here, each value is a posted message, typically a few hundred words. For each, we create a doc object, which is a version of the text processed by spaCy. This allows us to access part of speech tags and other information about each word in the document. For this example, we use this for its ability to parse sentences and words accurately to create counts of these, along with the number of stop words (the most common words in the language; for English this includes *and, then, the, if, but,* and so on). Measuring the nonstop words gives a sense of how much real content is in each message.

Listing 9.8   Extracting features from text using spaCy

```
import pandas as pd
import spacy
from spacy.lang.en.stop_words import STOP_WORDS
from spacy.lang.en import English
from sklearn.datasets import fetch_20newsgroups

data = fetch_20newsgroups(                                    ◁── Collects the data
        remove=('headers', 'footers', 'quotes'))
df = pd.DataFrame({"Content": data['data']})                  ◁── Generates simple
                                                                  features that do not
                                                                  require spaCy
df['Num Chars'] = df['Content'].str.len()
df['Num Unique Chars'] = df['Content'].apply(lambda x: len(set(x)))

nlp = spacy.load('en_core_web_lg')          ◁── Loads the package used by
stopwords = list(STOP_WORDS)                    spaCy to process text

num_words_arr = []                          ◁── Generates features based
num_unique_words_arr = []                       on spaCy's parsing
num_stop_words = []
num_sentences_arr = []
for v in df['Content']:
  doc = nlp(v)
  num_words_arr.append(len(doc))
  num_unique_words_arr.append(len(set([x.text for x in doc])))
  num_stop_words.append(len([x for x in doc if x.text in stopwords]))
  num_sentences_arr.append(len(list(doc.sents)))
df['Num Words'] = num_words_arr
df['Num Unique Words'] = num_unique_words_arr
df['Num Non-Stop Words'] = df['Num Words'] - num_stop_words
df['Num Sentences'] = num_sentences_arr
```

The first two rows are shown in table 9.5.

Table 9.5   Features engineered from the 20 Newsgroups dataset

Content	Num Chars	Num Unique Chars	Num Words	Num Unique Words	Num Non-Stop Words	Num Sentences
I was wondering if anyone out there could enli...	475	35	116	75	70	7
A fair number of brave souls who upgraded thei...	530	41	109	79	72	5

It may be useful to further engineer features along these lines, such as average number of characters per word, average number of words per sentence, and so on, to the extent extreme values in these would flag useful outliers.

spaCy also allows estimating the sentiment of each string, though this tends to work poorly for outlier detection purposes. For this, it is preferable to use more powerful language models, such as those available on Hugging Face Hub, which allow testing for toxicity, anger, and other sentiment-related properties of the text that may be relevant for some projects.

The relevant features will depend on the types of outliers you wish to find and the type of data. Your data may be more similar to a comments or description column or to the longer text in the 20 Newsgroups data—for example, if you are working with data such as email, text messages, or social media posts. Different again would be contracts, journal articles, or notes made in patients' medical records.

In cases where the values in the text field tend to use the same small vocabulary of words, we may look for unusual text in this regard. An example is shown in listing 9.9. For convenience, this again uses the 20 Newsgroups data, but this technique may be more useful in other types of data, depending on the goals. This starts by converting all strings to lowercase (to allow matching words that happen to be in different cases) and removing all nonalphabetic characters. We then determine the frequency of each word in the full set of newsgroup messages. For each message, we then find the frequency of its least-frequent word. This will help identify the use of unusually rare words.

> **Listing 9.9 Finding the frequency of the rarest word in each record**

```
import pandas as pd
from sklearn.datasets import fetch_20newsgroups
from collections import Counter
import statistics                                          Removes nonalphabetic
                                                           characters and convert
def clean_data(x):                                         to lowercase
    return [c.lower() for c in x.split() if c.isalpha()]

data = fetch_20newsgroups(
        remove=('headers', 'footers', 'quotes'))           Collects the data
df = pd.DataFrame({"Content": data['data']})

df['Cleaned Content'] = df['Content'].apply(clean_data)     Creates an array
                                                           with the data over
full_text = []                                             all messages
for v in df.index:
    full_text.extend(df.loc[v, 'Cleaned Content'])         Gets a count of each
                                                           word in the full corpus
c = Counter(full_text)
                                                           Loops over each message
min_frequency_arr = []                                     and calculates features
mean_frequency_arr = []
for v in df['Cleaned Content']:                        Handles where messages
    if len(v) == 0:                                    have no words
        min_frequency_arr.append(0)
        mean_frequency_arr.append(0)               Calculates the frequency of the least
    else:                                          used word and the average frequency
        min_frequency_arr.append(min([c[word] for word in v]))
        mean_frequency_arr.append(statistics.mean([c[word] for word in v]))
df['Min Frequency Word'] = min_frequency_arr
df['Mean Frequency Word'] = mean_frequency_arr
```

In the case of the newsgroups data, 121 documents (out of 11,314) had words that were only used once, making them unusual in this regard. However, with this dataset it may be more useful to instead search for the use of many rare words. The mean word frequency tracked here may also be meaningful, as this allows us to find documents that tend to contain an unusual proportion of rare words.

Other features that may be useful for some outlier detection projects include spelling quality, grammar quality, the use of active versus passive voice, and writing level (e.g., the Funning fog index). Most often, though, simpler methods will be more appropriate for outlier detection purposes, as text can be difficult to work with and it's easy to flag large numbers of false positives using complex methods. There are some exceptions, such as when working with large, complex documents—for example, contracts, patents, legislation, and so on. In these cases, more sophisticated tools will usually be needed. We present two here: topic modeling and clustering.

9.3.2 *Topic modeling*

It is often useful when working with text data to look at, in addition to the lengths of the strings, word counts, and similar features, the actual content. To support this, we can use a common technique in NLP, called *topic modeling*. This identifies the sets of topics discussed in a collection of documents and assigns each document a set of scores indicating how related it is to each topic. This allows us to find documents that are outliers by focusing on topics that are rarely covered by the other documents and to find unusual combinations of other features with the topics discussed.

Topics are found by identifying the words that tend to go together in documents. The comments for expenses may tend to contain "dinner," "restaurant," and "client" frequently together, which may then form a topic. Another topic may be "taxi," "cab," "hotel," and "plane." In this way, while the topics found in topic modeling tend to be sensible, they generally do not match any expectations we may have ahead of time regarding what topics may be found. With the 20 Newsgroups dataset, we may expect to identify 20 distinct topics corresponding to the 20 newsgroups but will usually find quite different, though still meaningful, results.

There are several tools available for topic modeling, including a tool for LatentDirichletAllocation (LDA, one algorithm for topic modeling) in scikit-learn, the Gensim library, and others. For this example, shown in listing 9.10, we use BERTopic (https://maartengr.github.io/BERTopic), which allows us to take advantage of a large language model called BERT. We simply load the data and pass it to BERTopic to create a set of topics. This may be installed with

```
pip install bertopic
```

Listing 9.10 Using `BERTopic` with the 20 Newsgroups dataset

```
from bertopic import BERTopic
from sklearn.datasets import fetch_20newsgroups

data = fetch_20newsgroups(subset='all',
```

```
                                remove=('headers', 'footers', 'quotes'))
topic_model = BERTopic()
topics, probs = topic_model.fit_transform(data['data'])
```

After executing this, we may call `topic_model.get_topic_info()` to get a description of the topics found, shown in table 9.6, though this shows only four of the columns provided. The topics are not named and are described only by the set of words that were found to frequently co-occur that were used to define the topic.

Table 9.6 Topics found in the 20 Newsgroups dataset using `BERTopic`

Topic	Count	Name	Representation
−1	6850	-1_to_the_and_you	[to, the, and, you, of, is, in, for, it, that]
0	1831	0_game_team_games_he	[game, team, games, he, players, season, hocke...
...	...	...	...
225	10	224_xterm_xterms_cursor_emu	[xterm, xterms, cursor, emu, blinking, blink, ...
226	10	225_mumble_article_sorry_ anouncementsmumble	[mumble, article, sorry, anouncements mumble, n...

We may also call `topic_model.get_document_info(data['data'])` to see the main topic assigned to each document, shown in table 9.7.

Table 9.7 Topics assigned to documents from the 20 Newsgroups dataset using `BERTopic`

	Document	Topic	Name	Probability
0	I am sure some bashers of Pens fans are pr.	0	[game, team, games, he, players, season, hocke...	1.0
4	I have an old Jasmine drive which I cann.	96	96_tape_backup_tapes_drive	0.53

In this case, topic −1 (unassigned) is fairly common, so it cannot be used to identify outliers but may be where this is rare. Outliers can also be found as those documents that are assigned a topic, but a rare topic, or where they are assigned with low probability, suggesting the document does not match any identified topics well. In the case of the staff expenses table, we can also identify outliers as rare combinations of the other fields, such as Department, Account, or Amount, with the topics—for example, an expense of $1,000 for a topic related to office supplies.

9.3.3 *Clustering text values*

As with other types of data, if text features are well clustered (having a reasonably small set of distinct types of values), it may be useful to first cluster the strings before performing outlier detection. We can then identify outliers as strings not similar to any of the clusters, strings that are within clusters but significantly different from the other strings in the cluster, or unusual combinations of cluster ID with other features in the table.

There are a few common ways to cluster strings:

- *Based on vectors representing word counts*—This applies well if the text feature has a limited set of words used or at least a small set of words that are used frequently. Here we transform the text feature to a set of numeric features, representing the counts of words in each string. For example, if there are 30 words that appear frequently in the column, we can create 30 columns giving the count for each of these words in each string. These may be useful features in themselves for outlier detection but can also be used to cluster similar strings.
- *TF-IDF transformation of this*—This is the same idea, but instead of using the count for each word, we perform a TF-IDF transformation on the data. This is outside the scope of this book, but it essentially normalizes the counts of each word in each record by considering how frequently the words are used in the full feature.
- *Based on topic modeling*—Here we generate features related to how similar to each topic each string is and cluster the strings such that those covering the same topics to the same degree tend to be clustered together.

An example of clustering messages based on their use of the most frequent 20 words in the corpus is shown in listing 9.11. This reads in the 20 Newsgroups dataset and extracts from each document only the nouns (using the `get_nouns()` function defined here), which are often, though not always, the most relevant words for analysis. We then identify the 20 most common nouns used and generate a feature for each of these, such that for each document we have a count of how many times it used each of these words. We then use Gaussian mixture model clustering to group the documents based on these features.

> **Listing 9.11   Clustering messages from the 20 Newsgroups dataset**

```
import pandas as pd
import numpy as np
import spacy
from collections import Counter
from sklearn.datasets import fetch_20newsgroups
from sklearn.mixture import GaussianMixture

data = fetch_20newsgroups(remove=('headers', 'footers', 'quotes'))
df = pd.DataFrame({"Content": data['data'], "Target": data['target']})
nlp = spacy.load('en_core_web_lg')

def get_nouns(x):
    content = ' '.join([c.lower() for c in x.split() if c.isalpha()])
    doc = nlp(content)
    return [x.text for x in doc if x.pos_ == 'NOUN']

df['Nouns'] = df['Content'].apply(get_nouns)
```

Extracts the nouns from a piece of text

```
full_text = []
for v in df.index:
    if (v%1000) == 0: print(v)
    full_text.extend(df.loc[v, 'Nouns'])
```

◄─── **Collects the full set of words used**

```
c = Counter(full_text)
common_words = [x[0] for x in c.most_common(20)]
```

◄─── **Counts the use of each word**

```
for common_word in common_words:
    df[common_word] = df['Nouns'].apply(lambda x: x.count(common_word))
```

```
best_score = np.inf
best_n_clusters = -1
for n_clusters in range(2, 20):
    gmm = GaussianMixture(n_components=n_clusters)
    gmm.fit(df[common_words])
    score = gmm.bic(df[common_words])
    print(n_clusters, score)
    if score < best_score:
        best_score = score
        best_n_clusters = n_clusters
```

◄─── **Clusters the documents based on their use of words**

```
gmm = GaussianMixture(n_components=best_n_clusters)
gmm.fit(df[common_words])
df['Cluster ID'] = gmm.predict(df[common_words])
```

After clustering, we have a cluster ID for each record, as shown in table 9.8.

Table 9.8 Cluster IDs generated from similar nouns in the 20 Newsgroups dataset

Content	Nouns	Cluster ID
I was wondering if anyone out there could enli...	[car, sports, doors, bumper, rest, model,...	3
A fair number of brave souls who upgraded thei...	[number, souls, si, clock, oscillator, experie...	8
well folks, my mac plus finally gave up the gh...	[ghost, weekend, life, way, market, machine, ...	3

For your data, you may need to use different parts of speech besides nouns, use a different number of most frequent words, or cluster in a different manner, but if the data is naturally clustered, you can likely use this or similar techniques to identify the clusters. Once done, the text field can be replaced with a field indicating the cluster ID for outlier detection.

For topic modeling, clustering, and other text processing, it may be useful to use not the actual words but their lemmas, which are the basic form of the word. For example, the words *do, doing, did,* and *does* all have the same lemma, *do,* a single token that represents all forms of the word. Using this allows us to treat all variations of a word as equivalent, which often makes more sense—words like *seminar* and *seminars* should be treated as the same word for many purposes. Lemmas can be found using spaCy, for example:

```
comment = "Purchased laptops to replace damaged laptops"
doc = nlp(comment)
comment = str(" ".join([i.lemma_ for i in doc]))
print(comment)
```

This will output

```
purchase laptop to replace damaged laptop
```

Ideally generating simple features, topics, and cluster IDs will be sufficient for most outlier detection purposes. Beyond these, it will likely be necessary to utilize large language models.

So far in this chapter we have looked at several types of data and examples of working with these, but it's important to take the general ideas and apply them to your more specific data. It's useful to engineer features that capture what is relevant and to format this in a way useful to the detector. Usually this means engineering a set of numeric and categorical features that describe the data in a way that allows outliers to stand out as rare or extreme values or as rare combinations when considered with other features.

Once these features are processed, we will have the original set of numeric and categorical features, as well as any engineered features created. This set of features will then require some further processing. We look next at working with this categorical and numeric data, which usually means converting the data to be either entirely numeric or entirely categorical.

9.4   *Encoding categorical data*

As the majority of detectors work with numeric data, encoding any categorical columns is commonly required. The set of choices for outlier detection is the same as for prediction, though the strengths and weaknesses of the different methods are somewhat different. Count encoding, for example, is more applicable and more common in outlier detection than in prediction. The two most popular are likely, as with prediction, one-hot and ordinal encoding.

An excellent library for encoding methods is Category Encoders (https://mng .bz/865K). This will likely cover any of the methods you will need. Many of the methods provided, such as Target and CatBoost, require a target column, which is normally not available with outlier detection. The majority, however, can usually be used.

Which encoding method works best will vary based on the dataset and the types of outliers you wish to find. And, in some cases, it may work best to use different encodings for different features. Unfortunately, as most outlier detection problems are unsupervised, it's very difficult to determine the best encodings. Where the system runs over time, it may be possible to collect labeled data and use this to evaluate different preprocessing methods including the encoding of the categorical columns. For most cases, though, the best approach is likely the use of synthetic data, as introduced in chapter 8. Here we will provide some description on how encoding methods behave, covering three methods.

9.4.1 One-hot encoding

One-hot encoding is very commonly used for outlier detection and can be a good choice when a feature has low cardinality. scikit-learn's documentation recommends ordinal encoding for IsolationForest, but one-hot tends to work well for most other detectors.

One-hot encoding creates a binary column for each unique value in the original feature. For example, encoding the staff expenses table, we would create a set of binary columns representing the department and another set representing the account, the two categorical features. The first several one-hot features are shown in table 9.9, covering the binary columns indicating the department. A similar set would be created for the account.

Table 9.9 Staff expenses one-hot encoded (showing only staff ID and department)

Row	Staff ID	Department Sales	Department Marketing	Department Engineering	Department HR	Department Communications
1	9000483	1	0	0	0	0
2	9303332	0	1	0	0	0
3	9847421	0	0	1	0	0
4	9303332	0	1	0	0	0

One-hot encoding may be suboptimal for some detectors because it creates a large number of features for each categorical feature in the original data and even more features for categorical features that happen to have higher cardinality. For example, with IsolationForest, the trees choose a random feature (from the one-hot-encoded data) at each step in constructing the trees. Where the original categorical features map to many one-hot features, these categorical features have an outsized influence in the model, as they will tend to be selected more than categorical features with fewer values and substantially more than numeric features.

One-hot encoding also results in categorical features being overrepresented in distance calculations for detectors that use these, though the effect is less severe than with IsolationForests. As an example, consider table 9.10, which shows a dataset with four rows and two features. The Color column has five values (with two present in the current data)—red, blue, green, white, and yellow—and two sizes—big and small.

Table 9.10 Dataset with color and size features

Row	Color	Size
1	Red	Big
2	Blue	Small
3	Red	Big
4	Blue	Big

The pair-wise distances between the four rows are shown in table 9.11, which shows only the unique distances above the main diagonal. Here we measure distance based on the number of values that are different. As a pair of rows can have zero, one, or two features that are different, these are the possible distances between rows.

Table 9.11   Distances based on match/not

	1	2	3	4
1	-	2	0	1
2	-	-	2	1
3	-	-	-	1
4	-	-	-	-

If we one-hot encode the data in table 9.10, we see the results in table 9.12.

Table 9.12   Dataset after one-hot encoding

Row	Red	Blue	Green	White	Yellow	Big	Small
1	1	0	0	0	0	1	0
2	0	1	0	0	0	0	1
3	1	0	0	0	0	1	0
4	0	1	0	0	0	1	0

If we calculate the pair-wise distances between the rows using one-hot encoding and either Manhattan or Euclidean distances, we have the distances shown in table 9.13. In this case, as all values are 0 or 1, the Manhattan and Euclidean distances are the same.

Table 9.13   Pairwise Manhattan/Euclidean distances

	1	2	3	4
1	-	4	0	2
2	-	-	4	2
3	-	-	-	2
4	-	-	-	-

Using Manhattan or Euclidean distance measures (table 9.13), the distances are proportional to when using a count of the number of values matching (table 9.11), but the values are double: when two values in the original data mismatch, there will be two cells in the one-hot encoding mismatched. This is not usually a problem when working with purely categorical data, but it does create an undesirable situation where we have mixed data. Consider table 9.14 with two features, Color and Weight, where Weight is numeric.

Table 9.14   Dataset with one categorical and one numeric feature

Row	Color	Weight
1	Red	0.1
2	Blue	0.1
3	Red	0.3
4	Red	0.9

Once one-hot encoded, we have table 9.15.

Table 9.15   One-hot encoding with one categorical and one numeric feature

Row	Red	Blue	Green	White	Yellow	Weight
1	1	0	0	0	0	0.1
2	0	1	0	0	0	0.1
3	1	0	0	0	0	0.3
4	1	0	0	0	0	0.9

Here, when we calculate Euclidean distances between the rows, we have the distances in table 9.16.

Table 9.16   Distances based on Euclidean distances

	1	2	3	4
1	-	1.4	0.2	0.8
2	-	-	1.4	1.6
3	-	-	-	0.6
4	-	-	-	-

Rows 1 and 2 differ in the color (having the same weight) and have a Euclidean distance of 1.4. Rows 3 and 4 are different in weight (having the same color) and have a Euclidean distance of 0.6. We can see the difference in color is more significant, though likely it should not be.

There are two factors that give categorical features more importance here than numeric. The first is that matches versus nonmatches affect two one-hot columns, while the differences in numeric values affect only a single column. The second is that distances in binary columns are larger than in numeric features. Here, row 1 and row 4 have Weight values of 0.1 and 0.9, which is a significant difference of 0.8 but is less than the difference in two mismatching categorical values, which will be (given two binary columns will mismatch) 2.0.

An example working with Manhattan and Euclidean distances is shown in listing 9.12. In the first case, we create a pair of vectors representing the first two rows from the previous data, with five one-hot columns for color and one column for weight. We then create another pair of vectors to simulate if the cardinality of Color were instead 2, using only two binary columns.

Listing 9.12   **Testing Manhattan and Euclidean distances**

```
from sklearn.metrics.pairwise import euclidean_distances, \
                                     manhattan_distances

row_1 = [1, 0, 0, 0, 0, 0.1]          ◀──── Creates data simulating
row_2 = [0, 1, 0, 0, 0, 0.1]                 two rows where five
                                             binary columns are used
print(manhattan_distances([row_1], [row_2]))  for one categorical
print(euclidean_distances([row_1], [row_2]))

row_1 = [1, 0, 0.1]                   ◀──── Creates similar data but
row_2 = [0, 1, 0.2]                          with two binary columns
                                             for one categorical
print(manhattan_distances([row_1], [row_2]))  column
print(euclidean_distances([row_1], [row_2]))
```

Interestingly, in both cases, the two rows have a Manhattan distance of 2.1 and Euclidean of 1.4: where we test using only two binary features for color instead of five, the distances are the same. Similarly, increasing the cardinality (using more than five binary features to represent color) does not affect the distance measures. There is, as noted, an imbalance between categorical and numeric features, but it is not made worse by the cardinality of the categorical features.

9.4.2 *Ordinal encoding*

Ordinal encoding avoids the explosion in the number of binary columns we see with one-hot encoding and can work well with some detectors, including Isolation Forest, but tends to work poorly for any detectors using distance metrics, as the ordinal values are arbitrary and not reflective of the actual distances between rows.

To look at why ordinal encoding does work well for Isolation Forest, consider the Department column of the staff expenses table (table 9.4). If there are 1,000 records for Sales, 500 for Marketing, and 50 for Engineering, then we will have three unique values in the column once ordinal encoded. Assume Sales is given value 0, Marketing 1, and Engineering 2: we have 1,000 records with value 0, 500 with value 1, and 50 with value 2. In constructing the isolation trees, these individual values will be initially isolated roughly as quickly as each other. But then, where nodes contain only duplicate values, isolation trees do not split these nodes further. Instead, they keep track of the number of duplicate training records that ended in each leaf node.

At predict time, when records are passed through the isolation trees, they may end in leaf nodes related to these values. In these cases, the trees will recognize that these nodes were not split further because they contained only duplicate values and will estimate the tree depth necessary to isolate points in these nodes. For any records ending in nodes related to Sales, given that Sales is very common, the isolation tree will estimate many more steps to isolate each point. For any records ending in nodes related to

Engineering, the tree will estimate only a few additional steps to isolate the point and hence more likely an outlier.

9.4.3 Count encoding

Count encoding can be useful in some outlier detection scenarios. As with ordinal encoding, each categorical column is mapped to a single encoded column, but here the encoding is not random; it represents the frequency of the value (rare values will be given small values and common values large values), which has some real information value when working with outlier detection.

If we have a distribution of Department values such as Sales: 1,000, Marketing: 500, Engineering: 100, HR: 10, Communications: 3, then these counts will be the encodings. That is, 1,000 records (those for Sales) will be given value 1,000, 500 will have value 500, and so on. This has the advantage that it can encode values such that rare values tend to be far from other values. In this case, the values 10 and 3 are close to each other, which means these 13 records will be close to each other, but they will be far from the other 1,600 records. The value 1,000 is distant from the other values, but there are 1,000 records with this encoding, which would then not be flagged as outliers.

In listing 9.13, using these values, we generate a simple, single-feature dataset representing the department and create a local outlier factor (LOF) detector (introduced in chapter 5) to assess this. When working with multiple columns, it is necessary to scale any count-encoded features to ensure all features are on the same scale, but as this example contains only a single feature, this step may be skipped. The LOF is able to correctly identify the rare values as outliers: the 13 rare values are given prediction −1, while all others are predicted as 1.

Listing 9.13 Identifying outliers in a single count-encoded column

```
import numpy as np
import pandas as pd
from sklearn.neighbors import LocalOutlierFactor

vals = np.array(['Sales']*1000 + ['Marketing']*500 + ['Engineering']*100 +
                ['HR']*10 + ['Communications']*3)
df = pd.DataFrame({"C1": vals})
vc = df['C1'].value_counts()
map = {x:y for x,y in zip(vc.index, vc.values)}
df['Ordinal C1'] = df['C1'].map(map)

clf = LocalOutlierFactor(contamination=0.01)
df['LOF Score'] = clf.fit_predict(df[['Ordinal C1']])
```

Creates a dataset with a single categorical column

Count-encodes the column

Uses LOF to determine the outliers in the column

9.5 Scaling numeric values

We discussed in chapter 4 the importance of scaling the numeric values for many detectors, particularly distance, density, and clustering-based detectors (though scaling is not necessary, for example, with Isolation Forest, Extended Isolation Forest, histogram-based outlier scores (HBOS), Entropy, Real versus Fake, or distance metric learning). Where scaling is necessary, this includes, as in the previous example, where the data is categorical and has been encoded using a method such as ordinal or count encoding (which can put the categorical features on a completely different scale than the numeric features).

The question will be: which is the best scaling method? Unfortunately, this is another place where the modeling choice can make a large difference, but it can be difficult to determine the best option. In lieu of labeled data that can be used for testing, we again have the use of synthetic data and methods such as doping, introduced in chapter 8, as likely the best means to decide. Complicating this, it is common to find different scaling methods work better for different detectors, even with the same data. The same scaling method should always be used for all features though.

The most common forms of scaling with outlier detection are min-max scaling, standard scaling (converting values to z-scores), and robust scaling. Normalizing by inter-quartile range, median absolute deviation (MAD), or similar metrics is also sometimes used. None of these alter the distribution of the data; the points remain, in relative terms, the same distances apart. Only the numbers change, so that the features are made comparable to each other.

Robust scaling works similar to standard scaling but is more robust to outliers in the data. Instead of using the mean and standard deviation, which can be affected by any extreme values, the median and interquartile range are used. Where the data does not contain extreme values, the two will work very similarly. Where there are extreme values, the scaled values using standard scaling can be less meaningful. Using robust scaling in this case, the extreme values remain extreme, but the other values remain as they would have been without the presence of the extreme values. Using robust scaling is almost always preferred to plain scaling for outlier detection.

To see why the choice of scaler is important, we test two methods in listing 9.14, `MinMaxScaler` and `RobustScaler`, on test data we've used previously, introduced in chapter 7. Using different scaling methods can actually alter which points are the nearest neighbors of others and the distances to their nearest neighbors. With detectors such as Radius, the choice of scaler can affect what other records, and how many other records, appear within any given radius.

Listing 9.14   Comparing min-max and robust scaling

```
from sklearn.preprocessing import MinMaxScaler, RobustScaler
from sklearn.neighbors import BallTree

df = create_four_clusters_test_data()            ← Creates test data using method defined in chapter 7

scaler = MinMaxScaler()                           ← Scales the data using a min-max scaler
df_minmax = pd.DataFrame(scaler.fit_transform(df), columns=df.columns)

scaler = RobustScaler()                           ← Scales the data using a robust scaler
```

```
df_robust = pd.DataFrame(scaler.fit_transform(df), columns=df.columns)

balltree = BallTree(df_minmax)
dist, ind = balltree.query(df_minmax.loc[0:0], k=10)
print(ind)
```
◄── **Finds the ten nearest neighbors of row 0 after min-max scaling**

```
balltree = BallTree(df_robust)
dist, ind = balltree.query(df_robust.loc[0:0], k=10)
print(ind)
```
◄── **Finds the 10 nearest neighbors of row 0 after robust scaling**

This produces a list of the closest neighbors for row 0 after min-max scaling and again after robust scaling. Both are shown here:

```
[[  0   3   2   4   1 757 691 663 676 501]]
[[  0   3   4   2   1 691 663 501 676 739]]
```

We can see that there is agreement on the two closest neighbors, but the balltrees provides different results after this point. For example, the sixth closest neighbor of row 0 when using min-max scaling is 757, while this is not even within the 10 nearest neighbors when using robust scaling. The effect is significantly stronger with more dimensions.

In listing 9.15, we use the same dataset but add a single row with the anomalous values [100, 100] and recalculate.

Listing 9.15 Adding a single outlier and recalculating the distances

```
df = pd.concat([df, pd.DataFrame({"A":[100], "B":[100]})])

scaler = MinMaxScaler()
df_minmax = pd.DataFrame(scaler.fit_transform(df), columns=df.columns)

scaler = RobustScaler()
df_robust = pd.DataFrame(scaler.fit_transform(df), columns=df.columns)

balltree = BallTree(df_minmax)
dist, ind = balltree.query(df_minmax.loc[0:0], k = 10)
print(ind)

balltree = BallTree(df_robust)
dist, ind = balltree.query(df_robust.loc[0:0], k = 10)
print(ind)
```

After adding a single outlier, the output is now

```
[[  0   3   2   4   1 757 691 642 676 446]]
[[  0   3   4   2   1 691 663 501 676 739]]
```

The nearest neighbors with the data transformed by a robust scaler are the same as previously, but the nearest neighbors when using min-max scaling are now slightly different. In this case, the outlier row that was added contained extreme values, which greatly affect min-max scaling. With extremely large values present, all other values will be pushed near 0.0. This will not occur when using robust scaling, though robust scaling may allow some very small or very large values after transformation. Extreme values will still be extreme after applying scaling and may have z-scores in the hundreds. This is not possible with min-max scaling.

One useful scaling method we have not looked at yet is the SplineTransformer, also available in scikit-learn. This is more complex, using a spline basis function, which effectively creates multiple features for each original feature. It is, though, often very effective for outlier detection.

The scikit-learn documentation includes a test comparing scaling methods for two datasets (forest cover and cardiography), which can be worth looking at (https://mng .bz/EOpq). For forest cover, MinMax does poorly, with RobustScaler, StandardScaler, and SplineScaler all doing well. For the cardiography dataset, MinMax and Robust perform similarly, with SplineScaler the strongest and Standard doing poorly. Again, there is no definitive best scaler, and the results will vary with your data and the type of outliers you are interested in. It may be worth trying multiple scalers, at least MinMax, Robust-Scaler, and SplineScaler.

9.6   *Binning numeric data*

We looked at options for binning data earlier when covering HBOS. The ideas there apply to any outlier detection method based on histograms as well as with any categorical outlier detectors, as they require binning all numeric features.

In general, when binning data for outlier detection, it is possible to use either equal-width or equal-count bins, though some other methods are occasionally used. Generally, equal-width bins are used when looking for univariate outliers, as this allows us to simply use the counts within each bin as a measure of how rare or common each value is.

When searching for multivariate outliers, we generally use equal-count bins; this assumes that univariate outliers are tested for elsewhere and we are focused on rare combinations. Both binning methods can be affected by outliers. With equal-width binning, the presence of one or more extreme values can create a bin containing only these few values, while all other values are pushed to the opposite leftmost or rightmost bin, leaving the bins in between empty, as shown in figure 9.1. This shows random data placed into either 20 or 50 bins.

The top row shows where 20 bins are used and the bottom row 50 bins. In both rows, the left pane presents a histogram of the data with no outliers (the data is a uniform distribution with all values between 0.0 and 1.0). The middle plot shows the histogram after a single outlier (with value 3.0) is added to the data. The right pane shows the histogram after a second outlier (with value 100.0) is added. The histograms are well-behaved with no outliers and with a single outlier. When the extreme outlier (100.0) is added, the other values are pushed to the leftmost bins, leaving the bins in between empty. In the case of using 20 bins, the 3.0 value is actually pushed into the same bin as the inliers, so is impossible to identify, though this does not occur with 50 bins. Using 50 bins, we have 3 populated bins (though this may be difficult to see in the plot): the first with almost all values, the second with the single 3.0 value, and the last bin with the single 100.0 value.

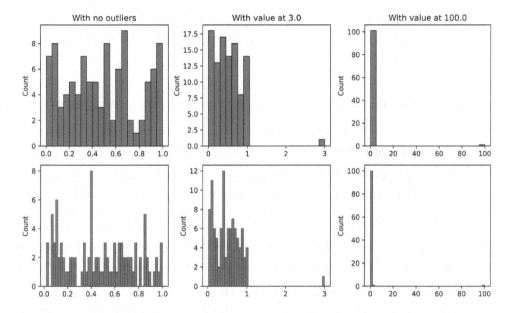

Figure 9.1 The effect of the number of bins. In the first row we see where 20 bins are used and in the second row, 50 bins. In each row we see a distribution of uniform data with no outliers (left pane), with a single outlier with value 3.0 (middle pane), and with a second outlier with value 100.0 (right pane). In the top-right pane we see, using 20 bins, the 3.0 value is placed in a bin with inliers. In the bottom-right pane we see, using 50 bins, the 3.0 value is in a separate bin with low count so will be recognized as an outlier.

This is an example of the potential issues using equal-width bins, as well as of the sensitivity of histograms to the number of bins used. Here using more bins removed the issue of the 3.0 value not being isolated well. In other cases, using more bins can cause the opposite problem, unnecessarily isolating values that are relatively normal.

One solution to this is to specifically separate extreme values into their own bins and perform equal-width binning on the remainder of the data. Where data is skewed, it can also work well to log-transform the data first and then perform equal-width binning.

With equal-count binning, the effects are less extreme, but where there are extreme values (and they are not separated into their own bins), they will be placed in either the leftmost or rightmost bin, creating an unusual range of values in these bins.

With binning data, the important question, besides the method used, is the number of bins. We saw in figure 9.1 that outlier detection methods can be quite sensitive to this, with rare values being included in bins with common values if too few bins are used, and moderately common values can be separated from common values if too many bins are used. Usually, the best number of bins will have to be found experimentally.

Again, testing with synthetic data is often the most practical approach. There is also a tool provided by PyOD to estimate the best number of bins to use for a given dataset. An example of this is shown in the following listing.

Listing 9.16   Using PyOD's utility to estimate the optimal number of bins

```
from pyod.utils.utility import get_optimal_n_bins
df = create_four_clusters_test_data()
get_optimal_n_bins(df)
```

The output for this is 7, indicating its estimate of the optimal number of bins to use for all numeric features in this dataset.

9.7   *Distance metrics*

Any outlier detectors that use distance measures will be sensitive to the distance metric used. So far we've seen several distance metrics, including Euclidean, Manhattan, Mahalanobis, the connectivity measure used by the connectivity-based outlier factor (COF), shared neighbors distances used by subspace outlier detection (SOD), and distance metric learning. Each will produce different measures between records, with some being more conducive to finding the results most useful to your project than others.

9.7.1   *Distance metrics for numeric data*

We'll look here at some additional options for distance metrics for numeric data. One that is used at times in outlier detection is the Canberra distance. The formula for this, where there are d features, is

$$d\,(row1,\ row2) = \sum_{i=1}^{d} \frac{|1i - 2i|}{|1i| + |2i|}$$

In the case where there are three features (here called a, b, and c), the distance between two rows, row 1 and row 2, would be

$$d\,(row1, row2) = \frac{|1a - 2a|}{|1a| + |2a|} + \frac{|1b - 2b|}{|1b| + |2b|} + \frac{|1c - 2c|}{|1c| + |2c|}$$

For example, if one record has values [0.1, 0.6, 0.2] and another record [0.5, 0.4, 0.7], as in table 9.17, their distance would be $(0.5 - 0.1)/(0.5 + 0.1) + (0.6 - 0.4)/(0.6 + 0.4) + (0.7 - 0.2)/(0.2 + 0.7)$. This is a sensible approach to measuring the distance: for each feature we examine the distance between the two values, relative to the scale of those two values, and sum over each feature, somewhat similar to the Manhattan distance. SciPy provides a method to calculate the Canberra distance between records, and scikit-learn and PyOD support it for most distance and density-based detectors, for example for KDE, KNN, and local outlier factor (LOF).

Table 9.17   Two rows with three numeric features

Row	a	b	c
1	0.1	0.6	0.2
2	0.5	0.4	0.7
Difference	0.4	0.2	0.5

Another useful metric is the Minkowski distance. This may be specified for the Ball-Tree class and for many of the detectors in scikit-learn and PyOD. This is actually a generalization of the Manhattan and Euclidean distances, allowing the distances between points to be raised to any power. Using the Minkowski distance and specifying the power as 1 is equivalent to using the Manhattan distance, and specifying the power as 2 is equivalent to using the Euclidean distance. Other powers may be specified as well. For, example, using the power of 3, we have the distances between two records (with three features) calculated as

$$d\left(row1, row2\right) = \sqrt[3]{(1a - 2a)^3 + (1b - 2b)^3 + (3c - 3c)^3}$$

Euclidean distances, compared to Manhattan distances, put more emphasis on the features with larger differences. In comparing the distance between two rows, the Manhattan distance looks only at the differences in each value, while the Euclidean distance looks at the squared distances, so any very large differences in a feature have more of an effect with Euclidean distances. Using larger powers will emphasize these large differences more so.

Taking this to its logical extreme (using an exponent of infinity), we have the Chebyshev distance, which can also be useful in outlier detection. Using this, the distance between two records is defined solely by the maximum difference between two records.

Consider the two rows in table 9.17. The Manhattan distance is the sum of the differences: $0.4 + 0.2 + 0.5$, or 1.1. The Euclidean distance is the square root of the sum of the squared distances, that is, the square root of $0.4^2 + 0.2^2 + 0.5^2$, or 0.67. The Minkowski distance, using a power of 3, is the cube root of $0.4^3 + 0.2^3 + 0.5^3$, or 0.58. The larger the power, the more relevant the largest difference, which in this case is 0.5. The Chebyshev distance here is 0.5—it simply uses the largest difference and nothing else. With Minkowski distances, on the other hand, using even a large power such as 5 or 6 would still include the smaller differences between the values in columns a and b to some extent. Chebyshev has some appeal, as it means two records are similar if all values are similar and dissimilar if any values are different. At the same time, Canberra and Manhattan distances, though in some sense the opposite, can also be quite sensible.

Euclidean distances appear natural when viewing the data as points in space, such as when examining scatterplots. But this is just one way to look at the data. When examining the actual tables of data and thinking about the difference in two rows, it is perhaps more natural (once the features are normalized), to simply take the absolute difference in each feature and sum these differences. If the columns represent dollar values, temperature, air pressure, or other such values, their squared differences don't intuitively have meaning. That is, the Euclidean distance is very useful but is not the only reasonable choice. Manhattan distances also have the significant advantage that they are more robust to the curse of dimensionality, followed by Euclidean and so on; the higher the power, the greater the effect of the curse of dimensionality.

scikit-learn and PyOD also allow specifying any decimal value for the exponent over 1.0. This means we can use, for example, 1.5 as the exponent, to create distance metrics somewhere between Manhattan and Euclidean distances. Using this with PyOD's KNN class, we could create the detector as

```
det = KNN(p=1.5)
```

9.7.2   *Gower's distance metric for mixed data*

In practice, most outlier detectors are either numeric or categorical, and so with outlier detection we normally work with either numeric or categorical distance metrics. This means, although most tabular data is actually mixed, it's rare to use distance metrics for mixed data. We will, though, briefly describe a very common metric for mixed data: the Gower distance.

This method is a little simplistic but can be effective. Given mixed data, such as the staff expenses table, once ordinal encoded and scaled, as shown in table 9.18, we calculate the distances between any two rows by calculating the sum of the distances over all cells. Where the values are numeric, we use the absolute difference (Manhattan distance) and where the values are categorical, we treat a match as 0 and a mismatch as 1. Considering the difference between rows 1 and 2, and skipping the Staff ID column, we have a difference of 1.0 for each of Department, Account, Date of Expense, Date Submitted, and Time Submitted and a difference of 0.09 (that is, 0.21-0.12) for the Amount, for a total Gower distance of 5.09.

Table 9.18   Staff expenses, with ordinal encoding and min-max scaling

Row	Staff ID	Department	Account	Date of Expense	Date Submitted	Time Submitted	Amount
1	1	1	1	2	3	9	0.12
2	2	2	2	3	5	10	0.21
3	3	3	1	4	5	10	0.93
4	1	2	2	4	7	11	0.76

A popular implementation of the Gower distance is the Gower library (https://github.com/wwwjk366/gower).

While the Gower distance is used only occasionally in outlier detection, it (and variations of it) should likely be used more frequently, as it allows us to work with numeric and categorical data together in a more natural way than transforming numeric data to categorical or vice versa. The Gower distance can be useful when you implement your own detection algorithms. It's also possible to use it with some other tools; for example, DBSCAN allows specifying metric = "precomputed," which allows precomputing pairwise distances between points with distances such as the Gower distance. The Gower distance also provides a good background for what we look at next: distance metrics for categorical data. Looking at these, we can address the main limitation of the Gower distance: that it puts more weight on categorical values than numeric. This is because the distances will always be 1.0, while the distances between numeric fields will always be less than 1.0 (assuming min-max scaling; if using robust scaling or other scaling methods, this may not be the case, but the relative importance of the categorical versus numeric features will still likely not be quite as is most appropriate).

9.7.3 *Distance metrics for categorical data*

As with the Gower distance, when working with categorical data, it's possible to measure the distance between two rows using 0.0 for a match and 1.0 for a miss. This is straightforward but doesn't necessarily capture the true difference well. For example, if matching two rows in the staff expenses table, if there are 1,000 records with Sales and 3 with Communications in the Department column, then matching two records with Communications is more significant than matching two with Sales. Also, if the Department column has 6 unique values and the Accounts column has 50 unique values, then matching on the Account is, at least generally, more relevant than matching on the Department feature.

Several metrics can be used with categorical features that take these into consideration, such as Eskin, Goodall, and Inverse Occurrence Frequency (IOF). Most will either count matches as 1.0 and give mismatches a score between 0.0 and 1.0 that considers the distribution or the opposite: they will give mismatches 0.0 and matches a score between 0.0 and 1.0 that considers the distribution.

One library to support these is the `categorical_similarity_measures` library (https://mng.bz/NBWE). This provides several distance measures, including four variations of Goodall, as well as Eskin, though in listing 9.17 I provide another implementation of Eskin distances that is somewhat more efficient. The Eskin distance measure is based on the number of unique values (n) in each feature and uses 1.0 for matches and $n_i^2 / (n_i^2 + 2)$ for mismatches. Listing 9.17 also includes an example collecting the pairwise distances using a sample of the staff expenses table.

Listing 9.17   Code for Eskin distance

```
import math
import pandas as pd

def eskin(df):
    n_rows = len(df)
    n_cols = len(df.columns)
    num_cat = [df[col_name].nunique() for col_name in df.columns]
    n_squared = [math.pow(x, 2) for x in num_cat]
```

Precalculates the
scores for mismatches
for each column

```
mismatch_score = [x/(x+2) for x in n_squared]
eskin_scores = np.zeros((n_rows, n_rows))         ◄──────  Initializes the matrix of
                                                           pair-wise distances
for i in range(n_rows-1):
  for j in range(1+i, n_rows):
    pair_distance = [1]*n_cols
    for k in range(n_cols):
      if df.loc[i, df.columns[k]] != \
          df.loc[j, df.columns[k]]:              ◄──────  Only updates the distance
        pair_distance[k] = mismatch_score[k]              for mismatches
    eskin_scores[i][j] = \
      (n_cols/sum(pair_distance))-1              ◄──────  Creates a normalized
    eskin_scores[j][i] = eskin_scores[i][j]              distance for each pair of
  return eskin_scores                                     rows based on the sum
                                                          over all columns
df = pd.DataFrame({"Department": [0, 1, 2, 0, 0],
                   "Account":[0, 1, 2, 1, 2],
                   "Date of Expence": [2, 2, 3, 4, 4],
                   "Date Submitted": [3, 5, 5, 7, 7]})
eskin(df)
```

This produces a table of pairwise distances between each row shown in table 9.19. The diagonal has 0.0 values as records have zero distance from themselves. The matrix is also symmetric across this diagonal, as the distance from row a to b is the same as from b to a.

Table 9.19   Eskin distances between staff expenses (five rows)

0.0	0.15	0.22	0.15	0.15
0.15	0.0	0.15	0.22	0.22
0.22	0.15	0.0	0.22	0.15
0.15	0.15	0.22	0.0	0.05
0.15	0.22	0.15	0.05	0.0

The Eskin distance is computationally much more expensive than numerical distances, as these are supported by data structures such as `BallTree`, which can optimize these calculations. Nevertheless, when working with categorical data, metrics such as this can be more meaningful in assessing which records are truly similar. This example uses Eskin, but other distance metrics may be more meaningful for some projects, such as Goodall, which considers the frequency of each value and not simply the counts of unique values per feature. Goodall is, though, even more computationally expensive.

9.7.4   *Using categorical distance metrics for mixed data*

The same ideas for categorical data, such as Eskin, Goodall, IOF, and so on, may be incorporated into distance metrics for mixed data. In general, if we have mixed data, we can define the distance between two rows as

$$w(\text{distances over numeric features}) + (1\tilde{\ }w)(\text{distances over categorical})$$

where w is the weight given to the numeric features and $(1 - w)$ the weight given to the categorical features. This removes any issues where categorical features may have greater weights than numeric features and allows us to choose the distance metrics used for the numeric features and for the categorical features separately. The weights may be set based on the relative importance of numeric compared to categorical features or simply based on the numbers of each.

Summary

- Null values may have information value, and we should be mindful how we fill these.
- With features that have a specific format, such as phone numbers, addresses, and dates, we can engineer features to identify anomalous values specific to these types of data.
- With high-cardinality categorical columns, we need to either engineer features from the values or reduce these to a smaller set of unique values.
- With text features, there is a lot of opportunity to use the information in these for finding meaningful outliers.
- Simple features extracted from text are often useful.
- More sophisticated features can be found with tools such as spaCy.
- Topic modeling and clustering are also useful with text features.
- There are cases where different categorical encoding methods, including one-hot, ordinal, count encoding, and others, are most appropriate.
- MinMaxScaler, RobustScaler, and SplineTransformer are often useful for scaling numeric values.
- Encoded categorical values are usually scaled in the same way as numeric features.
- Equal-width and equal-count binning can both be useful at times.
- Determining the ideal number of bins is equally important as the binning method.
- The distance metrics used will be important to any detectors that look at the distances between points.
- Using Canberra, Minkowski, or Chebyshev distances can be effective for some outlier detection projects.
- Gower distance is often used for mixed data though other options are possible.
- There are useful distance metrics for categorical data including Eskin distance, Goodall, IOF, and several others.

Handling very large and very small datasets

The cases we've looked at so far assume the data is of a manageable size, both in terms of the number of rows and number of features, but you may encounter datasets with sizes that are more challenging to work with. We saw in chapter 8 that different detectors can have very different training and prediction times for large datasets, and generally the best option when faced with very large datasets is to work with faster model types, though these may not provide sufficient accuracy in finding the types of outliers needed for your project. For example, univariate outlier tests will tend to be very fast but will miss rare combinations of values. It may be that the detector, or set of detectors, that best provides the outlier scores suitable for your project struggles with the volume of data it is required to assess.

In this chapter we look at some ways to work with large datasets, including dimensionality reduction, searching for relevant subsets of features, using samples, running outlier detection in parallel, and using tools designed for larger data volumes. We end by looking at the opposite problem: very small datasets.

10.1 Data with many features

We've seen before a few major problems working with datasets with many features. To recount from chapter 3:

- Due to the curse of dimensionality, many algorithms are not useable with high dimensions as the distance measures between records become meaningless.
- Some detectors can become very slow, both for training or for prediction.
- It's easy to find spurious results as some records may have unusual values in some features simply due to there being a large number of features.

Here we look at a couple ways to address these problems: dimensionality reduction and using feature subspaces (training multiple models, each on a subset of the full set of features). In all cases, the strategy is to reduce the set of features to a smaller set that can be evaluated for outliers efficiently and reliably.

10.1.1 Dimensionality reduction

One effective method to reduce the number of features is to apply dimensionality reduction techniques. Among the effective methods are principal component analysis (PCA), t-SNE (both provided with scikit-learn), UMAP (https://github.com/lmcinnes/umap), and auto-encoders (covered in chapter 16). These allow us to mitigate the curse of dimensionality, execute outlier detection often considerably faster, and, if we reduce the data to two or three dimensions, visualize the data.

An example is shown in listing 10.1. Here we generate two random datasets with 100,000 rows and 10 features. The first, `data_corr`, has strong associations between the features. We update the last row to contain some large (but not exceptionally large) values that deviate from the normal patterns between the features. We create another test dataset called `data_extreme`, which has no associations between the features. The last row of this is modified to contain extreme values in some features. This allows us to test with two well-understood data and outlier types. This example uses PyOD detectors, which requires first executing `pip install pyod` if this has not been done already.

> **Listing 10.1   Testing model accuracy and time with and without PCA**

```
import numpy as np
import pandas as pd
from sklearn.decomposition import PCA
from pyod.models.ecod import ECOD
from pyod.models.iforest import IForest
```

```
from pyod.models.lof import LOF
from pyod.models.hbos import HBOS
from pyod.models.gmm import GMM
from pyod.models.abod import ABOD
import time

np.random.seed(0)

num_rows = 100_000
num_cols = 10
data_corr = pd.DataFrame({0: np.random.random(num_rows)})

for i in range(1, num_cols):
  data_corr[i] = data_corr[i-1] + (np.random.random(num_rows) / 10.0)

copy_row = data_corr[0].argmax()
data_corr.loc[num_rows-1, 2] = data_corr.loc[copy_row, 2]
data_corr.loc[num_rows-1, 4] = data_corr.loc[copy_row, 4]
data_corr.loc[num_rows-1, 6] = data_corr.loc[copy_row, 6]
data_corr.loc[num_rows-1, 8] = data_corr.loc[copy_row, 8]

start_time = time.process_time()
pca = PCA(n_components=num_cols)
pca.fit(data_corr)
data_corr_pca = pd.DataFrame(pca.transform(data_corr),
                             columns=[x for x in range(num_cols)])
print("Time for PCA tranformation:", (time.process_time() - start_time))
```

Creates a dataset with one exception, with an unusual combination of values

PCA transforms this test set.

We now have the first test dataset, `data_corr` (with the last row deliberately set as an outlier) and have calculated the PCA transformation of this. We next do this for the other test dataset:

```
np.random.seed(0)

data_extreme = pd.DataFrame()
for i in range(num_cols):
  data_extreme[i] = np.random.random(num_rows)

copy_row = data_extreme[0].argmax()
data_extreme.loc[num_rows-1, 2] = data_extreme[2].max() * 1.5
data_extreme.loc[num_rows-1, 4] = data_extreme[4].max() * 1.5
data_extreme.loc[num_rows-1, 6] = data_extreme[6].max() * 1.5
data_extreme.loc[num_rows-1, 8] = data_extreme[8].max() * 1.5

start_time = time.process_time()
pca = PCA(n_components=num_cols)
pca.fit(data_corr)
data_extreme_pca = pd.DataFrame(pca.transform(data_corr),
                                columns=[x for x in range(num_cols)])
print("Time for PCA tranformation:", (time.process_time() - start_time))
```

Creates a dataset with one exception, with four extreme values

PCA transforms the second test set.

We now have both test datasets and will define a function that, given a dataset and a detector, will train the detector on the full dataset as well as predict on the same data, timing both operations. For the empirical cumulative distribution function (ECOD), we add special handling to create a new instance so as not to maintain a memory from previous executions:

```
def evaluate_detector(df, clf, model_type):          ◄─┐  Function to train and test
  if "ECOD" in model_type:                              │  a model and output the
    clf = ECOD()                                        │  times required
  start_time = time.process_time()
  clf.fit(df)
  time_for_fit = (time.process_time() - start_time)

  start_time = time.process_time()
  pred = clf.decision_function(df)
  time_for_predict = (time.process_time() - start_time)

  scores_df[f'{model_type} Scores'] = pred
  scores_df[f'{model_type} Rank'] =\
    scores_df[f'{model_type} Scores'].rank(ascending=False)

  print(f"{model_type:<20} Fit Time:    {time_for_fit:.2f}")
  print(f"{model_type:<20} Predict Time: {time_for_predict:.2f}")
```

The next function defined executes for each dataset and the variations on the dataset, calling the previous method for each:

Function to test one model
type for one dataset

```
def evaluate_dataset_variations(df, df_pca, clf, model_name):  ◄─┐
  evaluate_detector(df, clf, model_name)
  evaluate_detector(df_pca, clf, f'{model_name} (PCA)')
  evaluate_detector(df_pca[[0, 1, 2]], clf, f'{model_name} (PCA - 1st 3)')
  evaluate_detector(df_pca[[7, 8, 9]], clf, f'{model_name} (PCA - last 3)')
```

The final function defined is called for each dataset, along with the PCA transformation of this dataset. It executes the previous function for each detector tested here. For this example, we use six detectors, each from PyOD:

```
def evaluate_dataset(df, df_pca):                    ◄─┐  Function to take
  clf = IForest()                                       │  each model type and
  evaluate_dataset_variations(df, df_pca, clf, 'IF')    │  evaluate each

  clf = LOF(novelty=True)
  evaluate_dataset_variations(df, df_pca, clf, 'LOF')

  clf = ECOD()
  evaluate_dataset_variations(df, df_pca, clf, 'ECOD')

  clf = HBOS()
  evaluate_dataset_variations(df, df_pca, clf, 'HBOS')

  clf = GMM()
  evaluate_dataset_variations(df, df_pca, clf, 'GMM')

  clf = ABOD()
  evaluate_dataset_variations(df, df_pca, clf, 'ABOD')
```

We finally call the `evaluate_dataset()` method for both test datasets and print out the last rows (after sorting by scores):

```
scores_df = data_corr.copy()
evaluate_dataset(data_corr, data_corr_pca)
rank_columns = [x for x in scores_df.columns
                if type(x) == str and 'Rank' in x]
print(scores_df[rank_columns].tail())

scores_df = data_extreme.copy()
evaluate_dataset(data_extreme, data_extreme_pca)
rank_columns = [x for x in scores_df.columns
                if type(x) == str and 'Rank' in x]
print(scores_df[rank_columns].tail())
```

There are several interesting results. Looking at the fit times for the `data_corr` dataset in table 10.1 (the fit and predict times for the other test set were similar), we see that, similar to the timing tests in chapter 8, different detectors have quite different times. The tests were on Google colab, with times in seconds. The times to fit the PCA-transformed data are about the same as the original data, which makes sense given this data is the same size. We also test using only the last three PCA components (components 7, 8, and 9), and the fit times are drastically reduced in some cases, particularly for local outlier factor (LOF).

Table 10.1   Fit Times for the `data_corr` test dataset

	IF	LOF	ECOD	HBOS	GMM	ABOD
Full data	6.1	19.4	0.56	0.08	0.68	29.1
PCA	6.6	16.9	0.44	0.10	0.55	25.3
PCA (3 components)	7.4	1.4	0.13	0.02	0.25	14.6

In table 10.2, we see the predict times for the `data_corr` dataset (the times for the other test set were similar here as well). Again, we see a very sizable drop in prediction times using just three components, especially for LOF. With Isolation Forest (IF), as we train the same number of trees regardless of the number of features and pass all records to be evaluated through the same set of trees, the times are unaffected by the number of features. For all other detectors shown here, however, the number of features is very relevant.

Table 10.2   Predict Times for the `data_corr` test dataset

	IF	LOF	ECOD	HBOS	GMM	ABOD
Full data	3.2	20.8	1.1	0.06	0.06	26.1
PCA	3.1	15.3	1.0	0.05	0.09	22.7
PCA (3 components)	2.7	1.4	0.3	0.01	0.03	12.3

In terms of accuracy, all five detectors performed well on the two datasets most of the time, in terms of assigning the highest outlier score to the last row, which, for both test datasets, is the one known outlier. The results are shown in table 10.3. In most cases, the last row was given the highest or nearly highest rank, with the exception of IF, ECOD, and histogram-based outlier score (HBOS) on the first dataset. This is a good example where strong detectors such as IF can occasionally do poorly even for clear outliers.

Table 10.3 Rank of known outliers for five detectors on two test datasets with the original features

Dataset	IF rank	LOF rank	ECOD rank	HBOS rank	GMM rank	ABOD rank
1	2175	1	14973	7053	1	1
2	10	1	1	1	1	1

We also see a drastic improvement in accuracy when using PCA for these datasets and these detectors (table 10.4). This is not always the case, but it does hold true here. When the detectors execute on the PCA-transformed data, all rank the known outlier the highest on both datasets. When data is PCA-transformed, as discussed in chapter 6, the components are all unassociated with each other; the outliers are the extreme values, which are much easier to identify.

Table 10.4 Rank of known outliers using PCA with components

Dataset	IF rank	LOF rank	ECOD rank	HBOS rank	GMM rank	ABOD rank
1	1	1	1	1	1	1
2	1	1	1	1	1	1

Also interesting is that only the last three components are necessary to rank the known outliers as the top outliers (table 10.5), and, as we see in tables 10.1 and 10.2, fit and predict times are substantially shorter in these cases. This is where we can achieve significant performance improvements using PCA: it's often necessary to use only a small number of the components. It can vary how many and which are best to use, and some experimentation will be needed—again, likely using doped data. This experiment did cover two of the main types of outliers we can have with data: extreme values and values that deviate from a linear pattern, both of which are identifiable in the later components, though for some types of outliers (and to reduce noise) you may wish to use other components for some projects. Using only a small set of components will also reduce memory requirements.

Table 10.5 Rank of known outliers using PCA with the last three components

Dataset	IF rank	LOF rank	ECOD rank	HBOS rank	GMM rank	ABOD rank
1	1	1	1	1	1	1
2	1	1	1	1	1	1

Dimensionality reduction also has some advantages in that it can help visualize the outliers. For example, inspecting the last two components of the first test dataset, which contained unusual combinations of values, we can see the known outlier clearly, as shown in figure 10.1. However, it's somewhat questionable how informative this is, as the components themselves are difficult to understand.

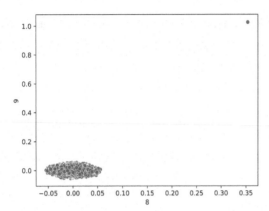

Figure 10.1   Scatterplot of the last two components of the PCA transformation of the first dataset, which contained an unusual combination of values. Here we see a single point in the top-right of the space. It is clear that the point is a strong outlier, though it is not clear what components 8 and 9 represent.

10.1.2 *Feature subspaces*

Where there are many features, a useful method to conduct outlier detection is to work with subspaces, which are subsets of the full set of features, as described in chapter 6. For example, if a dataset has 100 features, we may train 10 models, each covering 10 features. This has major advantages in terms of speed, mitigating the curse of dimensionality, and interpretability. For example, if a model using only 10 features scores a record high, we do not know the exact set of features that are relevant, but there are at least only 10 features that may be related to this. It also allows both training and predicting in parallel. Further, it allows the use of detectors such as ConvexHull, which struggle with high-dimensional data but do quite well in low dimensions.

It is, however, difficult to find the relevant subspaces. Assuming we are interested in unusual combinations, it can be difficult to know which sets of features will contain the unusual combinations. In creating 10 detectors, we may use the first 10 features for the first detector, the second set of 10 features for the second, and so on, If the first two features have some rows with anomalous combinations, we will detect this. But if there are anomalous combinations related to the first feature and any of the 90 features not covered by the same model, we will miss these. We can improve the odds of putting relevant features together by using many more subspaces, but it can be difficult to ensure all sets of features that should be together are actually together at least once, particularly where there are relevant outliers in the data based on three, four, or more features, which must appear together in at least one subspace to be detected.

There is also the question of how many features should be in each subspace. We can keep the subspaces small for greater interpretability. The most interpretable, using two features per subspace, also allows for simple visualization. However, if we have d features, we will need d × (d − 1)/2 models to cover all combinations, which can be intractable. With 100 features, we would require 4,950 detectors. In general, we need to use at least several features per detector. We wish to use enough detectors, and enough features per detector, that each pair of features appears together at least once and few enough features per detector, that the detectors have largely different features from each other. In terms of accuracy, using more subspaces is strictly better but is computationally more expensive.

There are a few broad approaches to finding useful subspaces:

- *Based on domain knowledge*—Here we consider which sets of features could potentially have combinations of values we would consider noteworthy.
- *Based on associations*—Unusual combinations are only possible if a set of features are associated in some way. In prediction problems, we often wish to minimize the correlations between features, but with outlier detection, these are the features that are most useful to consider together. The features with the strongest associations will have the most meaningful outliers if there are exceptions to the normal patterns.
- *Based on finding very sparse regions*—Records are typically considered as outliers if they are unlike most other records in the data, which implies they are located in sparse regions of the data. Therefore, useful subspaces can be found as those that contain large nearly empty regions.
- *Randomly*—This is the method used by FeatureBagging and, while it can be suboptimal, it avoids the expensive searches for associations and sparse regions and can work reasonably well where many subspaces are used.
- *Exhaustive searches*—This is the method employed by CountsOutlierDetector, which will be covered later in chapter 13. This is limited to subspaces with small numbers of features, but the results are highly interpretable.
- *Using the features related to any known outliers*—If we have a set of known outliers, and can identify why they are outliers (the relevant features), and are in a situation where we do not wish to identify unknown outliers, only these specific outliers, then we can take advantage of this and identify the sets of features relevant for each known outlier, and construct models for the various sets of features required.

We covered subspace outlier detection (SOD) and FeatureBagging in chapter 6, as both are provided by PyOD. Here we will look at some other algorithms that may be employed to find subspaces. Other than SOD and FeatureBagging, there are few open-source implementations of subspace discovery algorithms, which is unfortunate as this is an important part of outlier detection.

DOMAIN KNOWLEDGE

Let's take the example of the expenses table from chapter 2 (repeated here as table 10.6). Examining this, we can determine the outliers we would and would not be interested in. Unusual combinations of Account and Amount as well as Department and

Account may be of interest, whereas Date of Expense and Time would not be a useful combination. We can continue in this way, creating a small number of subspaces, each with likely two, three, or four features, which can allow for very efficient and interpretable outlier detection.

Table 10.6   Staff expenses

Row	Staff ID	Department	Account	Date of expense	Date submitted	Time	Amount
1	9000483	Sales	Meals	02/03/2023	02/03/2023	09:10:21	12.44
2	9303332	Marketing	Travel	02/03/2023	02/03/2023	10:43:35	41.90
3	9847421	Engineering	Meals	02/03/2023	02/03/2023	08:56:04	643.99
4	9303332	Marketing	Supplies	02/03/2023	02/03/2023	03:12:09	212.00

This can miss cases where we have an association in the data but where the association is not obvious. If so, the association can be worth investigating. We can discover associations, for example, testing where features can be predicted accurately from the other features using simple predictive models. Discovering these associations may be useful in itself, though it may or may not be useful for the outlier detection process. If there is a relationship between accounts and the time of the day, this may be due to the process people happened to use to submit their expenses, and deviations from this are possibly of interest but more likely are not.

RANDOM FEATURE SUBSPACES

Creating subspaces randomly can be effective if there is no domain knowledge to draw on. This is fast and can create a set of subspaces that will tend to catch the strongest outliers, though it can miss some important outliers too.

Listing 10.2 provides an example of code to create a set of random subspaces that all have the same number of features. There is also an advantage in having the subspaces cover different numbers of features, as this can introduce some more diversity, but there is strong diversity in any case from using different features (so long as each uses a relatively small number of features, such that the subspaces are largely different features). Having the same number of features simplifies tuning the model as many parameters depend on the number of features—if all subspaces have the same number of features, they can also use the same parameters. It also simplifies combining the scores, as the detectors will be more comparable to each other; using different numbers of features can produce different scores. For example, with k nearest neighbors (KNN), we expect greater distances between neighbors if there are more features.

Here the main loop executes once for each base detector, so will create one subspace each iteration. It starts by selecting the feature that so far has been used the least and adds features one at a time to the current subspace, such that it minimizes adding features that have already been matched with the features already in the subspace. Doing this, we create a set of subspaces that matches each pair of features roughly equally often. This example uses a set of eight features, named A through H.

Listing 10.2 Algorithm to select random subspaces

```
import pandas as pd
import numpy as np

def get_random_subspaces(features_arr, num_base_detectors,
                         num_feats_per_detector):
    num_feats = len(features_arr)
    feat_sets_arr = []
    ft_used_counts = np.zeros(num_feats)
    ft_pair_mtx = np.zeros((num_feats, num_feats))

    for _ in range(num_base_detectors):
        min_count = ft_used_counts.min()
        idxs = np.where(ft_used_counts == min_count)[0]

        feat_set = [np.random.choice(idxs)]

        while len(feat_set) < num_feats_per_detector:
            mtx_with_set = ft_pair_mtx[:, feat_set]
            sums = mtx_with_set.sum(axis=1)
            min_sum = sums.min()
            min_idxs = np.where(sums==min_sum)[0]
            new_feat = np.random.choice(min_idxs)
            feat_set.append(new_feat)
            feat_set = list(set(feat_set))

            for c in feat_set:
                ft_pair_mtx[c][new_feat] += 1
                ft_pair_mtx[new_feat][c] += 1

        for c in feat_set:
            ft_used_counts[c] += 1

        feat_sets_arr.append(feat_set)

    return feat_sets_arr

np.random.seed(0)
features_arr = ['A', 'B', 'C', 'D', 'E', 'F', 'G', 'H']
num_base_detectors = 4
num_feats_per_detector = 5

feat_sets_arr = get_random_subspaces(features_arr,
    num_base_detectors, num_feats_per_detector)
for feat_set in feat_sets_arr:
    print([features_arr[x] for x in feat_set])
```

- **Gets the set of features with the minimum count**
- **Picks one of these randomly and adds to the current set**
- **Finds the remaining set of features**
- **Updates ft_pair_mtx**
- **Updates ft_used_counts**

Normally we would create many more base detectors, but this uses four to keep the example simple. This will output the following subspaces:

```
['A', 'E', 'F', 'G', 'H']
['B', 'C', 'D', 'F', 'H']
['A', 'B', 'C', 'D', 'E']
['B', 'D', 'E', 'F', 'G']
```

FEATURE SUBSPACES BASED ON CORRELATIONS

Everything else equal, in creating the subspaces, it's useful to keep associated features together as much as possible. There are several ways to test for associations. We can create predictive models to attempt to predict each feature from each other single feature (this will capture relatively complex relationships between features). With numeric features, the simplest is to check for Spearman correlations, which will miss nonmonotonic relationships but will detect most strong relationships.

In listing 10.3, we provide an example of code to select subspaces based on correlations. To execute this, we first specify the number of subspaces desired and the number of features in each. This executes by first finding all pairwise correlations between the features. We then create the first subspace, finding the largest correlation in the correlation matrix (which adds two features to the subspace) and looping over the number of other features to be added to this space. For each, we take the largest correlation in the matrix for any pair of features such that one is currently in the space and one is not. Once this space has a sufficient number of features, we create the next space, taking the largest correlation remaining in the matrix, and so on.

We execute this on the baseball dataset, which turns out to contain some large correlations. The correlation, for example, of At bats and Runs is 0.94, indicating any values that deviate significantly from this pattern would likely be outliers.

Listing 10.3 Example code to identify subspaces based on correlations

```
def get_highest_corr():                                        Function to find the pair
    return np.unravel_index(                                   of features remaining in
        np.argmax(corr_matrix.values, axis=None),              the matrix with the
        corr_matrix.shape)                                     highest correlation

def get_correlated_subspaces(corr_matrix, num_base_detectors,  Starts each
                             num_feats_per_detector):          subspace as the
    sets = []                                                  two remaining
    for _ in range(num_base_detectors):      Loops through each features with the
        m1, m2 = get_highest_corr()          subspace to be created highest
        curr_set = [m1, m2]                                    correlation
        for _ in range(2, num_feats_per_detector):
            m = np.unravel_index(np.argsort(corr_matrix.values, axis=None),
                                 corr_matrix.shape)
            m0 = m[0][::-1]                   Gets the other
            m1 = m[1][::-1]                   remaining correlations
            for i in range(len(m0)):
                d0 = m0[i]                                     Adds the pair if either
                d1 = m1[i]                                     feature is already in
                if (d0 in curr_set) or (d1 in curr_set):       the subset
                    curr_set.append(d0)
                    curr_set = list(set(curr_set))
                    if len(curr_set) < num_feats_per_detector:
                        curr_set.append(d1)
                        curr_set = list(set(curr_set))   Removes duplicates
            if len(curr_set) >= num_feats_per_detector:
                break
```

```
            for i in curr_set:
                i_idx = corr_matrix.index[i]
                for j in curr_set:
                    j_idx = corr_matrix.columns[j]
                    corr_matrix.loc[i_idx, j_idx] = 0
            if len(curr_set) >= num_feats_per_detector:
                break

        sets.append(curr_set)
    return sets

import pandas as pd
import numpy as np
from sklearn.datasets import fetch_openml

data = fetch_openml('baseball', version=1)
df = pd.DataFrame(data.data, columns=data.feature_names)

corr_matrix = abs(df.corr(method='spearman'))
corr_matrix = corr_matrix.where(
    np.triu(np.ones(corr_matrix.shape), k=1).astype(np.bool))
corr_matrix = corr_matrix.fillna(0)

feat_sets_arr = get_correlated_subspaces(corr_matrix, num_base_detectors=5,
                                    num_feats_per_detector=4)
for feat_set in feat_sets_arr:
    print([df.columns[x] for x in feat_set])
```

Updates the correlation matrix, removing the features now used in the current subspace

This produces

```
['Games_played', 'At_bats', 'Runs', 'Hits']
['RBIs', 'At_bats', 'Hits', 'Doubles']
['RBIs', 'Games_played', 'Runs', 'Doubles']
['Walks', 'Runs', 'Games_played', 'Triples']
['RBIs', 'Strikeouts', 'Slugging_pct', 'Home_runs']
```

ONGOING OUTLIER DETECTION PROJECTS

One thing to be aware of when constructing subsets, if they are formed based on correlations or on sparse regions, is that the relevant subspaces may change over time as the data changes. New associations may emerge between features and new sparse regions may form that will be useful for identifying outliers, though these will be missed if the subspaces are not recalculated from time to time.

Using PCA and creating subspaces can be useful for outlier detection even where data volumes are not large and speed is not a major concern, as they can result in greater accuracy, and subspaces can increase interpretability. Nevertheless, where data volumes are very large (in terms of number of rows), even using both methods, the system may be too slow or consume too much memory to be usable. In fact, problems with large numbers of rows, though exacerbated by large numbers of features, can occur even with few features. We look at this next.

10.2   Data with many rows

Having large volumes of data is in some ways a benefit. It allows us to create models that represent the data very accurately, which results in better assessments of what is typical and what is unusual. It also allows the option of deep learning-based approaches, which tend to require very large volumes of data. Large datasets, though, can be slow to work with, can exceed memory resources, and can be difficult to evaluate; even when flagging only a small fraction of the records, detectors may flag, in terms of the actual count, a very large number of records.

Here we'll separate the concerns of training versus predicting. Both steps, when working with large data volumes (for example, in the millions or billions of rows), can be very slow. We saw in chapter 8 the results of some timing experiments. Some detectors remain very fast even with large volumes, but many can become impracticably slower. In some cases, the parameters may be adjusted (such as n_neighbors for LOF, bandwidth for kernel density estimation (KDE), number of bins for HBOS, number of iterations for Nearest Sample, and so on), which can improve execution times but can also affect the accuracy.

10.2.1   Training and predicting on data samples

In most scenarios, training can be done relatively infrequently and can be executed on a sample of the data, which can greatly reduce the training times. How large of a sample is used is a tradeoff between accuracy and speed. The more features present and the more complex the interactions between the features, the more rows needed to train a reliable model. You may be able to create a reliable model with just hundreds or thousands of records, though you may need many more as well. The best way to estimate this will often be testing with manipulated records (the doping process introduced in chapter 8). As you train with larger datasets, you will likely be able to detect synthetic outliers with more reliability. Doing this, you will be able to measure the relationship between sample size and training time and find a suitable balance. An example of this was shown in chapter 8.

Building models based on smaller samples will also, in some cases, allow prediction to execute faster. This will not affect, for example, Isolation Forest, Extended IF, distance metric learning, or methods based on predicting Real versus Fake but will affect any that evaluate records using distances to reference sets, such as LOF, KNN, Radius, local distance-based outlier factor (LDOF), and so on. The more records in the reference set to calculate distances to, the longer (though more accurate) the prediction process.

With prediction, we do not usually have the luxury of using a sample; we usually need to execute the model on every record to find any outliers in the data. There can be exceptions though: where it is sufficient to spot-check the data (where we want to ensure only that it is largely free of major anomalies, not necessarily completely free) or where we wish to identify only as many anomalies as can be followed up by the people available; in this case identifying more outliers may have little value, as there will not be people available to examine them.

10.2.2 *Testing models for stability*

Another advantage of large datasets, at least for ongoing projects, is they allow the opportunity to better test the model. Although we likely do not have a ground truth to test against, we can at least test if the model is stable: we can test if the model produces similar results when trained on different data. If we have, say, 100 million rows and know we will need to regularly retrain the model as new data arrives, we can experimentally determine how many records appear to be necessary to train on each time. We can assume we will need well less than 100 million, but the training size that best balances accuracy with execution time will need to be determined experimentally.

In listing 10.4, we work with the KDD Cup dataset, introduced in chapter 5. This loads in approximately 100,000 records. We test using training set sizes ranging from 100 rows to 25,000. For each size, we train on 10 different samples of that size and examine the consistency in prediction among the 10 trials. As more data is used for training, the predictions from the 10 trials become more consistent, and eventually we can determine that the training size, at least in this respect, is big enough; that is, we can determine the point where, if we train on more data, the results will become slightly more consistent but this does not warrant the additional execution time.

We use two measures of consistency. For the first, we look at the top 50 records predicted in each trial and determine how consistent these are from trial to trial. If perfectly consistent, all trials will select the same top 50 and there will be only 50 unique records selected. If completely inconsistent, all 10 trials will select 50 different top-scored records, and 500 unique records will be selected in all. The second is a correlation measure introduced in chapter 8—here taking the Pearson correlation among the top-scored records each trial, defined as those with scores at least 2.0 standard deviations above the mean after robust scaling. In this case, clustering-based local outlier factor (CBLOF) is used for the detector.

Listing 10.4 Testing a model for stability

```
import pandas as pd
import numpy as np
from sklearn.datasets import fetch_kddcup99
from sklearn.preprocessing import OrdinalEncoder

np.random.seed(0)

X, y = fetch_kddcup99(subset="SA", percent10=True, random_state=42,
                      return_X_y=True, as_frame=True)
y = (y != b"normal.").astype(np.int32)

enc = OrdinalEncoder()
X = pd.DataFrame(enc.fit_transform(X), columns=X.columns)
```

We have now loaded and ordinal-encoded the KDD Cup data. We next define the code to test training on a range of sample sizes:

```
from sklearn.preprocessing import RobustScaler
from pyod.models.cblof import CBLOF
import matplotlib.pyplot as plt
import seaborn as sns
import warnings
warnings.filterwarnings('ignore')
np.random.seed(0)

training_set_sizes = [100, 250, 500, 1_000, 1_500, 2_000, 2_500, 3_000,
                      4_000, 5_000, 10_000, 15_000, 20_000, 25_000]
number_unique_arr = []
corr_arr = []
for train_size in training_set_sizes:
    top_results = []
    scores_df = pd.DataFrame()
    for trial_number in range(10):
        det = CBLOF()
        det.fit(X.sample(n=train_size, random_state=trial_number))
        pred = det.decision_function(X)
        top_results.extend(np.argsort(pred)[:50])
        scores_df[trial_number] = pred

    top_results = list(set(top_results))
    number_unique_arr.append(len(top_results))

    for col_name in scores_df.columns:
        scaler = RobustScaler()
        scores_df[col_name] = scaler.fit_transform(
            np.array(scores_df[col_name]).reshape(-1, 1))
        scores_df[col_name] =\
            scores_df[col_name].apply(lambda x: x if x > 2.0 else 0.0)

    corr_arr.append(scores_df.corr().mean().mean())
```

- Loops through each training set size
- Loops through 10 trials of each training set size
- Collects the set of the top 50 predictions for each trial
- Saves the full set of predictions
- Determines how many unique records were in the top 50
- Determines the correlation among the top-scored records from each trial

Plots of the consistency over the trials compared to the size of the training set are shown in figure 10.2. Using both measures, we can see increased agreement among the detectors as the training set size is increased. By 10,000 or 20,000 there is not complete agreement, but the process is reasonably stable.

It is still useful to test with doped data to estimate the accuracy of the models, but this process also allows us to estimate the stability of the model, which is also very important when it will be regularly retrained.

10.2.3 Segmenting data

One useful approach when working with very large datasets is to segment the data: to break it into a set of smaller datasets that can each form a smaller, simpler model. For example, consider the staff expenses table from chapter 2, repeated here as table 10.7. It's possible to create a model to represent the full normal behavior for staff expenses, which needs to capture how different departments and different accounts tend to work—the model will have to capture some complex behavior. It may be simpler to

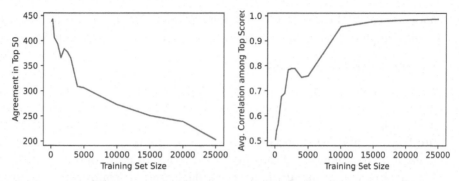

Figure 10.2 **Two measures of stability given different training set sizes. With outlier detection, other than when testing with synthetic data, we typically do not have a ground truth to test against, but we can determine how stable the model is given different training set sizes. This helps determine an appropriate sample size to train with. The left pane shows over 10 trials for each training set size, the number of unique records placed in the top 50 over the trials. Less is better, and ideally all 10 trials would select the same top 50. In the right pane we see the Pearson correlation among the top-scored records. Higher is better, with 1.0 being complete agreement.**

create a separate model for each account type, where each model attempts to model the normal behavior for only that one type of account.

Table 10.7 Staff expenses

Row	Staff ID	Department	Account	Date of expense	Date submitted	Time submitted	Amount
1	9000483	Sales	Meals	02/03/2023	02/03/2023	09:10:21	12.44
2	9303332	Marketing	Travel	02/03/2023	02/03/2023	10:43:35	41.90
3	9847421	Engineering	Meals	02/03/2023	02/03/2023	10:56:04	643.99
4	9303332	Marketing	Supplies	02/03/2023	02/03/2023	11:12:09	212.00

Although this will result in more models, it may be that each can use a simpler algorithm and can be trained on a smaller sample. The total training time will not likely decrease, though this is possible if significantly simpler detectors may be used. Prediction time will also decrease for some models (KNN, LOF, ODIN, and so on—models that use reference datasets) though will be roughly the same for other models.

The same may be accomplished by first clustering the data, but as clustering may be as expensive as outlier detection, there may not be any decrease in time, especially as clustering can be difficult to perform well and may take some number of iterations to become effective. It will often be more expedient (and interpretable) to manually segment the data and to quickly create useful subsets of the data to work with.

Using multiple, smaller models may also help mitigate any memory limits that you may face when working with the full dataset. Having multiple models adds overhead in terms of testing but can also make tuning the models more practical: when tuning the model for meals, there's no risk of damaging the model for travel expenses. The use of multiple models also facilitates training in parallel, which we look at next.

10.2.4 *Running in parallel vs. in sequence*

Where hardware resources allow, executing training in parallel will be a very effective means to reduce training time, though this is only possible with some model types. PyOD supports parallel training for several detectors, including COPOD, ECOD, Feature Bagging, and Isolation Forest, through setting the n_jobs parameter. The documentation describes specifically how this is used for each, but the idea is similar to n_jobs parameter frequently used with scikit-learn: this controls the number of processes that are executed simultaneously.

Where multiple detectors are trained, parallelism can certainly be used. That is, we may not be able to train a single detector in parallel, but if the system uses multiple detectors, these can be trained simultaneously. Although in predictive models, ensembles of models are often sequential (such as with boosted or stacked ensembles), in outlier detection the detectors are almost always completely independent, so they may be trained separately. Parallel training may be done simply by using Python tools such as Python's multiprocessing library or by using the Scalable Framework for Unsupervised Outlier Detection (SUOD) as described in chapter 6.

PREDICTION IN PARALLEL

Prediction may almost always be done in parallel. Where multiple detectors are used, it is possible to send the current batch of records for prediction to each detector at once and combine the results once all detectors are complete. It is also possible to divide the current batch of records to be predicted into smaller batches, which may each be executed in parallel, as long as the detectors have separate train and predict steps, which is true of almost all detectors other than ConvexHull and Entropy.

Lising 10.5 provides an example of predicting in parallel using the KDD Cup dataset. This can be particularly useful when data arrives in large batches and must be evaluated quickly.

> **Listing 10.5   Executing prediction in parallel**

```
import numpy as np
import pandas as pd
from sklearn.datasets import fetch_kddcup99
from sklearn.preprocessing import OrdinalEncoder
from pyod.models.iforest import IForest
import concurrent
import warnings
warnings.filterwarnings('ignore')

np.random.seed(0)

X, y = fetch_kddcup99(subset="SA", percent10=True, random_state=42,
                      return_X_y=True, as_frame=True)
```

```
enc = OrdinalEncoder()
X = pd.DataFrame(enc.fit_transform(X), columns=X.columns)       ◄──┐ Ordinal encodes the
det = IForest().                                                   │ data and fits an IF
det.fit(X)

                                                          Defines the number
num_splits = 5                                      ◄──┘ of parallel processes

def evaluate_subset(df):                            ◄──┐ Defines a method to evaluate
    return det.decision_function(df)                   │ each subset against the IF

process_arr = []
full_results = []                                                  ┌ Loops through
rows_per_subset = len(X) // num_splits                             │ each subset of the
with concurrent.futures.ProcessPoolExecutor() as executor: ◄──┘ data in parallel
    for dataset_idx in range(num_splits):
        print(f"Starting process for dataset: {dataset_idx}")
        start_row = dataset_idx * rows_per_subset
        end_row = (dataset_idx + 1) * rows_per_subset
        print(start_row, end_row)
        f = executor.submit(evaluate_subset, X[start_row: end_row+1])
        process_arr.append(f)
    for f in process_arr:                              ◄──┐ Collects and consolidates
        full_results.extend(f.result())                    │ the results
```

PREDICTION IN SEQUENCE

However, with respect to total processing time, in some cases it may actually be possible to organize the outlier detection system such that it is faster to execute the detectors in sequence. For example, in a system where we have found a set of three detectors (and parameters for each) that work well and have determined that it is useful to flag the records that are scored highly by all three, then it is possible to execute these in sequence, such that the first detector scores all records, with only those scoring relatively high being passed to the second detector, which passes only the top-scoring subset of these to the third detector. In the end, this will flag as an outlier only records scored at least moderately high by each detector.

Ideally, this would be set up such that the fastest detectors are executed first and the slowest last (as these need to process only a small number of records), though this is actually difficult to arrange. This setup requires that the first detectors identify a broad set of outliers, including any subtle outliers, while the very fastest tend to be univariate outlier tests, such as HBOS and ECOD, which detect only specific types of outliers. It may work better to use detectors such as IF, which detect a reasonably broad collection of outliers and operate quickly, in the early stages, possibly passing a large fraction of the data (perhaps the top 10% or 15% of the data in terms of scores) to the next detectors. This may take some tuning, but the general idea of running in sequence with later detectors examining fewer and fewer rows can allow significantly reduced total execution times.

An example is shown in figure 10.3 using the KDD Cup dataset and three detectors: IF, LOF, and GMM. Using this setup can require substantially less processing than executing all detectors of the full dataset.

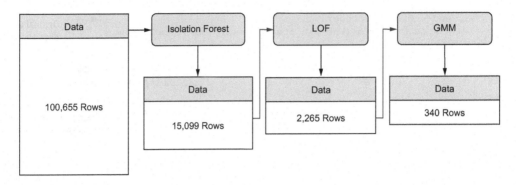

Figure 10.3   Flow diagram of sequential processing of the KDD Cup dataset given three detectors. Where we wish to flag only records scored the highest by all three, we may run the detectors in sequence to reduce total execution time. Similar approaches can also be taken in more complex workflows. Here, the IF must work with the full dataset but all other detectors with substantially fewer records.

Listing 10.6 provides a code example of this process. Here we take the top 15% of rows at each stage, passing these to the next stage. The row counts are shown in figure 10.3. We start with 100,655 records and end with 340 in the final set, the set scored at least relatively high by all three detectors. This can easily be adjusted to return more or less as required.

Listing 10.6   Executing detectors in sequence on the KDD Cup dataset

```
import numpy as np
import pandas as pd
from pyod.models.iforest import IForest
from pyod.models.lof import LOF
from pyod.models.gmm import GMM
from sklearn.datasets import fetch_kddcup99
from sklearn.preprocessing import OrdinalEncoder

np.random.seed(0)
df, _ = fetch_kddcup99(subset="SA", percent10=True, random_state=42,
                    return_X_y=True, as_frame=True)
enc = OrdinalEncoder()
df = pd.DataFrame(enc.fit_transform(df), columns=df.columns)

outliers_df = df.copy()                         Executes the IF on
clf = IForest(contamination=0.15)               the full dataset
pred = clf.fit_predict(outliers_df)
outliers_df = outliers_df[pred == 1]

clf = LOF(contamination=0.15)                   Executes the LOF on the top 15%
pred = clf.fit_predict(outliers_df)             of the data as scored by the IF
outliers_df = outliers_df[pred == 1]

clf = GMM(contamination=0.15)                   Executes the GMM on the top
pred = clf.fit_predict(outliers_df)             15% of what that LOF evaluated
outliers_df = outliers_df[pred == 1]
```

10.2.5 *Tools for working with large datasets*

When working with large volumes of data, the methods covered here will be useful, but it may also be necessary to look at using different tools or platforms. There are excellent tools available to handle data at scale, which can be helpful for different stages of the outlier detection process. These are particularly worth looking into when it is necessary to routinely process large volumes of data.

FASTER PAIRWISE DISTANCE CALCULATIONS

As many outlier detectors, as well as many other tasks in computer science, rely on pairwise distance calculations between points, there has been a great deal of research into approximate algorithms and data structures to allow this to be performed quickly. Though little is available for categorical distances calculations, there are excellent tools for numeric data.

One tool is provided in the datasketch library (https://github.com/ekzhu/datasketch), the Hierarchical Navigable Small World (HNSW) data structure. This allows for very fast, approximate nearest neighbors searches. It is somewhat more complex to use than `BallTree` but is still simple to use and well documented. An example is provided in listing 10.7. This creates a random set of data with 1,000 rows and 10 features and then inserts this into an HNSW object, looping through the data and inserting the items one at a time. We then call `query()` to find the 10 nearest neighbors for a given point—in this example, the first record in the data.

Listing 10.7 Example using HNSW for nearest neighbors queries

```
from datasketch.hnsw import HNSW          Creates a random
import numpy as np                        set of data

data = np.random.random_sample((1000, 10))          Inserts the
index = HNSW(distance_func=lambda x, y: np.linalg.norm(x - y))   data into a
for i, d in enumerate(data):              HNSW object
    index.insert(i, d)
                                   Finds the 10 nearest
index.query(data[0], k=10)         neighbors of the first row
```

There are several other tools for approximate nearest neighbors queries as well, with an overview of these provided at https://github.com/erikbern/ann-benchmarks. Some of the tools pointed to, such as Faiss (https://github.com/facebookresearch/faiss) from Meta also support faster clustering, which can be very useful to increase the performance with any outlier detection methods based on clustering.

H20

When working with very large datasets, it may be necessary to use tools specifically designed to work with data at scale. We look broadly at a few of these next, starting with H20. H20.ai (https://h2o.ai/) is an open-source platform for scalable machine learning. It's a large system that provides a great deal of functionality for machine learning, including predictive models, deep neural networks, large language models, PCA, and quite a bit more. It's available in Python as well as other languages. One advantage of using H20 is it works with technologies well suited for big data, such as Hadoop and Spark. H20 also provides two outlier detector algorithms, IF and Extended IF, though any others can be used with H20.

SPARK

When working on outlier detection projects with large volumes of data, the process of fitting and executing the model may be only a small portion of the total time required; much more time may be needed for collecting and cleaning the data, along with engineering the relevant features. Most of the examples in this book use pandas, and pandas can be an excellent tool where the data size allows it, but it can hit limits with larger data volumes. Tools such as Spark (https://spark.apache.org/) can be very useful here. Working in Python, PySpark may be installed with a pip install.

Using Spark, it's possible to work with data in dataframes, similar to pandas. As with pandas, many univariate outlier tests (e.g., tests based on z-score, interquartile range, or median absolute deviation) can be done directly in Spark data frames. These can be simple outlier detection tests in themselves, or filtering to remove strong outliers before exporting to numpy and using other outlier detection algorithms, such as the detectors covered in previous chapters.

One interesting project that may be worth looking at is spark-iforest (https://github .com/titicaca/spark-iforest). This provides Isolation Forest in a manner similar to scikit-learn and PyOD but allows working with large volumes of data quickly using parallel execution. spark-iforest uses scala, but the project also provides a PySpark wrapper, allowing you to work strictly in Python. Another implementation of IF for Spark, provided by Microsoft, is SynapseML (https://github.com/microsoft/SynapseML).

DASK

Dask (https://www.dask.org/) is another alternative to pandas, which, like Spark, can handle much larger volumes of data and can provide some basic univariate outlier tests. As with Spark, this may be used to support collecting and preprocessing the data, though not the outlier detection itself, other than basic tests.

Listing 10.8 shows a simple example working with Dask to identify the records with the largest values, after scaling using RobustScaler. Normally the data would be read from disk or a database, but for simplicity here we use the KDD Cup dataset and read this from OpenML, first into a pandas dataframe, and then we create a Dask dataframe from this. Dask uses similar APIs as pandas, though they are somewhat different. The major advantages are that this work can be spread over a distributed system and can execute where the data exceeds memory limits. Before executing this, we must install dask, which can be done with

```
pip install dask
```

Listing 10.8   Identifying univariate outliers in Dask

```
import pandas as pd
import numpy as np
import dask.dataframe as dd
```

```
from sklearn.preprocessing import RobustScaler, OrdinalEncoder
from sklearn.datasets import fetch_kddcup99

X, y = fetch_kddcup99(subset="SA", percent10=True, random_state=42,
                      return_X_y=True, as_frame=True)

enc = OrdinalEncoder()
df = pd.DataFrame(enc.fit_transform(X), columns=X.columns)

dask_df = dd.from_pandas(df, npartitions=2)
transformer = RobustScaler().fit(dask_df)
vals = transformer.transform(dask_df)
dask_df = dd.from_array(vals, columns=df.columns)

dask_df['Max Value'] = dask_df.max(axis=1)
dask_df.compute().sort_values(['Max Value'])
```

Collects the data

Creates a Dask dataframe from the data

Uses sklearn's RobustScaler to scale the data

Uses the maximum scaled value per row as a simple outlier score

Sorts the data from least to most anomalous

HOSTED SOLUTIONS

When working with very large collections of data and frequently performing analysis on the data, it may be more practical to use hosted resources than to set up the hardware and databases necessary internally. We won't look closely at hosted solutions here but will note that they are often the most practical approach to deal with large data volumes, as most are designed with this in mind, and provide multiple tools to store and process data at scale. For most hosting solutions as well, data storage is extremely cheap.

Some hosted solutions provide tools specifically for outlier detection, generally for analysis of streaming time series data (for example, https://mng.bz/Dpey), as these are the types of problems that tend to have especially large data volumes. Another interesting service is Amazon Fraud Detector (https://aws.amazon.com/fraud-detector/), which can simplify creating fraud detection systems, especially where scales can be large.

10.3 Working with very small datasets

A challenge we are sometimes faced with in outlier detection is the opposite problem of what we've discussed so far in this chapter, working with datasets with very few rows, possibly in the order of thousands, or even only hundreds of rows. In these cases, we may still perform outlier detection but must be very cautious about any findings. In this setting, both false positives and false negatives are quite likely. Rows that appear to be unusual may only appear so because more examples similar to them happen to be missing from the data available. At the same time, rows that would normally be considered outliers may not be flagged: where many records erroneously appear as outliers, this can mask the truly unusual records—the inliers may be as rare, or almost, as the outliers in a small sample.

Where the outlier detection is performed on a one-time basis and any findings are manually evaluated, it may still be feasible to perform some outlier detection. If this is useful depends on the purpose of using outlier detection, but if the goal is to simply find the records that are most unusual relative to the available set, we can, to some degree, do this. This is with the understanding that, while the records flagged may or may not be true outliers, the scores are certainly not accurate: with small volumes of data, we cannot gauge well how unusual any given record is.

Where the model will be run on an ongoing basis, any models built based on a small sample will be unreliable, at least initially. It may be possible, though, to start with a weak outlier detector and tune it gradually over time as more data arrives, eventually creating a more accurate system.

With few rows, the problem is exacerbated when there are also many features. The chances of spurious results in this case become very high. If outlier detention is done at all, it's safest to limit any analysis to only a small number of the most relevant features, use only univariate outlier detection, and flag only extreme outliers. It may also be useful to perform PCA on the data (if linear patterns are strong) and perform outlier detection on just a small number of components, reducing again the chance of spurious results.

Summary

- Datasets may be very large both in terms of the number of rows and number of features.
- Working with very large datasets can create challenges, such as long fit and predict times and exceeding memory limits.
- When data has many features, it can be useful to run dimensionality reduction, which can often actually increase the accuracy of the models as well.
- It is also useful to train multiple models, each on subsets of the features, known as subspaces.
- Subspaces can be found in several ways, including randomly or based on correlation.
- Where there are many rows, we can train on samples of the data or segment the data into separate subsets, each with its own model.
- It can speed execution to perform fitting and/or prediction in parallel.
- In some cases, we may wish to execute prediction in sequence (as opposed to parallel) to reduce the total workload.
- Several tools are available to provide fast, approximate nearest neighbors searches, which are the basis of many outlier detection algorithms.
- Numerous tools are available to work with big data, which may be employed to collect and preprocess the data, including H2O, Spark, and Dask. These may make processing faster and/or avoid memory issues.
- Small datasets are unreliable to work with, though some outlier detection can be done if not excessively small. The results do need to be treated with more caution in this case.

11

Synthetic data for outlier detection

This chapter covers

- Creating realistic data to better understand detectors
- Creating more effective synthetic data tune and test detectors
- Using histograms and Gaussian mixture models to generate data
- Using simulations to generate data
- Using synthetic data to train detectors

We've seen already that synthetic data is very useful in outlier detection for at least a few purposes. First, it helps us experiment with detectors to better understand their behavior. We saw examples of this in chapters 6 and 7 when introducing new detectors and in chapter 8 when examining techniques to visualize how detectors work. In these cases, we worked primarily with small, 2D datasets, which were limited but quite useful—in this chapter we will look at more realistic synthetic datasets, which can provide further value.

A second purpose is tuning and testing models; we saw examples of this in chapter 8 using doped data. Synthetic data is especially important for this, as there are often few other good options available to evaluate detectors, at least until a large body of well-labeled data is collected. We'll look here at other ways to generate doped data, as well as other forms of synthetic data that may be used for this purpose.

Third, synthetic data is used to train some types of detectors. This applies to any detectors that internally use classifiers to distinguish real from synthetic data. We've seen examples with the Real versus Fake detector in chapter 3 and distance metric learning (DML) in chapter 7.

In this chapter we'll look more closely at using synthetic data for each of these purposes, as well as different techniques to create synthetic data, including using histograms and Gaussian mixture models (GMMs), and creating simulations.

11.1 Creating synthetic data to represent inliers

So far most of the synthetic data we've created has been simple 2D datasets, which are very useful to start with as they are easy to understand and visualize. This type of simple dataset allows us to assess, among other things, which types of data the detectors are suited for, how the preprocessing and parameters affect the detectors, and how the outliers are scored. For example, some detectors score the strongest outliers with the highest scores, while some do the reverse; some give scores for outliers only slightly higher than the scores for inliers, while others give scores that are orders of magnitude higher.

Normally, after we have experimented with simple datasets and understand these properties of the detectors, we would start testing the detectors with the real data along with synthetic test data. To do this, we may, as described in chapter 8, generate synthetic data (where this data is assumed to be outliers), test the models with both the real and synthetic data, and check that the synthetic records are consistently scored higher than the real data. The synthetic data here can be doped data, as we used in chapter 8, or data generated using other methods described in this chapter.

11.1.1 Testing with realistic inlier data

However, there is a step in between that can also be very useful: working with data somewhat like the simple 2D sets we've used (in that both the inliers and outliers are purely synthetic) but where the synthetic data mimics the real data. This step is not normally included in outlier detection projects and may not be necessary for your work. When it is used, however, it can be very informative and can help debug outlier detection systems that are often difficult to understand otherwise. It allows us to further explore (beyond the 2D toy sets we may start with) the behavior of the detectors, preprocessing, and parameters in an environment that is realistic (though somewhat oversimplified) and is much easier to understand than working with real data, as the real data can be noisy and can contain an unknown number of true outliers.

This requires creating synthetic data that, unlike most synthetic data we would generate, is actually designed to replicate inliers and not outliers. To create this data, we create a simple model of the real data and generate inlier data strictly following this. The synthetic data is, then, very similar to the real data but likely much simpler and cleaner. We would next also generate synthetic outliers, likely by hand, though another script may be used as well.

When the real data has some complexity, it is difficult to generate realistic synthetic data, so this process is limited to generating very typical data and may not cover the full range of what may be considered inliers. This would, though, generate data with the same number of rows, number of features, distributions within each feature, and to some extent, the associations between features. For example, if the real data is clustered, the synthetic data would mostly be generated close to the cluster centers; if the real data has linear relationships between the numeric features, these would be replicated, and so on.

Working with this, we can start to tune and test the detectors in a situation that is not quite realistic yet but quite similar and, importantly, understandable. Visualizations of the 1D and 2D spaces, as shown in chapter 8, may be helpful to determine what the detectors are able to flag. Initially, the outliers should be created to be very strong outliers, created with extreme values, or very rare combinations. We can first ensure the detectors work well in this environment before moving gradually to progressively more realistic and challenging outliers.

An overview of the major steps working with synthetic data is shown in figure 11.1. This is divided into three steps, though there are other ways to view this process. Projects will not necessarily require all these steps, but they can each be helpful. Where done, they will generally each be repeated multiple times with different synthetic datasets, to get greater value from each step and to be less reliant on any single synthetic dataset representing inlier or outlier data well. Once these steps are complete, we will have a set of outlier detectors (along with the preprocessing and parameters used by each) that appear to be the most effective for the data and goals we have. We would typically then drop the use of synthetic data and train and predict using strictly the real data.

Considering the second step, there are a few ways to generate realistic inlier data we'll look at in this chapter: creating the data feature-wise in a left to right manner, using GMMs, and creating simulations. Once this data is created, we would train the models using the synthetic inliers and test on both these and the simulated outliers, checking that the known outliers receive significantly higher scores. The detectors can be tuned until this is the case. A more challenging and more realistic situation can then be studied, where some number of outliers are included in the training data, to evaluate how robust the system is to contaminated data.

After spending some time working with this synthetic inlier data, we would then usually proceed to the third step: working with the actual data along with synthetic data generated to represent outliers, possibly occasionally returning to the synthetic inlier data where we wish to use it to help debug detectors. Interestingly, the methods to generate realistic inlier synthetic data and realistic outlier synthetic data can be fairly similar and are often distinguished only by degree: how realistic the data produced is.

Step 1: Experiment with 2D toy data

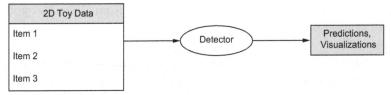

Step 2: Experiment with realistic synthetic data and strong synthetic outliers

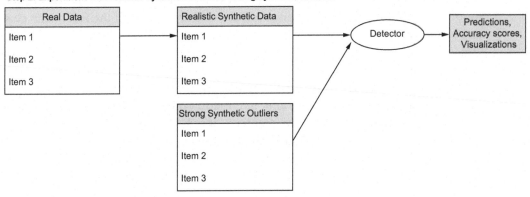

Step 3: Test with real data and realistic synthetic outliers

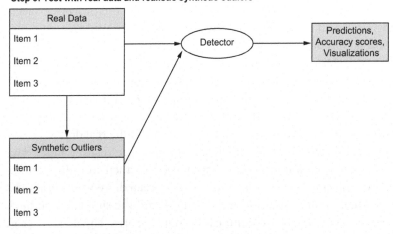

Figure 11.1   The major steps in working with outlier detection. In the first step, we simply seek to understand the detectors themselves. This step may have little relationship to the real data. This is usually unnecessary in subsequent projects other than when introducing new detectors, parameters, or preprocessing. In the second step, we test creating outlier detectors with purely synthetic data, where the inliers are very similar to the real data but are more consistent and likely actually stronger inliers than the real data and the outliers are typically hand-crafted to be very strong outliers. In the third step, we test with the real data along with synthetic data. The synthetic data in this step will also be realistic but less so than in the second step, such that the detectors can still reasonably distinguish it from real data.

11.1.2 *Using realistic synthetic inliers for training*

Other than this early form of modeling (the second of the three steps in figure 11.1), synthetic data that simulates inliers is rarely used. Though this data is very clean and potentially useful to train models, it may not actually model the real data well, so there is some risk in using it to train models that are used in production. Likely the individual rows will each be reasonably typical, but this is not certain, and the distribution produced may not be realistic. Nevertheless, synthetic inlier data will typically capture the major patterns well (even if not all the patterns in the data) and any deviations from these, even if legitimate, can quite likely be considered statistical outliers. And so, though not done commonly, using this data to train models may be useful in some cases.

We can view this data generation process as a strong form of cleaning. If we are able to generate synthetic inlier data that replicates the major patterns well, training a detector on this will fit a detector to an ideal version of the data, as opposed to a realistic version of the data. This may be preferable for the same reason that cleaning the data is useful: the detectors will not attempt to fit contaminated data. It will also allow us to generate any volume of data, which allows the detectors to assess in a more stable way how unusual records are, at least relative to the models created.

In practice, cleaning is done much more often by removing clear outlier rows than by generating clean synthetic data, though where the data is highly contaminated, cleaning may require removing a large portion of the data, which is not a problem with synthetic data. If models trained on synthetic data are used, they would likely be used simply as a piece of a larger ensemble of detectors, primarily trained on real data. In these cases, we would also generate multiple models trained on different synthetic data to mitigate the risks of unrepresentative synthetic data.

11.2 *Generating new synthetic data*

When generating synthetic data, there are two broad approaches: creating doped data and creating new data. I'm using "new" here to indicate data that is not based on any specific real data. This is as opposed to doped data, which is composed of variations of the real data: each row in the doped data corresponds to one (or potentially multiple) rows in the real data, modified in some way. New data corresponds only to the general patterns in the real data. Both types of synthetic data can be quite useful.

The most common uses of synthetic data are training detectors such as Real versus Fake or DML and tuning and testing detectors. For these purposes, the synthetic data is treated as known outliers, and either doped data or new synthetic data may be used. The less common, but also important, purpose for synthetic data we look at in this chapter is to create realistic inlier synthetic data. For this, generating new synthetic data is the sole option; the doping process, by design, modifies data such that it is likely no longer typical and can only be considered outliers.

When training detectors (that internally use classifiers) or tuning and testing detectors, it can vary whether using doped or new data is preferable, though it will generally be best to use a combination of both. To test detectors, for example, we wish to generate a variety of types of outliers, which is achieved best by using multiple means to generate the outliers, including both new and doped data. The only way we can be confident the system will catch one in a million events is to test with many one in a million events, which requires generating a large and diverse set of outliers.

A major advantage of creating new synthetic data (true with doped data as well), is it allows us to test with a range of types of outliers and levels of difficulty. It is useful to create, for each type of outlier, not a few records but an entire test dataset of some significant size. This allows us to test well how each detector performs with each type of known outlier, as these are each evaluated separately. We may combine these into a final score in order to select the best final detectors, but we can assess much better in this way how each detector handles each type of outlier. For example, if one test dataset is created to have extreme values in a certain column, another to have internal outliers in that column, and others with other types of outliers, we can determine which detectors identify each best. Where each test set has a substantial number of rows, we can estimate this with some confidence.

There are a few ways to generate new data we look at in this chapter. We saw one simple method in chapter 3. There, the features were created independently, each based on the mean and standard deviation of the feature in the original data. Here we'll look at variations of this that can be used to create more realistic data, as well as a method using GMMs. First, though, we'll look at some libraries that may be used to generate synthetic data.

11.2.1 *Libraries to generate new synthetic data*

Many libraries provide methods to generate synthetic data, and these can be useful, but they are not intended to be similar to your dataset and so do not have the ability to help set up a working outlier detection system for your data. They are, though, helpful when generating initial toy datasets you may experiment with, corresponding to step 1 in figure 11.1.

scikit-learn, for example, provides methods such as `make_classification()`, `make_blobs()`, and several others. These are designed to create normal data and so require manually inserting outliers to test. PyOD provides a method, `generate_data()`, which can be useful. This is similar to some of the simple synthetic data generated in earlier examples in this book, here using a multivariate Gaussian distribution for inliers and a uniform distribution for outliers. It has a couple convenient properties: the outliers are labeled, and the data is predivided into train and test rows. PyCaret (covered in chapter 7) also provides a method, `get_data()`, which may be used with the `dataset` parameter set to"anomaly" to generate data to experiment with. Faker (https://github.com/xfxf/faker-python) is a useful tool as it supports creating many types of features (names, addresses, text, IP addresses, and so on).

Overall, though, it is best to generate your own synthetic data to fully understand the detectors, train Real versus Fake and DML detectors, and tune and test the outlier detection system. For each of these purposes, we will require realistic synthetic data, similar to our real data, though with the latter two purposes we do want to be able to distinguish real data; for the first purpose, trying to understand the detectors, the data does not need to be distinguishable from real data, but it is preferable the data is reasonably simple.

11.2.2 *Using patterns between features*

A straightforward method to create new synthetic data that mimics a real dataset is to generate the data one feature at a time, from left to right. There are a few variations of this, which allow us to control how realistic the synthetic data generated is:

- As with the example in chapter 3, create each feature independently, considering the distribution of that feature in the real dat, but ignoring any associations between the features.
- Generate the left-most feature as in the previous method, but for each subsequent feature, predict the values based on the features already populated. So the values in the second feature would be based on the values generated for the first feature; the values in the third feature would be based on those generated for the first two; and so on. This creates data that is realistic both in the sense of having typical values in each column and of maintaining the associations between the columns.

We'll look at examples of both these methods, as well as methods that can be considered in between these two, resulting in data more realistic than with the first method but less than with the second.

CREATING THE FEATURES INDEPENDENTLY

In the example in chapter 3, we used an approach where each feature was created independently, in that case based on a Gaussian distribution approximating each feature's actual distribution. A similar method, classifier-adjusted density estimation (CADE), uses a uniform distribution for each feature. More accurate methods may create a histogram or kernel density estimation (KDE) for each feature and generate new values from these, which will mimic the real data's distribution more faithfully. Listing 11.1 shows an example using a histogram (specifically, numpy's `histogram` method).

In this example, we use 10 bins, which represent the data closely, though more may be needed for some datasets. The `histogram()` method returns the bin edges and frequency of each bin. As there are 11 edges, we average each pair of edges to determine the center of each bin. We then add some jitter to each value to create continuous values (and to not generate only 10 distinct values in each numeric feature). Varying the amount of jitter may also be used to adjust how realistic the data is.

This example uses the baseball dataset first seen in chapter 4 and creates synthetic data somewhat similar to this, though data that may safely be considered, largely, outliers.

Listing 11.1 Generating features individually using histograms

```
import pandas as pd
import numpy as np
from sklearn.datasets import fetch_openml
```

```
data = fetch_openml(
        'baseball', version=1, parser='auto')                          Collects
df = pd.DataFrame(data.data, columns=data.feature_names)               the data
df['Strikeouts'] = df['Strikeouts'].fillna(df['Strikeouts'].median())

cat_features = [x for x in df.columns              Specifies the categorical columns as
               if df[x].nunique() <=10]            any with 10 or fewer unique values
num_features = [x for x in df.columns
               if x not in cat_features]           Loops through each numeric
                                                   column and creates synthetic values

synth_data = []                                    Creates a histogram
                                                   to represent the
                                                   distribution of values
for num_feat in num_features:                      in the real data
    hist = np.histogram(df[num_feat], density=True)
    bin_centers = [(x+y)/2 for x, y in zip(hist[1][:-1], hist[1][1:])]
    p = [x/sum(hist[0]) for x in hist[0]]
    vals = np.random.choice(bin_centers, p=p, size=len(df)).astype(int)
    vals = [x + (((1.0 * np.random.random()) - 0.5) * df[num_feat].std())
            for x in vals]
    synth_data.append(vals)                        Loops through each
                                                   categorical column and
for cat_feat in cat_features:                      creates synthetic values
    vc = df[cat_feat].value_counts(normalize=True)
    vals = np.random.choice(list(vc.index), p=list(vc.values),
                            size=len(df))
    synth_data.append(vals)                        Selects a random set of
                                                   values, proportional to the
synth_df = pd.DataFrame(synth_data).T              frequency of each value in
synth_df.columns = num_features + cat_features     this column in the real data
```

Executing this, we will ensure each feature follows the same distribution in the synthetic data as the real data, but the associations will not be maintained, as shown in figure 11.2. We see in the left pane that the distribution for At_bats is almost identical for the real and the synthetic data; this is true of the other features as well. In the middle and right panes, we contrast the joint distribution of At_bats and RBIs for the real compared to the synthetic data; the linear association between the features is not maintained, which ensures the synthetic data consistently contains reasonably strong outliers.

Simply creating each feature individually may create data that's too unusual, in the sense of being significantly more unusual than most real outliers would be, as well as too easy for most outlier detectors. In this case, the synthetic data would have limited ability to test the system, though it still may eliminate some possible detectors. It may also allow the use of interpretable detectors where these outliers are still plausible—for example, as data artifacts.

CREATING THE FEATURES TO MAINTAIN ASSOCIATIONS

Listing 11.2 shows a method to generate data that is very realistic, generating the features left to right, with each predicted (in this case using a RandomForest) from the generated features to the left.

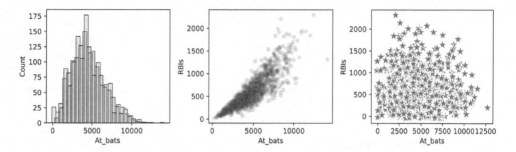

Figure 11.2 The distribution of `At_bats` is shown in the left pane for both the real and synthetic data. The distributions are almost identical. The middle pane shows the joint distribution of `At_bats` and `RBIs` in the real data, and the right pane shows the same two features in the synthetic data. The relationship between these features is not maintained in the synthetic data.

Listing 11.2   Generating data from left to right

```
import pandas as pd
import numpy as np
from sklearn.datasets import fetch_openml
import matplotlib.pyplot as plt
import seaborn as sns
from sklearn.ensemble import RandomForestRegressor, RandomForestClassifier

data = fetch_openml('baseball', version=1, parser='auto')
df = pd.DataFrame(data.data, columns=data.feature_names)
df['Strikeouts'] = df['Strikeouts'].fillna(df['Strikeouts'].median())

cat_features = [x for x in df.columns if df[x].nunique() <=10]
num_features = [x for x in df.columns if x not in cat_features]
synth_data = []

feature_0 = df.columns[0]                                           ◄─┐ Sets the left-most column
hist = np.histogram(df[feature_0], density=True)                      │ based on its distribution only
bin_centers = [(x+y)/2 for x, y in zip(hist[1][:-1], hist[1][1:])]
p = [x/sum(hist[0]) for x in hist[0]]
vals = np.random.choice(bin_centers, p=p, size=len(df)).astype(int)
vals = [x + (((1.0 * np.random.random()) - 0.5) * df[feature_0].std())
        for x in vals]
synth_data.append(vals)
synth_cols = [feature_0]

for col_name in df.columns[1:]:                                     ◄─┐ Loops through the features
    print(col_name)                                                   │ after the left-most
    synth_df = pd.DataFrame(synth_data).T
    synth_df.columns = synth_cols

    if col_name in num_features:
        regr = RandomForestRegressor()                              ◄─┐ Trains a Random
        regr.fit(df[synth_cols], df[col_name])                        │ Forest on real data
```

```
        pred = regr.predict(synth_df[synth_cols])
        vals = [x + (((1.0 * np.random.random()) - 0.5) * pred.std())
                for x in pred]
        synth_data.append(vals)

    if col_name in cat_features:
        clf = RandomForestClassifier()
        clf.fit(df[synth_cols], df[col_name])
        synth_data.append(clf.predict(synth_df[synth_cols]))

    synth_cols.append(col_name)

synth_df = pd.DataFrame(synth_data).T
synth_df.columns = synth_cols

sns.scatterplot(data=df, x="At_bats", y="RBIs", color='blue', alpha=0.1)
sns.scatterplot(data=synth_df, x="At_bats", y="RBIs",
                color='red', marker="*", s=200)
plt.show()
```

Predicts on the synthetic data created so far

Adds jitter so that there are not only a small number of unique values

This starts by creating the first feature based on its distribution in the real data. Each subsequent feature is created based on the features already created. Random Forests are strong models and can usually capture patterns in the data as well as any detector, so this creates very realistic data. Using other models, or tuning the Random Forest parameters, can be used to adjust how realistic the data is and to add diversity to the data sets created. We see in figure 11.3, the joint distribution between `At_bats` and `RBIs` is well maintained. This is true of every combination of features, even those spanning many dimensions.

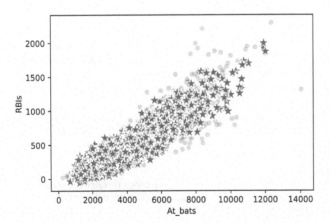

Figure 11.3 The distribution of `At_bats` and `RBIs` for both the real data (shown as dots) and the synthetic data (shown as stars) created when using a left-to-right method. Here the joint distributions are well-preserved.

We may face a couple of problems when generating data in this manner. First, even attempting to create very realistic data, the data may not be realistic enough and it may be easy for detectors to distinguish from real data; there are often many constraints in data that are hard to capture when creating the data, which detectors may be able to exploit. If we know these constraints, they can be coded into the generating process. However, it is usually unnecessary to create synthetic outliers that are more realistic: in most cases, realistic synthetic data is very challenging for outlier detectors to distinguish from real.

We may also have the opposite problem: we may create data that is too close to the real data and too challenging for any detector—it may be that the most realistic data generated cannot be distinguished as outliers by any of the detectors. In fact, any very realistic data created may be no more outlier-ish than the real data, or only slightly more so, and so correctly not flagged as outliers.

In most cases, though, we will create, not a single dataset, but a collection, ranging from very easy to distinguish to very difficult. To achieve this, we will use the first approach (having no associations between the features), as well as a range of variations on the second approach: when populating each column, instead of considering all features created to the left, we consider only some of these. The more that are used and the more they are associated with the current column, the more realistic the data will be. Given a range of datasets, it will not be a problem if some of datasets created are too simple, or some too challenging, for any of the detectors, as long as we have a good collection of datasets that range in difficulty. The interesting sets, though, will be the datasets where some, but not all, detectors are able to distinguish the synthetic data from the real. Consequently, given a good collection of datasets, we will be able to identify the most useful detectors for the current dataset.

An example of varying the number of features used is shown in listing 11.3. This takes some of the code from listing 11.2 and places it in a parametrized function, which allows us to control how many previous features are used to predict the appropriate values for the current feature and whether we use the left-most or right-most of these. Calling this multiple times with different parameters will allow us to create a diversity of datasets. Other variations on this, as well as generating the features in different orders (the columns order may be shuffled before calling this), can also work well and add diversity to the test sets generated. This assumes df has been created as in listing 11.2.

Listing 11.3 Function to generate data using only some prior columns

```
from sklearn.ensemble import RandomForestRegressor, RandomForestClassifier

def generate_dataset(df, max_cols_used, use_left):
    feature_0 = df.columns[0]
    hist = np.histogram(df[feature_0], density=True)
    bin_centers = [(x+y)/2 for x, y in zip(hist[1][:-1], hist[1][1:])]
    p = [x/sum(hist[0]) for x in hist[0]]
    vals = np.random.choice(bin_centers, p=p, size=len(df)).astype(int)
    vals = [x + (((1.0 * np.random.random()) - 0.5) * df[feature_0].std())
            for x in vals]
    synth_data = []
    synth_data.append(vals)
    synth_cols = [feature_0]
```

```
for col_name in df.columns[1:]:
    print(col_name)
    synth_df = pd.DataFrame(synth_data).T
    synth_df.columns = synth_cols
    if use_left:
        use_synth_cols = synth_cols[:max_cols_used]
    else:
        use_synth_cols = synth_cols[-max_cols_used:]

    if col_name in num_features:
        regr = RandomForestRegressor()
        regr.fit(df[use_synth_cols], df[col_name])
        pred = regr.predict(synth_df[use_synth_cols])
        vals = [x + (((1.0 * np.random.random()) - 0.5) * pred.std())
                for x in pred]
        synth_data.append(vals)

    if col_name in cat_features:
        clf = RandomForestClassifier()
        clf.fit(df[use_synth_cols], df[col_name])
        synth_data.append(clf.predict(synth_df[use_synth_cols]))

    synth_cols.append(col_name)

synth_df = pd.DataFrame(synth_data).T
synth_df.columns = synth_cols
return synth_df

synth_df = generate_dataset(df, max_cols_used=2, use_left=False)
```

Trains the Random Forest using only a specified set of features ◀ (annotation pointing to `if use_left:` block)

The remainer of the code is the same as previously. ◀ (annotation pointing to `if col_name in num_features:` line)

The same two features shown in figure 11.3 are shown in figure 11.4. Here the association between the features is largely maintained but is less correct than in figure 11.3. The synthetic data (stars) cover a broader range, extending outside of where the real data (dots) are located.

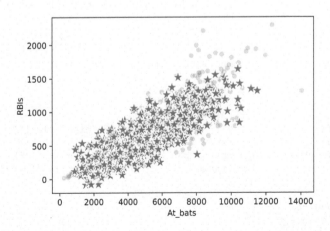

Figure 11.4   The same features as in figure 11.3 but generated using a weaker association between the features. In this case, each feature is generated based on the right-most two previously generated features (as opposed to all previously generated features). The association between the features is maintained but not as well as seen in figure 11.3.

11.2.3 Using GMMs

Given that GMMs are generative models, they are useful not only to evaluate data but to generate new data and may be used to create data that is very much like the real data. To do so, the GMM must first be fit to the real data. It is then able to generate any quantity of new data (behind the scenes, doing this one new record at a time). For each new record, the GMM first selects a Gaussian center randomly, proportional to the weight of that cluster, then generates a point using the multivariate Gaussian for that cluster. The following listing shows an example, again using the baseball dataset and generating a very clean version of this dataset.

Listing 11.4 Generating data from a GMM

```
import pandas as pd
import numpy as np
from sklearn.datasets import fetch_openml
import matplotlib.pyplot as plt
import seaborn as sns
from sklearn.mixture import GaussianMixture
from sklearn.ensemble import IsolationForest

data = fetch_openml('baseball', version=1, parser='auto')      ← Loads the data
df = pd.DataFrame(data.data, columns=data.feature_names)
df['Strikeouts'] = df['Strikeouts'].fillna(df['Strikeouts'].median())
df = pd.get_dummies(df)

np.random.seed(0)
clf_if = IsolationForest()                 ← Cleans the data of strong outliers
clf_if.fit(df)
pred = clf_if.decision_function(df)
trimmed_df = df.loc[np.argsort(pred)[50:]]

best_score = np.inf                        ← Determines the best number of clusters to use
best_n_clusters = -1
for n_clusters in range(2, 10):
    gmm = GaussianMixture(n_components=n_clusters)
    gmm.fit(trimmed_df)
    score = gmm.bic(trimmed_df)
    if score < best_score:
        best_score = score
        best_n_clusters = n_clusters

gmm = GaussianMixture(n_components=best_n_clusters)      ← Fits a GMM
gmm.fit(trimmed_df)

samples = gmm.sample(n_samples=500)        ← Uses the GMM to generate synthetic data
synth_df = pd.DataFrame(samples[0], columns=df.columns)

sns.scatterplot(data=df, x="At_bats", y="RBIs", color='blue', alpha=0.1)
sns.scatterplot(data=synth_df, x="At_bats", y="RBIs",
                color='red', marker="*", s=200)
plt.show()
```

As with generating features left to right (using a predictor for each feature), using GMMs generates data that is very realistic, respecting the associations between features well. Figure 11.5 shows a similar plot as figure 11.3, in this case with data generated by the GMM.

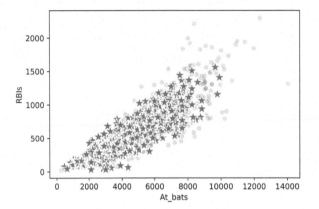

Figure 11.5   Scatterplot of two features from the baseball dataset (At bats and RBIs). Real data is shown as dots and the synthetic data as stars. We can see the synthetic data follows the same distribution and tends to be, at least with this pair of features and the volume created, more typical than some of the actual data.

Working with categorical data is slightly more involved, as we have to convert the numeric values generated by the GMM to categorical values. If the data is, for example, one-hot encoded, we can take the binary column with the highest value as the generated value; if count encoded, we take the value with the count closest to the generated value.

Used in this way, GMMs are well suited to generate realistic data but not anomalous data. Most of the data generated will be very typical and so can only be used to simulate strong inliers. However, it is also possible to modify the means of the clusters and their covariance matrices, which will allow the GMMs to generate data that is distinctly different. In listing 11.4, we may add code such as the following after fitting the GMM and before calling `sample()`:

```
for i in range(len(gmm.covariances_)):
    for j in range(len(gmm.covariances_[i])):
        for k in range(len(gmm.covariances_[i])):
            gmm.covariances_[i][j][k] *= 20.0
```

This multiplies each value in the covariance matrices for each cluster by 20.0; it may be useful to use a smaller or larger value in different cases, but again, this may be adjusted to create a range of synthetic datasets for testing. This produces synthetic data as shown in figure 11.6, though here (for clarity) the alpha value for inliers is set to 1.0 and for the outliers to 0.1.

Other tools that model the density of the data space may be used to generate data in a similar way. For example, scikit-learn's `KernelDensity` works very similarly as this, also providing a `sample()` API. Other methods, such as multidimensional histograms, are also possible to model the real data and generate synthetic data to match.

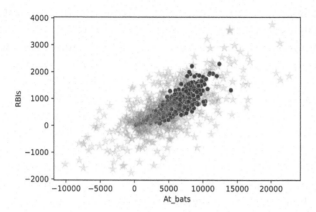

Figure 11.6 Output of the GMM after modifying the covariance matrices for each cluster. Real data are shown as dots and synthetic as stars. The range of the synthetic data is much larger in all directions compared to the real data and can be assumed to contain a large proportion of outliers.

Now that we've taken a closer look at some methods that can be used to generate new synthetic data, it's useful to also do this for doped synthetic data, which we do next.

11.3 Doping

The doping process was introduced in chapter 8 and, like new synthetic data, is often an effective means to tune and test outlier detectors and ensembles of detectors. One property of doping is that it is open-ended regarding how the records are modified. We saw in chapter 8 an example where values were set to random values (in that case, a random value either above or below the median). It's also possible to vary the data in a similar but more deterministic and consistent manner—for example, altering each (scaled) numeric value by a consistent amount. In this case, the relevant section of listing 8.3 is

```
if doped_df.loc[i, col_name] > med_val:
    doped_df.loc[i, col_name] = \
      clean_df[col_name].quantile(np.random.random()/2)
  else:
    doped_df.loc[i, col_name] = \
      clean_df[col_name].quantile(0.5 + np.random.random()/2)
```

We may replace this, for example, with

```
if doped_df.loc[i, col_name] > med_val:
    doped_df.loc[i, col_name] = doped_df.loc[i, col_name] - 0.2
  else:
    doped_df.loc[i, col_name] = doped_df.loc[i, col_name] + 0.2
```

This has the advantage that the magnitude of the changes is known, which is especially useful when creating many test sets—each with specific forms of doping and levels of difficulty. We can assume that the more the values are modified, the easier the synthetic data will be to detect as outliers. This allows us to understand best where the system works well and where is does not and helps to better identify the redundant detectors: the detectors that score similarly for most forms of doped data.

Any number of variations of these may be used. We can, for example, base the modifications on multiple feature values or on other modifications made to the same row. Generally, with doping, we adjust at least the number of features altered in each row and the degree to which each is altered, and control whether the new value can be outside the range of values in the real data. For categorical features, this controls if categorical values in the doped data must be in the set of unique values for that feature in the real data; for numeric, this controls if the values in the doped data can be below the minimum or above the maximum values found in that feature in the real data. All these data modifications have the advantage of being quite simple and relatively easy to understand, though when we modify any value, it's not clear how many associations between features this will upset. Nevertheless, we have some estimate of the outlierness, assuming the more features changed, and the larger the changes, the more outlier-ish the new data. Figure 11.7 shows a set of test datasets created by multiple doping processes conducted on a real dataset.

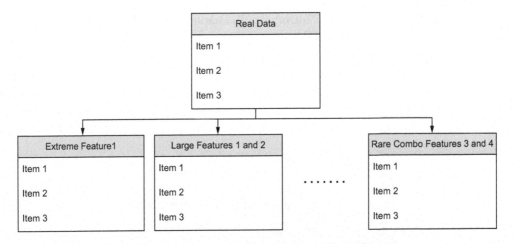

Figure 11.7   A set of test datasets created by multiple doping processes conducted on a real dataset. As with using new synthetic data, when using doped data to simulate outliers, we wish to create each test dataset with known properties to help us understand where each detector performs well and where it does not. In this example, we introduce extreme values in some columns, moderately large values in multiple columns, rare combinations in some columns, and so on. It is important to cover, as well as is practical, the range of outliers you are interested in and not to include outliers that are not of interest.

Listing 11.5 provides another example of doping—this time using a Random Forest, though in this case to ensure each inserted value is anomalous. Here we loop through each row in the doped data and for each select a set of columns to modify. We ensure the data modification is done such that the new value is unlike both the actual and the predicted value. For brevity, we do not show the categorical case here, but for categorical data we simply select a value that is neither the actual nor the predicted value. In this case, the data is one-hot encoded, so each of the corresponding one-hot columns for each categorical column would be updated appropriately.

For numeric features, we determine the quartiles of both the actual and predicted values and select a value in another quartile, which ensures the new value is anomalous. Here we are able to use all features, and not simply features to the left, to train each Random Forest as we are maintaining the bulk of the existing data values. Because the process is slow, this example creates only a small set of doped records, but in practice we would create a much larger set.

Listing 11.5 Doping using a Random Forest

```
import pandas as pd
import numpy as np
from sklearn.datasets import fetch_openml
from sklearn.preprocessing import RobustScaler
import matplotlib.pyplot as plt
import seaborn as sns
from sklearn.ensemble import RandomForestRegressor, RandomForestClassifier
import random
from scipy import stats

np.random.seed(0)

data = fetch_openml(
        'baseball', version=1, parser='auto')      ◄──── Collects the data
df = pd.DataFrame(data.data, columns=data.feature_names)
df['Strikeouts'] = df['Strikeouts'].fillna(df['Strikeouts'].median())
df = pd.get_dummies(df)
df = pd.DataFrame(RobustScaler().fit_transform(df), columns=df.columns)

cat_features = [x for x in df.columns if df[x].nunique() <=10]
num_features = [x for x in df.columns if x not in cat_features]

min_cols_per_modification = 1
max_cols_per_modification = 5      ◄── Defines the minimum and maximum
doped_df = df.copy().head(20)           number of features to modify each row
for i in doped_df.index:           ◄── Loops through each row
    num_cols_modified = -1                                              ◄── Determines
    while (num_cols_modified < min_cols_per_modification) or \              the set of
      (num_cols_modified > max_cols_per_modification):                      columns to
        num_cols_modified = int(abs(np.random.laplace(1.0, 10)))            modify
    modified_cols = np.random.choice(df.columns, num_cols_modified,
                              replace=False)

    for col_name in modified_cols:
        other_cols = df.columns.tolist()
        other_cols.remove(col_name)
        if col_name in num_features:
            regr = RandomForestRegressor()
            regr.fit(df[other_cols], df[col_name])
            pred = regr.predict(
```

```
        pd.DataFrame(doped_df.iloc[i][other_cols]).T)[0]
    pred_quantile = stats.percentileofscore(
        df[col_name], pred) // 25
    cur_val = doped_df.loc[i, col_name]
    cur_val_quantile = stats.percentileofscore(
        df[col_name], cur_val) // 25
    q1 = doped_df[col_name].quantile(0.25)
    q2 = doped_df[col_name].quantile(0.5)
    q3 = doped_df[col_name].quantile(0.75)
    quantiles_list = list(range(4))
    np.random.shuffle(quantiles_list)
    for q in quantiles_list:
        if q != pred_quantile and q != cur_val_quantile:
            break
    doped_df.loc[i, col_name] =\
        ((0.25) * q) + 0.125 + \
np.random.random()/20
```

Selects a random quantile such that neither the actual nor the predicted value is in that quartile ◄

Generates a random value within the selected quartile ◄

Generating new and doped data does have one limitation, which is that the rows are generated independently. This is not a problem for most purposes but does preclude testing for certain types of outliers. We look next at simulations, a technique to create data that can be more realistic and allows for inserting different types of outliers, such as rows that are unusual given the rows that have preceded them.

11.4   *Simulations*

The most sophisticated (and difficult) means to create synthetic data is by creating simulations. These are processes where the data is created one row at a time, each representing an action or state at some point in time. When there is an order to the data, simulations can create much more realistic data than can be created generating the records independently of each other.

As an example, we look at a simulation of a company: buying and selling goods and maintaining an inventory of each type of item. In a realistic setting, we would not expect to see many purchases for goods that have not been selling, sales for goods not in inventory, and so on. That is, each row (each transaction in this example) has to make sense given its context—the state of the world at that time (which is created by the previous rows). Any exceptions to these should be flagged as outliers.

Simulations mimic the behavior of separate agents (in this example, purchasers buying items and sales agents selling items), each acting as independent processes but acting based on their knowledge of the world at that time. Taking the idea, introduced in chapter 1, that outliers are data that appear to have been created by separate mechanisms (or processes), we may create simulations with multiple processes, most creating both many records and normal records, with a small number of outlier processes creating records, or sets of records, that are both rare and significantly different.

While the individual records generated by a simulation may be similar to those generated with the previous methods, the collection of records as a whole, to the extent the simulation models the true behavior well, will be much more realistic. That is, the records will appear in a sensible order, and each will be realistic (other than those created by outlier processes) considering the prior records. This allows us to create outliers that are different than the outliers we've looked at so far; we can create outliers that are unusual sets of rows or unusual given the set of rows that precede them. We will look at ways to identify these soon, particularly collective outlier tests in chapter 12 and time series analysis in chapter 17, but for now we describe how a simulation can create realistic datasets with small numbers of known anomalies.

Listing 11.6 shows snippets of code for a simple simulation, where we have a set of purchasers (including one rogue purchaser, which will introduce some known anomalies into the data) and a sales process, which together create a set of sales and purchase transactions. This loops over a specified time period—in this case, one year. At each minute, every purchaser and the sales process may randomly purchase goods or make sales, each considering the time of day and the current inventory levels. Most purchases are made from suppliers at random and at random unit prices. The rogue purchaser, however, does not purchase product 0, and on the 28th day of each month makes unusually large purchases of product 5 from supplier 10.

The full code is available at https://mng.bz/lrjj. Here we show part of the code for the normal purchase agents and the rogue purchase agent. The remainder of the code covers the sales process and a loop, which every minute, over the range December 15, 2022, to December 31, 2023, prompts each purchaser to consider making a purchase and the sales process to consider making a sale. The sales process randomly decides if it will make a sale that minute. If so, it chooses a product and quantity randomly and, if a sufficient quantity is in inventory, makes a sale, which reduces the inventory for that product. The sales process tends to make sales for small volumes, while the purchases are for larger volumes, resulting in many more sales than purchase transactions.

Listing 11.6 Simulation representing one company for 1 year

```
class Purchacer:
    def consider_purchase(self):            ← Simulates a normal
        global inventory                      purchase agent
        global transactions
        if (current_datetime.hour < 9) or \   Only makes purchases
        (current_datetime.hour > 17):         between 9 AM and 6 PM
            return                          ←
        if np.random.random() > 0.01:       ← Randomly decides if
            product_id = np.random.choice(range(num_items_in_inventory))   will make a purchase
            if inventory[product_id] > 1000:   ←
                return                         Does not buy if there is
            supplier_id = \                    sufficient in stock
                np.random.choice(range(num_suppliers))   ←
            unit_cost = np.random.exponential() * 20.0    Chooses a supplier,
            num_purchased = np.random.randint(10, 200)    number bought, and
            total_cost = num_purchased * unit_cost        unit cost randomly
            inventory[product_id] += num_purchased
            transactions.append([
                    'Purchase', self.staff_id,
                    supplier_id, product_id,
```

```
        current_datetime.strftime("%Y-%m-%d %H:%M"),
        num_purchased, unit_cost, total_cost,
        inventory[product_id]])
```

This skips some of the code available on Github but covers the main idea: each time the purchaser agent's `consider_purchase()` method is called, it randomly decides if it will make a purchase and then selects a product, supplier, unit price, and number purchased randomly, though considering the current inventory level. The rogue purchaser has a similar but different purchasing process. On the 28th day of each month, it makes an unusual purchase of product 5 from supplier 10. It also avoids product 0, which is unusual, and tends to buy more units at a time than other purchasers.

```
class RoguePurchaser:                                    ◄──┐ Simulates a rogue process
    def consider_purchase(self):
        if (current_datetime.hour < 9) or (current_datetime.hour > 17):
            return
        if (current_datetime.day == 28) and \
            (current_datetime.month not in \              The 28th of each month it
                self.extra_purchase_months):     ◄──┘    makes an unusual purchase.
            product_id = 5
            supplier_id = 10
            unit_cost = np.random.exponential() * 250.0
            trend_factor = np.log2(current_datetime.month+1) + 1
            num_purchased = int(np.random.randint(50, 60) * trend_factor)
            total_cost = num_purchased * unit_cost
            inventory[product_id] += num_purchased
            transactions.append([
                    'Purchase', self.staff_id, supplier_id,
                    product_id,
                current_datetime.strftime("%Y-%m-%d %H:%M"),
                    num_purchased, unit_cost, total_cost,
                    inventory[product_id]])
            self.extra_purchase_months.append(current_datetime.month)

        elif np.random.random() > 0.01:
            product_id = np.random.choice(range(num_items_in_inventory))
            if product_id == 0:                      ◄──┐ This agent does not
                return                                     buy product 0.
            if inventory[product_id] > 1000:
                return
            supplier_id = np.random.choice(range(num_suppliers))
            unit_cost = np.random.exponential() * 20.0
            num_purchased = np.random.randint(10, 200)   ◄──┐ Tends to buy more
            total_cost = num_purchased * unit_cost             units at once than
            inventory[product_id] += num_purchased             other purchasers
            transactions.append([
                    'Purchase', self.staff_id, supplier_id, product_id,
                    current_datetime.strftime("%Y-%m-%d %H:%M"),
                    num_purchased, unit_cost, total_cost,
                    inventory[product_id]])
```

One thing to note about most simulations, including this, is that there is an early period (referred to as the *burn-in period*) that tends to not be realistic and can usually be discarded. In this example, there are many purchase records per day at the beginning until a normal inventory level is reached that you would not normally see in the real world. In this case, we could initialize the inventory to a realistic level, but there is still often some burn-in process. For this example, we start the simulation 2 weeks prior to the year we wish to simulate.

Creating a good simulation is difficult, as it is necessary to capture a lot of real-world incentives and constraints. It is usually an iterative process, where the simulation generates data, we check if it is similar to real-world data, and then we tune it until it is. For example, we can check if the simulated data, compared to real data, has similar numbers of purchases, a similar distribution of amounts, a similar distribution of times of the day, and so on. It's not necessary, though, to perfectly match the real data—only to largely match it. Once they are substantially similar, any deviations in the real data may be considered outliers (likely quite legitimate but nevertheless statistically unusual and potentially interesting).

If desired, the simulation can be made more realistic, particularly if maintained over time and the places where it deviates from the real world become clearer. In this simulation we could, for example, define different prices for different items; define specific times of the day, week, and year when sales are higher; simulate suppliers charging different rates, suppliers running out of stock, and so on. Once the simulation is sufficiently accurate, we can then run it to generate a realistic dataset with known anomalies.

Simulations are most useful when the concept of time is very important to the data. When there is no significance to time (or other sense of order, such as physical location) and the rows are completely independent of each other, there will be less value in simulations, but there is still some real benefit: if the simulations are accurate, we can use these to evaluate outliers in real data. To achieve this, we run the simulation not just once but many times, each time creating a simulated world. Once this is done, to determine how unusual a record is, we can gauge it not just against the currently available real data (which is simply a sample of the full population of potential data) but also against a large collection of simulated worlds.

This allows us to gauge more accurately how probable certain occurrences are, as we can determine how many simulated worlds they occur in. Outliers, then, are events that occur in an unusually small number of worlds compared to other events. For example, if a purchaser makes, say, 10 purchases of the same item in a single day, we can (using the real data) determine specifically how frequently this has occurred in the past, and this may be unusual given our current data. But we can also, using simulations and encoding certain assumptions about the real-world processes, determine how frequently this will occur randomly. Further, we can adjust the parameters used by the simulation to determine how often this occurs given different assumptions, which may help point to possible explanations for the anomaly.

This is less necessary when we have a large set of reliable data to compare against, but this is not always the case. Given that, there are really two powerful benefits to simulations: creating datasets that can include anomalous collections of records and evaluating real outliers against many simulated worlds.

Once we have a good collection of simulated data, the next step is to train and test entirely using this data, which will indicate how well the detectors are able to find the known outliers. In this example, we wish to flag the records generated by the rogue purchaser, but in general records generated by any process that runs infrequently and anomalously.

In this case, we could also generate, and test if we can detect, for example, cases where purchases are made despite there being a large inventory; many purchases in the same day for the same staff; unusual levels of sales for a given hour, day, or month, and so on. Most of these examples can be detected only by tests for collective outliers, and simulations are often the only practical means to test and tune these sorts of detectors. In fact, in chapter 12, where we examine collective outliers, we use the data generated by this simulation.

Once the detectors are tuned so that they can reliably detect the sort of outliers we are interested in, we can be reasonably confident they will do so on real data as well. We would then typically retrain on the real data and execute the detector either on that same real data or on any subsequent data that arrives. The data generated by simulations is usually strictly used as a way test that the sorts of outliers they can produce are detected well. It is also useful because anything identified as an outlier can be compared against a large set of simulated worlds to help quantify how unusual it is.

Simulations can also generate data used to tune and test any detector. However, where we are strictly interested in outliers that are single records (and not anomalous sets of records), it is more practical to use the methods described previously to generate test data than to use simulations. Simulations can work quite well but are more difficult to create and may not warrant the additional effort.

One of the limitations of simulations is that it is difficult to know when they truly match real-world behavior, especially given we have only one real-world dataset to compare to. Domain experts can confirm if the behaviors encoded are sensible, but it can be difficult to determine if anything is missing.

Simulations similar to this may be created to simulate processes for many types of projects. For example, simulations may be used to simulate big bath frauds (described in chapter 1), credit card fraud, insider trading, network intrusions, information operations on social media, industrial systems with failing equipment or failing sensors—all of these may exhibit unusual patterns on the part of a small number of independent agents (in these examples, people or equipment) over time. In these cases, simulations could be created and then executed many times to determine experimentally the range of normal and abnormal behavior. Taking the big bath fraud as an example, we can run a simulation that spans many years, including a set of consecutive years where the fraud is executed. Most processes would run normally, covering various business processes, but one or more processes would also run, attributing revenue or expenses to inappropriate years, attempting to put all losses for the fraudulent time period into a single year.

11.5 Training classifiers to distinguish real from fake data

The idea of training a classifier to distinguish real from fake data was introduced in chapter 3. Now that we have a fuller understanding of the process of creating synthetic data, we can look at this idea more closely. We've seen how to generate more realistic data in a left-to-right manner (which can preserve the associations between features and generate much more realistic data than the method in chapter 3), how to use a modified GMM (or KDE and similar generative models), how to create doped records, and how to create simulations, all of which can be used to create the synthetic data necessary for this type of detector.

There is a strong correspondence between Real versus Fake outlier detection, at least when we use a Random Forest as the classifier, and DML, as both create models to distinguish real from synthetic data. The difference is that the Real versus Fake method uses the prediction to estimate the outlierness of each record, while DML uses the set of leaf nodes the predicted records end in. The process of generating the synthetic data is the same—though when optimizing both detectors, we may actually use different synthetic data and may tune the Random Forests (or other models, if used by Real versus Fake detectors) differently. In the remainder of this section, we will focus on Real versus Fake detectors, as these are more commonly used, but the ideas apply to DML as well.

When training the classifier used by a Real versus Fake detector, we train on real and synthetic data, with the data labeled as such. For any Real versus Fake detector we train, we will likely use the same real data; we only have the real data we have. Where Real versus Fake detectors can vary is in the classifier used (and parameters they use) and the synthetic data used.

Generating good synthetic data for Real versus Fake detectors can take some experimentation and some back and forth. As we'll see in chapter 16, this is similar to how generative adversarial networks (GANs) work, though a GAN uses a pair of neural networks to alternate between generating synthetic data and learning to discriminate this from real data, while here we would manually tweak the script to generate the synthetic data and would usually use a simpler predictive model than a neural network to discriminate between real and synthetic. Boosted models (e.g., LGBM, XGBoost, and catboost) tend to be the most accurate with tabular data, though we may be able to use interpretable models such as decision trees or simple logistic regression models for Real versus Fake detectors as well, which is a major advantage where possible.

In a simple scenario, we would create not a single Real versus Fake detector but two detectors based on two sets of synthetic data. We may create one that contains fairly obvious outliers, probably ignoring the associations between features and possibly including extreme and very rare values. We may create a second that respects the associations between features well and contains only subtle outliers. In this way, when outliers are flagged, we have some information given which detectors identified the outliers: when outliers are found by the first detector, we know they are fairly clear and likely strong outliers; if they are found only by the second detector, we know they are likely more subtle and will be harder to interpret. In practice, however, we would likely create not just two, but a series of detectors in the same way we often create a series of synthetic datasets for testing. In addition, we can vary the strength of the classifiers used, with some being simple, interpretable models such as decision trees and others more complex, powerful models, such as Random Forest, KNN classifiers, boosted machines, or others.

Detectors based on classifiers can be very effective. They are, however, limited both by the range of real data and the range of the synthetic outliers they were trained on, so they may not be as robust in identifying outliers (especially unknown outliers) in future data as other detectors. In fact, even within the existing data, where the synthetic data does not match the real outliers, detectors based on classifiers may not detect these as well as other detectors, and it will be preferable to use an ensemble of different detectors. On the other hand, where our interest is strictly in detecting specific outliers (outliers that have known properties), a classifier trained in this way may often work very well and may be sufficient.

There is, though, one danger to note in using this type of detector and also using synthetic data to test the process. Goodhart's law states: "when a measure becomes a target, it ceases to be a good measure." That is, we risk using the same process both to identify the outliers and to evaluate how well we found the outliers. It could be analogous to, for example, using an Entropy detector to identify the outliers and also using entropy to test the process (measuring the entropy before and after the outliers are removed) or using KDE as the outlier detector and then using the average log likelihood estimated by a KDE of the data to evaluate the process.

This is a real concern. However, there are few means to tune and test outlier detection systems other than using synthetic data—at least until there is a significant collection of labeled data. In addition, detectors based on classification tend to work well but may not be the strongest detectors. In both cases—where they are and where they are not the strongest detectors tested—we will likely use an ensemble of multiple detectors in any case, which will provide diversity to the outlier detection system. When we do use Real versus Fake or DML detectors, though, we should evaluate them in a different manner, such as by inspection, or at a minimum using a very different type of synthetic data.

Summary

- Synthetic data may be used for at least a few purposes with outlier detection:
  - To help understand detectors. For this we may use toy 2D datasets, as well as synthetic data that is very similar but cleaner and simpler than the real data. This is easier to work with than real data for early modeling, though we will need to work with real data once this stage is complete.
  - To tune and test detectors. For this we need data that is similar to the real data but at least slightly different so that we can test that this data is largely scored higher than the real data by the detectors.
  - To train some outlier detectors that internally use classifiers, such as Real versus Fake and DML detectors.

- Methods to create synthetic data include creating the data feature by feature based on the distributions found in the training data, GMMs, KDEs, doping, and simulations.

- Creating synthetic data one feature at a time, we can either create the features independently or use some means (such as a predictor) to model the joint distribution.

- Creating synthetic data one feature at a time, using GMMs or KDEs, and doping all allow us to adjust how realistic the data is.

- GMMs and KDEs work similarly to each other and are limited to creating typical data unless modified. Once modified, they will generate data with a fraction of outliers, proportionate to how greatly they were modified.

- For all three purposes for synthetic data covered here, it is useful to create a range of synthetic data, from data very different from the real data (and easy for detectors to flag) to data very similar to the real data (and difficult for detectors to flag).

- Simulations are a powerful tool to create synthetic data but are more difficult to set up.

- Once created, simulations allow us to create test data that includes unusual sets of data or data that is unusual given the records that proceeded it.

- Simulations also allow us to create many simulated worlds, which allow us to evaluate effectively how unusual certain events are.

- Real versus Fake and DML detectors can take advantage of largely the same methods to generate synthetic data as those used to evaluate detectors.

- Avoid using the same means to identify outliers as to evaluate the system.

Collective outliers

12

This chapter covers

- Testing for unusual duplicates or gaps in the data
- Identifying anomalous entities
- Identifying anomalous time periods
- Finding items that are unusually common, as opposed to unusually rare
- Anomalous trends or distributions of values

Often when analyzing data, we're interested in finding not just unusual individual records, but any unusual patterns in the data. For this, an important step in outlier detection is searching for what are called *collective outliers*. These are cases in which individual rows are not necessarily unusual but sets of rows are. For example, in network logs a failed password attempt is likely not unusual, but a large number in a short period would be. With credit card records, a large purchase may not be unusual for the cardholder, but many large purchases in a short period may be very unusual. With collective outlier tests, we identify sets of records that collectively are unusual. In these examples, the set of records related to the failed passwords and the set of records related to the large credit card purchases would, when considered together, form outliers.

To find collective outliers, in most cases we will start with tables of data as we have so far, but we will aggregate the data in different ways, creating new sets of tables that can then be analyzed using standard univariate and multivariate tests. Doing this, we find different types of outliers—sometimes that are much more relevant, as they may indicate issues that are occurring on a large scale.

12.1 *Purchases data*

When creating a system to search for collective outliers, as with any outlier detection work, it's very useful to have test data to ensure the process works well and to, where necessary, support tuning the system until it is effective. There are different ways we can generate test data for this purpose. We may, for example, deliberately generate known collective outliers by duplicating real rows many times (such that they appear unusually often in the data), deleting large numbers of related rows, and so on. This is similar to doping but is done on sets of records as opposed to individual records. For this chapter, we will use a simulation, specifically the simulation of a business described in chapter 11.

There are some significant advantages to using simulations to generate test data for collective outliers. They allow us to create test data where certain segments of the data (a single purchaser in this example) are different, in aggregate, from other segments, even where the individual records are not necessarily unusual. Simulations also allow us to assess well what can and cannot be reliably detected, particularly when testing with many datasets generated by the simulation. Simulations typically use some random processes in generating the data, so they allow us to create large volumes of similar (and plausible) test sets, each a bit different.

If we are instead simply duplicating, deleting, or otherwise modifying the records, it will not generally be clear what the implications of these operations are and what collective outliers we should expect to find. But with simulated data, we have a known ground truth related to the anomalous behavior. The purchases data includes a rogue purchaser, who had a number of known characteristics, such as an escalating pattern of a certain type of purchase and typically larger purchases. We know that the records for this purchaser, while not necessarily individually unusual (none are drastically larger), are, as a set, different than those of the other purchasers. It would be possible, though more difficult, to reliably generate test data where that is true other than through a simulation.

As with any type of test data used, for the testing process to be effective we need to ensure that the data generated by the simulation represents real-world data well (that it is plausible), that the simulation data covers a large number of anomalies, and that the known anomalies are outliers we would be interested in identifying. Once this is in place, we will have a very effective test set, or preferably, suite of test sets. Later, as we work with this, we may think of additional types of outliers we would wish to identify, and it may be necessary to adjust the simulation to cover additional test cases.

For the examples here, we use a subset of the data created in the simulation, which created both sales and purchase records. For simplicity, we will look here at only the purchases. For a fuller examination of the data, however, the sales and inventories should also be considered, as these provide more context to identify unusual behavior. The purchases data can be isolated with

```
purchases_df = transactions_df[transactions_df['Type']=='Purchase'].copy()
purchases_df = purchases_df.drop(columns=['Type'])
```

This assumes the `transactions_df` dataframe has been created by the simulations code (available at https://mng.bz/Bgav). The first few rows of the purchases data are shown in table 12.1. The full table covers 9,415 rows and represents the set of purchases for one company for a year for several purchasers, suppliers, and products.

Table 12.1 Purchase records

Staff ID	Supplier ID	Product ID	Datetime	Count	Unit cost	Total cost	Inventory
4	9	9	2023-01-01 09:35	113	27.66	3,125.66	1,106
7	6	11	2023-01-01 09:56	83	61.82	5,131.54	1,082
8	15	3	2023-01-01 10:14	95	14.18	1,347.34	1,092

It's important to first check the table for unusual individual purchases, which may be done using any of the outlier tests we've looked at so far. As the table contains both categorical and numeric features, we may wish to use either numeric or categorical detectors, though a combination of both will usually be preferable. Outliers identified as individual records are referred to as *point anomalies*. Here this may include unusual total costs, unusual times of day, unusual staff IDs, unusual combinations of product code and unit cost, and so on. Once these are found (and any data artifacts identified possibly removed), we can search for collective outliers.

This dataset contains three types of entities—staff, suppliers, and products—which allows us to identify anomalous examples of each of these. We can find staff that are unusual relative to other staff, suppliers unusual relative to other suppliers, and products unusual relative to other products. Taking staff as an example, there are many ways we can compare the staff to each other, all based on aggregating the set of records we have for each staff into a set of statistics describing each. We can look at their average unit prices paid for each product, the average number of purchases they make per day, the suppliers they tend to use, the times of day they make purchases, and so on.

Testing for collective outliers, we can also look for unusual time periods. For example, there may be days that are significantly different from the other days in the data—similarly for hours, weeks, months, and so on.

Given this, we can use collective outlier tests to identify numerous types of anomalies in the purchases data that could not be detected otherwise, including data errors, inefficient purchases (where too many of certain items were purchased), unusually high prices being consistently paid, and other issues that appear to be inefficiencies, errors, or fraud. For example, we may find where certain suppliers are favored by some purchasers despite having higher prices, which may suggest kickbacks or other issues.

12.2 Preparing the data

Before we begin the process of searching for collective outliers, we will usually need to process the existing table a little. This is similar to what would be done when we are searching for point anomalies. In this case (listing 12.1), we break the Datetime field into separate columns, which will make aggregating easier later.

> **Listing 12.1 Preparing the data for tests for collective outliers**

```
purchases_df['Date'] = pd.to_datetime(purchases_df['Datetime']).dt.date
purchases_df['Year'] = pd.to_datetime(purchases_df['Datetime']).dt.year
purchases_df['Month'] = pd.to_datetime(purchases_df['Datetime']).dt.month
purchases_df['Day'] = pd.to_datetime(purchases_df['Datetime']).dt.day
purchases_df['Hour'] = pd.to_datetime(purchases_df['Datetime']).dt.hour
purchases_df['Minute'] = pd.to_datetime(purchases_df['Datetime']).dt.minute
purchases_df = purchases_df.drop(columns=['Datetime'])
purchases_df = purchases_df.reset_index(drop=True)
purchases_df.insert(0, 'Purchase ID', purchases_df.index)
```

This updates the table to the format are shown in table 12.2 (due to space limitations, not all columns are shown).

Table 12.2 Inventory purchases reformatted

Staff ID	Supplier ID	Product ID	Count	Unit cost	Total cost	Inventory	Date	Year	Month	Day	Hour	Minute
4	9	9	113	27.66	3,125.66	1106	2023-01-01	2023	1	1	9	35
7	6	11	83	61.82	5,131.54	1082	2023-01-01	2023	1	1	9	56
8	15	3	95	14.18	1,347.34	1092	2023-01-01	2023	1	1	10	14

We can now start reformatting this data in various ways to test for unusual entities and unusual time periods, but we'll first check for some other important anomalies that span sets of rows: duplicates, gaps in time, and missing combinations. These may all be considered forms of collective outlier: each, if sufficiently unusual, is an anomaly, but none can be identified by looking for unusual individual records. In each case, we need to aggregate the data and look at it somewhat differently to find the outliers. This is another simple but important example of the general idea that looking at the data from more perspectives can help turn up outliers we would otherwise miss.

The examples here assume a one-off project, where it is useful to examine the data manually, creating plots and segmenting the data in different ways. For ongoing projects, the process would be similar but slightly different in that we would automate looping through each test and scoring the results of each.

12.3 *Testing for duplicates*

Duplicate records often indicate an issue. In some datasets, it may be the case that all rows should be completely unique and any duplicates indicate an error, and in other cases some duplicates would be reasonable, but we will still wish to test for unusual numbers of duplicates.

Duplicates can be defined based on different sets of features, which allows us to check for these, sometimes, in multiple ways. In this case, it is unusual for the same purchaser to buy the same product more than once per day. Duplicates in the same hour (as are checked in listing 12.2) would be suspicious and likely either errors or fraud (duplicate transactions are sometimes created to circumvent controls, where it can be erroneously believed the transactions have already been checked). Checking by minute instead of by hour would produce outliers that are more suspicious but would miss those duplicates created more than a minute apart (but within same hour), so it may be worth checking both.

This example uses pandas's `groupby()` method to get the count of each combination of staff, product, and hour and uses `value_counts()` to display these. In production, a simple rules-based system with a threshold would likely be sufficient to identify the duplicates that may be worth checking.

Listing 12.2 Testing for duplicates

```
duplicates_test_df = (pd.DataFrame(
        purchases_df.groupby(
            ['Date', 'Hour', 'Staff ID', 'Product ID']
        ).size(),
        columns=['Count']
    )).reset_index()
duplicates_test_df['Count'].value_counts()
```

Looking at longer periods such as days or weeks may be useful as well. With this dataset, we expect multiple purchases for the same product for the same purchaser per day, so if looking at days (or at periods longer than a day), any findings would not be considered duplicates per se; we would be performing a different, though also useful, test. We may, in this way, be able to identify unusually low or high numbers of similar purchases in the same day or week.

In this case, there are 74 cases in which there were two matching purchases in the same hour and none where there were three or more in an hour. With the cases found, we would generally try to identify patterns in the duplicates, such as if there are specific purchasers, suppliers, products, times, and so on where these tend to occur more often. In this example, we can also examine the data more closely by considering the supplier and testing for duplicates in the sense of multiple purchases for the same staff, product, and supplier in the same hour:

```
duplicates_test_df = (pd.DataFrame(
        purchases_df.groupby(
            ['Date', 'Hour', 'Staff ID', 'Supplier ID', 'Product ID']
        ).size(),
        columns=['Count']
    )).reset_index()
duplicates_test_df['Count'].value_counts()
```

Using this test, there are five cases where there were two duplicate purchases within an hour, which we may wish to investigate further. These appear to be anomalies, though; as with any type of outlier, what is interesting depends on the context, and many outliers may be innocuous.

12.4 Testing for gaps

A common data quality issue problem is gaps in the data. These can occur due to problems collecting the data at source or in processing the data, such as SQL errors. These can be clear, such as ranges of dates completely missing, but they can also be more difficult to spot—for example, where there are no records for some purchasers or suppliers for certain periods. These will normally be legitimate, such as staff vacations or suppliers temporarily shutting down, but if statistically unusual, they are likely worth noting. In some cases, these may be data artifacts or indications of unusual behavior.

Here we test if there are any dates entirely missing by sorting the data by date and using pandas's `diff()` method to find the difference in dates between consecutive rows:

```
purchases_df = purchases_df.sort_values(['Date'])
purchases_df['Date'].diff().dt.days.value_counts()
```

The results are

```
0.0    9051
1.0     363
```

We see that in all cases the difference is either zero (for two consecutive records on the same day) or one (for records on consecutive days), with no larger gaps found, so there are no gaps in this regard but there may be more subtle gaps, which can be worth checking for as well. Part of this is testing for missing combinations, which we look at next. This provides some examples, but it's important to determine where missing data would be of interest with your data.

12.5 Testing for missing combinations

As well as gaps in time in the data, there may be values or combinations of values that are not present. Often the absence of data is as informative as the presence of rare data, and this is only possible to detect using collective outlier tests: normal outlier detection can identify where there are few instances of something but not where there are zero. In listing 12.3, we check for each combination of Staff ID and Product ID, which indicates that the purchaser with Staff ID 10 does not purchase product 0. This is less likely to be a data collection problem, though that is still possible. More likely it is an anomaly of another type and possibly relevant. Here we use pandas's `crosstab` method to get the sum (in numbers of units purchased) of each combination.

Listing 12.3 Checking for missing combinations

```
counts = pd.crosstab(index=purchases_df['Staff ID'],
    columns=purchases_df['Product ID'],
    values=purchases_df['Count'],
    aggfunc='sum')
counts = counts.fillna(0)
sns.histplot(counts.values.flatten(), bins=30)
plt.show()
```

The `counts` dataframe produced is easy to examine, though it is too large to display here. We flatten the dataframe and render a histogram of the sums of each combination, shown in figure 12.1. We can see from the dataframe, and also from the histogram, that counts of 0 are highly unusual for this pair of features. To measure specifically how unusual, we need to consider, as introduced in chapter 2, the marginal probabilities; some combinations of product and staff may be rare simply because there are few records for the product and/or staff, so the combination can be expected to be rare.

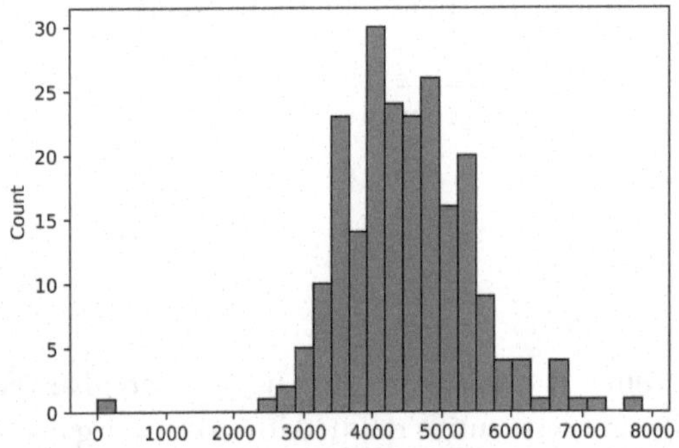

Figure 12.1 Distribution of the counts of the unique combinations of Staff ID and Product ID

Doing this, we have found an anomaly, which, having no records, would have been impossible to find as a point anomaly. A similar process can be used to find unusually low or high counts of combinations of other pairs or triples of features. In this case, the data is not likely large enough to examine combinations of more than three features, but this is feasible with sufficiently large datasets.

Now that we've looked at tests for unusual duplicates, gaps in time, and missing combinations, we're ready to look at detecting what we more normally associate with collective outliers: unusual entities and unusual time periods.

12.6 Creating new tables to capture collective outliers

For the most part, searching for collective outliers requires creating new tables such that each row represents the concept we are interested in (likely an entity or a time period), and each feature contains statistics about these, calculated by aggregating the original data. The art of detecting collective outliers is in aggregating the data in effective ways. Outlier detection systems cannot discover the relevant metrics, and so these features must be engineered by the data scientists working on each project.

How we do this depends on the type of data we have and the types of anomalies that would be interesting. For example, examining logs of user activity from a social media platform, we may be interested in identifying any inauthentic accounts based on records of the messages sent. Comparing the users, we can identify any users that are unusual enough to be suspicious. For this, we can create a table, with a row for each user and with the features containing the statistics we feel are most relevant to describe them. We want these features, either on their own or when compared with the other features, to highlight the unusual sorts of behavior we would be interested in. Some users may post large numbers of messages, post in very intense bursts, or post 24 hours a day for days at a time (highly unusual for accounts that aren't bots). It's necessary to shape the data and engineer features such that these may be exposed. We may, for example, generate features for each user to indicate the average number of posts per day, maximum per hour, and maximum number of unique hours per day where they post at least one message.

Table 12.3 shows an example with features generated to describe three users. User 2 stands out as having once posted 403 messages in a day and user 3 for having once posted at least one message per hour for at least 24 hours.

Table 12.3   Example table of social media accounts

User ID	Avg # posts per day	Max # posts per day	Max # posts per hour	Maximum # unique hours per day	Avg # unique hours per day
1	0.4	10	7	4	1.1
2	30	403	10	3	2.0
3	0.2	8	2	24	1.9

Ultimately, the new tables created will be organized such that each row in the new table summarizes a set of rows in the original data (in this example, the set for each user). Running univariate and multivariate tests on the new tables will find the unusual records in the new tables, which indicate unusual *sets of records* in the original data. With the purchases data, we would likely create a table for staff (with a row for each individual staff), another table for suppliers, and another table for products, as well as possibly tables for various time periods, such as months, weeks, days, and hours, trying to create features that expose the most anomalous of these.

12.6.1 Aggregating by entity

In general, there are three main types of anomalies we can find aggregating the data by entity:

- *Where a set of records are not necessarily individually unusual but there's an unusual number of them* (very few or very many)—In the case of the social media accounts, each of user 2's posts may be normal, but having 403 in a single day is unusual. With the purchases data, we may have some purchasers buying more items than is normal or using certain suppliers more than is normal, even where the individual purchases are typical.

- *Where the records in a set are each slightly unusual, but likely would not be flagged using point anomaly tests*—For example, the rogue purchaser pays slightly more for items, but this is not detectable when considering each purchase on its own. It can be clearer, though, if aggregating over many purchases.

- *Where the set of records are unusual as a set*—With social media accounts, the posts for one user may be unusual only when considered together. For example, they may be spaced exactly 1 hour apart (with unusual consistency) or unusually repetitive in their content. With the purchases data, the purchases for one staff may be, for example, unusually consistent day to day or unusually variable.

Looking at the purchases data, we start with an example aggregating by Product ID. This may be done, for example, using pandas's `groupby()` method:

```
purchases_df.groupby(['Product ID']).agg({
    'Count': ['mean', 'sum'],
    'Unit Cost': ['mean', 'sum'],
    'Total Cost': ['mean', 'sum'],
    'Hour': ['mean', 'min', 'max'],
    'Purchase ID': ['count']})
```

This creates a new dataframe (table 12.4) on which we simply run outlier detection tests the same as we would on the original data, here finding unusual products. Often simple univariate tests are sufficient, such as those shown in chapter 2, or histogram-based outlier score (HBOS), empirical cumulative distribution function (ECOD), Entropy, and so on. We may also benefit from multivariate tests such as Isolation Forest (IF), local outlier factor, k nearest neighbors, outlier detection using in-degree number (ODIN), DBSCAN, Real versus Fake, and others to detect unusual combinations of values.

Table 12.4   Table representing each product

Product ID	Count		Unit cost		Total cost		Hour			Purchase ID
	mean	sum	mean	sum	mean	sum	mean	min	max	count
0	103.4	48,784	15.2	7,190.7	1,541.8	727,734.8	13.1	9	17	472
1	103.3	49,675	16.6	8,007.5	1,724.5	829,466.8	13.2	9	17	481
2	101.5	50,439	16.6	8,230.5	1,688.9	839,378.9	13.1	9	17	497

In this case, none of the products stand out as anomalous. The rogue purchaser is paying larger unit prices for product 5, and this is visible if plotted (figure 12.2) but not in a way that would likely qualify it as an outlier.

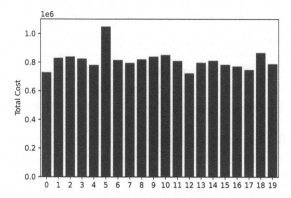

Figure 12.2 **Distribution of the sum of Total Costs for each of the 20 products. Product 5 has the highest total costs but not likely to an anomalous degree. In this case, it will be necessary to view the data more closely to reliably identify any anomalies.**

In the same way, we can engineer tables to represent staff or suppliers. We can also create tables where each row represents the combinations of two or more entities, which we look at next.

12.6.2 *Aggregating by two or more entity types*

As well as creating tables for each staff, each product, and each supplier, we can also create tables for combinations of these. For example, we can look at each combination of staff and product and generate statistics related to each, likely using similar statistics to those shown in table 12.4 but possibly others if relevant. This allows us to determine where the specific combinations are anomalous even if the entities on their own, on the whole, are not. As with checks for single entities, when testing combinations of entities, we would check for unusual counts, cases where the original records related to the combination are consistently unusual in some way (even if only moderately), and cases where the set itself may be unusual.

In the case of the purchases data, we know from the simulation that product 5 is generally normal and that purchaser 10 (the rogue purchaser) is generally normal but the combination is not. Given that, examining just the products or just the staff may not reveal anything unusual or, as in figure 12.2, something just slightly unusual. Examining combinations of entities instead, we can tune the system (engineering features and trying different outlier detectors) until we can identify known anomalies with these reliably. We can examine staff and products together with similar code such as

```
agg_df = purchases_df.groupby(['Staff ID', 'Product ID']).agg({
    'Count': ['mean', 'sum'],
    'Unit Cost': ['mean', 'sum'],
    'Total Cost': ['mean', 'sum'],
```

```
'Hour': ['mean', 'min', 'max'],
'Purchase ID': ['count']})
```

As well as unusual average unit costs and so on, looking at each combination allows us to find simply how frequent each combination is. Here we achieve this by counting the number of Purchase IDs for each combination. This code will cover only the existing combinations so will not detect missing combinations but will identify the very rare and very frequent combinations.

Rare combinations may be detected with point anomaly tests on the original records in any case, but there is a strong benefit in testing for rare combinations here as well: the outliers found are usually more interpretable when found with collective outlier tests. We get information about how rare the combination is and context about how rare other combinations are.

Still, where collective outlier tests are particularly powerful is in detecting where combinations are entirely missing (as in the previous test) or where they have unusually large counts. We can then identify anomalies that are somewhat the opposite as with outlier detection for point anomalies: we can find what is unusually frequent, while tests for point anomalies will detect only what is unusually rare.

In this case, once aggregated, we can perform outlier detection on the new table:

```
from sklearn.ensemble import IsolationForest

det = IsolationForest()
det.fit(agg_df)
agg_df['IF Scores'] = det.decision_function(agg_df)

agg_df.sort_values(['IF Scores'])
```

This produces the table shown in table 12.5, though some columns are removed here.

Table 12.5   Table representing each combination of staff and product

Staff ID	Product ID	Count		Unit cost		Total cost		Purchase ID	IF score
		mean	sum	mean	sum	mean	sum	count	
10	5	182.6	7,850	29.5	1,269.9	9,303.3	40,0041.4	43	−0.3
10	12	95.3	2,669	12.8	358.8	1,042.5	29,190.2	28	−0.2
2	0	106.5	3,941	17.4	644.7	1,940.2	71,786.6	37	−0.1

The combination of staff 10 and product 5 is scored strongest (most negative, with a score of −0.3), which suggests it may be worth looking more closely at these.

12.6.3   Aggregating by time

Aggregating by time works very similarly to aggregating by entity. In the case of the purchases data, we can aggregate by minute, hour, day, week, month, or other periods.

With other types of data, other periods may be relevant; with mobile network data, for example, it may be useful to analyze the data on the level of seconds or 10-second intervals. But, each level of analysis will highlight certain types of anomalies that would likely be missed looking at the data at another level of granularity. For example, with the purchases data, there may be cases where there are unusual days but each hour within the day is fairly normal: it could be that most hours had large numbers of purchases—that are each not particularly unusual, but when summed over the full day, the day as a whole was notably unusual. In addition, averaged in with the other days of the month, the month may not stand out as noteworthy; only examining the data by day will reveal this particular anomaly. In the same way, there may be other anomalies that only stand out when looking at other time periods.

Consequently, it is useful to examine the data at multiple time scales, though in many cases we should be mindful that doing so may find some anomalies simply due to the large number of periods examined. For example, with mobile network data where the data spans many days, examining data at the level of seconds may find anomalous seconds simply because a large number were checked. This is particularly true if there are few records per second, in which case the statistics produced for each second may not be stable.

In the case of the purchases data, we can examine by month. On average, each month has 785 records, which is good, but there are only 12 months, which makes comparing them to each other less reliable. Examining each day, there are a good number of days (364) but each has only 26 records on average. Both are usable, but we need to be cautious of any findings and likely follow up only with very strong outliers. Testing for collective outliers does require more data than testing for point anomalies. When a sufficient amount of data is available, however, collective outlier tests can be more stable than point anomaly tests, as each record in the aggregated data may be based on a large number of records from the original data.

In listing 12.4, we create a new dataframe where each row represents one day. Here we engineer seven features based on the counts per purchase, unit costs, total costs, and the total number of purchases per day. This provides a useful table to compare the days to each other, but it is also possible to aggregate in other ways or to engineer otherfeatures that should also be considered.

Here the values are fairly consistent each day. The counts are also too low to be used reliably for some analysis, but given how consistent they are, if any very large values were present, they may be worth further investigating. In this case, no day stands out as unusual.

Listing 12.4 Creating a table where each row represents one day

```
purchases_df.groupby(['Date']).agg({
    'Count': ['mean', 'sum'],
    'Unit Cost': ['mean', 'sum'],
    'Total Cost': ['mean', 'sum'],
    'Purchase ID': ['count']})
```

In table 12.6 we see the first few rows of the aggregated data, where each row represents 1 day.

Table 12.6   Daily summary of purchases data

	Count		Unit cost		Total cost		Purchase ID
Date	mean	sum	mean	sum	mean	sum	count
2023-01-01	121.4	2,670	21.8	479.9	2,502.6	55,057.5	22
2023-01-02	98.1	2,846	16.8	486.4	1,656.8	48,046.1	29
2023-01-03	93.6	2,152	17.2	394.6	1,763.2	40,554.4	23

Examining this shows nothing unusual, but we can look at the data in other ways and possibly discover something noteworthy. We can also look at the days of the week, days of the month, hours of the day, and so on to see if there are other unusual differences in these. Aggregating, similar to listing 12.4, but by the Day feature (instead of Date), we get statistics for each day of the month. Plotting these out, we can see the 28th day of each month stands out. For example, plotting the sum of Total Cost by day of the month (figure 12.3), we see a noticeably higher level of sales on the 28th day of each month. We also see the 31st day has lower counts, but this is simply due to not all months having 31 days.

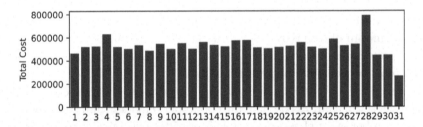

Figure 12.3   The sum of purchases in dollars for each day of the month. The 31st is low simply because it appears in only some months. The 28th day stands out as unusually high. It is not a strong outlier but may be worth examining further.

Once we've identified the 28th day of the month to appear as unusual, it's useful to drill down and determine more specifically what makes this different from other days of the month. We can create a subset of the data representing just transactions on the 28th day of the month and examine this more closely. We can create this with

```
day_28_df = purchases_df[purchases_df['Day'] == 28]
```

Once this is created, we can test for point and collective anomalies and determine which entities or time periods are overrepresented in the data in order to try to determine the root cause of the unusual statistics for the 28th day. We can also look at aggregating by day of the month along with other features to determine why there is a spike on the 28th day of each month. We'll look next at the latter approach, creating more specific subsets, where any anomalies may stand out more clearly.

12.6.4 *Aggregating by entity and time*

In general, where there is sufficient data, it is useful to aggregate both by entity and time. It may be that there are unusual time periods for certain entities or for certain combinations of entities. In addition, where potential anomalies are found when examining specific entities or time periods, it may be worth looking at the data more granularly to determine the source of the discrepancy.

Aggregating by entity and time, we create a table where each row represents one entity for one time period. In this example, we look at each staff for each day of the month and create six features to describe each. The table created uses the count, mean, and sum for a set of original features, as well as the 95th percentile for the Total Cost. Using statistics such as minimum and maximum is sensitive to outliers, which, when looking for outliers, is often desirable, but we also want to be able to compare each segment of the data to its peers in a robust, meaningful way, and using percentiles can be preferable to do this. In this case, the 95th percentile indicates the large values for each staff for each day of the month without being affected by any extreme values. Other aggregation functions may be more useful in some situations, such as other percentiles or the standard deviation (which can measure how consistent or variable the values in different groups are):

```
def p95(x):
    return x.quantile(0.95)

purchases_df.groupby(['Staff ID', 'Day']).agg({
    'Count': ['mean', 'sum'],
    'Total Cost': ['mean', 'sum', p95],
    'Purchase ID': ['count']})
sns.histplot(purchases_df.groupby(['Staff ID', 'Day'])['Total Cost'].sum())
plt.show()
```

The results are shown for the Total Cost, summed for each staff member for each day, in figure 12.4. We can see one value stands out as a very strong outlier, which is for staff 10, for the 28th day of the month.

A histogram is possible here as we expect all staff and days of the month to be equivalent, and any exceptions are noteworthy. In cases where this is not true (where some staff make more purchases than others or different days of the month have more purchases than others), we will need to consider their marginal probabilities as described in chapter 2.

One property of aggregating by both entity and time is that the peers each combination will be compared to will include other time periods for the same entity, other entities for the same time period, and other combinations of both. This is often very useful, but we do need to ensure these are reasonably comparable. It may be useful, for example, to simply compare each entity to itself from prior periods or to only compare each entity to others for the same time period.

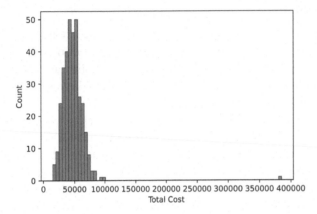

Figure 12.4   **Histogram of values for the sum of Total Cost, grouped by Staff ID and day of the month**

This form of test, examining each subset of the data for each time period, will also allow us to identify outliers such as described at the beginning of the chapter, where there are many failed logins for a user, or many large credit card purchases for a cardholder, in a short time period. With network logs, for example, we can create a table with a row for each user action (including login) by minute, along with statistics such as the number of successful calls and number of unsuccessful calls for each user and minute. For credit card records, a table may represent purchases per cardholders per hour, along with features for each, such as number of purchases, total spent, number of unique locations, number of items, average price per item, and so on for each hour. These will then allow simple outlier tests to identify these anomalies in the generated tables.

12.6.5 *Merging in additional information*

So far we've looked at reshaping the data available in the original data in order to identify anomalies in different ways, but it may also be useful to bring in more information from other tables. For example, with the purchases data, if the staff are in different divisions, it may be useful to merge this information into the original table, creating a new feature for this. When looking for point anomalies, this provides more context, but it also allows us to find collective outliers in more ways. We can, in this example, determine if any divisions may be considered anomalous in regards to their purchasing, if certain combinations of supplier and division are unusual, and so on.

We do need to be mindful, though, as incorporating additional features may identify outliers that are of less interest and will increase the likelihood of identifying entities that are unusual simply by chance. Where large numbers of combinations are examined, we are less likely to miss important issues in the data, but we also need to contend with more false positives: entities or time periods that are statistically unusual but due to random variation and not anomalous in an interesting way.

12.7 Identifying trends

To identify anomalous entities, it's useful to look not just at the type of statistics for entities we've looked at so far but also at any relevant timelines for each entity. With industrial equipment, for example, we may have records related to many pieces of equipment. It may be that some have extreme values for some sensor readings and we can identify these as point anomalies; but we also have a history of readings for each piece of equipment, which can be very useful. For some equipment, the individual sensor readings may all be quite normal, but there may be, for example, an unusual upward trend, unusual volatility or other unusual patterns over time, suggesting failure in the near future.

We will look at examining time series in more detail in chapter 17; in this section we will look at simpler methods, engineering simple features that represent trends over time for each entity.

With the purchases data, the rogue purchaser has an escalating pattern. This is common in fraud scenarios, as those committing the fraud, if not detected early, become more confident and brazen. In fact, as discussed in chapter 1, looking for escalations in certain behaviors is an important test for fraud detection. So we look in this example for upward trends, but it can also be useful to look for unusually low or high variability, unusual repeating patterns in the timelines, and so on.

Similar to creating statistics for each time period in the previous section, when we examine timelines for each entity, we can aggregate the data by minute, hour, day, week, or other period, and we may find different results for each. Intuitively, if we are concerned with fraud, errors, or inefficiencies in purchasing, we are looking for patterns over the full year and likely aggregating over each day, each week, or both. If aggregating by day, then each point on the timeline will represent a summary of the data per entity per day—for example the number of purchases per day, total spend in dollars, average unit prices, and so on for each purchaser.

Using these methods, we may be able to narrow down a search to staff 10, day 28, and product 5. We may also be able to identify this combination as anomalous after looping over many combinations and testing each timeline for unusually strong upward trends or for other anomalous timelines. Listing 12.5 shows an example that plots some timelines for this specific combination. This has 12 points for each plot, as the data is plotted by day but filtered to cover only the 28th day of each month.

Listing 12.5 Plotting the trends for staff 10, day 28, product 5

```
sub_df = purchases_df[(purchases_df['Staff ID']==10) & (purchases_
    df['Day']==28) & (purchases_df['Product ID']==5)]

fig, ax = plt.subplots(nrows=1, ncols=3, figsize=(10, 3))
s = sns.lineplot(data=sub_df, x='Date', y='Count', ax=ax[0])
```

```
s.set_xticklabels([])
s = sns.lineplot(data=sub_df, x='Date', y='Unit Cost', ax=ax[1])
s.set_xticklabels([])
s = sns.lineplot(data=sub_df, x='Date', y='Total Cost', ax=ax[2])
s.set_xticklabels([])

plt.tight_layout()
plt.show()
```

The timelines are shown over the 12 months in figure 12.5. The left pane shows a strong upward pattern for counts (the number of items bought in each purchase) but a less-clear pattern for the other metrics plotted.

For any timeline to be considered anomalous, we need to compare it to comparable timelines—in this case, other combinations of staff, day of the month, and product. In addition, it can be very useful to compare timelines for certain entities (or combinations of entities) not to their peers but to themselves in earlier time periods. For example, we might compare the timeline by month for staff 10, day 28, and product 5 for 2023 to the equivalent timeline for 2022.

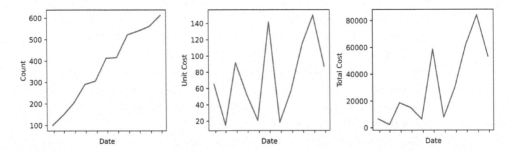

Figure 12.5   Timelines for Count (number of items per purchase, left pane), Unit Cost (middle pane), and Total Cost (right pane) for Staff ID 10, Product ID 5, on day 28 of the months. There is a clear upward trend for counts, which is suspicious. This can be compared to other segments of the data to confirm how unusual it is. The middle does not show an upward trend. The right pane shows some upward trend and appears to increase in variability over time, though this may be due to chance.

We can compare the timelines themselves, and discuss this in chapter 17, but it is simpler to generate statistics that describe each timeline. Doing this, the statistics created do conceptually have a different meaning from statistics not related to time but may be treated similarly. An example of some features created to describe each combination of staff, day of the month, and product (with respect to their timelines) is

```
import statistics

def trend_func(x):
    return statistics.mean(x[-3:]) / statistics.mean(x[:3])
```

```
purchases_df = purchases_df.sort_values(['Staff ID', 'Product ID', 'Date'])
staff_product_day_df = purchases_df.groupby(
    ['Staff ID', 'Product ID', 'Day'], as_index=False).agg(
    {'Purchase ID': 'count',
     'Count': ['first','last', trend_func],
     'Unit Cost': ['first','last', trend_func],
     'Total Cost': ['first','last', trend_func]
    })
staff_product_day_df['Count Diff Last to First'] = \
    staff_product_day_df[('Count', 'last')] -  \
        staff_product_day_df[('Count', 'first')]
staff_product_day_df
```

As each combination of staff, product, and day of the month has at most one instance in this dataset, we can simply execute this over the full purchases dataframe, which we do here for simplicity. Generally, however, we would need to first combine all transactions for each combination. This groups by each combination of staff, product, and day of the month; for each tracking statistics about the trends in Count, Unit Cost, and Total Cost; as well as the number of purchases. For each original feature, we calculate the first and last values (the values in January and December), which allows us to subtract these to get an estimate of the overall trend over the year. There is one example of this after the groupby, creating a feature to represent the difference from the start of the year to the end in the count of items per purchase. This may be able to capture upward trends to some extent but is sensitive to the values of those two specific months and ignores the months between. To be more robust, we also add a function, trend_func(), which calculates the average values for the first three and last three months and takes their ratio. Other similar functions may also be useful, such as taking the ratio of the mean of the last six months to the first six months, the slope of a regression line through the data, or other statistics summarizing the trend over time. Again, once this table is generated, any outlier detection tests may then be executed on this.

A portion of the output table is shown in table 12.7. There is a row for each combination of staff, product, and day of the month, along with trend information about each. In the two rows shown here, the trend_func value is 1.0, indicating the Total Costs were similar for the last three months as the first three months. Combinations with very strong upward or downward trends will stand out with extreme values in this feature. In this case, almost all combinations have a ratio close to 1.0. Staff 10 for product 5 on the 28th day of the months has a ratio of 7.3, which matches figure 12.5 (left pane).

Table 12.7 Table representing each staff, product, day of the month, with trend features

Staff ID	Product ID	Day	Total Cost		
			first	last	trend_func
0	0	1	1,026.4	768.8	1.0
0	0	3	4,968.4	687.3	1.0

12.8   *Unusual distributions*

As well as unusual statistics and unusual trends for subsets of the data, it's possible to check for unusual distributions of values. In listing 12.6, we look at the distributions of suppliers used by each purchaser, plotting these first over the full dataset and then for three different purchasers. This example compares staff to each other (seeing if there are any that have an unusual distribution in their use of each supplier), but it is also possible to compare each staff to themselves from prior time periods. Comparing the staff, we can examine these visually to see if anything stands out. Some may have, for example, more variability than others, suggesting the staff are favoring certain suppliers more than is typical. In this case, there is nothing visually obvious.

Listing 12.6   Distribution of suppliers

```
fig, ax = plt.subplots(nrows=2, ncols=4, figsize=(23, 3))
sns.countplot(data=purchases_df, x='Supplier ID', ax=ax[0][0])
sns.countplot(data=purchases_df[purchases_df['Staff ID']==0],
              x='Supplier ID', ax=ax[0][1])
sns.countplot(data=purchases_df[purchases_df['Staff ID']==1],
              x='Supplier ID', ax=ax[1][0])
sns.countplot(data=purchases_df[purchases_df['Staff ID']==10],
              x='Supplier ID', ax=ax[1][1])
plt.show()
```

The distributions are shown in figure 12.6. The distributions for the three staff shown fluctuate more than for the full data (in the top left pane), which is expected given the data sizes are smaller. They are similar to each other, with no obvious differences in their distribution. Staff 10 (the rogue purchaser, shown in the bottom right) has higher values for supplier 10 but not likely to the extent to be considered anomalous.

As well as examining the data visually, we can compare the distributions to each other in a more objective way, which means creating one or more statistics to describe each distribution. To do this, we can create an array for each staff, storing the fraction of their sales associated with each supplier. Using fractions instead of raw counts allows us to compare the shapes of the distributions as opposed to the magnitudes of the values. To be comparable, each array should be ordered in the same way, likely either by supplier ID or by frequency. Listing 12.7 has an example, ordering by supplier: each array lists the same suppliers in the same order.

Once we have a set of distributions, we can compare these pairwise to determine if any are consistently different from the other distributions. This is similar to the idea of comparing records pairwise, as is done with k nearest neighbors (KNN), local outlier factor (LOF), outlier detection using in-degree number (ODIN), and so on, using metrics such as Manhattan, Euclidean, and Canberra distances. When comparing distributions, though, we usually use a statistical distance measure, such as KL-Divergence, Wasserstein, and so on, though Manhattan and Euclidean can also be used. In listing 12.7 we use a measure called the Jensen-Shannon divergence.

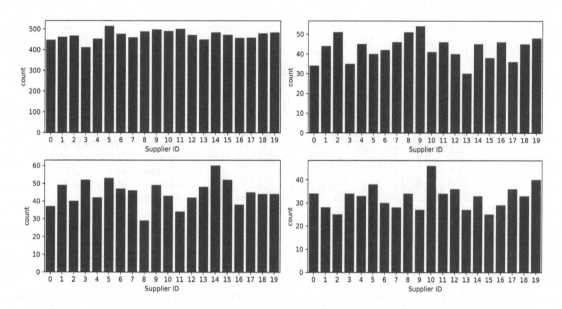

Figure 12.6 Distribution of suppliers for all staff (top left pane), staff 0 (top right pane), staff 1 (bottom left pane), staff 10 (bottom right pane). There are no clearly unusual distributions examining these visually.

Calculating every pairwise distance between the distributions is expensive. To avoid this, we determine the average distribution and compare each distribution to this. This creates a set of numeric scores indicating how anomalous the distributions are compared to those of the average among its peers. A threshold can be set for this based on, for example, the median absolute deviation, as shown in chapter 2. As discussed in chapter 7, using cumulative distributions can be more stable as well and are often useful. They do not apply here, as there is no natural order among the suppliers, but they can be useful if ordering by frequency.

Listing 12.7 Examining the statistical differences

```
from scipy.spatial import distance

base_distribution = purchases_df.groupby('Supplier ID')['Count'].count()/11
for staff_id in sorted(purchases_df['Staff ID'].unique()):
    distrib = purchases_df[purchases_df['Staff ID']==
        staff_id].groupby('Supplier ID')['Count'].count()
    print(distance.jensenshannon(base_distribution, distrib, 2.0))
```

In this case, there's no significant outliers in the distances. All are about 0.06, as shown in figure 12.7.

We repeat this, examining only the data for day 28 in listing 12.8, this time plotting some of the distributions.

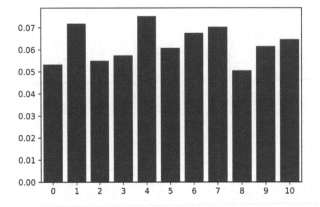

Figure 12.7 The statistical distances of the distributions of suppliers for each staff from the average distribution. All are roughly similar.

Listing 12.8 Examining the differences in suppliers for day 28

```
day_28_df = purchases_df[purchases_df['Day'] == 28]

fig, ax = plt.subplots(nrows=2, ncols=2, sharey=True, figsize=(8, 5))
sns.countplot(data=day_28_df, x='Supplier ID', color='blue', ax=ax[0][0])
sns.countplot(data=day_28_df[day_28_df['Staff ID']==0], x='Supplier ID',
              color='blue', ax=ax[0][1])
sns.countplot(data=day_28_df[day_28_df['Staff ID']==1], x='Supplier ID',
              color='blue', ax=ax[1][0])
sns.countplot(data=day_28_df[day_28_df['Staff ID']==10], x='Supplier ID',
              color='blue', ax=ax[1][1])
plt.tight_layout()
plt.show()
```

The results are shown in figure 12.8. In some cases, we wish to identify subsets that are significantly different than the overall pattern. However, in cases such as this, the pattern over the full dataset is suspicious, and we wish to identify the source of that pattern. That is, we want to find the subsets most, not least, like the overall distribution and particularly those with spikes for supplier 10, as with staff 10 here.

Staff 10 (figure 12.8, bottom right pane) may be more focused on a single supplier than is normal: the shape of the distribution is significantly more skewed than for the other staff. Assuming, as in this case, that all purchasers use the same suppliers, they should have roughly similar distributions, though staff with fewer purchases will have more variability. In this case, we have found an outlier, staff 10, who is anomalous in this sense.

12.9 *Rolling windows features*

Most of the examples so far have created new tables to test for collective outliers. These tests are effective and are very often useful for outlier detection work, but it is also possible to engineer similar features to add to the existing table, which may expose similar types of outliers and also allow for multivariate tests with the existing features.

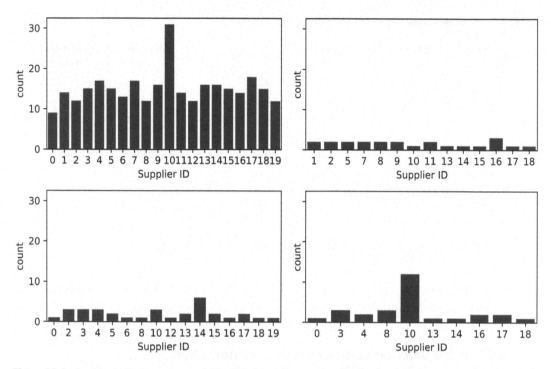

Figure 12.8 Looking only at purchases on the 28th day of the months: distributions of suppliers used for the full dataset (top left pane), and for staff 0, 1, and 10 in the other plots. Staff 10 (bottom right pane) stands out as having an unusual distribution relative to the other staff. It may explain the unusual shape of the full dataset, which also has a spike for supplier 10.

The following code snippet shows a couple of examples where we calculate the rolling average of the unit cost over the previous 10 records (this allows us to compare each unit cost paid relative to the normal costs just prior to that purchase), and the daily cumulative total cost (which allows us to identify where large purchases are made when there has already been a large amount of spending that day):

```
purchases_df = purchases_df.sort_values(['Date', 'Hour', 'Minute'])

purchases_df['Avg Unit Cost Prev 10'] =\
    purchases_df['Unit Cost'].rolling(window=10).mean()

purchases_df['Daily Cummulative Total Cost'] =\
    purchases_df.groupby('Date')['Total Cost'].cumsum()
```

The new features can be seen in table 12.8 (with some other columns removed to allow fitting on the page). The rolling window feature uses a window of size 10, which means it is impossible to calculate for the first 10 records (which are shown as NaN). It can, however, be calculated for all rows after these.

Table 12.8   Purchases table with additional features

Staff ID	Supplier ID	Product ID	Unit cost	Total cost	Year	Month	Day	Avg unit cost prev 10	Daily cumulative total cost
4	9	9	27.7	3,125.7	2023	1	1	NaN	3,125.7
7	6	11	61.8	5,131.5	2023	1	1	NaN	8,257.2
8	15	3	14.2	1,347.3	2023	1	1	NaN	9,604.6

We may also wish to track a rolling average of unit prices to individual products, which can be added with

```
purchases_df = purchases_df.sort_values(
    ['Product ID', 'Date', 'Hour', 'Minute'])

purchases_df['Rolling Mean'] = purchases_df.groupby(
    'Product ID')['Unit Cost'].rolling(10).mean().values
```

Many features of this sort can be added to the table, providing more context for the purchases and more information for multivariate outlier detection performed on the original data.

12.10 *Tests for unusual numbers of point anomalies*

An important use of collective outlier tests is to determine the entities or time periods where there are higher than normal rates of point anomalies. For example, in an industrial setting, it may be relatively common to have an anomalous sensor reading, but having unusually many anomalous readings within a minute would be a significantly higher concern. Tracking point anomalies over time also makes it possible to identify upward trends in anomalies, which can be informative.

Listing 12.9 shows an example with the purchases data. We perform outlier detection in this example using an Isolation Forest on the original purchases data (though on a subset of features), which identifies the unusual purchases. We then examine which staff (the same may be done for suppliers, products, days, and so on) are most represented in the top outliers. If the outliers are assigned randomly to each entity or time period, we would expect a roughly Poisson distribution of these.

Listing 12.9   Examining point anomalies by staff

```
from sklearn.ensemble import IsolationForest

det = IsolationForest(random_state=0)
df = purchases_df.copy()
subspace_df = df[['Count', 'Unit Cost', 'Total Cost']]
det.fit(subspace_df)
df['IF Scores'] = det.decision_function(subspace_df)
df = df.sort_values(['IF Scores'])
df.head(10)['Staff ID'].value_counts()
```

This outputs

```
10      6
1       2
8       1
3       1
```

Six of the top 10 outliers relate to staff 10. In fact, the six highest-scored outliers belong to staff 10, which makes staff 10 an outlier in terms of the number of point outliers found, further emphasizing that this staff member is functioning in an atypical manner.

It would be possible to measure the staff regarding their point anomalies in other ways as well—for example taking into consideration the average outlier score for each staff. As described in chapter 8 (when considering the correlations between detectors), we should include in the average only the records given high scores (possibly setting all others to a score of zero) so as not to average in the scores from records that may be considered inliers.

We can also consider the proportion of records that are flagged as outliers for each staff, as opposed to the raw count. Some staff may have more outliers simply because they have more purchases. In this case, it is possible to compare counts as we expect all staff to have similar numbers of purchases, but in general, a staff who has, say, 5% of their transactions scored highly likely warrants further investigation more than a staff with 0.5%, even if the latter has significantly more outliers.

Summary

- Collective outliers refer to unusual collections of records.
- Checking for collective outliers can identify anomalies that will not be detected when checking for unusual individual rows.
- The absence of data can be as interesting as the presence of rare data.
- Collective outlier tests can detect unusually common as well as unusually rare items.
- Usually, to test for collective outliers, we create new tables and perform standard outlier detection on these.
- Once the tables are created, often simple univariate tests, such as tests for very small and very large values, can be sufficient.
- It is also possible to perform multivariate outlier detection on the new tables.
- To compare entities to each other, it is useful to look at timelines and distributions associated with each entity.
- It is also possible to add features, such as rolling averages, cumulative sums, and so on, to the original data, which provide context to the records and allow the detection of similar types of outliers as collective outlier tests.
- It can be useful to look for entities or time periods with unusually many point anomalies.

Explainable outlier detection

This chapter covers

- Introducing eXplainable AI (XAI)
- Describing XAI in outlier detection
- Presenting methods to explain black-box outlier detectors
- Presenting interpretable outlier detectors not covered previously

When performing outlier detection, it's often important to know not just the scores given to each record but *why* the records were given the scores they were. There are at least two situations where this is necessary. The first is in assessing the detectors, as was introduced in chapter 8. During this step, we determine if the detectors produce sensible scores for the known outliers that we test with, but we also wish to know why the records were given these scores. To be confident that we have a useful outlier detection system, and that the detectors will produce reasonable scores for future data as well, we want to know the detectors are not only correct but correct for the right reasons.

Once we establish that a detector, or set of detectors, works well and they are put in production, as any records are flagged by the detectors, we will typically wish to understand why they were. To see why this is the case, consider the purposes we may have for performing outlier detection, such as those described in chapter 1. If searching for indications of financial fraud, for example, we may run one or more outlier detection algorithms on a collection of financial transactions and follow up with the records that scored the highest: the most atypical records are often the records most likely to have issues, and so auditors will investigate to determine if there is anything inappropriate with any of these. To do this efficiently, we must know what may be suspicious about each record. For example, if a journal entry is posted by a staff member who is significantly more senior than the staff that typically post entries, this may suggest an attempt to alter the financials for the company. But an auditor would need to know that it's the seniority of the staff that caused the high score to be able investigate this; otherwise, they are simply faced with a flagged transaction, possibly with a large number of features, and must deduce this on their own.

In some cases, it may be clear why these were scored as they were, but quite often it is not, particularly if they are scored highly for multiple reasons or based on unusual combinations of many features. Trying to reverse-engineer the outlier detection system can be time consuming and error prone. Having explanations of each score removes a significant amount of labor in ascertaining this. It also allows us to group transactions together that are flagged for the same reasons, which can further allow us to process these more efficiently.

Looking at other uses of outlier detection, such as scientific discovery, again, it is much more practical to investigate any novelties found in data where they are explained—similarly for business discovery, where it is hoped to learn new things about a business by searching the data for outliers. These can only add to our understanding of the business if the nature of the outliers is well understood.

In real-time environments, the need to quickly assess any outliers found is especially acute. With, for example, credit card fraud, monitoring of e-commerce sites, network intrusion, or industrial processes, anything flagged highly enough will usually be sent to a team to investigate. Where the outliers indicate real problems, we wish to understand this and implement procedures to mitigate the problems as quickly as possible. And, where these are not problems (simply statistically unusual events), we wish to remove any measures already put in place during the investigation as quickly as possible—machinery may have been shut down, credit cards set as inactive, user accounts locked out of websites, network access restricted, and so on.

Even considering situations where time is not a pressing concern, such as checks for data quality or estimating maintenance schedules with equipment, it is important to be able to understand the outliers found to more easily investigate the anomalies, track occurrences of specific anomalies over time, and tune and improve the system.

There are some exceptions to this—cases where the outlier detection system does not have to be interpretable. One example may be where outlier detection is run simply as a step to clean data for downstream machine learning tasks, such as clustering or prediction. In this case, detecting and removing strong outliers may form part of a pipeline and can be tuned automatically without the need to understand it well. The outlier detection and removal steps are then similar to other preprocessing steps such as scaling, filling null values, and so on. The best outlier detection method and parameters can be found experimentally, cross-validating the process, without a need to know which records are removed or why. Another example may be flagging anomalous images: it will often be clear if the images are of interest or not without the need to explain the outlier scores assigned, at least in contexts where only small numbers of images are identified as anomalous.

In most cases, however, we will wish to follow up with the outliers found to determine if they are truly issues or are simply statistically unusual, and explanations are quite important. Unfortunately, despite the importance of understanding outlier detectors and their results, most outlier detection tools provide little insight into this, simply returning a score or label for each record.

To address this, we can look to an important field of research in machine learning, known as *eXplainable AI* (XAI). This field is concerned with making machine learning models and their predictions comprehensible. XAI is now well studied, and though it is far from a solved problem, we have made some significant advances in this field. Almost all of the research in XAI, unfortunately, has been in explaining predictive models, with relatively little attention so far in other areas, including outlier detection. Nevertheless, many of the ideas developed in this field may be applied equally to outlier detection, including some of the main techniques used in XAI: feature importances, proxy models, forms of plotting specific to XAI, and counterfactuals, which we will examine in this chapter.

13.1 Introducing XAI

The motivation behind XAI is that very often in machine learning, the most powerful tools for the tasks at hand are essentially black boxes and we don't know how they are operating internally. As most of the XAI research is focused on prediction problems, this typically relates to attempts to explain the behavior of neural networks, boosted models, random forests, and other predictive models. Given that these models are not fully understandable (the algorithms are usually understood but the specific predictions are typically not), there are quite often questions in terms of robustness and fairness. For example, we often wish to determine if a model is biased regarding gender, race, or other such properties of people, which is difficult to do without understanding specifically why the model makes each prediction. Other biases in the model (for example, being trained on data unrepresentative of the true population or the model being under- or overfit) may not have implications for fairness but may still affect the robustness of the model on future data and should be understood so that they may be corrected.

In outlier detection, we face roughly the same problems: the models are often black boxes and we do not understand exactly why they behave as they do, which leaves questions about how robust and how fair they will be going forward, even after testing. And, similar to predictions made by predictive models (where we may wish to know why specific predictions were made), we will wish to see why certain records are considered outliers by the detectors and others are not, which requires techniques to try to explain in human-understandable terms why this is the case.

13.1.1 *Interpretability vs. explainability*

There are two general approaches to creating outlier detection systems that can be understood. The first approach relates to what's called *interpretability*. This uses models that are inherently interpretable (such as association rules or Real versus Fake detectors). The second approach relates to what's called *explainability*. Here, models that are not inherently interpretable are used, and we use various techniques to attempt to explain why the detector scores as it does. We look at both of these approaches as both can be very useful.

INTERPRETABLE MODELS

Unfortunately, there are relatively few interpretable models in outlier detection. The most interpretable are univariate tests that simply flag very small and very large values, for example interquartile range, interdecile range, and median absolute deviation covered in chapter 2 or histogram-based outlier score (HBOS) and empirical cumulative distribution function (ECOD) covered in chapter 6. With these, it's relatively easy to understand why records received high scores where they do: they are the rows with more, and more extreme, very small and very large values. Even with these, though, if there are many features it can be difficult to see why one row received a higher score than another if both have several very low or very high values. But overall these are quite interpretable: in each row it's easy to see which values are particularly extreme and how they compare to other values in those columns.

Frequent pattern outlier factor (FPOF) and association rules may also be considered interpretable. With FPOF, we can see which frequent item sets are most common in the data, along with statistics about these; and can see statistics about each flagged row with regard to the frequent item sets they do and do not contain, which provides a decent understanding of each outlier. With association rules, we can see each association rule that is and is not respected (cases where the lefthand side is true and the righthand side is or is not true), along with statistics about these. Real versus Fake detectors may also be interpretable, at least where the model used to distinguish real from fake records is an interpretable classifier, such as a shallow decision tree or very simple logistic regression.

Quite often, using interpretable detectors will provide a sufficient level of accuracy, speed, and interpretability. Where this is the case and understanding the predictions is important, this will be the preferred approach. However, it can be difficult in some projects to achieve the desired level of accuracy when limiting the set of detectors used, and so it is also often common to use the full set of detectors available and then attempt to understand their predictions as well as possible, which we cover next.

EXPLANATIONS OF MODELS

With explainable approaches, instead of using interpretable detectors, we use what are called *post hoc* explanations. Here, the outlier detector model itself may be a black box, but we attempt to explain, after the fact (post hoc), the scores it assigned, at least approximately. Given that most detectors [for example, Isolation Forest (IF), k nearest neighbors (KNN), Radius, One-class Support Vector Machine, Convex Hull, angle-based outlier detection (ABOD), principal component analysis (PCA), connectivity-based outlier factor (COF), subspace outlier detection (SOD), FeatureBagging, and most others covered in this book] are largely uninterpretable, the promise of finding explanations for their scores after the fact is appealing. It is, however, a challenging problem and, as we'll see when going through the available methods for post hoc explanations, we can only approximate the actual explanation.

We've actually already seen some examples of explanations in the forms of 2D plots we looked at in chapter 8. As discussed there, these are quite useful and provide some sense of how the model works but not a full picture, particularly with respect to outliers in three or more dimensions. Before we look at some other approaches to understanding models, though, it's important to understand two main types of explanations we wish to find: global and local explanations, which we look at next.

13.1.2 *Global vs. local explanations*

In the context of XAI, the terms *global* and *local* have related but somewhat different meanings than in outlier detection. With XAI, a global explanation refers to how the outlier detector as a whole evaluates the records, while a local explanation refers to why an individual record received the score it did.

Global explanations describe the main patterns discovered by the detector, how these are used to score the records, and the properties of these patterns most associated with the highest outlier scores on the data available. How much information is presented and how comprehensible this is can vary a great deal. For example, with an Isolation Forest, a complete global explanation of the detector could be a presentation of the set of isolation trees created or some comprehensible summary of these. With distance and density detectors, a global explanation could be information about the distributions of distances between records and the features most contributing to these distances. Whether these are useful explanations or comprehensible, or if there are better global explanations is quite subjective.

As well as for assessing the systems, global explanations can be valuable when debugging outlier detection systems—where clear, accurate explanations can be found, they can point to anomalies the system is missing and anomalies it is overemphasizing. Global explanations are also useful for forming ensembles, as they can aid the process of seeing where certain types of relevant outliers will be picked up by some and not other detectors.

A local explanation, on the other hand, would specify why each individual row scored as it did. For example, if using an Isolation Forest, this would require describing the sparse spaces it was found to be in (possibly the relevant features and some descriptions of the distribution of data in these). This is difficult to do, but the methods we'll look at here will provide some insight into the scores assigned.

13.2 Post hoc explanations

In this section, we examine the main approaches to XAI. Some other XAI techniques may be used as well, though these typically are designed to explain specific types of detectors, such as neural networks, or specific types of predictions, such as object recognition in image data. We will limit our discussion to techniques useful for any outlier detection work.

In listing 13.1 we create an Isolation Forest detector, trained on the abalone dataset, using one-hot encoding for the single categorical feature (Sex, which has three values). After calling `fit()` and `score_samples()`, the IF has calculated scores for all records in the training data. In the remainder of this section, we will look at techniques to explain why the records have the scores they do. This is tricky, as it is actually a combination of understanding both what is truly anomalous and what the IF considered anomalous.

Listing 13.1 Creating a model to be explained

```
import pandas as pd
import numpy as np
from sklearn.datasets import fetch_openml
from sklearn.ensemble import IsolationForest

np.random.seed(0)

data = fetch_openml('abalone', version=1, parser='auto')   ◄─┐ Collects and one-hot
df = pd.DataFrame(data.data, columns=data.feature_names)      │ encodes the data
df = pd.get_dummies(df)
orig_features = list(df.columns)      ◄──────  Saves the original features, as they are
                                              useful later to ensure we work only with
                                              the original features for outlier detection
det = IsolationForest(random_state=0)   ◄──
det.fit(df)
df['IF Score'] = det.score_samples(df)    Creates an IF and gets
                                          the training scores
```

The distribution of scores can be seen in figure 13.1. Looking at this, we may consider −0.6 as a reasonable cutoff and therefore any records scored below this as outliers. The question, then, is what the IF focused on with these records—why were they considered anomalous?

13.2.1 Feature importances

Where outlier detectors flag certain rows, it can be useful to simply know which features were most relevant to its score. We saw in chapter 6 that PyOD provides explanations, in the form of feature importances, for three of its detectors; for iForest, it provides global feature importances, and for empirical cumulative distribution function (ECOD) and copula-based outlier detection (COPOD) it provides local feature importances. This does help us understand the outliers, but we should note that feature importances do not provide a full explanation of the scores assigned. With some detectors such as ECOD and COPOD, feature importances are likely sufficient

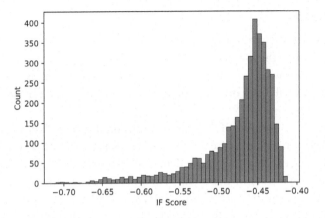

Figure 13.1   Distribution of outlier scores from a scikit-learn IF with default parameters on the abalone dataset. Using `score_samples()`, the most anomalous records have the lowest (most negative) scores.

explanations, as these detectors check only for extreme univariate outliers. With other detectors, though, feature importances provide only a partial explanation. For example, if it is found that two features are responsible for the high score in a given record, it's not clear if each had an unusual value or if the combination of the two was unusual. Internal outliers are also often difficult to assess simply from feature importances. But, despite these caveats, knowing the relevant features, especially with datasets with many features, is a significant improvement over having no knowledge of this.

There are several techniques available to determine feature importances. We'll use here a library called SHAP (https://github.com/shap/shap), which is considered the most accurate system for estimating feature importances, though it can also be slower than some alternatives. This is installed with

```
pip install shap
```

In listing 13.2 we create an instance of a class provided by SHAP, `Explainer` (passing the detector created in listing 13.1), which is able to explain most machine learning models. The data is sorted to put the highest-scored record first, which is convenient later when we look at local explanations for this row.

Listing 13.2   Determining the SHAP global feature importances

```
import shap

df = df.sort_values('IF Score')          ◄── Orders such that the most
explainer = shap.Explainer(det)              anomalous are first
explanation = explainer(df[orig_features])   ◄── Creates an Explainer object, which
                                                 can provide feature importances for
                                                 the detector passed as a parameter
```

Once this is executed, we can begin displaying plots to provide global and local feature importances. We start with the global importances, which can be displayed using

```
shap.initjs()
shap.plots.bar(explanation)
```

Normally SHAP would be used within a notebook, and the call to `initjs()` is made in each cell where we render a SHAP plot (though this is not always necessary). The results are shown in figure 13.2. This uses a bar plot, though a number of other options are also available. Here one-hot encoding can be convenient, even if Isolation Forests can sometimes be less accurate using this encoding than Ordinal encoding, as it allows us to view the global importance of each value. Sex with value I is rare (compared to M or F) and is given the highest importance, followed by Height.

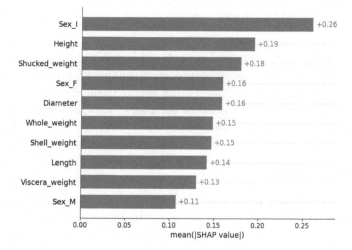

Figure 13.2 Global feature importances for an IF executed on the abalone dataset

This does leave the specific relationship between each feature and the outlier score unspecified. Further information can be found using a beeswarm plot, created with

```
shap.initjs()
shap.plots.beeswarm(explanation)
```

The results of this are shown in figure 13.3. Beeswarm plots do not show the complete relationship between each feature and the target, and they can be a little more effort to read than some other plots, but they do provide quite a bit of information. The plot is actually comprised of a set of dots, each representing one instance in the data for each feature. Unfortunately, this relies on color, and it can be difficult to see in black and white versions of this book, but the idea should still be clear, and experimenting with this in a notebook will show the full colors. The color of the dot represents the value for that record for that feature (blue for low values, purple for average values, and red for high values). Here we can see that for most features, high values affect the outlier score more than low values, though for Length the opposite is true.

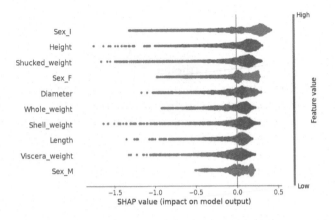

Figure 13.3   Beeswarm plot of the global feature importances. This indicates which features are most important but also where low values or high values tend to contribute more to the outlier scores.

To get local explanations, similar plots are available as for global explanations (though some plots are available for only global or only local explanations) and are called specifying a specific row, as opposed to passing the full explanation object as was done in the previous examples. Here we show another bar plot to explain the most relevant features for records scored the most anomalous by the IF. This may be created with

```
shap.initjs()
shap.plots.bar(explanation[0])
```

This produces the bar plot shown in figure 13.4. For this row, Shucked_weight is the most relevant feature, followed by Viscera_weight. The bars to the left of the center line (blue) indicate the features that contributed to its strong score and the bars to the right of the center line (red) those that would suggest another target value—where the target value was made despite, not because of, these feature values.

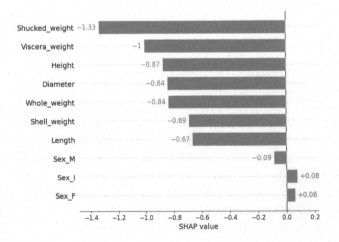

Figure 13.4   Local explanation for the row scored most anomalous by the IF

To contrast the feature importances calculated by PyOD, we collect and plot these in the following listing.

Listing 13.3 Plotting the features importances calculated by PyOD

```
from pyod.models.iforest import IForest
import matplotlib.pyplot as plt
import seaborn as sns

pyod_clf = IForest()
pyod_clf.fit(df)

s_list = sorted(list(zip(pyod_clf.feature_importances_, df.columns)),
                reverse=True)
importance_score, col_names = zip(*s_list)
sns.barplot(orient='h', y=np.array(col_names),x=np.array(importance_score))
plt.show()
```

We can see (figure 13.5) that the global feature importances are significantly different. Where possible, it is preferable to use SHAP, though other feature importance estimates can often provide a decent sense of the feature importances.

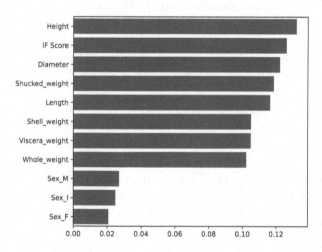

Figure 13.5 Feature importances as reported by PyOD. The features are ordered differently here than in figure 13.2. The PyOD feature importances are more approximate than SHAP and in this case scored the numeric features almost identically to each other, which may not be correct.

A major limitation of feature importances is that they don't easily look at the interactions between features. In the case of abalone, the height feature may have different relationships with the outlier score depending on the length, for example, which is difficult to see simply by looking at feature importances. One way to address this is to replace the original features with engineered features that may be more interpretable on their own, such as the ratio of height and length. It also may be addressed with proxy models, which we look at next.

13.2.2 *Proxy models*

The idea of a proxy model (also known as a *mimic model* or a *surrogate model*) is to create an interpretable predictive model that estimates the predictions that will be made by a black-box outlier detector. With the Isolation Forest created earlier, for example, we do not know why it will assign the scores it does to records but we are able to collect the scores given by the IF for any given set of rows and use these to train an interpretable model to estimate the scores the IF will give to any row. Though the proxy model will be (by necessity) simpler than the actual model, it may be possible to create the proxy that's able to estimate the behavior of the detector reasonably well.

The same models that would be considered interpretable in a prediction context, or when used for outlier detection within a Real versus Fake detector, would be considered interpretable proxy models for outlier detection. There are, unfortunately, few good options, but there are there are a small number that often work well. Likely the models available would be

- *Decision trees*—These can get quite difficult to interpret if allowed to grow to a large size, but if kept reasonably small, with perhaps 10 or fewer leaf nodes, they can be quite manageable to read. If accurate, they can provide clear explanations of outlier scores.

- *Rule sets or rule lists*—These are lists of rules such as those described in chapter 4. As with decision trees, these are very interpretable if kept to a minimal size or pruned such that they are a small size (relatively few rules, each with a modest number of terms). Any decision tree may easily be converted to a set of rules, so the difference between these is not large, though different tools are used to generate trees versus rules, and different audiences may find one or the other more intelligible.

- *Linear/logistic regression*—These models can also become difficult to read if not restricted, but using Lasso regularization, they may be kept to a small number of terms. These are often found to be more comprehensible where integer (as opposed to floating point) coefficients are used, though, again, this depends on the audience. Working with linear or logistic regression models, we can either scale the features or keep them at their original scales. Scaling the values allows us to see clearly the relative importance of each feature, while using the original values may allow the coefficients to be more intelligible in some cases.

- *Generalized additive models*—This model type works by treating each feature individually and determining a function relating each feature to the target (assuming the feature and target are both numeric, this can be represented visually with a line plot) and combining the predictions over each feature. A good implementation of this for python is the Explainable Boosted Machine (https://interpret .ml/docs/ebm.html), available with the interpretML library (https://github .com/interpretml/interpret).

These last two alternatives were developed by myself to increase the options available for interpretable predictive models.

- *AdditiveDecisionTrees*—The AdditiveDecisionTrees model (https://github.com/Brett-Kennedy/AdditiveDecisionTree) is a variation on standard decision trees that is designed to provide more interpretability though more concise and more comprehensive rules.

- *ikNN*—This is a form of interpretable kNN classifier based on ensembles of 2D spaces (https://github.com/Brett-Kennedy/ikNN). As it uses 2D subspaces, each may be visualized, which allows understanding the predictions, very similar to approaches discussed later in this chapter for outlier detection based on 2D subspaces.

DECISION TREES AS PROXY MODELS

In this section, we discuss an example using a decision tree as a proxy model to approximate the Isolation Forest created in listing 13.1. In listing 13.4 we first test training a decision tree with default parameters to estimate the IF scores. We are able to get quite accurate results: the R2 scores on the three test folds are 0.90, 0.91, and 0.88 (your results may vary somewhat as the cross validation is random in this example). However, as this uses default parameters, the trees that are built will be quite deep, which will eliminate any interpretability. We next set the maximum number of leaf nodes to 10, which creates quite interpretable models though also, in this case, significantly reduces the accuracy; the cross validation scores are now 0.74, 0.77, and 0.74. It may be worth trying other model types or experimenting further with the hyperparameters, but this is likely nearly as well as we can do with a decision tree.

> **Listing 13.4 Creating an IF and a decision tree to mimic its behavior**

```
from sklearn.tree import DecisionTreeRegressor
from sklearn.model_selection import cross_validate
import matplotlib.pyplot as plt
import seaborn as sns

np.random.seed(0)

regr = DecisionTreeRegressor(random_state=0)
cv_results = cross_validate(regr, df[orig_features], df['IF Score'], cv=3)
print(cv_results)

regr = DecisionTreeRegressor(max_leaf_nodes=10)
cv_results = cross_validate(regr, df[orig_features], df['IF Score'], cv=3)
print(cv_results)

regr = DecisionTreeRegressor(max_leaf_nodes=10)
regr.fit(df[orig_features], df['IF Score'])
df['DT Prediction'] = regr.predict(df[orig_features])

sns.scatterplot(data=df, x='IF Score', y='DT Prediction')
plt.show()
```

Fits a decision tree with default parameters to predict the output of the IF and evaluates

Fits a decision tree with a maximum of 10 leaf nodes and evaluates

Fits the final decision tree

Plots the actual IF scores vs. the predicted scores

We plot the relationship of the actual scores to the predicted scores, which is shown in figure 13.6. There is a strong relationship, but it is far from perfect. This is a property of regression decision trees: each split in the tree tends to lead to a closer estimate of the true value, but it can require a very deep tree to produce precise numeric predictions.

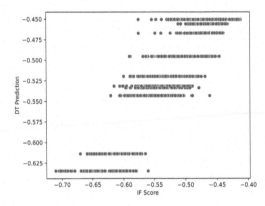

Figure 13.6 The relationship of the actual IF scores to the decision tree predictions of the scores. As we limit the number of leaf nodes to 10 for interpretability, only 10 unique values may be predicted by the tree, reducing its fidelity.

To try to create a more accurate proxy model, we next look at using a binary classifier instead of a regressor. As these predict only two values, they typically do not require the depth that an accurate regression model would. The code is shown in listing 13.5. This assumes the previous listings have run. It first creates a binary label, using −0.60 as the threshold for outliers. It then creates a decision tree classifier, which is displayed to indicate the rules discovered by the tree.

Listing 13.5   Using a classifier to predict a binary form of the detector score

```
from sklearn.tree import DecisionTreeClassifier
from sklearn import tree

clf = DecisionTreeClassifier(random_state=0)

df['IF Binary'] = df['IF Score'] < -0.60          ◁── Creates a binary target

cv_results = cross_validate(clf, df[orig_features], df['IF Binary'], cv=3,
                            scoring='f1_macro')    ◁
print(cv_results)                                      Tests the accuracy using
                                                       default parameters

clf = DecisionTreeClassifier(random_state=0, max_leaf_nodes=10)   ◁
cv_results = cross_validate(clf, df[orig_features], df['IF Binary'], cv=3,
                            scoring='f1_macro')
print(cv_results)                                  Tests the accuracy
                                                   limited to ten leaf nodes

clf = DecisionTreeClassifier(random_state=0, max_leaf_nodes=10)   ◁
clf.fit(df[orig_features], df['IF Binary'])
df['DT Binary Prediction'] = clf.predict(df[orig_features])
print(tree.export_text(clf, feature_names=orig_features))    Creates and
                                                             exports the
                                                             final model
```

This provides F1 macro scores of 0.93, 0.94, and 0.88 over the three test folds, which is pretty good. Notably, the scores were almost as high for a decision tree restricted to 10 leaf nodes as for the unrestricted decision tree (0.95, 0.97, 0.87). The scores are likely preferable to the accuracy found with the regressor, though it is difficult to compare regression to classification metrics. We also have (as is normal with outlier detection) very few examples of high outlier scores, which makes the estimates of the accuracy themselves only very approximate. The rules found are

```
|--- Whole_weight <= 1.96
|    |--- Shucked_weight <= 0.02
|    |    |--- Viscera_weight <= 0.01
|    |    |    |--- class: True
|    |    |--- Viscera_weight >  0.01
|    |    |    |--- Diameter <= 0.14
|    |    |    |    |--- class: True
|    |    |    |--- Diameter >  0.14
|    |    |    |    |--- class: False
|    |--- Shucked_weight >  0.02
|    |    |--- Shell_weight <= 0.01
|    |    |    |--- class: True
|    |    |--- Shell_weight >  0.01
|    |    |    |--- class: False
|--- Whole_weight >  1.96
|    |--- Diameter <= 0.56
|    |    |--- Whole_weight <= 2.15
|    |    |    |--- Viscera_weight <= 0.43
|    |    |    |    |--- class: False
|    |    |    |--- Viscera_weight >  0.43
|    |    |    |    |--- class: True
|    |    |--- Whole_weight >  2.15
|    |    |    |--- class: True
|    |--- Diameter >  0.56
|    |    |--- Height <= 0.17
|    |    |    |--- class: False
|    |    |--- Height >  0.17
|    |    |    |--- class: True
```

Exporting the tree provides a global explanation of the detector. We can see from this that the Whole_weight, Shucked weight, Viscera weight, Diameter, Length, Height, and Sex features are used by the decision tree to estimate the behavior of the Isolation Forest, and we can get some sense of how they interact. From this, it is also possible to get local explanations: to explain any given row, we can step through the rules and see how each decision is made. It's also possible to use the decision tree's `decision_path()` method to get the decision path for any record or to call the `apply()` method to get the leaf nodes for each prediction. This can be useful, as well, to group the predictions into sets. As this decision tree has 10 leaf nodes, each record will be grouped into one of these, some of which will be associated with high outlier scores and others with low. An example is

```
df = df.sort_values('IF Binary')
nodes = clf.tree_.apply(df.loc[:,orig_features].values.astype(np.float32))
```

```
df['Leaf Node'] = nodes
sns.countplot(data=df, x='Leaf Node', hue='IF Binary')
plt.show()
```

This will output the leaf node for each prediction as shown in the left pane of figure 13.7 (though the plot is enhanced to use patterns to make viewing in black and white easier). The vast majority of records are inliers and are placed in leaf node 12. To see the remainder of the predictions better, in the right pane we hide leaf node 12 and see that leaf nodes 1, 8, 14, 16, and 17 are primarily associated with outliers.

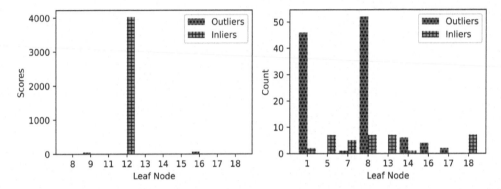

Figure 13.7   Distribution of binary labels per leaf node. Predictions for outliers are shown with a dotted pattern. Inliers are shown with a hash pattern. The majority of the rows are inliers and are placed in leaf node 12. The right pane shows the same results but excluding node 12 so that the other values may be seen clearly. The other nodes distinguish the remaining records. Several nodes are associated primarily with outliers, particularly nodes 1 and 8. In cases like this, we may find the different nodes associated with outlier predictions represent different types of outliers.

One significant limitation of decision trees as proxy models is that decision trees will indicate only one reason a record was scored highly, while there may actually be multiple reasons. We should be aware of this when using decision trees—even where very accurate, they may not provide a full picture of why a record is unusual, and it's common for the most relevant records to be unusual for multiple reasons. In the previous example related to tests for fraud in financial records, a decision tree may identify that a journal entry was entered by a staff member with unusually high seniority, but it may also be that the entry was entered, for example, overnight or for a seldom-used account, where it would also be important to investigate the transaction. However, having the seniority highlighted by a decision tree's explanation can at least be a valuable starting point for investigation.

RULES AS PROXY MODELS

Rules work similarly as decision trees as proxy models and often have a similar level of accuracy and interpretability. In any given case, though, decision trees or rules may work better than the other, so it may be worthwhile to test both. For this example, we use

PRISM rules, which can be installed by copying the `prism_rules.py` file from https://mng.bz/dZpD. There are several other Python libraries to generate rules as well; one that is good to work with is imodels (https://github.com/csinva/imodels). This has a simple pip install and once installed includes several rule discovery algorithms including RuleFit, Skope Rules, Bayesian Rule Lists, and CORRELS. FIGSClassifier, also included with imodels, is similar to a decision tree, though it is slightly more powerful (utilizing multiple trees internally) but also slightly more complex. We use PRISM rules in this example as they tend to be quite interpretable.

PRISM creates a set of rules for each class; in the case of outlier detection, this will generate a set of rules to explain inliers and a set of rules to explain outliers. The rules for each class will be listed in order, such that the first rule will explain as many rows of that class as possible, with the next rule explaining as many of the remaining rows as possible, and so on. Each row is explained, where it can be explained, by the first rule it matches. A (configurable) minimum coverage and support is required for each rule so that only relevant rules will be displayed. Assuming the PrismRules code has been placed into the current file or imported, we may execute the tool as in listing 13.6. This divides each numeric feature into three bins. It then generates a set of rules: first to explain inliers and then outliers.

Listing 13.6 Using PRISM rules to explain the IF

```
df['IF Binary'] = df['IF Score'] <= -0.6

prism = PrismRules(nbins=3)
_ = prism.get_prism_rules(df[orig_features + ['IF Binary']], 'IF Binary')
```

In this case, as is common, no reliable rules could be produced for the outliers, as there is no consistent pattern for outliers. Generally, each is relatively unique, and patterns related to rows being flagged as outliers can be difficult to impute without a very large collection of data. Using the data available, it is possible to generate rules for the inliers. These include

```
Target: False
Height = Med
    Support:  The target has value: 'False' for 100.000% of the 1449 rows
              matching the rule
    Coverage: The rule matches: 1449 out of 4073 rows for target value:
              'False'. This is:
        35.576% of total rows for target value: 'False'
        34.690% of total rows in data

Shucked_weight = Med
    Support:  The target has value: 'False' for 100.000% of the 552
              remaining rows matching the rule
    Coverage: The rule matches: 552 out of 2624 rows remaining for target
              value: 'False'. This is:
        21.037% of remaining rows for target value: 'False'
        13.553% of total rows for target value: 'False'
        13.215% of total rows in data
```

```
Shell_weight = Med
    Support:  The target has value: 'False' for 100.000% of the 127
              remaining rows matching the rule
   Coverage: The rule matches: 127 out of 2072 rows remaining for target
             value: 'False'. This is:
     6.129% of remaining rows for target value: 'False'
     3.118% of total rows for target value: 'False'
     3.040% of total rows in data
```

This shows the first three rules, which provide patterns that describe the inliers found in this dataset. We see where the height is medium, the shucked weight is medium, or the shell weight is medium, the data is entirely inliers. However, we should be careful, as these describe only the inliers in the current data and in future data records with medium values in these features could be outliers.

As with decision trees, using rules for proxy models has the advantage that, if reasonable rules to describe the outliers are found, even where they do not quite correspond to what the outlier detector is doing, they may be converted to rules that are used as part of the outlier detection system itself, as described in chapter 4.

RULES AS PROXY MODELS USING DOPED DATA

Looking at the problem where it can be difficult to generate reliable rules for outliers, one solution is to generate a large volume of synthetic data, either randomly or with specific outlier patterns we wish to test. We may then pass this through the IF, which should flag many of these synthetic records as outliers. We can next use this larger set of labeled data to generate rules that describe the behavior of the IF. We should note, though, depending on how the synthetic data was generated, this may include many rules not related to realistic outliers. In addition, this is useful only to produce a global explanation of the IF; it will not necessarily produce rules that describe any of the real records that were flagged as outliers. We provide an example in the following listing using doped data, specifically modifying the Height feature.

Listing 13.7   Generating PRISM rules, modifying the Height feature

```python
import pandas as pd
import numpy as np
from sklearn.datasets import fetch_openml
from sklearn.preprocessing import RobustScaler, OrdinalEncoder
from sklearn.ensemble import IsolationForest
import warnings

warnings.filterwarnings(action='ignore', category=FutureWarning)
np.random.seed(0)

data = fetch_openml(                                      ◄─── Collects and ordinal
        'abalone', version=1, parser='auto')                   encodes the data
df = pd.DataFrame(data.data, columns=data.feature_names)
df = pd.DataFrame(OrdinalEncoder().fit_transform(df), columns=df.columns)
orig_features = list(df.columns)
                                                         ◄─── Creates and fits an
det = IsolationForest(random_state=0)                          IF on the real data
```

```
det.fit(df)
```

Creates doped data, modifying the Height feature to be out of line with the other features ◄

```
doped_df = df.copy()
for i in doped_df.index:
  if doped_df.loc[i, 'Height'] > df['Height'].median():
    doped_df.loc[i, 'Height'] = doped_df.loc[i, 'Height'] / 10
  else:
    doped_df.loc[i, 'Height'] = doped_df.loc[i, 'Height'] * 2

df['Doped'] = 0
doped_df['Doped'] = 1
test_df = pd.concat([df, doped_df])
```

Creates a single test dataset from the original and doped data ◄

```
test_df['IF Binary'] = \
        det.predict(test_df[orig_features])
```

Gets scores for the test data from the IF ◄

```
prism = PrismRules(nbins=3)
_ = prism.get_prism_rules(test_df[orig_features + ['IF Binary']],
                    'IF Binary')
```

Creates PRISM rules to explain the outliers found in the doped data ◄

Here we are able to generate rules for the outlier class, such as

```
Target: -1
Height = Low AND Whole_weight = High
    Support:  the target has value: '-1' for 100.000% of the 1358 rows
              matching the rule
    Coverage: the rule matches: 1358 out of 5007 rows for target
              value: '-1'. This is:
        27.122% of total rows for target value: '-1'
        16.256% of total rows in data


Height = High AND Whole_weight = High
    Support:  The target has value: '-1' for 100.000% of the 35 remaining
              rows matching the rule
    Coverage: The rule matches: 35 out of 3220 rows remaining for target
              value: '-1'. This is:
        1.087% of remaining rows for target value: '-1'
        0.699% of total rows for target value: '-1'
        0.419% of total rows in data


Height = High AND Shell_weight = Low AND Sex = 2.0
    Support:  The target has value: '-1' for 100.000% of the 226 remaining
              rows matching the rule
    Coverage: The rule matches: 226 out of 3181 rows remaining for
              target value: '-1'. This is:
        7.105% of remaining rows for target value: '-1'
        4.514% of total rows for target value: '-1'
        2.705% of total rows in data
```

ASSESSING THE EXPLANATIONS FROM PROXY MODELS

Quite often it's possible to find a proxy model that can describe a black-box outlier detection system satisfactorily. We should be aware, though, that there are some significant limitations with using proxy models:

- The proxy models will not have 100% accuracy so will often predict incorrectly what the detector will output: the proxy may predict the detector will give a record a high score when it assigns a low score or the opposite. In these cases, there's no valid explanation available for the records. More often, the proxy model will predict scores similarly but somewhat differently from the scores given by the detector, and it will be less clear if there is a valid explanation.
- The proxy models may predict the output of the detector well, but the predictions made by the proxy models may nevertheless be for different reasons than for the predictions of the detector. The more accurate the proxy model, the more likely its logic is to be concordant with that of the detector, but this is never completely certain.
- Proxy models, to the extent they mimic the detector well, explain how the detector actually behaves, not how it *should* behave. We should be careful to not consider explanations of the detectors' scoring as justification.
- Proxy models can be very difficult to train where there are only small numbers of each type of outlier. This is less of an problem in prediction environments (where the class imbalance tends to be less extreme), but with outlier detection the outliers are, by definition, rare, and it can be challenging to create an accurate model, especially for the rarest of the outliers.
- In general, classifiers work on the assumption that each class is located in a single (or a small number of) distinct locations in the space, which is not the case with outliers, as they are spread in small numbers throughout the dataspace making classifiers challenging to create until either a large number of outliers are collected or relevant synthetic data is generated.

In XAI, there is an important concept to understand: that of the *just-so* story, which refers to an explanation that is plausible and appears convincing but isn't correct. The proxy can, in some cases, predict reasonably well what the detector will predict but not for the same reasons. For example, a record may have two unusual feature values; while the detector scores the record high because of the first feature, the proxy model predicts the detector will score it high because of the second feature. This can be a problem in some situations. Where we are tuning the outlier detection system, for example, it's important to properly understand the behavior of the detectors. However, where we are following up with the outliers, particularly in a low-risk environment, it may be the case that it's only necessary to see why the record is unusual in some way, not necessarily why the detector flagged it as unusual. This will result in missing some anomalies in the follow-up, but in some situations, this may be acceptable. In any case, when using proxy models we have to accept that these will only approximate the true explanations.

As with outlier detection generally, it's useful to test the proxy models with synthetic data and select proxy models that appear to mimic the detectors reasonably closely. Here we would generally create a dataset comprised of real data along with synthetic outliers (created using any of the methods described in chapter 11). With this we know the true nature of the outliers. Though we do not know why the detectors scored these highly (where they do, in fact, flag the known outliers), we at least know why they *should* have scored these highly and can check the proxy models are consistent with this.

Where creating strong proxy models proves difficult, we may wish to increase the feature selection performed. The fewer features involved, the more possible it is to identify why records were scored as they were. It also may be useful to explain, not single detectors, but ensembles of detectors. Often, using ensembles can increase the breadth of outliers found, which will make them more difficult to explain, but ensembles can also make the scoring more stable (as described in chapter 14), which can simplify any XAI processes on the results.

Despite these limitations, and though they are used less often with outlier detection than for prediction, proxy models are one of the more common methods used in XAI for outlier detection. For example, H20's documentation provides, as an example explaining an Isolation Forest, code to generate a Random Forest proxy model to mimic the IF. Nevertheless, it can sometimes be difficult to create a reliable proxy model and, unlike the other post hoc XAI techniques covered here, it can be impossible to create reliable proxy models in some cases.

13.2.3 Plotting

There are a few visualizations that can be useful to help understand the behavior of detectors: Partial Dependence Plots (PDP), Individual Conditional Expectation (ICE), and Accumulated Local Effects (ALE). These are actually variations of the same idea, which is to plot the relationship between each feature to the outlier scores. This provides a global explanation of the detector in terms of how each of the features relate to the outlier scores.

Alibi (https://github.com/SeldonIO/alibi) is an excellent library for XAI in general and has several useful tools, including ALE plots, as well as SHAP, and one other tool we look at later this chapter: counterfactuals. Alibi also has quite good documentation and is generally a good resource for explainable AI. It may be installed with

```
pip install alibi
```

In listing 13.8, we use its implementation of ALE plots to help explain the behavior of the IF created in listing 13.1. scikit-learn provides ICE and PDP plots, which look similar but, given the development of ALE plots, are no longer likely useful—ALE plots are faster to create and more accurate. Creating ALE plots requires only creating an `ALE` object, calling its `explain()` and `plot_ale()` methods.

Listing 13.8 Generating ALE plots to explain the IF

```
from alibi.explainers import ALE, plot_ale
import warnings

warnings.filterwarnings(action='ignore', category=DeprecationWarning)
warnings.filterwarnings(action='ignore', category=UserWarning)
```

```
if_ale = ALE(det.score_samples, feature_names=orig_features,
            target_names=['IF Score'])
if_exp = if_ale.explain(df[orig_features].values)
plot_ale(if_exp, n_cols=4, fig_kw={'figwidth':14, 'figheight': 7})
```

The results are shown in figure 13.8, which shows how each feature relates to the outlier scores. With scikit-learn's Isolation Forest, lower scores indicate more anomalous records. For most features, we see a nonlinear relationship, with values at the extremes being more associated with stronger predictions from the IF of outlierness.

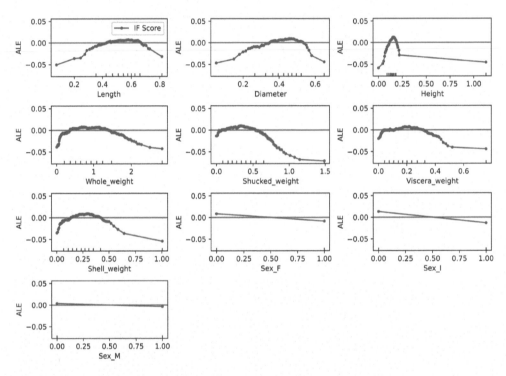

Figure 13.8   ALE plots explaining the predictions of the IF on the abalone dataset. In most cases we see a nonlinear relationship between the feature and the target.

13.2.4 *Counterfactuals*

Another important idea in XAI is the concept of counterfactuals. With these we find the minimum changes to a row necessary to produce a different prediction. In the case of classification, this is the minimum change (the fewest features changed and the smallest changes to each feature) to predict a different class; for regression, the minimum change to predict a significantly different numeric value; and for outlier detection, the minimum change to an outlier record such that it would be considered an inlier.

The Alibi library provides four algorithms to identify counterfactuals, but for this example we use the interpretML library's DiCE tool (https://github.com/interpretml/DiCE), as shown in listing 13.9. DiCE may be installed with

```
pip install dice-ml
```

Note this may downgrade your version of pandas, so a virtual environment is safest to use.

DiCE expects a `predict_proba()` function, which IsolationForest does not provide, so we wrap the `IsolationForest` class in another class that provides this. We specify the categorical and numeric features; as the data has been encoded, all are numeric in this example. We then create and list the counterfactuals for a single record—one scored as an outlier but close to the threshold for an inlier. When working with DiCE, it is easier to use ordinal encoding, which we do here, as well as scale the values to help ensure the magnitude of changes in each column are comparable.

Listing 13.9 Generating counterfactual explanations using DiCE

```
import pandas as pd
import numpy as np
from sklearn.preprocessing import RobustScaler, OrdinalEncoder
from sklearn.datasets import fetch_openml
from sklearn.ensemble import IsolationForest
import dice_ml

np.random.seed(0)

data = fetch_openml('abalone', version=1, parser='auto')      ◀──  Collects and ordinal
df = pd.DataFrame(data.data, columns=data.feature_names)            encodes the data
df = pd.DataFrame(OrdinalEncoder().fit_transform(df), columns=df.columns)
df = pd.DataFrame(RobustScaler().fit_transform(df), columns=df.columns)
orig_features = list(df.columns)

det = IsolationForest()                     ◀──  Creates an IF
det.fit(df)
df['IF Score'] = det.score_samples(df)

                                            Defines a wrapper
class IF_wrapper:                     ◀──   class for the IF
    def __init__(self, det, cutoff):
        self.det = det
        self.cutoff = cutoff

    def predict_proba(self, x):                        Creates an instance of
        return self.det.score_samples(x) < self.cutoff  the wrapped detector

if_wrapped = IF_wrapper(det, -0.6)          ◀──  Converts the scores
                                                 to binary labels

df['IF Outlier'] = df['IF Score'] < -0.6    ◀──

                                                 Creates a dataset that
d = dice_ml.Data(                          ◀──   can be used by DiCE
    dataframe=df[orig_features + ['IF Outlier']],
    continuous_features=['Sex', 'Length', 'Diameter', 'Height',
```

```
                    'Whole_weight', 'Shucked_weight',
                    'Viscera_weight'],
        outcome_name='IF Outlier')

m = dice_ml.Model(model=if_wrapped, backend='sklearn')
exp = dice_ml.Dice(d, m, method='random')
query_instance = df.loc[2810:2810][orig_features]
dice_exp = exp.generate_counterfactuals(
        query_instance, total_CFs=4, desired_class="opposite")  ◄── Generates
dice_exp.visualize_as_dataframe()                                    counterfactuals
                                                                     for one outlier
```

Displaying the counterfactuals for an outlier, we first see the original row, shown in table 13.1.

Table 13.1　The original values for an outlier flagged by the IF

Sex	Length	Diameter	Height	Whole_ weight	Shucked_ weight	Viscera_ weight	Shell_ weight
0.5	1.06	0.96	1.30	1.14	1.41	1.66	0.79

Table 13.2 shows three counterfactuals created as variations of this row, where the IF Binary value will be changed from 1 to 0. This is stochastic, and your results may vary.

Table 13.2　Three counterfactuals created for a single outlier

Sex	Length	Diameter	Height	Whole_ weight	Shucked_ weight	Viscera_ weight	Shell_ weight
0.5	1.06	0.96	1.30	1.14	1.41	1.13	0.79
0.5	1.06	0.96	1.30	1.14	0.89	1.66	0.85
0.5	0.0	0.96	1.30	1.14	1.41	1.66	0.79

Generally, a small number of counterfactuals is sufficient to explain the various ways a row may be anomalous. In this example, as with many outliers, the counterfactuals modify only a single feature each—in this case the Length, Shucked_weight, or Viscera_weight features, which makes understanding these relatively straightforward. With stronger outliers, however, usually multiple features will need to be altered to create a modified record that would be considered an inlier by the detector.

The difficulty with producing counterfactuals is creating alternatives to the current record that are realistic. To achieve this, counterfactual algorithms focus on changes that are as small as possible, with the idea that values close to the original will be more likely realistic than values far from the original. Using counterfactuals to explain outlier detection systems, as opposed to with prediction problems, has an advantage, as the underlying detector will specifically evaluate how realistic the counterfactuals are.

As well as tools such as DiCE, most proxy models can also be useful for identifying counterfactuals for any outlier. Take the tree generated by listing 13.5. For any record flagged as an outlier, we can determine its path through the tree and so can determine, for each node it passes through, if changing the values of the record would result in ending in leaves associated with inliers. As the tree is simply a proxy and not the true detector, we would need to confirm these changes with the actual detector. We can also evaluate the counterfactuals found logically—determining if the records could reasonably be considered inliers if the changes suggested by analyzing the decision tree were made.

13.2.5 General notes on post hoc explanations

Depending on the explanation technique used, the outlier detector, and the dataset, how accurate the explanations are, and how comprehensible they are, can vary. A major finding in XAI research is that what is interpretable depends a great deal on the audience and the purpose for understanding the outliers. Some audiences, for example, are more comfortable with plots, while others benefit more from table or text explanations; some people think much more visually than others, and people have different backgrounds. In addition, there is a large difference in the amount of detail that is preferred. Often explanations for outliers are presented to nontechnical audiences, and we must be careful to provide clear explanations but not lose the nuances involved, particularly around the subjective nature of outlier detection. In general, to have decent understanding of the output of an outlier detector, we should have at least

- *An understanding of the algorithm*—A complete understanding of the algorithms is not always necessary, but it's useful to have a good sense of how they evaluate data and, therefore, what types of records may be flagged as outliers.
- *Scores (as opposed to labels)*—Scores provide more information not only about how the outliers rank relative to each other but in terms of which records are very strong outliers and which are likely noise or other weak outliers.
- *Interpretable features*—While it's possible to explain outliers in terms of rare values or rare combinations of values, our understanding of the outlier scores will be limited to our understanding of what the features mean.
- *What features contributed the most to the score*—Generally, even the most anomalous records have a majority of typical values, with a small number of features being the most relevant to the outlier score. While feature importances are only one method for XAI, any good understanding of an outlier does require knowing the relevant features.
- *An idea of how the features interacted to form the outlier score*—For example, with the abalone dataset, we may know that some records may have high outlier scores due to the whole weight and diameter values, but it may not be clear how they interact, and simply knowing the weight and diameter were involved does not tell the full story.

The first three points are unrelated to the XAI technique used and are necessary to establish before we even start to explain the detectors, but the last two are what we hope to capture with the explanations. We've seen that proxy models, if they can be made simple and yet accurate enough, provide very good explanations, as can counterfactuals. Feature importances and ALE plots provide less complete explanations but are still quite valuable. A good explanation would likely require several of these techniques. However, even with this, we will not generally have a full or completely reliable picture of the detector. Using interpretable models, if possible, is preferred.

13.3 Interpretable outlier detectors

We now take a look at models that are inherently interpretable (and post hoc explanations are unnecessary). As with explanations of black-box models, which models are found to be comprehensible by which audiences can vary, but in this section we'll go through some of the main options available for interpretable outlier detectors. We'll look at a method to make any detector interpretable by running on sets of 2D subspaces, followed by the introduction of three new outlier detectors. Each of these is generally useful and may be used for outlier detection even where interpretability is not necessary, but they have been saved for this chapter as they're particularly useful as interpretable detectors.

13.3.1 Outlier detection on sets of 2D subspaces

A useful method to ensure any detector can be made interpretable is to execute the model on a set of 2D subspaces. As described in chapter 10, this is infeasible where there are many features, but where there are a small number of features or this process is limited to pairs of features that are highly related, it can work very well. It does preclude detecting any outliers in three or more dimensions, but it allows us to find any outliers in one or two dimensions and for these to be clearly understood.

This method is not necessary for detectors such as FPOF, association rules, Real versus Fake, and so on that are interpretable in any case but is useful for most other detectors. It also allows us to use contour plots, as described in chapter 8, which are very useful for further understanding the predictions of each detector. The following listing shows an example using a KNN detector to score the abalone dataset (using the full set of features), as well as a series of KNN models based on 2D subspaces of the abalone dataset.

Listing 13.10   Calculating outlier scores with a set of 2D KNN models

```
import pandas as pd
import numpy as np
from sklearn.datasets import fetch_openml
from sklearn.preprocessing import RobustScaler, OrdinalEncoder
from pyod.models.knn import KNN
import matplotlib.pyplot as plt
import seaborn as sns

np.random.seed(0)

data = fetch_openml('abalone', version=1, parser='auto')      ◄─── Collects and preprocesses the data
df = pd.DataFrame(data.data, columns=data.feature_names)
df = pd.DataFrame(OrdinalEncoder().fit_transform(df), columns=df.columns)
df = pd.DataFrame(RobustScaler().fit_transform(df), columns=df.columns)
orig_features = list(df.columns)
```

```
det = KNN()
det.fit(df)
df['KNN Score'] = det.decision_function(df)
```
Executes a KNN on the full dataset

```
combo_id = 0
scores_df = pd.DataFrame()
scores_2d_cols = []
for col_name_1_idx, col_name_1 in enumerate(orig_features):
    for col_name_2_idx, col_name_2 in enumerate(
            orig_features[col_name_1_idx+1:]):
        print(col_name_1, col_name_2)
        det = KNN()
        det.fit(df[[col_name_1, col_name_2]])
        scores_df[str(combo_id)] = det.decision_function(
            df[[col_name_1, col_name_2]])
        scores_2d_cols.append((col_name_1, col_name_2))
        combo_id += 1
```
Executes a KNN on each 2D subspace

```
scores_df['Final Score'] = scores_df.sum(axis=1)
scores_df = scores_df.sort_values('Final Score')
df['KNN 2D Scores'] = scores_df['Final Score']
```
Calculates the final scores as the sum of scores on the 2D spaces

```
sns.scatterplot(data=df, x='KNN Score', y='KNN 2D Scores')
plt.show()
```
Visually compares the scores given using both methods

```
df = df.sort_values(['KNN 2D Scores'])
max_row = df.iloc[-1:]
top_row_index = max_row.index[0]
top_feature_pairs_idxs = np.argsort(
    scores_df.loc[top_row_index])[::-1][1:5].values
```
Finds the row with the highest score using 2D subspaces

```
fig, ax = plt.subplots(nrows=2, ncols=2, figsize=(8, 8))
for pair_idx, pair_id in enumerate(top_feature_pairs_idxs):
    col_pairs = scores_2d_cols[pair_id]
    s = sns.scatterplot(data=df, x=col_pairs[0], y=col_pairs[1], alpha=0.3,
                        ax=ax[pair_idx//2][pair_idx%2])
    s = sns.scatterplot(data=max_row, x=col_pairs[0], y=col_pairs[1],
                        ax=ax[pair_idx//2][pair_idx%2], color='red',
                        marker='*', s=200)
    s.set_title(f"{col_pairs[0]} \nAND \n{col_pairs[1]}")
plt.tight_layout()
plt.show()
```
Plots the four subspaces most responsible for its final score

This first displays the relationship between the scores calculated using the full data and those created using an ensemble of 2D subspaces, shown in figure 13.9. We can see the scores using both methods are well correlated with each other. In other cases, where using a single detector and using multiple 2D detectors have different results, it's not usually clear which is more correct, and it may take some investigation to determine. Often both are reasonable and simply different, though in some cases using the full set of features may suffer from the curse of dimensionality; in other cases, the scores from the individual 2D models may not be combined optimally. We take a closer look at combining scores in chapter 14.

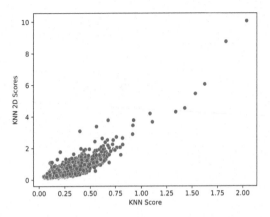

Figure 13.9 The outlier scores calculated on the abalone dataset using a KNN on the full data and an ensemble of 2D models. The scores in this example generally correspond closely. The high scores agree, which is the most relevant.

We then display an explanation of the top-scored row using the four subspaces that contribute most to its final score, shown in figure 13.10.

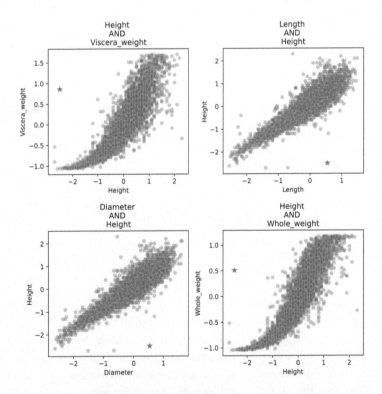

Figure 13.10 An explanation of the top-scored record in the dataset given an ensemble of 2D models. In all four subspaces, the record (shown here as a star) is distinctly anomalous. In this example, each subspace includes the Height feature, suggesting its value is incongruous with the other values for this record.

This method, where applicable, provides useful local explanations for each outlier in terms of the pairs of features most responsible for their outlier scores. It's also possible to aggregate these to provide global explanations listing the features most associated overall with the outliers found in the available data. As well, we may reduce the data to 2D spaces using dimensionality reduction, such as PCA, but as this transformation is itself uninterpretable, this would generally not be considered an interpretable model.

13.3.2 *Bayesian Histogram-based Anomaly Detection*

Bayesian Histogram-based Anomaly Detection (BHAD) (https://github.com/AVoss84 /bhad) is an interpretable outlier detector, similar to histogram-based outlier score (HBOS) in that it performs univariate outlier tests on each feature and scores each row based on the sum of these tests. HBOS has one major advantage over BHAD in that it's included in PyOD: it uses PyOD's standard API and can be used with Scalable Framework for Unsupervised Outlier Detection (SUOD) (described in chapter 6) and other PyOD tools. BHAD does, however, provide a simple pip install and a straightforward interface, making it easy to work with as well. It has a couple of benefits over HBOS: it is able to estimate the optimal number of bins for each feature, and it provides explanations in the form of feature importances. Given the detector uses only univariate tests (and is unable to detect unusual combinations of values), feature importances can be considered complete explanations: providing statistics about each bin is sufficient to explain each outlier score. Both local and global feature importances are available with BHAD. BHAD may be installed with

```
pip install bhad
```

Listing 13.11 shows an example running on the abalone dataset. The main classes are the discretizer, BHAD itself, and the Explainer. The discretizer determines the optimal number of bins for each feature based on a sophisticated Bayesian analysis (which tends to favor fewer bins to aid with interpretability). Here we run the disretizer and BHAD together using a scikit-learn pipeline. Once the model is fit, we create an Explainer object, which can provide feature importances. We plot out the global feature importances and show an example of the local explanations.

Listing 13.11 Running BHAD on abalone

```
import pandas as pd
from sklearn.datasets import fetch_openml
from sklearn.pipeline import Pipeline
from bhad.model import BHAD
from bhad import explainer
from bhad.utils import Discretize
import matplotlib.pyplot as plt
import seaborn as sns
                                                          Collects the data
data = fetch_openml('abalone', version=1)          ◄──┘
abalone_df = pd.DataFrame(data.data, columns=data.feature_names)
```

```
cat_cols = list(abalone_df.select_dtypes(                          Specifies the numeric and
    include=['object', 'category']).columns)                      categorical columns
num_cols = list(abalone_df.select_dtypes(include=['float', 'int']).columns)

pipe = Pipeline(steps=[                                            Creates a
    ('discrete', Discretize(nbins = None, verbose = False)),      pipeline that
    ('model', BHAD(contamination = 0.01, num_features = num_cols, both
                cat_features = cat_cols))])                        determines
                                                                   the number
y_pred = pipe.fit_predict(abalone_df)                              of bins and
                                                                   evaluates data
local_expl = explainer.Explainer(pipe.named_steps['model'],
                    pipe.named_steps['discrete']).fit()
abalone_df = local_expl.get_explanation(nof_feat_expl = 5)
print(abalone_df.loc[4, 'explanation'])                            Displays the explanation
                                                                   of one row
global_feat_imp = local_expl.global_feat_imp
scores = pipe.score_samples(abalone_df)                            Determines the global
                                                                   feature importances
fig, ax = plt.subplots(nrows=1, ncols=2, figsize=(8, 3))
s = sns.barplot(orient='h', y=global_feat_imp.index,
                x=global_feat_imp.values.flatten(), ax=ax[0])
s.set_ylabel("")
sns.histplot(scores, ax=ax[1])
plt.tight_layout()
plt.show()
```

The explanation of row 4 (with spaces added for clarity) is given as

```
Length          (Cumul.perc.: 0.078): 0.33
Diameter        (Cumul.perc.: 0.087): 0.26
Height          (Cumul.perc.: 0.081): 0.08
Shell_weight    (Cumul.perc.: 0.083): 0.06
Viscera_weight  (Cumul.perc.: 0.089): 0.04
```

Each row is explained in terms of either percentile or, in this example, cumulative percentile. The global feature importances and the distribution of scores are shown in figure 13.11. We can see the Length feature contributes most to final outlier scores over the full dataset and Sex the least.

BHAD appears to be competitive with other outlier detectors and should be expected to perform similarly to HBOS or ECOD, though it may work better or worse for any given project. The explanations may be useful, though those provided by PyOD for ECOD and COPOD are similar and may be preferable for some purposes.

13.3.3 CountsOutlierDetector

We'll finish the chapter with two outlier detectors I created, motivated by the lack of options for interpretable outlier detection. The first of these is CountsOutlierDetector (COD) (https://mng.bz/r1lg), a multidimensional histogram-based detector. In chapter 3, I indicated that this type of approach can break down in high dimensions due to

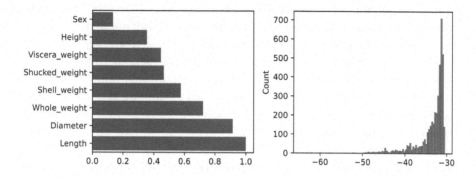

Figure 13.11 Output of BHAD analysis of the abalone dataset. The left pane shows the global feature importances. The right pane shows the distribution of scores.

the curse of dimensionality—given enough dimensions, almost all bins will be empty, and most records will appear in bins with few other records. COD avoids this by limiting analysis to a maximum of six dimensions at a time. This ensures each subspace considered is safe to examine (the algorithm will also decline to examine any dimensionalities where there are not enough records in the data to support this). It also allows for faster execution, as only a restricted number of subspaces need to be examined.

In general, histograms are quite interpretable; which bin each record is in is straightforward, as is the relative counts of each bin. For example, if a low value for Height and a high value for Diameter are rare, this is simple to describe. Restricting the dimensionality ensures explanations are more interpretable, as, for most outliers, only a small number of features are needed to describe why the values or combination of values are rare.

In creating the tool, testing was also performed to examine the number of outliers that exist in higher dimensions, and it appears to be quite small, which makes intuitive sense. It would be unlikely for a record to be an outlier if considering, say, seven dimensions, that is not an outlier in any six-dimensional space. It can occur but is infrequent, and any such outliers would tend to be difficult to interpret, likely not relevant, and statistically difficult to even establish as truly outliers, given that all combinations are rare when considering many dimensions. Consequently, COD restricts itself to outliers in lower dimensions and fills a useful gap between univariate detectors and detectors that work with all features at once.

COD first identifies all records that are outliers in a single feature, then all outliers in each pair of features, then each set of three features, and so on up to, at most, sets of six features. To avoid searches to determine the relevant subspaces (as described in chapter 10) and to avoid missing any informative subspaces, COD exhaustively checks every subspace for each dimensionality covered.

For each subspace tested, the space is divided into cells. Outliers are identified as those appearing in one or more cells in some subspaces with very low counts. This does mean there can be some arbitrariness, as with HBOS and any histogram-based method, where the number of bins can affect the outlier scores. However, this is mitigated by the fact that each record is compared against a very large number of subspaces, over a range of dimensionalities, and errors in this regard tend to average out.

COD, when examining each dimensionality, considers the outliers found in lower dimensionalities. For example, if a record has an unusual value in Feature A (found when examining the 1D subspaces), then when examining 2D spaces, there is no reason to consider, for this record, any pair of features that includes Feature A. Given the row has an unusual value in Feature A, it will necessarily have an unusual pair of values in any pair of features that includes Feature A (as described in chapter 2). Similarly, when looking at sets of three or more features. COD will, though, continue to examine this row for other sets of features, which may expose other anomalies.

Excluding outliers already found has two benefits. First, it removes double-counting of anomalies. In the case of a row with an unusual value in Feature A, this is simply counted as one anomaly for the records, and unusual combinations of Feature A and other features are not counted for this row. Second, it ensures the explanations of each outlier are as simple as possible: they are based on as few features as are necessary to describe the anomaly.

Each record is scored based on how many subspaces it had rare values in, or combinations of values in, which results in a straightforward scoring. The main benefit of COD, with respect to interpretability, though, is its ability to plot the 1D and 2D spaces and to plot the distribution of counts for higher dimensions. For example, with 4D subspaces, though the subspaces themselves cannot be plotted, COD can present a bar plot of the counts of each 4D cell within the subspace.

As the numeric data is divided into small numbers of bins, the cells themselves are interpretable. For example, if three bins are used, we can think of these as low, medium, and high values; and where five bins are used, as very low, low, medium, high, and very high. Using three bins, as in the example here, a rare combination may be something like low Height, low Diameter, high Whole_weight.

Listing 13.12 provides an example with the abalone dataset. The code for Counts-OutlierDetector itself is available as a single .py file, which may be copied into the file or saved in its own file and imported where needed. This executes the predict() method to determine the outliers and then outputs some explanations of these.

Listing 13.12   Executing COD on the abalone dataset

```
import pandas as pd
import numpy as np
from sklearn.datasets import fetch_openml
                                                              Collects the data
data = fetch_openml('abalone', version=1, parser='auto')
df = pd.DataFrame(data.data, columns=data.feature_names)
print(df.head())                                    Creates an instance of the
                                                       CountsOutlierDetector
det = CountsOutlierDetector(n_bins=3, max_dimensions=6, threshold=0.25,
                            verbose=True)
```

```
results = det.fit_predict(df)

print(det.get_most_flagged_rows().head())
most_flagged = int(det.get_most_flagged_rows().index[0])
det.explain_row(most_flagged)
```

COD provides a method to get the most flagged rows.

COD provides a method to explain a specified row.

The most unusual records found are displayed in table 13.3.

Table 13.3   **The most unusual records as scored by the COD outlier detector on the abalone data**

Sex	Length	Diameter	Height	Whole_ weight	Shucked_ weight	Viscera_ weight	Shell_ weight
M	0.455	0.365	0.095	0.5140	0.2245	0.1010	0.150
M	0.350	0.265	0.090	0.2255	0.0995	0.0485	0.070
F	0.530	0.420	0.135	0.6770	0.2565	0.1415	0.210
M	0.440	0.365	0.125	0.5160	0.2155	0.1140	0.155

An example of the 2D spaces found is shown in figure 13.12. In this example, each feature is divided into three bins and so each 2D space into nine. The 2D space based on the features Diameter and Viscera_weight are shown here both as a scatterplot and as a heatmap. The point being explained is shown as a star. We can see, in this case more clearly in the heatmap, that it is in a relatively sparse cell. For any specified row, the set of subspaces that best explain the outlier score assigned are displayed.

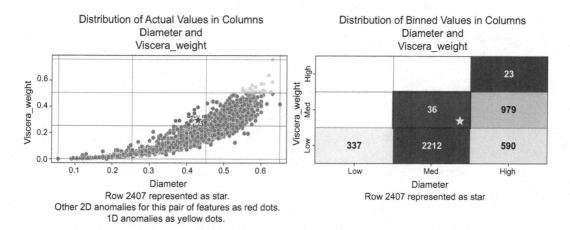

Row 2407 represented as star.
Other 2D anomalies for this pair of features as red dots.
1D anomalies as yellow dots.

Row 2407 represented as star

Figure 13.12   Part of the explanation for the outlier score for a single row, shown here as a star, in the context of one 2D subspace in which it was found to be in a sparse region, Diameter and Viscera_weight. The colors will not appear in black and white version of this book, but when using the tool, the colors clearly indicate the sparseness of each cell. In both the scatterplot and the heatmap, darker red is used for the sparse regions (but only the non-empty cells—those containing outliers), darker blue for the most populated cells, and medium tones for the moderately populated cells. The cells with counts of 23 and 36 can be clearly identified in both plots, providing context for the current row.

Figure 13.13 shows an example of an explanation for a 3D subspace. COD shows how the combination of values for this record compares to other combinations of values. The record is in the third last cell (shown in red) and appears in a cell with a notably low count.

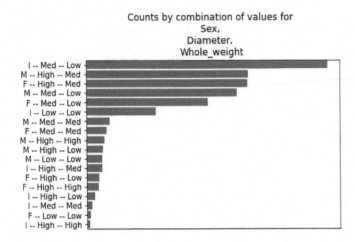

Figure 13.13 Example of 3D outliers found. This provides information about one 3D subspace where the specified row was scored highly. Outliers in 4 to 6 dimensions are shown similarly.

We can also get the counts of each combination with

```
det.explain_features(['Sex', 'Diameter', 'Whole_weight'])
```

Table 13.4 shows a subset of the returned table, including the row for Sex = I, Diameter = Med, Whole_weight = Med, which is only 12.

Table 13.4   COD explanations of a specified subspace

Sex	Diameter	Whole_weight	Count
I	Med	Low	976
M	High	Med	656
F	High	Med	652
...			
I	Med	Med	12
...			

As covered in chapter 2, a histogram cell (or set of categorical values) may have a low count for two reasons. First, it may be that the values in the record are unusual in all dimensions covered by this subspace, so the combination of these will necessarily also be rare. Second, the record may have fairly normal values in each feature but the combination is unusual. These are both legitimate but different types of outliers, which can be distinguished by calculating the expected count of each cell given the marginal probabilities. COD provides an option to consider this, using the `check_marginal_probs` parameters in the class constructor.

COD also provides an option to limit the dimensionalities examined. For example, limiting the process to 1D and 2D spaces will produce the most interpretable outliers while also limiting the outliers found to what may, at least in some cases, be the most relevant outliers.

Testing COD using doping with a large collection of datasests available on OpenML has shown COD to perform favorably compared to Isolation Forest. It's a generally useful outlier detection but is also among the more interpretable. Where there are large number of features, though, feature selection must be performed first to keep execution times manageable.

13.3.4 *DataConsistencyChecker*

The DataConsistencyChecker (DCC) (https://mng.bz/V2rX) is a tool designed for both exploratory data analysis and interpretable outlier detection. DCC takes a different approach to outlier detection than any other detector I'm aware of. As opposed to simply examining the magnitude of each numeric value or the frequency of each categorical value, DCC looks closer at the values themselves. For example, if a column of numbers contains values such as 10, 50, 16, 43.2233, and 43, then DCC would identify the 43.2233 value as having an unusual set of decimals (assuming this is unusual in the full column), even though the magnitude of the value is quite normal. Other tests check where one column's values may be predicted from other values in the row using a simple decision tree or linear regression, where two or more columns tend to have zero and nonzero values in the same rows (there are also similar tests for null values and negative values), where one column tends to be the sum (or product, ratio, difference, minimum, maximum, or mean) of two or more other columns, where numeric values tend to be rounded to a certain degree, and so on. The general idea is to find the common patterns within the columns and between the columns and then flag any exceptions to these. To do this, it executes over 150 simple (and interpretable) tests on each row.

As the tool is intended for understanding datasets, finding their major patterns, and interpreting any exceptions to the patterns, there are a large number of APIs to facilitate processing the data efficiently. As with the example in listing 13.13, though, in most cases it's possible to simply create a `DataConsistencyChecker` object, call `init_data()` with the data we wish to examine in a pandas dataframe, and call `check_data_quality()` to analyze the data. To display the results, we may either use `display_detailed_results()` or `display_next()`. The former will output all findings. This can be large for some datasets; in these cases, parameters may be set to reduce the output to the results that are of most interest. The `display_next()` API will output the results of each test one at a time, which makes it easier to examine the results and, in a notebook environment, keeps the output size manageable. There are also APIs to provide summaries of the findings and to examine the most highly scored results.

For brevity, in this example we simply output the results for a single test, LARGER, which checks if one column is typically larger than another. This example assumes the `check_data_consistency.py` file has been copied from GitHub and is placed in the same directory.

Listing 13.13   Example executing DataConsistencyChecker

```
import pandas as pd
import numpy as np
from sklearn.datasets import fetch_openml
import sys

sys.path.insert(1, '..')
from check_data_consistency import DataConsistencyChecker

data = fetch_openml('abalone', version=1, parser='auto')
df = pd.DataFrame(data.data, columns=data.feature_names)

dc = DataConsistencyChecker(verbose=0)
dc.init_data(df)
dc.check_data_quality()
dc.display_detailed_results(test_id_list=['LARGER'])
```

Though we display only one example here, the tool actually finds a number of anomalies in the abalone dataset. For each pattern found, DCC lists a set of rows as examples both of the general pattern as well as any exceptions. Most tests, including the LARGER test, also provide visual descriptions of each pattern or exception. These are shown in figures 13.14 and 13.15. In the case of the LARGER test, DCC found one instance where Diameter is larger than Length, though the opposite is normally true.

Most tests provide one or more visualizations to help explain the outliers found, as in figure 13.15.

DCC also provides tests for correlated values and for values in sparse 2D regions, which means it is possible to detect some issues such as this in multiple ways, though in practice this tends to be minimal.

Outlier scores are simply the counts of the number of tests that flagged each row. For example, a row may have rare values in some columns or very large values in

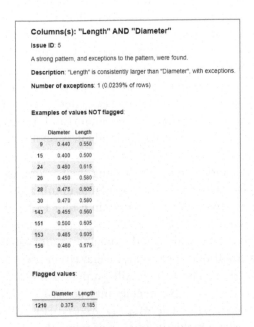

Figure 13.14   Explanation of the outlier found in row 1210. The Diameter value is normally smaller than the Length but in this case is larger.

others and may be an exception to a general pattern that one column is the inverse of another column. In this case, we simply count the number of these exceptions for the row, which provides a very interpretable scoring system.

DCC has an advantage over most other detectors in that it treats data natively: as binary, categorical, numeric, or date. This removes the normal requirement that data be converted from one format to another, which inevitably loses some information. For example, as date values are treated as dates, DCC is able to examine the data for unusual days of the week, days of the month, gaps between two date columns, and so on,

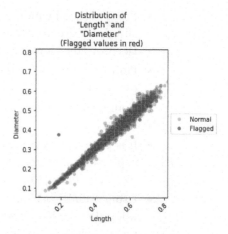

Figure 13.15 Visual representation of the outlier displayed in figure 13.14. This flags the point well above the main body of points.

as well as find cases such as where there are unusual numeric values in another column given the date values in a date column.

Another major advantage of using DCC is that it tends to check for forms of outliers not covered by other detectors so will have little redundancy with other detectors. There are some exceptions (DCC includes tests for rare, very large, very small values, and so on), but the majority of tests covered by DCC are unique to it. At the same time, DCC does not include tests that cover the full range of multidimensional outliers. Given that, DCC is often useful to complement other forms of outlier detection.

Summary

- Most outlier detector algorithms produce outlier scores that are difficult or impossible to interpret.
- Some exceptions exist, such as univariate tests, FPOF, association rules, and Real versus Fake detectors.
- XAI is an active area of research, focusing on predictive models, with little research in interpretable outlier detection.
- The ideas from XAI for predictive models, nevertheless, can often be applied to outlier detection.
- A common approach to outlier detection is to use black-box models and then perform post hoc analysis on these to provide an approximate explanation of the outlier scores produced.
- Common forms of post hoc explanations are feature importances, proxy models, plotting, and counterfactuals.
- SHAP is a common and useful tool to determine feature importances.

- Proxy models include decision trees, rules, linear and logistic regression, generalized additive models (GAM, such as Explainable Boosted Machine), Additive-DecisionTrees, and ikNN.
- Plotting methods include PDP, ICE, and ALE plots, with ALE plots being preferred.
- Counterfactuals present a set of minimal changes necessary to consider an outlier an inlier.
- It is preferable, everything else equal, to use interpretable models to post hoc explanations, but often the uninterpretable detectors produce the most useful scores, requiring the use of explanations.
- Using 2D subspaces allows any detector to be interpretable but is only applicable when the number of features is relatively small or when a small number of features can be selected for this type of outlier detection.
- BHAD, CountsOutlierDector, and DataConsistencyChecker also provide interpretable outlier detection and are generally useful as outlier detectors even where interpretation is not necessary.

Ensembles of outlier detectors

14

This chapter covers

- The benefits and tradeoffs in creating ensembles
- Selecting the detectors for ensembles
- Scaling the scores from the detectors
- Combining the scores from each detector for a
  final score

Often when evaluating outlier detectors, we're able to identify a number of detectors that appear to work well, though none work perfectly. We may also have cases where we appear to detect the known outliers that we test with well but are not confident we will detect the full range of outliers we may encounter in the future. In most cases, the solution in these situations is to use multiple outlier detectors, combining them into an ensemble. This is a powerful technique, and it's very common to use ensembles for outlier detection problems.

This is similar to the idea of creating ensembles with prediction problems, where ensembling is well understood to be a very powerful technique. In fact, with tabular data, the strongest models tend to be ensembles, for example XGBoost, LGBM, and CatBoost, which are ensembles of decision trees. In addition, the strongest autoML tools, such as AutoGluon, focus on creating ensembles of models as the most effective means to create highly accurate predictive systems.

However, the goals of creating ensembles are actually a bit different with outlier detection than with prediction, and these are important to understand. It's easier to understand ensembles in terms of outlier labels (as opposed to scores), so we'll look first at outlier detection in this form. The goal in this case is to label the records as inliers and outliers, with as few errors as possible. There are two types of errors that can be made: *false negatives* and *false positives*—here "positive" refers to a record that is truly an outlier and "negative" to a record that is not. False negatives are cases where we miss an outlier—a record is falsely labeled as negative (as an inlier when it is actually an outlier)—and false positives are cases where a record is falsely labeled as an outlier (as positive when it is actually an inlier). Creating ensembles of detectors allows us to reduce both errors and so create outlier detection systems that are overall more accurate.

It may sound odd to describe records as being *truly* outlier or not, given the subjective nature of outlier detection, but here we are referring not to statistical outliers but to records that are useful given the purpose you have for outlier detection. In practice, we will never be able to assign each record a true label: there are likely far too many records to examine and too many features to examine them accurately. Further, it's impossible for humans to consistently label even what they can assess. But in theory, each record does have a true label (an indication if it is relevant for your project), and this may be estimated correctly or incorrectly by the system.

To reduce missing outliers, it's useful to simply use more, and more diverse, detectors. This is especially true as it's generally accepted that, unless there is a quite specific set of known outliers you are interested in, no one detector will likely find everything.

To reduce false positives, on the other hand, the focus may be less on using additional detectors (though this may also be done) and more on how the findings of each detector are combined. For example, false positives can be substantially reduced by having the ensemble flag records as outliers only where they are scored high by all, or by most, of the detectors. Doing this will greatly reduce the cases where rows are inappropriately flagged as outliers, as it's very unlikely multiple detectors will incorrectly flag any given inlier as an outlier. However, there is always a tradeoff between false positives and false negatives. Setting stringent requirements to label a record as an outlier will reduce false positives but also increase false negatives: many legitimately anomalous records will be missed.

Similar to the idea of false positives and false negatives is an issue relating to the specific scores given. Detectors may correctly flag outliers but may assign unreasonably high or low scores, possibly resulting in more attention being paid to less relevant than to more relevant outliers. Given this, the benefits of creating ensembles with outlier detection are

- It allows us to assign more reliable scores to each record. Combining the scores assigned to each record by multiple detectors can provide more stable scores than would be found relying on a single detector. This can also be viewed as making the system more future-proof. It will likely be more robust to the unexpected types of outliers we may face in the future: while some detectors may miss these as outliers entirely and others may assign unreasonably high scores, the scores will tend to average out well, at least more so than when depending on a single detector.

- The second benefit is much more concerned with reducing false negatives—that is, not missing outliers. As each type of detector will flag different outliers, using many detectors allows us to detect more outliers than would be possible using only a single detector.

The first benefit is common to predictive models. If we have, for example, a classification problem and we have, say, 10 classifiers where one classifier predicts one class and the other nine another class, we would normally simply take the prediction of the nine that agree. This will tend to produce the most reliable predictions.

However, with outlier detection problems, we also wish to receive the second benefit, detecting more outliers, which requires giving greater credence to the detectors that flag certain records as anomalous, even where they are in the minority. There is no concept of this benefit with predictive models; the first benefit listed here is, actually, the sole purpose for ensembling in predictive models. But with outlier detection, we also wish to detect outliers missed by the majority of detectors: it's quite possible these records are anomalous in a manner the other detectors do not check. Here, if nine detectors predict a record is an inlier and one predicts it is an outlier, to receive the first benefit, we would take the opinion of the nine that agree. But for the second benefit, we would take the opinion of the one—allowing this record to be flagged even though the other nine missed it.

In this way, the two goals of creating ensembles can be at odds with each other. The first seeks to create stable, reliable scores, while the second seeks to ensure few outliers are missed. Creating ensembles, then, relates to balancing these to get the set of outliers, and the scoring, most suitable for your current project. This can take some tuning, but once done, there are significant advantages to creating ensembles of outlier detectors—we need to balance them but can receive both benefits to some degree.

There is, as well, a third benefit to ensembling. This applies only to ongoing projects but can be an appealing property of ensembles in these cases. Using ensembles can make it easier to tune the system as we develop a better sense of which outliers we are interested in and which we are not. Where certain detectors within an ensemble tend to identify outliers that are the most useful, we can increase their importance in the ensemble (for example, if the ensemble is based on a weighted average of scores, we can increase their weights) and where detectors tend to produce few useful outliers (or if they produce more outliers that are not useful, depending on our tolerance for false positives and false negatives), we can decrease their importance. While this is very useful, it is also fairly straightforward, and the remainder of the chapter will focus on the first two benefits, which can take a little effort to balance well though the techniques covered here make the process manageable.

Note there are some costs with creating ensembles in terms of execution time and possibly with respect to interpretability. Where a single detector is used, it may be possible to use an interpretable detector, but where many are used, it is less likely that they will all be interpretable, and including any black-box models will make the ensemble more difficult to interpret—the final scores may or may not be related to the scores produced by the interpretable models (it's possible the black-box detectors are a larger factor in the final scores). There will also often be cases where the interpretable models disagree with the ensemble as a whole or, if multiple interpretable detectors are used, with each other. But while using an ensemble of detectors (even if including interpretable models) will tend to lower interpretability relative to using a single interpretable model, using an ensemble with one or more interpretable models is still preferable to using a single black-box model. This allows at least some insight into the predictions of the ensemble.

As described in chapter 13, we may also wish to identify some post hoc explanations for an ensemble, such as feature importances, proxy models, Accumulated Local Effects (ALE) plots, and counterfactuals. This can be done with ensembles as with single detectors, though it will generally require wrapping the full ensemble in a single object, as with the wrapper class used in the counterfactuals example in chapter 13.

One case where it may not be advantageous to create an ensemble is where we are concerned only with specific outliers (as described in chapter 4) and a single detector is able to reliably detect these. In this case, adding additional detectors would only add overhead without benefit. Most of the time, however, there is some interest in finding unknown outliers (in which case, the larger and more diverse a collection of detectors used, the better, everything else equal), and even where our interest is strictly with specific, known outliers, it typically requires multiple detectors to find these consistently. Further, when looking for specific outliers, it may be that you are able to identify a set of detectors that can each detect these reasonably well but none score the outliers well. In these cases, combining the scores of many detectors may produce a more reliable overall scoring than using any one of the detectors.

14.1 *Overview of ensembling for outlier detection*

As common and useful as it is in outlier detection to create ensembles, it is sometimes difficult to do so optimally. It's necessary to both select a good set of detectors and to combine their scores effectively. In general, there are a few steps to creating strong ensembles:

- *Test individually each combination of detector, feature selection, preprocessing, and parameters and store the scores given by each of these to each record.* For the remaining steps, we will not need to re-execute the detectors—only to work with the scores they produced.
- *Select a set of these for the final ensemble.* It may be ideal, in terms of accuracy, to use a large number of detectors, but to be practical (to maintain reasonable train

and predict times), we will usually select a smaller set of these. To create strong outlier detection ensembles, we select a set of detectors that complement each other well—that are all reasonably accurate, but where they are wrong, they are wrong for different rows, and that, between them, cover all the outliers we would be interested in (that is, that balance the two benefits of ensembles listed previously).

- *Scale the scores from each detector.* This is necessary to make the scores from the different detectors comparable, as each detector generates scores with quite different scales and different distributions.

- *Combine the scores using some formula.* So far, we've usually simply taken the sum of their scores, which can often work well, but we'll look in this chapter at other techniques that can, in some cases, be more effective.

We covered the first step, testing the detectors on their own, in previous chapters, but we'll look at each of the next three steps in this chapter: selecting the detectors, scaling their scores, and deriving a final score for each record. An example can be seen in figure 14.1. Here we have a set of records that are each scored by three detectors. This shows the scores for three records, A, B, and C. The three detectors create scores on quite different scales, but it is possible (though nontrivial) to combine these into a final set of scores for each record. The final scores (2.4 for A, 0.02 for B, and 1.3 for C) are also shown. Ideally these scores are more appropriate than those assigned by any individual detector. Here we see some inconsistencies in the scores of the individual detectors—for example, the first detector assigns a higher score to B (0.8) than to C (0.2). Often, though, when combining the scores of multiple detectors, we can create final scores without such inconsistencies.

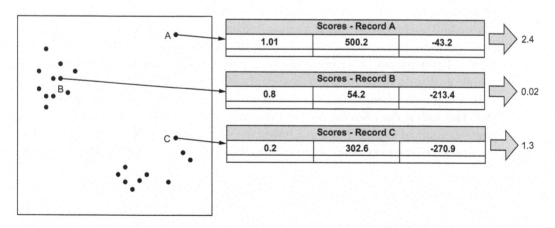

Figure 14.1 Example of an outlier detection ensemble. Here three detectors are used, each scoring all records. The scores for three points, A, B, and C, are shown as well as their final scores, which are based on the scores given by the three detectors.

As a simple example, consider where we have run the three outlier detectors: inter-quartile range (IQR), z-score, and Isolation Forest (IF). The first two are similar to each other and the third is a bit different, but they all make intuitive sense as outlier detectors, and they all have a long history of use. If you run all three, they will flag different rows, which is the nature of outlier detection: some rows will be outliers in one sense and not another, but any flagged are outliers, at least in some regard. Most of us would likely agree that, everything else equal, those flagged by all three algorithms are most likely the strongest outliers, followed by those flagged by two, followed by those flagged by only one.

However, any record flagged by just one of these may still be very unusual. Isolation Forest, for example, may flag unusual combinations of values, which the other two detectors would miss, and these are likely useful outliers. At the same time, the Isolation Forest may score some records highly that are not useful as outliers: including the Isolation Forest scores may result in some false positives. Considering the scores of the IQR and z-score detectors as well as the IF scores (assigning the highest final scores to records that are also flagged by the IQR and z-scores tests) will dampen this effect.

Overall, we wish to combine their scores in such a way that the IQR and z-scores (being probably quite correlated) do not count more than the Isolation Forest and such that we flag the records scored highly by even only one of the detectors but usually do not assign final scores as high as for those scored highly by two or three detectors. This is the challenge of creating strong ensembles.

We look closer now at another example, using six detectors (each with default parameters) on the baseball dataset we saw first in chapter 4. This shows the most basic form of ensembling, which we've seen previously in this book. We simply scale the scores and take their sum (which is equivalent to taking their mean, though slightly less computationally expensive).

In this example, we create a single final score for each record, but note in other projects you may wish to create multiple scores for each record—for example, where you are looking for outliers for more than one purpose, possibly searching for data artifacts, specific outliers, and unknown outliers (and wish to score each record in all three senses). For simplicity, though, in the remainder of this chapter we will assume there is a single goal and a single final score assigned to each record.

In listing 14.1, we simply collect the data, which is used in most of the following examples. This uses Robust Scaling on the numeric features and one-hot encoding for the single categorical feature, Position. However, it's common when creating ensembles to use a variety of preprocessing methods, as each may produce valid, but different, results.

Listing 14.1 Collecting the data

```
import pandas as pd
from sklearn.datasets import fetch_openml
from sklearn.preprocessing import RobustScaler

data = fetch_openml('baseball', version=1, parser='auto')
```

```
df = pd.DataFrame(data.data, columns=data.feature_names)
df['Strikeouts'] = df['Strikeouts'].fillna(df['Strikeouts'].median())
df = pd.get_dummies(df)
scaler = RobustScaler()
df = pd.DataFrame(scaler.fit_transform(df), columns=df.columns)
orig_features = df.columns
```

Next, in listing 14.2, we create six detectors and collect their outlier scores. This uses the four detectors provided with scikit-learn, as well as Nearest Sample and Radius (using the implementations from https://mng.bz/x6o8). These may be copied into the same file or into separate files and imported in.

As the scikit-learn detectors score the most anomalous records as the most negative scores, these are reversed to be consistent with the scoring using by Nearest Sample and Radius, which give the most anomalous records the highest scores (both systems work fine—the important point is to be consistent).

Listing 14.2   Executing six detectors on the baseball dataset

```
from sklearn.ensemble import IsolationForest
from sklearn.neighbors import LocalOutlierFactor
from sklearn.svm import OneClassSVM
from sklearn.covariance import EllipticEnvelope

scores_df = df.copy()

det_if = IsolationForest()
det_if.fit(df)
scores_df['IF Scores'] = (-1)*det_if.score_samples(df)

det_lof = LocalOutlierFactor()
det_lof.fit(df)
scores_df['LOF Scores'] = (-1)*det_lof.negative_outlier_factor_

det_ee = EllipticEnvelope()
det_ee.fit(df)
scores_df['EE Scores'] = (-1)*det_ee.score_samples(df)

det_ocsvm = OneClassSVM()
det_ocsvm.fit(df)
scores_df['OCSVM Scores'] = (-1)*det_ocsvm.score_samples(df)

det_ns = NearestSampleOutlierDetector()
det_ns.fit(df)
scores_df['Nearest Samples Scores'] = det_ns.decision_function(df)

det_radius = RadiusOutlierDetector()
scores_df['Radius Scores'] = det_radius.fit_predict(df, radius=4.0)
```

In this example, all six detectors do well. Elliptic Envelope is possibly the strongest on this dataset, but all do well enough to reasonably be considered for inclusion in an ensemble. This example uses six detectors, but note that outlier detection systems will often use dozens of detectors. In other cases, it's common to use only two or three, depending on the nature of the project. Figure 14.2 shows the distribution of scores.

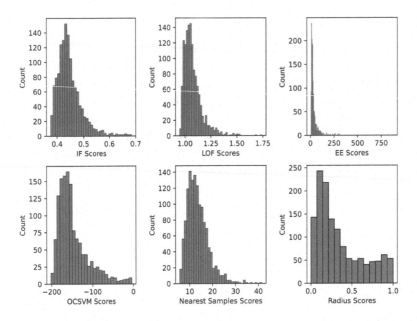

Figure 14.2   Distribution of outlier scores for six detectors. These show similar shapes, though some are more skewed than others. The OCSVM scores are negative but are ordered such that the highest scores are the most anomalous.

The distributions have very different scales but (in this case) similar shapes. Elliptic Envelope is, though, much more skewed in its scores than the others and Radius much less.

In listing 14.3 we look at combining the scores from each into a final score. This scales the scores using RobustScaler and sums the scores, which is among the easiest and safest methods.

Listing 14.3   Combining the scores using RobustScaling

```
from sklearn.preprocessing import RobustScaler

scores_cols = \
        list(set(scores_df.columns) - set(df.columns))

for col_name in scores_cols:
    scores_df[col_name] = RobustScaler().fit_transform(
        scores_df[col_name].values.reshape(-1, 1)).reshape(1, -1)[0]
scores_df['Score'] = scores_df[scores_cols].sum(axis=1)
```

Gets the set of columns from scores_df related to the scores

Uses RobustScaling to scale the scores in each score column

Sums the scaled scores to get a final score for each record

This works well in this case, but there are some questions we should consider. We used RobustScaling to scale each score and used their sum to combine the scores. It's not clear if either of these are the best choice. If our goal were to identify the most complete set of outliers we can, then using sum to combine the scores would actually hinder this. The scores for records flagged by only one or two detectors would be watered down by the detectors giving these records low scores. We would be better off, in this scenario, to use the maximum of the scores, also commonly used in outlier detection ensembles. To determine the best method, we will likely need to evaluate the process. As before, synthetic data may be the only realistic option, at least for new projects before we have labeled a large volume of real data.

14.2 Accuracy metrics with ensembles

When working with ensembles, having a meaningful accuracy metric to evaluate the ensemble is likely much more relevant than when working with a single detector. With a single detector, it's necessary to tune the feature selection, prepreprocessing, and parameters. There may be a significant number of combinations tested, but it may be, to some degree, manageable to select the best configuration by manually examining the output of each. With ensembles, however, there are many more combinations.

When creating ensembles, we seek to create the strongest overall ensemble, which is not necessarily created by using the detectors that are individually the strongest. Instead, we look for the combination that works best as a whole, likely including some detectors that are not among the strongest but that complement the others well. This requires testing many more combinations than simply taking the top-performing detectors. Further, for each combination of detectors, we also have multiple methods for scaling the scores and for combining the scores to test. Tracking the results from each combination may be difficult, and it will likely be infeasible to make a judgment call on the best set of results produced by manually examining the results.

To develop a strong ensemble, it's usually necessary to automate looping through many combinations, comparing each using a single metric that has been determined to be the most relevant (possibly Area Under Receiver Operator Characteristic Curve (AUROC), precision at k, or another), typically evaluated against a synthetic test set, unless sufficient labeled real data is available. Using what's called a *pseudo-ground truth* is also a useful option and is covered below.

A discussion of the best choices for metric is included in chapter 8; the same considerations apply for ensembles as for single detectors, though the execution times related to fitting and predicting may be more relevant for ensembles, as these may be longer than when using a single detector. In addition, though a single metric must be used to select the best ensemble, it is useful to measure the accuracy with multiple metrics if multiple are relevant, to ensure the final system performs reasonably well in all regards.

14.3 Methods to create ensembles

We first create a set of detectors and then select some subset of these for the final ensemble. To create the set of detectors for an ensemble, we may use different methods such as the following:

- Types of detectors
- Preprocessing
- Hyperparameters
- Sets of the original features
- Engineered features
- Training rows

We look at each of these in more detail next. Often, though, when constructing ensembles, we will use a combination of these techniques to create a more robust collection of detectors.

14.3.1 *Different model types*

Listing 14.2 shows an example of using different model types. This is straightforward and can be the most effective way to create ensembles, as different detectors are often very different and diversity is central to a strong ensemble.

While not all the detectors that are tried will necessarily be included in the final ensemble, it is usually worthwhile to test a large number of types of detectors. However, it's not necessary that all detectors are very different. For example, we may test both local outlier factor (LOF) and Local Outlier Probability (LoOP), which work similarly. Testing both, we may select just the stronger of these. It might even be advantageous to select both. We do need to be mindful, however, that if there are many detectors that are similar to each other in the final ensemble, this may overemphasize the types of outliers they tend to detect. This is not a problem in all cases, as it may be that these are the types of outliers most of interest. However, we will generally wish for the detectors to be as distinct (with low correlations in the top scores) from each other as possible, everything else equal.

14.3.2 *Different preprocessing*

Using different preprocessing, such as different methods to handle nulls (or other missing values), categorical encoding, scaling, and binning, can produce different but equally useful outlier detectors. It can, therefore, be useful to use a variety of preprocessing methods and include these in the final ensemble. We've also seen that principal component analysis (PCA) transformations (or other dimensionality reduction methods) can be useful for outlier detection and that using different components will identify different types of outliers. Using several variations on these may be advantageous in an ensemble. Using different forms of cleaning the data may also add some diversity.

14.3.3 *Different hyperparameters*

Often using different hyperparameters will produce different but equally (or nearly) valid results. We've seen previous examples such as varying the eps parameter with DBSCAN, the number of clusters with clustering-based detectors, and the k parameter with k nearest neighbors (KNN). Using a variety of distance metrics can also be useful where this may be specified as a parameter. Most detectors have some parameters, and including the same detector type with a variety of parameter values will tend to work better than relying on a single set of values, as was covered in chapter 8. This is true even when the detectors have been well tested with real or synthetic data. In fact, when testing to determine the best hyperparameters, we often find a range of values, and not a single value, that appear to work well, and we can take advantage of this when creating ensembles.

14.3.4 Sampling the original features

The process of sampling the features refers to creating subspaces, which we've seen with subspace outlier detection (SOD) and FeatureBagging in PyOD and with other methods in chapter 10. We've also seen in chapter 13 that this can allow more interpretable outlier detection if restricted to small numbers of features—ideally two (which may then be plotted). This method is unnecessary when working with datasets with very few features or where we limit the analysis to univariate tests (e.g., creating an ensemble based on, say, IQR, median absolute deviation, histogram-based outlier score (HBOS), empirical cumulative distribution (ECOD), and Entropy) but is generally useful in other cases.

We may also wish to specifically consider features that have especially low or high relevance. For any given dataset, there may be some features that appear to be less relevant for outlier detection and that lead to flagging records we are not interested in; these should likely be removed entirely and not included in any of the detectors in the ensemble. We may also have features that are the opposite—that relate to relevant, but very strong, outliers that overwhelm the other features, causing the system to miss anomalies associated with other features. With these features, we wish to ensure they appear in some but not all of the detectors. Ensembles may be used in this way to reduce masking effects.

14.3.5 Different engineered features

In some cases, we may wish to create engineered features to better capture the outliers. For example, with the baseball dataset, we may create features to represent `At_bats/ Games_played`, `Games_played/Number_seasons`, `Home_runs/At_bats`, and so on. Different detectors may use different of these, which will then detect and emphasize different types of outliers. Usually when adding engineered features of this type we will also remove the related original features to avoid overemphasizing these.

14.3.6 Sampling rows

Creating multiple detectors, each trained on a different random sample of the records, is equivalent to the idea of bagging used by some predictive ensembles, such as Random Forest. Some detectors also take advantage of this idea, such as Isolation Forest and Nearest Sample, with IF using different samples for each tree and Nearest Sample using a different sample for each iteration. The idea is that different subsets of records have slightly different distributions, which are each possible to compare the records against. Each detector trained on a sample of rows will be weaker than a detector trained on the full set of rows, but combining many such detectors in an ensemble may create a system that is, overall, more accurate.

While we've looked at most forms of creating different detectors previously in the book, we've not looked at sampling rows, other than in discussing IF and Nearest Sample, so we examine this now. To test this, we first create a simple doped dataset in the following listing.

Listing 14.4   Creating a test dataset

Creates a small number of doped records

Loops through each record in the doped data

Selects a random column to modify

Modifies the selected column

```
doped_df = df.sample(n=50)
for i in doped_df.index:
    row = doped_df.loc[i]
    col_name = np.random.choice(doped_df.columns)
    doped_df.loc[i, col_name] = doped_df.loc[i, col_name] * -0.9
df['Doped'] = 0
doped_df['Doped'] = 1
full_df = pd.concat([df, doped_df])
full_df = full_df.reset_index(drop=True)
```

With the doped data created, we are ready to test creating an ensemble using different samples of the full data. When creating an ensemble in this way, it can be difficult to determine an appropriate sample size: how many rows do we train each detector on? Similar to selecting the number of features for subspaces (covered in chapter 10), selecting few records per sample results in less correlation among the detectors but less reliable detectors; more records per sample allows more reliable detectors but also more correlation. As it can be difficult to choose an appropriate sample size, it might be best to use different sizes for each sample, each chosen randomly.

Varying the number of records per sample can also add diversity in the sense that many parameters (for example, k with k nearest neighbors) relate to the number of rows; so varying the number of rows has the same effect as modifying the parameters. However, it may also be the case that some parameter values are put beyond the range of what is effective for the given number of rows and different parameters will be appropriate for samples of different sizes.

The following listing shows an example of training multiple detectors, in this case One-class Support Vector Machine (OCSVM) models, each on a different random set of rows, here between 300 and 1,300 records each.

Listing 14.5   Using OCSVM with multiple samples of different sizes

```
from sklearn.metrics import roc_auc_score

ocsvm_scores_df = pd.DataFrame()
for i in range(50):
    sample_size = np.random.randint(300, 1300)
```

```
        sample_df = df.sample(n=sample_size)
        det_ocsvm = OneClassSVM(nu=0.2)
        det_ocsvm.fit(sample_df.values)
        ocsvm_scores_df[f'Scores {i}'] = \
            (-1)*det_ocsvm.score_samples(full_df.values)

ocsvm_scores_df['Scores'] = ocsvm_scores_df.sum(axis=1)
print(roc_auc_score(full_df['Doped'], ocsvm_scores_df['Scores']))
```

This results in an Area Under Receiver Operator Characteristic Curve (AUROC) score of 0.754, a very small improvement over using a single OCSVM trained on the full dataset (which is about 0.752), though cross validation (skipped here for brevity) is necessary to determine if there is truly a gain. In addition, there is some randomness in the sampling, so your results may vary slightly.

Several things make it difficult to see significant increases in accuracy with bagging. If the data is fairly clean, with simple, consistent relationships among the features, the samples will often tend to be similar to each other: while each is weaker than using the full dataset (due to having a smaller size), there is little gain in this case from diversity. Most systems that use bagging, such as Random Forest for prediction or Isolation Forest for outlier detection, do not rely solely on sampling the rows and do this only to add some additional diversity. For example, Isolation Forest achieves the bulk of the diversity between the isolation trees by selecting random features and random split points. Generally, the other methods listed here for creating ensembles will tend to work better; using samples of rows can be worth trying but primarily as a means to increase the diversity found through other methods.

14.4 Selecting detectors for an ensemble

Once we have created a few detectors, we need to select a subset of these for the final ensemble. Logically, this would be the next step; however, in practice we may actually first choose the methods to scale and combine the results and then select the set of detectors used. This allows us to test different combinations of detectors. For example, if we've established a good synthetic test set, accuracy metric, scaling method, and combining method, we may loop through different subsets of the detectors to find the strongest combination (using synthetic data, this is the set of detectors that best scores the synthetic data higher than the real data). It is also possible to do this the other way: to first determine the subset of detectors used and then the best means to combine their scores. In either case, this is often an iterative approach—first selecting one, then adjusting the other and repeating, with as many iterations as is practical to achieve the accuracy required for the project. In the next examples, we assume we have selected the initial scaling and combining methods and wish to next select the set of detectors.

To evaluate each potential ensemble, we will need some ground truth to test against. Where a large body of labeled data or of reliable synthetic data is available, we may use this. We look in this chapter at another approach that may also be useful for many projects: creating what's called a *pseudo-ground truth*. This refers to assigning inlier/

outlier labels to the records where the labels may not be perfect but are reliable enough we may use them to construct a strong ensemble. We look specifically at two methods to establish pseudo-ground truth labels: manually inspecting the set of records flagged by at least one detector and taking the consensus of many detectors. We then look at several methods to select the set of detectors to best match the labels used (using pseudo-ground truths for these examples, though synthetic data or true labels, if available, may also be used).

14.4.1 *Manually inspecting the superset of many detectors*

The first method we look at to establish a pseudo-ground truth for the records is based on the idea that running many detectors (especially if diverse) will identify the full (or nearly full) set of outliers of interest in a dataset. That is, they may flag records that are not of interest, but if many detectors are used, they will likely miss very few. Ideally a small enough set will be flagged that they can be manually inspected to determine which are, in fact, of interest. To do so, execute the following process:

1 Run a large number of outlier detectors (with different preprocessing and parameters).
2 Run PyThresh, or in some way establish the records from each that appear to be considered the outliers by that detector—the records with the unusually high scores.
3 Collect these records into one set of potential outliers (the set of records identified by at least one detector).
4 Remove any duplicates.
5 Manually examine these and determine which can actually be considered relevant outliers (records useful to flag for the current project). This is the set of known outliers in the current data. There may be other outliers, but realistically it may be that no other outliers can be detected with the tools available. Nevertheless, it may be worthwhile to also check the records that are scored just below the thresholds, as some of these could possibly be considered outliers as well. Though they may not be realistic to detect with any individual detector (without also incorrectly flagging many inliers), it may be possible that an ensemble can detect these—for example, where they are slightly unusual—but in many ways, an ensemble may be able to detect this. Inspect these records and add any that are appropriate to the set of known outliers.
6 Tune the system such that this set of known outliers is scored higher than all other records as much as possible, using as few detectors as necessary.

An example of collecting the set of records flagged by at least one detector is shown in listing 14.6. This takes the raw (unscaled) scores from the six detectors (set in listing 14.2) and finds the set of rows that were given a high score by any of the detectors. In this case, it simply takes the top 10 records from each detector, but other methods may work better for some projects.

Listing 14.6 Collecting a superset of high-scored records

```
def get_top_scored(df, scores_col):
    cutoff = sorted(df[scores_col])[-10]
    return scores_df[scores_df[scores_col] >= cutoff].index.tolist()

scores_cols = set(scores_df.columns) - set(df.columns)    ◀── Gets the set of columns
top_rows = []                                                  related to the scores
for scores_col in scores_cols:
    res = get_top_scored(scores_df, scores_col)    ◀── Gets the top-scored
    top_rows.extend(res)                               records for each detector
top_rows = list(set(top_rows))    ◀── Removes duplicates
```

Once we have this set of flagged outliers, we can manually inspect them and label the ones that are relevant to the current project. We can assume anything not flagged in this way is not relevant to be flagged (or is impossible to flag with the detectors available).

14.4.2 Taking the consensus of many detectors

Another method to establish a pseudo-ground truth may also be used where we do not take a superset of the outliers found by the detectors, but the consensus of the detectors. This may not establish as strong of an approximation of the ground truth, but it does save the step of manually inspecting the flagged outliers and so can be more practical.

This method executes the same as listing 14.3 (though it would generally use many more detectors and many variations of each). We assume a scaling method and combining method and then create a final score using all detectors. This works on the assumption that most detectors work reasonably well and that combining their scores will produce a sensible final score.

We may, once we have this pseudo-ground truth, seek to create an ensemble that can approximate this score but using fewer detectors, so we are operating with less overhead. We won't likely be able to match the scoring exactly, but we can assess how similar each subset of detectors is and make a judgment call as to which subset of detectors best balances accuracy (similarity to the pseudo-ground truth), training time, prediction time, and robustness. Robustness is hard to estimate and realistically can only be tested with synthetic data, but in general, having more, and more diverse, detectors will tend to be more robust. In lieu of extensive testing, it may be best to simply favor more diverse sets of detectors.

Having looked at a couple of methods to establish a pseudo-ground that we will try to replicate with a smaller set of detectors, we next look at methods to select the detectors to do so.

14.4.3 Testing random subsets of detectors

A straightforward method to identify subsets of detectors that are effective as an ensemble is to simply test random subsets. This may sound expensive, but the detectors do not need to be run more than once, and we consider only combining their scores in different ways. In listing 14.7, we provide a simple example. This assumes listing 14.3 has executed and is used as the pseudo-ground truth. We then wish to find a smaller, more efficient set of detectors that can approximate this.

This code loops through each possible size of ensemble and attempts to find, for each size, the best set of detectors. For each size of ensemble tested, this looks at a maximum of 50 combinations. This may be set higher, but we probably wish to limit this to some manageable number.

We may then pick a subset, balancing the number of detectors with agreement with the pseudo-ground truth (though may also wish to consider execution time and interpretability). This provides a simple method to compare the scores produced by a subset of detectors to that of the full set (taking the Pearson correlation, considering only scores over 2.0 after applying Robust Scaling) and several other methods may be used, as described in chapter 8. In general, we wish to find agreement between the top-scored records while assigning little or no weight to agreement between the low-scored records.

> **Listing 14.7   Code to randomly test subsets of detectors**

```
import math
import itertools

def test_agreement(df, detector_cols, truth_col):     ◀── Defines a means to
    temp_df = scores_df.copy()                             evaluate the agreement
    temp_df['Test Score'] = temp_df[detector_cols].mean(axis=1)   between two ensembles
    temp_df['Test Score'] = temp_df['Test Score'].apply(
        lambda x: x if x > 2.0 else 0)
    temp_df[truth_col] = temp_df[truth_col].apply(
        lambda x: x if x > 2.0 else 0)
    corr = temp_df[['Test Score', truth_col]].corr().loc['Test Score',
                                                          truth_col]

    if corr != corr:
        return 0.0
    return corr


scores_cols = list(set(scores_df.columns) - set(df.columns))
scores_cols.remove('Score')
                                        Loops through each possible number of
for num_detectors in range(1, 6):    ◀── detectors up to, but not including, the full set
    best_agreement = -1
    best_set_detectors = []
    num_combinations = math.comb(6, num_detectors)      Tests up to 50 random
    max_trials = 50                                  ◀── subsets of detectors
    detector_cols_arr = itertools.combinations(scores_cols, num_detectors)
    if num_combinations <= max_trials:                                      ◀──
        for detector_cols in detector_cols_arr:
            res = test_agreement(df, list(detector_cols), 'Score')
            if res > best_agreement:                      If only a small number of
                best_agreement = res                      subsets of the current size
                                                          are possible, tests them all
```

```
                best_set_detectors = detector_cols
        else:
            for _ in range(max_trials):
                detector_cols = np.random.choice(a=scores_cols,
                                                 size=num_detectors)
                res = test_agreement(df, detector_cols, 'Score')
                if res > best_agreement:
                    best_agreement = res
                    best_set_detectors = detector_cols
        print((f"\nUsing {num_detectors} detectors, the best set of "
               f"detectors found is: \n{best_set_detectors} with an "
               f"agreement score of {best_agreement}"))
```

If a large number of subsets of the current size are possible, tests a random set of these

This produces:

```
Using 1 detectors, the best set of detectors found is:
('EE Scores',) with an agreement score of 0.88

Using 2 detectors, the best set of detectors found is:
('OCSVM Scores', 'EE Scores') with an agreement score of 0.89

Using 3 detectors, the best set of detectors found is:
('OCSVM Scores', 'EE Scores', 'IF Scores') with an agreement score of 0.87

Using 4 detectors, the best set of detectors found is:
('OCSVM Scores', 'LOF Scores', 'EE Scores', 'IF Scores') with an agreement
     score of 0.86

Using 5 detectors, the best set of detectors found is:
('OCSVM Scores', 'LOF Scores', 'Radius Scores', 'EE Scores', 'IF Scores')
 with an agreement score of 0.86
```

In this case, the best option is possibly using two detectors, which will use OCSVM and Elliptic Envelope (EE). This approach will not work as well as Bayesian optimization or some other approaches to finding an optimal subset of detectors for an ensemble, but it is simple and can often work reasonably well.

Once we have found a good, small set of detectors, the question is whether there is benefit in adding any additional detectors. This may add overhead to the system and may potentially lower the quality of the final scores, though this can be balanced by increasing the breadth of the outliers found. This is a judgment call and really comes down to the goals of the outlier detection system.

14.4.4 Greedy methods to identify a set of detectors

In this section we look at two other methods to select a set of detectors, again matching a pseudo-ground truth. In the first, we start with an empty set and add detectors one at a time until we have a set of final scores that approximate the pseudo-ground truth sufficiently well. In the second, we start with the full set and remove detectors one at a time until we no longer have a sufficient match—at that point we take the subset immediately before this. These are both greedy approaches, and so are reasonably efficient though less thorough than other methods, such as the random search covered previously.

An example of the additive method is shown in listing 14.8. We start with an empty set, find the detector that best matches the pseudo-ground truth, add that to the ensemble, and then find the detector that, when combined with the detector already in the ensemble, best creates an ensemble that matches the pseudo-ground truth, and so on. In general, at each step we will have a set of detectors that, combined, better matches the pseudo-ground truth than the previous step, though it is possible for some steps to actually move away from this. This uses the test_agreement() method defined in listing 14.7.

Listing 14.8   Greedy method to create an ensemble

```
scores_cols = list(set(scores_df.columns) - set(df.columns))
scores_cols.remove('Score')

detectors_used = []                              ◄──  Initially, no detectors
detectors_not_used = scores_cols.copy()               are in the set.

                                                 ◄──  Each iteration adds one
for num_detectors in range(6):                        detector to the ensemble.
    best_next_detector = ""
    best_agreement = -1                          ◄──  Tests adding each detector that
    for detector in detectors_not_used:               is not yet in the ensemble
        potential_set = detectors_used + [detector]
        res = test_agreement(scores_df, potential_set, 'Score')
        if res > best_agreement:
            best_agreement = res
            best_next_detector = detector
    detectors_used.append(best_next_detector)
    detectors_not_used.remove(best_next_detector)
    print((f"Using {num_detectors}, the best set is: "
           f"{detectors_used} with an agreement score of "
           f"{best_agreement}"))
```

This produces

```
Using 1, the best set is: ['EE Scores'] with an agreement score of 0.88

Using 2, the best set is:
['EE Scores', 'OCSVM Scores']
with an agreement score of 0.89

Using 3, the best set is:
['EE Scores', 'OCSVM Scores', 'IF Scores']
with an agreement score of 0.87

Using 4, the best set is:
['EE Scores', 'OCSVM Scores', 'IF Scores', 'LOF Scores']
with an agreement score of 0.86

Using 5, the best set is:
```

```
['EE Scores', 'OCSVM Scores', 'IF Scores', 'LOF Scores',
'Radius Scores']
with an agreement score of 0.86
```

It is possible to set a stopping criteria, but this is generally efficient enough to consider every case from using a single detector up to using all but one of the initial detectors. After this is executed, it is possible to examine the results printed and determine the best set of detectors, again balancing the number of detectors with the overall accuracy and any other concerns such as execution time and interpretability.

14.4.5 *Selecting detectors to minimize correlation*

While it is possible to use synthetic data or a pseudo-ground truth to optimize the set of detectors selected, it is also possible to simply select a set of detectors that ensures we have the greatest diversity (that have the lowest correlation). It is always a goal of ensembling to have diverse detectors—including multiple detectors that have a very high level of agreement in an ensemble has little value. And while the correlations between detectors may be less relevant than their accuracies, the correlations can be measured with greater certainty.

However, selecting detectors purely to minimize correlations can, in some cases, lead to weak ensembles, as detectors may be uncorrelated because one has poor accuracy. Including correlation in the consideration of what detectors to add can be useful but should be balanced with the primary concern, which would likely be either matching a pseudo-ground truth or identifying synthetic outliers. Listing 14.9 provides an example similar to 14.8 but including code to weight the importance of (1) maximizing agreement with the pseudo-ground truth and (2) minimizing agreement with the existing ensemble. In this example, the weights are set to 0.7 and 0.3, meaning the decision is based 70% on accuracy and 30% on correlation.

Listing 14.9 Including a test to minimize correlation

```
weight = 0.7
scores_cols = list(set(scores_df.columns) - set(df.columns))
scores_cols.remove('Score')

detectors_used = []
detectors_not_used = scores_cols.copy()

for num_detectors in range(6):
    best_next_detector = ""
    best_agreement = -1
    for detector in detectors_not_used:
        potential_set = detectors_used + [detector]
        agreement_target = test_agreement(
            scores_df, potential_set, 'Score')
        if len(detectors_used) > 0:
            agreement_ensemble = test_agreement(
                scores_df, detectors_used, detector)
        else:
            agreement_ensemble = 0.0
```

Sets the relative importance of matching the pseudo-ground truth compared to minimizing correlation

If there are no detectors in the ensemble yet, goes strictly by agreement with the pseudo-ground truth

```
        res = (weight*agreement_target) + (1.0-weight)*agreement_ensemble
        if res > best_agreement:
            best_agreement = res
            best_next_detector = detector
    detectors_used.append(best_next_detector)
    detectors_not_used.remove(best_next_detector)
    print((f"Using {num_detectors}, the best set is: "
        f"{detectors_used} with an agreement score of "
        f"{best_agreement}"))
```

Finds the best option for this iteration considering the weighted sum of both scores

14.5 Scaling scores

As we see in figure 14.2, the scores of different outlier detectors can be on quite different scales. For example, the IF scores range from about 0.3 to 0.7, while the Elliptic Envelope's range from about 0 to 1000. In outlier detection projects that use a single outlier detector, scaling can be convenient to help understand the scores but is usually not necessary. With ensembles, however, scaling the scores is almost always necessary; without this, there is no way to determine if a record given a score of 0.6 by an IF or a record given a score of 900 by an Elliptic Envelope is a greater outlier.

There are some exceptions where scaling the scores is not necessary, such as where all detectors are of the same type and are simply trained on different samples of rows or sets of features. In these cases it is reasonable to treat the scores as-is; in fact, scaling the scores may actually cause you to lose some information. However, in the great majority of cases, we will need to adjust the scores produced by each detector so that they are comparable.

The choices to scale scores are similar to the choices available to scale the data itself before using distance, density, or clustering-based detectors. We revisit these here, looking at them in the context of combining detectors. We also look at some additional methods that can be useful for this purpose.

14.5.1 Min-max scaling

Using min-max scaling for scores is similar to using this for the data: all scores will be translated to values between 0.0 and 1.0. If any scores are extremely high (it is common for some detectors, LOF for example, to assign scores for some records orders of magnitude higher than others), all other scores will be pushed toward 0.0, and so many moderately strong outliers will end up with scores that are effectively 0. This is a concern but not necessarily a major problem so long as many detectors are used and most do not have this behavior. In this case, we will simply have the few records that are given extremely high scores by one detector assigned more weight in the final score (as that detector does not contribute to the final scores of any other records), which is consistent with the findings for that detector.

14.5.2 z-scores (standard scaling)

Using z-scores translates each score to the number of standard deviations it is from the mean score for that detector. z-scores can work well so long as the detectors all produce scores without extreme values. If there are any extreme scores, these may compromise the ability to score the other records, as the extreme values affect the mean and standard deviation of the scores for that detector.

14.5.3 Robust scaling

As with scaling data, using robust scaling is usually preferred to plain scaling for scores. For robust scaling, instead of using the mean and standard deviation, which can be affected by any extreme scores, the median and IQR are used. While this will prevent extreme scores from affecting other scores, it does still result in extreme scores remaining extreme after scaling. Where this occurs, these scores may completely dominate the final scores, possibly negating much of the benefits of ensembling.

14.5.4 MAD scaling

Here scores are translated to indicate the ratio of their distance from the median score to the median distance from the median score, as described in chapter 2. Similar to robust scaling, this is robust in the sense that extreme scores do not affect the scores given to other scores, but they do remain extreme themselves.

14.5.5 Ranking

With the previously described methods, the values of the scores are adjusted so that the scores from each detector are within similar ranges. These methods did not, however, adjust the distribution of the scores: the shape of the distribution of scores remains the same. As indicated, this can be a problem where some detectors produce extreme scores but is also a problem generally where the distributions are quite different.

The remaining methods we look at—ranking and Box Cox—not only scale the scores but also change the distributions so that the scores of all detectors have the same scales and distributions. The order of the scores remains the same, but the gaps between the scores will be modified. This can be useful, for example, where some detectors score outliers only slightly higher than inliers and other detectors score outliers considerably higher. The gaps between the scores may have very different meanings for each detector, and there's often no consistent way to interpret these gaps. This makes it most reasonable to adjust the scores so that all detectors have the same distributions: the same gaps between the scores. It can also be the simplest and safest method to scale scores where some detectors produce extreme scores. Using the rank is the simplest form of this, as we consider only the order each record is scored in by each detector.

We should highlight though, as with the correlations between detectors (covered in chapter 8), it is strictly the high scores produced by each detector that are relevant; it is not relevant how the scores of the inliers are distributed. Consider figure 14.3 (left pane) where we see the four highest scores produced by three detectors. These have different distributions (gaps between the scores), and it's not obvious how to best combine these, as these gaps may or may not be comparable from one detector to another. In most cases, we assume the gaps are both meaningful and comparable, and so we simply scale the data and then combine them (using the mean, maximum, or other

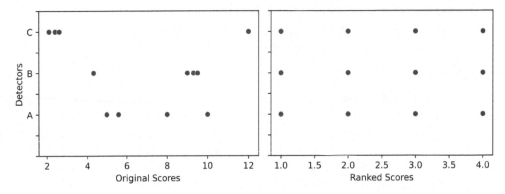

Figure 14.3   Left pane: examples of a set of high scores produced by three detectors, A, B, and C. Right pane: the same scores after applying rank ordering. The scores are now evenly spaced for each detector.

function). But this assumption may not hold, and it's also possible to use the rank order of these (right pane), which loses information about how separated the scores are but also removes any distortions that may be due to some detectors scoring differently.

Detector C has one score far above the next three scores it gives. B has a smaller range of scores though also a significant gap between its third and fourth highest scores. In the right pane, we have the same scores after rank transformation. The top four records for each detector are now evenly spaced, and there is no sense of how much more anomalous the detectors thought the records were compared to the other top-scored records but also no effects from different detectors producing different distributions simply as an artifact of their algorithm.

To give another example, consider the scores shown in figure 14.4 for the Isolation Forest and Elliptic Envelope, here plotted as rank plots. We can see the distributions of scores are different, with IF (left pane) giving the top outliers similar scores and EE (right pane) creating large differences between the top scores.

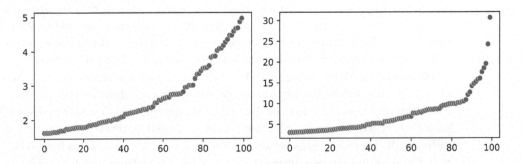

Figure 14.4   IF (left pane) and EE (right pane) scores as rank plots. The EE has much larger gaps between its top scores than the IF.

Taking the rank ordering for the IF and EE scores, we do lose the sense of which records the detectors considered strong versus moderate outliers, but we would also remove any effects from the fact that the two algorithms score differently. In other cases, ranking may not work as well. For example, consider where a detector assigned the scores to a series of six records: 1.0, 1.1, 1.2, 1.3, 0.9, 0.8. In this case, there are no outliers (all scores are roughly the same), but a ranking scheme would simply translate the scores to ranks: 4, 3, 2, 1, 5, 6, (where rank 1 is given to the highest scores), which loses the sense that there are no outliers.

In the following listing, we look at the scaling methods covered so far, scaling the scores from the IF on the baseball data. This produces the plots shown in figure 14.5.

Listing 14.10 Scaling the IF scores

```
import matplotlib.pyplot as plt
import seaborn as sns
from sklearn.preprocessing import MinMaxScaler, StandardScaler, \
                        RobustScaler

scaler = MinMaxScaler()                              Applies min-max
scores_df['MinMax IF'] = scaler.fit_transform(       scaling to the IF scores
    scores_df['IF Scores'].values.reshape(-1, 1)).reshape(1, -1)[0]

scaler = StandardScaler()                            Applies standard
scores_df['Standard IF'] = scaler.fit_transform(     scaling
    scores_df['IF Scores'].values.reshape(-1, 1)).reshape(1, -1)[0]

scaler = RobustScaler()                              Applies robust
scores_df['Robust IF'] = scaler.fit_transform(       standard scaling
    scores_df['IF Scores'].values.reshape(-1, 1)).reshape(1, -1)[0]

scaler = RobustScaler()                              Applies robust scaling
scores_df['Rank IF'] = scaler.fit_transform(         to the rank order
    scores_df['IF Scores'].rank().values.reshape(-1, 1)).reshape(1, -1)[0]

fig, ax = plt.subplots(nrows=2, ncols=2, figsize=(8, 6))
sns.histplot(scores_df['MinMax IF'], ax=ax[0][0])
sns.histplot(scores_df['Standard IF'], ax=ax[0][1])
sns.histplot(scores_df['Robust IF'], ax=ax[1][0])
sns.histplot(scores_df['Rank IF'], ax=ax[1][1])

plt.tight_layout()
plt.show()
```

With min-max, standard, and robust scaling, the shape does not change from the original distribution of scores—only the scale. Where previously the IF scores ranged from roughly 0.3 to 0.7, after min-max scaling, they will be between 0.0 and 1.0. With standard and robust scaling, they will be centered at zero; they may extend to any minimum or maximum value, but with most datasets the maximum will be around 4.0 or 5.0 (with far greater values possible where detectors produce extreme scores). In this case,

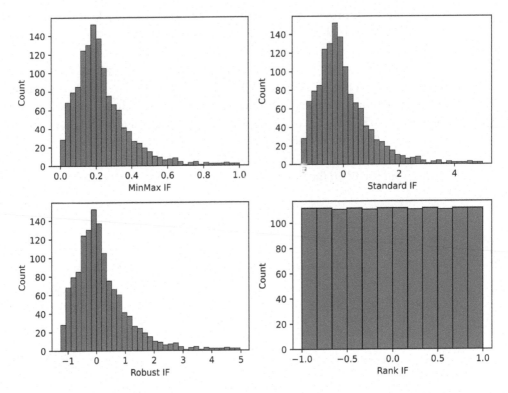

Figure 14.5   The IF scores after min-max, standard, and robust scaling, and rank transformation

the data is well behaved, and standard and robust scaling produce similar results. With ranking, we end up with a uniform distribution of scores, with even spacing between each score. In this example, the ranked scores are also scaled, as this makes the scores easier to interpret, but this is not necessary.

We look next at the Elliptic Envelope scores, which had a different shape to start with than that for the Isolation Forest. We do not show the results of the rank transformation in this example, as this will look the same regardless of the distribution we begin with. Here we do, however, include a log transformation. In this example, performing the log transformation on the Elliptic Envelope creates a distribution that may be comparable to the other detectors. This won't usually be possible, but in this case, using this on this one detector may be sufficient to ensure the detectors are comparable once scaled. More often, though, a transformation such as rank order will be necessary. The plot in figure 14.6 shows the Elliptic Envelope scores after min-max, standard, and robust transformations, as well as after log transformation.

14.5.6 Box Cox

The Box Cox transformation is another technique to adjust the scores of multiple detectors to make them comparable, such that they have similar scales and distributions

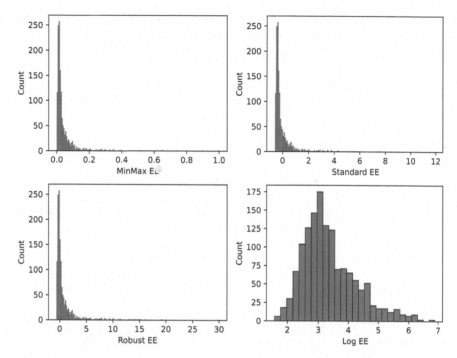

Figure 14.6 **The Elliptic Envelope scores after min-max, standard, and robust scaling, as well as log transformation**

as each other. A Box Cox transformation is somewhat similar to using rank values in that the order of the scores is preserved but the distances between the points is altered. Instead of a uniform distribution as we get with rank transformations, Box Cox produces a normal distribution. This means very high scores (for example the score of approximately 12.0 given by detector C in figure 14.3) remains well separated from the other points but possibly less so (and possibly more so) than in their original distribution—they will be spread out as is dictated by a Gaussian distribution.

Listing 14.11 shows an example of performing a Box Cox transformation on the Isolation Forest scores, which transforms the scores to have a Gaussian shape. We use a method provided by SciPy for this. To make the scores from each detector comparable, we also ensure each has a mean of 0.0 and standard deviation of 1.0.

One thing to note about the Box Cox method is that all scores must be positive, with the minimum values being close to 0.0. If this is not the case, the data can be shifted to ensure this is true: if there are negative values, the data can be shifted to the right by adding the minimum value to all values, and if the minimum is larger than 0.0, the data can be shifted left by subtracting the minimum value from all values.

The Box Cox transformations will not support all distributions that may be produced by outlier detectors. It's common for the scores of outlier detectors to follow an exponential distribution (as, visually examining the plots, the detectors in this case appear to have produced), which Box Cox can support well with default parameters, but in other cases it may be necessary to adjust its lambda or alpha parameters or to use another transformation, such as Yeo-Johnson.

Listing 14.11   Transforming IF scores with Box Cox

```
from scipy import stats

det_if = IsolationForest()
det_if.fit(df)
scores_df['IF Scores'] = (-1)*det_if.score_samples(df)

fig, ax = plt.subplots(nrows=1, ncols=3, figsize=(10, 3))
data_box_cox = stats.boxcox(scores_df['IF Scores'])[0]
sns.histplot(data_box_cox, ax=ax[0])

std = data_box_cox.std()
data_box_cox = data_box_cox / std
sns.histplot(data_box_cox, ax=ax[1])

mean = data_box_cox.mean()
data_box_cox = data_box_cox - mean
sns.histplot(data_box_cox, ax=ax[2])

plt.tight_layout()
plt.show()
```

Performs the Box Cox transformation to put the data in a Gaussian shape

Divides by the standard deviation to ensure the data has a standard deviation of 1.0

Moves the data by subtracting the mean, to ensure it has a mean of 0.0

The results are shown in figure 14.7. The first pane shows the scores in a Gaussian distribution though with an unspecified mean and standard deviation. In the middle pane we show the data slightly adjusted, with a standard deviation of 1.0, and in the right pane the data shifted to have a mean of 0.0. If this is done for all detectors, the scores will be comparable.

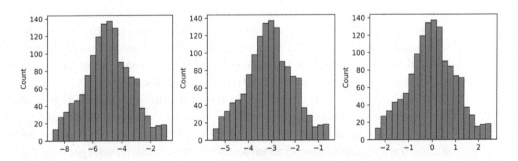

Figure 14.7   Transforming the IF scores to a Gaussian distribution with mean 0.0 and standard deviation 1.0. The first pane shows the data after the Box Cox transformation. The middle pane shows data after dividing by the standard deviation. In this case, the standard deviation was close to 1.0 already, so the scale is almost the same. We then shift the data to the right, to have a mean of 0.0.

After performing a Box Cox transformation and adjusting the data to have 0.0 mean and a standard deviation of 1.0, you should see a symmetric, unimodal distribution, with values ranging from about roughly –3.0 to 3.0, though the more data, the wider the range.

Box Cox is typically preferred to rank transformations, as it can be desirable to emphasize the highest scores, which Box Cox does by spreading them out more so than rank order. However, different projects may benefit most from any of the methods listed here or others.

As discussed previously, one thing to check for is cases where detectors appear to have detected no outliers: where they have no scores that are unusually large. However, to determine this, it's necessary to be familiar with the distributions normally produced by the detector, likely using (both realistic and atypical) synthetic data. Angle-based outlier detection (ABOD), for example, can produce distributions quite different from other detectors. Where it does appear that the detector has identified no outliers, it may be best to simply set the scaled scores to 0.0 for all records.

14.6 Combining scores

Once the scores for each detector are scaled, we have the question of how to combine them. For the moment, we will assume we have also selected the detectors to be used. As we saw in chapter 2, even very simple detectors, such as tests for z-scores (or other univariate tests for extreme values), if performed on multiple columns, leave the question of how to best combine the scores to create an overall score for each record. For example, in one row (with four features), there may be values, after z-score scaling, of 4.1, 4.2, 3.3, 3.5, while another row has 15.1, 0.8, 0.3, 1.1. The first row has unusual values in all four features (z-scores over about 3.0 can be considered fairly high), while the second row has an extreme value in the first feature (with a z-score of 15.1) but quite typical values in the other features (with z-scores close to 0.0 or 1.0). When examining this, we need to ask, for the current project, which record should be scored highest overall? Much of this relates to how much we want the score of 15.1 to dominate.

When working with multiple detectors, as opposed to a single detector run on each feature, the issues are similar but a bit different. If we instead assume the four scores given to each row are given by four different (multivariate) detectors, then the 15.1 may be suspected to be an errant value, as the other three detectors gave the same record scores reflecting an inlier. It also may be that the first detector identified a legitimate anomaly the others missed; both are possible. But where we use a single test (such as z-score) on every feature, this is not a possibility—we know the extreme score is as legitimate as any other score; the question is simply how strongly to weight it. For the remainder of this section, we assume multiple detectors and so a situation where we do not know if all scores are reliable and so do not know if extreme scores should always be treated as legitimately extreme outliers, but the more detectors that also score this record high, the more confident we can be that it is truly an outlier.

How we combine the scores relates to the relative importance of false positives compared to false negatives and the two goals we may have for using an ensemble: creating more stable scores and detecting more outliers. In addition, we need to consider how much trust should be given to any one detector. In this example, how confident would we be, if a single detector produced a score such as 15.1 (where most detectors scored the same row close to 0.0), that this should be given a high score overall? As with much of outlier detection, there is no definitive answer generally, but there will be a solution that best suits your project.

If the concern is minimizing false positives (we do not wish to flag anything that is not very likely an outlier), then there are a few approaches we can take:

- We may consider only records that are scored extremely high by at least one detector, with the idea that any rows given extreme scores may not be as outlier-ish as the scores suggest but are very likely at least outliers. In this case, we would flag only the second row, which has one score of 15.1, though the other scores for that row are low.

- We may consider only records that are scored at least moderately high by many detectors, with the idea that it is unlikely many detectors would incorrectly score an inlier as an outlier. In this case, we would flag only the first record, which is given high scores by all four detectors.

- We may consider either case but such that if few detectors gave it a high score, they must be very high, and if its highest scores are not exceptionally high, it must be given a high score by many detectors.

If the concern is instead minimizing missing any outliers, we would likely flag any records given a moderately high score by at least one detector. In that case, we would flag both rows. However, we are likely still concerned that the scores are well ranked, as it may be that there are limited resources to investigate each outlier. The risk is that if we flag too many records and they are not well ranked, the most significant may be lost. To score the records well we have to balance the same two approaches we have to minimize false positives (relying on very high scores and relying on consensus). However, we will do so in possibly a different way if missing outliers is more of a concern, likely giving more emphasis to the high scores produced by a small number of detectors. It may be, though, that we would actually use a similar means to combine the scores in both cases and simply use different thresholds on the final scores to balance the concerns of false positives and false negatives.

The two clearest, and most used, approaches to combine the scores are both quite simple: to take the mean and the maximum, which we look at closer next.

14.6.1 *Mean vs. maximum*

Consider the scores produced by four detectors (D1, D2, D3, and D4) as in table 14.1. Here the first two records are the example we saw earlier, along with three other rows. In some cases, we see some low scores, while others, such as rows 1 and 3, have consistently high scores. Using the mean, row 3 would get the highest final score, and if using max, row 2 would get the highest final score. Note as well that with row 2, though it received only one high score, as that score is very high, the mean of its four scores is also quite high. This is not the case using the median, also shown in table 14.1.

Table 14.1 Scores given by a set of four detectors and various options for the final scores

Row	D1	D2	D3	D4	Mean	Max	Median
1	4.1	4.2	3.3	3.5	3.8	4.2	3.8
2	15.1	0.8	0.3	1.1	4.3	15.1	0.9
3	6.5	6.4	6.6	11.1	7.6	11.1	6.6
4	2.1	1.3	1.7	0.4	1.4	2.1	1.5
5	5.4	4.3	0.8	0.2	2.7	5.4	2.6

Using the maximum value relies on a single detector, which can be risky, though less so if we are confident in each detector used. Using the mean is somewhat safer but does average in the scores from detectors that considered the record to be an inlier—for example the scores of 0.8 and 0.2 given to row 5. Using the median has this weakness as well. Using the mean also invites bias where the detectors are correlated, essentially weighting some outlier detection approaches more highly than others. This is not a problem using the maximum.

Choosing the best method to combine the scores can be found by trying to match a pseudo-ground truth, by achieving the best test results with synthetic data, or simply by examining scenarios such as in table 14.1 and making a judgment call as to what is the best approach for the task at hand. There are also some general guidelines we can look at, which won't always apply but can be useful, specified in terms of how the ensembles are formed. If the ensemble is based on different model types or different preprocessing, using either mean or max may be valid. Other methods of creating ensembles are as follows:

- If ensembling based on using different subspaces of features, in most cases we would prefer using maximum. The idea of checking many subspaces is that some will expose outliers while others will not. We wish to identify the subspaces, if there are any, that have the highest outlier scores; the other subspaces that do not identify outliers are not relevant and should not be averaged into the final scores.
- If ensembling based on varying the parameters, we may use either mean or max but more likely the mean, as was shown in chapter 8. The idea here is to use many parameter values and to average these together to smooth out the effects of using less ideal parameters in some cases. We wish to down-weight any extreme scores that are found only when using some parameters, as these are possibly spurious. The strongest outliers are likely those that are scored high given multiple parameter settings and not those for only a single setting.
- If ensembling based on different samples of rows, we would likely use the mean. In this case, ideally all detectors would give each row the same score or nearly.

There may be some variation (due to quirks in the data that appear in only some subsets), which we would wish to smooth out, and this is best done using the mean function.

Besides using the mean or max, other combining methods may be preferable. For example, row 5 in table 14.1 has two very high scores, which is likely more reliable than a single high score and so should possibly be given a higher score than would be given using mean or max (or median). We next look at some alternatives that better consider cases such as this.

14.6.2 *PyOD ensembling methods*

We look here at the options provided by PyOD's combination module, which supports the following methods:

- Mean
- Median
- Max
- Majority vote
- Average of maximum
- Maximum of average

Most of these are straightforward, other than the last two, which warrant some explanation. Average of maximum works by dividing the detectors into subgroups, taking the maximum score within each subgroup, and then taking the average of these. Maximum of average works similarly, dividing the detectors into subgroups, taking the average of each, and then taking the maximum of these. In both cases we generate final scores that provide a compromise between using the mean and the maximum. As with any system for combining, this requires the scores first be scaled. More information about these can be found at https://github.com/yzhao062/combo. The package may be installed with

```
pip install combo
```

In listing 14.12, we assume listing 14.2 has been executed and this is executed next. We first scale the scores, in this case using Robust Scaler. We then use the Average of Maximum (aom) method to create a final score for each record, using subgroups of size two.

Listing 14.12 Using PyOD combination to combine models

```
from sklearn.preprocessing import RobustScaler
from pyod.models.combination import aom

scores_cols = list(set(scores_df.columns) - set(df.columns))
scores_cols = [x for x in scores_cols if 'Scores' in x]
for col_name in scores_cols:                              ◁─── Scales the scores
    scaler = RobustScaler()
    scores_df[col_name] = RobustScaler().fit_transform(
```

```
            scores_df[col_name].values.reshape(-1, 1)).reshape(1, -1)[0]

comb_by_aom = aom(scores_df[scores_cols], 2)

sns.histplot(comb_by_aom)
plt.show()
```

Gets the combined scores

The final scores using this are shown in figure 14.8.

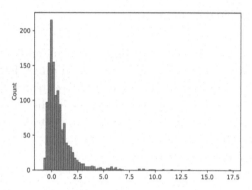

Figure 14.8   Distribution of final scores using the aom method

14.6.3   *Variations of mean and maximum*

We look here at some additional methods to combine the scores of multiple detectors. Each of these is a simple formula, but more complex formulas or rules (with IF-ELSE logic) may be used as well, and it can be useful to incorporate, where PyOD detectors are used, the confidence scores produced by these, as shown in chapter 6. For each of these, we assume we have a set of scores in the `scores_df` dataframe and that these have been scaled in some manner.

90TH PERCENTILE OF THE SCORES

Using the 90th percentile (or some such high percentile) is similar to using the maximum but is more robust, as it is not determined by a single detector. If we have, say, 100 detectors, this uses the 10th-highest score given to each record. In the example in table 14.1, there are only four detectors, so we could take, instead, the 75th percentile, which is the second-highest score received by the record. Getting a percentile across scores may be done with code such as

```
scores_df['perc_90'] = scores_df[scores_cols].quantile(0.90, axis=1)
```

25TH PERCENTILE OF THE SCORES

Using a low percentile, such as the 25th, has a similar effect as using the mean or using the median (50th percentile): for any record to be given a high final score, it must be scored high by a significant number of detectors, though it is not necessary that every detector scored the records highly.

It's possible to set the percentile used to any value that best balances the two goals of ensembles for the current project. The lower the percentile used, the more emphasis put on consensus; the higher the percentile, the more emphasis on at least a small number of detectors scoring the record particularly high. It is, however, not recommended to use a very low percentile. If we're using many detectors, almost no records, even strong outliers, will be scored high by every detector, and the scores given by detectors that did not identify anything anomalous in the records can be somewhat arbitrary. Using a very low percentile will tend to focus on these more arbitrary scores, while we normally wish to minimize their effect on the final scores.

MEAN OF THE TOP N DETECTORS

The next few approaches we look at are variations on using the mean, and each tries to reduce the influence of detectors that consider the row to be an inlier. The mean of the top n is similar to using a percentile but incorporates all scores from the top n detectors, as opposed to taking only the nth highest. In table 14.1, where there are four detectors, we may take, for example, the mean of the top two detectors, which will ensure any rows must either be scored highly by at least two or have a very high score in at least one detector. An example, using the mean of the top three is

```
import statistics

def get_mean_top_n(x, n):
  return statistics.mean(sorted(x)[-n:])

scores_df['mean_top_three'] = \
  scores_df[scores_cols].apply(get_mean_top_n, n=3, axis=1)
```

This can still be affected by a single detector, which may or may not be desirable. If not, capping the scores at a certain limit before taking the mean may be preferable.

MEAN, WITH ALL SCORES BELOW A THRESHOLD SET TO ZERO

The approach here—setting all scores below a given threshold to zero—is similar to some methods to calculate the correlation between detectors shown in chapter 8. To choose the threshold, we can use PyThresh or simply set a threshold based on our judgment. We then set all scores below this to zero, and take the mean of the remaining scores.

When doing this, for each row examined, if some detectors consider the row to be an outlier, we will use their specific scores, and if some detectors consider the row to be an inlier, we do not. We then take the mean over all detectors, so the final scores are affected largely by how many detectors considered the row an outlier, but the specific scores they gave are also relevant. Given this, the initial distributions of scores are relevant, in that these determine where the threshold is placed, but once this is used and lower values are set to zero, it is only the distribution of scores above this point that are relevant.

An example of keeping all scores (after z-score scaling) above 3.0 is

```
import statistics

def get_mean_over_t(x, t):
```

```
    return statistics.mean([s if s >= t else 0 for s in x])

scores_df['mean_over_2'] = \
    scores_df[scores_cols].apply(get_mean_over_t, t=3.0, axis=1)
```

MEAN OF SQUARED SCORES

It can be a bit crude to simply set a single threshold, with everything above remaining as is and everything below set to zero. Ideally, this would be done more smoothly, without a single threshold, where lower scores count for less and higher scores for progressively more. This can be done by using the squares of the scores and taking the mean of these. This way high scores count more toward the final score and low scores less, but all are included, weighted by the score itself. The general idea may be applied using other powers as well, for example using a power of 3 to further increase the importance of higher scores or 1.5 to reduce this.

Tables 14.2 and 14.3 show some examples of possible final scores using various means to combine the scores for the five rows from the four detectors. Looking at this, it may be possible to assess what would be most sensible for your project, potentially one of these or possibly another function. In this example, the highest scores still go to row 2 or row 3, though other rows are in some cases the second-highest scored. For example, row 1 gets the second-highest score using the 25th percentile, and row 5 does if using the 75th percentile or Mean of Top 2.

Table 14.2 Additional options for the final scores

Row	D1	D2	D3	D4	25th Percentile	75th Percentile	Mean of top 2	Mean of top 3
1	4.1	4.2	3.3	3.5	3.5	4.1	4.15	3.9
2	15.1	0.8	0.3	1.1	0.8	1.1	8.1	5.7
3	6.5	6.4	6.6	11.1	6.5	6.6	8.85	8.0
4	2.1	1.3	1.7	0.4	1.3	1.7	1.9	1.7
5	5.4	4.3	0.8	0.2	0.8	4.3	4.85	3.5

Table 14.3 provides additional examples for the same five rows.

Table 14.3 Additional options for the final scores

Row	D1	D2	D3	D4	Mean of squared scores	Mean of cubed scores	Mean with values below 3.0 set to 0.0
1	4.1	4.2	3.3	3.5	14.40	55.45	3.78
2	15.1	0.8	0.3	1.1	57.49	861.20	3.78
3	6.5	6.4	6.6	11.1	62.49	547.97	7.65
4	2.1	1.3	1.7	0.4	2.29	4.11	0.0
5	5.4	4.3	0.8	0.2	12.08	59.37	2.42

14.6.4 *Weighting based on accuracy*

Another simple method to combine the scores is to create a weighted average over the
scores, weighted by the overall accuracy of each detector (gauged by using synthetic
data or comparing the scores to pseudo-ground truth labels). An example is shown
in listing 14.13. Here we train and test all six detectors and then assess the accuracy of
each, assuming the doped records are outliers and the real records are not. To keep
the example simple, this creates a single, very simple set of synthetic data, but more
extensive testing would be used in practice. As covered in chapter 11, the doped data
should be created in a way to consistently be records we would be interested in flagging
and such that they cover a wide range of such outliers.

One benefit of this approach is it can remove the need to select the best detectors,
as we simply use all the detectors, weighting each by its overall accuracy. It is possible,
though, to remove any detectors that would receive a very low weight in any case.

Listing 14.13 **Creating an ensemble based on a weighted average**

```python
from sklearn.metrics import roc_auc_score

doped_df = df.sample(n=50)                          # Creates a set of doped data that may
for i in doped_df.index:                            # be used to assess the detectors
    row = doped_df.loc[i]
    col_name = np.random.choice(doped_df.columns)
    doped_df.loc[i, col_name] = doped_df.loc[i, col_name] * -0.9
df['Doped'] = 0
doped_df['Doped'] = 1
full_df = pd.concat([df, doped_df])
full_df = full_df.reset_index(drop=True)
doped_df.head()

scores_df = pd.DataFrame()

np.random.seed(1)
                                                    # Makes predictions
                                                    # using each detector
det_if = IsolationForest()
det_if.fit(full_df)
scores_df['IF Scores'] = (-1)*det_if.score_samples(full_df)

det_lof = LocalOutlierFactor()
det_lof.fit(full_df)
scores_df['LOF Scores'] = (-1)*det_lof.negative_outlier_factor_

det_ee = EllipticEnvelope()
det_ee.fit(full_df)
scores_df['EE Scores'] = (-1)*det_ee.score_samples(full_df)

det_ocsvm = OneClassSVM()
det_ocsvm.fit(full_df)
scores_df['OCSVM Scores'] = (-1)*det_ocsvm.score_samples(full_df)

det_ns = NearestSampleOutlierDetector()
det_ns.fit(full_df)
```

```
scores_df['Nearest Samples Scores'] = det_ns.decision_function(full_df)

det_radius = RadiusOutlierDetector()
scores_df['Radius Scores'] = det_radius.fit_predict(full_df, radius=4.0)

total_accuracy = 0                          ◄──── Measures the accuracy
accuracy_dict = {}                                 of each detector
for col_name in scores_df.columns:
    auroc = roc_auc_score(full_df['Doped'], scores_df[col_name])
    accuracy_dict[col_name] = auroc
    total_accuracy += auroc

accuracy_dict = {x: accuracy_dict[x]/total_accuracy for x in accuracy_dict}

mod_scores_df = pd.DataFrame()              ◄──── Creates another dataframe with the scores
for col_name in scores_df:                         scaled by the accuracy of each detector
    scaler = RobustScaler()
    mod_scores_df[col_name] = scaler.fit_transform(
    scores_df[col_name].values.reshape(-1, 1)).reshape(1, -1)[0]
    mod_scores_df[col_name] = \
      mod_scores_df[col_name] * accuracy_dict[col_name]
mod_scores_df['Score'] = mod_scores_df.mean(axis=1)
```

Figure 14.9 compares the scores given by the Isolation Forest and by the Nearest Samples detector to the final scores. In both cases, we can see there is a strong correlation but also a number of records that are given high final scores, but not by these detectors, likely due to being outliers with respect to other detection algorithms.

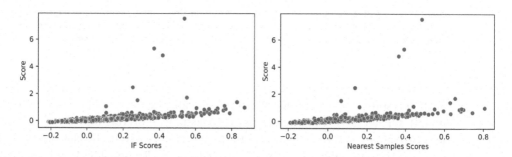

Figure 14.9   Plotting the IF and Nearest Samples scores against the final scores

14.6.5 Stacked ensembles

One deficit of weighting based on accuracy is it does not consider the correlations between the detectors. If there are multiple detectors that are very accurate but almost the same, they will both be given large weights, and they will likely have a combined importance higher than is appropriate. Another deficit of weighted averages is that they look only at the overall accuracy of the detectors and do not learn where some can be strong in certain cases and weak in others.

Another solution is to create what's called a stacked ensemble (see figure 14.10), which uses a classifier to determine how best to combine the scores for a final score. The term "stacking" is used more with prediction problems, where the outputs of multiple predictors are given to another predictor to determine how best to combine their results. The same can be done with outlier detection, where a classifier learns how best to combine the results of many outlier detectors. If a ground truth can be provided, we can train a classifier, which will learn how to best combine the scores from multiple detectors into a binary prediction. With most binary classifiers, a probability for the positive class can also be calculated, which may then be used as an outlier score.

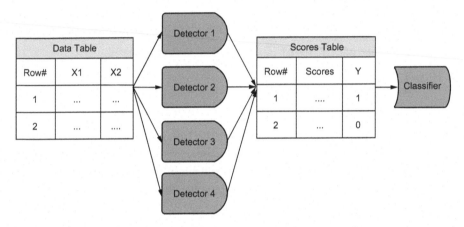

Figure 14.10   A stacked ensemble. This works by first fitting a set of detectors to a given dataset. Each detector will then create an outlier score for each row, and these may be saved to another table. This table, along with a ground truth label, will then be used to train a classifier.

An example is given in listing 14.14. This uses a Random Forest classifier, but any classifier that is sufficiently accurate will work (this can be confirmed by cross-validating the model). Once this is done, we can use the classifier to predict outliers using the classifier's probability as the outlier score. In this example, we train the classifier only on the detector scores but including the original features is also possible. In this case, we used synthetic data, but pseudo labels as created earlier in this chapter may also be used.

Listing 14.14   Creating a stacked ensemble

```
from sklearn.ensemble import RandomForestClassifier

clf = RandomForestClassifier()
clf.fit(scores_df, full_df['Doped'])
outlier_scores = clf.predict_proba(scores_df)
```

Stacking can learn from the data how much weight to give to cases where only a minority of the detectors scored certain records highly and also handles better where detectors are correlated. It does, however, rely on having good, and representative, examples of both classes. Without this, the classifier may learn to optimize for cases that are unrepresentative of real data.

The major concern, though, is that classifiers can learn only to predict well for data similar to what they have been trained on. This is always a limitation of classifiers—they cannot reliably generalize well to data that is unlike data they have seen, and the very nature of outlier detection is handling data that is unlike other data. If outliers are found that are completely novel, even though some of the detectors in the ensemble may recognize this, it's possible the classifier will assign these a low probability of being an outlier. It is, given this, useful to complement this method of combining scores with other methods covered previously to ensure that any records that are given a sufficiently high score by sufficiently many detectors are still flagged. Stacking in this way will, though, tend to give accurate scores where it is able to recognize the outliers. Often this can be safer after the system has run for some time and we are more aware of the types of outliers we can expect to encounter. We look further at this approach in the next chapter, where labeled data may be used.

This chapter covered a range of methods to select detectors, scale their scores, and combine scores, which will likely cover your needs for most projects, but it hopefully also provided you with the background to look into other schemes where necessary for other projects.

Summary

- Each outlier detector identifies only specific types of outliers, though we typically wish to find many types of outliers.
- Quite often in outlier detection it is best to use, not a single, but multiple outlier detectors.
- Using multiple detectors allows us to have more stable scores than relying on a single detector, as well as to detect more outliers.
- To create an effective ensemble, we need to choose a subset of the detectors that were tested.
- It is also necessary to put the scores from each detector on the same scale.
- We may also wish to adjust the distribution of scores for each detector. In some cases, the distributions have meaning and we wish to preserve these, while in other cases it is best to apply the same distribution to the scores of all detectors.
- Once we have a set of detectors selected and have scaled their scores such that they are comparable, we must create a single final score for each record.
- Combining the scores of multiple detectors may be done using the mean, maximum, or other function of the scores produced by each detector.
- It is also possible to combine the scores using a weighted average based on the accuracy of each detector or using a classifier, forming a stacked ensemble.
- Creating an ensemble is often iterative, and we may loop through this process multiple times.

Working with outlier detection predictions

This chapter covers

- Processing the output produced by outlier detection systems
- Improving outlier detection systems over time
- Taking advantage of labeled data to create more effective ensembles

Once outlier detection systems are put in production, they will begin to identify outliers. If run on a large body of data or if run over a long period of time, they may flag a very large number of outliers, even if this is only a small fraction of the total data examined. It's usually necessary to examine the output, not only to investigate the outliers found, but also to ensure that the system is working well (particularly for new systems, but even for established systems, which may degrade in effectiveness over time). It's important that both of these may be done efficiently.

In addition, where the outlier detection system tends to repeatedly identify certain types of outliers (for example, abuse of meal allowances when examining staff expenses, unusually high temperature readings in industrial equipment, specific attack signatures in networks, or overbilling in sales records), it's useful to be able to track these over time. This allows us to identify, for example, where they are becoming more common (which may be a concern) or the opposite, reducing in frequency (which may be due to a diminished ability of the outlier detection system to detect these, or masking effects from the presence of other outliers). The main concern, though, is usually the ability to efficiently investigate the outliers that were flagged.

To get to this point, we need to understand the outliers, and a large portion of this is categorizing them. For example, working with financial data, we may classify the outliers as data artifacts, staff errors, inefficiencies, inconsistencies, and fraud, and we will likely wish to subdivide each of these into more specific categories as well. Fraud may include round-tripping, overordering, bogus staff, bogus suppliers, and any other cases that have been, or reasonably may be, seen. Once we establish the categories and are able to label the outliers found, we are better able to ensure the system is working well, investigate outliers, and track the appearance of outliers over time. We will look at several other benefits in this chapter as well. To understand more fully the ideas related to following up with the outliers found, let's consider some of the most common types of processes that may be used with outlier detection:

- *The flagged items will be sent to a team for follow-up.* The system simply attempts to identify a set of items for follow-up such that the most relevant items are scored highest. The team will then examine as many as time allows. Here it is often most important that the outlier scores are well ranked in terms of their relevance. In other cases, if many similar outliers can be grouped together and processed in bulk, it may be more important to cover a broad range of the outliers identified in the data.

- *The data is examined by the outlier detection system in real time, and strong outliers are immediately turned into alerts and sent to a team.* In this case, it is important to send out relevant alerts quickly and with sufficient information to understand the anomalies. This includes the context: what is normal, the recent history, and so on. It is also important to not overreport, as people may learn to ignore the alerts. Here the system needs to be able to estimate the importance of the outliers found and estimate their similarity to the outliers associated with recent alerts (to avoid multiple alerts for the same issues). The team will also likely need to be able to assess these outliers quickly, which requires understanding why they were flagged.

- *The flagged items are acted on automatically and immediately without human intervention.* For example, the system may automatically shut down access to a web service for a user or stop an assembly line. A team will generally then investigate these. There may be an immediate investigation to determine if there is a real issue, as well as a more thorough investigation later. The initial investigation needs to be very efficient, which requires a clear understanding of the anomalies associated with the flagged items.

- *The results are used by a downstream machine learning task, such as training a regression or classification model or recommendation system, or for clustering.* Where outlier detection is used as a step within larger machine learning processes, it is possible to tune the process experimentally. In this case, it is not relevant if the items flagged would be considered outliers by a person evaluating them—only if the downstream process functions measurably better where the outliers are removed.

In all cases, other than the last, there is some follow-up, even if some time after the outliers are flagged. In some cases, a team will follow up with all high-scored records and, in other cases, only as many as there is time to check. As indicated, the team will wish to both investigate the outliers and check that the records being flagged are, in fact, largely relevant outliers (i.e., check if the system itself is running well). We also wish to check, as much as time allows, the opposite: that the records not being flagged are not outliers. Finding useful outliers that were missed can be difficult, but we can check the cases where missed outliers are most likely:

- *Where records are given moderately high scores but under the threshold for items that are followed up.*
- *Where records are given a high score by one or more detectors in an ensemble but do not receive a high final score.* This can be checked using either the detectors in the current ensemble or by other detectors that are used strictly for testing.

Checking the output in this way, we can test if the system is working well and get a good sense of what tends to be flagged most often. We can then start to identify how we want to categorize the outliers. Efficiently following up with the outliers, and efficiently monitoring the system, hinges on our ability to sort the outliers found into specific categories. This will almost always require some hand-labeling of the data. Often this requires little additional work, though, as the outliers are followed up for investigation in any case. The trick may simply be to label any items investigated in a clear and consistent manner and to reliably store these labels (along with the flagged records) over time. Once we have these labels, they have several purposes, particularly

- More efficiently investigating flagged outliers.
- Filtering out outliers that are not necessary to investigate.
- Tracking the appearance of each type of outlier over time.
- More effectively testing changes to the outlier detection system to ensure any modifications we make do not affect it negatively.
- Creating more powerful ensembles than we can without this labeled data. We saw this in chapter 14 and will look further at this here.
- Sending more appropriate and effective alerts.
- Developing rules and classifiers that may become part of the outlier detection system, supplementing the detectors used.

Once we have a good collection of labeled data, we can create a system to automatically sort subsequently flagged outliers. Categorizing the flagged outliers gives us a starting point to investigate the outliers and allows us to group similar outliers together so that they may be investigated more efficiently in bulk. Knowing the counts for the different categories of outliers is also useful information that may help the investigation. For example, if an outlier relates to a website user leaving unusually negative product reviews, it may be informative to know how many similar outliers there are for this user account and how many outliers of this type there are generally. It may help determine, for example, if this is malicious or coordinated with other users, or merely represents negative reviews. If the outlier is related to overpurchasing goods from certain suppliers, it is, again, useful to know how common this is. This gives a sense of how relevant the outlier is and may point to sources of the anomaly. As covered in chapter 1, fraud tends to escalate over time, so this is useful to specifically watch for.

A large benefit of categorizing outliers is the ability to filter out outliers that do not require follow-up. There are a couple of common scenarios where the outlier detection system may, even after re-tuning some number of times, continue to flag outliers that are known to be unnecessary to investigate. One is where there is no practical way found to set the system to not flag these that won't also result in it missing other outliers that are of interest. Another is where we do not need to investigate these outliers (it may be that they have been investigated already and are well understood) but we do wish to track their appearance over time. In these cases, it is useful to be able to filter these out from consideration for investigating and direct our time to other anomalies. An example may be where sensors in an industrial system detect vibration in a certain piece of machinery. If the readings are unusual but have been seen before and are known to not indicate an immediate problem, we may wish to track the appearance of this pattern but do not need to investigate each occurrence.

Considering where the detection of outliers triggers automatic actions (such as alerts or shutting down systems), knowing the type of outlier is helpful. It can help reduce overalerting: if two outliers are known to be of different types, it is more likely reasonable to send alerts for both. And it is easier to gauge the significance of the outlier. The outlier scores indicate how statistically unusual the record is, not how relevant, which is better determined by considering both this score and the type of outlier. For example, consider where outlier detection is part of monitoring an e-commerce website and a very low price was entered in error, resulting in lost income. The outlier detection system may detect this, possibly with checks for unusual prices or for unusually high sales. The system may also detect at the same time very unusual visitor navigation of the site. Unusual visitor behavior may suggest, for example, the presence of bots and may be worth investigating, but the pricing error is likely more relevant and should be investigated first, even if the user behavior is statistically more unusual.

Another important purpose of categorizing the flagged outliers, as covered in chapter 4, is to create rules and classifiers that are able to form part of the outlier detection system. It's common to rely heavily on outlier detection when monitoring systems are first put in place and then over time develop rules and classifiers to perform the bulk of the work (detecting the most common and most relevant specific outliers), with outlier detectors being used only to catch any outliers missed by these. As we can develop more rules and classifiers, which capture increasingly more of the records that are of interest, we will have a more reliable and interpretable system. We will, though, likely always have some statistical outliers. These will be progressively less common and harder to explain but likely more interesting.

We look in more depth in the remainder of this chapter at categorizing the flagged outliers, creating more effective outlier detection systems using a technique called *semisupervised learning*, and setting up a system (based on a method called *regression testing*) to ensure the system can improve in accuracy over time.

15.1 *Hand-labeling output*

Before we take a look at how we can label (i.e., categorize) the flagged outliers, we'll take a quick look at the labels themselves. While we should, at minimum, label each record examined as being of interest or not, it is much preferable to assign each record both (1) a more specific label indicating the type of outlier (as in the previous example for financial data, possibly indicating data entry error, bogus staff, bogus suppliers, and likely dozens of other categories), and (2) a score indicating how important the outlier is to flag. We look at both of these but first consider quickly the case where only binary labels are produced during hand-labeling. This is less useful but may be the most practical in some projects.

If binary labels are used, what is labeled is not if the records are statistically unusual but if they are relevant to your specific project; outlier detection is not an end in itself but simply a means to find the records that are useful. This will usually require the work of both the data scientists and the domain experts involved. Note that we should be careful in this regard: a record may be investigated and found to be a nonissue, but this does not indicate that we wish for the system to no longer flag similar records (or to filter them out from investigation). Consider the example of a financial journal entry entered by an unusually senior staff in chapter 13. If this were investigated and found to be a nonissue, we likely would still wish to flag similar records in the future, as they could still easily be inappropriate and worth investigating.

15.1.1 *Hand-labeling specific types of outliers*

As described previously, it's best to use specific labels to define each type of outlier, at least for the outliers that are frequently recurring and for the most relevant. When investigating the outliers, this will require making a judgment as to which type of outlier they are (or possibly which *types*—some may be in multiple categories and should receive multiple labels). For the labels to be useful, they need to be well defined and applied consistently. For example, with a financial transaction entered by an unusually senior staff, there may be a category for "unusual or inappropriate staff for transaction."

Records that are found to not be of interest (and merely statistically unusual) can be labeled as well—again, in this case, as specifically as is practical. For example, with sales data there may be records flagged as outliers due to unusual combinations of items sold and time of day. It may be, after investigating some occurrences of this, that we can determine these are not interesting and are simply rare events due to random chance. We can create a category for, say, "rare time of day for item sold." Going forward, it may be useful to tune the models (so we can deemphasize these or, ideally, not flag them at all) or to filter out these outliers as not requiring investigation.

15.1.2 Hand-scoring the outliers

As well as labeling each examined record with a label related to the type of outlier, it is preferable to also label each with a score. These would indicate not how statistically unusual the outliers are (which is still best determined by the detectors) but the significance of the outliers. For all the reasons we have for labeling data (tracking outliers over time, sorting flagged outliers for investigation, re-tuning the system, and so on), it is preferable to understand which records are most of interest and which are of some interest but less pressing. It allows us, for example, to tune the system such that, as much as can be achieved, the high-importance outliers receive higher scores than the medium-importance ones, which receive higher scores than those with low importance. And, in production, where outliers are flagged but time is limited, it will be easier to determine which outliers we should focus our investigation efforts on. Another application of these scores is in sending alerts: if we can learn to estimate the relevance of each outlier detected, we can more appropriately send alerts (adjusting the frequency sent, urgency indicated, set of recipients, and so on).

Applying numeric scores will not likely be practical, and it may be more realistic to use labels such as low, medium, and high importance. Even with these, it will be necessary to define these precisely for the flagged outliers to be labeled consistently, but where this can be done, it is quite valuable.

15.2 Examining the flagged outliers

Now that we have a sense of the properties of the labels we wish to apply to the outliers, we'll look more closely at determining what the specific labels are for the dataset at hand and applying these labels to each outlier.

Determining the relevant categories requires understanding what the anomalies in each flagged outlier are, though in some cases it may not be obvious on inspection why they were flagged. In this section, we will look at a few methods to help us understand the flagged results where this is not clear. Once the outliers are understood, much of the remaining work analyzing them is determining which anomalies appear to be flagged repeatedly and which are relevant for the current project.

With an understanding of what is flagged frequently (if anything—it may be that all outliers found are distinct from each other, but this is actually not too common), we can next establish a set of categories that we wish to sort the flagged outliers into. This will likely evolve and expand over time, but we can try to start with a simple, but useful, set of categories. We wish to find the categories that are most useful to support: investigations, tracking over time, re-tuning, and the other purposes listed previously. To support investigations well, for example, the categories should be clear to the team investigating the outliers, and the outliers in the category should be reasonably consistent. If a set of outliers from a collection of sensor readings are labeled as "readings unusually low and flat over time" and "readings unusually dissimilar to other sensors at the same time," investigators will know to look first for failing sensors.

We may then develop a system (likely a set of coded rules, but quite possibly classifiers) to automate sorting the flagged outliers, as well as possible, into these categories. This is with the understanding that many, particularly novel, outliers will not fit into any category and will be left unlabeled unless labeled by hand. Even once a set of tools is created to sort the flagged outliers into categories, it will nevertheless usually remain necessary to hand-label some outliers or at least confirm if the tools categorized them properly. There will likely be some categories that the tools do not yet support, and the categorization cannot always be done completely correctly.

Many of the benefits of labeling the outliers (e.g., tracking categories of outliers over time, re-tuning the system) can be done well as long as we apply the labels consistently, even if this is done strictly manually and we do not have tools to do this automatically. However, once we do have these tools, we may be able to label far more outliers than can be labeled by hand, and processing the outliers found can usually be much more efficient.

To start with an example, in listing 15.1 we read in the KDD Cup dataset and run an Isolation Forest (IF) on this data. We will, in the next few sections, look at ways to try to create categories to describe the outliers the IF detects, specifically manual inspection, using interpretable detectors and examining subspaces of features. We later look at systems to automate sorting the outliers into these categories.

Listing 15.1 Collecting data and evaluating with IF

```
import numpy as np
import pandas as pd
from sklearn.datasets import fetch_kddcup99
from sklearn.preprocessing import OrdinalEncoder
from pyod.models.iforest import IForest

np.random.seed(0)

X, y = fetch_kddcup99(subset="SA", percent10=True, random_state=42,    ◄── Collects the data
                      return_X_y=True, as_frame=True)
y = (y != b"normal.").astype(np.int32)
df = pd.DataFrame(OrdinalEncoder().fit_transform(X), columns=X.columns)
orig_feats = X.columns
                                                    Uses IF to generate
clf_if = IForest()                                  the outlier scores
clf_if.fit(df[orig_feats])           ◄──
df['IF Scores'] = clf_if.decision_scores_
```

15.2.1 *Manual inspection of the outliers*

Determining the categories used may be done in several ways, including taking advantage of any interpretable detectors or post hoc explanations, but it likely involves manually inspecting the flagged outliers. This is, in fact, an exploratory process, similar to what may be done with the original data prior to running any outlier detection, described in chapter 4. We are looking to identify patterns in the outliers. We may use clustering, frequent item set mining, association rules, or simply, as in this example, examining the output. Here we are looking for things that occur regularly in the flagged outliers but are rare in the majority of the data.

As an example of identifying categories, we start by looking at some of the records scored highest by the Isolation Forest. This can be done simply by sorting by the IF Scores column and viewing the last several rows. Looking at these rows, we may notice the features relating to error rates seem to be particularly high. Table 15.1 shows some top-scored rows with a few columns related to error rates.

Table 15.1   Sample of highly scored records from the KDD Cup dataset

Row	dst host serror rate	dst host srv serror rate	dst host rerror rate
99,649	27	0	69
100,246	23	0	76
65,050	5	8	55

These may be among the more important features, and these rows appear to have unusual values, at least in a univariate sense. Creating one or more categories related to high error rates may be useful. Examining other features in this way will likely be useful as well. By simply viewing the top-scored records, it is possible to find a simple explanation such as this, but more complex patterns may also be found, spanning multiple features.

15.2.2   *Executing interpretable detectors*

It may also be possible to reproduce some of the results found by the Isolation Forest using interpretable detectors. For this, we can begin with simple univariate tests, such as z-score, interquartile range, interdecile range, median absolute deviation, and others described in chapter 2, or with empirical cumulative distribution function (ECOD), copula-based outlier detection (COPOD), and Bayesian Histogram-based Anomaly Detection (BHAD), described in chapters 6 and 13. These will explain well the flagged outliers that can be understood in terms of extreme values. Listing 15.2 shows an example where we use an ECOD detector to evaluate the same rows that were evaluated by the Isolation Forest. In this case, the scores relate well, and explanations from the ECOD detector can be taken as being often at least partial explanations of the Isolation Forest scores.

Listing 15.2   Executing ECOD on the KDD Cup dataset

```
import matplotlib.pyplot as plt
import seaborn as sns
from pyod.models.ecod import ECOD

clf_ecod = ECOD()
```

```
clf_ecod.fit(df[orig_feats])
df['ECOD Scores'] = clf_ecod.decision_scores_

sns.scatterplot(data=df, x='IF Scores', y='ECOD Scores')
plt.show()
```

The relationship between the IF and ECOD scores is shown in figure 15.1. Though they are well correlated, the IF is likely picking up multivariate anomalies that ECOD will miss. However, we know the explanations provided by ECOD will at least partially explain many outliers.

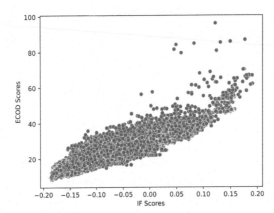

Figure 15.1   The relationship between the IF and ECOD scores on the KDD Cup data. The scores are well correlated, though not perfectly.

Given that ECOD scores can be useful to understand the outliers identified by the IF, we can take advantage of ECOD's explainability with code such as

```
fig, ax = plt.subplots(figsize=(15, 4))
clf_ecod.explain_outlier(65050)
```

This is run on row 65,050, which is the row given the highest score by the Isolation Forest. This produces the plot shown in figure 15.2, which indicates the first and third features (duration and service) are the most anomalous features for this row; these are the features most outside of the cutoff band (as described in chapter 6). We may wish to create categories related to these or a single category related to their combination, depending on which makes the most sense for the current project.

Given that ECOD will miss any multivariate outliers that the Isolation Forest finds, it's also useful to use an interpretable multivariate detector, such as Real versus Fake, FPOF, association rules, or, as in listing 15.3, CountsOutlierDetector (COD, introduced in chapter 13; https://mng.bz/AaMp). In this example, we also have the COD explain the row given the highest IF score, 65,050. This assumes the code for CountsOutlier-Detector is included in the source or has been imported. We use the default settings in this example, which will search for outliers in subspaces up to six dimensions.

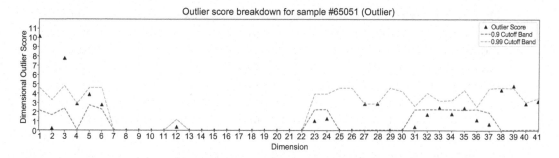

Figure 15.2 ECOD explanation of row 65050 of the KDD Cup dataset. This shows how anomalous each of the 41 features are for this row. Features 1 and 3 are the most unusual as measured by ECOD.

Listing 15.3 Comparing the results of COD with IF

```
det = CountsOutlierDetector()
results = det.fit_predict(df[orig_feats])
det.explain_row(65050)
```

This displays several plots. Like ECOD, it identifies some single features that have unusual values, including duration (at 2,349.0 s) and dst_host_srv_serror_rate (at 8.0). It also finds some unusual combinations of values, such as shown in figure 15.3, which presents the combination of values in dst_host_same_srv_rate and dst_host_srv_rerror_rate. In this case, neither of the values for these features are especially rare—only the combination. In this example, COD uses the default 7 bins per feature, which results in 49 bins per 2D space. The bin that row 65,050 is in for this 2D space has only 18 elements (for comparison, as shown in the right pane, the most common of the 49 bins has 72,135 rows).

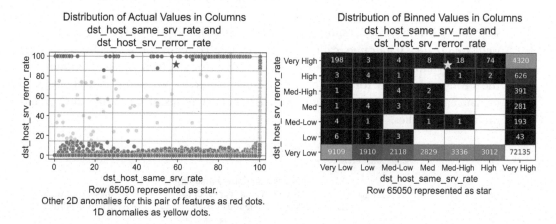

Figure 15.3 Example of an unusual pair of values detected by the COD for row 65,050, which is shown as a star. This is a combination that occurred only 18 times, though the values for both features are fairly common.

Here we are in effect using interpretable models as proxies of the actual models, similar to using classifiers as proxy models (described in chapter 13). But the purpose here is different. We are not trying to determine why the detectors scored records as they did but why the records are anomalous. These ideally will be the same, but this may not always be the case. In this case, ECOD and COD (and possibly other detectors) can explain why many of these rows are unusual, though possibly for reasons the Isolation Forest missed. And they may not identify all the anomalies in the records the IF found. Any anomalies found in this way will be interpretable and quite possibly worth investigating, but we do need to be mindful that there may be other anomalies with the flagged records as well.

15.2.3 *Examining subspaces of features*

To help us understand the anomalies found, it is often helpful to create many simpler versions of the detectors used, each using a small number of features. This will likely use 2D models or possibly models based on three or four features. Though more dimensions can also be used, the fewer dimensions, the more interpretable the results and the faster the process. If testing, for example, every 2D and 3D space, we can iterate through each unique pair and each unique triple of features and create a simple model using just those features. This is an approach similar to COD, though here we may use any detector on the subspaces (Isolation Forest in this example) and not necessarily a multidimensional histogram approach, as is used by COD.

The set of simple models created, even collectively, will likely not replicate the results exactly but may be sufficient to explain why many of the flagged records are unusual (the majority of anomalies can usually be explained with a small number of features) and can be a good starting point for investigation. With any records that cannot be explained well in this way, we know they have more complex anomalies, which is still informative.

In listing 15.4 we create a set of 2D versions of the Isolation Forest (similar code may be used to examine subspaces with three or more features). Doing this, it may be possible to discover a set of 2D subspaces that explain at least some of the flagged outliers well. We create a dataframe, called `scores_df`, that contains the scores from each 2D space. For simplicity, in this example we look only at the single 2D space that identified the strongest anomaly for each row. However, in practice we would typically seek to explain each outlier with not a single but a series of 2D spaces, at least where the row has multiple anomalies.

Listing 15.4 Creating 2D spaces to identify outliers

```
scores_df = pd.DataFrame()
col_map = {}
c = 0
for i_idx in range(len(orig_feats)):
    for j_idx in range(i_idx+1, len(orig_feats)):
```

Defines a dictionary mapping the columns in scores_df to the pairs of features used

Defines a counter for each pair of features

Loops through each pair of features

```
        col_name_i = orig_feats[i_idx]
        col_name_j = orig_feats[j_idx]
        clf = IForest()                                    ◄─── Creates an IF for the
        clf.fit(df[[col_name_i, col_name_j]])                   current two features
        scores_df = pd.concat(
          [scores_df, pd.DataFrame({f'Scores_{c}': clf.decision_scores_})],
            axis=1)
        col_map[c] = [col_name_i, col_name_j]
        c += 1

def get_max_cols(x):
    return col_map[np.argmax(x)]                           Finds the pair of features
                                                           that identified the largest
scores_cols = scores_df.columns                     ◄───   outlier for each row
max_scores = scores_df.max(axis=1)
scores_df['Max Cols'] = scores_df.apply(get_max_cols, axis=1)
scores_df['Max Score'] = max_scores
```

Plotting the distribution of the maximum 2D scores, we have the plot shown in figure 15.4 (left pane). This appears to separate the outliers well. It may be useful to examine the highest scored of these, perhaps any over about 0.4 or 0.5. In the right pane we see the relationship between the IF scores and the maximum of the 2D IF scores. There is a relationship, but the IF scores are not fully explained by any single 2D spaces. It is, however, a straightforward place to begin. We may next look at records with at least moderate scores in multiple 2D subspaces; these may further help us understand what the full Isolation Forest is flagging.

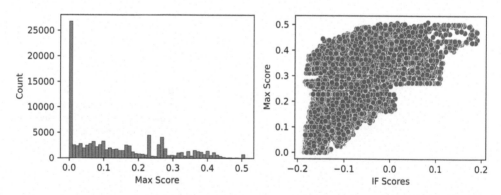

Figure 15.4   Left pane: distribution of the maximum scores from each pair of features, creating an IF for each pair of features in the KDD Cup dataset. Right pane: the relationship of the IF scores to the maximum 2D IF scores. There is a relationship, though the maximum 2D scores are far from a complete explanation of the IF scores when run on the full data.

Given the Max Score column for each record contains the maximum score given in any 2D subspace, we may identify the records with the highest maximum 2D scores with code such as

```
top_scored = scores_df[scores_df['Max Score'] > 0.5]
top_scored['Max Cols'].value_counts()
```

We may then examine these records more closely. For example, we can see which pairs of features identify the strongest 2D outliers:

```
[dst_host_serror_rate, dst_host_srv_serror_rate]      737
[num_root, dst_host_serror_rate]                        2
```

Almost all the top-scored records, going by the 2D subspaces, relate to only two features. These features may be particularly useful for developing rules.

In this example, we used pairs of features; these are beneficial in that we can plot any of the subspaces found that scored the record highly. Checking again row 65,050, we see the pair of features that has the highest 2D Isolation Forest score (a score of 0.43) is dst_host_serror_rate and dst_host_srv_serror_rate. This can then be plotted as in figure 15.5. This shows row 65,050 as a star and all other points in the dataset as dots. We see here that the great majority of points are in the lower left, while this row is outside this dense region, though it is less extreme than many other points. Viewing other 2D spaces would further explain how this row is anomalous, though it may not fully explain the anomalies detected by the IF, as some anomalies may relate to three or more features.

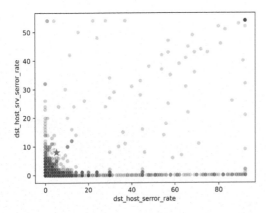

Figure 15.5   Scatterplot of the 2D space that most flagged row 65,050 as an outlier. Row 65,050 is shown as a star; all other records are dots.

Once we understand why the records are anomalous, we will next need to map them to the set of specific labels we have created for the current project. This should be relatively straightforward; often understanding why the records are anomalous is the more difficult part.

15.3   *Automating the process of sorting outlier detection results*

In the previous steps, we will have determined the set of categories we wish to use to group the outliers and will have hand-labeled some examples of each. We will next wish to create some rules or classifiers that can automatically sort the outliers into these categories.

It may be that we can hand-label all of the flagged outliers while examining them. In this case, tools to sort the flagged outliers will still be useful to sort any outliers later flagged. If not all the flagged outliers were hand-labeled, the tools created can then sort these.

The process of creating these rules and classifiers is somewhat similar to creating rules and classifiers to identify the outliers, as covered in chapter 4, but here we assume the outliers have already been identified. In some cases, rules may be easier to create and in other cases classifiers, but everything else equal, rules would tend to be preferred as they are more interpretable.

15.3.1 *Rules to sort the output of detectors*

For the KDD Cup dataset, we may wish to create categories for the outliers including "unusually long sessions," "unusual combination of protocol_type and service," "unusually high error rates," and likely several others. If we start with "unusually high error rates," we can create rules based on the error rate features shown in table 15.1. As there are several error rate features (seven features related to error rates in all), we look here at a means to create simpler and more accurate rules. It seems that each of the error rate features are relevant. We may add code to collect their sum, with the idea that having high values in any one of these features may relate to useful rules but that having a high total of these may as well. Assuming listing 15.1 has run and `df` contains the KDD Cup data, we may create a Total Error Rate feature for each record with the following listing.

Listing 15.5 Engineering a Total Error Rate feature

```
error_cols = [x for x in df.columns if 'error_rate' in x]
df['Total Error Rate'] = df[error_cols].sum(axis=1)
sns.scatterplot(data=df, x='Total Error Rate', y='IF Scores')
plt.show()
```

The output is shown in figure 15.6. With any features in the data, or features that we engineer such as this, it may be useful to plot these. We can look, for example, at the relationships between individual features and the final scores as in figure 15.6, which indicates the Total Error Rate is related to the total IF scores. We see that when the Total Error Rate is high, the IF Score is high as well, though there may be high IF Scores without high Total Error Rates: there are also, as we would expect, other patterns related to the IF scores.

Examining the data and the plots, we may wish to determine some thresholds for any rules created. This is another place where judgement is necessary. For Total Error Rate, a threshold of 200 may be reasonable; most records with a Total Error Rate of 200 or more have at least moderately high scores. Plotting duration against the IF scores in figure 15.7, we can see that longer durations are associated with higher scores. Here a

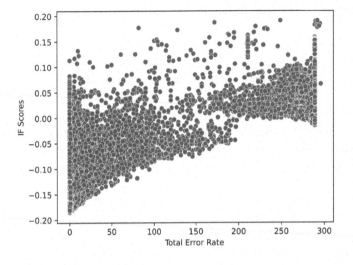

Figure 15.6   Relationship between Total Error Rate and IF scores

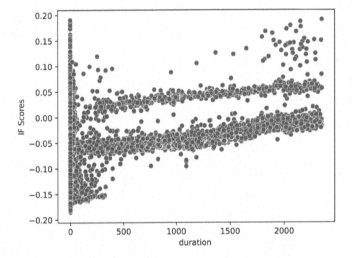

Figure 15.7 Relationship between duration and IF scores

threshold of 2,000 may be reasonable, though this may take some tuning to ensure the rules work well to sort the outliers.

A simple set of rules is shown in listing 15.6. Realistically, a much larger and more complex set of rules would likely be used, but this gives some indication how we may look for different types of issues. Over time, these can ideally relate more to the root causes (e.g., specific attack types) and less to the symptoms (e.g., high error rates). For simplicity, the rule related to error rates checks only the total error rate, but we would likely have one or more rules related to individual error rate features as well. This example attempts to give each outlier as many explanations as are applicable and a numeric importance score based on the number of known anomalies it contains.

> **Listing 15.6 Sorting outliers detected in KDD Cup dataset**

```
top_scored_df = df[df['IF Scores'] > 0.1].copy()
top_scored_df['Total Errors'] = top_scored_df[error_cols].sum(axis=1)

top_scored_df['Label'] = 'Unknown'
top_scored_df['Importance'] = 0
for i in top_scored_df.index:
    row = top_scored_df.loc[i]
    expl = ''
    importance = 0
    if row['duration'] > 1500:
        expl += "Unusually long sessions. "
        importance += 1
    if row['Total Errors'] > 200:
        expl += "Unusually high error rates. "
        importance += 2
    if len(expl):
        top_scored_df.loc[i, 'Label'] = expl
        top_scored_df.loc[i, 'Importance'] = importance
```

It is also possible to assign each specific category an importance and use these to set the total importance for each record, for example, creating a dictionary such as

```
importances_dict = {"Unusually long sessions. ": 1,
                    "Unusually high error rates. ": 2}
```

We may then test the rules created on the records flagged by the system (and ideally those not flagged by the system—particularly those just below the threshold and those scored highly by at least some detectors) to determine how well they work. Once they work well, they may be used to help sort any subsequent outliers that are flagged. Well-formed rules should help determine for each: why was it flagged as an outlier, if this of interest, and how pressing it is.

The rules found in this way will likely never cover all the outliers found but may cover many. Once they are reliable, they may, as indicated, be used as part of the outlier detection system itself. Another use can be as part of the cleaning process done before training the outlier detectors: these rules may be useful to remove the strongest and most common outliers, allowing the detectors to be trained on cleaner (less contaminated) data.

15.3.2 Classifiers to sort the output of detectors

We've seen classifiers used in several different ways already in this book. In chapter 3, we introduced the Real versus Fake detector, which learns to distinguish real from synthetic data. In chapter 4, we covered their use in identifying outliers, acting as form of outlier detector. In chapter 13, we saw an example where interpretable classifiers (such as decision trees), used as proxy models, could be used to explain the predictions made by a detector.

Here we look at a similar application, where a classifier is used to classify the types of outliers found by an outlier detection system (to place them into the predefined categories). However, we will first take a closer look at something indicated earlier in the book regarding classifiers. Though very useful, they do have a significant limitation: they can only learn to classify data that is similar to the data they have been trained on. This does not mesh well with the nature of outliers, in that outliers are often novel—unlike anything we have seen previously or at least seen frequently. This creates a substantial limit for the use of classifiers for all these purposes.

Likely the most significant implication of this is: we typically cannot create a general binary classifier to distinguish statistically normal from abnormal records (only detectors may do this) or to distinguish outliers of interest from outliers not of interest. Real versus Fake detectors attempt to do this and can become accurate enough to be useful (often very useful) if trained on sufficient synthetic data, but this is very rarely feasible training with real data.

Classification relies on several assumptions, including what are known as the *smoothness assumption* (we assume records near each other are the same class) and the *clustering assumption* (we assume each class is in a single cluster or a small number of clusters; that is, we assume each class is in a small number of specific locations). With outlier detection, these, particularly the clustering assumption, rarely hold. Outlier regions are spread throughout the dataspace (wherever normal data is not), and outliers are never together in clusters. In fact, if outliers were together in a large, dense cluster, they would then, by definition, no longer be considered outliers (with an exception where the cluster was not present during training, appearing only in subsequent data).

In figure 15.8 (left), we see the synthetic dataset introduced in chapter 7. This has data in three large clusters, and likely any points outside of these could be considered

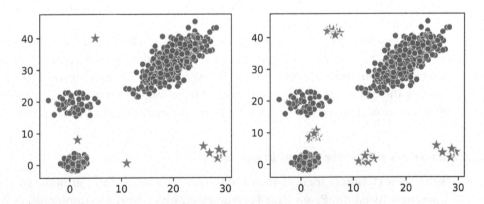

Figure 15.8   Left pane: dataset with known outliers. Inliers are drawn as dots and outliers as stars. Conceivably, we can create a classifier to separate these, but as the outliers are distributed throughout the space, it is not clear where to draw the decision boundary. This is much more of a problem in higher dimensions. Right pane: where there are many examples each of a small number of specific outliers, it is more feasible to classify these.

outliers. Points along the fringes of the three large clusters may be statistical outliers and may or may not be of interest for any given project; for this example, we assume they are not. The eight known outliers, drawn as stars, could be used for training a classifier, but subsequent outliers may be in almost any location other than the three large clusters. If we were to attempt to train a classifier on this data, the classifier may draw boundaries anywhere between the eight currently known outliers and the three clusters of inliers.

As we saw in chapter 5, it can be quite feasible to create a one-class model to model the inlier class. In this case, it would ideally model the three large clusters, drawing a tight boundary around these. Binary classifiers, on the other hand, simply trained on the inliers and the small number of outliers, would unlikely be able to create a similar boundary. This is due partially to the small number of training examples for the outlier class but primarily to the violation of the clustering assumption.

However, our goal here is not to create a general binary classifier to detect outliers (to classify any given record as being an outlier or not), but to create classifiers to distinguish specific types of outliers. This is quite feasible. If a sufficient number of a specific type of outlier are found, as in figure 15.8 (right), and these are clustered in one or a small number of regions (in this example, four regions), it may be possible to create a classifier to detect these, which may then be useful to sort the results of an outlier detection system. With a situation such as in the right pane, we may be able to train a classifier to sort outliers into four categories, representing the four types of outliers seen here. This can be quite useful but does have the limitation that any novel outliers will likely be misclassified and predicted as either being inliers or one of the four types of outliers seen here.

Another solution to this is to train a one-class model for each specific category of useful outlier. A One-class Support Vector Machine (OCSVM) will attempt to model this set of records as tightly as possible, such that anything similar to these will be classified as being of this type and anything not similar as being not of this type. In this example, there are four categories of known useful outliers, so we can train four OCSVM models. Any records that are not classified as being similar to any of these categories may be considered unclassified outliers. In listing 15.7, we train an OCSVM to recognize one of the types of outliers in figure 15.8, the small cluster in the bottom right. In this example they happen to be the first five records in the dataset; we separate and use these to train the OCSVM. The code for `create_four_clusters_test_data()` appears in chapter 7.

Listing 15.7 OCSVM to identify non-useful outliers

```
from sklearn.svm import OneClassSVM

df = create_four_clusters_test_data()
clf = OneClassSVM()
clf.fit(df[['A', 'B']].loc[:5])
df['OCSVM Pred'] = clf.predict(df[['A', 'B']])
```

This creates a decision boundary as shown in figure 15.9, which ideally will reliably isolate records with this form of anomaly.

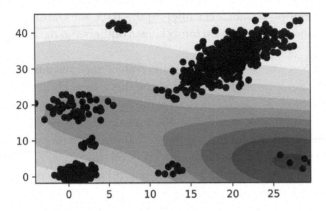

Figure 15.9   Decision boundary of an OCSVM model created to identify a specific type of known, useful outlier, in this case, the small cluster in the bottom right

Interestingly, this is the opposite of how we would normally use a OCSVM with outlier detection. There we would train on all data and use the OCSVM to detect outliers—the points outside the decision boundary. But here we are not looking for outliers; we are looking for *specific interesting outliers*, so we train on only the interesting outliers and try to isolate each specific category of these, at least for the most common cases. We then identify the outliers *inside* the decision boundaries as being of these types of outliers.

15.3.3 *Executing rules and classifiers on flagged outliers*

Though the tools used to categorize the flagged outliers may not be complete and may not be perfectly accurate, they may be a practical method to process large numbers of results. And, in many cases, the tools may be able to accurately categorize the outliers found. In this way, investigation of the outliers can be more directed and more efficient.

One thing to be mindful of when executing the rules and classifiers on the flagged outliers is that we will need to identify where records appear to have additional anomalies. To check for this, when testing flagged outliers with these tools, it is important to also check the scores of the records. For example, if a record is flagged because of a high value in feature B given the value in feature A, and this is relatively common among the outliers flagged so far, a rule or classifier may classify it as being this category of outlier (if that will be meaningful to a team investigating these; otherwise, a more intelligible label should be used, such as "abuse of meals allowance"). What's important to check is if its score is higher than most other outliers in this category. Once we have determined all the known anomaly patterns associated with a row, if these do not fully explain its score, there may then be additional unknown anomalies associated with the record. It may also potentially be explained simply by having extreme instances of the known patterns. In either case, this is not a problem but is something investigators need to be aware of.

Earlier we listed several benefits of labeling the outliers, including more efficiently investigating the outliers, prioritizing outliers for investigation, tracking outliers over time, and so on. The benefits of these are much greater if we are able to automate the categorization of the outliers. Another benefit of rules and classifiers, once they are performing well, is they provide a powerful form of testing. Where we have tools that are able to sort records into the categories of outliers we have identified, we may then, when new data is available and scored by the outlier detectors, execute these and determine how many of each category were found. This allows us to perform some testing on the most recent (and likely most relevant) data, even where no hand labels are yet available. If substantially more or less of any category is found, this may suggest a change: either in the data, or in the system's sensitivity to this type of outlier. This is, though, only possible when working with large enough volumes of data that this can be assessed reliably.

Once we have an established system, we can also start to look for the root causes of the outliers. In some cases, there may be a small number of sources for many outliers, even outliers that appear to be of different types (a single issue may manifest in many ways in the data). For example, with financial data, we may have cases where senior staff have manipulated the finances of the company, recognizing revenue from sales that are not certain. This may turn up as unusually high revenue, unusually smooth year-to-year growth, unusual individual sales, unusually short intervals between revenue recognition and the anticipated cash collection, an unusual customer, and unusual bonuses paid to the senior staff. These outliers may appear, on the surface, quite different but have, in this case, a single root cause.

As these root causes are identified, they can be incorporated into the outlier detection system either as additional features the detectors can take advantage of or as rules. This may help us further improve the system, but it can also get to the very purpose of many outlier detection systems: finding the sort of issues that may be considered root causes may be why the detection systems were created in the first place.

15.4 *Semisupervised learning*

There is another major advantage to labeling the outliers we've not looked at so far: it can make the system significantly more accurate. An important phenomenon in outlier detection is that, once we have a large set of labeled data indicating what is relevant versus what is not, we can use a set of techniques called *semisupervised learning*.

These methods work, in a sense, similarly to supervised systems: as binary classifiers that distinguish relevant outliers from other records. Despite the caveats listed previously related to creating binary classifiers to distinguish records of interest from records not of interest, semisupervised methods work a little bit differently, and they can be very effective. They do, though, have a major limitation that we will have with any system based on classification: they cannot handle novel data well. Classifiers can be very powerful, but with outlier detection, we always need to be mindful of this limitation.

However, for outliers similar to what we have seen before, they can create very effective tools (providing more accurate scores) and may be at least part of the full system, which may be supplemented with other tools focused more on novel outliers.

We've not looked at semisupervised methods previously, as they not only take advantage of labeled data but also require labeled data, which may not be available in the early stages of outlier detection but will generally be later. This is commonly true for long-running systems, but even with one-off projects, we will likely spend some time hand-labeling records as they are flagged by one or another outlier detector (or nearly flagged—we may label those just below any thresholds as well). In some cases, it may be possible to label a sufficient quantity of data to use semisupervised methods. We will, though, often require thousands of labeled outliers to create a strong semisupervised system.

Before looking at how semisupervised methods may be used with outlier detection, we'll take a minute and describe what semisupervised methods are. Semisupervised methods are used not only in outlier detection but in other areas of machine learning, particularly prediction, in cases where we have both labeled data and (often substantially more) unlabeled data. With semisupervised learning, we train a model on the labeled data to predict a target, the same as would be done with supervised machine learning. The term "semisupervised" refers to the fact that we also, in one way or another, take advantage of the unlabeled data. With prediction problems where the bulk of the data is unlabeled, there is often a sense that there must be a good way to take advantage of the unlabeled data, as it contains valuable information about the distribution of the data. Sometimes this is possible and sometimes not, as the overall distribution of the data may or may not be relevant to the prediction problem, but it is very often possible with outlier detection, as the overall distribution is fundamental to outlier detection.

With outlier detection, this is very powerful, as there can be substantially more unlabeled than labeled data. For example, if you have 100,000 rows of data and run a set of detectors on this data, they may flag 200 rows. You can then manually assess these and will then have 200 rows of data labeled as being of interest or not. You may also spot-check and label another 100 rows that were not scored above the threshold, so you may have 300 rows of labeled data in total. It may be possible to train a reliable classifier using only 300 rows of labeled data but it more likely will not be, due to the small data volume and likely violations of the smoothness and clustering assumptions.

However, we can take advantage of the unlabeled data. As we have run a set of outlier detectors on all 100,000 rows, we have outlier scores for each record. These may then be used as a set of additional features that describe each record, and these are likely very powerful features. Assuming the outlier detection system works well (the statistical outliers it finds tend to be largely the sort you are interested in finding), then these outlier scores will be very predictive of the target label. So, though the 99,700 rows of unlabeled data cannot be used directly to train a classifier, they can be used to generate very predictive features that can be used by the classifier on the 300 labeled rows (their outlier scores are only accurate because of the strong sense of what is normal versus abnormal provided by running the detectors on the full dataset).

Most feature engineering modifies a single feature (for example, extracting the day of the week from a date) or combining two features (for example, taking the ratio of two numeric features). Using outlier scores as features, though, describes the rows as a whole. And these features are quite powerful. While each individual outlier detector will provide a good but imperfect estimate of how interesting each record is, their combined scores will likely be very predictive.

We then train a classifier, still using only the 300 labeled records but where these are enhanced to have these very powerful additional features: the outlier scores. In fact, the original features may not be necessary, and we may be able to use only the detector scores. This process can help create a very strong scoring system. It learns, with respect to the existing labels, to best combine the scores from the various detectors into a final score. As indicated, this may miss novel outliers, but when using the detector scores as the features, as opposed to the original features, this is less likely: the system will most likely learn to assign any records flagged by any detector at least some score. Nevertheless, additional checks for one or more high outlier scores, as covered in chapter 14, may be useful.

Using a semisupervised system, then, allows us to score the records better: they are scored with respect to how likely interesting they are for the current project and not how statistically unusual they are. Though it may, if used alone, miss some outliers, the scores assigned will tend to be meaningful and the statistical outliers that are not of interest will tend to receive low outlier scores, at least where similar outliers have been seen before and labeled as being not of interest.

In comparison, a strictly supervised model for this example would be limited to using the 300 labeled records, without taking advantage of the unlabeled data. And a strictly unsupervised model would be able to assign outlier scores to all rows but would not be able to learn from the labels we collect over time (as data is assessed and labeled or from synthetic data that has reliable labels). Semisupervised techniques can provide a way to receive the benefits of both.

For many projects, it can be worthwhile to look into semisupervised methods, particularly where it is possible to label some significant portion of the data, ideally 1% or more (semisupervised methods may struggle with small numbers of labeled records). As we indicated earlier, many projects may initially rely primarily on outlier detection and then later more supervised methods (rules and classifiers used to detect specific outliers once larger volumes of data are labeled). However, it's also possible to progress from primarily unsupervised methods, to semisupervised, to supervised. In either case, unsupervised outlier detection will remain necessary to detect any unknown outliers.

A useful resource for semisupervised outlier detection is the ADBench website, which we first saw in chapter 8 (https://github.com/Minqi824/ADBench). This provides some discussion of unsupervised, semisupervised, and supervised outlier detection and points to some methods, including one we look at in this chapter, Extreme Gradient Boosting-based Outlier Detection (XGBOD).

15.4.1 *Using labeled data to create a stacked model*

The simplest means to implement semisupervised outlier detection is to create a stacked model. This is the same idea as an example shown in chapter 14, though that used synthetic data while this uses labeled data. In both cases, the code is very simple: we simply create a dataframe with both the outlier scores from each detector for each record and the labels that were assigned to each record. We then train a model to predict the labels. The labels used to train the model may be binary labels indicating if the records are of interest or not or, preferably, scores indicating how relevant they are. It will be best to also test with synthetic data (this will cover a broader range of outliers than are probably available in the labeled data), and it is best to cross-validate the process to ensure it works well. An example is shown in listing 15.8, which assumes labels (likely from hand-labeling) are available in the Label column. This can default all unexamined rows to Inlier (or to zero) and use the true labels for any records that have been examined.

Listing 15.8   Stacked ensemble of detectors

```
from sklearn.ensemble import RandomForestClassifier

clf = RandomForestClassifier()
clf.fit(scores_df[scores_cols], full_df['Label'])
```

In the next section, we look at a tool provided by PyOD, called XGBOD, which is designed for this purpose and is useful, but it is also useful to be able to create your own stacked model where necessary. Creating your own allows greater flexibility—for example, allowing you to include models that are not part of PyOD. In general, the more detectors and the more diverse the detectors used, the better. Chapter 14 covers methods to create a wide range of detectors.

15.4.2 *XGBOD*

XGBOD is a model provided by PyOD that works in the same way as previously discussed but has the advantage of being part of PyOD. Internally, XGBOD uses XGBoost as the classifier (a boosted ensemble of decision trees and generally a very strong classifier) and a series of outlier detectors to generate outlier scores for all records. The outlier detectors may be specified, but if not, a default set will be used (k nearest neighbors, local outlier factor (LOF), IF, OCSVM, and histogram-based outlier score (HBOS), each with a range of parameters). XGBOD also accepts several parameters related to the XGBoost model used—for example for the tree depths and the learning rate. XGBOD works by executing the following steps:

1 Run the outlier detectors. This step is unsupervised (does not require labels) and so will be run on the full dataset. In all, 107 combinations of detectors and parameters are used by default.
2 Select the relevant detectors.

3 Combine the new features (the outlier scores) into a new table, along with the original features for the data.

4 Fit XGBoost on the labeled data.

5 Make predictions for all records (labels are necessary only for training and not for prediction).

Listing 15.9 shows an example using XGBOD. This does require labeling (hand-labeling or labeling in some reliable way) a large set of records, which is not shown here (for this example, we fill it with random values). Other than this labeling step and passing the labels as the y parameter to the fit() method, using XGBOD is as simple as any other PyOD detector.

> **Listing 15.9 Predicting the relevant outliers using XGBOD**

```
from pyod.models.xgbod import XGBOD

y = np.random.choice([0, 1], len(df))

clf = XGBOD()
clf.fit(df, y=y)
```

15.5 *Regression testing*

As discussed in chapter 4, with ongoing outlier detection systems, it's necessary to retrain from time to time to handle changes in data and changes in our goals for outlier detection and, whenever we have substantially more labeled data, to take advantage of this. Each time we do so, it's necessary to ensure the system continues to behave well with respect to any synthetic data we may test with but more importantly, with respect to the labeled data we've managed to collect since beginning running the system.

To ensure the system continues to work well, it's necessary to create what are called *regression tests*. These are common in software development, and, while they are often difficult to implement in other areas of machine learning, such as predictive models, they can be useful and easy to create in outlier detection. Regression testing refers to tests that check if things that used to work properly still do; if they do not, we say the system has *regressed*. In the case of outlier detection, we check that the real data records that were correctly flagged as outliers are still scored highly.

To support this, we maintain a set of labeled data of both classes: records we are interested in and records we are not. Ideally, these records will also be scored as well as labeled with more specific labels (representing specific types of outliers), but at minimum, they should be given binary labels. We can then ensure that the outlier detection system continues to score highly the known outliers we have found in the data without scoring highly too many of those labeled as being not of interest. Regression tests with outlier detection, then, are quite simple: they are generally just lists of records that have been assigned each label.

When retraining the detectors, we may simply train on more recent data (using the same detectors, preprocessing, distance metrics, parameters, etc. as previously), or we may make more substantive changes, such as changing the detectors used, the features, the parameters, or the method to combine results from multiple detectors (where ensembles are used). The more significant the changes made, the more we can expect different results to be produced. We hope not to introduce many new false positives or false negatives when retesting with older data. We will, though, almost certainly see at least some of both, and we have to assess if there is a net improvement or not.

When working with outlier detection, what may also occur from time to time is we discover a new type of outlier we are interested in, add this to the set of regression tests, and discover the current system does not flag these well. This may then require re-tuning the system, possibly adding more detectors, adjusting the parameters, or increasing the weights of any detectors in an ensemble that do detect this well. When doing this we need to ensure we do not create other problems while fixing this one, which is exactly what regression tests are designed to do. We will tune the system until, as much as possible, the full set of regression tests are performing well—all known outliers are scored highly, with few other records scored as high.

Over time, the set of outliers labeled will grow, which will allow the regression tests to become increasingly more reliable. We should be careful though: many of the outliers will be equivalent to each other, and simply counting the number of known outliers scored highly may not be the most effective means to evaluate the results of the regression tests. This is where it is useful to have more specific labels for the outliers, at least for the outliers that we wish to flag, as we can ensure that each category of these is covered well. It is also useful to have scores (at least an indication of low, medium, and high) to better evaluate the quality of the system.

During this process, it's quite possible for the detectors to flag records that have not been flagged previously. These will be unlabeled, and it will not be clear if they are of interest or not so will require manual inspection and labeling. In this way, re-tuning the system can take some time, but it does often result in having more labeled data and consequently a more powerful set of regression tests.

We should also take note that some previously labeled data may relate to types of outliers we are no longer interested in collecting, and these should be relabeled before running the regression tests. Overall, though, we tend to want to identify the same types of outliers over time, and it is useful to test if the system continues to flag the same items.

As outlier detection systems run, they will flag many records that are statistically unusual but not of interest, and these would be labeled as such. This means, over time, we will likely have a large collection of these negative examples. Ideally the outlier detectors can be tuned to not flag these, but it may be acceptable if some are flagged, as long as they do not mask the outliers that are of most interest and they can be later filtered out as not requiring investigation. It is a judgment call if regression tests should be specifically written to check that these are not flagged or if we simply test that the known outliers are flagged and that there are relatively few other records that are scored as high. If we do not create regression tests related to specific categories of uninteresting outliers, having labels for these can still be useful. As they are repeatedly flagged each time we run the regression tests, it saves us manually reevaluating whether they are relevant. Whether we do have regression tests for the noninteresting records comes down largely to the best balance of false positives and false negatives. Regardless, when creating each version of the system, we must check that we are not flagging substantially more inliers as outliers than previously.

The re-tuning process will tend to not be perfect, and there will often be two steps forward and one step back. To measure how the new scoring compares to the old, it is likely most expedient to report something like the following:

- The number of records labeled as outliers that were reported as outliers both in the previous version and in the new version
- The number of records labeled as outliers that were reported as outliers in the previous version but (incorrectly) as inliers in the current version

This carries on for the eight combinations of the true label, if they were flagged in the previous version and if they are flagged in the current version. Preferably, if possible, we would break this down by category of outlier and score. To capture the consistency in the system from previous versions, we can also measure the correlation, as was done to compare two different detectors in chapter 8.

While it's still useful to test with synthetic data each time the model is re-tuned, and this can cover a far broader range of outliers than is possible with real data, the real data will have more meaning and is important to save for this purpose. Also, as real outliers are identified, we can use them to update the system to generate synthetic data to ensure it covers the cases we now know we can expect, with some possibility, to reappear in future data.

In this way, labeled data can be extremely valuable: even where we do not have enough to support supervised or semi-supervised methods, we can use the data for testing. Given this, we can expect the system to steadily improve over time.

Summary

- It is very useful, for several reasons, to label the output of outlier detectors. This includes future re-tuning of the models, tracking the presence of certain types of outliers over time, and efficiently processing the outliers detected—where there are multiple outliers of the same type, they may be investigated together, reducing the total time required for investigation.
- It is also important to be able to filter out the types of outliers that are known to not be important, or at least not necessary to investigate.
- Creating the labels usually requires hand-labeling, though this may not add additional work where the outliers are investigated in any case.
- Labeling relates to whether we wish for records of this type to be scored highly in the future, not to whether they are statistically unusual, or if investigation found them to be important.
- Once we have labeled data, we can create rules or train classifiers, which can then help sort any subsequent outliers flagged by the system.

- These rules or classifiers may become part of the outlier detection system itself.
- Rules and classifiers are limited to known forms of outliers.
- Labeled data also has the advantage that it may be used to train semisupervised models, which can score records more reliably than unsupervised models (though they still require the use of unsupervised outlier detectors), at least once there is a sufficient collection of labeled data to train these well.
- Labeled data is useful in creating regression tests, which may be simply lists of known, real outliers that we want to continue to score highly. These can be very useful when re-tuning the models.

P art 4 covers deep learning and two other modalities you may work with: time-series and image data.

In chapter 16 we describe deep learning-based methods for tabular and image outlier detection. This includes cutting-edge techniques based on self-supervised learning.

In chapter 17 we introduce outlier detection for time-series data.

Deep learning-based
outlier detection

16

This chapter covers

- The general concepts of deep learning-based outlier detection
- Some of the options available in standard libraries
- Outlier detection for image data
- The state of the art in outlier detection today

Deep learning-based outlier detection techniques can be very powerful for many types of problems. For tabular data, they are typically still not as useful as the methods we've looked at so far in this book, but as a data scientist, you may also often work with time series, text, image, video, audio, network, or other types of data, and for many of these, deep learning-based methods can be very effective. In fact, for many types of data, including image, video, and audio, there really are no other viable options available today.

Deep learning-based outlier detection can work in a variety of ways, but all use deep neural networks in one way or another. Deep neural networks have some significant advantages as models and have proven themselves to be able to handle many types of problems that are unsolvable using other means. At the same time, they do

467

have some costs associated with them. They tend to require a very large amount of data to train, are slower to work with, and are more difficult to tune. Still, they've made phenomenal progress in many fields in the last several years, even with tabular data, and we will certainly see them become increasingly powerful in years to come.

Most of what we've covered in the book so far has been relatively stable for many years—some methods for decades. Deep learning, on the other hand, especially as applied to outlier detection, is much newer and much more in a state of flux. I suspect we will continue to see major advances in deep learning-based outlier detection, at least with image, video, audio, and text. With tabular data, though, it's not clear if there will be similar advances in deep learning-based outlier detection. It's also not clear if there will be significant advances with more traditional machine learning tools [methods akin to Isolation Forest (IF), k nearest neighbor (KNN), angle-based outlier detection (ABOD), and so on] or in any other form for tabular data. If there are, I believe they are most likely to come from deep learning, but outlier detection on tabular data using deep neural networks does appear to be a fundamentally difficult problem to solve.

The reasons for this are described in this chapter, but tabular data lends itself less to deep learning methods than other modalities (such as image, video, or audio). Nevertheless, there are some effective deep learning methods for tabular data available today, largely based on concepts we'll describe soon: autoencoders (AEs), variational auto encoders (VAEs), and generative adversarial networks (GANs). While these do not tend to be any stronger than the methods we've looked at so far (and they tend to be slower and more difficult to tune), they can, for many projects, be effective and are very often useful for inclusion in ensembles: they are quite different than the methods we've looked at so far and consequently are able to add diversity. They also have the advantage that they can support not just tabular but any form of data.

Although it's not clear if deep learning will become the most effective tool for tabular outlier detection generally, there are a couple scenarios where it appears to hold a great deal of promise, at least where large amounts of data (that is, many rows of data) are available. One is where the tables also have many features. Most traditional models, other than univariate tests, can struggle with datasets with many features. Deep neural networks, though, appear to be able to handle even enormous numbers of features quite well.

The other scenario where deep learning may be the most effective method for tabular outlier detection is where the outliers are based on very complex relationships among the features. These would tend to be missed by other methods. Deep neural networks, though, at least with sufficient data, can learn the relationships between the features well, even where these are very subtle and spread over many features. The implication may be that the tools we've seen so far in this book will continue to be the models best suited for detecting most outliers, while more nuanced anomalies will only be possible to detect with deep learning-based methods (though only where we have large quantities of data to train on).

In this chapter, we'll look at deep learning methods for tabular and image data. We'll examine some of the most established models for outlier detection using deep neural networks: auto encoders, variational encoders, and GANs. We'll also explore some methods based on an important concept in deep learning called *self-supervised learning*, which is currently used extensively in most domains of outlier detection other than tabular (and is sometimes used with tabular as well) and may hold the most promise for deep learning-based outlier detection in the future. In addition, we'll look at a few libraries for deep learning-based outlier detection, including in two libraries we've seen previously in this book, PyOD and alibi-detect (introduced in chapter 7). We'll focus on these and an additional library, DeepOD. PyOD covers tabular; DeepOD covers tabular and time series; and alibi-detect covers tabular, image, and time-series data.

16.1 Introducing neural networks

To understand deep learning-based outlier detection, it's important to have some understanding of neural networks. These are used for a number of purposes in machine learning but quite often as predictive models. In this case, they are used in effectively the same way as decision trees, Random Forest, and other predictive models, though they are often much more powerful.

Figure 16.1 shows an example of a neural network. The input (which is given to the network, both during training and during prediction, one object at a time) is shown as the squares at the left. This shows only a small number of elements, but for image data, there would be as many as there are pixels per image and for tabular data as many as there are features in the table. The circular points are known as *neurons*. These take numeric input from the initial input or the other neurons to their left, combine the numeric values in some way (which the network learns to do as it is trained), and pass the resulting numeric values to the neurons to the right, eventually resulting in values in the final neuron(s), the rightmost neurons of the network, which represent the

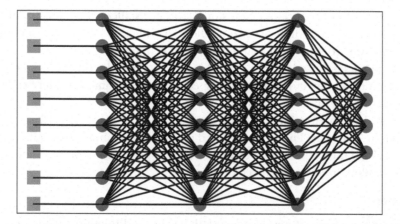

Figure 16.1 Example of a neural network. The square points at the left are the input. The circular points are neurons. During prediction, as input is given to the neural network and neurons calculate their values (floating point numbers each neuron will contain) one layer at a time (left to right) based on the input, with the final (rightmost) layer containing the prediction for the input.

prediction for the current input. For example, in a classification problem with four classes, the four neurons would represent the probability assigned to each of the four classes.

If we have a collection of images and there are four types of items (e.g., cat, dog, horse, and goat), then the neural network can learn to predict each of these classes. Once the neural network is trained, as a picture is given to the network, the neurons in the first layer will calculate their values based on an arithmetic combination of the pixel values in the input. Each subsequent layer will calculate a value based on the layer to its left. Neural networks may have some randomness during training but are deterministic during prediction, so for each input, each neuron will calculate a specific value. The last layer represents the predictions. In this example, these would represent the probabilities of the image being a cat, dog, horse, or goat. The term "deep" is applied to networks with more than a few layers. Deep networks can be much more powerful than networks with only a small number of layers, though they also require much more data to train.

16.2 PyOD

We've covered PyOD extensively already, but it also has some deep learning-based methods we haven't seen yet that we'll look at in this chapter. These follow the standard PyOD API, so they can be used interchangeably with the methods we have seen previously (Gaussian mixture models (GMMs), kernel density estimation (KDE), Local Outlier Probability (LoOP), local outlier factor (LOF), and so on). As is standard, the detectors are fit to the training data and then may be used to evaluate either this or separate test data, which generates a score for each record.

Almost all deep learning in Python today (including outlier detection) is done with either TensorFlow/Keras (Keras is a library that runs on top of TensorFlow) or PyTorch, and these are both used by PyOD (each individual detector will use either PyTorch or TensorFlow). Consequently, using the deep learning methods with PyOD does require having either TensorFlow/Keras or PyTorch installed. On Google Colab and some other environments, these are preinstalled, so using these requires installing only PyOD; in other environments you will need to install one or both of these (depending on which detectors are used). Once everything is installed, the detectors can be used similarly to any other detector. Other than specifying the parameters, there is little difference from the other PyOD detectors

PyOD provides autoencoder, variational autoencoder, and GAN, as well as some similar methods we'll look at. These are included in some other libraries as well, including alibi-detect. Using these libraries is convenient, but in practice people also often implement these models directly in PyTorch or Keras.

16.2.1 Autoencoders

Autoencoders are a form of neural network that were traditionally used as a compression tool, though they have been found to be useful for outlier detection as well. Autoencoders take input and learn to compress this with as little loss as possible, such that it can be reconstructed to be close to the original. For tabular data, autoencoders are given one row at a time, with the input neurons corresponding to the columns of the table. For image data, they are given one image at a time, with the input neurons corresponding to the pixels of the picture. However, as we'll see later, the images may also be given in what's called an *embedding* format.

Figure 16.2 provides an example of an autoencoder. This is a specific form of a neural network that is designed not to predict a target but to reproduce the input given to the autoencoder. We can see that the network has as many elements for input (the leftmost neurons of the network) as for output (the rightmost neurons of the network), but in between, the layers have fewer neurons. The middle layer has the fewest; this layer represents the *embedding* (also known as the *bottleneck* or the *latent representation*) for each object. The size of this layer is the size to which we attempt to compress all data, such that it can be recreated (or almost recreated) in the subsequent layers. We'll look at the concept of embeddings in more detail later, but it is essentially a concise vector of floating-point numbers that can represent each item. In the case of autoencoders, it is the set of values that appear in the neurons in the middle layer for each item as it is passed through the neural network.

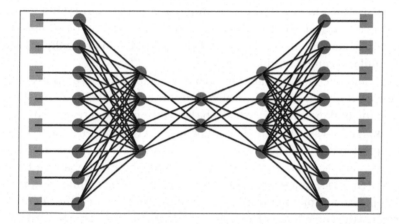

Figure 16.2 Example of an AE. The neural network learns to condense any input to as many elements as appear in the middle layer and then reconstruct the data to its original values.

Autoencoders have two main parts: the first layers of the network are known as the *encoder*. These layers shrink the data to progressively fewer neurons until they reach the middle of the network. The second part of the network is known as the *decoder*: a set of layers symmetric with the encoder layers that take the compressed form of each input and attempt to reconstruct it to its original form as closely as possible.

If we are able to train an autoencoder that tends to have low reconstruction error (the output of the network tends to match the input very closely), then if some records have high reconstruction error, they are outliers—they do not follow the general patterns of the data that allow for the compression. Compression is possible because there are typically some relationships between the features in tabular data, between the words in text, between the concepts in images, and so on. When items are typical, they follow these patterns, and the compression can be quite effective (with minimal loss). When items are atypical, they do not follow these patterns and cannot be compressed without more significant loss. This is similar to the ideas we've seen before, where outliers are records that do not tend to contain frequent item sets, do not fit into clusters, or otherwise do not follow the main patterns.

The number and size of the layers is a modeling decision. The more the data contains patterns (regular associations between the features), the more we are able to compress the data, which means the fewer neurons we can use in the middle layer. It usually takes some experimentation, but we want to set the size of the network so that most records can be constructed with very little, but *some* error. If most records can be recreated with zero error, the network likely has too much capacity—the middle layer is able to fully describe the objects being passed through. We want any unusual records to have a larger reconstruction error but also to be able to compare this to the moderate error we have with typical records; it's hard to gauge how unusual a record's reconstruction error is if almost all other records have an error of 0.0. If this occurs, we know we need to scale back the capacity of the model (reduce the number or neurons) until this is no longer possible. This can, in fact, be a practical means to tune the autoencoder—starting with, for example, many neurons in the middle layers and then gradually adjusting the parameters until you get the results you want.

In this way, autoencoders are able to create an embedding (compressed form of the item) for each object, but we typically do not use the embedding outside of this autoencoder; the outlier scores are usually based entirely on the reconstruction error. This is not always the case though. The embeddings created in the middle layer are legitimate representations of the objects and can be used for outlier detection. Figure 16.2 shows an example where we use two neurons for the middle layer, which allows plotting the latent space as a scatterplot as in figure 16.3. The x dimension represents the values appearing in one neuron and the y dimension in the other neuron. Each point represents the embedding of an object (table row in this example). Any standard outlier detector (e.g. KNN, IF, Convex Hull, Mahalanobis distance, etc.) can then be used on the latent space. This provides an outlier detection system that is somewhat interpretable if limited to two or three dimensions, but, as with principal component analysis (PCA) and other dimensionality reduction methods, the latent space itself is not interpretable.

To calculate the reconstruction error, any distance metric may be used to measure the distance between the input vector and the output vector. Often Cosine, Euclidean or Manhattan distances are used, with a number of others being fairly common as well. In most cases, it is best to standardize the data before performing outlier detection, both to allow the neural network to fit better and to measure the reconstruction error more fairly. Given this, the outlier score of each record can be calculated as the reconstruction error divided by the median reconstruction error (for some reference dataset).

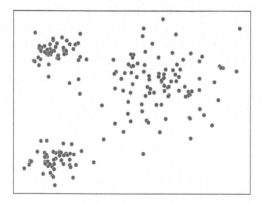

Figure 16.3 Example of latent space created by an AE with two neurons in the middle layer. Each point represents one item. It is straightforward to visualize outliers in this space, though the 2D space itself is not intelligible.

Another approach, which can be more robust, is to not use a single error metric for the reconstruction but to use several. This allows us to effectively use the autoencoder to generate a set of features for each record (each relating to a measurement of the reconstruction error) and pass this to a standard outlier detection tool, which will find the records with unusually large values given by one or more reconstruction error metrics.

In general, autoencoders can be an effective means to locate outliers in data, even where there are many features and the outliers are complex, spanning many features. One challenge of autoencoders is they do require setting the architecture (the number of layers of the network and the number of neurons per layer), as well as many parameters related to the network (the activation method, learning rate, dropout rate, and so on), which can be difficult to do. Any model based on neural networks will necessarily be more finicky to tune than other models. Another limitation of AEs is they may not be appropriate with all types of outlier detection. For example, with image data, they will measure the reconstruction at the pixel level (at least if pixels are used as the input), which may not always be relevant. Interestingly, GANs can perform better in this regard.

We next look at an example using an autoencoder provided by PyOD. First, though, we load in the KDD Cup dataset in the following listing, which is used for later examples as well.

Listing 16.1 Loading the KDD Cup dataset

```
import numpy as np
import pandas as pd
from sklearn.datasets import fetch_kddcup99
from sklearn.preprocessing import OrdinalEncoder

np.random.seed(0)
X, y = fetch_kddcup99(subset="SA", percent10=True, random_state=42,
                      return_X_y=True, as_frame=True)
y = (y != b"normal.").astype(np.int32)
enc = OrdinalEncoder()
X = enc.fit_transform(X)
```

PyOD provides two implementations of the autoencoder detector: one based on Ten-sorFlow/Keras and one on PyTorch. Listing 16.2 uses the TensorFlow version. This example fits on the full KDD Cup dataset (in the X variable) and makes predictions for all rows. This example uses the `predict_proba()` method but, as with other PyOD detectors, the `decision_scores_` attribute or `predict()` method may also be used.

Listing 16.2   Example using the PyOD AE detector

```
from pyod.models.auto_encoder import AutoEncoder

np.random.seed(0)
det = AutoEncoder(epochs=5, random_state=0)
det.fit(X)
pred = det.predict_proba(X)[:, 1]
```

This sets the number of epochs (the number of iterations the detector goes through the data) as five; using more will require more time but may result in higher accuracy. This can be one of the more important parameters to set, along with the number of layers and the number of neurons per layer. This will usually need to be found experimentally.

As with all outlier detection (other than when using interpretable models), the output can take some time to examine, usually using techniques such as those described in chapters 8 and 15, including plotting, creating rules to sort the results, comparing to other detectors, also running interpretable detectors, and so on.

16.2.2 *Variational autoencoders*

Variational autoencoders (VAEs) are a similar idea to AEs though somewhat more complicated. However, the differences (though very powerful) actually don't tend to affect how outlier detection is performed: VAEs have a similar architecture as AEs and also usually use the reconstruction error to estimate the outlierness of each input.

The main difference between a VAE and a standard AE is that while AEs are designed to compress data, VAEs are designed to be generative models: they can produce new content. There are a few differences in how they are formed to support this. First, the latent space (the middle layer) isn't a fixed encoding. For an AE, any given input will result in a specific, reproducible set of values at each subsequent layer, including the middle layer. But for a VAE, this is probabilistic: the middle layer actually represents a mean and variance of each value, not a fixed value. There is also a difference in how VAEs are trained. While AEs are trained specifically to minimize the reconstruction error for the training data, VAEs are trained both to minimize this and to maintain a well-formed latent space, which is necessary to support their use in generating new, realistic content.

However, VAEs are generally not used to generate data when used for outlier detection and are usually simply another means to attempt to compress and reconstruct data, such that anomalous data will tend to have larger reconstruction errors. As they do work slightly differently than AEs, VAEs may be more suited to some datasets and goals than AEs, while in other cases AEs may perform better.

Although a VAE is somewhat more complicated of a model than an AE, PyOD's implementations use almost the same set of parameters. An example is shown in listing 16.3. This again assumes listing 16.1 has executed and collected the data.

Listing 16.3   Example using the PyOD VAE detector

```
from pyod.models.vae import VAE

np.random.seed(0)
det = VAE(epochs=5, random_state=0)
det.fit(X)

pred = det.predict_proba(X)[:, 1]
```

To determine if this works better than an AE or other detectors, or if other parameters work better, it is generally best to test using the methods covered in chapter 8, particularly testing with synthetic data, or by establishing a pseudo-ground truth, as described in chapter 14. Once well tuned, it may be advantageous to include both AEs and VAEs, as well as some of the other model types covered in this chapter, in an ensemble.

16.2.3 *Generative adversarial networks*

GANs, similar to VAEs, are generative models, though unlike VAEs, they use their generative process when applied for outlier detection. A GAN is actually a pair of networks, known as *generator* and a *discriminator*. A description is shown in figure 16.4, presenting the generator as G and discriminator as D. Given a set of training data (X), the generator learns to generate realistic synthetic data (data similar to the training data) and the discriminator learns to distinguish the real data from the synthetic. Training begins with the generator producing near-random data that is fairly easy for the discriminator to distinguish from real. Training then proceeds with the generator becoming more and more skilled at producing realistic data (such that the discriminator has difficulty

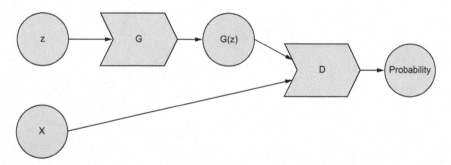

Figure 16.4   GAN network. This includes two neural networks: the generator (G) and discriminator (D). The generator learns to take random input (z) and convert this to synthetic data (G(z)) that is very similar to real data (X). The discriminator learns to distinguish synthetic data generated by G from the real data. They are trained together such that over time both become more powerful, with the generator being able to produce increasingly realistic data and the discriminator being able to detect increasingly subtle deviations from real data. Once trained, both the generator and discriminator may be used for outlier detection.

telling it from real) and the discriminator becoming more and more skilled at telling real from synthetic.

This is similar to the process used in creating Real versus Fake detectors, though it is more automated (with Real versus Fake detectors, usually a person will repeatedly manually adjust the creation of the synthetic data and the parameters used by the classifier until the detector is well-tuned) and can become, if sufficient data is available, progressively more sophisticated in its ability both to generate realistic data and distinguish generated data from real. In the end, GANs can produce very realistic data—usually more so that can be produced with a VAE—but are more difficult than VAEs to train as they require balancing training two networks.

The generator takes as input random noise (z, also called the *latent vector*—it plays a similar role as the latent space with an autoencoder), which is usually from a uniform or Gaussian distribution. The generator then learns to map this noise to realistic data (G(z)). The discriminator learns to distinguish G(z) from X. Usually the generator and discriminator are trained until they reach an equilibrium, though other stopping criteria may be used.

GANs may be used in a variety of ways to identify outliers. One simple method, equivalent to what is done with Real versus Fake detectors, is to pass data through the discriminator network. Any real data that receives a prediction that it is fake (or a prediction that it is real, but with low confidence) may be considered an outlier.

However, for outlier detection, we usually, though not always, use a slightly more complicated process and a slightly more complicated form of GAN called a bidirectional GAN (BiGAN). An example is shown in figure 16.5. BiGANs include a third neural network, called an *encoder* (or *inverse mapper*), which learns to map the inverse of the generator (map from G(z) to z, to identify the data in the latent space that resulted in G producing the current data). It therefore plays a similar role as the encoder in an AE network. In practice, we may alternate training G, E, and D, improving each a step at a time as opposed to training all three at once.

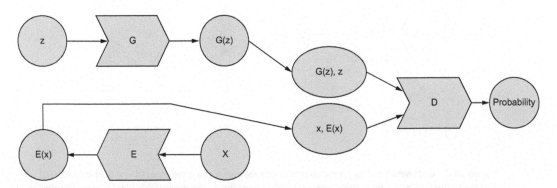

Figure 16.5   BiGAN network shown during training D. E is the inverse of G. X and G(z) should be similar (real or realistic synthetic data). z and E(x) should also be similar (the type of data that can be given to G to produce realistic output). The discriminator is often given the latent representation of the data as well (it is given z along with G(z), and E(x) along with x) and learns to distinguish these.

Once we have the full BiGAN (G, E, and D) trained, we can use this for outlier detection, as shown in figure 16.6. We use E to perform an inverse mapping on the real data (x). This will map the real data to E(x), which will be in the latent space, the same as z. The idea is that the encoder will only be able to predict the input (E(x)) for normal data. We can then take any object (any element of X), pass it through E (to estimate the input, z that G would have seen to produce this), and pass that through the generator. For normal data, G(E(x)) should be very similar to x. We can then look at the reconstruction error, similar to what is done with AE and VAE networks. We can also use the probability produced by the discriminator as part of the outlier score.

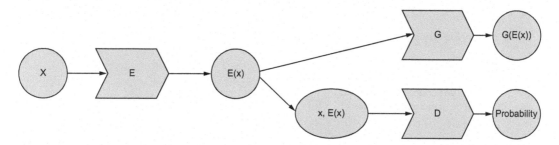

Figure 16.6 BiGAN network at predict time to estimate the outlierness of real data X. The data is encoded and passed through the generator G, as well as through the discriminator D. This allows us to measure both the reconstruction error and the probabilities estimated by the discriminator.

Note that while AE, VAE, and GAN-based models can be useful for outlier detection, VAEs and GANs can also be quite useful to generate synthetic data, similar to the methods described in chapter 11 such as GMMs and KDEs and may also be useful for outlier detection in this capacity.

ANOGAN

PyOD provides a few GAN-based detectors. The first one we look at is AnoGAN, a GAN designed specifically for anomaly detection. This predates BiGANs and works in the way described in figure 16.4. AnoGAN first fits a GAN, such that we have a trained generator and discriminator. Once this is fit, for every test point, we evaluate its outlierness using the reconstruction error as well as the discriminator prediction. As with most other GAN-based models, AnoGAN is based on the assumption that normal data have good representations in the latent space and that these can be discovered. Once this point is discovered, it is passed through the generator to determine the reconstruction error.

AnoGAN uses a method based on gradient descent to estimate, for each test point, the location in the latent space associated with the point. This is far less efficient than using a BiGAN. This search approximates what the inverse mapper in a BiGAN does but can be prohibitively slow and must be repeated for every test point. I've found AnoGAN to be slow enough to be unworkable for most projects, especially where tuning is necessary (and the process needs to be run many times) and would tend to recommend favoring other detectors, such as adversarially learned anomaly detection (ALAD; covered next), for most projects where deep learning tools are effective.

ALAD

ALAD is another GAN-based model provided by PyOD, in this case backed by TensorFlow. ALAD employs a BiGAN architecture so is substantially faster than AnoGAN. ALAD also provides some improvements over AnoGAN in the construction of the GAN itself, developed since the introduction of AnoGAN. ALAD uses the reconstruction error as the outlier score. An example is shown in the following listing.

Listing 16.4   Example using the PyOD ALAD detector

```
from pyod.models.alad import ALAD

det = ALAD()
det.fit(X)
pred = det.decision_scores_
det.plot_learning_curves()
```

16.2.4 SO_GAAL

The generative adversarial learning (GAAL) approach is very similar to the GAN models discussed previously. Internally it uses a generator and a discriminator—the generator generates synthetic data, and the classifier (discriminator) learns to distinguish real from fake. Where GAAL is different is it seeks to generate the outliers (the synthetic data) with a specific objective: not to fool the discriminator but to help the detector identify the boundary between normal and abnormal data. These are informative outliers. We want the outliers to be similar, but not too similar, to the real data, such that an effective classifier can be created, and this may be used as an outlier detector. PyOD provides two forms of a GAAL model, called single-objective GAAL (SO_GAAL) and multiobjective GAAL (MO_GAAL). We look first at SO_GAAL.

As with a GAN, part of the trick of creating a strong SO_GAAL model is to tune it until it is powerful but not too powerful. If it learns to identify even very subtle deviations from real data, it may tend to overreport on future real data, which may also deviate from the current distribution but possibly in trivial ways that we would not wish to be flagged. The main parameter for SO_GAAL associated with this is stop-epochs, with a default value of 20. This controls how long the model is tuned for and how powerful it becomes.

PyOD's implementation of SO_GAAL is based on that of another library, https://mng.bz/ZVnm. Either may be used to execute the code, but the link shown here points to documentation relating to the GAAL method. This library also provides the MO_GAAL detector, covered next. An example using SO_GAAL in PyOD is shown in the following listing.

Listing 16.5 Example using the PyOD SO_GAAL detector

```
from pyod.models.so_gaal import SO_GAAL

det = SO_GAAL()
det.fit(X)
pred = det.decision_scores_
```

Again, this will return an estimated outlier score for every record in the KDD Cup dataset.

16.2.5 *MO_GAAL*

MO_GAAL has a similar approach as SO_GAAL but was designed to address a problem that can occur with SO_GAAL. SO_GAAL can reach a state where the informative outliers generated are all the same. This is a common problem with GANs known as *mode collapse*, where a generator repeatedly creates a single type of output. To avoid this, MO_GAAL is expanded from SO_GAAL (which uses a single generator) to use k generators, so it is referred to as being *multiobjective*, as opposed to *single-objective*. Where SO_GAAL does perform well, it may be unnecessary to take on the extra complexity using MO_GAAL. However, as with outlier detection generally, it is usually useful to try multiple models. An example using this detector is shown in the following listing.

Listing 16.6 Example using the PyOD MO_GAAL detector

```
from pyod.models.mo_gaal import MO_GAAL

det = MO_GAAL()
det.fit(X)
pred = det.decision_scores_
```

16.2.6 *DeepSVDD*

DeepSVDD is a deep learning-based tool designed specifically for outlier detection. This makes it different in this regard from AE, VAE, or GAN models, which were designed primarily for compression and generation and were later applied to outlier detection. DeepSVDD is designed for deep one-class classification, so it may be used as an outlier detector in the same way as a one-class Support Vector Machine (OCSVM). The deep neural network backing, though, allows it to extend to many more dimensions than is possible with OCSVM. It works by attempting to find a neural representation of the items in the training data such that a hypersphere drawn around them may be as tight as possible. An example using DeepSVDD is shown in the following listing.

Listing 16.7 Example using the PyOD DeepSVDD detector

```
from pyod.models.deep_svdd import DeepSVDD

det = DeepSVDD()
det.fit(X)
pred = det.decision_scores_
```

Other implementations of SVDD outside of PyOD are available as well, including https://github.com/lukasruff/Deep-SVDD-PyTorch, which will be more appropriate when working with image data.

16.2.7 Deep IF

Deep IF (DIF) is similar to Isolation Forest but uses a neural network to represent the space and identify isolated areas within this, which allows it to identify nonlinear spaces. Similar to Extended Isolation Forest (covered in chapter 7), this can be more powerful than the axis-parallel splits possible with standard Isolation Forest. An example is shown in the following listing.

Listing 16.8   Example using the PyOD DIF detector

```
from pyod.models.dif import DIF

det = DIF()
det.fit(X)
pred = det.decision_scores_
```

16.3 Image data

Outlier detection with image data is a major field in itself and is one of the very interesting, and very active, areas in outlier detection research today. Looking at this is useful in itself but also provides a glimpse into some of the most advanced outlier detection techniques being developed today.

Outlier detection with image data can work somewhat differently than with tabular and other modalities. Most of the time, we're focused on the single, main object shown in an image, and the goal of outlier detection is not to determine if this object is anomalous in any way but specifically to determine if it is a type of object not encountered (or possibly very rarely encountered) during training: most of the time with image data, we are looking for what is known as *out of distribution* (OOD) data (meaning outside of the distribution used for training). Though we do on occasion, it's rare to look for unusual colors, angles, shading, background, or other properties of the pictures. Much more often, we look for novel objects.

This relates to a couple of the purposes for outlier detection in image data we looked at in chapter 1: finding items that are truly novel and managing the confidence we should have in any predictions related to the types of objects seen in images. For example, with self-driving cars, where an object is detected by a camera and the system makes a prediction as to what type of object it is, the system may assign a high confidence to the prediction, even if the object is out of distribution. This can be quite a serious problem—the vehicle may conclude that a novel object (such as a type of vehicle it did not see during training) is an entirely other type of object, likely the closest match visually to any object type that was seen during training. It may, for example, predict the novel vehicle is a billboard, phone pole, or another unmoving object. But if an outlier detector, running in parallel, recognizes that this object is unusual (and likely OOD), the system as a whole can adapt a more conservative and cautious approach to the object and any relevant fail-safe mechanisms in place can be activated.

Another common use of outlier detection with image data is in medical imaging, where anything unusual appearing in images may be a concern and worth further investigation. Again, we are not interested in unusual properties of the image itself—only if any of the objects in the images are OOD: unlike anything seen during training and therefore rare and possibly an issue.

As detecting OOD objects in images is key to outlier detection in vision, much of the training and testing done tends to relate specifically to this. Often with image data, an outlier detection system is trained on images from one data collection, and testing is done using another similar dataset, with the assumption that the images are different enough to be considered from a different distribution. For example, training may be done using a set of images covering, say, 100 types of birds, with testing done using another set of images of birds. We generally assume that, if different sources for the images are used, any images from the second set will be at least slightly different and may be assumed to be OOD, though labels may be used to qualify this better as well: if the training set contains, say, European Greenfinch and the test set does as well, it is reasonable to consider these as not OOD.

16.3.1 *Techniques for outlier detection with image data*

Though the goals with outlier detection with images can be different than with other forms of data, the methods used to find outliers tend to be similar as with other types of data where deep learning is used. The main approaches to outlier detection with image data are:

- *Reconstructive*—Here we use a model, such as an AE, that compresses the data and use the reconstruction error to estimate the outlierness.
- *Generative*—Here we use generative models such as VAEs and GANs. There are several variations on this, including, as we saw with the BiGAN example previously, where we attempt to regenerate data.
- *Confidence scores*—Here we consider where a classifier is used, and the confidence associated with all classes is low. If a classifier was trained to identify, say, 100 types of birds, then it will, when presented with a new image, generate a probability for each of those 100 bird types. If the probability for all these is very low, the object is unusual in some way and quite likely out of distribution.
- *Feature modeling*—Here embeddings (described later) are created for each object and standard outlier detection (e.g., IF, KNN) is used on the embeddings. As discussed later, embeddings created to support classification or regression problems do not tend to work well in this situation, but we look later at some research related to creating embeddings that are more suitable for outlier detection.
- *Testing with perturbed data*—Here we modify the data in some way, such as rotating the image. We may, for example, take an image, rotate it four different ways, and

for each of these four, predict how it was rotated. With normal data, the system should be able to predict all four correctly and with high confidence. For unusual data, there will be more errors and lower confidence. Other modifications may include discoloring the data, cropping, stretching, and so on.

These methods tend to work well with image data. With image data, we are well-positioned to take advantage of deep neural networks, which can create very sophisticated models of the data. One of the important properties of deep neural networks is that they can be grown to very large sizes, which allows them to take advantage of additional data and create even more sophisticated models. This is in distinction from more traditional models such as frequent pattern outlier factor (FPOF), association rules, KNN, IF, LOF, Radius, and others we've looked at: as they train on additional data, they may develop slightly more accurate models of normal data, but they tend to level off after some time, with greatly diminishing returns from training with additional data beyond some point. Deep learning models, on the other hand, tend to continue to take advantage of access to more data, even after huge amounts of data have already been used.

This is an area where image data is more suitable for deep learning than tabular data. It is usually easy to collect more image data, and it's also possible to generate more by perturbing the existing data: when we take a picture of a cat and rotate, crop, discolor, or stretch it, it remains a valid picture of the same cat. But with tabular data, each table only has the rows that it has (it is not possible to collect more rows), and perturbing them in any way will quite not likely result in equivalent rows.

Note that although there has been a great deal of progress in outlier detection with images, it is not yet a solved problem. It is much less subjective than with other modalities, at least where it is defined to deal strictly with out of distribution data (though it is still somewhat vague when an object really is of a different type than the objects seen during training—for example, with birds, if a Jay and a Blue Jay are distinct categories). Image data is challenging to work with, and outlier detection is still a challenging area. But the ideas used in outlier detection for images are quite useful, and you may be able to apply some to other forms of data as well.

16.3.2 *Astronomaly*

Before looking at using general purpose tools for deep learning-based outlier detection and their support for image data, we look quickly at a tool related to a subject alluded to in chapter 1: examining images specifically in an astronomy context. An example of a very interesting tool for this is Astronomaly (https://github.com/MichelleLochner/astronomaly). Modern telescopes produce phenomenal quantities of data daily, far more than could be inspected manually. The images that are of most value for scientific discovery are those that are most anomalous, which Astronomaly is designed to identify. It provides some tools to preprocess the images (cropping, converting to grey scale, color correcting, resizing, etc.), but much of it consists of feature extraction (using AEs and a number of other tools) and then running outlier detection, specifically IF or LOF, both provided by scikit-learn.

Astronomaly also utilizes what's called *active learning*, a process that keeps a human in the loop to help label the data to distinguish interesting (e.g., new phenomena) from uninteresting anomalies (e.g., instrument artifacts). As covered in chapter 15, having labeled data can be very valuable, but it's not always clear what data is most important to label. In chapter 15, we worked on the assumption that the records that are scored highest by an outlier detector (or ensemble of detectors) are the most relevant to hand-label, and this is usually true, but with astronomical data, even limiting hand-labeling to images with very high scores can result in more manual labor than is feasible. Active learning seeks to identify the items such that knowing if they are of interest or not helps the system learn what is most interesting.

For anyone interested in experimenting with Astonomaly, checking the Galaxy Zoo dataset (a set previously labeled through citizen science) can be an interesting place to begin.

16.4 *alibi-detect*

The alibi-detect library was introduced in chapter 7, but we take another look at it here, as its deep learning tools are where it is particularly valuable, especially for tabular, image, and time series-data. For time-series data, it provides a couple models, including a wrapper around an important times-series tool, Prophet (covered in chapter 17). For image and tabular data, it provides an AE and a VAE class, as well as some other interesting tools: a deep AE Gaussian mixture model (AEGMM) and VAE Gaussian mixture model (VAEGMM), which to my knowledge, are supported only by alibi-detect.

The autoencoder GMM works by first using an AE, which creates a low-dimensional representation of the input (and examines the reconstruction error) and then passes this embedding to a GMM, which also evaluates it for outliers. Normally an AE is trained to minimize the total reconstruction error and a GMM (as described in chapter 5) is trained for expectation maximization (finding the parameters that maximize the probability of the training data). What is interesting is that with AEGMM, the AE and GMM are trained together, with a shared objective, which allows it to create a more optimal system than where these are fit separately. VAEGMM works similarly.

Before using alibi-detect, it is necessary to install, which can be done with

```
pip install alibi-detect
```

As with PyOD, alibi-detect requires TensorFlow or PyTorch, and at least one of these must be installed. Where convenient, this can be done with `pip install alibi -detect[tensorflow]` or `pip install alibi-detect[torch]`.

alibi-detect does require some more coding when creating detectors than PyOD. This can be slightly more work but also allows more flexibility. alibi-detect's documentation provides several examples, which are useful to get you started. Listing 16.9 provides one example, which can help explain the general idea, but it is best to read through the documentation and examples to get a thorough understanding of the process. Listing

16.9 uses an AE outlier detector. As alibi-detect can support image data, we provide an example using this, using a commonly used image dataset, CIFAR10. Using this method, or other image outlier detection methods provided by alibi-detect, we are able to identify the outlier images in the dataset. CIFAR contains 60,000 images, covering 10 classes (airplane, car, ship, truck, bird, cat, deer, dog, frog, horse). The images are $32 \times 32 \times 3$ (32 pixels by 32 pixels, covering three colors) so are quite low resolution.

Working with deep neural networks can be slow. For this, I'd recommend using GPUs if possible. The code in listing 16.9, for example, takes about 1 hour on Google Colab using a CPU runtime but about 3 minutes using the T4 GPU runtime.

This example starts by first using Keras to create the encoder and decoders used by the AE and then passing these as parameters to the OutlierAE object alibi-detect provides. As is common with image data, the neural network includes what are called convolutional layers. These are used at times with other types of data as well, including text and time-series, though rarely with tabular. It also uses what's called a dense layer, which is a layer of the sort we've seen previously. We then call `fit()` and `predict()`. For fit, we specify five epochs. Using more may work better but will also require more time. alibi-detect's OutlierAE uses the reconstruction error (specifically, the mean squared error of the reconstructed image from the original image).

Listing 16.9   Evaluating the CIFAR10 image dataset

```
import matplotlib.pyplot as plt
import numpy as np
import tensorflow as tf
tf.keras.backend.clear_session()
from tensorflow.keras.layers import Conv2D, Conv2DTranspose, \
    Dense, Layer, Reshape, InputLayer, Flatten
from alibi_detect.od import OutlierAE

train, test = tf.keras.datasets.cifar10.load_data()        ◄──── Loads the data used

X_train, y_train = train
X_test, y_test = test
X_train = X_train.astype('float32') / 255
X_test = X_test.astype('float32') / 255

encoding_dim = 1024
                                                       Defines the encoder
encoder_net = tf.keras.Sequential([            ◄──── portion of the AE
    InputLayer(input_shape=(32, 32, 3)),
    Conv2D(64, 4, strides=2, padding='same', activation=tf.nn.relu),
    Conv2D(128, 4, strides=2, padding='same', activation=tf.nn.relu),
    Conv2D(512, 4, strides=2, padding='same', activation=tf.nn.relu),
    Flatten(),
    Dense(encoding_dim,)])

decoder_net = tf.keras.Sequential([            ◄──── Defines the decoder
    InputLayer(input_shape=(encoding_dim,)),        portion of the AE
    Dense(4*4*128),
    Reshape(target_shape=(4, 4, 128)),
```

```
        Conv2DTranspose(256, 4, strides=2, padding='same',
            activation=tf.nn.relu),
        Conv2DTranspose(64, 4, strides=2, padding='same',
            activation=tf.nn.relu),
        Conv2DTranspose(3, 4, strides=2, padding='same',
            activation='sigmoid')])

od = OutlierAE(threshold=.015,                          ◄─────── Specifies the threshold
            encoder_net=encoder_net,                            for outlier scores
            decoder_net=decoder_net)
od.fit(X_train, epochs=5, verbose=True)

                                                    ┌── Makes predictions on
                                                    │   the first 500 records
X = X_train[:500]                              ◄────┘
od_preds = od.predict(X,
                    outlier_type='instance',
                    return_feature_score=True,
                    return_instance_score=True)
print("Number of outliers with normal data:",
    od_preds['data']['is_outlier'].tolist().count(1))
```

This makes predictions on the first 500 rows used from the training data. None are outliers. We next look at deliberately adding an outlier to the dataset and predicting again. To do this, we could take another type of object (besides the 10 classes the model was trained on) or perturb an existing image, which we do here in listing 16.10. This takes an image of a ship (the eighth record in the data) and adds random noise. alibi-detect provides a method to perturb data, but the process is fairly simple so is coded directly here.

Listing 16.10   Predicting outliers with and without perturbing the data

```
idx = 8
fig, ax = plt.subplots(ncols=2, figsize=(8, 3))     ◄────┐ Plots image 8 and the
X = X_train[idx].reshape(1, 32, 32, 3)                    │ reconstructed version of this
X_recon = od.ae(X)
ax[0].imshow(X.reshape(32, 32, 3))
plt.axis('off')
ax[1].imshow(X_recon[0])
plt.axis('off')
plt.show()

im = X_train[idx]                              ◄────┐ Adds random noise
im.shape                                            │ to image 8
for _ in range(500):
  i = np.random.choice(list(range(32)))
  j = np.random.choice(list(range(32)))
  k = np.random.choice(list(range(3)))
  im[i][j][k] = 0
                                               ┌── Makes the predictions again
                                               │   for the first 500 records,
X = X_train[:500]                         ◄────┘   including image 8
od_preds = od.predict(X,
                    outlier_type='instance',
                    return_feature_score=True,
```

```
                        return_instance_score=True)

X_recon = od.ae(X).numpy()
X = X_train[idx].reshape(1, 32, 32, 3)
X_recon = od.ae(X)

fig, ax = plt.subplots(ncols=2, figsize=(8, 3))
ax[0].imshow(X.reshape(32, 32, 3))
plt.axis('off')
ax[1].imshow(X_recon[0])
plt.axis('off')
plt.show()

print("Number of outliers with normal data:", od_preds['data']['is_outlier'].
    tolist().count(1))
```

◄─ **Plots the modified image 8 and its reconstruction**

For this example, we pick a random image to perturb. Figure 16.7 shows this before modifying it and its reconstruction produced by the AE. As this image is typical of ships, the AE was able to reconstruct it quite well.

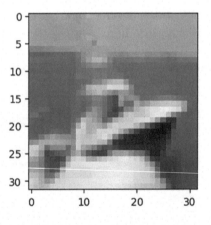 

Figure 16.7   The left pane shows image 8, an image of a boat. The right pane shows the reconstructed image. The reconstruction is quite close to the original.

Figure 16.8 shows image 8 with random noise and the reconstructed version of it, which is quite different. Given the high reconstruction error, we can say the modified version of image 8 is an outlier.

In general, many of the methods we've looked at here, provided by alibi-detect, PyOD, or other libraries, do well with image and many other formats and can perform adequately, though slowly, with tabular data. You would likely use these most of the time when using deep learning-based outlier detection, but self-supervised methods, as indicated earlier, are what may hold the most promise and are proving themselves

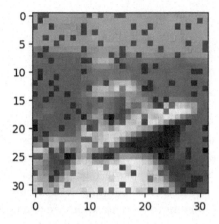 

Figure 16.8 The left pane shows image 8 with random noise added. The right pane shows the reconstruction of this. Here the reconstruction error is high, and the image in the left pane is flagged as an outlier.

very valuable with image and other modalities, even if they are not quite competitive for tabular data. We will look at these further next.

16.5 *Self-supervised learning for outlier detection with tabular data*

As indicated earlier, self-supervised learning is common for outlier detection with most types of data other than tabular and is possibly where we'll see the most advances in outlier detection in the future (including possibly with tabular data). Self-supervised learning is also very common in deep learning generally, particularly for prediction.

Self-supervised learning was developed to address an issue we often have with supervised deep learning: the models tend to require very large numbers of labeled examples—far more than is practical to label by hand. Self-supervised learning provides a way to automatically create labels for data, which is extremely useful. Before looking further into self-supervised learning, though, it's important to better understand embeddings, which we talk about next.

16.5.1 *Introducing embeddings*

We saw one example of embeddings with AEs, but for most models, embeddings are created quite differently, although the central idea is the same. Embeddings are vectors of floating-point numbers, usually between about 50 and 3,000 elements long (though often shorter or longer), which each represent an object. For example, with the images of mugs in chapter 1, we could create an embedding to represent each image. The vectors would describe (not in a way a person can understand, but in some way) the properties of each image, so would likely describe the colors, the lighting, the orientation, the size of the mug, the background, and so on. For example, the embeddings of the images may look like the two examples shown in table 16.1.

Table 16.1   Embeddings of images of mugs

V1	V2	V3	V4	V5	V6	V7	V8	V9	V10
0.232	-0.230	-0.837	-0.269	0.976	0.356	0.543	-0.486	0.432	-0.222
0.234	0.468	-0.075	-0.864	0.098	-0.738	-0.553	-0.322	-0.447	0.344

In this example, each image is represented by a vector of only 10 elements (having hundreds or thousands of elements is more typical), but it gives some sense of what embeddings look like. The idea is: each object (a video, text document, audio clip, table row, or other object—an image in this example) has a finite number of properties, which can be represented numerically and that together describe the object reasonably well. The embeddings are not sufficient to recreate an image of a mug, but they are sufficient to describe the image for many purposes, usually other machine learning applications such as classification or regression.

To create embeddings, we use deep neural networks. This can be done in several ways, but a common method is to train a network to predict a certain target. This target usually isn't one we actually wish to predict—it's created solely for the purpose of training a neural network and to create the embeddings, so it is often called a *proxy task* or *pretext task* (that is, we create the neural network on the pretext we are interested in the target it predicts). It will be a target for which it's possible to collect a large amount of labeled data and where predicting the target forces the network to understand the objects well enough to make good predictions.

To do this, we generally collect a large volume of unlabeled data and use self-supervised learning to generate labels. That is, we label the data in a manner that does not require hand-labeling. An example may be where we take a large set of images (there are many large collections of images used for machine learning research available online, but it's also possible to simply scrape many from the internet) and rotate the images some number of degrees (often one of 0, 90, 180, or 270 degrees). In this example, we start with some number of images, say 100,000, then rotate each four ways, so we have 400,000 images, all accurately labeled as to their rotation. We may then train a classifier neural network that predicts, for each image, how it was rotated: it predicts one of four classes for each image. Learning to predict this forces the neural network to develop some understanding of the content of the images, and this understanding may then be applicable for other purposes.

An example of a neural network is shown in figure 16.9. The image is identical to figure 16.1, but here we can imagine the network is trained to predict the rotation for each image and the four output neurons represent the predicted probability that the image has been rotated 0, 90, 180, or 270 degrees.

There may be any number of layers of neurons, and each layer may have any number of neurons; setting these appropriately is part of the process of tuning a neural network. Once the network is trained well (it is able to accurately predict the labels), we may pass data through the network, not for the purpose of getting a prediction, but rather to get the embeddings: the values in the second-last layer. Using other layers is actually possible, and sometimes done, but the second-last is usually used; this has a good representation of the object being encoded and tends to be sufficient input for the final neurons to make an accurate prediction.

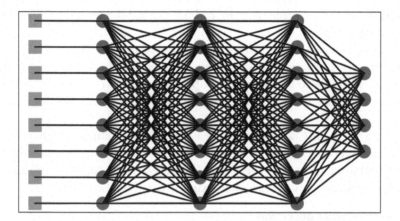

Figure 16.9 Neural network to predict the rotation of images. The input is likely the pixels of the image though may be embeddings representing the images created by another neural network. The output neurons predict the four types of rotation used in this example. Any number of rotations, or other modifications of the images, may also be used. The second-last layer may be used as embeddings for the images.

Much of deep learning relates to generating high-quality embeddings for objects (referred to as *representation learning*—finding good representations for objects). The embeddings are then typically used as input to other models—for example, classifiers or regressors. These are usually other neural networks, though they can be any strong predictive model, such as XGBoost or CatBoost.

Different pretext tasks will produce different embeddings. In the case of images, other commonly used forms of self-supervised learning include cropping, discoloring, stretching, and otherwise modifying pictures—again such that the neural network can learn to estimate which transformations were applied.

Self-supervised learning is usually used in this way to train neural networks that can create good, general-purpose embeddings for objects. Often the motivation for this is that we have other prediction problems we wish to solve but there is no practical way to hand-label sufficient data and there is no self-supervised means to label the data. If we have good embeddings to represent each object, though, this may make the prediction problem much simpler—ideally requiring only a small amount of labeled data. The idea is that by creating good representations of the objects, we've done much of the work necessary to generate predictions related to the objects. The embeddings tend to capture well the most relevant high-level concepts in the items (images, videos, audio clips, etc.).

This means we want the embeddings to be generally useful to represent the items so that they are useful for a variety of models. For example, we may be interested in finding pictures of damaged mugs (a real application of outlier detection is examining images of manufactured items where most items will appear typical but items with defects will be flagged as outliers). We may not have enough images of damaged mugs to train a network from scratch to identify these. This would require training a network to understand damaged mugs, starting from the raw pixels. But it is much easier to learn to do this starting with a good representation of the images that tend to capture the high-level concepts of the picture.

Good embeddings will be good representations of the objects generally and not only for one specific purpose. If we can create good embeddings to represent pictures of mugs, we may be able to use the same embeddings to train other models as well—for example, to estimate the size of the mugs or to identify where the mugs appear to be full.

In fact, even where it is possible to train a neural network from scratch to predict these different targets, we often simply use the embeddings created from another neural network and learn to predict the target from these embeddings, as training each neural network can, in many cases, be very expensive and time-consuming.

16.5.2 *Embeddings for outlier detection*

Given that embeddings can be generated to represent items well, and these can then be useful to support a range of prediction problems, intuitively they should be useful for outlier detection as well. They often are and can be used in several ways, but I'll first explain why the most obvious method (treating the embeddings equivalently to tabular data and performing standard tabular outlier detection, such as Isolation Forest or KNN, on these) actually tends to work poorly. We then look at other options that appear to have much more promise.

As the embeddings are usually quite large (often with hundreds or thousands of elements), we face the curse of dimensionality. In addition, embeddings often contain many elements that are irrelevant to outlier detection. With prediction, this is not a problem, as the predictors can learn which elements are relevant for each purpose. But with outlier detection, each feature is treated equally, and irrelevant features can create noise. While embeddings are very powerful for many tasks, they are (with some exceptions) not designed for outlier detection and do not perform well for this.

For tabular data especially, using embeddings for outlier detection tends to have limited value. To understand why, imagine an image being converted to an embedding as in figure 16.7, though with many more inputs and many more neurons. The images may have 1000×1000 (1 million) pixels but be reduced to embeddings of, say, 500 elements, which is a considerable degree of compression. But a row from a table may have only, for example, 50 columns. Expanding it to any vector of 50 or more elements results in a representation that is no more concise. In addition, given the embeddings can only be approximations of the original data, they also lose information. This is not a problem with images, where we usually wish to represent the content of the picture (or often simply the single main object in the picture) at a high level, so we are fine to lose information about the individual pixels or other smaller details.

However, with tabular data, the conversion to embeddings tends to not be productive. Embeddings simply stretch the data space and may add some number of irrelevant features if the neural network has more capacity than necessary (the second-last layer has more neurons than are necessary so some may contain noise). In fact, if the embeddings have more dimensions than the original data, they can be counterproductive. Some researchers have found that using embeddings for outlier detection can work best where useful subspaces of the features can be found, though these are difficult to find. An exception—where transforming table rows to embeddings is effective—is where the data has very many dimensions and the embeddings have significantly fewer dimensions, as with AEs.

Another key point about embeddings is they can actually be not just unhelpful for outlier detection but actually antithetical. As they are based on the idea of compression (historically they have been used primarily for images, text, audio, and other types of data where each item is much larger in terms of bytes than the embeddings that are created from them), they are created to minimize redundancy. However, redundancy is where we are able to find anomalies (other than univariate outliers), as this is where we can have relationships between the features and therefore exceptions to these relationships. This is why, as described in chapter 10 when searching for subspaces, we often search specifically for related features. With principal component analysis (PCA) transformations, we are also left with data with no relationships between the features, but this is done in such a way that we can search for extreme values in the new space, which is not necessarily effective with embeddings.

16.5.3 *Transfer learning*

Transfer learning is another important concept in deep learning and relates to another reason deep learning methods tend to work well for image and some other data but poorly for tabular. Significant research in deep learning-based outlier detection with image data began many years before similar research with tabular data, which is part of the reason there is still hope the progress we've made with image data can be extended to tabular data. But some things do appear to be fundamentally different, including that transfer learning is more possible with image than table data.

The idea of transfer learning is that when we train a neural network to do one task, we can often train another neural network to perform another task for substantially less effort than was needed to train the first neural network. For example, if we train a neural network to distinguish images of cats from images of dogs (the first network is often called a *foundation model*, particularly if it was trained on a pretext task), we may be able to train another neural network (using a process called *fine-tuning*), based on the first network to distinguish, for example, different types of dogs. This is the benefit of using embeddings created by one network as input for another.

The reason this works is that many of the features relevant to both problems have already been learned by the first neural network. For the second model, we may only need to retrain the last layer of the first model or perhaps add an additional layer. This has a couple substantial advantages: (1) it allows us to train the first neural network in a self-supervised manner, which allows us to create enormous amounts of labeled data (creating pretext targets along the lines of predicting the rotations of images), and (2) it can save a great deal of time and money, as it is usually extremely slow and expensive to train the first neural network, but subsequent models require substantially less training; they are starting with embeddings that are already close to what is necessary.

With tables, though, this is very difficult to do. Generally, each table is very different: there isn't the commonality between tables that there is between images (or between text documents, audio files of spoken language, or other areas where deep learning tends to work very well). With images, much of what the foundational neural network is learning basic concepts, such as edges, shapes, shadows, and so on, that apply to virtually any image. With text, a foundational neural network will learn vocabulary, grammar, and other elements of language that will transfer to other documents (impressively, even often to documents in other languages). But the features in a table and the relationships between features may have almost no commonality from one table to another. We can imagine some of the tables we've looked at in this book, such as the KDD Cup, abalone, baseball, or speech datasets—these are all quite unique, and the patterns discovered in one are likely not applicable to other tables. It appears (though this may turn out not to be true) that anything learned in any one of these tables will simply not apply to another. The implication is that transfer learning is much less applicable for tabular data, and almost every project using tabular data needs to train entirely from scratch for each table.

This applies to outlier detection as well as prediction. With text, image, video, and other formats, we can develop a sense of what's normal and abnormal on one set of data and require only fine-tuning to apply this to another dataset, but this appears not possible with tables. I suspect, if there are major advances in deep learning for tabular outlier detection, it will be in learning to transfer knowledge from one table to another. This is currently an active area of research and may produce useful techniques. If so, this could drastically change the nature of outlier detection on tabular data, though it also may simply provide an additional set of useful tools to complement the existing options.

To summarize, deep learning-based outlier detection works quite well for many types of data, including image data. As of today, though, it does not usually work as well for tabular data as the other methods covered in this book. However, some methods, particularly AEs, VAEs, and GANs, can work satisfactorily; they are slower and more difficult to tune but can often provide strong results. These three approaches, though, are not based on self-supervised learning, which is very often used for images and other forms of data. Self-supervised learning with tabular data is currently an active research area and may provide more effective outlier detection in the future. We look further at this next.

16.5.4 *Self-supervised methods for tabular data*

As discussed previously, self-supervised learning is the main method used for deep learning generally, and it is a commonly used method for deep learning-based outlier detection for most types of data. The exception is with tabular data, where it remains a stubbornly difficult problem to apply effectively. There are, though, a few reasons to look further at this: it helps us understand why self-supervised methods do work well for other modalities; it gives us a view of the cutting edge of outlier detection research today; and for some problems (as indicated at the beginning of the chapter, where we have huge tables and either many features or complex relationships among the features), these can be the best methods available today.

Given the promise of self-supervised learning, a focus of outlier detection research has been identifying good embeddings for table rows that lend themselves well to outlier detection. The belief is that this most likely hinges on identifying effective pretext tasks. Good pretext tasks are easy to identify for image data; we've seen several examples previously, based on rotating images, cropping, stretching, discoloring, and so on. They are much more difficult to develop for tabular data, as any small change in any cell value in a table row may cause the row to be very different semantically. There are no transformations, as there are with images, that are known to transform one table row to another such that it has different content but essentially the same meaning. There are several approaches to self-supervised learning, though, that may prove effective. Three of the main approaches are

- Predicting transformations
- Contrastive learning
- Masked learning

We describe each of these quickly before looking at specific implementations. The first of these, predicting transformations, we've seen already with image data and have indicated that this is more difficult with tabular data, though there are some approaches. One is to apply transformations similar to those we've seen with images, including arithmetic operations on the numeric fields. Another method is to shuffle the cells (once the data has been scaled so that all columns are on the same scale). The neural network then learns to predict the correct order of the cells in a scrambled row, which forces it to learn the relationships between the features. Once a strong sense of the relationships between the features is established, we may be able to identify any deviations from these as outliers.

With contrastive learning, we seek to ensure that embeddings for similar items are very similar to each other and that embeddings for dissimilar objects are dissimilar to each other. With images, this can be done by starting with a collection of real images and, for each of these images, creating many variations (again, cropping, rotating, stretching, and so on). Once altered, the new images may look quite different, but they represent the same object so should be given similar embeddings. We then train a neural network specifically to do this while giving other sets of images substantially different embeddings (though, again, similar to each other if they are simply different views of the same object). This is much harder to do with tabular data, as any change to a value in a row may represent a significantly different object. We do, though, look at one method for this later that can work well, called ICL.

With masked learning, the idea is to hide (or mask) certain portions of the item and train the neural network to estimate these. If you are familiar with large language models for text, you understand the idea of estimating words based on the surrounding words. With image data, one or more sections of an image may be blacked out, and the neural network may learn to predict the content of these areas. With tabular data, one or more cell values may be hidden, and a neural network learns to estimate the values in these missing cells.

We next look at the DeepOD library, which provides several implementations of these ideas.

16.5.5 DeepOD

The DeepOD library (https://github.com/xuhongzuo/DeepOD) provides tools for both tabular and time series data. There is some overlap with PyOD (some detectors, such as DeepSVDD and DIF are provided in both), but DeepOD has several additional detectors, including two we look at here called general anomaly detection (GOAD) and internal contrastive learning (ICL). DeepOD is not as well documented as PyOD but does tend to include more cutting-edge tools. In all, 27 algorithms are provided, covering both unsupervised and semisupervised methods. We look here at its support for tabular data and for time-series data in chapter 17. Although many of the detectors are designed for tabular data, they may also be used for any data that may be converted to table or embedding format.

CLASSIFICATION-BASED ANOMALY DETECTION FOR GENERAL DATA (GOAD)

GOAD is a method for tabular outlier detection based on predicting transformations in table rows (specifically, a mathematical technique known as *affine transformations*, roughly equivalent to rotations and stretches with images). The idea is that with normal data we will be able to apply numerous transformations to a row and correctly predict in each case, which was applied, while with unusual records, we will not be able to.

There are several implementations of GOAD (including https://github.com/lironber/GOAD), but we look at the implementation in DeepOD here in listing 16.11. GOAD takes the approach of applying many transformations to each object, estimating the transformation for each and aggregating the scores—again with the idea that the more normal the data, the better the tools will be able to determine each transformation that was applied to it. DeepOD uses the same API as PyOD and works in the same way. In this example, assuming X contains the KDD Cup data, each record will receive an outlier score.

Listing 16.11 Using DeepOD's GOAD with the KDD Cup dataset

```
from deepod.models.tabular import GOAD

clf = GOAD()
clf.fit(X)
scores = clf.decision_function(X)
```

This does require a large amount of RAM and special hardware, so may not be possible to execute in all environments.

INTERVENTIONAL CONTRASTIVE LEARNING (ICL)

ICL is possibly the best-known contrastive learning method for tabular data. A description of the process is shown in figure 16.10. To create two versions of the same table row, ICL takes two subsets of the features and attempts to train a neural network such that the two embeddings for these subsets are similar to each other, but the embeddings for other table rows are different. Once trained, to estimate the outlierness of a table row, we can examine how similar the embeddings for two subsets of it are, with the idea that typical rows (rows where the features relate to each other in normal ways) will have two embeddings (one per subset of features) that are similar to each other and that atypical rows will not.

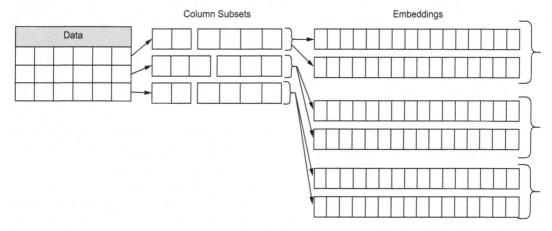

Figure 16.10 **ICL. For each row in the dataset, we create subsets of features and an embedding for each subset. As the subsets for a given row represent the same object, they should have similar embeddings but they should be different from the embeddings for other rows. The neural network learns to create embeddings for each subset of features such that this is as true as possible.**

In general, using embeddings with machine learning, once embeddings are created, they will be used for another machine learning task, such as prediction or outlier detection. In fact, when working with most modalities other than image or text (for example, video, audio, text), embeddings will almost always be used as the input. With images, either embeddings or the raw pixels may be used, but typically we would use raw pixels for the foundational model and the embeddings created by these for other models: models that have applied transfer learning to the foundational modals to perform more specific tasks. With tabular data, using the raw features is far more common than using emdeddings (both for prediction and outlier detection), but as indicated, using methods such as ICL, it is possible to create embeddings that can be useful for outlier detection. An example using this with DeepOD is shown in the following listing.

Listing 16.12   Using DeepOD's ICL with the KDD Cup dataset

```
from deepod.models.tabular import ICL

clf = ICL()
```

```
clf.fit(X)
scores = clf.decision_function(X)
```

This provides an introduction to deep learning-based outlier detection. As this field is fairly new, other tools become available from time to time, and it can be useful to check sources such as arXiv and GitHub if you are interested in keeping up to date.

Summary

- Deep learning-based outlier detection methods each use deep neural networks in some way, though there are a variety of specific approaches.
- Common methods are AEs, VAEs, and GANs.
- There are several other more recent methods as well, based on various self-supervised learning schemes.
- These tend to work well for images and some other forms of data but can struggle with tabular data.
- For image, video, audio, and some other data formats, deep learning-based methods are the only viable tools for outlier detection available today.
- For tabular data, deep learning-based methods usually do not compare favorably to established methods, such as statistical methods and traditional machine learning methods. The accuracy can be similar or lower, and the process is usually substantially slower.
- Some datasets, particularly with very large numbers of records, can be exceptions to this and lend themselves well to deep learning-based outlier detection.
- The field is progressing, and we may see similar advances as we've seen with other modalities with tabular data.

Time-series data

Though we've focused on tabular data so far in the book, another type of data you may often work with, and may need to perform outlier detection with, is time-series data. Time-series data is useful to look at in itself but is also a good example of an important concept in outlier detection: converting data from one format to another. Often, though certainly not always, tabular data can be treated as time series, and time-series data can usually be converted to table format. In general, with outlier detection, any item we examine may be typical in most ways but may, nevertheless, be unusual (and possibly unusual in an interesting way) in one or more other respects. To find these anomalies, we need to look at the data from different perspectives, and an important method to support this is converting data to another format. Although we'll look specifically at time-series data, this concept can be extended to other types of data as well. First, though, we'll take a closer look at what time-series data is and how it relates to the tabular data we've looked at so far.

17.1   *Cross-sectional, panel, and time-series data*

Three of the main types of data that you may work with are known as *cross-sectional*, *panel* (also known as *longitudinal*), and *time series*. Cross-sectional data is what we've seen primarily in this book. This is tabular data where there is no concept of time: each row simply represents one entity. For example, in the baseball dataset (first seen in chapter 4, with a sample repeated here as table 17.1), each row represents one player.

Table 17.1   Sample of baseball data set prior to scaling

Number seasons	Games played	At bats	Runs	Hits
23	3298	12364	2174	3771
13	1165	4019	378	1022
13	1424	5557	844	1588

It may be possible to add date columns to the baseball dataset—for example, representing each player's date of birth or first year in a major league—but these would be properties of the player and not timestamps of the records, and this would not be considered time-series data.

  With time-series data, we are not looking at many objects but at a single entity, measured at regular time intervals. Time-series data usually measures only a single variable for this entity, and so time-series data often has only two columns: one for the time of the measurement and one for the measurement itself. Table 17.2 shows an example of time-series data taken from https://mng.bz/RNDj, a good source of time-series datasets. Other datasets on this site relate to NYC taxi usage tracked over time, histories of server CPU usage, and so on. This table is part of a data collection that tracks the number of mentions of publicly traded companies (UPS in this table) on Twitter, with counts taken at 5-minute intervals. This dataset is used in a number of the examples in this chapter so is useful to download if you wish to execute the examples here.

Table 17.2   Time-series data representing mentions of UPS on Twitter

Timestamp	Value
2015-02-26 21:42:53	2
2015-02-26 21:47:53	2
2015-02-26 21:52:53	4
2015-02-26 21:57:53	3

Panel data is a combination of cross-sectional and time-series data. With this type of data, we have multiple entities and each is recorded at multiple points in time. An example of this is the sales and purchase data created in the simulation in chapter 11. A sample of this dataset (covering just six columns) is shown in table 17.3. Considering for a moment just the purchases, we have multiple staff, each making purchases, each at a specific time. In this example, the times are not evenly spaced (as is required with time-series and panel data), but we can make them so by aggregating by purchaser and some time frame—for example by hour or by day (setting the count to zero where there are no purchases for that purchaser that hour or day). If aggregating by hour, we will have a record for each staff for each hour.

Table 17.3 Sample of sales and purchases data created by the simulation in chapter 11

Type	Staff ID	Product ID	Datetime	Count	Inventory
Purchase	4	9	2023-01-01 09:35	113	1106
Purchase	7	11	2023-01-01 09:56	83	1082
Purchase	8	3	2023-01-01 10:14	95	1092

In chapter 12, we treated this dataset as panel data, which allowed us to create a timeline per staff, per supplier, and per product. This allowed us, then, to compare these entities to each other. It is also possible to examine the full data, which can allow for more powerful time-series analysis. If considering only, for example, specific suppliers, each may only have a short history (each may only be used by the company for a portion of the time period we are interested in), and each supplier may only have a small number of records associated with them. If we look at larger time series—for example, the full set of sales or the full set of purchases (or possibly the full history of inventory levels)—we will likely have a longer and larger collection of data.

In listing 17.1 we collect the full sales and purchases time series. This assumes the code to generate the data (https://mng.bz/2g28) has executed and the full set of purchase and sales records are in `transactions_df`. We create a time series for purchases tracking the count of purchases per day and a similar series for sales, tracking the counts of sales per day.

Listing 17.1 Converting sales and purchases data to time series

```
import pandas as pd
import matplotlib.pyplot as plt
import seaborn as sns

purchases_df = \
        transactions_df[transactions_df['Type'] == 'Purchase']
purchases_df = purchases_df.set_index(
    pd.DatetimeIndex(purchases_df['Datetime']))
purchases_df = purchases_df[['Count']]
purchase_days_df = purchases_df.resample('1d').sum()

sales_df = \
        transactions_df[transactions_df['Type'] == 'Sale']
sales_df = sales_df.set_index(pd.DatetimeIndex(sales_df['Datetime']))
sales_df = sales_df[['Count']]
sales_days_df = sales_df.resample('1d').sum()

total_days_df = purchase_days_df.copy()
```

Separates out the purchase transactions

Aggregates the data by day

Separates out the sales transactions

Combines the daily sales and daily purchases

```
total_days_df.columns = ['Purchases']
total_days_df['Sales'] = sales_days_df['Count']                    Plots the data

fig, ax = plt.subplots(nrows=2, ncols=1, sharex=True, figsize=(15, 5))
sns.lineplot(data=total_days_df, ax=ax[0])
total_days_df['Diff'] = total_days_df['Purchases'] - total_days_df['Sales']
sns.lineplot(data=total_days_df['Diff'], ax=ax[1])
plt.tight_layout()
plt.show()
```

This example uses daily summaries. Similar to the discussion in chapter 12 when looking at time series per entity, it can make a significant difference what time intervals we look at. There can be outliers that are clear when aggregating the data by hour, by day, by week, or by another period that aren't visible otherwise. It's usually worth examining the data in multiple ways.

The purchases and sales data can then be seen as time-series data, shown in figure 17.1. We show the sales and purchases together in the top pane, which can help us identify any relationships between these and any anomalies related to their relationship (logically, they should be related, with purchases ideally anticipating sales but possibly simply lagging the sales). In the bottom pane, we see their difference, which appears to be fairly stable.

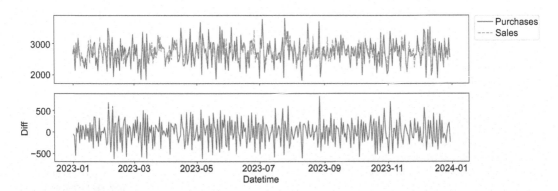

Figure 17.1   Top pane: daily purchases (solid line) and sales (dashed line); Bottom pane: their difference, also represented as time-series data

Here we have much more data to work with than when examining the data by entity; in general, it's fairly common with time-series data to have a large collection of data. For example, time-series data often comes from Internet of Things sensors, health monitoring, business processes, network traffic, web logs, and similar sources. Very often the data goes far back in time and is recorded at very small intervals. If we have sensor readings collected every 5 minutes for 31 days, we have 8,640 points of data. This is significant, but it's also common to have data collected more frequently or to have longer histories of data. If data is collected, for example, every minute for a year, we have 525,600 data points.

In general with time-series data, it's not feasible to specifically check for every rare event that may occur. We often look for a small set of known patterns (related to specific relevant anomalies), but, similar to tabular data, we also rely on outlier detection to flag any unusual patterns.

As covered in chapter 12 (with respect to collective outliers), when any time-series outliers are identified, we will likely wish to drill down into the data to identify the source of these. In this case, this probably means looking at specific purchasers, suppliers, or products to try to identify the source of the anomalies.

We next take a look at the sorts of anomalies we may find in time-series data.

17.2 Types of time-series outliers

When looking for anomalies in time-series data, we are usually looking either for unusual single values (point anomalies) or unusual sequences of values. We'll describe each of these here, as well as some of the specific types of each.

17.2.1 Extreme values

Extreme values are probably the simplest form of outlier in time-series data. These can be found easily where the data is stable over time (where it has a relatively constant average value and constant variability). Often, working with such time series, we calculate the mean and standard deviation and flag any points that are more than a specified number of standard deviations from the mean. Listing 17.2 provides a similar example but uses the interquartile range (IQR), as this is more robust to outliers. Using the interdecile range or median absolute deviation can also work well. This uses a coefficient of 2.2 to set the limits, but this would need to be set appropriately for the project to best balance under- and overreporting. Here we continue the example in listing 17.1, take the sales data, and deliberately add a single unusual value. We then plot the data along with the lower and upper limits, highlighting any values outside this range.

Listing 17.2 Identifying extreme values in sales data

```
daily_median = sales_days_df['Count'].median()          ◄──┐ Calculates the IQR
q1 = sales_days_df['Count'].quantile(0.25)                 │ thresholds for daily sales
q3 = sales_days_df['Count'].quantile(0.75)
iqr = q3 - q1
lower_limit = q1 - 2.2*iqr
upper_limit = q3 + 2.2*iqr

jan_sales_df = sales_days_df[:31].copy()               ──┐ Deliberately adds a known
jan_sales_df.loc['2023-01-15'] = 4033           ◄────────┘ outlier to the data

flagged_vals = []                               ◄──┐ Checks the data
for i in jan_sales_df.index:                       │ for extreme values
    v = jan_sales_df.loc[i]['Count']
    if v < lower_limit or v > upper_limit:
        flagged_vals.append((i, v))
```

```
fig, ax = plt.subplots(figsize=(15, 2.5))
ax.axhline(lower_limit)
ax.axhline(daily_median)
ax.axhline(upper_limit)
ax.fill_between(jan_sales_df.index, lower_limit, upper_limit, alpha=0.1)
sns.lineplot(data=jan_sales_df)
sns.scatterplot(x=[x[0] for x in flagged_vals],
                y=[x[1] for x in flagged_vals], marker='*', s=500)
plt.show()
```

Plots the daily sales, drawing any extreme values as a star

Plots the region between the lower and upper limits

The results are shown in figure 17.2. The shaded area represents the area between the lower and upper bounds, which we consider normal. The known outlier is outside this range and is straightforward to detect.

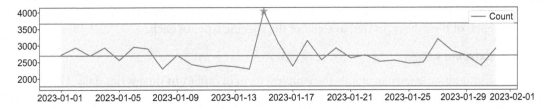

Figure 17.2 Extreme values in daily sales data. For clarity, this plot shows only the January sales, but the outlier is anomalous relative to the full year of data. The shaded area shows the expected region, with a lower bound of the first quartile minus 2.2 * IQR and the upper bound the third quartile plus 2.2 * IQR.

Tests such as this may be considered simple rules, and generally time-series data lends itself well to creating rules along these lines. This is a convenient property of time-series data not true of many other data formats, such as image, video, or audio data. In fact, defining rules is often more straightforward with time series than with tabular data. Where rules can be easily formulated, they should be used as they will execute reliably and efficiently and will produce interpretable results.

How the rules are best constructed depends on the project. As covered in chapter 2, there are expected and unexpected outliers. Expected outliers are unusual but we can anticipate them occurring at least occasionally, and unexpected outliers we would expect to never occur; if they do, there is either something extremely unusual in the data or a data collection error. We gave the example in chapter 2 of measuring human heights, with 7' being rare but expected and 70' being unexpected and assumed to be an artifact.

Using IQR with a coefficient of 4.0, we'd expect the odd value to exceed this, and we would likely take notice only if very many do. But if a point is, say, 50 times the IQR above q3, this is unexpected and a much more significant anomaly. With the sales data in this example, the median daily sales counts is about 2,600 and most days are between about 1,600 and 3,600. Daily sales of 5,000 would be unusual and possibly worth looking at, but sales of 50,000 would be almost implausible and certainly worth examining.

Where alerts are sent, we may wish to set the limits fairly high or to use multiple limits. For example, we may wish to send an alert only when events more than q3 + 5.0 * IQR occur – likely extreme values are always worth investigating. We may also wish to send alerts for less extreme events (for example, more than q3 + 3.0 * IQR) but only if many occur within a short time frame. We may as well if there is an escalating pattern to the anomalies.

Techniques such as this are often used in monitoring industrial systems or business processes where we expect roughly consistent behavior over time, and any extremely small or large values are likely worth investigating. This does, however, not work well, at least in the simple form presented here, where there are significant cycles or trends in the data, which we will look at later.

17.2.2 *Contextual point outliers*

Another type of outlier we often look for is known as a *contextual point outlier*. These are points that may have normal values considering the full range of data but are unusual for their specific time period. When examining data offline (sometime after it has arrived), this relates to finding points that are unusual given the set of points just before and just after them. In streaming environments, data is usually examined in real-time so can only be compared to prior data; in this case, contextual outliers are values that are unusual relative to the recently proceeding data. Where there are trends or cycles (covered later), these form part of the context for each value as well, but for simplicity we consider data without trends or cycles for the moment.

Figure 17.3 shows an example of a contextual outlier (shown with a dot). Comparing this value to the previous 10 or 20 seconds, it clearly stands out, though comparing it to the previous 100 seconds, it is quite normal. This example highlights that it's important to compare points to an appropriate reference period. If we look back too far, we are not necessarily looking at the window that is relevant to compare to, and if we go back not far enough, we may have too little data to reliably compare to.

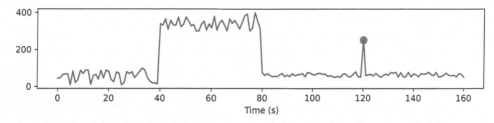

Figure 17.3 **Example of contextual point outlier. The x-axis indicates time values in seconds. The point indicated with a dot at 120 seconds is unusual considering the context of its immediate neighborhood of values, though it has a normal value considering the full range of data shown.**

Often contextual outliers can be identified as cases of a large change from the previous values. For example, if monitoring industrial equipment we may detect a sudden, and unusual, increase in vibration, even if the level is still within the range of normal. In the case of the point at 120 seconds in figure 17.3, the point will be detected easily by checking its difference from the prior value. This is an increase of about 200 points, which is unusual, though does occur once before this, at 40 seconds. The point at 120 seconds, though, is a spike, as opposed to a jump: it has a very different value than the points both right before and right after it, and the values before and after it are similar to each other. It may be useful to check specifically for unusual spikes such as this; the jump we see at about 40 seconds is also interesting but a different phenomenon than the spike at 120 seconds. For the rest of this section, though, we will assume we are comparing each value only to previous values.

There are a couple of common ways to check for contextual outliers. One is to compare each value to the individual values a small number of time steps before them. In this example, we can compare the value at 120 seconds to the values at, possibly 110, 115, and 119 seconds (going back 1, 5, and 10 seconds). We can also compare each value to the mean for some comparable period of time. The value at 120 seconds can be compared, for example, to the mean value for the previous 10 seconds—in this case to the mean value between 110 and 119 seconds. Similarly, we may compare a value to the median, to the mean and standard deviation (determining how many standard deviations from the prior mean each point is, as opposed to the absolute difference), and so on.

Comparing a point to the points immediately before or after can, in some cases, be somewhat unstable, as these points may also be outliers, or at least not representative of the relevant time period. A more stable approach can be to compare to a smoothed line that represents the general trend. Listing 17.3 provides a simple method to create a smoothed version of the data, where each point is represented by the average of the point itself, the two points before, and two points after. Many variations of this are used, but this provides the general idea of smoothing. In this example, each point in the smooth line is based on the average of five points in the original data; the more points used in the calculation, the smoother it becomes (the more small perturbations in the time series are averaged out).

Given that each point in the smoothed form of the data is based on some number of points before and after each point in the original data, there are no defined values for the very first or very last time points in the smoothed line. In listing 17.3, we simply extend the first defined point back to the beginning of the time range and similarly for the last defined value. Once this is done, we have a smoothed line covering the full time range, and each point in the original data may be compared to this smoothed line to estimate its outlierness.

Listing 17.3   Creating a smoothed version of time-series data

```
values = vals1 + vals2 + vals3 + [250] + vals4
smooth_values = []
for v in range(2, len(values)-2):
```

```
smooth_values.append(
    (values[v-2] + values[v-1] + values[v] + values[v+1] + \
    values[v+2])/5)
smooth_values.insert(0, smooth_values[0])
smooth_values.insert(0, smooth_values[0])
smooth_values.extend([smooth_values[-1], smooth_values[-1]])
```

**Calls this twice to add two points
to the beginning of the series**

The output is shown in figure 17.4.

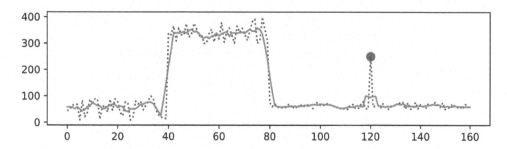

Figure 17.4 The original time series (drawn as a dotted line) and the smoothed version of the data (drawn as a solid line). As an alternative to comparing each point to other points in the original data, they may be compared to this smooth line, which may be a more stable reference.

17.2.3 Outliers based on decomposition

Finding extreme values or contextual outliers can be more difficult if the data contains what are known as *trends* or *cycles*, both of which are common in time-series data. In the sales and purchases data we've looked at, the data is stable over time, but it's more realistic that over time these would be either increasing or decreasing (that is, that there is some long-term trend, though the term *trend* also allows for more complex trends and is better understood as a highly smoothed version of the data). Figure 17.5 is similar to figure 17.3, but has a strong upward trend over time. To detect outliers, we need to take this into consideration. A value that is considered normal at 10 seconds may be considered unusually low at 160 seconds.

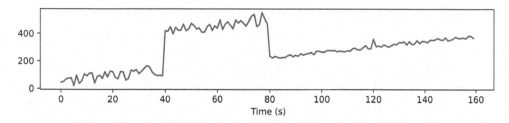

Figure 17.5 Time series similar to figure 17.3 but with an upward trend

Cycles are also common in time-series data. When tracking outdoor temperatures, for example, there are clear daily and yearly cycles. With computer network traffic, there may be times of the day as well as days of the week when traffic is higher or lower. With sales data, sales may tend to be higher certain times of the day, days of the week, days of the month, or times of the year. To determine if sales for a given day, for example Wednesday April 17, 2024, are unusually low or high, it may be best to consider sales on recent Wednesdays, days around the middle of the month for recent months, and days during April from recent years. This history, as well as the recent days, can be an important part of the context.

The spike seen in figure 17.3 would be an outlier if it occurs rarely but would not be if it occurred regularly—for example, every 10 seconds as in figure 17.6. In fact, if this were the case, seeing the value at 120 seconds *without* this spike may be considered an outlier.

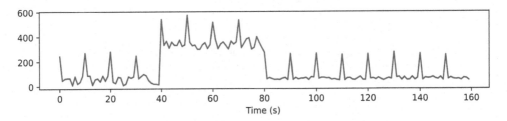

Figure 17.6   Time series similar to figure 17.3 but with a spike every 10 seconds. Here we expect a spike at 120 seconds, and it would be an anomaly if there wasn't one.

There is also a concept in time-series analysis called *seasonality*, which is similar to the idea of cycles though is more regular and more tied to the calendar—for example, relating to weekly sales patterns (seasonality can be on any time scale and does not necessarily relate to annual patterns). The term *cycles*, on the other hand, refers to repeating patterns that can be less regular and vary in length, such as business cycles. As this pattern appears regularly every 10 seconds, it may be considered a form of seasonality.

To take trends and seasonality into consideration, we can identify the trends and seasonality that exist in the data and then subtract these from the time series. What is left is known as the *residuals*. This is effectively the time series ignoring the effects of the larger trends and the seasonality. For example, in figure 17.6 we can consider the value at 120 seconds, subtracting the effect of the regular spikes every 10 seconds to see if the point is otherwise anomalous. In this case it is not, shown in figure 17.7.

Another example is shown in listing 17.4. This creates a simple synthetic test set using the sine function to create a regular cycle and then calls `statsmodels.tsa` (time-series analysis) `seasonal_decompose()` method to break this into the trend, seasonality, and residuals. For this, statsmodels uses a form of smoothing known as LOESS to calculate the trend. statsmodels provides the trend, seasonality, and residuals in the `results`

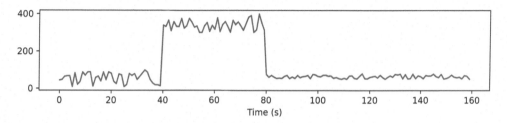

Figure 17.7 This presents figure 17.6 with the regular spikes subtracted.

variable, which allows us both to analyze and plot these. Examining these, the residuals are usually the focus, though there may be anomalies in the trend or seasonality as well.

Listing 17.4 Using statsmodels for time-series decomposition

```python
import numpy as np
import pandas as pd
import matplotlib.pyplot as plt
from statsmodels.tsa.seasonal import seasonal_decompose

np.random.seed(0)
n_points = 2000
dates = np.array('2005-01-01', dtype=np.datetime64) + np.arange(n_points)
data = 12*np.sin(4 * np.pi * np.arange(n_points)/365) + \
       50.0*np.array(range(n_points))/n_points + \
       np.random.normal(12, 2, n_points)
df = pd.DataFrame({'Values': data}, index=dates)

result = seasonal_decompose(df, model='additive', period=365)
result.plot()
plt.show()
```

This does require specifying the size of the periods—in this case, 365 days. The results are shown in figure 17.8.

As well as trends and cycles, when looking for outliers, it can be useful to consider special events—for example, holidays, scheduled maintenance, electrical blackouts, rare price discounts, and so on. Many of us doing data analysis now have to be careful when handling time-series data that includes the COVID period, given that many things were distinctly different during this time. This makes it more difficult to identify outliers during this period but also makes it more difficult to detect outliers *after* this period. Normally with outlier detection, we compare values to the time before it (as well as to prior periods related to any relevant cycles). But immediately after a special event, we may not be able to compare subsequent points to values during this time. For example, in figure 17.3, we should not conclude the value at 121 seconds is an outlier because it is significantly different from the value at 120 seconds. If we would normally compare

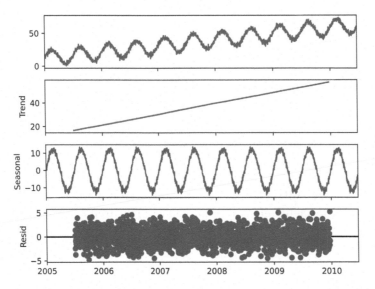

Figure 17.8   Time-series decomposition produced by statsmodels. Top pane: the original data; Second pane: the trend (not considering seasonality); Third pane: the seasonal pattern (not considering the trend); Bottom pane: the residuals (the values after taking into consideration the trend and seasonality). Here the values appear quite random, without any pattern or extreme values.

points to the value immediately before, in the case of 121 seconds, we may need to skip this test or instead use the point two steps before (at 119 seconds).

17.2.4 *Ruptures*

Another type of anomaly we often look for in time-series data is what is known as a *rupture* (also known as a *regime change, level change, change point,* or *breakpoint*). This occurs when the data shows a change, such as a jump to a higher level or a change in volatility but the change is not short-lived; it appears to be the new normal, though it is possible the data will eventually return to the previous levels. An example is seen in figure 17.3, where the level changes between 40 seconds and 80 seconds and then returns to nearly the previous level, making this time period possibly anomalous, or at least noteworthy.

While the regime change itself is likely worth flagging as an outlier (assuming these are rare), we also need to be careful, after the regime change, to compare points to comparable points; that is, we should compare each point to other points within their regime. The point at 120 seconds, which stands out as an outlier, does so only if it is compared to the regime it is within, which covers roughly 80 seconds to 160 seconds. This regime has a different level and different (lower) variance than other periods, making it likely invalid to compare a point during this period to other periods.

One tool to detect such changes is called ruptures (https://github.com/deepcharles/ruptures/), which may be installed with

```
pip install ruptures
```

Listing 17.5 provides an example using this. ruptures provides a number of algorithms to identify regime changes. This uses Pelt (linearly penalized segmentation), which is a relatively simple technique. This starts by calling a method ruptures provides, `pw_constant()`, to generate synthetic data. It then examines this data using Pelt and identifies a set of change points. We then take advantage of ruptures's `display()` method to render the data with the change points highlighted.

Listing 17.5 Generating test data and detecting ruptures

```
import pandas as pd
import numpy as np
import matplotlib.pyplot as plt        Creates test data with 1,000 points,
import ruptures as rpt                     1 dimension, 4 breakpoints, and a
                                            standard deviation of 4.0

signal, bkps = rpt.pw_constant(n_samples=1000, n_features=1, n_bkps=4,
                               noise_std=4, seed=42)

model = rpt.Pelt(model="rbf")          Creates a ruptures object
model.fit(signal)                       Fits the model to the series

result = model.predict(pen=10)          Predicts where the
                                        breakpoints are

rpt.display(signal, [], result)
plt.show()                              Displays the results
```

The output (figure 17.9) shows the original series along with dashed vertical lines where each breakpoint was identified. In each case, we can see where there is, within each regime, a new mean established, which persists for some time until another breakpoint is reached.

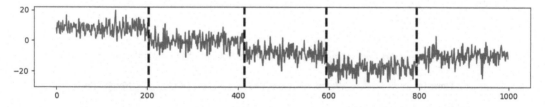

Figure 17.9 Output of ruptures on test data using the ruptures library. Here the data was created with four ruptures, and these were properly identified and plotted.

Note that testing for ruptures is imperfect, and the human eye can see patterns in the data differently than a tool such as this; ruptures may detect changes a person would miss and may also miss changes a person would not. Where feasible, it is preferable to check the data visually. But where systems run on an ongoing basis, as is common with time-series analysis, it's necessary to set up the system to run as well as possible and then check it periodically and tune as necessary, possibly adjusting the parameters used. For example, we used "rbf" as the model here, though other options are possible and may work better. There is also a `pen` parameter with the `predict()` method, which controls how sensitive the tool is to small nonlinear patterns. As with outlier detection generally, it's best to test with both real and synthetic data to ensure the system works well.

17.2.5 *Outliers based on tabular representations*

As mentioned at the beginning of the chapter, it can be useful in outlier detection to convert data from one format to another to gain new perspectives on it, and one method to identify outliers in time-series data is to convert it to table format. This is a similar idea as was introduced in chapter 12, where a number of additional features were created for each point in time, representing the history up until that point. As an example, we start with table 17.2 (repeated here as table 17.4).

Table 17.4   Time-series data representing mentions of UPS on Twitter

Timestamp	Value
2015-02-26 21:42:53	2
2015-02-26 21:47:53	2
2015-02-26 21:52:53	4
2015-02-26 21:57:53	3

We can engineer a set of additional features as in table 17.5. This provides a lag from the previous value, the difference from the previous value, and the mean of the previous two values. Some calculated values will be null in the first one or two rows where there are not enough prior rows to define them properly. Any number of similar features may also be created. The idea is to create features that capture sufficient context about each record to be able to determine, using only the values in each row, if the record is unusual.

Table 17.5   Time series from table 17.2 with additional features for historical context

Timestamp	Value	Lag 1	Diff 1	Mean Prev 2
2015-02-26 21:42:53	2	–	–	–
2015-02-26 21:47:53	2	2	0	–
2015-02-26 21:52:53	4	2	-2	2
2015-02-26 21:57:53	3	4	1	3

Although there are useful tools that work specifically with time-series data and that treat the data as a sequence of values, evaluating each value relative to its position in the series (some of these tools are covered later), it can also be useful to construct tables such as this. Doing this, each row ideally captures the full relevant context (history to that point) of the record's original value, and the rows may then be considered independently; that is, they may be considered in any order. This allows us to then use standard tabular outlier detection on the data.

Some additional features may include the following:

- Lags of longer periods—for example, the values 10, 20, or more time steps prior. This is similar for the difference features. We may also add lag features to capture cycles. If there is a strong daily cycle, we may add a lag of one day (and possibly of two, three, or more days), which allows us to compare to values the same time of the day one, two, or three days prior.

- The differences may be calculated as percent differences, as opposed to numeric differences, from the prior values. For example, from the second row to the third, the value increases from 2 to 4, which is an increase of 100.0 percent.

- The minimum or maximum values from various windows prior to the current time point. For example, we may wish to capture the maximum value in the previous hour. Outliers may be detected as values well above this maximum (or well below the minimum). We may also track percentiles for previous windows—for example tracking the 90th percentile of the values in the previous hour. An outlier is then a point well above this 90th percentile (which can be more robust, though more expensive to calculate, than using the maximum).

- If we track various lag, difference, mean values, and so on, we can also determine how the current value compares to these, taking the ratio of the value to these values. For example, we may calculate the ratio of the current value to the maximum for the previous hour, the ratio of the current value to the mean of the previous 100 values, the ratio of the current value to the standard deviation of the previous 50 values, and so on.

- We may similarly add features to put the size of the difference features in context. For example, we may track the average size of a difference between two consecutive values in the previous 1 hour.

- The day of the week, day of the month, month of the year, and similar.

Ideally the features would capture the recent values, trends, cycles, and ruptures well. Once this table is created, it's possible to use standard univariate or multivariate tests, as with any tabular data.

17.2.6 *Forecasting-based time-series outlier detection*

Another common method to identify point anomalies is to attempt to forecast each value from previous values and flag any that are significantly different from what has been forecast. This has strong intuitive appeal: outliers are points that deviate significantly from what we expected. This has the advantage that the forecast can consider recent values, ruptures, trends, and cycles. It also provides a straightforward outlier score: the difference between the forecast and the actual value. Normally, we would present this error relative to the normal forecast errors, such as the difference from the median error divided by the median absolute deviation of the errors. In figure 17.3, if we predict a value of, say, 50 for 120 seconds and the actual value is 240, then the error is 190. If most forecast errors are around, perhaps, 10 or 20, then this is a significantly larger deviation from the forecast value than normal and can be considered an outlier.

Many methods can be used for forecasting in Python. One common method is Auto Regressive Integrated Moving Average (ARIMA). There are actually numerous variations on this as well, with similar names, such as SARIMA and SARIMAX. These are provided by, among other tools, statsmodels. ARIMA is usually the first, or one of the first, methods we would try for forecasting, along with another called Exponential Smoothing. ARIMA is roughly a linear regression based on prior values—though that's actually an oversimplification, and it's well worth looking closer at this method if you work with time-series data. It's an interesting, but quite easy to understand, idea.

In listing 17.6, we generate synthetic test data. In this, each point is based on the previous value, the day of the week, and some randomness. In the subsequent examples, we look at forecasting this data.

Listing 17.6   Generating test data

```
import numpy as np
import pandas as pd
import matplotlib.pyplot as plt
import seaborn as sns
import datetime

np.random.seed(42)                                        Specifies the date range
n_points = 2000                                           of the synthetic data
dates = np.array('2005-01-01', dtype=np.datetime64) + np.arange(n_points)
d_df = pd.DataFrame(dates)

base_value = 100
values = []
prev_value = base_value                                   Loops through the dates and
for i in range(n_points):                                 generates a random value for each
    dow = d_df.loc[i, 0].dayofweek
    r = (np.random.rand() * 2) - 1
    v = (0.8)*prev_value + (0.02)*(r * base_value) + \
        (0.8)*(dow+1)
    values.append(v)
df = pd.DataFrame({'Values': values}, index=dates)

fig, ax = plt.subplots(figsize=(15, 2))
sns.lineplot(df['Values'], color='blue')
plt.show()
```

Listing 17.7 shows an example using ARIMA. For this we use an excellent library for time-series analysis called Darts (https://github.com/unit8co/darts). This has many tools besides ARIMA that are worth investigating as well. In this example, we convert the dataframe to a TimeSeries object, which is a class Darts works with. We then create and fit an ARIMA model using all but the last 60 values. This has several parameters that require tuning, which normally needs to be done experimentally. We then predict the last 60 values and plot these. We must first install darts with

```
pip install darts
```

Listing 17.7 Forecasting values using Darts with ARIMA

```
from darts import TimeSeries
from darts.models import ARIMA

df['timestamp'] = df.index
series = TimeSeries.from_dataframe(df, "timestamp", "Values")

model = ARIMA(p=7, d=2, q=2)
model.fit(series[:-60])
pred = model.predict(60)

pred.plot(label="forecast", low_quantile=0.05, high_quantile=0.95)
plt.legend()
plt.show()
```

Converts the dataframe to a format darts uses

Creates and fits an ARIMA model

Predicts the last 60 values

Plots the predictions

The forecast is shown in Figure 17.10.

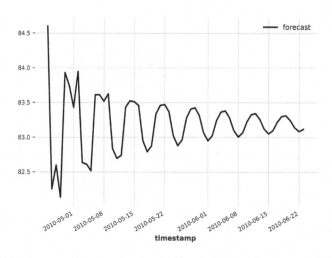

Figure 17.10 Forecast of the last 60 days based on prior data using the ARIMA tool in Darts. This maintains the weekly pattern but relies more on the mean value when predicting further into the future. The accuracy of the model is dependent on tuning the parameters used.

It's also possible to perform forecasting using the same type of regression models we normally use for prediction. Doing this, we would usually create a dataframe where each row covers one value from the time series, along with features summarizing the history of values up until that point in time.

In listing 17.8 we use a Random Forest. We start with engineering features. If we believe there may be weekly, monthly, or annual cycles, we can engineer features related to these; in this example, these are created in the form of several lag values. This includes lags of 7, 14, and 21 days to capture weekly cycles. We also use 360 and 364 days to capture annual cycles. 360 is divisible by 12 so will also respect any monthly cycles, and 364 is divisible by 7 so will respect any weekly cycles. As the dataframe includes information about recent values and values from prior cycles, it ideally has enough information to make accurate forecasts such that any values deviating from the forecasts can be reasonably considered outliers.

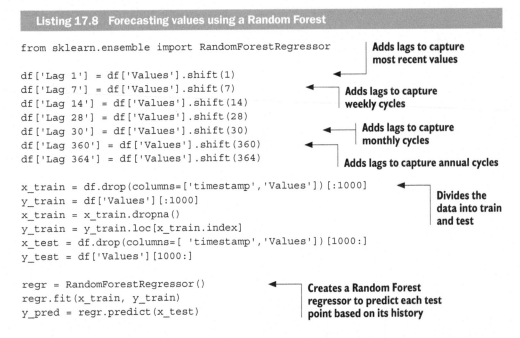

Listing 17.8 Forecasting values using a Random Forest

```
from sklearn.ensemble import RandomForestRegressor          Adds lags to capture
                                                            most recent values
df['Lag 1'] = df['Values'].shift(1)
df['Lag 7'] = df['Values'].shift(7)                    Adds lags to capture
df['Lag 14'] = df['Values'].shift(14)                  weekly cycles
df['Lag 28'] = df['Values'].shift(28)
df['Lag 30'] = df['Values'].shift(30)                 Adds lags to capture
df['Lag 360'] = df['Values'].shift(360)               monthly cycles
df['Lag 364'] = df['Values'].shift(364)
                                                      Adds lags to capture annual cycles

x_train = df.drop(columns=['timestamp','Values'])[:1000]
y_train = df['Values'][:1000]                              Divides the
x_train = x_train.dropna()                                 data into train
y_train = y_train.loc[x_train.index]                       and test
x_test = df.drop(columns=[ 'timestamp','Values'])[1000:]
y_test = df['Values'][1000:]

regr = RandomForestRegressor()                    Creates a Random Forest
regr.fit(x_train, y_train)                        regressor to predict each test
y_pred = regr.predict(x_test)                     point based on its history
```

We plot the actual and forecast values just for the last 60 days in figure 17.11 and can see the forecast is fairly accurate: the gap between the actual and predicted values (shown as the shaded area) is fairly small. In this example, the model performs better than the ARIMA model, but this may not be true if the ARIMA model were well-tuned.

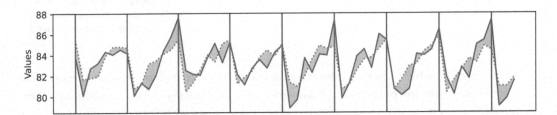

Figure 17.11   Actual (solid lines) and forecast values (dotted lines) from the test time-series data. The vertical lines indicate weeks. We can see a regular pattern over each week with some randomness. The predictions are consistently reasonably accurate.

This can also be measured using an error metric such as mean absolute error or mean squared error. Mean absolute percentage error (MAPE) is also commonly used in time-series forecasting; this measures the error in each point forecast relative to the size of the actual value. This error metric has the appealing property that it is very interpretable; it's easy to understand a MAPE of, say, 0.14: on average the forecasts are off by 14%. An implementation is provided in listing 17.9. Using this, we can determine if the accuracy is reasonably high (the average error is low). We can also take the most accurate model where multiple models are tested. Testing should be done on multiple test months, similar to cross-validation as is done with cross-sectional data.

Listing 17.9   Determining the MAPE for the prediction

```
import numpy as np
def mape(y_true, y_pred):
    return np.mean((abs(y_true - y_pred)/y_true)*100.0)

mape(y_test, y_pred)
```

We next test adding the following line to listing 17.6 immediately after defining the dataframe:

```
df.iloc[1980]['Values'] = df.iloc[1980]['Values'] * 1.1
```

This adds a known outlier to the 1980th value. Training and predicting again, we have the results in figure 17.12, which shows a large forecast error at this point (shown with a dot and a vertical dashed line). Similar to the average error, we can measure outliers based on absolute errors or percent errors relative to the forecast value.

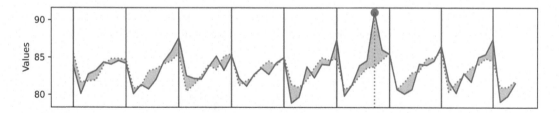

Figure 17.12   The same as figure 17.11 but with a single known outlier deliberately added. A dot and dotted vertical line indicate the position of this value. We can see the forecast value is substantially less accurate than normal for this point.

It is only possible to identify outliers in this manner if the forecasts are reasonably strong. If not, it may be possible to engineer more predictive features or to use a stronger model than RandomForest, such as XGBoost or CatBoost. It is also possible to use other tools designed specifically for time-series forecasting, such as Prophet (covered later) or one of several others provided by Darts. One advantage they all have is they are able to extrapolate any trends present in the data into the future, which predictive models based on decision trees (including Random Forests, XGBoost, and CatBoost) cannot do; they are able only to predict values similar to what they have seen during training. For example, if the data looked similar to figure 17.13, we see the same weekly cycle, but the trend leads to increasingly higher values, which tree-based models cannot predict. For this, we use other models such as linear models (including ARIMA and variants) or models based on neural networks.

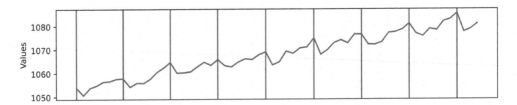

Figure 17.13   Similar data with upward trend. Future values cannot be predicted from prior values using a tree-based predictor as they are unlike any previous values.

Where the data is predictable, techniques such as this can be used to find point anomalies. It may also be quite relevant to identify where there are many point anomalies within a short time window, suggesting that time period is anomalous in some way. If, on the other hand, no techniques are able to forecast the data accurately, the data is likely random and there is no concept of outliers in the sense of deviations from forecasts. It may still be productive to check for extreme values, unusual jumps, spikes, and so on but not to check forecasts.

In listing 17.8, we included a lag of one, which allows us to include the immediately previous values in the forecast. In some cases, we may wish to exclude features that are this close to the forecast value. Figure 17.14 shows a time series that is fairly stable and

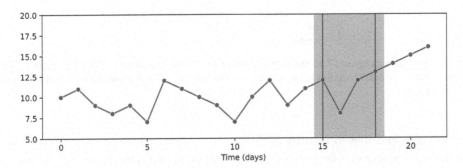

Figure 17.14   Example forecasting using a gap between the train and predict period. This ensures the forecasts cannot rely entirely on only recent values.

appears random until about day 18; after this point, we see an escalating set of values. These are taking on values that are unusually large with respect to the full time series but are still each quite predictable from the values immediately before them. If the data represents daily sales, the sales by day 21 are unusual but still very predictable based on the sales on day 20. Figure 17.14 also shows a gap that may be added to help mitigate this effect. This would slide across the data as we forecast each point. In this example, if forecasting the value on day 19, we would forecast based on the values between days 0 and 14 only—the gap represents the data not used for the forecast. When forecasting the value on day 20, we would slide this window by one day so would predict based on values between day 0 and day 15 (though we may also slide the start date used for the forecast so would forecast based on day 1 to day 15). Doing this, predictions are based on the recent past for each point but not the values only a couple time steps previous, which allows us to better detect patterns such as we see starting day 18 as anomalous.

There are many methods to create forecasts for time series, and this is something we can take advantage of. Where we use multiple forecasts and a point is unusually different from most or all the forecasts, we can be more confident it is truly an outlier. In addition, using multiple forecasts allows us to combine them—for example, taking their average. As with creating ensembles generally, this can result in more accurate forecasts, which are more meaningful to compare actual values against.

One important thing to notice with forecasting is that each value is forecast based on prior values—usually values shortly before the point being predicted (and values in the same place in the cycle for previous cycles). If these values are themselves anomalous, they can affect subsequent forecasts. In fact, an important application of outlier detection for time-series data is to improve forecasting by removing outliers (for example, values associated with one-time events or data artifacts) and replacing them with more expected values so that later forecasts are not thrown off by these. Similarly, with outlier detection in time series, it's useful to replace outliers once they are detected; this allows us to better support outlier detection on points later in time in the series. For example, with the point identified as an outlier at 120 seconds in figure 17.3, we may replace this with the value that would be forecast for 120 seconds; this may allow us to more reliably detect outliers in the subsequent period. We do, though, need to be careful, as we risk overwriting current patterns and perpetuating previous patterns in the analysis if we are too aggressive.

In this section, we've looked at identifying outliers as points that are very different from what would be predicted. It is also often important to look for time-series data that is *too* predictable. With most processes we assume a certain level of randomness, and it may be suspicious if this is not present. For example, one important test for financial fraud, indicated in chapter 1, is to check for revenue or profit numbers that are unusually predictable from previous values, suggesting manipulated values.

17.2.7 *Unusual shapes of windows in timelines*

So far we've looked at techniques to locate anomalous point values, but it can also be useful to identify periods of time that have unusual sequences of values even if the individual values are all normal. This has several applications—for example, detecting where machinery is unusually volatile or where financial data is unusually smooth. We may also find anomalous sequences where there are strong cycles: we can detect where the data, for some periods, deviates from these cycles. The example in figure 17.15 shows a very regular weekly pattern, but one week deviates from this, having a flat sequence of values for several days. This pattern is fairly common in time-series data, occurring for example where the process shuts down (for example, a store closes for a week) or the process for collecting and storing the data breaks (for example, staff fail to properly record the sales).

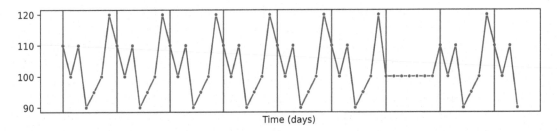

Figure 17.15   Time series with regular weekly pattern. One week has a flat pattern for most of the week, representing a divergence from the norm, though all individual values are normal.

Listing 17.10 demonstrates a simple method to determine the normal shape of each week. This loops through each week, then over each day in the week, determining how the values relate to the week as a whole. This allows us to capture weekly cycles even where the weeks are at different levels from each other. Given this, we may then compare the actual shape of each week to this and in this way identify any unusual weeks.

Listing 17.10   Describing the regular shape of time period

```
avg_frac_dict = {x:[] for x in range(7)}          Initializes a dictionary that tracks the
for i in range(0, len(df), 7):                     relative values of each day in each week
  week_df = df.iloc[i: i+7]
  avg_val = week_df['Values'].mean()               Loops over each week
  for j in range(len(week_df)):
    avg_frac_dict[j].append(week_df.iloc[j]['Values'] / avg_val)
avg_frac_dict = {x:np.mean(avg_frac_dict[x])       Loops over each day
                for x in avg_frac_dict.keys()}     in the current week
```

In the case of the graph shown in figure 17.5, this produces: [1.06, 0.96, 1.06, 0.86, 0.91, 0.96, 1.25], indicating how each day of the week typically relates to the average of the week. Any weeks substantially different from these ratios can be considered outliers.

We may also wish to engineer features that describe the amount of volatility in each period. In listing 17.11, we consider each month and engineer a few features to describe the month in terms of how much variability there is. Many features may be used for this purpose. This example uses the standard deviation of the values, the fraction of values that are larger than the previous (which gives a sense of how often the amounts tend to increase vs decrease), and the fraction of values that are peaks (larger than the values on either side).

Listing 17.11 Engineering features for the volatility each month

```
import statistics

df['Lag -1'] = df['Values'].shift(-1)
df['Bigger'] = df['Values'] > df['Lag 1']
df['Peak'] = (df['Values'] > df['Lag 1']) & (df['Values'] > df['Lag -1'])

df['YM'] = df.index.strftime("%Y%m")
df.groupby(['YM'])['Values'].std()
df.groupby(['YM'])['Bigger'].mean()
df.groupby(['YM'])['Peak'].mean()
```

These features may then be examined per group, in this case by month. Figure 17.16 shows the distribution of standard deviations within the months. In this case, there is a roughly normal distribution, and none of the months stand out as having very low or very high standard deviations.

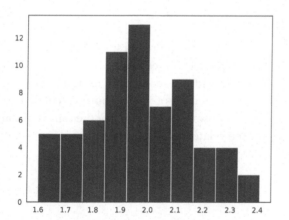

Figure 17.16 Histogram of the standard deviations found within each month. None stand out as unusually volatile (having high standard deviation) in this example.

17.2.8 *Tabular outlier detection on windows of data*

Where there is strong seasonality, it's possible to reorganize the data such that each row represents one period and the features represent the values for each element of the period. This may be done using only the original data (though additional features may also be added where useful). In listing 17.12 we take the data created in listing 17.6 and reshape it so that each row represents one week, with seven features for the values in the seven days each week.

Listing 17.12   Creating a dataframe for each period

```
weekly_arr = []
for i in range(0, len(df), 7):                    ← Loops through each
    week_df = df.iloc[i: i+7]                        week in the data
    weekly_arr.append([i] + week_df['Values'].values.tolist())
weekly_df = pd.DataFrame(
        weekly_arr,
        columns=['Week', 'Mon', 'Tues', 'Wed', 'Thur',
        'Fri', 'Sat', 'Sun'])
weekly_df = weekly_df.dropna()
weekly_df
```

This creates the table shown in table 17.6, with a row for each week.

Table 17.6   Dataframe organizing the weeks as rows

Week	Mon	Tues	Wed	Thur	Fri	Sat	Sun
0	84.2	87.4	81.7	81.9	81.9	81.8	82.2
7	86.2	86.0	81.6	79.6	84.2	84.5	82.8

Once this is created, standard multivariate tabular outlier detection can be executed to identify any unusual weeks.

17.2.9   *Mulivariate time-series outliers*

So far we've looked primarily at examples where there is a single value we are tracking, but time-series data may also have multiple sequences of data, all recorded at the same time intervals. One example is the sales and purchases data in figure 17.1 (repeated here as figure 17.17), which are two sequences of values, both calculated daily. We may also have cases where two or more sensors are monitoring the same equipment or where two or more statistics are tracked related to an e-commerce website. We can look

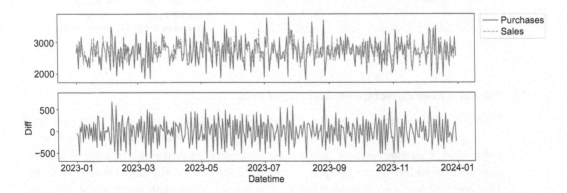

Figure 17.17   Sales and purchases data

for anomalies in each of the series, but, where the series tend to have a relationship to each other, it's also possible to look for deviations from this.

A simple test in this case is to take their difference, as in the bottom pane of figure 17.17, and examine this for unusual differences, or unusual sequences of differences, in the two series. In listing 17.13 we load in a dataset related to air quality, which can be found at https://mng.bz/1a21. This tracks a number of metrics, but we look at three specifically in this example: PM2.5, PM10, and SO2.

Listing 17.13   Displaying the Beijing Multi-Site Air Quality dataset

```
import pandas as pd
air_quality_df = pd.read_csv(
    'PRSA_Data_Aotizhongxin_20130301-20170228.csv')
(air_quality_df[air_quality_df['year']==2017][['PM2.5', 'PM10', 'SO2']].
    plot(subplots=True, sharex=True, figsize=(10,10)))
plt.show()
```

Figure 17.18 shows the series for 2017 for the three metrics related to air quality. We can see these are largely in sync though not completely. Any cases where they diverge substantially can likely be considered outliers.

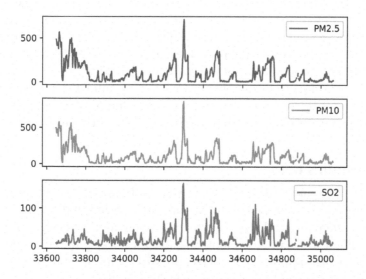

Figure 17.18   Three columns from the Beijing Multi-Site Air Quality dataset, PM2.5, PM10, and SO2 for 2017. We can see these are correlated. Though not perfectly in sync, it may be considered anomalous where one is very different from the others.

In listing 17.14 we add a set of features that measure the pairwise distances between the time series. We first scale the data so that each feature is comparable. We may then simply take the numeric differences between the original features.

Listing 17.14   Calculating pairwise differences between features

```
from sklearn.preprocessing import RobustScaler

df = air_quality_df[air_quality_df['year']==2017]
df = df[['PM2.5', 'PM10', 'SO2']]
scaler = RobustScaler()
df = pd.DataFrame(scaler.fit_transform(df), columns=df.columns)

for col_idx_i in range(len(df.columns)):
    col_name_i = df.columns[col_idx_i]
    for col_idx_j in range(col_idx_i+1, len(df.columns)):
        col_name_j = df.columns[col_idx_j]
        df[f"Diff {col_name_i} vs {col_name_j}"] = \
            df[col_name_i] - df[col_name_j]
```

Once this is executed, we have a dataframe where each row represents one point in time and includes the values for each measurement as well as the pair-wise differences between them. We can run standard tabular outlier detection on this dataframe. In this case, S02 is different from PM2.5 and from PM10 during the early part of the year. This can be seen in the plot, but encoding this allows us to automate the act of finding such outliers.

In some cases, there should be a direct relationship between the series being measured. In figure 17.18 we expect PM2.5 and PM10 to rise and fall at about the same times. But in other cases, there may a strong relationship but a lag. For example, with sales and purchases records, where the purchases simply replenish the goods sold, the purchases may follow behind sales by some number of days. With economic data, there are often leading indicators (for example, the Consumer Confidence Index) that proceed other time series by some interval. In these cases, the previous techniques can work, though they require either shifting one or more series to put them in line, or engineering the features to consider the lags.

17.3   *Tools for time-series data*

We've now gone over some of the basic ideas with outlier detection with time series. This is a major area of study in itself, but it has hopefully given you the background to code simple tests where this works best and to explore the tools available where this is the best option. There are many good tools available for working with time-series data in Python and many that support outlier detection. We can, unfortunately, cover only a few of these here, but these will give you a good background.

17.3.1   *Anomaly Detection Toolkit*

A very good tool for time-series outlier detection is the Anomaly Detection Toolkit (ADTK; https://github.com/arundo/adtk). This is intended for unsupervised and rules-based outlier detection in time series. It may be installed with

```
pip install adtk
```

Listing 17.15 provides a very simple example. This loads in the data shown in table 17.2 related to mentions of UPS on Twitter. To execute this, it's necessary to download the .csv file and place it in a folder where this code may access it (though any file with time-series data will work as well). ADTK provides a method `validate_series()`, which can be used to check the data is loaded properly. It also provides a `plot()` method, which is called here on the original data and again with the anomalies found. Here we simply set high and low thresholds (flagging anything under 0 or above 150).

Listing 17.15   Using ADTK as a simple method to detect extreme values

```
import pandas as pd
from adtk.data import validate_series
from adtk.detector import ThresholdAD
from adtk.visualization import plot
import matplotlib.pyplot as plt

df = pd.read_csv('Twitter_volume_UPS.csv')        ◄──┘  Reads in the data
df['timestamp'] = pd.to_datetime(df['timestamp'])     ┐  Sets the timestamp feature as
df = df.set_index('timestamp')                    ◄──┘  the index of the dataframe
s_train = validate_series(df)

plot(s_train)                ◄──┘  Plots the original data
plt.show()
                                          ┐  Collects the anomalies,
                                          │  defined as any over the
threshold_ad = ThresholdAD(high=150, low=-1)   │  specified threshold
anomalies = threshold_ad.detect(df)        ◄──┘
plot(df, anomaly=anomalies, ts_linewidth=1, ts_markersize=3,
    anomaly_markersize=5, anomaly_color='red', anomaly_tag="marker")  ◄──┐

                                                   Plots the data with the
                                                   anomalies highlighted
```

The output with the flagged anomalies is shown in figure 17.19.

This used a hard-coded limit, which can work well in some cases, but it is more robust and easier to set up using a method such as IQR, which we do in listing 17.16. This uses the same code as listing 17.15 but replaces the import, the line to create the anomaly detection object, and the line to execute the `detect()` method. This example uses a coefficient of 20.0 as the data contains many extreme values.

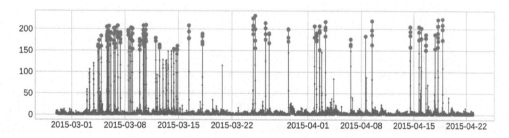

Figure 17.19   ADTK's `plot()` method shown with anomalies on the Twitter Volume UPS dataset

Listing 17.16 Using ADTK with a threshold based on the IQR

```
from adtk.detector import InterQuartileRangeAD

iqr_ad = InterQuartileRangeAD(c=20.0)
anomalies = iqr_ad.fit_detect(df)
```

The output is shown in figure 17.20. This uses a slightly different (lower) threshold than in figure 17.19, and so more points are flagged as extreme values.

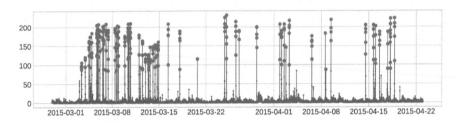

Figure 17.20 This is the same as figure 17.19 but uses IQR with a coefficient of 20.0 instead of a hardcoded limit.

This provides only a simple example, but ADTK offers several other tools as well, checking for deviations from seasonal patterns, spikes, level shifts (ruptures), and changes in volatility.

17.3.2 DeepOD

DeepOD (https://github.com/xuhongzuo/DeepOD) was first introduced in chapter 16 where we looked at its support for outlier detection in tabular data. We look at it again here as it also supports several deep learning-based methods for time-series outlier detection. This includes implementations of Deep Isolation Forest and Deep SVDD (both introduced in chapter 16) created specifically for time series, as well as several other quite sophisticated deep outlier detection tools. We look here (listing 17.17) at one method supported, TimesNet. This uses an interesting approach where a 1D time-series dataset is first expanded (using a complex neural network model) to a 2D matrix. This is similar to some of the feature engineering we've seen already, but it is much more involved and more abstract. As with other deep learning-based models, it's able to model multiple periodicities very well. TimesNet is considered among the stronger deep learning-based tools for time-series outlier detection, though for any given project, other tools may work preferably.

TimesNet is based on PyTorch, so this must be installed as well. As with any deep learning-based tool, it will be considerably slower to execute than most other approaches. To execute this code, it is necessary to have access to one or more GPUs. Before executing, we can install it with

```
pip install deepod
```

As with many Python libraries, installing this can conflict with other installations, and using a virtual environment is safer.

Here we again use the dataset of mentions of UPS on Twitter. For simplicity, we train and test on the full dataset. We set outliers to be any records with a score over 1,000. We then plot the full data, highlighting any records flagged as an outlier.

Listing 17.17 Using TimesNet to detect outliers

```
import numpy as np
import pandas as pd
from deepod.models.time_series import TimesNet
import matplotlib.pyplot as plt
import seaborn as sns                                    Collects the data

df = pd.read_csv('Twitter_volume_UPS.csv')          ◀──┘    Formats the data
df.index = df['timestamp']                           ◀───── as TimesNet requires
df = df.drop(columns=['timestamp'])
                                                     Creates a model, fits, and gets
clf = TimesNet()                                 ◀──┘ outlier scores for each record
clf.fit(df)
scores = clf.decision_function(df)
                                                 Reorganizes the data
df['x'] = range(len(df))                      ◀── to make plotting easier
df1 = df.loc[scores<=1000]
df2 = df.loc[scores>1000]                            Plots the data, highlighting
                                                                   the outliers
sns.scatterplot(data=df1, x='x', y='value', color='blue', s=5)    ◀──
sns.scatterplot(data=df2, x='x', y='value', marker="*", s=70, color='red')
plt.xticks([])
plt.show()
```

The output is shown in figure 17.21. The outliers tend to be the larger values, though some more moderate values are flagged as well, likely due to deviations from seasonality or large differences from prior values.

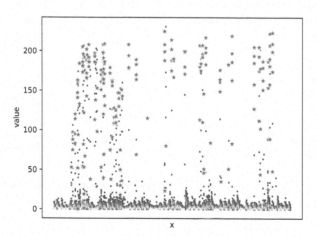

Figure 17.21 Output of TimesNet run on mentions of UPS on Twitter. This shows outliers as stars and other points as dots.

17.3.3 *Prophet*

Prophet (https://github.com/facebook/prophet) is one of the more popular time-series tools today. It does not include outlier detection, but it does include very powerful methods for forecasting and so is well worth looking into for this. Prophet also provides decomposition into trends, cycles, and residuals and change point (rupture) detection. Prophet has some appealing properties, including the ability to take holidays into consideration.

Here we provide an example using Prophet for forecasting, followed by detecting outliers as points that deviate from these forecasts. What's very useful for outlier detection is that Prophet (as with ARIMA models and many other tools, but not all) provides a confidence range for each prediction, which means it's possible to detect outliers as points outside of the confidence range. However, we should be careful doing this: where we predict for a range of time, the times furthest into the future will always have the widest confidence range. This, though, is not relevant for outlier detection and is simply an outcome of the fact that predicting further into the future is harder than predicting the near future. To avoid this, when evaluating each data point, we would ideally train on all data up until this point in time and then predict only this value, repeating this for each value we wish to evaluate. However, this is computationally expensive, so in practice we would tend to predict moderately sized batches at each step.

In listing 17.18 , for simplicity, we simply train on the full dataset and predict on this as well. This can be sufficient in situations where we wish only to evaluate a single series and it is not necessary to generalize. To execute this, we need to first install Prophet with

```
pip install prophet
```

Alternatively, Prophet is also provided with Darts and with alibi-detect, so installing either of these will work as well. In this example, we use the Twitter data again. Prophet requires all data be placed in a dataframe with two columns: "ds" representing the date and "y" representing the value that is tracked. We collect the forecasts and flag as outliers any values above the upper limit of the forecasts. Here we use the default 0.95 for the confidence range, meaning the range where the model is 95% confident the true value will fall within.

Listing 17.18 Forecasting with Prophet

```
import pandas as pd
from prophet import Prophet                              Collects the data

df = pd.read_csv('Twitter_volume_UPS.csv')              Ensures the data
df = df.rename(columns={'timestamp':'ds', 'value':'y'}) is in the format
                                                         Prophet requires

m = Prophet()                    Creates a Prophet model and predicts the
m.fit(df)                        values for all records in the dataframe
forecast = m.predict(df)
m.plot(forecast)
```

```
outliers = []
for i in range(len(df)):
    if df.iloc[i]['y'] > forecast.iloc[i]['yhat_upper']:
        outliers.append(df.iloc[i]['ds'])
```

Collects the outliers as all values above the upper limit of the forecast

The forecast object returned by the predict() method is a dataframe with a rich set of features describing the fit model and the forecast. Three features are particularly interesting for outlier detection: y_hat, y_hat_upper, and y_hat_lower, which are respectively the forecast value, the upper limit of the forecast, and the lower limit. In this example, we populate the outliers array with a list of timestamps where the value was above the upper bound of the confidence interval.

Prophet also supports plotting, which is shown in figure 17.22. This shows a confidence range around the predictions (the shaded areas) as well as a set of points well outside this, when there were unusually many mentions of UPS on Twitter.

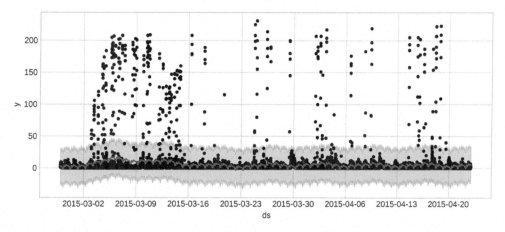

Figure 17.22   Mentions of UPS on Twitter. The actual data is shown as dots and the predicted values as a line, along with the confidence range, shown as a shaded region.

Summary

- Some data is naturally in table format but can be converted to time-series format to examine in other ways.

- Similarly, some data is naturally in time series but can be converted to tabular.

- Examining data from other perspectives allows us to find anomalies that may be missed otherwise.

- There are several types of outliers we often look for in time-series data, including extreme values, contextual outliers, ruptures, deviations from forecasts, and unusual shapes.

- We may also look for multivariate time-series outliers, where two or more series tend to have a certain relationship and deviations from this relationship may be considered outliers.

- There are many tools for outlier detection in time-series data, including many based on simple concepts (such as extreme values or deviations from seasonal patterns) and many based on deep learning.

- There are also many time-series tools that do not directly support outlier detection but do provide tools for forecasting, which allows us to detect outliers as points that are significantly different from the forecasts.

- When detecting outliers based on forecasts, it's preferable to use tools that provide confidence intervals around the predictions as this provides more context.

index